A Journey Through

Africa, Asia and the Pacific Realm

TEACHER'S EDITION

VOLUME 2

Gibbs Smith, Publisher
Salt Lake City

NC STATE UNIVERSITY

This series is dedicated to Burt and Pauline Beers for their dedication to history and social studies education, but most importantly for their dedication to North Carolina's students.

Published by
Gibbs Smith, Publisher
P.O. Box 667
Layton, UT 84041
800-748-5439
www.NCJourneys.com

Cover Design: Jeremy C. Munns

Printed and bound in China
ISBN 978-1-4236-0324-5

13 12 11 10 09 08 07 10 9 8 7 6 5 4 3 2 1

Gibbs Smith, Publisher wishes to thank all the contributors to the second and third editions of this series.

Gibbs Smith, Publisher

Julie Dumont Rabinowitz
Managing Editor

Christopher Harlos, Ph.D.
Editor

Susan A. Myers, Aimee Stoddard
Copy Editors

Jeremy C. Munns
Lead Designer

Michelle Brown, Alan Connell, Robert Jones, John Vehar
Designers

Janis J. Hansen
Photo Editor

Lynn P. Roundtree, Wendy Knight
Photo Researchers

Content Specialists

Writers

Linda Scher
Raleigh, North Carolina

Elisabeth Gaynor Ellis
New York, New York

Area Specialists

Joel Cline
Meteorology, National Weather Service
Raleigh, North Carolina

David P. Gilmartin, Ph.D.
South Asia
North Carolina State University

Akram F. Khater, Ph.D.
Islam
North Carolina State University

Tom Parker
Terrorism Consultant
Bard College

Tony K. Stewart, Ph.D.
South Asia
North Carolina State University

Kenneth P. Vickery, Ph.D.
Africa
North Carolina State University

Douglas C. Wilms, Ph.D.
Geography
East Carolina University

Curriculum Specialists

Mary Vann Eslinger
Social Studies Consultant
Morehead City, North Carolina

Jacqueline Boykin
Social Studies Consultant
Williamston, North Carolina

Candy Beal, Ph.D.
Middle Grades Social Studies Education
North Carolina State University

Consulting Teachers

Susan O. Collatz
Mooresville, North Carolina

Rose H. Cooper
Carthage, North Carolina

Karen Fichter
Zebulon GT Magnet Middle School
Cary, North Carolina

Greg Giles
Raleigh, North Carolina

Ann Hamzé
C. M. Eppes Middle School
Greenville, North Carolina

Leah Harkness
Apex, North Carolina

Amy L. Hayden
Apex, North Carolina

Kevin C. Martin
Teacher Consultant
Raleigh, North Carolina

Barbara B. Massey
Thomas Jefferson Middle School
Winston-Salem, North Carolina

Margaret Parrish
Raleigh, North Carolina

William E. Pitts
Educational Consultant
Wake Forest, North Carolina

Arvil R. Sale
Boone, North Carolina

Stacey Anne Samuel
Wilmington, North Carolina

Judy Simpson
Mt. Airy, North Carolina

Rebecca Stevens
Greensboro, North Carolina

Sue Trent
Charlotte, North Carolina

Laurie Walsh
Teacher Consultant
Bend, Oregon

Karen Watts
Wilkesboro, North Carolina

NC State University

Humanities Extension/Publications

James W. Clark, Ph.D.
Director & Professor of English

Burton F. Beers, Ph.D.
Editor Emeritus
Humanities Publications &
Professor of History

Regina Higgins, Ph.D.
Editor
Humanities Publications

James Alchediak
Chief Videographer & Lecturer
in Communications

Pamela H. Ellis
Administrative Assistant

Lisa Morgan
Bookkeeper

Zachary H. Jackson
Editorial Assistant
Humanities Publications

Pallavi Talwar
Editorial Assistant
Humanities Publications

Frances Higgins
Editorial Assistant
Humanities Publications

Editorial Support

Bryan Smithey
Copy Editor
Warrenton, North Carolina

Contents

Volume 1

Volume 2

Contents

Unit 4 South Asia

This unit begins with an 1850 painting from Kotal, India, showing an elephant procession, and an account by Mark Twain of his 1896 visit to India. As your students discover South Asia in this unit, they may very well agree with Twain that this is the "Land of Wonders."

Home to seven countries, South Asia is located on a vast peninsula. South Asia has a long and rich history. India, the largest and most influential nation, shares the region with Islamic Pakistan and Bangladesh. Along the region's rim, your students will also find four smaller countries— Afghanistan, Nepal, Bhutan, and Sri Lanka.

UNIT LESSON PLAN

	LESSON 1	LESSON 2	LESSON 3
CHAPTER 15 The Lands of South Asia	South Asia is a giant peninsula extending southward from the Asian continent. It is a land apart from the remainder of Asia. **Essential Question:** What are the physical characteristics of the region of South Asia? **Suggested Time:** 1 day	South Asia is located in the low hot latitudes. Even so, climates vary. Different types of vegetation grow there. **Essential Question:** What climate zones are found in South Asia, and how do they affect vegetation in the area? **Suggested Time:** 1 day	South Asia's population is growing rapidly. Giant India has had more success in meeting the needs of its people than its neighbors have. **Essential Question:** How have South Asian countries met the needs of a rapidly growing population? **Suggested Time:** 1 day
CHAPTER 16 South Asia's Enduring Traditions	South Asia's religions, languages, politics, and culture are rooted in its ancient past. **Essential Question:** How has South Asia's historical foundations influenced its daily life? **Suggested Time:** 2 days	Family and village are the foundations of Indian life. **Essential Question:** What are the foundations of daily life in South Asia? **Suggested Time:** 1 day	Most of South Asia was ruled by the British from the 1800s until 1947. After independence, the subcontinent was divided into several nations. **Essential Question:** What impact did colonization have on South Asia? **Suggested Time:** 1 day
CHAPTER 17 Modern India	India has a constitutional government that ensures democratic rights. **Essential Question:** How does India's constitutional government protect the rights of its citizens, and what are these rights? **Suggested Time:** 1 day	India has industry and commerce. Still, nearly half the people are poor. **Essential Question:** What factors contribute to the high poverty rate in India? **Suggested Time:** 1 day	India is a leader in modern entertainment. Yet traditional entertainment and foods remain popular. **Essential Question:** How does Indian culture reflect a blend of the modern with the traditional? **Suggested Time:** 1 day
CHAPTER 18 Other Nations of South Asia	Pakistan is South Asia's second largest nation. It is a developing nation under Islamic leaders. **Essential Question:** What role does Islam have on the government of South Asia's second largest country, Pakistan? **Suggested Time:** 1 day	Bangladesh is an Islamic nation with rich agricultural resources in South Asia. Bangladesh faces environmental challenges. **Essential Question:** What environmental challenges face the Islamic nation of Bangladesh? **Suggested Time:** 1 day	Four small nations are located on the rim of South Asia. **Essential Question:** What nations are located on the rim of South Asia? **Suggested Time:** 1 day

Unit Planner

Preparing the Unit

- Worksheets, assessments, and reproducibles for this unit are found in the Teacher's Resource Guide.
- See the list of Cultural Resources in the Teacher's Edition.
- Review the resource list and find as many materials as possible from the suggestions to have available in your classroom for your students.
- As you prepare your daily lessons, refer to the suggested goals listed in the unit plan for selecting the specific objective(s) that you plan to cover in each lesson. Refer to the North Carolina Standard Course of Study for the specific objectives covered under each goal.
- Share the art and music activities with your cultural arts teachers so that they might help you integrate the curriculum.

Unit Teaching Strategies

- Use posters, artifacts, maps, and other items to decorate your room to help give students a visual effect of South Asia.
- Review the suggested activities and select the ones that are most appropriate for your classroom. Plan ahead by collecting the materials for the activities.
- If time is an issue, focus your attention on Chapters 15–17 and use the suggested group work activity for Chapter 18 on page 352B.
- Prepare some area foods for the students to sample. If you have a South Asian restaurant in your area, visit it and see if you can set up a time for a class visit or if the restaurant can come to you.
- Check the Web site, **NCJourneys.com,** for updates and materials.

Unit Projects

Assign students a South Asian nation and have them complete the research checklist. After completing the research, have them complete one of the project choices.

PROJECT CHOICES

OBJECTIVES: 1.01, 2.01, 9.02, 11.01

Travel Brochure

Use your research to create a travel brochure based on your country. The brochure should be well planned with typed, accurate information and colorful pictures that would encourage tourists to visit your country.

"ABC" picture book

Design and create an "ABC" picture book or digital story about your country. For each letter of the alphabet, write one term and its definition based on geography, culture, animals, plants, or other aspects. and include a picture that illustrates the word.

Map Poster

Make a poster-size map of your country including the information from your research. A title and key should be part of your map.

Diorama

Design a diorama depicting a typical scene from your country and include facts on the outside of the box.

Poster

Design a poster illustrating your country using the research as a guide.

Presentation

Create a PowerPoint presentation or digital story of your country highlighting the facts from your research.

Extra Credit

For additional credit, you may research an authentic recipe and prepare the dish for your classmates to sample. Be sure to include a copy of the recipe, plates, serving utensils, napkins, and forks and/or spoons.

Extension ELL students should use an ELL-friendly Web site for research without the research sheet. Instead of a brochure, assign them an ABC book or diorama (PowerPoint may be good if students are computer literate but not fluent in English). A recipe may be a good way to let your ELL students "show off" as well as involve their parents. Most of the time, they love to share pieces of the culture.

Research Checklist

Directions: While researching your country, make sure that you find information about the following topics.

Name of country	Location
Type of government	Population
Leader	Capital city
Major landforms	Bodies of water
Neighboring countries	Major crops
Major industries	Religion
Art	Entertainment
Clothing	Tourist attractions
Education	Flag

How do most people make a living?
What do their houses look like?
How do they travel from place to place?

Bulletin Board Ideas

South Asian Rain Forests

Use green construction paper cut in large fringed pieces to represent the rain forests of South Asia. Have students draw or research and photocopy pictures of animals found in the jungles. Have them put names, habitats or environmental preferences, whether or not the animal is endangered, and population or numbers of those animals left on index cards. Display information along with pictures.

South Asian Current Events

Do a current events bulletin board with a particular focus such as weather, population, or transportation in one particular country of South Asia (such as weather in Bangladesh). Have students clip or print newspaper articles or photocopy magazine articles and display them. Use a map of the country as the background.

Monsoons

Create a bulletin board depicting the monsoon wind patterns of South Asia. Use a large map of the area and cut out arrows and cardinal directions to show the directions of the monsoon.

Introductory Activity

The Subcontinent

OBJECTIVES: 2.01, 2.03

Give each student a blank map of South Asia and a few Hershey kisses. Ask them to pretend that the Hershey kisses are the Himalayan mountains and ask them to position the mountains in the correct location on their blank map. Refer students to page 293 for the location. Before you allow the students to enjoy the candy, ask them to explain how the Himalayas might affect this region. After discussing their ideas, explain that South Asia is known as a subcontinent because it is separated from the rest of Asia by the mountains.

Culminating Activity

Building a Newspaper

OBJECTIVES: 1.01, 1.02

Students will create a newspaper about a country from the region studied in this unit, as they did in Unit 1. This will be issue number four of their newspaper.

Refer to the Unit 1 Culminating Activity on page 14C in the Teacher's Edition for specific directions and references on how to create and organize the newspaper. Remind students that the newspaper should feature two articles on the front. The back of the newspaper should include a map, a box displaying vital statistics, an article about something special or current events, and a puzzle. The students should use their newspapers from the previous unit as a model, and thus the students should be able to complete it in similar or slightly less time.

Share the newspapers with others in the class. Have the students keep each of their newspapers. At the end of the year, bind each student's newspapers together so he or she will have their own volume of newspapers covering the regions studied throughout the year. Use copies of all students newspapers to organize a class volume according to region.

Technology Activity

Indian Current Events

OBJECTIVES: 6.01, 9.02, 11.01

Have the students find some recent newspaper or magazine articles about India. Or, if possible, go to a newspaper site online and search "India." Put the students into groups and have them share their findings with one another. See if they can relate the stories in any way. How many are about computers? Have each group report to the class. Then with the entire class discuss what general conclusions might be drawn from all the articles combined.

Science Activity

Natural Disasters in South Asia

OBJECTIVES: 2.02, 3.01

Floods, typhoons, cyclones, and earthquakes are some of the natural disasters that occur in the countries of South Asia. Have students research the ways in which people of these countries adapt to their climate. Ways that people adapt will include the crops that are grown, the homes that they live in, the occupations that people have, etc. This project can be coordinated or co-taught with the science teacher.

Extension Their product should be a poster, diorama, or PowerPoint presentation (if students are computer literate but not fluent in English), not a report.

Math Activity

Estimating Percentages

OBJECTIVES: 1.02, 4.01

The total population of South Asia is approximately 1.37 billion.

The following chart is a breakdown by country in millions.

Country	Pop. (in millions)	Percentage
India	1,013.7	74.0
Pakistan	156.5	11.5
Bangladesh	129.2	9.4
Nepal	23.9	1.7
Afghanistan	22.7	1.6
Sri Lanka	18.8	1.3
Bhutan	2.1	0.14

Have the students consider 137 people as the total population of South Asia with each country having the number of people listed below. (It might make it easier to combine Sri Lanka and Bhutan to a total of 2, and Nepal and Afghanistan to a total of 5). Now have them estimate the percentage breakdown. List some of the answers on the board and have the students explain the method of estimation they used.

Total	137	Estimated %
India	101	
Pakistan	16	
Bangladesh	13	
Nepal/Afghanistan	5	
Sri Lanka/Bhutan	2	

Unit Resources

Books

India

Bosse, Malcolm. *Ordinary Magic.* Sunburst, 1993. ISBN 0374425175.

Collins, Larry and Dominque Lapierre. *Freedom at Midnight.* New York: Simon and Schuster, 1975. ISBN 0671220888.

Jaffrey, Madhur. *Seasons of Splendor: Tales, Myths, and Legends of India.* New York: Atheneum, 1985. The author intersperses the tales with childhood recollections of festivals.

Jhavbala, Ruth Prawer. *Out of India: Selected Stories.* New York: Simon & Schuster/Fireside, 1987. ISBN 1582430527. Jhabvala writes fiction that explores the effect of the subcontinent on visiting Europeans.

King, Clive. *The Night the Water Came.* New York: Harper, 1982. On an island off Bangladesh, eleven-year-old Apu struggles to survive the aftermath of a cyclone that has destroyed his home.

Kipling, Rudyard, *Kim.* Dell Pub. Co., 1959. ISBN 0812565754. Kim's early years as an orphaned beggar in India lead to an exciting career in the British Secret Service.

Nonfiction

Kapoor, Sukhbir Singh. *Sikh Festivals.* Vero Beach, Florida: Rourke Publications, 1989. Photographs and descriptions of Sikh holy days and celebrations.

McClure, Vimala. *Bangladesh: Rivers in a Crowded Land.* Minneapolis: Dillon, 1989. Presents folktales, recipes, a biography of the nation's first woman pilot, and a discussion of Bangladeshis in the United States.

Scarsbrook, Ailson, and Alan Scarsbrook. *A Family in Pakistan.* Minneapolis: Lerner, 1985. Focuses on fourteen-year-old Assim Mahmood and his family.

Seuss, Dr. *The Sneetches and Other Stories.* Random House, 1989. ISBN 0394800893.

Other Resources

Maps

National Geographic Society. Each is available as an uncirculated back issue with supplement map, many double-sided. Contact: *National Geographic* Back Issues. (800) 777-2800, Fax: (813) 979-6685. Cost: ranges between $5 and $10 (shipping included).

December 1984—South Asia (political map/peoples of South Asia).

May 1997—India (political map/historical, land use, population distribution)

Web Sites

Go to **NCJourneys.com** for links to the following Web sites:

Asia (General)

- Asia Society Presents Ask Asia
- Association for Asian Studies
- Coombsweb–Asian Studies online research facility, The Australian National University
- South and Southeast Asia Studies, Columbia University Libraries
- Internet Modern History Sourcebook (primary source documents), Fordham Universiy

South Asia

- The Caste System and the Stages of Life in Hinduism
- Interactive Map of Asia South Asia
- The Literature and Culture of the Indian Subcontinent
- Monsoon Magazine, Journal or South Asian Culture
- South Asia Culture, Historyteacher.net
- South Asian History: India, University of California at Berkeley
- South Asian History

Paideia Seminar

The Sneetches

The Sneetches and Other Stories by Dr. Seuss (Random House, 1976. ISBN 0394800893.)

The Sneetches is a story about a society of haves and have-nots in which access to things is determined by whether or not Sneetches have a star on their belly.

Opening Questions

- What do you think this story is about?
- Do think this story is funny?
- Is there anything not funny about it?

Core Questions

- How would Sneetches define quality?
- What does this story have to say about being happy?
- What in Man's nature makes him feel that he has to be superior?

Closing Questions

- What does this story have to say about human relations?
- Is it possible to be different without being better?
- How do the themes of this story apply to India's caste system?

Map Activity

South Asia's "Funnel"

NATIONAL GEOGRAPHY STANDARDS: 2

GEOGRAPHIC THEMES: Location

OBJECTIVES: 1.02, 2.02

Using the Robinson world map projection with South Asia, including Sri Lanka, highlighted in red, ask students to notice the funnel shape of Pakistan, Nepal, Bhutan, India, and Bangladesh. Also have students imagine Sri Lanka as a drop of liquid falling from this funnel. The bulge Pakistan creates in this image may be compared to a finger/thumb handle on the funnel.

Have students describe other visual images they see in the overall image of this Asian region.

Have students speculate about how the funnel might suggest population density to them.

Unit 4 South Asia

The American writer Mark Twain visited India in 1896. Twain was awed by India. It was, he exclaimed, a

> Land of dreams and romance, of fabulous wealth and fabulous poverty, of splendor and rags, of palaces and hovels, of famine and disease, of tigers and elephants, the cobra and the jungle, and the country of a hundred tongues.

An American tourist visiting India today might echo Twain's observations. The nation still has these qualities, but it offers even more to impress a visitor. It is a land of modern cities, big business, and advanced science and technology. In the end, today's visitor and Mark Twain might agree that India could only be called "the Land of Wonders."

1850 painting of Kotal, India, elephant procession

290

Career Feature

Social Studies at Work: High-Tech Researcher

A high-tech researcher uses scientific and mathematical principles to improve or invent new technologies such as computers, cellular phones, medical equipment, fiber optics, machinery, and other important devices.

Meet Pallav Sudarshan

High-tech researcher at North Carolina State University.

Southern hospitality is one of the things that Indian-native Pallav Sudarshan likes best about North Carolina. Having grown up in the bustling city of New Delhi, India, he was surprised and pleased to discover that courtesies like saying hello to passersby are commonplace in his new hometown of Raleigh.

Sudarshan hopes to someday return to India to marry and raise a family. In the meantime, however, he is part of a university research team looking to develop faster, clearer, and less expensive wireless communication systems. The results of their work are expected to improve Internet and cellular phone technologies all over the world.

Degrees in electrical engineering and communications from top universities in India helped prepare him for this job. Now he is pursuing a doctorate degree at North Carolina State University.

Sudarshan says that some people are surprised to find out that he speaks English so well. However, since there are 325 languages native to India, 67 percent of Indians are bilingual, with English being the language that ties them together. This is particularly

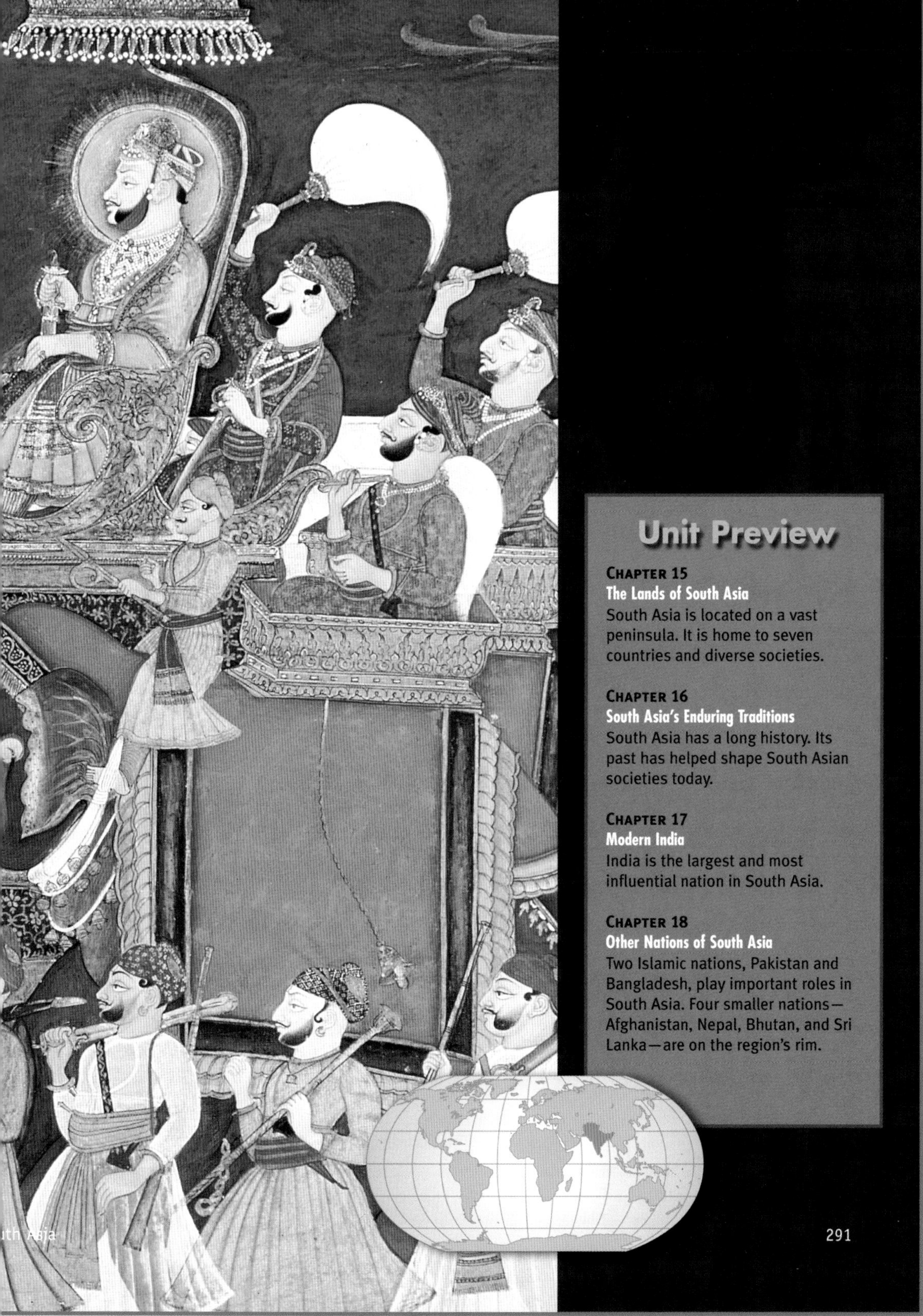

Unit Preview

Chapter 15
The Lands of South Asia
South Asia is located on a vast peninsula. It is home to seven countries and diverse societies.

Chapter 16
South Asia's Enduring Traditions
South Asia has a long history. Its past has helped shape South Asian societies today.

Chapter 17
Modern India
India is the largest and most influential nation in South Asia.

Chapter 18
Other Nations of South Asia
Two Islamic nations, Pakistan and Bangladesh, play important roles in South Asia. Four smaller nations—Afghanistan, Nepal, Bhutan, and Sri Lanka—are on the region's rim.

291

true in the educational system and in all things technical and official. When at home with his family at friends, Sudarshan speaks Hindi, but otherwise his English skills are as good as most Americans.

Questions, and lots of them, were the first clues that directed Sudarshan toward his high-tech future. He says he's always been inquisitive. He started finding answers to his questions in his first physics class. Now he uses the laws of physics and other complex principles to make life simpler for everyone.

High-Tech Researcher for a Day

Most middle school students can relate to the problem of lugging around heavy backpacks all day. Your job is to use technology (either real or imaginary) to come up with a solution. How can students gain easy access to textbooks and assignments without breaking their backs? Sketch out your plan with notes on how your new technology would work and why it would be a good solution.

The Lands of South Asia

Social Studies Strands

Geographic Relationships
Climate

Cultures and Diversity
Population

North Carolina Standard Course of Study

Goal 2 The learner will assess the relationship between physical environment and cultural characteristics of selected societies and regions of Africa, Asia, and Australia.

Goal 3 The learner will analyze the impact of interactions between humans and their physical environments in Africa, Asia, and Australia.

Goal 6 The learner will recognize the relationship between economic activity and the quality of life in Africa, Asia, and Australia.

Goal 11 The learner will recognize the common characteristics of different cultures in Africa, Asia, and Australia.

Teaching & Assessment

- English Language Learner Modified Lesson Plans for this chapter are found in the Teacher Resource Guide.
- *ExamView® Assessment Suite* is provided at **NCJourneys.com.** It includes customizable assessments for all chapters. Paper tests are also available in the Teacher Resource Guide. See pages T16–T17 for information about how to use the assessments and the Scoring Guide.

Worksheets

Worksheets and answer keys are found both in the Teacher Resource Guide and at **NCJourneys.com**, including Reading Guides, Reading Strategies, Chapter Reviews, English Language Learner and others.

ACTIVITIES AND INTEGRATIONS

SOCIAL STUDIES
▲ Map Study, p. 292B
South Asia's Extremes and Characteristics, p. 293
● Tectonic Movement, p. 294
▲ ■ Topography, p. 298
● Vegetation Zones, p. 303
Skill Lesson: Comparing Subregions in South Asia, p. 309

READING/LANGUAGE ARTS	READING/LANGUAGE ARTS OBJECTIVES
"The Blind Men and the Elephant," p. 292B	2.01
Analogies, p. 292B	2.01
▲ ■ Activator: *One Grain of Rice,* p. 292	1.03
Writing Prompt: Seasons in India, p. 292	3.03
★ ■ The Hindu Religion, p. 296	1.03
Writing Prompt: Pedicab Writing, p. 304	1.01
★ Describing the Ganges, p. 306	1.01
Almanac Comparison, p. 307	2.01
Go to the Source: Analyzing Historic Documents, p. 311	2.01, 4.01, 4.02

SCIENCE	SCIENCE OBJECTIVES
Climograph, p. 299	3.05
South Asia's Ecosystems, p. 302	3.01
Which Way Do the Winds Blow?, p. 300	3.05

MATHEMATICS	MATHEMATICS OBJECTIVES
Estimating Percentages, p. 290C	1.02
▲ ■ Distance Word Problem, p. 295	1.02
Climograph, p. 299	4.01, 4.05
● Crops and Rainfall, p. 301	4.01
★ Population Cartogram, p. 305	1.03, 4.01
▲ ■ Temperature Word Problem, p. 306	1.02
Database Table, p. 308	4.01, 4.05

TECHNOLOGY	TECHNOLOGY OBJECTIVES
South Asia's Ecosystems, p. 296	3.01, 3.03, 3.10
Climograph, p. 299	3.01, 3.10
★ Almanac Comparison, p. 307	3.01, 3.03, 3.10

VISUAL ARTS	VISUAL ARTS OBJECTIVES
● ▲ ■ Daruma Dolls, p. 292B	2.04, 5.02
▲ ■ Hindu Diwali Festival, p. 297	2.05, 4.01
Connections Cartoon, p. 307	1.02, 4.04

CHARACTER AND VALUES EDUCATION	TRAITS
Writing Prompt: Seasons in India, p. 292	good judgment, integrity
What Would You Do?, p. 306	respect, responsibility

● Basic Activities ★ Challenging Activities ▲ English Language Learner Novice ■ English Language Learner Intermediate

Chapter Activities

Introductory Activity

"The Blind Men and the Elephant"

OBJECTIVES: 11.03

Find the poem "The Blind Men and the Elephant." This is widely available online (see NCJourneys.com for links).

Read "The Blind Men and the Elephant" aloud. Have students discuss how looking at one aspect of an object might create misconceptions. Divide them into six groups. Give each group a set of the photographs. Have them draw conclusions about India based solely on the pictures. They are not only to look at the individual pictures but also to see what might be a common theme among them. Each group will share their observations and pictures with the class. After all have presented, go back and have the class reflect on how this activity relates to the story.

Extension Have the students think of a TV show or movie. How might someone from another country get a biased view of the United States if they based their opinion solely on the show or movie?

Have intermediate ELL students write descriptions as simple sentences.

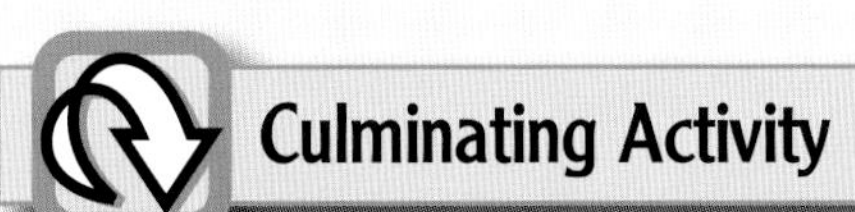

Culminating Activity

Map Study

OBJECTIVES: 1.02, 1.03, 2.01

Laminate a class set of outline maps of South Asia. These maps do not need to include the political boundaries. The laminated maps will be traced by students as often as necessary for various activities.

Have students locate South Asia on a globe and a flat map, then have them trace one of the laminated maps. They should add the physical features of South Asia to the map using colors, symbols, or shading.

Students should identify India, Sri Lanka, Pakistan, Bangladesh, Nepal, Bhutan, and Afghanistan. Use the laminated maps as a base to make topographic models. Use papier maché or modeling clay to represent different countries to scale. Students can work in cooperative groups.

Extension Ask ELL students to show their country of origin. (Consider creating a bulletin board with ELL students' names located on a map identifying their native country.)

Art Activity

Daruma Dolls

OBJECTIVES: 1.01, 4.03, 8.01, 11.01

Daruma are dolls named after an Indian priest called Dharma, credited with creating Zen Buddhism. Generally, three faces are depicted on Dharma dolls: a face with no eyes (wishing Dharma), a face with one eye (for making a wish), and a face with two eyes (for when the wish comes true).

Materials two old tennis balls cut in half; tape: masking tape or plastic; plaster of paris; water; mixing container; mixing spoon/wooden paddle-stick; variety of colored construction paper; handout of the cone pattern found in the Teacher's Resource Guide; stapler; colored markers; glue

Procedure Pour 1 cup of plaster and ½ cup of water into mixing container, and mix to a heavy, thick consistency. Pour about ¼ cup of plaster into each tennis ball half. Let it harden completely. Using cone patterns, form doll's head for tennis ball to fit in circle of cone's base. Cut out a small face from a piece of construction paper and glue it near the rounded end of the cone. Decorate the face—without eyes—with markers. Glue the cone together. Set the cone on top of the tennis ball half and tape securely. As students make a wish, they should put one eye on their doll. Only when the wish comes true should they put a pair of eyes on the doll.

Analogies

OBJECTIVES: 1.02, 2.01

Analogies are useful to help students make associations with prior knowledge. Read the analogies aloud and ask students to identify the relationship between the terms. As an extension, ask students to write their own analogies using key terms or places discussed in the chapter. Identify on a map or globe when possible.

subcontinent : continent :: subplot : plot :: subculture : culture (is below/lesser than)

Mount Everest: world :: Mount Mitchell : North Carolina (is the highest mountain peak in)

Banares/Varanasi : Hindus :: Jerusalem : Christians :: Mecca : Muslims (is the holy city of)

Northern Plain : India :: Great Plains : United States (is the breadbasket of)

Vindhya Mountains : north and south India :: Mississippi River : east and west United States :: Ural Mountains : Europe and northern Asia (divide[s])

vegetarian : plants :: carnivore : animals (eats)

cotton : Deccan Plateau :: jute : Bangladesh (is the major crop of)

mahogany : Central Africa :: teak, sandalwood : South Asia (is exported from)

Teaching Strategies

Before students can understand the culture of South Asia, they must first understand the geography of the region. Allocate time for students to learn about the landforms and physical features of the region.

Discussion Questions

1 What are some cities you consider special?

2 What qualities make them special?

Activator

OBJECTIVES: 11.02

Activators are great tools to use in order to "hook" the attention of the students. Reading picture books or stories is an excellent way to build interest in the subject and is also a great way to integrate language arts into the social studies curriculum.

One Grain of Rice: A Mathematical Folktale by Demi (Scholastic Press, 1997. ISBN 059093998X.)

Writing Prompt

OBJECTIVES: 2.01, 2.03

Evaluative

India has three seasons that shape the everyday lives of people in the country. Are North Carolinians ruled by the seasons to the same extent as Indians? After reading Chapter 15, write an essay to give your opinion and explain your answer.

As you write your paper, remember to

- clearly state your position.
- give at least three reasons and explain your reasons fully.
- give examples to support your reasons.
- write in complete sentences and paragraph form.
- organize your ideas and include an introduction and a conclusion.
- use good grammar, spelling, punctuation, and capitalization.

CHAPTER 15

The Lands of South Asia

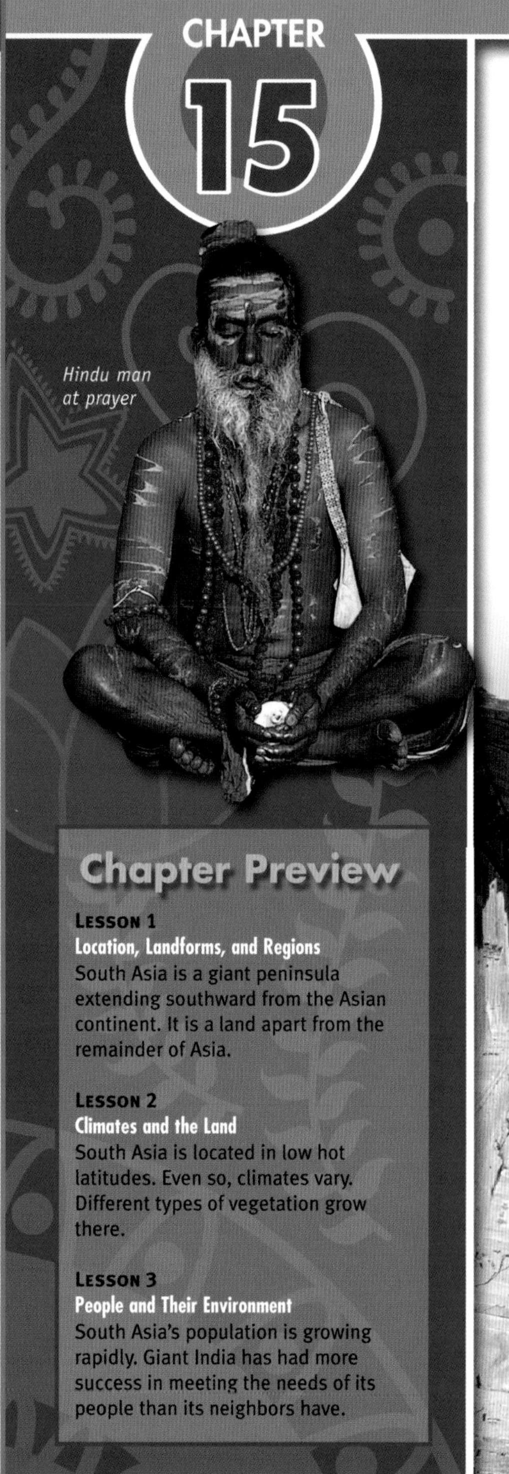

Hindu man at prayer

Many of the world's most spectacular natural features, including high mountain ranges, vast plateaus, and majestic river basins lie in South Asia. High mountain ranges are the dominant landforms of the northern countries, the Deccan Plateau is India's dominant landform, and the delta of the Ganges is the dominant landform in Bangladesh.

The lands of South Asia support some of the world's most densely populated nations. But they are also home to a great diversity of people, religions, and cultures.

Cattle pull a cart on a city street in Pakistan

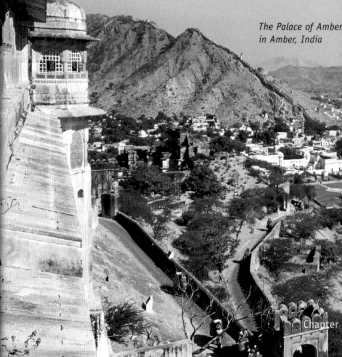

The Palace of Amber in Amber, India

Chapter Preview

Lesson 1
Location, Landforms, and Regions
South Asia is a giant peninsula extending southward from the Asian continent. It is a land apart from the remainder of Asia.

Lesson 2
Climates and the Land
South Asia is located in low hot latitudes. Even so, climates vary. Different types of vegetation grow there.

Lesson 3
People and Their Environment
South Asia's population is growing rapidly. Giant India has had more success in meeting the needs of its people than its neighbors have.

292

Chapter

Chapter Resources

Print Resources

Fiction

Bash, Barbara. In the Heart of the Village: The World of the Indian Banyan Tree. Gibbs Smith, Publisher. Salt Lake City, Utah. ISBN 1578050804

Nonfiction

Demi. *One Grain of Rice: A Mathematical Folktale.* Scholastic Press, 1997. ISBN 059093998X.

India (Welcome to My Country). Franklin Watts Ltd., 2005. ISBN 0749660155.

Khoo , Eileen.Welcome To Bangladesh (Welcome to My Country). Gareth Stevens Publishing, 2005. ISBN 083683125X.

Kwek, Karen and Jameel Haque. Welcome to Pakistan (Welcome to My Country). Gareth Stevens Publishing, 2003. ISBN 0836825527.

Pollard, Michael. *The Ganges.* Benchmark

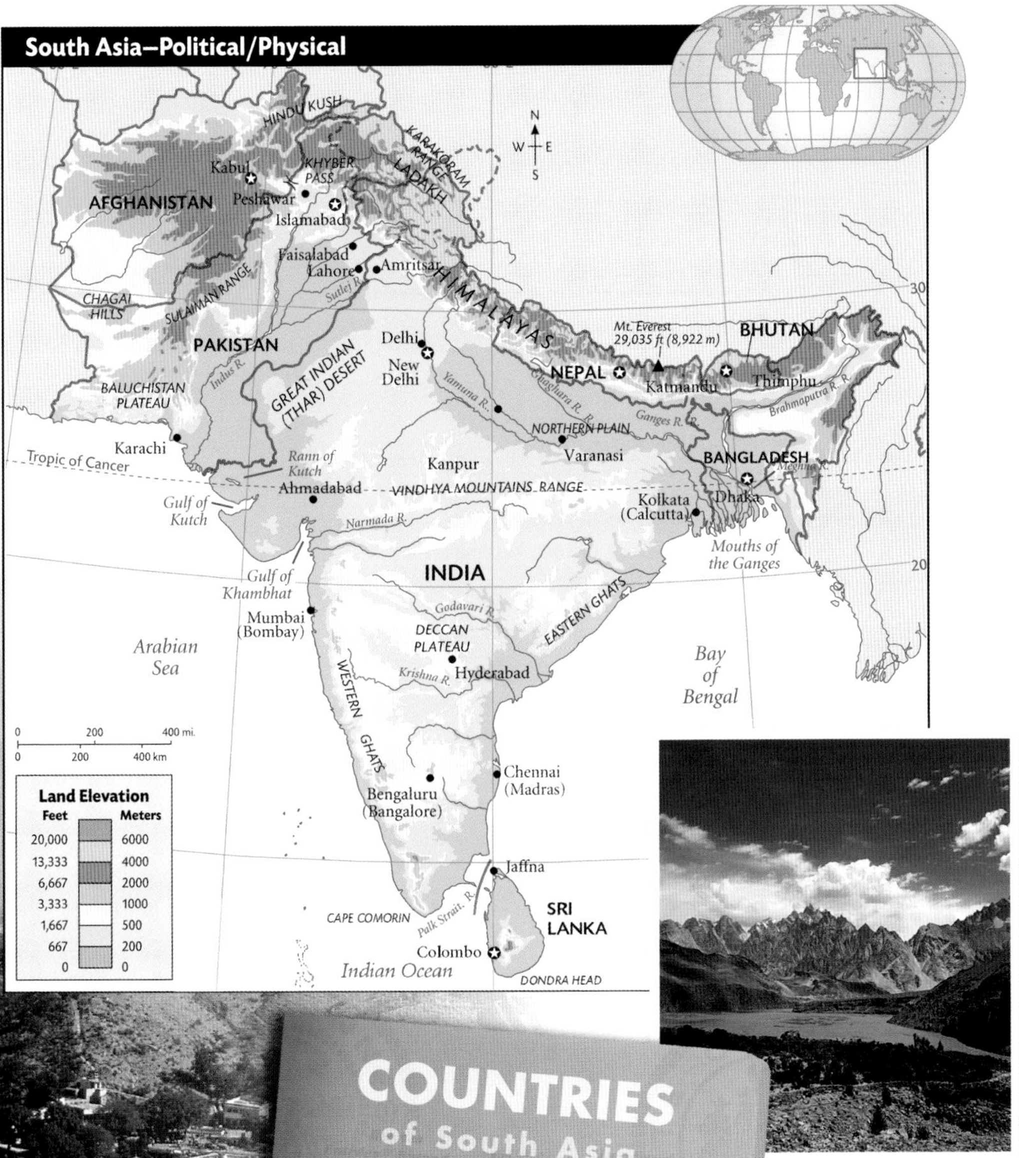

South Asia—Political/Physical

A pass in the Hindu Kush

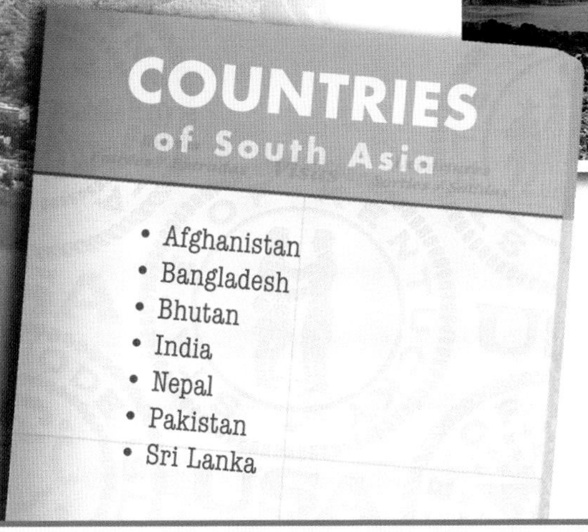

COUNTRIES of South Asia

- Afghanistan
- Bangladesh
- Bhutan
- India
- Nepal
- Pakistan
- Sri Lanka

The Lands of South Asia

293

Map Activity

South Asia's Extremes and Characteristics

NATIONAL GEOGRAPHY STANDARDS: 1, 3, 4, 17

GEOGRAPHIC THEMES: Location, Place, Region

OBJECTIVES: 2.01

Introduce some of this region's unique characteristics. South Asia is a land of extremes:

1. Earth's highest elevation: *Mount Everest* (29,035 feet)
2. Earth's highest lake: *unnamed glacial lake near Mount Everest (19,300 feet)*
3. One of the earth's rainiest/wettest locations: *Cherrapunji (about 450 inches per year)*
4. Earth's only subcontinent: *South Asia's peninsula*

Assign students to identify which South Asian nation is characterized below:

1. Asia's invasion route location: *Afghanistan (particularly with Khyber Pass)*
2. Cyclone central: *Bangladesh*
3. Land of the thunder dragon: *Bhutan*
4. World's subcontinent and largest democracy: *India*
5. World's only Hindu kingdom and roof of the world: *Nepal*
6. Cradle of one of Asia's oldest civilizations (Indus): *Pakistan*
7. Serendib ("serendipity") to Arab spice traders: *Sri Lanka*

Books, 1998. ISBN 0761405046. Traces the course of this famous river in India and describes its physical features, history, and importance.

Web Sites

Go to **NCJourneys.com** for links to the following Web sites:

- Census of India
- Climate Change, India's Ministry of Environment and Forests
- Mt. Everest Crown of the Earth Thinkquest
- Mt. Everest Panorama View

OBJECTIVES: 2.01, 2.02, 3.01

Discussion Questions

1 What geographic features helped isolate parts of North Carolina in its past?

Caption Answer

A subcontinent is a distinct landmass that is smaller than a continent.

ELL Teaching Tips

English and Native Language Literacy Connection

Building native language literacy is important. Students who are literate in their native language will be more likely to become literate quickly in English. ELLs will use strategies learned in their native language to help them in reading English.

Activity

Tectonic Movement

OBJECTIVES: 3.04

Using small and large paper plates, students design tectonic "plates" (African, Antarctic, Arabian, Caribbean, Cocos, Eurasian, Indian, Australian, Nazca, North American, Pacific, Philippine, Somali, South African) with a simple outline shape of each "plate" sketched onto paper plates. Paper plates are positioned on a flat surface in the basic pattern that matches the Supercontinent map on page 28 of the pupil text.

Roll one-fourth cup of soft dough/clay to the radius of a small paper plate and place it on lower portion of the Eurasian "plate" as the Himalayas. Place an old iron on top of the Arabian and Somali paper plates, push them gently into the Eurasian paper plate to illustrate how the tectonic plate movement in the continental drift theory gradually is increasing the elevation of the Himalayas. Have the students speculate what will occur over millions of years of plate movement if the subcontinent of South Asia continues to push upward into the Eurasian plate. Is it possible for the Eurasian plate to eventually become the European and Asian plates in billions of years?

LESSON 1 Location, Landforms and Regions

KEY IDEAS

- South Asia is a large landmass set apart from the rest of Asia.
- South Asia has three major physical regions. Its landforms have influenced life in the subcontinent.
- Three great river systems in the north bring water to millions of people.

KEY TERMS

Hindus
South Asia
subcontinent

Landforms, such as towering mountains in the north of South Asia, offer some of the most awesome sights. A daring traveler riding along a high mountain road recalled his feelings when his jeep rounded a bend and a tiny village came into sight. "I glimpsed irrigated plots of corn. This lush oasis of green was so startling amid the lunar landscape that I caught my breath."

South Asia—A Land Apart

The wonder that is India can first be explained by its location and landforms. India is located on a vast peninsula called ***South Asia.*** The peninsula is large enough to be called a subcontinent. A ***subcontinent*** is a distinct landmass that is smaller than a continent.

An arc of mountains to the north separates South Asia from the Asian continent. Dense jungles and mountains to the east mark the border with Southeast Asia. Mountainous terrain and deserts to the west isolate South Asia from Southwest Asia. To the south, the peninsula narrows like a giant arrowhead that points into the Indian Ocean.

At its widest, South Asia stretches 2,000 miles (3,220 km) west to east from the Arabian Sea to the Bay of Bengal (see map, page 293). South Asia reaches about an equal distance from its northern mountains to its southern cape.

These geographic features have set South Asia apart from its neighbors. The isolation has helped South Asian civilization develop unique characteristics.

In Mark Twain's time, as you read in the Unit 4 opening on page 210, most of South Asia was ruled by the United Kingdom. Under British rule, nearly all of South Asia was named India.

Today, several independent nations exist in South Asia. India occupies the most land, but South Asia also includes the independent nations of Pakistan, Bangladesh, Afghanistan, Nepal (nay·PAWL), Bhutan (boo·TAHN), and Sri Lanka (sree·LANG·kuh).

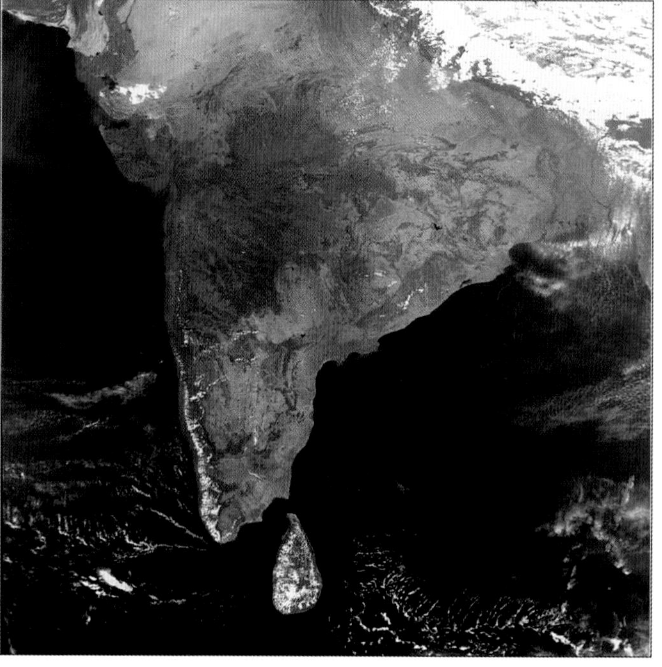

The South Asian subcontinent is a peninsula that extends into the Indian Ocean. **What is a subcontinent?**

ubregions
f South Asia

Headlines announced stunning news in ay 1953. Two men, Edmund Hillary of ew Zealand and Tenzing Norgay of epal, had "conquered" Mount Everest. e two determined mountaineers had ttled brutal winds, bitter cold, and thin r to reach the highest point on earth. ey were the first to climb Everest.

Mount Everest soars to 29,035 feet ,711 m) above sea level. It is the highest ak in the highest mountain range in the orld—the Himalayas. The Hindu Kush d the Karakoram ranges have peaks most as high as those in the Himalayas.

These towering walls of rock and ice e one of many environments in South ia. The mountains contrast with coastal in forests. Deserts of Pakistan differ om the low-lying marshlands of ngladesh.

Geographers divide the region of uth Asia into three physical bregions—northern mountains, a wide est-to-east plain south of the mountains, d a southern area occupied by a ateau, mountains, and coastal plains (see ap, page 293). Each subregion has aped a different way of life.

Mountains

The mountains of northern South Asia influence climate and vegetation and affect movement. The Himalayas extend west to east across South Asia in a 1,500-mile (2,415-km) curve. Parts of the range run 200 miles (322 km) north to south. Aircraft fly over the mountains, but movement through them remains difficult. Mountain passes do cut between the peaks, but few passes are below 15,000 feet (4,500 m). That high elevation creates thin air—air that lacks enough oxygen for people to breathe easily. Also, the passes are usually blocked with snow.

Movement through the Hindu Kush is easier. The peaks are nearly as high as those in the Himalayas, but the passes among the peaks are lower and wider. Even in ancient times, invaders and traders reached India through the passes of the Hindu Kush. The traditions that they brought shaped the civilization of South Asia.

The mountains influence the subcontinent's climates and vegetation. The northern slopes protect South Asia from dry winds blowing out of Central Asia. Moisture-bearing winds are blocked by the mountains' southern slopes. The warm air rises, creating clouds that drop their precipitation onto the northern plains. The rain feeds the sources of South Asia's great rivers.

e village of Mussoorie, India, sits at 6,600 et (1,980 m)—in the Himalayas. **What is the lative location of South Asia's northern ountain region?**

Mount Everest is the world's highest mountain. **What are some of the landforms of South Asia?**

Discussion Questions

1 How do the Appalachians of North Carolina compare to the mountains of South Asia?

2 Do they have the similar effects?

Caption Answer

It is the northernmost region of the subcontinent, north of the plain and the plateau. It runs from west to east across South Asia, dividing the subcontinent from the Asian continent.

Caption Answer

Mountains (Himalayas, Hindu Kush, Vindhya, Western Ghats and Eastern Ghats), plateaus (Deccan), rivers (Indus, Ganges, Brahmaputra), and plains.

Math Activity

Distance Word Problem

OBJECTIVES: 1.02

Use the map on page 293. Find the distance in miles from Kabul, Afghanistan, to Colombo, Sri Lanka.

Answer 2,017 miles

Extension Assist ELL students by setting up the problem.

Name Origin

Bangladesh "Land of the Bengal," from when it was a portion of the Bengal Province of the British Empire.

Bhutan From a local language meaning "the end of Tibet."

India Named after the Indus River. (Indus is a Sanskrit word meaning "river.")

Nepal Named after the Nepal Valley.

Pakistan Urdu for "land of the pure."

Sri Lanka Sinhalese language for "glorious land."

Tibet Mongolian for "the country."

Colombo (Sri Lanka) In a local language, "Kolamba" meant port. The Portuguese changed the spelling and pronunciation slightly to honor Christopher Columbus.

Himalayas Sanskrit word meaning "Snow Abode."

Mount Everest Named after Sir George Everest, the surveyor who fixed its height in 1841.

K-2 The second highest mountain in the world, was also the second to be surveyed in the Karakorum Range in 1856. Its unofficial name is Mount Godwin Austen, after the surveyor.

Activity

The Hindu Religion

OBJECTIVES: 12.01

Invite an Indian ELL student's parent or adult friend to come to your class and discuss the Hindu religion. There may also be a Hindu temple in your community that you may contact to ask about a guest speaker.

India's Holiest City

The British called it Benares, but the ancient name of Varanasi is its most common name. With the Ganges flowing by and a long history as a center of Hindu temples, Varanasi is known as India's holiest city.

Followers of the Hindu religion— ***Hindus*** — come from all over the world to bathe in the Ganges River at Varanasi. Broad steps, or ghats, lead down to the water where thousands go daily into the river. Hindus believe bathing in the Ganges will purify them.

This "city of a thousand temples" sits on the two tributaries of the Ganges. Believed to be one of the oldest cities in the world, Varanasi was the capital of the kingdom of Kasi. Under Muslim occupation in the MIddle Ages, Varanasi declined and many of its ancient temples were destroyed.

Behind the miles of ghats lining the shores of the Ganges (below) are narrow streets where shops sells religious items. The Banaras Hindu University is a center of Hindu learning.

Selling sugarcane juice in the Varanasi market

296 Chapter

Background Information

Ganges River

At 1,560 miles (2,511.6 km), the Ganges is one of the world's longest rivers. It begins high in the Himalayas and empties into the Bay of Bengal. The Gangetic Plain through which the river flows is fertile, densely populated, and intensively cultivated. Some of India's largest cities, such as Kolkata (Calcutta) and Kanpur, lie along the riverbanks. The Ganges is also a sacred river to Hindus. Each year thousands of Hindu pilgrims travel great distances to visit such holy cities as Varanasi and Allahabad on the banks of the Ganges. For them, bathing in the river is a religious experience that cleanses and purifies. Pilgrims often take home vials of river water. Bathers that are sick or disabled come hoping that the water will heal them. Many elderly Hindus come to the river to die, believing that those who drink of the Ganges before dying go to paradise.

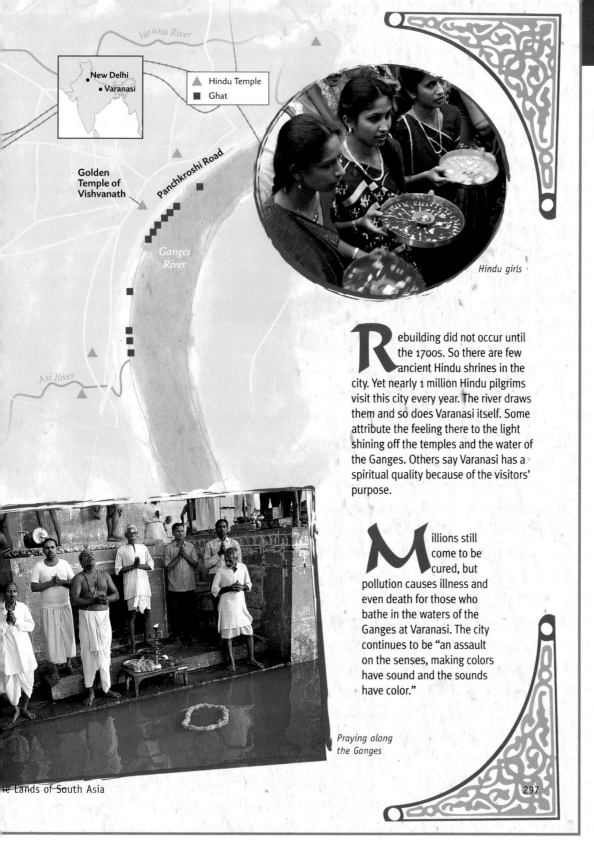

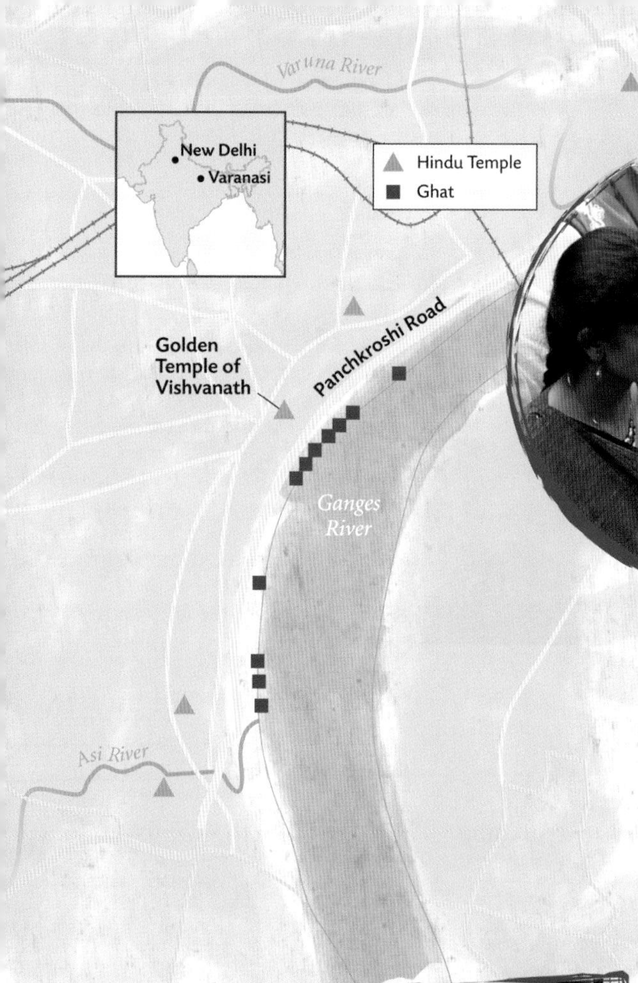

Hindu girls

Rebuilding did not occur until the 1700s. So there are few ancient Hindu shrines in the city. Yet nearly 1 million Hindu pilgrims visit this city every year. The river draws them and so does Varanasi itself. Some attribute the feeling there to the light shining off the temples and the water of the Ganges. Others say Varanasi has a spiritual quality because of the visitors' purpose.

Millions still come to be cured, but pollution causes illness and even death for those who bathe in the waters of the Ganges at Varanasi. The city continues to be "an assault on the senses, making colors have sound and the sounds have color."

Praying along the Ganges

Eyewitness Activity

Hindu Diwali Festival

OBJECTIVES: 12.01, 12.02

During October or November (depending on the Hindu calendar), Diwali, the festival of lights, is held. Small earthenware bowls are filled with oil and wicks called dipa lights. These are lit in front of a home altar with many placed on the edges of the roofs of buildings at dusk. Many dipas are lit in Hindu temples, such as the Golden Temple of Vishvanath, taken down the ghats (broad steps), and placed in the waters of the sacred Ganges River to float until extinguished. Make dipa lights with the class.

Materials small, clean, flat can or jar lid (tuna fish or sardines can or baby food jar); clay (recipe below); glue; small candle or votive; plastic knife and other clay tools (for making designs); and gold spray enamel paint

Flatten the clay and mold it evenly around the can/lid. Smooth the clay and use tools to decorate it. Make a candleholder from one band of clay. Place candle in center of candleholder. Carefully remove candle. Allow this to dry. Center and glue the candle holder on the inside of the bottom of can/lid. Spray the entire dipa with gold paint. Allow paint to dry thoroughly. Insert candle into candleholder. Remind students to have an adult light candle carefully.

Clay Recipe

2 cups all-purpose flour
1 cup salt
½ to 1 cup water
2 tablespoons vegetable oil

Combine all ingredients in mixing bowl and knead until smooth. Place finished projects on waxed paper if drying them; they will air dry in a few days. Use aluminum foil if baking them at low heat.

Teacher Notes

Name Changes

India has officially changed the names of several of its cities from the "British" versions to native pronunciations and spellings. On our maps and in our text, the former names are referred to in parentheses. For example, Calcutta is now Kolkata, Bombay is now Mumbai, and Madras is now Chennai.

Mount Everest

New satellite imaging technology and the use of the space shuttle to measure points on earth has resulted in a new height for Mount Everest. This new height, 29,035 feet, is seven feet higher than the previous measurement.

Discussion Questions

1 How would you compare the northern plain to the Piedmont region of North Carolina?

2 Compare the Deccan Plateau with the Coastal Plains of North Carolina.

Caption Answer

The Western and Eastern Ghats rise close to the coast.

Activity

Topography

NATIONAL GEOGRAPHY STANDARDS: 1, 7, 8, 14

GEOGRAPHIC THEMES: Place, Human-Environmental Interaction

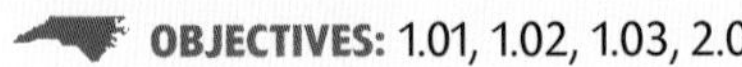 **OBJECTIVES:** 1.01, 1.02, 1.03, 2.01

Have cooperative groups of students make topographic models of South Asia using a laminated map as a base. Have students try to categorize the words below according to landforms, bodies of water, countries, and crops. Do not tell them the category types until after they have worked for 10 minutes.

Bodies of Water: Arabian Sea, Bay of Bengal, Indus, Ganges, Brahmaputra
Countries: India, Pakistan, Bangladesh, Afghanistan, Nepal, Bhutan, Sri Lanka
Mountains: Himalayas, Hindu Kush, Mount Everest, Vindhya, Western Ghats, Eastern Ghats
Crops: wheat, rice, peanuts, pepper, spices, cotton, jute , timber

The Kerala Province in southwest India is part of the coastal plain of South Asia. **Why are the coastal plains narrow in the region?**

Northern Plain

The Indus, Ganges, and Brahmaputra Rivers flow south out of mountain streams onto the broad northern plain. The lowland sweeps east from Pakistan through Bangladesh. Water drawn from the rivers and rainfall irrigates farmland. The rivers often flood, spreading rich soil across the plain.

The fertile northern plain produces so much food it is called India's "breadbasket." It is home to one of the world's largest concentrations of people. India's population officially topped 1 billion in May 2000. Almost two thirds of that population live in the northern plain subregion. Most are villagers who farm. Millions more live in such cities as Delhi, India; Kolkata, India; Karachi, Pakistan; and Dhaka, Bangladesh.

Deccan Plateau and South India

A low mountain range called the Vindhya (VIN·dyuh) separates the norther plain from southern India. This subregion has a more varied terrain. The Deccan (DECK·en) Plateau, an area of mostly level land that rises high above sea level, takes up most of the south. Along each side of the Deccan Plateau stand mountain range known as the Western Ghats (GATS) and Eastern Ghats. The Ghats are lower than the Himalayas, but they do affect the climate by keeping rain from reaching most of the Deccan. The plateau often suffers drought. It has fewer rivers that can be used for irrigation. Farmers grow crops that do not require much moisture.

Narrow plains lie between the Ghats and the coastlines. These coastal plains average less than 50 miles (81 km) wide along the western coast. Along the easter coast, they are a bit broader. Despite thei small size, these plains have favorable climate and soil for farming. Warm temperatures and rainfall produce abundant crops. This food supply supports large populations.

LESSON 1 REVIEW

Fact Follow-Up

1. Describe the size and relative location of South Asia.
2. What nations occupy the South Asian subcontinent?
3. What physical regions lie within South Asia?
4. Which region is called the "breadbasket" of India? Why?
5. What are the major rivers in South Asia?

Talk About It

1. How are the northern mountains both a benefit and a burden to people living on the northern plain?
2. If you could visit one of South Asia's subregions, which one would you choose? Why?
3. How are the rivers of South Asia both a benefit and a threat to people? Which affects life more—the benefits or threats?

LESSON 1 REVIEW

Fact Follow-Up Answers

1. At its widest point, South Asia stretches 2,000 miles west to east (four times the size of the east-west span of North Carolina) and extends about the same distance north to south. South Asia lies south of the Asian continent, west of Southeast Asia, and east of Southwest Asia. To the south, the peninsula juts into the Indian Ocean (locate on map).
2. India, Pakistan, Bangladesh, Afghanistan, Nepal, Bhutan, and Sri Lanka occupy the subcontinent.
3. There are three physical regions: northern mountains, a wide west-to-east plain south of the mountains, and a southern area occupied by a plateau, mountains, and coastal plains.
4. The northern plain is called the "breadbasket" of India because its fertile farmland produces so much food.
5. The Indus, Ganges, and Brahmaputra Rivers are the major rivers of South Asia.

Talk About It Answers

1. The northern mountains shield the plains from dry winds blowing out of Central Asia. Moisture-bearing winds blocked by the mountains' southern slopes create clouds that drop precipitation on the northern plains, bringing needed water for crops. The mountains, however, make transportation difficult.
2. Important points: Students should choose one region to visit and explain why they chose it. Note: The mountains may generate interest.
3. Important points: Students should state both advantages and disadvantages, then state which affects life more, explaining why. Note: People need water, but too much can bring disaster.

LESSON 2 Climates and the Land

Many outsiders think South Asia is hot all year. A British resident once joked that India had three climates—"hot, hotter, and hottest." That description is not accurate. :limates vary greatly across the subcontinent (see the climate map in he appendix).

:limate and Location

It is true that some places are very hot. aytime temperatures in the Thar Desert f the northwest can top 115° F (46° C). 1uch of southern India also has arid or emiarid climates. Yet the high mountains e cold. The northern plains can be cool.

Travel brochures often show South sia as a lush green land. They advertise ick jungles where tigers and other wild imals roam. Yet those images are not pical, either. Some of South Asia is dry. those areas the landscape is brown and eeless, and water is a precious resource.

Why do climates vary so much? In outh Asia, as elsewhere, location fluences climate. The British resident should have expected hot weather when he went to live in South Asia, a subtropical region near the Equator. Higher temperatures are normal when a region is located near the Equator. Sri Lanka and the southern tip of the South Asian mainland lie in the Tropics between latitudes 5°N and 10°N.

The cooler northern subregion has a humid subtropical climate, sometimes called subtropical monsoon. Temperatures are also lower because of South Asia's mountains. They protect some areas from high heat. Elevation blocks hot winds from Central Asian deserts. Wind patterns that change by season also affect climate by determining the time and quantity of rainfall.

KEY IDEAS

- Seasonal winds—called monsoons—are a key feature of South Asian life.
- Although climates vary within the subcontinent, much of South Asia has three seasons: dry, wet, and cold.
- South Asia's lands and climates produce many kinds of agricultural products.

KEY TERMS

jute
monsoon
vegetarian

Camel herds gather in the Thar Desert in India's Rajasthan Province. **What other climate regions does the subcontinent have?**

OBJECTIVES: 2.01, 2.02, 3.01

Discussion Questions

1 Based on where we live, how would you describe the climate of North Carolina? Is this an accurate assessment for the whole state?

Caption Answer

Besides arid climate regions, the subcontinent also has tropical, semiarid, and humid subtropical climate regions.

Science Activity

Climograph

OBJECTIVES: 1.01, 1.02, 1.03

Given climactic data for South Asia, have students design climographs for each location. Design rainfall as a vertical bar graph in the lower half of the graph as shown below (use blue color reference as the international color key for water). Plot temperature with dots connected as a line graph in the upper half of the graph (use red as a visual color reference to some mercury in thermometers).

1. Compare and contrast the monthly, seasonal, and yearly rainfall characteristics.
2. Analyze the seasonal and yearly temperature patterns.
3. Determine why various locations have their particular climate feature based upon their relative location.
4. Evaluate why latitude creates differences between Raleigh and India.

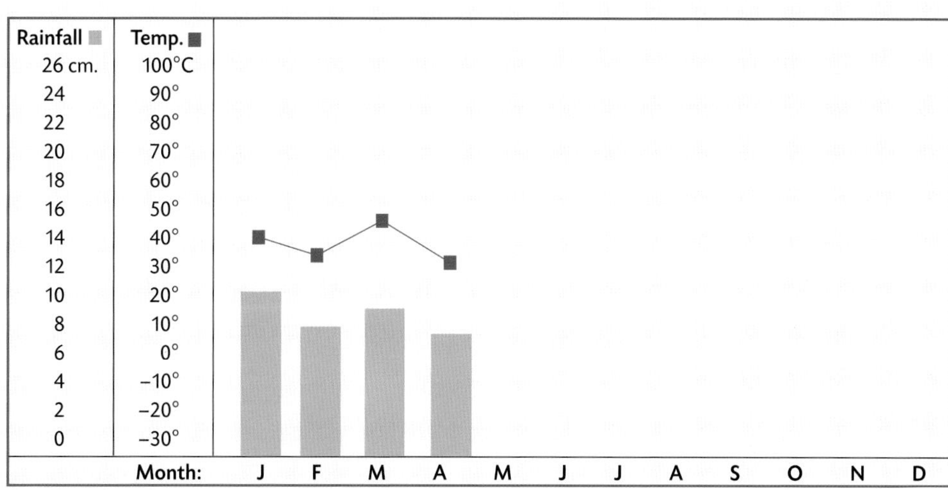

Discussion Questions

1 What would be some problems if the monsoons did not come when they were expected?

Caption Answer

The Thar Desert rarely receives rain from the monsoons. Much of the Indus Valley also remains dry. In southern India, the Western Ghats keep the Deccan from receiving much rain.

Science Activity

Which Way Do the Winds Blow?

NATIONAL GEOGRAPHY STANDARDS: 1, 4, 7, 8, 15

GEOGRAPHIC THEMES: Location, Place, Human-Environmental Interaction, Region

OBJECTIVES: 2.01, 3.04

Define winds with students: horizontal movement of air in response to differences in atmospheric pressure. Note that monsoons are seasonal winds (not the precipitation associated with these winds). Discuss with students that the Beaufort scale measures wind speeds. Students to answer the following questions:

1. Summer monsoon winds blow from what body of water onto India? *Arabian Sea*
2. Winter monsoon winds blow from what direction? *northeast*
3. What physical feature impacts South Asia's summer monsoon season? *Western Ghats*
4. Which physical feature in northwest South Asia is not affected by the summer monsoon winds? *Thar Desert, Indus Valley*
5. In what direction—clockwise or counterclockwise—do the monsoons blow? *counterclockwise*
6. What is the primary cause of monsoons? *difference in annual temperature patterns over land and water*

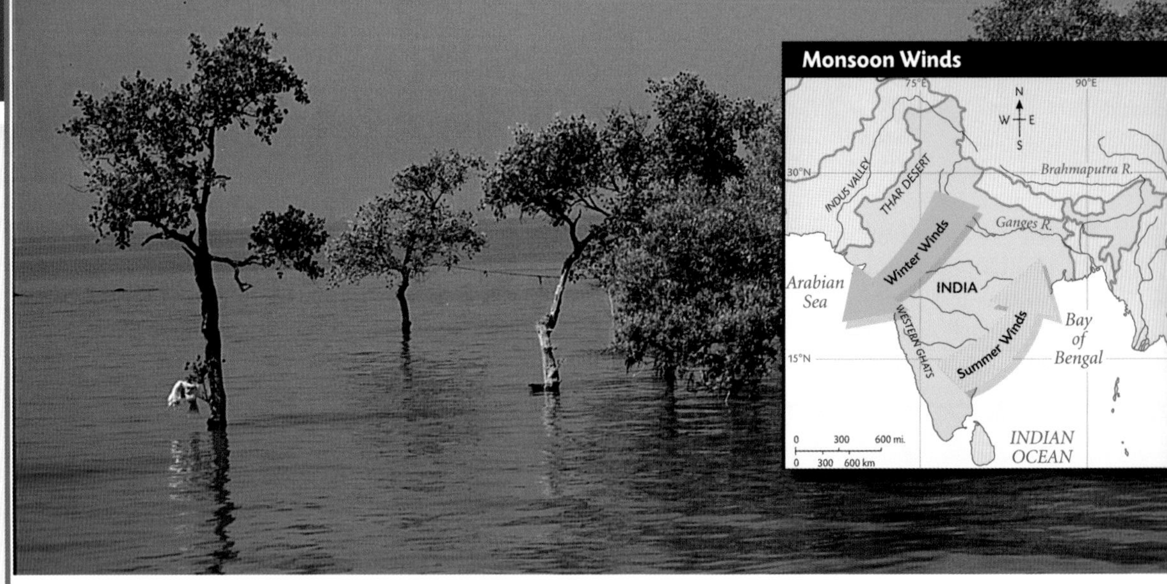

The coast of southwest India often floods during monsoon season. **What other places flood? Where is it dry in South Asia? Why?**

Climate and Rainfall

Much of the subcontinent has three seasons: dry, wet, and cool. The seasons, influenced by rainfall, rule everyone's life.

March, April, and May bring hard times. No rain falls for months. The thermometer soars. The air becomes still. A thick blanket of humidity presses on the land. Wealthy families flee to cool mountain resorts.

As the land heats up, rivers in the Deccan Plateau dry to a trickle. Plants shrivel and the ground is baked hard. By June, all eyes are on the huge, dark clouds that pile up from the south. They will bring rain and restore vegetation.

The dark clouds are the first sign of the summer, or wet, ***monsoon.*** A monsoon is a seasonal wind that blows between the ocean and nearby land. In summer, the monsoon blows over the land from the southwest. It brings heavy rains that last on and off until September. By November, the winds have reversed. They blow from the northeast. This winter, or dry, monsoon brings cool, dry air. Much of South Asia experiences pleasant weather. By April, the land heats up, and the cycle starts again.

Rainfall varies across South Asia. The summer monsoon hardly touches the northwest. The Thar Desert rarely receives rain. Much of the Indus Valley is also dry, so farmers have to irrigate crops. In southern India, the Western Ghats keep the Deccan from receiving much rain. Th monsoon drenches the southwestern coas of India.

The delta of the Ganges-Brahmaputra and nearby highlands in northeast India receive huge amounts of rain because monsoon winds pick up moisture as they cross the Bay of Bengal. One of the wettest places on earth is Cherrapunji, a town in northeastern India. It averages about 450 inches (11.4 m) of rain a year—ten times the amount that falls in most of North Carolina. In the Ganges Valley, 80 percent or more of the year's rain falls between June and August.

Word Origins

Monsoon is an Arabic word. It means the "time" or "season." In the days of sailing ships. Arab merchants crossed the Arabian Sea and Indian Ocean to carry on trade with East Africa and India. They had to wait for the "monsoon," the season when favorable winds blew either from the northeast or the southwest.

7. From what direction does a monsoon blow—cold toward warm or warm toward cold? *cold toward warm*
8. The Indian Ocean has a monsoon current. Speculate where this surface current is located. *Northern Indian Ocean—Indian North Equatorial Current/Northeast Monsoon Drift*
9. There is a tropical forest called a monsoon forest (also identified as dry forest, tropical deciduous forest). Where on this map would you predict this would be found? *Western Ghats*

Remind students that monsoons affect western Africa and northern Australia, and that Eurasian monsoons are limited to tropical and subtropical locations around the periphery of this huge landmass.

Extension You are a writer for *Monsoon* magazine. Write an informative caption to accompany this map to be included with your magazine story.

CONNECTIONS • GEOGRAPHY & LANGUAGE ARTS •

Describing Monsoons

India feels bone-dry before the monsoon. Then Moisture-bearing winds blowing off the Indian Ocean hit India's southwest coast. It takes about a month for rains to reach the north. When the summer monsoon arrives with its drenching downpours, people celebrate. All work stops.

The Indian writer Khushwant Singh describes the beginning of the monsoon:

> *There is a flash of lightning. The wind fills the black sails of the clouds. A profound shadow falls on the earth. There is another clap of thunder. Big drops of rain fall and dry up in the dust. A fragrant smell rises from the earth. Another flash of lightning and another crack of thunder like the roar of a hungry tiger. It has come!*

The rains are welcome even though they can bring disaster. "Wells and lakes fill up and burst their bounds," writes Singh. "In towns, gutters get clogged, and streets become turbid streams. In villages, mud walls of huts melt in the water and thatched roofs sag."

Rain-swollen rivers flood the land. They sweep away roads, livestock, homes, and even entire villages. If the rains are too heavy, many people will drown. Yet the rains renew the land. "Almost overnight grass begins to grow and leafless trees turn green," Singh writes. In fields everywhere, crops begin to grow.

Before and after a monsoon

Activity

Connections Cartoon

 **OBJECTIVES:** 2.01, 2.02, 2.03

Have students draw a series of cartoon or story frames and illustrate Khushwant Singh's description.

Activity

Crops and Rainfall

 **OBJECTIVES:** 1.01, 2.03, 3.01

Trace a laminated map of South Asia. Indicate where the following crops grow in Asia: rice, jute, sugarcane, wheat, grain sorghum. Create a key showing the amount of rainfall in each of the three regions. Explain the relationship between the amount of rainfall and the type of crops that grow in South Asia.

Background Information

Deadly Storms in Bangladesh

Bangladesh makes up the eastern two thirds of the Ganges–Bhramaputra (Brah • ma • POOH • tra) delta that empties into the Bay of Bengal. In April and May and late in the monsoon season from September through November, violent storms with winds of more than 100 miles per hour (161 km per hour) create 20-foot (6 m)-high waves, the height of a nine-story building, in the Bay of Bengal. These waves come crashing down onto the coastal areas. Their impact and the subsequent flooding often cause massive damage. In October 2000, more than 700,000 Bangladeshi were left homeless by the worst monsoon flooding in more than 100 years.

Discussion Questions

1 What are some crops grown in North Carolina?

2 How do our absolute and relative locations influence the agricultural products we grow?

Caption Answer

Wheat, rice, peanuts, pepper and other spices, and jute.

Science Activity

South Asia's Ecosystems

OBJECTIVES: 1.01, 1.02, 2.02

An ecosystem is made up of living things interacting with their environment in a certain place. Divide students into jigsaw groups (one each for location, climate, plants, animals, and challenges). Using the maps on 293 and 303 and other resources, fill in the data retrieval chart below on South Asia's ecosystems.

Jigsaw with one member of each original group, sharing with each of the other groups to complete chart. Debrief, noting areas that lack data and discuss why. Give additional attention to problems speculating cause(s), solution(s), and environmental impact.

Although many farmers use machines to pick tea leaves, some people still do the job by hand, as this woman in Sri Lanka is doing. **What are some of the other crops grown in the region?**

Land—A Basic Resource

Land is South Asia's most valuable resource. Most people in Pakistan, India, and Bangladesh are farmers. Almost three of every four people work the land. Yet farm life is difficult. Crops can fail if the monsoon rains come too late or too briefly.

Food Crops

South Asian farmers grow crops that vary from place to place. In the dry area west of the northern plain (including mo of Pakistan), farmers produce large whea crops on irrigated land. In the east and c the southwestern coast, heavy monsoons bring enough precipitation for farmers to grow rice. India ranks among the world's largest wheat and rice producers.

Farmers on the Deccan Plateau produce peanuts. Most of these are crushed and turned into cooking oil. Pepper and other spices grow well on the slopes of the Western Ghats. Tea grows i mountainous areas of India and Sri Lank South Asia leads the world in tea production.

Other Agricultural Products

South Asia is home to millions of cows, goats, and sheep. The region does not have livestock industries similar to those found in North and South America Hinduism, the most common religion in India, teaches respect for all life. Most Hindus are ***vegetarian,*** meaning they do not eat meat. Cattle are not slaughtered for food. Instead, they are allowed to roam the land and even the city streets. Cows are a traditional sign of wealth, valued for both milk and dung, which ha been used for fuel.

Muslims and people belonging to other religious faiths do eat meat. For these South Asians, goats and sheep are valued for food. Sheep also produce woo that herders either sell or spin themselves The long hair of goats raised in Kashmir in northern India can be woven. The expensive wool fabric is called cashmere. Cotton was first grown in South Asia more than 4,000 years ago. Today, the Deccan Plateau is a major cotton-producing region.

Jute is a major crop in Bangladesh. The coarse fibers of the jute plant are use to make burlap bags, rope, and carpets. Bangladesh sends jute to mills in India, where the fiber is turned into finished products and exported.

Ecosystem	Locations	Climate	Plants	Animals	Challenges
Tropical rain forest					
Mid-latitude deciduous forest					
Mixed forest (deciduous & coniferous)					
Tropical grassland					
Temperate grassland					
Desert scrub					
Highlands					

Sheep are raised in parts of South Asia where crops are not easily grown. Look at the map below. **Where would you expect herding areas to be in South Asia?**

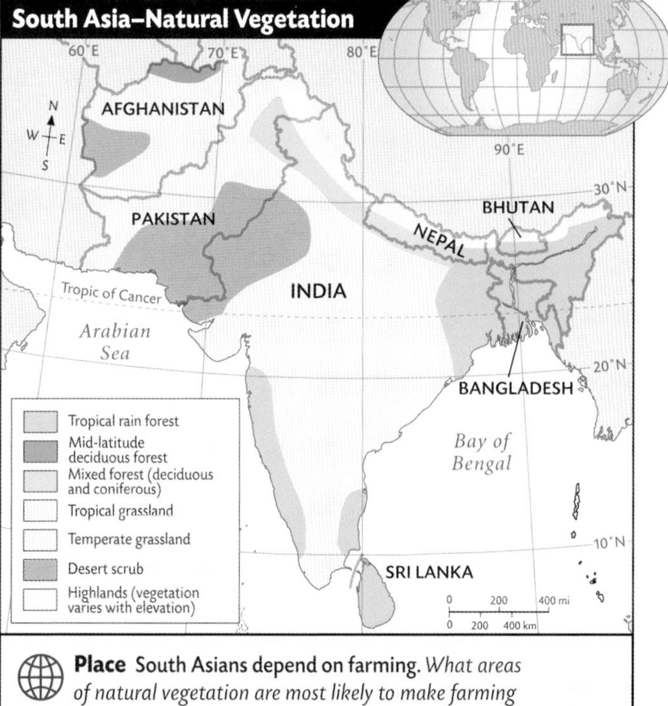

Place South Asians depend on farming. *What areas of natural vegetation are most likely to make farming more profitable? Why?*

imber

Long ago, South Asia's northern plain as densely forested. Gradually, a growing opulation cleared the land, using timber r building and fuel.

Today, only about a fifth of the ıbcontinent is forested. South Asia has aluable resources in the forests that main. Sri Lanka, Bangladesh, and India ontain tropical rain forests. The climate ıpports rare woods such as teak, ebony, ıd sandalwood, much of which is xported to furniture manufacturers. ecause they need the land for crops, llagers rarely replant trees, leading to osion during the monsoon.

LESSON 2 REVIEW

Fact Follow-Up

1. Describe the variations in climate in South Asia.
2. What is a monsoon? When and why do monsoons occur?
3. What animals and food crops are produced in South Asia?
4. What nonfood crop was first grown in South Asia?

Talk About It

1. Which climate region of South Asia would you most like to visit? Explain why.
2. How are monsoons both a disadvantage and an advantage to people of South Asia?
3. Why is there such great variation in climates in South Asia?
4. Why is erosion a problem?

Discussion Questions

1 Should there be an economic boycott on products made from these woods in order to preserve them? Keep in mind the land is used for crops, and the income is needed

In the temperate grassland

Tropical grassland because of adequate rainfall and better soil than tropical rain forest.

Vegetation Zones

NATIONAL GEOGRAPHY STANDARDS: 1, 3, 8

GEOGRAPHIC THEMES: Region, Place

OBJECTIVES: 1.02, 2.01

Answer the following questions using the map on this page.

1. Which vegetation zone covers most of South Asia? *tropical grassland*
2. Sri Lanka and Bangladesh are entirely in this vegetative area. *tropical rain forest*
3. Which zone are the Himalayas in? *highlands*
4. Northwest India and Southeast Pakistan are in this zone. *desert scrub*
5. Which nation has an area of deciduous forest? *Afghanistan*

LESSON 2 REVIEW

Fact Follow-Up Answers

1. The southern tip of the subcontinent is tropical, but the northern mountains are humid subtropical. Temperatures are cooler at high elevations. The northwest and southeast are arid and semiarid. Much of the subcontinent has three seasons: dry, wet, and cool.
2. A monsoon is a seasonal wind that blows from the ocean over nearby land. In summer, the monsoon blows over the land from the southwest, bringing heavy rains that last on and off until September. By November the winds have reversed. They blow from the northeast and bring cooler, dry air.
3. South Asians raise cattle, sheep, and goats. They grow wheat, rice, peanuts, peppers and other spices, and tea.
4. Cotton was first grown in South Asia.

Talk About It Answers

1. Important points: Students should choose one climate region and explain their choice. Note: The climate varies by month as well as by region. The northern mountains are cool and dry during the hot months of March, April, and May.
2. Monsoons bring needed rain to agricultural regions, but they often cause flooding.
3. Differences in elevation and variations in seasonal winds produce a variety of climates.
4. Villagers rarely replant the trees that are cut down for furiture making because they need the land for crops. The bare land erodes during the monsson.

OBJECTIVES: 2.02, 6.01, 11.04

Discussion Questions

1 What might be some problems a government of such a rapidly growing country would face?

Caption Answer

Newcomers keep pouring in from the countryside.

Activity

Pedicab Creative Writing

OBJECTIVES: 3.01, 4.01

Assign students the following prompt: Imagine you are the owner of a pedicab like the one pictured on page 304. Invent a story telling of a day as a pedicab driver in your hometown.

LESSON 3 People and Their Environment

KEY IDEAS

- South Asian nations face the problems of freeing their people from poverty and providing adequate education and health care.
- India has had some success in improving the lives of its people.

KEY TERMS

Green Revolution
population density
population explosion

A young man pedals his pedicab—a bicycle taxi—through the packed streets of Delhi, India. He bumps through potholes, dodging trucks and buses. He ignores the heat, dust, and swarms of people.

The pedicab driver works in one of the most crowded cities in the world. Delhi's population grows by thousands every day. Newcomers pour in from the countryside. The pedicab driver is lucky to have a job because many people do not. Life in the city is hard, but it is harder still in poor rural villages. South Asian cities offer dreams to millions. All hope to improve their lives. The ***population explosion*** —the dramatic multiplication of people—makes these dreams harder to reach.

Densely Settled South Asia

Delhi's millions are merely a small part of the more than 1.6 billion people living in South Asia. The subcontinent is home to one of the heaviest concentrations of the 6.5 billion people living on earth. One out of every four persons in the world lives in a South Asian nation.

The population continues to grow. India's population increases at a rate of 1.6 percent a year. It surpassed 1 billion i[n] May 2000. India will outrank China as the world's most populous nation by 2050.

South Asia's population patterns are similar to Africa's. Both have large cities, many villages, and large, almost empty, spaces. People are not evenly distributed throughout South Asia. Few live in the northern mountains. Most live in farming

Pedicab drivers pedal their passengers through the crowded streets of Delhi, India. **Why are South Asian cities steadily growing?**

llages, but the number and size of the llages vary. Bangladesh is almost exactly e same size as North Carolina, yet its pulation is nearly half that of the nited States.

Population density—the number of ople living in a square mile or kilometer land—is greater in Bangladesh than in kistan. Bangladesh has ample rain and od soil. The nation has little land left r new farms. Much of Pakistan is so dry at it cannot be farmed. Large areas of kistan are empty.

his plantation in Bangladesh grows bananas. **Why do so many people live in this nation?**

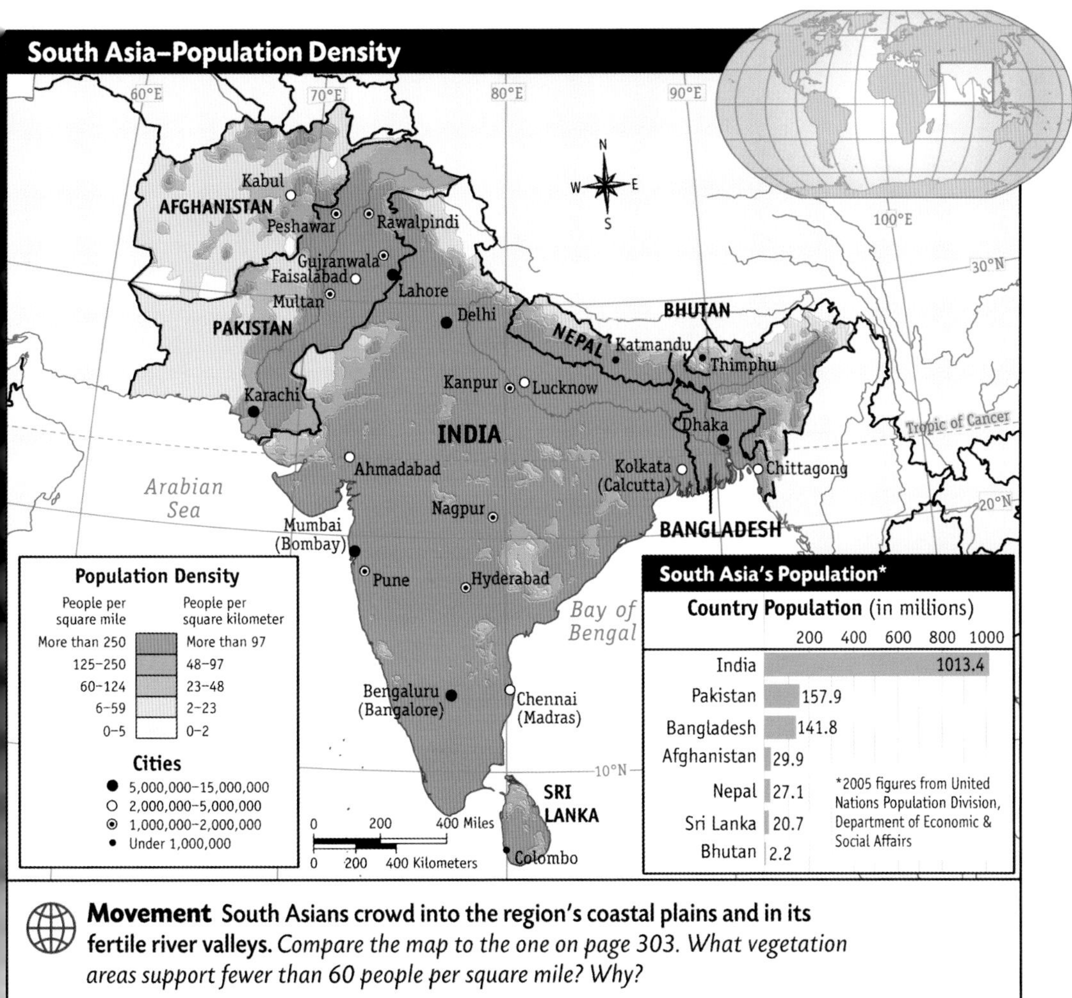

Movement **South Asians crowd into the region's coastal plains and in its fertile river valleys.** *Compare the map to the one on page 303. What vegetation areas support fewer than 60 people per square mile? Why?*

Desert scrub, highlands and some tropical rain forest. These areas cannot support many people because they are not agricultural.

Discussion Questions

1 Why would fewer people live in the northern part of India?

Bangladesh has ample rain and good soil.

Population Cartograms

OBJECTIVES: 1.01, 1.02, 1.03

A cartogram is a map showing information with the size of the land areas in proportion to the information being given. Cartograms can be used to show population. On a cartogram, each country is drawn in proportion to its size of population rather than its area. So a country having a large population will be shown as larger than another country with a smaller population. A country with a large land area will not necessarily look large on a cartogram. Have students make a cartogram of the South Asian region using the most recent statistics for the population of each of the seven countries.

Estimate with students about which country will require more paper/coloring to represent its population on a cartogram (India). Given 1 inch equals 2 million people, have students calculate approximately how many inches will be needed for each South Asian nation:

India: 507 Pakistan: 79
Bangladesh: 71 Afghanistan: 15
Nepal: 14 Sri Lanka: 10
Bhutan: 1

Designate one color for each country. Using graph paper with 1-inch grids, let each inch represent 2 million people. Color that area on the graph paper. (India will require a lot of inches, at least six 8½ by 11-inch-size sheets of graph paper, and it will be more sensible to color an entire sheet of graph paper for this country than inch by inch.)

Display cartogram graph paper inches in the shape of each country's political boundary in a scheme giving each country's location within South Asia.

Discussion Questions

1 What role do you think education could have in slowing the rapid population growth?

Caption Answer

For centuries, South Asians have seen large families as protection. Farmers need families to help them work the land.

Activity

Temperature Word Problem

OBJECTIVES: 2.02

The deserts of South Asia sometimes reach high temperatures of 115° Fahrenheit and the mountains fall to temperatures as low as 30° F below zero. What is the range of the temperature?

Answer 145° F

Extension Assist ELL students by setting up the problem.

Activity

Describing the Ganges

OBJECTIVES: 4.03, 12.01

Assign students the following prompt: Pretend that you have taken a trip to see the Ganges River. Describe for someone who has never seen it what it looked like. Include sights, sounds, and people you may have seen. Include at least one simile or metaphor to describe part of this scene.

A group of Indian boys are reading. **Why have Indians tended to have large families?**

Why South Asia's Population Grows

Most South Asian families traditionally had many children. The total population, however, did not grow much. Disease and food shortages caused people to die about as fast as new babies were born.

By the 1920s, people were living longer. Medical care improved. Food supplies increased, and railways moved food to regions suffering from food shortages.

These changes caused the population to grow. Then India's government tried to encourage people to plan smaller families. These efforts have had limited success.

Farm families, especially those living in productive regions, are responsible for much of South Asia's population growth. These families continue to have large numbers of children.

Farmers have only a few tools to cultivate the land, so they depend on the family for help. Children tend animals, weed, or collect fuel. Older children care for aging parents.

For centuries, South Asians have seen large families as protection. Despite government efforts, they have a hard tim[e] believing their lives will be better with fewer children.

What would YOU do?

In India and Africa, expanding human populations and wildlife often collide. In India, wild tigers have become an endangered species. Until the 1880s, India's forests were home to thousands of these magnificent animals, but today only a few are left. Many were killed by hunters. Others could not survive the cutting of forests. Do you think wild tigers ought to be saved? If you do, what would you do to save them?

Background Information

Population Slowdown in India

India has succeeded in slowing population growth and lowering the birth rate with the help of family planning programs. However, even though India's rate of population growth has dropped, its absolute increases in population are greater than ever. With more than 1 billion people, India adds more than 18 million people yearly, even with its declining rate of population growth. Today one out of every six people in the world lives in India. Only China has more people. Pakistan has been less successful in curbing population growth. Its population has risen not only because of natural increase but also due to the war in neighboring Afghanistan in the 1980s, which brought 3.5 million Afghan refugees into Pakistan. More refugees fled the Taliban and the United States War on terror, too.

mproving Daily Lives

Skyrocketing population growth poses allenges. Each child needs education and od. All South Asian nations struggle to eet these basic needs. Too many people e too poor to have enough food, medical re, or even permanent homes. Among uth Asia's nations, India has had more ccess in meeting some needs.

uilding Industry

India's determination to build industry s largely benefitted its people. Leaders ew that industry is central to creating a ong nation. The opening of factories, ines, and businesses has provided jobs. dia's industrial capacity is immense cause of its many natural resources and rge workforce. People's lives will ntinue to improve as India manufactures ore and more goods for world markets.

In the 1950s, India's leaders began anning for economic expansion. India rrowed money from wealthier nations d private investors. It built oil and sugar fineries and wood-processing plants. ctories produced textiles, automobiles, comotives, cement, fertilizers, and paper.

India then built factories that oduced such consumer goods as TVs, deo recorders, computers, and watches. the 1990s, India had become one of the n largest industrial nations in the world. any people moved to cities to work.

nproving Agriculture

At the same time, India also set out to ise agricultural production and improve llage life. Its large population needed all e crops farmers could produce. Indian rmers feed far more people today than ey did 60 years ago. Wheat production India has tripled since 1967. angladesh exports rice to Japan.

Improvements in agricultural yields ere due in part to the ***Green Revolution.*** ientists developed disease-resistant, high-elding plants. Agricultural specialists ught farmers improved cultivation ethods. Rivers were dammed and lldozers dug farm ponds. Water supplies for irrigation increased. Crop yields increased dramatically.

Quality of Life

Better standards of living have come from basic changes—a better food supply, cleaner water, improved village sanitation, vaccination programs, and more available healthcare. Life expectancy—the age at which people are expected to die—has shot upwards. Sixty years ago, the average villager might have lived 32 years. In contrast, a baby girl born in 2005 has a life expectancy of more than 65 years. Infant mortality has declined.

Irrigation projects have improved food production. **How has that success caused population to increase?**

Customs

In every country or culture people have special ways of greeting one another. One formal greeting in India requires each person to put his or her own palms together, holding the hands beneath the chin. As palms touch, each person gives a slight nod of the head toward the other.

Discussion Questions

1 What steps has India taken to industrialize and modernize?

Caption Answer

More and better quality food has helped people live longer.

Research Activity

Almanac Comparison

 **OBJECTIVES:** 1.01, 1.02, 1.03

Have students use an almanac (print or online) to compare the United States to nations of South Asia. Create a table or spreadsheet with these nations written on the top row: United States, India, Pakistan, Afghanistan, Nepal, Bhutan, Bangladesh. Compare the nations using the following categories listed down the first column of the table:

Topics to be compared
Population, population density, per capita GDP, literacy rate, male life expectancy, female life expectancy, monetary unit, GNP, area, government, economy chief crops, economy chief minerals, and economy chief industries

Have students answer the following questions based on the information from the above activity:

1. What is the average literacy rate among South Asian countries? How does this average compare to the literacy rate of the United States?
2. What is the predominant form of government in South Asia?
3. What would explain the low GDP of Nepal? If you were the finance minister of Nepal, what would you do to improve the GDP of your people?

Discussion Questions

1 How has a better standard of living been a mixed blessing in India?

Caption Answer

Irrigation, training in agriculture, and improved water supplies have also helped South Asian villagers.

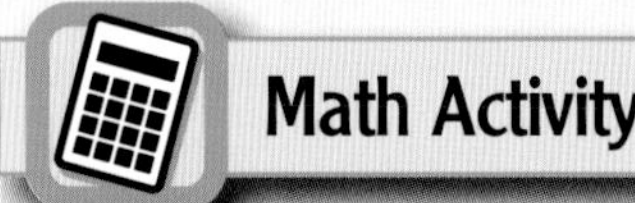

Math Activity

Database Table

OBJECTIVES: 1.01, 1.02, 1.03

Have students create a database comparing information about India with other nations. Have students research the data.

List vertically: country, population, square miles, population density, GNP, per capita GDP, cars, TV, radios, telephones, male life expectancy, births/1,000, deaths/1,000, literacy percentage, years of education required, female life expectancy, and infant mortality

List horizontally: China, Japan, Singapore, India, Taiwan, Hong Kong, Bangladesh, North Korea, South Korea, and the United States

Children study at a primary school in Andhra Pradesh. **What other government programs have helped South Asian villagers?**

Village Life

India has benefited from a better educational system. Most villages now have a primary school. In 1950, only 16 percent of the nation could read. Today, about 60 percent of the nation is literate. Educated citizens make better workers and strengthen a nation.

Other government programs have helped farm families add to their incomes. Programs encourage villagers to expand production of hand-made goods. Jewelry, pottery, and brass housewares are manufactured in small factories. Textiles are woven on household looms. Leather goods are tanned in village workshops. Most of these products are then sold in markets outside the villages.

Despite these efforts, village life continues to be hard. Millions of villagers remain poor. Those villagers who have received more nutritious diets, health services, and some education have a chance for a better life.

LESSON 3 REVIEW

Fact Follow-Up

1. Describe population growth and population density in South Asia.
2. What projects has the Indian government undertaken to improve industry and agriculture?
3. What is the Green Revolution? How has it affected South Asia?
4. Describe improvements in education in India.

Talk About It

1. Why does South Asia have a population problem?
2. Which government effort do you think was most necessary to deal with the population problem? Why?
3. Suppose India had concentrated all its efforts on industrial growth. Would that have solved its population problems? Explain your answer.

LESSON 3 REVIEW

Fact Follow-Up Answers

1. South Asia is home to one of the heaviest concentrations of people on earth. One out of every four persons in the world lives in a South Asian nation. The population density is greatest in cities, along the coasts, and in the river valleys.
2. In the 1950s, India's leaders borrowed money from wealthy nations and private investors to expand industry. Factories began producing consumer goods. By the 1990s, India had become one of the ten largest industrial nations in the world. In agriculture, scientists developed disease-resistant, high-yielding plants. The government built dams, dug farm ponds, and improved irrigation. Wheat production in India has tripled since 1967.
3. The Green Revolution refers to the rise in crop yields from government-sponsored improvements in agriculture. Life expectancy has risen. More people enjoy a better standard of living.
4. Most villages now have a primary school. By 1995, almost half of the nation could read.

Talk About It Answers

1. Life expectancy has risen, but people are still having large families. With an ever-growing population, it is difficult to make resources available to everyone.
2. Important points: Students should choose one government program and explain their choice. Note: Education about the importance of the problem is important.
3. Important points: Students should take a position and explain the position they have taken. Note: Most industrialized nations show a decrease in population as people become more prosperous. Over time, the rate of population growth declines.

Analyzing, Interpreting, Creating, and Using Resources and Materials

Comparing Landform Subregions in South Asia

SKILL GOALS NORTH CAROLINA SOCIAL STUDIES skill

When you need to make sense of a great deal of information, a data retrieval chart or graphic organizer is often helpful. You have already worked with these charts. By now, you have a variety of them to choose from. Which will enable you to organize information so you can make comparisons, identify relationships, and make summaries?

If Mark Twain could feel awed by India, how do you feel as you try to figure out the gigantic puzzle that South Asia sometimes seems to be? The subcontinent is so large with so many people, nations, landforms, climate variations, and other features that it is difficult to remember "what goes where."

To select the most appropriate graphic organizer, you need first to decide what information will be organized. In this case, you will be organizing information about the three physical subregions of South Asia: the northern mountains, the broad plains south of the mountains, and the southern subregion of a plateau, mountains, and coastal plains.

A web chart might be used. Examine the sample shown that lists features of the mountain subregion.

Suppose you were to construct a web chart for each of the three subregions. How easy would it be to use the three charts to make comparisons or to make summaries?

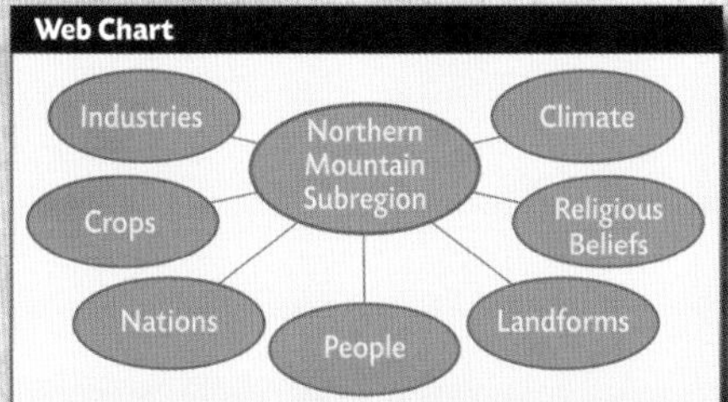

A data retrieval chart like the one below might be better. Notice that this chart directs you to record (and organize) information in certain categories such as "Crops." Once you have organized information in these ways, it is easy to make comparisons.

Complete the data retrieval chart, adding categories you think are needed, and see how easy it is to compare South Asia's subregions!

Comparing the Three Subregions of South Asia

Categories	Northern Mountains	Plains/Flatlands	Southern Subregion
Nations			
Landforms			
Climate			
Crops			
Industry			
Religion			
People			

Skill Lesson Review

1. Which graphic organizer do you think is more useful when you need to compare two or three items—a web chart or data retrieval chart? Why? *A data retrieval chart arranges a limited amount of information very clearly.*
2. When do you think a web chart is more useful than a data retrieval chart? *A larger amount of information, or information that is less easily categorized, works better with a web chart.*
3. How many categories did you have in your data retrieval chart? Did you have too many, too few, or just the right number? *Students should compare answers.*
4. Look ahead to Chapters 16–18, skimming the pages for new topics. If you keep your web and data retrieval charts, could you add to them for an in-depth study of regions or subregions? *Yes. Students should keep their charts and add to them.*
5. What are some other useful and convenient ways of organizing information such as you used in this skill lesson? Would one of these be better than the ones used here? Why? *Charts arranged by topic and subregion would create different connections.*

Teaching This Skill Lesson

Materials Needed textbooks, paper, pencils, reference books, overhead projector, acetate, marking pens, transparency of data retrieval chart on page 309 (enlarged)

Classroom Organization whole class, small group, pair or individual

Introducing the Lesson Have students look at the map on page 305. Ask them to tell you how Afghanistan and Sri Lanka are different; ask what the two nations have in common.

Refer to the two charts on page 309, discuss how each might be used. Ask such questions as: Which looks easier to use? Which would be better for analyzing one nation? Which would be better for comparing nations. Note that students will be comparing not nations but the three subregions of Asia in this skill lesson.

If possible, enlarge the data retrieval chart on page 309 and make a transparency of it or sketch it on acetate. Using the overhead projector, help students fill in the Nations category using the map on page 305.

Lesson Development Tell students they will be completing the data retrieval chart for homework. Distribute large sheets of paper and allow students to draw their charts, cautioning them to leave plenty of space for entering information. They are to use information from Chapters 15–18 and any available reference books.

Conclusion When students return with their data retrieval charts, divide the class into small groups to compare charts and help each other complete charts. Have students use their charts to answer questions such as the following:

1. Which subregion has the most industry? the least?
2. What is the major religion in the Northern Mountains? the Southern Region?
3. What nations are in the plains/flatlands?

Ask again how Afghanistan and Sri Lanka are alike and different. Have students comment on the ease of answering such a question now that the data retrieval charts are complete. Post students' charts.

CHAPTER 15 REVIEW

Lessons Learned

LESSON 1
Location, Landforms, and Regions
South Asia's physical characteristics have played an important role in shaping the lives of its people. Mountains along the region's northern edge have helped isolate it from surrounding people. Yet within the giant peninsula, different landforms have provided a variety of environments.

LESSON 2
Climate and the Land
All of South Asia is located in the lower, hot latitudes of the Tropics. Yet differences in elevation and variations in seasonal winds provide a variety of climates. Heavy rainfall that comes with shifts in winds have been essential to life in South Asia.

LESSON 3
People and Their Environment
Most of South Asia has experienced rapid population growth. No nation in the region has had the resources to provide vital services for all its people. India, however, has generally been more successful than others in providing for its people.

Talk About It

1. How have mountains influenced the movement of people, goods, and ideas in South Asia?
2. How would life be different in South Asia if there were no monsoons?
3. Which has been more important to life in South Asia—mountains or monsoons? Explain your answer.
4. Suppose you could spend a month in one region of South Asia. Which region would you choose? During which month would you visit? Why?
5. Why is rapid population growth a problem for South Asian nations?
6. Imagine that you are an advisor to a South Asian government. What advice would you give with regard to population growth? Explain why you would give this advice.

Mastering Mapwork

HUMAN-ENVIRONMENTAL INTERACTION

Use the map on page 293 to answer these questions:

1. Locate Bangladesh. What environmental features would you expect to affect the lives of people living in this country?
2. Locate Nepal and Bhutan. Do people influence the environment or does the environment influence people more in these countries? Explain your answer.
3. Locate New Delhi and Madras. Would you expect the patterns of human-environmental interaction to be the same in these two places? Why?
4. How would you expect patterns of human-environmental interaction to be different in the Northern Plain and in the Great Indian (Thar) Desert?

310 Chapter 1

Talk About It

1. The northern mountains have isolated the people of South Asia from the Asian continent. Movement is easier through the lower passes of the Hindu Kush in the northwest. People, goods, and ideas from Europe and Southwest Asia came to the subcontinent by this land route.
2. Important points: Students should be encouraged to suggest a number of ways in which life would be different. Note: The rivers would not be filled every year, and the subcontinent might be desert.
3. Important points: Students should choose either mountains or monsoons and explain their choice. Note: The monsoons bring needed rain for crops over much of the subcontinent. The mountains, however, have made monsoons possible, are the source of the major rivers of the subcontinent, and have been a barrier to movement, isolating the subcontinent for much of its history.
4. Important points: Students should choose both a region and a month and give reasons for their choices. Note: Students should be aware that the monsoons bring great changes to regions. April in the mountains would be cool and dry.
5. All South Asian nations are struggling to provide food, education, medical care, and housing for more and more people.
6. Important points: Students should state what advice they would give and explain why they would give that advice. Note: Education may be the most direct method of dealing with the problem.

Mastering Mapwork

1. Most of Bangladesh lies between 0 and 667 feet (200 meters) above sea level. Many mouths of the Ganges River empty into the Bay of Bengal in Bangladesh. Flooding is a strong possibility.
2. Important points: Students should take a position and explain it. Note: Most of Nepal and nearly all of Bhutan are located in an area of very high mountains. It is likely that the environment would influence the lives of people more than people would influence the environment. Transportation and farming would be difficult in these areas.
3. Important points: Students should state a position and support it with reasons. Note: New Delhi lies south of the Himalayas, is located in a flat, dry area, is at a higher latitude than Madras. Madras is located on the Bay of Bengal in a flat area, is at a lower latitude than New Delhi.
4. The Northern Plain is well watered from major rivers and lies south of the Himalayas within the monsoon area. The Thar Desert is at a higher elevation; the term "desert" implies little rainfall.

Go to the Source

Analyzing Historic Documents

Read the letter below from Great Mughul Jahangir to James I, King of England and Scotland (1617). Answer the questions using specific references from the text. Jahangir ruled the Mughal Empire from 1605 until 1627.

When your Majesty shall open this letter let your royal heart be as fresh as a sweet garden. Let all people make reverence at your gate; let your throne be advanced higher; amongst the greatness of the kings of the prophet Jesus, let your Majesty be the greatest, and all monarchies derive their counsel and wisdom from your breast as from a fountain, that the law of the majesty of Jesus may revive and flourish under your protection.

The letter of love and friendship which you sent and the presents, tokens of your good affections toward me, I have received by the hands of your ambassador, Sir Thomas Roe (who well deserves to be your trusted servant), delivered to me in an acceptable and happy hour; upon which mine eyes were so fixed that I could not easily remove them to any other object, and have accepted them with great joy and delight.

Upon which assurance of your royal love I have given my general command to all the kingdoms and ports of my dominions to receive all the merchants of the English nation as the subjects of my friend; that in what place soever they choose to live, they may have free liberty without any restraint; and at what port soever they shall arrive, that neither Portugal nor any other shall dare to molest their quiet; and in what city soever they shall have residence, I have commanded all my governors and captains to give them freedom answerable to their own desires; to sell, buy, and to transport into their country at their pleasure.

For confirmation of our love and friendship, I desire your Majesty to command your merchants to bring in their ships of all sorts of rarities and rich goods fit for my palace; and that you be pleased to send me your royal letters by every opportunity, that I may rejoice in your health and prosperous affairs; that our friendship may be interchanged and eternal.

Your Majesty is learned and quick-sighted as a prophet, and can conceive so much by few words that I need write no more.

The God of heaven give you and us increase of honor.

Questions

1. Why does Moghul Jahangir write this letter? Who is his intended audience?
2. Why do you think Jahangir, a Muslim, mentions Jesus in his letter?
3. Why do you think Portugal is mentioned in this letter?
4. Who is Sir Thomas Roe?
5. What do you think "tokens of your good affection" refer to?
6. What is Jahangir asking James I to do?
7. Why do you think that the Moghul Jahangir is allowing the English to trade?
8. What is the tone of this document? How do you know?

Go to the Source

Go to the Source

OBJECTIVES: 4.01, 4.02, 5.01, 5.04, 7.01, 7.02, 8.01, 11.02, 11.03; Skills 1.01, 1.08, 2.01, 3.05, 4.03, 4.06

On February 6, 1613, a treaty was arranged between the English and Jahangir. Per this agreement, an English ambassador was to reside at the Moghul Court. It also granted the English permission to establish a factory in Surat. Sir Thomas Roe was the first English Ambassador at the Court of the Great Moghul. He laid the foundation of trade with India. A link to this document can be found at **NCJouneys.com.**

ANSWERS

1. It is a response to the English request to open trade in India. Jahangir is allowing the English to come and trade in India. James I is his intended audience.
2. He possibly is appealing to the Christian king of England, James I.
3. Portugal was a rival to England for trade in the region.
4. James I's ambassador or representative
5. James I sent the Moghul gifts. This was the custom of the time to exchange gifts as a sign of respect or to hopefully gain favor of someone.
6. "Bring in their ships of all sorts of rarities and rich goods fit for my palace."
7. To increase his own wealth and riches
8. The tone is quite friendly. The Moghul is thanking James I and praising him. He is allowing the English to come in and trade and offers to protect the English.

How to Use the Chapter Review

There are three sections in the Chapter Review: Talk About It, Mastering Mapwork, and Go to the Source. Use the Vocabulary Worksheets and the Chapter Review Worksheet in the Teacher's Resource Guide for additional reinforcement and preparation for the Chapter Assessments. The chapter and lesson reviews and the Chapter Review Worksheets are the basis of the assessment for each chapter.

Talk About It questions encourage students to speculate about the content of the chapter and are suitable for class or small-group discussion. They are not intended to be assigned for homework.

Mastering Mapwork has students apply one or more of the Five Themes of Geography to maps within the chapter.

Go to the Source activities allow students to analyze a primary source that relates to the content of the chapter. The questions and activities familiarize students with different types of primary sources and also build content-reading skills.

South Asia's Enduring Traditions

Social Studies Strands

Cultures and Diversity
Religions of South Asia

Historic Perspectives
Imperialism
Independence
Nonviolence

Individual Development and Identity

Government and Active Citizenship

North Carolina Standard Course of Study

Goal 4 The learner will identify significant patterns in the movement of people, goods, and ideas over time and place in Africa, Asia, and Australia.

Goal 8 The learner will assess the influence and contributions of individuals and cultural groups in Africa, Asia, and Australia.

Goal 11 The learner will recognize the common characteristics of different cultures in Africa, Asia, and Australia.

Goal 12 The learner will assess the influence of major religions, ethical beliefs, and values of cultures in Africa, Asia, and Australia.

Teaching & Assessment

- English Language Learner Modified Lesson Plans for this chapter are found in the Teacher Resource Guide.
- *ExamView® Assessment Suite* is provided at **NCJourneys.com.** It includes customizable assessments for all chapters. Paper tests are also available in the Teacher Resource Guide. See pages T16–T17 for information about how to use the assessments and the Scoring Guide.

Worksheets

Worksheets and answer keys are found both in the Teacher Resource Guide and at **NCJourneys.com**, including Reading Guides, Reading Strategies, Chapter Reviews, English Language Learner and others.

ACTIVITIES AND INTEGRATIONS

SOCIAL STUDIES
● Gandhi's Scrapbook, p. 312B
Geography of Buddhism and Hinduism, p. 317
▲ ■ Kinesthetic Caste, p. 320
Mapping Investigation, p. 323
Divali Festival, p. 324
★ The East India Company, p. 324
Jewel of the British Empire, p. 325
Skill Lesson: Change Through Nonviolent Resistance, p. 329

READING/LANGUAGE ARTS	READING/LANGUAGE ARTS OBJECTIVES
Analogies, p. 312B	2.01
▲ Activator, p. 312	1.03
Writing Prompt: Gandhi, p. 314	3.03
★ Language Diffusion, p. 314	6.01
★ Travel Brochures, p. 314	2.02
Create a Game, p. 316	2.01
▲ ■ In My Next Life, p. 319	3.01
● To Drink or Not To Drink, p. 320	3.01
Debate About Marriage, p. 321	1.03
● ■ Satellite Dish, p. 322	4.01
Imperialism Compare and Contrast, p. 325	2.02
★ Colonial Role Play, p. 326	2.01
Ganghi's Salt March, p. 327	2.01
Interview, p. 328	1.03
Go to the Source: Understanding Protest Movements, p. 331	2.01, 3.01, 3.02

MATHEMATICS	MATHEMATICS OBJECTIVES
Population Growth, p. 312B	1.01, 1.02, 1.03
Diffusion of Language, p. 313	4.01

TECHNOLOGY	TECHNOLOGY OBJECTIVES
Travel Brochures, p. 314	3.01, 3.07
Gods and Godesses of Hinduism, p. 318	3.01, 3.10
● Mughal Rule, p. 323	3.01, 3.11

VISUAL ARTS	VISUAL ARTS OBJECTIVES
▲ ■ Puppetry from India, p. 312B	2.04, 6.01
▲ ■ Taj Mahal Freestyle, p. 315	2.04, 7.02
▲ ■ Taj Mahal Paper Model, p. 315	2.04, 7.02
Model Indian Village, p. 321	1.02, 4.01

CHARACTER AND VALUES EDUCATION	TRAITS
Writing Prompt: Gandhi, p. 312	respect
What Would You Do?, p. 322	self-discipline, integrity

● Basic Activities ★ Challenging Activities ▲ English Language Learner Novice ■ English Language Learner Intermediate

Chapter Activities

Population Growth

OBJECTIVES: 1.01, 1.02, 1.03, 2.02

The class may be divided into one small group per country for this activity.

Option A

Use the rate of population increase to determine the approximate length of time it will take for the population of your country to double. (Note: You may use the Rule of 72 to determine the approximate length of time it will take for the population to double. By this rule, the rate of increase may be divided into 72 to give the length of time it will take for a number to double.)

Option B

Use the following population doubling time information to determine the number of years before population will double.

Annual growth rate

0.5%	139 yrs.	2.5	28
1.0	69	3.0	23
1.5	46	3.5	20
2.0	35	4.0	17

	Annual growth rate percentage	Years before population will double
Afghanistan	3	24
Bangladesh	1.64	44
Bhutan	2.12	34
India	1.26	32
Maldives	2.27	32
Nepal	1.83	39
Pakistan	1.98	36
Sri Lanka	.67	107

Option C

Each group should determine the effect of rapid population growth on their country. What would happen to population density? Students should design a graph labeled "years" on the horizontal axis and "population growth" on the vertical axis. Plot population growth.

Prepare a presentation for the people of each country explaining what needs to be done and why.

Gandhi's Scrapbook

OBJECTIVES: 8.01

Using information from the book as well as additional information about Mohandas K. Gandhi, have students make a scrapbook or digital story/PowerPoint presentation representing important events and dates from his life. Use a variety of visuals to enhance the scrapbook, including diplomas, certificates, pictures, letters, and mementos that you create to fill the pages of the scrapbook.

Extension ELL students should use ELL-friendly Web sites to find information and visuals for the scrapbook.

Puppetry from India

OBJECTIVES: 12.02, 12.03

Puppetry from India dates back 1,000 years. It spread in popularity throughout Southeast Asia.

Materials matte board or thick paper, scissors, metal brads, ¼-inch wooden dowels (various lengths), tape, glue, pencils, drawing paper, tempera paint or markers, hole puncher

Students will create a character(s) for a puppet show. On drawing paper, they should practice drawing the character. On matte board or heavy paper have them draw the character to desired size (at least 18 inches is recommended). Where the body bends (shoulder, elbow, hand, waist, knee, and ankle) should be the spots where the body of the puppet will be separated. Students should cut the puppet up into the different parts. Paint with tempera paint or color the parts with markers. Punch holes at all the joints. Connect with metal brads. Attach one wooden dowel to the back of the puppet with tape or glue. Attach another to the shoulder or to one of the hands.

OBJECTIVES: 8.01, 12.01

Analogies are useful to help students make associations with prior knowledge. Read the analogies aloud and ask students to identify the relationship between the terms. As an extension, ask students to write their own analogies using key terms or places discussed in the chapter.

reincarnation : Hindu/Buddhist :: resurrection : Christian/Muslim (is believed by)

caste : birth :: class : achievement (is based on)

Dalit : lowest caste :: Brahmins : highest caste (are in the)

abolish : establish :: end : begin (is opposite of)

burden : relief :: pain : comfort (is the opposite of)

water buffalo : South Asia :: cattle : Masai :: camel : Bedouin (is prized animal of)

partition : divide :: union : unite (noun to verb)

Mohandas K. Gandhi : India :: Martin Luther King : United States (civil rights leader of)

majority : minority :: 60 percent : 40 percent (is greater than)

Teaching Strategies

In this chapter, students will study the history and culture of India. Because of the large amount of material in this chapter, you will need to allocate more time for this chapter to ensure understanding.

Discussion Questions

1 What have you heard about Mohandas K. Gandhi?

Activator

OBJECTIVES: 12.01

Activators are great tools to use in order to "hook" the attention of the students. Reading picture books or stories is an excellent way to build interest in the subject and is also a great way to integrate language arts into the social studies curriculum.

Buddha, by Demi (Henry Holt, 1996. ISBN 0805042032.)

OR

Reincarnation Activator

Explain that reincarnation is an important concept in the Hindu religion. Briefly explain that reincarnation is the idea that the soul is reborn after death into a human or other form of life. Students can refer to page 316 for more information. After students have an understanding of the concept, ask them to choose a form that they would like to be reborn in if they were a Hindu and have them give reasons to support their choice. Be sure to remind students that reincarnation is one of the most sacred tenents of Hinduism and should therefore be discussed only with respect.

Writing Prompt

OBJECTIVES: 8.01

Evaluative

Mohandas Gandhi was given the title Mahatma, meaning "Great One." Read Chapter 16, then write an essay explaining either why he deserved this title or why he did not deserve it.

As you write your essay, remember to:

- clearly state your position.
- give at least three reasons and explain your reasons fully.
- give examples to support your reasons.
- write in complete sentences and paragraph form.
- organize your ideas and include an introduction and a conclusion.
- use good grammar, spelling, punctuation, and capitalization.

CHAPTER 16

South Asia's Enduring Traditions

The first civilization in South Asia rose in the fertile Indus River valley. By 2500 B.C., two great cities—Harappa and Mohenjo-Daro—had emerged. The cities were well planned. Wide streets were laid out on a regular pattern. The wealthy lived in large homes that boasted bathrooms and kitchens. Elaborate sewage systems carried off waste water. Then after 1,000 years, the Indus River cities declined. They were buried and forgotten. Who built these cities? Why were they forgotten?

Priest of Mohenjo-Daro

Chapter Preview

LESSON 1
History's Impact on South Asia
South Asia's religions, languages, politics, and culture are rooted in its ancient past.

LESSON 2
Family and Village Life
Family and village are the foundations of Indian life.

LESSON 3
South Asia Divided
Most of South Asia was ruled by the British from the 1800s until 1947. After independence, the subcontinent was divided into several nations.

312

Mohenjo-Daro ruins

Chapter Resources

Print Resources

Fiction

Demi. *Buddha.* Henry Holt, 1996. ISBN 0805042032.

Nonfiction

Ali, Daud. *Ancient India* (Step Into series). Anness Publishing, Incorporated, 2000. ISBN 0754806588.

Dhanjal, Beryl. *What Do We Know About Sikhism?* Peter Bedrick Books, 1999. ISBN 0872263878. An illustrated guide to Sikhism.

Ganeri, Anita. *What Do We Know About Buddhism?* Peter Bedrick Books, 1997. ISBN 0872263894.

__. *What Do We Know About Hinduism?* Peter Bedrick Books, 1995. ISBN 0872263851.

Severance, John B. *Gandhi, Great Soul.* Clarion Books, 1997. ISBN 039577179X. A biography of Mohandas K. Gandhi.

Language Arts: Writing Connections

Story Starters on Ancient India. Heinrich Enterprises. Takes a time period and helps students develop a story.

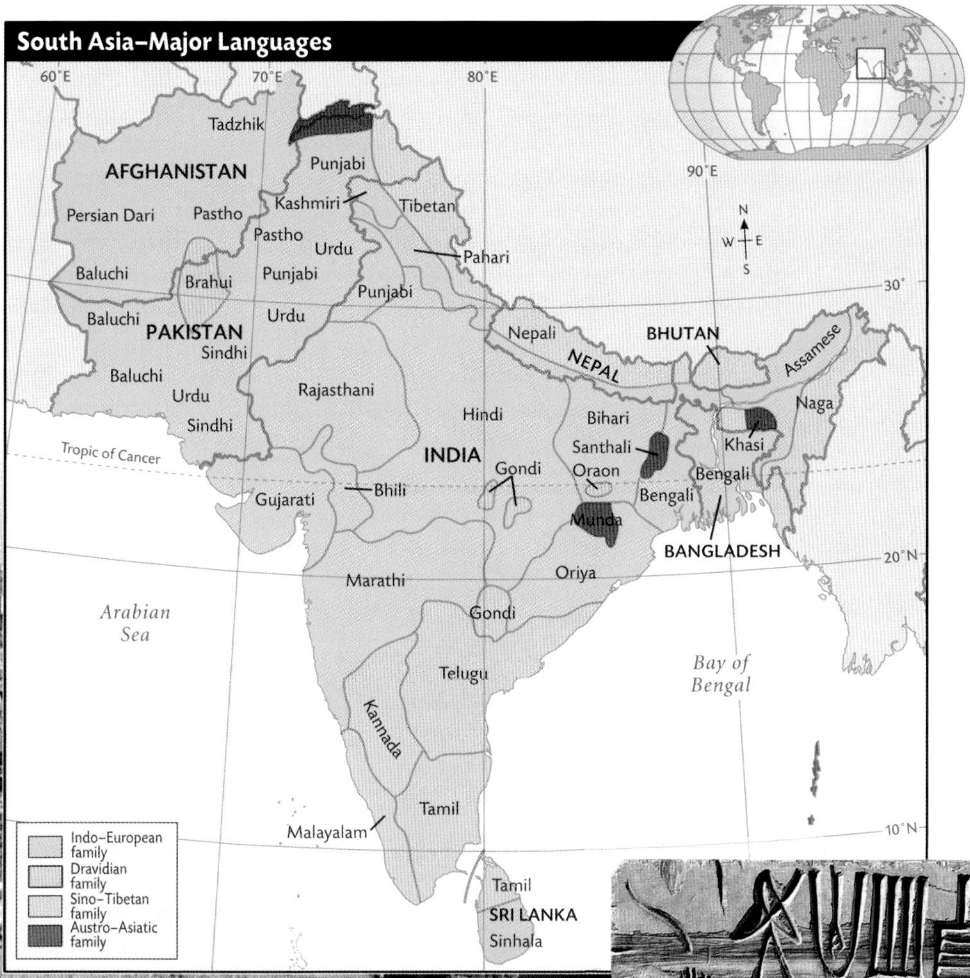

South Asia–Major Languages

Royal seal of Mohenjo-Daro

Discussion Questions

1 A country is polyglot when it is formed from a mixture of cultural groups with different languages and an official language is needed. Name a country in South Asia that is polyglot. (India is an example of this, with English being the official language since Britain colonized this part of South Asia.)

2 Indo-European is the largest of the world's language families. This includes Hindi, Urdu, Baluchi, Dari, Bangla, Punjabi, Sinhalese, English, Greek, Russian, Spanish, and Portuguese. Which of these are spoken in South Asia?

3 Sino-Tibetan is the second largest of the world's language families. It includes Dzongkha, Nepali, and Chinese. Which of these are spoken in South Asia? (Sino is often used to refer to something about China.) Why do you think this is so?

4 The sixth largest of the language families of the world is Dravidian, which includes Tamil. This is spoken in what parts of South Asia?

Map Activity

Diffusion of Language

NATIONAL GEOGRAPHY STANDARDS: 1, 4, 9

GEOGRAPHIC THEMES: Location, Place, Movement, Region

OBJECTIVES: 1.01, 1.02, 1.03, 12.03

It is estimated that there are as many as 6,500 languages spoken in the world. Of the 12 most widely spoken, Hindi, English, and Bengali are prominent in South Asia.

Have students graph the dominant languages below on seven small circle graphs. Assign students to identify which language family contains each of the official/majority languages spoken in each South Asian country.

- Afghanistan: 50% Dari (Indo-European)
- Bangladesh: 98% Bangla (Indo-European)
- Bhutan: 50% Dzongkha (Sino-Tibetan)
- India: 30% Hindi (Indo-European)
- Nepal: 58% Nepali (Sino-Tibetan)
- Pakistan: 64% Punjabi (Indo-European)
- Sri Lanka: 72% Sinhalese (Indo-European)

Back issues of magazines

Ashoka: India's Philosopher King. Cobblestone Publishing Company. ISBN 03822445155.

Buddhism. Cobblestone Publishing Company. ISBN 0382406060.

Hinduism. Cobblestone Publishing Company. ISBN 038240596X.

Audiovisual

Gandhi. Granada Video, 1990. ISBN 1556077785. 40 minutes. Contains original footage tracing Gandhi's role.

Varanasi: City of Lights. United Learning. ISBN 1560076550. 25 minutes. Excellent video for Hinduism.

Web Sites

Go to **NCJourneys.com** for links to the following Web sites:

- Ancient India Tales
- The Ghandi Foundation
- Harappa
- The Heart of Hinduism
- Mahatma Gandhi
- Religion and Ethics: Buddhism
- Religion and Ethics: Hinduism

OBJECTIVES: 9.01, 11.01, 12.01

Caption Answer

They suggest that migrants from the Caspian area entered South Asia from the Hindu Kush about 4,500 years ago.

ELL Teaching Tips

Encourage Social Interaction

ELLs need to interact with real speakers of English. Give them a variety of activities. Limit the amount of time ELLs spend completing nonverbal tasks. Acceptance is an excellent motivational tool.

Writing Activity

Language Diffusion

OBJECTIVES: 12.03

Many people who study languages think there are two explanations of how Indo-European languages spread from their core: conquest and agriculture. Hypothesize what these two explanations are by knowing the definition of each key word. *Conquest:* spread when one group conquered another. *Agriculture:* spread with farmers migrating to find better/more farmland.

Have students compose a point of view essay using this prompt:

Diffusion of languages has become more associated with political influences and global economics instead of the relocation of cultural groups in recent centuries.

LESSON 1 History's Impact on South Asi

KEY IDEAS

- South Asia's civilization is one of the world's oldest.
- Many people migrated into South Asia, creating today's mix of languages and religions.
- South Asian nations today have had problems in building political unity.

KEY TERMS

Buddhism
castes
caste system
Dalit
karma
rajahs
reincarnation
Sanskrit

Archaeologist are beginning to solve some of the mysteries surrounding the Indus Valley civilization. It was one of the world's earliest civilizations, whose great cities prospered at the same time as those along the Nile, Tigris, and Euphrates Rivers.

The achievements of Harappa and Mohenjo-Daro were not lost whe the cities were abandoned. Dravidians—the name of the people living in the Indus Valley—moved southward. Some residents of the Deccan Plateau and the southern tip of India may be descendants of the Indus people. No one knows exactly why the Indus Valley civilization declined Excavations have unearthed more than 1,500 archeological sites from th period. Artifacts suggest connections with later Hindu traditions, but many cultural elements are found nowhere else in South Asia.

Patterns from the Past

Indus Valley remains suggest that about 4,500 years ago, migrants from the Caspian Sea area entered South Asia through the Hindu Kush to mix with local people. They brought with them the beginnings of a language called ***Sanskrit,*** which is the basis for most languages of South Asia's northern plains. The languages that grew out of ancient Sanskrit include modern Hindu-Urdu, the world's second largest spoken language, and Bengali, the sixth largest spoken language. Each language has a different script.

The language family spoken in the south of the subcontinent, Dravidian, is completely different. Tamil, the oldest o these languages, has a literature dating back well over 2,000 years. Each of the Dravidian languages also has a unique script.

When people speak different languages, they develop different cultures. With so many languages being spoken across the subcontinent, it is ea to see why South Asia is so diverse and complex.

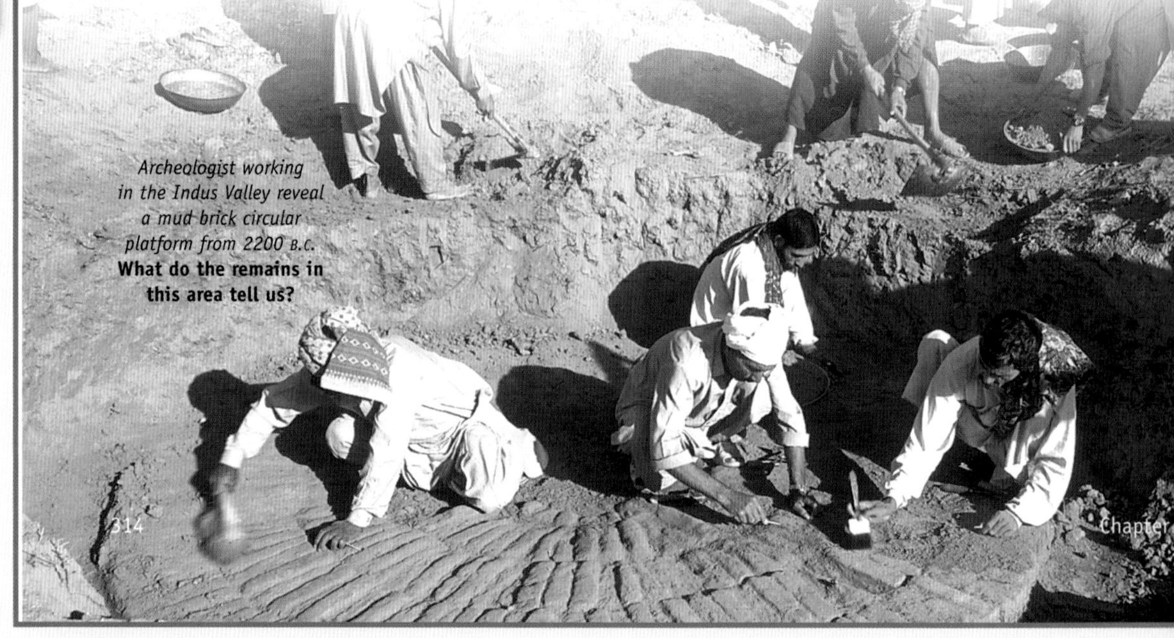

Archeologist working in the Indus Valley reveal a mud brick circular platform from 2200 B.C. **What do the remains in this area tell us?**

Research Activity

Travel Brochures

OBJECTIVES: 8.02

Have students research Mohenjo Daro and Harappa using the Internet. They should create travel brochures, PowerPoint presentations, or digital stories for each, include a catchy slogan. Enrichment: Create a commercial for travel to one of the cities.

Extension ELL students should use an ELL-friendly Web site for research and create a poster instead of a brochure

CONNECTIONS • GEOGRAPHY & THE ARTS •

The Taj Mahal

Three hundred years after the completion of the Taj Mahal (below), the identity of its architect is unknown. What is known is that the gleaming white marble structure stands as a monument to a husband's grief. It is also a symbol of how India blends several ideas from the many people who settled India. A Muslim built it using Islamic and Persian styles of architecture.

Only the best artisans of the time were brought in by Shah Jahan to build the tomb for his wife, Mumtaz Mahal, who died while giving birth to her fourteenth child.

Stonecutters and masons, engineers and sculptors, gold inlayers and calligraphers—37 in all—made up the group of artisans. Work began in 1632. More than 20,000 people labored 22 years to bring Shah Jahan's vision to reality.

Teams of 30 oxen pulled huge marble blocks. The builders used marble everywhere—for the 58-foot (17-m) diameter dome, for the walls inlaid with precious stones, and for window coverings carved thinly to allow light to shine through.

An archway leads to the mausoleum, or crypt. A three-storied gateway with sandstone and inlaid marble marks the entrance. Pure white marble changes with the changing light. Soft curves, straight lines, and the distribution of solids and empty spaces make the Taj Mahal pleasing to the eye.

A visitor in 1670 said that it was "arches upon arches." Another declared that the mind saw "an entire harmony of parts, a faultless congregation of architectural beauties on which it could dwell forever without fatigue."

The Taj Mahal started out as a wooden model that was studied and altered until all the changes were made for construction. What is built this way today?

)ivision and Unity

South Asia has a long, rich history. The ıbcontinent was seldom united. Indo-ryan rulers, also known as ***rajahs,*** ›tablished small kingdoms across the ›rthern plain. Rival rajahs often turned the plain into a battlefield. Sometimes, a strong rajah united the north. These rajahs were not able to extend their power into the south. The Deccan Plateau's rugged terrain usually stopped them. Meanwhile, small competing kingdoms dominated southern South Asia.

Discussion Questions

1 Oil is a limited energy source for the United States, just as wood is in South Asia. What alternate fuel sources might be available to South Asia or to the United States?

2 How would the inability to unite affect the development of South Asian culture?

Taj Mahal Model Freestyle

OBJECTIVES: 1.01

Have students study the architecture of the Taj Mahal. Have them make a model of the Taj Mahal using a variety of materials, such as cardboard, Legos, sugar cubes, cakes, gingerbread, paper, or others.

Taj Mahal Paper Model

OBJECTIVES: 1.01, 2.1, 12.02, 12.1

Materials handout of the Taj Mahal cube pattern (found in the Teacher's Resource Guide); scissors; colored pencils, markers, crayons; rulers; protractors; compasses; glue/glue sticks or transparent tape

Procedure Using basic cube pattern with dome and archway features, have students cut out pattern, carefully cutting the space inside the archway. The cube is folded on all lines, with tabs temporarily folded inside cube. Students must gain perspective of which side of the cube becomes exterior walls on the Taj Mahal. Paper is unfolded for students to decorate the exterior walls of this famous landmark. Symmetry is an important architectural feature of this monument so students must demonstrate this in their decoration. Additional arches can be cut, calligraphy and arabesque designs should be incorporated, as well as mosaic inlays. When students are satisfied with their exterior wall decorations the cube must be reformed and glued with tabs on the interior of the Taj Mahal.

Discussion Questions

1 What do you think is the most important idea in Hinduism?

2 Does Hinduism have any ideas in common with the monotheism of Southwest Asia?

3 What are the basic beliefs of Hinduism?

Caption Answer

There are religious festivals, temples, and stalls selling pictures of gods and holy men.

Activity

Create a Game

OBJECTIVES: 4.03, 7.02, 8.02, 8.03

India's Gupta dynasty accomplished much during a four-hundred-year reign. Have students use the following information to create a simulation or game.

Art/architecture
- height of Buddhist style, revival of Hindu style
- expensive, richly decorated temples featuring paintings and sculptors.
- metallurgy advances with iron forged to be rust-proof
- dance with bharata natyam and kathak
- music with sitar, tabla, and tambura

Language/literature
- Sanskrit (from which Hindi evolved)
- animated fables
- fairy tales
- folktales
- plays (Sakuntala: love story about king and beautiful bride)
- poetry

Mathematics
- Arabic numerals refined
- zero invented
- infinity defined
- decimal system created
- value of p (pi)

Medicine
- diagnosis and treatment of many illnesses
- cleanliness preventing infection
- surgery setting bones
- plastic surgery correcting malformations
- Caesarean section delivery of babies

Politics
- dynasty ruled with divine right to promote dharma
- village councils (panchayat) encouraged
- land taxes based on percentage of crops raised

Occasionally, powerful rulers did unite large parts of the subcontinent. In 321 B.C., for example, the Maurya (MAWR·yah) Empire conquered nearly all of South Asia. Mauryan rule lasted for about 150 years.

Much later, the Gupta Empire expanded across South Asia. It lasted from A.D. 320 to 535. After the Gupta Empire collapsed, South Asia was again divided for about 1,000 years into small kingdoms.

Religious Traditions

South Asia is home to many religions. Their importance may be seen in countless religious festivals and the towering temples that soar skyward in every large city. Hindu temples are covered in elaborate carvings of gods, goddesses, animals, and plants. More modest templ stand at the entrance to smaller towns. Nearby stalls sell pictures of gods and holy men. The faithful buy flowers and food to be presented to the gods. They hope such offerings create a bond with their gods.

This bronze carving of Shiva Nataraja, a Hindu god, decorated a temple. **What are other signs of religions' influence in India?**

Hinduism: One and Many

Most of India's festivals, temples, an worshippers are Hindu. More than 80 percent of the population follow this fait Hinduism is one of the world's oldest living religions. Its origins are in 5,000-year-old Aryan religious beliefs.

"God is one," says a Hindu proverb "The wise speak of it in different ways." The proverb reflects a Hindu belief in a single all-powerful, unchanging Universa Spirit. The Spirit, Hindus believe, exists every living thing—in trees, plants, insec animals, and people—and is seen in hundreds of gods. People may worship one or many of them. Hindus believe all of these gods help the faithful reach enlightenment.

Hindus respect all life. They believe th Universal Spirit lives in every creature. Because all living things have souls, they should be treated with respect. Hindus especially honor cows as a sacred animal. Cows roam freely. Hindus do not kill cow In fact, most Hindus do not eat any meat.

Hindus also believe in ***reincarnatio*** the idea that the soul is reborn after death into a human or other form of lif The cycle of birth, death, and rebirth continues until the soul becomes perfec and is unified with the Universal Spirit.

Word Origins

Early Aryan rulers took the title of **rajah.** Translated from Sanskrit the word means "king." Much later, as the British took control of India, some local rulers were allowed to retain some authority. These men took the title Maharajah (great king).

South Asia–Buddhism and Hinduism to A.D. 500

Movement The map shows the movement by A.D. 500 of the two religions that began in South Asia–Hinduism and Buddhism. *Where did Buddhism spread? Where did Hinduism spread?*

nduism and Caste Hinduism became ɔsely linked to the *caste system,* a ɡid social structure that emerged over ousands of years. Hindus believe that e gods created four social groups, or *ıstes.* Over many centuries, each caste me to have a well-defined position. ıose at the top were seen to be closest spiritual perfection. The others were ought to be less spiritually pure. Here their organization:

- Brahmins had the highest standing. Brahmins were well-educated priests.
- Kshatriyas were warriors and rulers.
- Vaisyas were merchants, craftsworkers, and farmers.
- Shudras were the lowest caste. Most were laborers and tenant farmers.

Beneath the Shudras were the *Dalit.* They were the poorest, most ill-treated people in Hindu society. Dalits were considered to be spiritually unclean. They farmed tiny plots or did work—sweeping streets or carrying away wastes—that others were forbidden to do. Today, Dalits are joining together to fight for better treatment.

Through reincarnation, Hindus believe, an individual is born into one of these groups. A person's status comes from ***karma,*** or the law of deed. This means that a person's every action affects his or her fate in the next life. Bad actions can lead to rebirth in a lower form. Those who act correctly acquire good karma. Their souls are rewarded in the next life.

Discussion Questions

1 To a Westerner, the traditional caste system probably seems terribly unfair, yet it has persisted for thousands of years. Compare and contrast the negative aspects of the caste system (from a Western point of view) with the possible benefits to a member of Indian society.

Caption Answer

Buddhism spread south as far as Java, north into Mongolia, east to Japan, and west to the border of Afghanistan. Hinduism spread throughout India, Pakistan, and northeast toward China.

Map Activity

Geography of Buddhism and Hinduism

NATIONAL GEOGRAPHY STANDARDS: 1, 3, 5, 9

GEOGRAPHIC THEMES: Location, Place, Movement, Region

OBJECTIVES: 1.03, 4.01, 4.03, 12.03

Explain that when arrows noting movement are placed on maps they are usually called flow-line maps. These arrows note the spread and movement of Buddhism from its origin in Nepal in South Asia into other countries of South Asia, parts of Southeast and East Asia. Using maps of Asia in the textbook's atlas, have students itemize every nation where Buddhism was found in these three regions of Asia by A.D. 500. Carefully emphasize that countries exist today that did not in A.D. 500.

Have students research Hinduism's original location and its spread throughout Asia. Using large-scale blackline master map of Asia, assign students to design flow-line map showing the movement and spread of Hinduism. Overhead transparency maps can be designed for the movement of Buddhism and Hinduism using the same scale to overlay while students note similarities and differences on a graphic organizer.

Background Information

Equal Rights for Dalit

The Harijans, the preferred name for the Dalit (Untouchables), are considered to be the lowest people by the Hindu caste system. They are considered so low as to actually be "outside" of a caste. By tradition, they were denied land ownership, required to drink and eat from separate utensils, and barred from wells, schools, and temples. In 1949 in India and 1953 in Pakistan, new constitutions declared the use of the term "untouchable" and the social restrictions associated with it illegal. While the Indian government has passed laws forbidding discrimination and instituted affirmative action programs to give Dalit access to greater political and educational opportunities, attitudes are slow to change. Human rights activists argue that laws need to be more aggressively implemented and enforced to overcome centuries of discrimination.

Discussion Questions

1 Why has the caste system lasted so long in Hinduism?

2 The idea of someone being classified as Dalit is now officially illegal in India. Why has it been so difficult for it to actually end?

3 What is the most important area of difference between Islam and Hinduism? What would you propose as a means to reconcile this difference?

4 Is there such a thing as fate?

Dalit were outside the caste system.

Gods and Goddesses of Hinduism

OBJECTIVES: 12.01, 12.02

Have pairs of students research Hindu deities using the Internet or reference books. Using unlined paper, each pair should illustrate their god or goddess and briefly explain the deity's role in Hinduism.

Extension ELL students should use an ELL-friendly Web site for research. Assign a peer tutor to assist.

Many of India's poorest people are considered to be part of the Dalit. **Where in the order of castes were the Dalit before the caste system was outlawed in India?**

Individuals know what is bad or good, because over thousands of years Hinduism has developed rules of behavior for everyone.

Islam in South Asia

After Hinduism, Islam has the largest number of followers in South Asia. Pakistan was created as a home for Indian Muslims. Bangladesh is also a Muslim country. About 456 million Muslims live in South Asia, about 44 percent of the world's Muslim population. More than 174 million live in India.

Traders and invaders from Southwes[t] Asia first brought Islam to the subcontinent. Between 1100 and 1600, Muslim rulers conquered much of India. Some Hindus converted to Islam. They hoped to win jobs in Muslim governme[nt] or to escape the caste system. Today the[re] are conflicts between Hindus and Musli[ms] in India. Their religions differ greatly.

Contrasts Between Islam and Hinduism	
Islam	**Hinduism**
Belief in one God	Belief in many gods and goddesses
The Quran provides same rules for everyone.	Different rules for different castes
Muslims have a duty to convert others to Islam.	No effort to convert others; individuals are born into Hinduism.
All believers are equal before God.	Individuals unequal; spiritual status revealed by membership in caste/Dalit
Cows (but not pork) may be eaten for food.	Cows are sacred.
No human or animal images or music in worship	Music; elaborately carved images of gods and animals

LESSON 1 REVIEW

Fact Follow-Up Answers

1. The Dravidians inhabited the Indus River Valley around 2500 B.C. About 4,000 years ago, the Aryans, herders from the Caspian Sea, migrated into the northern plain and might have pushed out the Dravidians. The Dravidians moved into southern India.
2. Hindus believe in a single, all-powerful Universal Spirit found in every living thing, including hundreds of gods. Because the Universal Spirit is present in every living thing, Hindus respect all life. One way Hindus show this respect is by not eating meat. They also believe in reincarnation. The cycle of birth, death, and rebirth continues until the soul becomes perfect and is unified with the Universal Spirit. Every deed in this life affects the next, and determines position in the caste system, a hierarchical social structure.
3. The caste system is a rigid social structure determined by Hindu belief. The Brahmins, well-educated priests, have the highest standing. Next are Kshatriyas, made up of warriors and rulers. Below that are Vaisyas, merchants, craftsworkers, and farmers. Shudras occu[py] the lowest caste and are laborers and tenant farmers. Beneath the Shudras, and outside the caste system, a[re] the Untouchables, the poorest and most ill-treated people in Hindu society. Because they are considered unclean by followers of the caste system, they do the

Buddhism and the Middle Way

Prince Siddhartha Gautama grew up in Nepal in his father's palace. As the story goes, he was sheltered from seeing unhappiness or misery. One day, he saw a sick man, an old man, and a dead body. For the first time, he realized people experienced suffering.

Greatly troubled, Gautama became a wandering holy man, searching for the cause of suffering and death. After many hardships, he gained understanding. Through his teachings, Gautama then became known as the Buddha, "the Enlightened One." He founded ***Buddhism*** in the sixth century B.C.

At the heart of Buddhism are the Four Noble Truths:

- Life is full of suffering.
- The cause of suffering is desire.
- The cure for suffering is to overcome desire.
- The way to end desire and achieve salvation is to follow the Middle Way.

The Middle Way was a guide to correct conduct. It included ethical, or moral, rules.

Buddhist beliefs grew out of Hinduism. Buddhists believe in reincarnation and nonviolence. The Buddha rejected caste and taught that all people were equal. The Buddha and his followers spread his beliefs through sermons, stories, and examples of how people should live.

For centuries, Buddhism had many followers in its South Asian homeland. Buddhism lost most of its following in India after Islamic armies invaded in the eleventh century. The destruction of Buddhist monasteries contributed to the religion's decline in India. By then, missionaries had spread Buddhism to Sri Lanka, Southeast Asia, China, Korea, and Japan. It remains an important religion in those parts of Asia (see map, page 317).

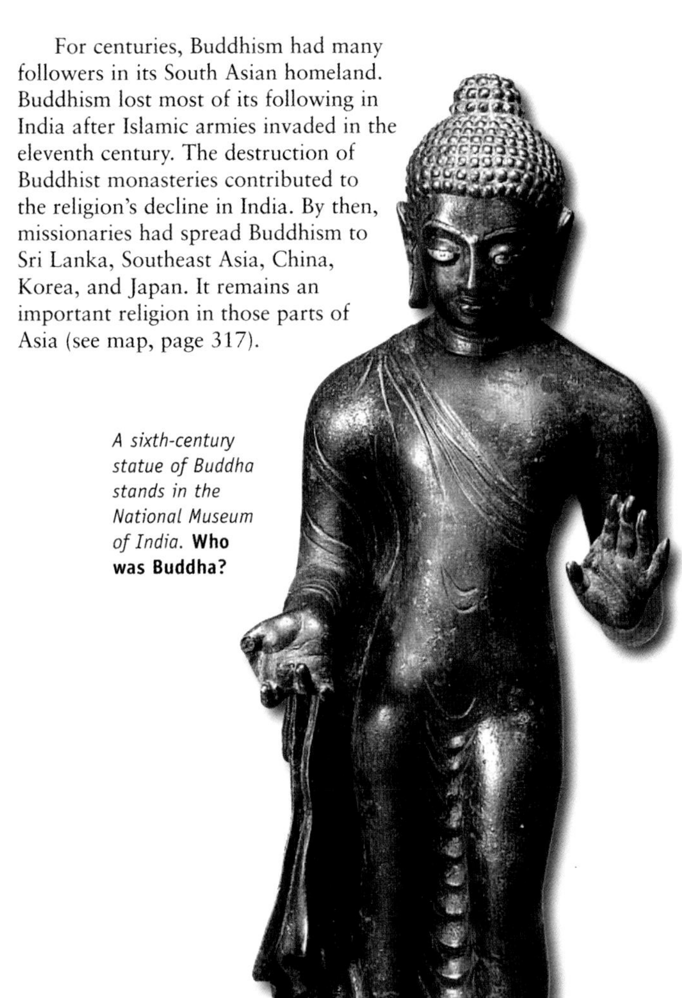

A sixth-century statue of Buddha stands in the National Museum of India. **Who was Buddha?**

LESSON 1 REVIEW

Fact Follow-Up

1. Who were the Aryans and Dravidians? Where did they come from? Where in South Asia did they settle?
2. Describe the basic beliefs of Hinduism.
3. What is the caste system? What are the four castes?
4. Compare the beliefs of Hinduism, Islam, and Buddhism.

Talk About It

1. How did the landforms of India discourage unity?
2. How did India and Hinduism give birth to Buddhism?
3. How did both Buddhism and Islam challenge Hinduism?
4. Who are the Dalit?

Discussion Questions

1. Why do you think Buddhism never was fully accepted in India?
2. To what groups would Buddhism appeal the most?
3. What do you think is the basis for most of the suffering in the world?

Caption Answer

Prince Siddhartha Gautama was a holy man who became known as the Buddha.

Writing Activity

In My Next Life

OBJECTIVES: 12.01

Have students reread the paragraph on reincarnation. On a piece of unlined paper have students illustrate what they will be in their next life. After adding color to their illustrations, students should write a paragraph explaining why they will exist in this new form in their next life.

Extension Novice and intermediate ELL students should draw illustrations with simple descriptions (words or sentences) about what the illustration is

dirty work others are forbidden to do.

4. Like Hindus, Buddhists believe in nonviolence and reincarnation. Buddhism, however, rejected the caste system, and proclaimed the equality of all believers. Islam, unlike Hinduism, has a belief in one God. Like Buddhists, Muslims hold all believers to be equal. Buddhism and Hinduism include music and images in worship. Islam forbids music and images in worship. Hindus do not eat beef and many are vegetarians. Muslims avoid pork but eat other kinds of meat.

Talk About It Answers

1. Mountains and rugged terrain divided people as did vast distances and deserts.
2. Buddhism grew out of Hinduism, which arose in India. Prince Siddhartha saw the suffering of people in India and began a spiritual journey that resulted in his founding of Buddhism. Buddhists believe in reincarnation and nonviolence, but the Buddha rejected the caste system and taught that all people were equal.
3. Both Buddhism and Islam proclaimed the equality of all believers and rejected Hinduism's caste system.
4. In the Hindu caste system, the Dalit were the poorest and most ill-treated people in society.

OBJECTIVES: 4.03, 10.04, 11.01

Caption Answer

Loyalty to family, the traditions of Hinduism, caste, and the preference of boys over girls remain strong customs in Indian villages.

Writing Activity

To Drink or Not to Drink

OBJECTIVES: 11.02

Assign students the following prompt: Put yourself in Sastri's shoes. Do you drink from the well? Do you try to educate your father and others? Do you just decide to follow tradition?

Activity

Kinesthetic Caste

OBJECTIVES: 11.01, 12.01

Materials slips of paper with a number from 1 to 5 printed on each slip (note that you need more slips with the numbers 1, 2, and 3 on them than 4 and 5); pitcher of iced water with 4–6 large, nice, glasses; pitcher of cold water without ice and 4–6 smaller glasses; plastic pitcher with 4–6 paper cups; serving tray (optional)

Prior to the activity, choose three students and privately explain to them that they will be "observers" of some kind of interaction. They must describe what they have seen, although they won't know in advance what to look for.

Next, have the rest of the class go out into the hall. Invite them back into the room, giving each student a number as they enter. Explain that you have a special activity for them and you need help from students with number 4 slips. Ask students with a number 1 slip to raise their hand. Prepare a large glass of water for each of them. Instruct the number 4 students to serve students with their hands raised. Make a big deal that it is iced water and that you brought nice glasses for them.

LESSON 2 Family and Village Life

KEY IDEAS

- The family is the basic unit of South Asian society. Family interests come before an individual's wishes.
- Most South Asians live in villages. Villages follow traditional ways of life.
- The caste system remains strong in Indian villages. It is less rigid in cities.

Sastri, a recent university graduate, returned to his village for a visit with his family. While walking along a village street with hi[s] father, Sastri stopped at a well for some water. The day was hot, and Sastri was thirsty.

His father watched silently for a moment. Then he angrily ordered his son away from the well. The older man was outraged because his son wa[s] about to drink from a well that was set aside for a lower caste. The rules of Sastri's caste forbade him from eating or drinking with members of another caste. According to Hindu beliefs, he would pollute himself and his entire family. Everyone's *karma* would be harmed.

Sastri no longer accepted the caste system. He knew that in 1950 India's constitution had abolished the caste system. With millions of others, Sastri believed that the constitution was right. At his university and in the city where he lived, caste distinctions were disappearing. Yet Sastri also knew that deep-rooted customs remained strong in his village. He stepped away from the well.

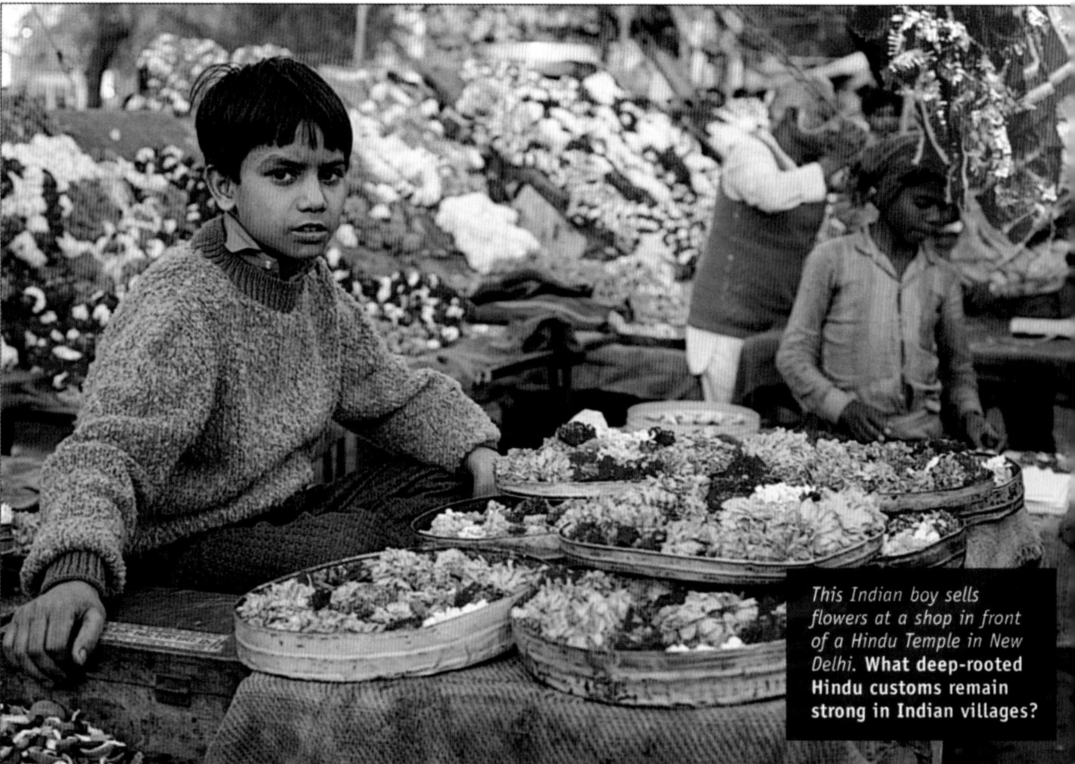

This Indian boy sells flowers at a shop in front of a Hindu Temple in New Delhi. **What deep-rooted Hindu customs remain strong in Indian villages?**

Once students with number 1 slips have been served, have students with number 2 slips raise their hand. Prepare each a glass of cold water without ice. Once again, have the number 4 students serve them. Make sure that the class sees that the glasses are different and that the water is from a different pitcher. Follow the same procedure for students with a number 3. Have the number 4 students serve them water from the plastic pitcher in paper cups.

Ask students with a number 5 slip to go pick up trash or take the trash can around the room. If your students are good sports, you could play up the "untouchability" of the number 5 students.

Read the lesson opener on page 320 about the drink of water. Thank the class for being good sports and make sure that you have a treat for all of them, especially the ones who were given number 4 or 5 slips. Explain the caste system.

Ask the observers to describe (without judgment) what they observed. Have the class consider why this type of practice may have evolved in India. Why is it important in their culture?

Lead a class discussion about customs in the United States that provide barriers to groups or classes (example: preference to children of alumni in college admissions).

Extension Intermediate ELL students can explain a system similar to the one in their country and be part of some of the groups.

'amily Ties

Sastri's action tells you a lot about oday's India. The young man had lived in city where he had met and studied with tudents from other castes. Some of his lassmates came from families classified as)alit. Sastri believed that these new ways f living were better than old ones. Yet he ad learned never to question his father's ommands.

Sastri had returned home to a raditional family headed by the oldest nale. He is thought to be the wisest, nost experienced family member. In amily affairs, his word is law. The amily's well-being is in his hands. Sastri vas expected to obey his father.

Today, as in the past, the family eaches children to respect and obey heir elders. Parents decide how much chooling their children will have and vhat skills they will learn. Even as dults, children know that their family's nterests will come first.

They also learn that in India boys are alued over girls. Only boys, Hindus elieve, can perform the rituals for the ouls of their fathers after death. Sons re seen as more useful for farmwork. 'hey are expected to marry and have randchildren. Sons provide security for arents, caring for them in old age.

Girls are loved by their parents. Yet ney are seen as a burden. A girl has to e fed, clothed, and protected until she narries. Weddings are expensive because amilies are criticized if daughters are ot married properly. Families sometimes pend a year's income on a wedding.)nce married, a girl's contributions to er family end. Her talents go to her usband's family.

'illage India

Why have traditional families emained so strong in India? One answer s found in India's villages. Most people ve in villages, not in cities. More than alf a million villages dot the ubcontinent. Daily life there supports amily traditions.

A woman chops fiber from coconuts in a village near Kerala. **How does village life support traditional families?**

Villages vary across India. Each region has its own customs because of varying landforms and ethnic groups. Yet villages everywhere share similar features. A typical village is surrounded by fields. Dusty paths and cart tracks cut through the land. Small plots of land are worked by hand.

Villagers live in small houses with few windows. Walls are made of packed earth or sun-baked bricks. Houses are used mainly for sleeping. They have little furniture. The family spends much of its time in a courtyard next to the house.

The courtyard serves many purposes. Chickens and goats are raised there. If the family has a water buffalo, that prized beast will be kept behind the courtyard's walls for protection.

Customs

In rural India, girls usually marry at an early age, often in their teens. After the marriage, the bride moves into the home of her husband's family. There, she is expected to serve and to obey her mother-in-law. After she produces sons, she gains more respect. When her sons marry, she becomes a mother-in-law and teaches her new daughter-in-law how to behave.

Discussion Questions

1 Why would old traditions such as the caste system last longer in villages than in larger cities?

2 Many Indians are now living in the United States. What potential conflicts do you see in the traditional roles of the family?

3 How does our society favor one group over another?

4 How is village life still traditional?

5 How will modernization in villages affect traditional life?

Daily life, especially the division of work, supports traditional families.

Model Indian Village

OBJECTIVES: 1.01, 2.01

Have students construct a model of an Indian village including such major components as houses, wells, courtyards, cows, fields, and so forth, using any material of their choice.

Debate About Marriage

OBJECTIVES: 11.01, 11.03

To generate a great class discussion about arranged marriages ask the students questions similar to these. Do you plan to get married? Do you have a brother or sister who is married? What are some ways to meet your marriage partner? Is it your parents' responsibility to find your marriage partner? How would you feel if your parents chose your husband/wife?

After a class discussion, divide the class into two sides. Pose the debate topic "Arranged marriages should still be practiced in modern India." One side should come up with benefits to having arranged marriages and the other side should come up with benefits to having free choice for marriage partners. See the Guide to Student Debates in the front of the Teacher's Edition.

Background Information

India Idol

Today many rural Indian villages have at least one television set because cable TV comes to them by satellite. Fewer than half of Indian households, about 70 million, have TVs, but those that do can find everything from news, music videos, movies, and sports to children's programming on cable TV.

Whereas in China restrictions on foreign broadcasts limit viewers to a few channels, Indian viewers can get more than 85 cable or satellite channels. Despite this, they watch much less TV than Americans. They average about 80 minutes a day. One of the most popular shows in India is "Indian Idol." Many millions of viewers tune in to watch this program modeled after the popular show "Pop Idol" in the United Kingdom and "American Idol" here.

Caption Answer

Since there is no electricity in many villages, work must be done by hand. An absence of refrigeration requires long daily preparation of food. More villages are beginning to get electricity.

Activity

Satellite Dish

OBJECTIVES: 8.03, 11.04, 12.03, 13.02

Break students into groups to imagine they live in an Indian village and the local café has installed a satellite dish. Each night they go to the café and watch shows transmitted from around the world. What impressions would they have of life in the United States from American programs? To answer this question, each group should come up with five programs that show the true nature of the United States and five that give a false impression of the United States. The groups should explain why they chose those programs to represent American values and culture. Have them imagine they are in an Indian village watching the programs they chose to represent the United States. From their perspective as a villager, how is life in the United States different from their own nation?

Extension As an alternative, have ELLs record a portion of their favorite TV show. Let the class have a "window to another culture" to see what it is like to watch a program you do not understand (culturally and linguistically).

Village girls wash their family's laundry. **Why does most village work take a lot of time? How is this changing?**

Daily Routines

Young children are allowed freedom to play until they are about seven years old. Older children may attend the local primary school. For most family members, days are filled with the hard work of farm life.

Work begins before dawn when the air is still cool. A boy takes the water buffalo to a nearby pond or the water tank that serves as the village reservoir. As daylight breaks, men and boys trudge to the fields. They work until midday, when they rest during the afternoon heat. Later, they return to the fields and work until dark. The family's water buffalo helps with some of the hardest tasks. Almost everything else is done by hand, because villagers often cannot afford machines.

Women and girls also do their work by hand. They carry heavy clay jars of water from the village well. They collect firewood or dried manure to burn as fuel. During daytime hours, women tend pots over a low grill. Nearby is the vegetable garden. Food preparation takes all day because of the lac of refrigeration and processed foods.

Changing Ways

Village life revolves around planting, harvesting, or waiting for the monsoon. It has changed little for centuries. Yet the modern world is affecting old ways. Paved roads instead of dirt tracks link some villages to towns and cities. Larger villages may have electricity to power lightbulbs o pumps. Families with relatives working in a city may have money to buy such luxuries as radios or cassette players. A prosperous villager might own a bicycle o even a motorbike.

More and more villages have TVs and satellite dishes. At night, people gather to watch television dramas and dream of a better life for their children. So far, these outside influences have not made dramatic changes in the lives of village families.

What would YOU do?

A village craftworker pounds a brass bowl wit a hammer. Each bowl will be different. Many people who work in factories earn more mone Often their work is repetitious and does not require the craftworker's skills. Would you favc learning a craft and making it your life's work even if the income were less than a factory worker? Which would you choose?

LESSON 2 REVIEW

Fact Follow-Up

1. Describe traditional family life in India.
2. What factors are changing traditional family life in India?
3. Describe a typical Indian village and life in it.
4. Compare the roles of boys to the roles of girls in a family.

Talk About It

1. If you had been Sastri, would you have acted as he did? Explain your answer.
2. Compare traditional Indian families with your own.
3. If you could choose to be either a female or male in a traditional Indian family, which responsibilities would you prefer? Explain your answer.

322 Chapter 1

LESSON 2 REVIEW

Fact Follow-Up Answers

1. Indian families are headed by the oldest male, who is obeyed by everyone else. The family's interest comes before the individual's wishes. Boys are more valued than girls, for religious and social reasons. Girls are married very young and go to live with their husbands' families.
2. The spread of transportation and communication to the remote villages is bringing changes. Paved roads, electricity, and television are introducing new ideas into village life.
3. A typical village is surrounded by fields, where small plots of land are worked by hand. Villagers live in small houses with few windows. Walls are made of packed earth or sun-baked bricks. Young children play freely and older children might attend a primary school. The men and boys work in the fields, and the women and girls carry water and wood and prepare food. People work all day, pausing only to rest during the afternoon heat.
4. In the morning, boys take the water buffalo to a nearby pond or water tank to drink. Boys work in the fields the rest of the day. Girls carry heavy clay jars of water from the village well. They collect firewood and dried manure to burn for fuel. Girls also help prepare food.

Talk About It Answers

1. Important points: Students should choose how they would have acted and explain why. Note: The choice is between affirming justice and respecting his father.
2. Important points: Students should compare roles of men and women, family responsibilities, positions of girls, importance of the caste system.
3. Important points: Students should state a choice of male or female and explain their reasons for the choice. Note: This question might lead to a classroom discussion about gender and roles.

LESSON 3 South Asia Divided

n 1498, Vasco da Gama, a Portuguese explorer, sailed around Africa to reach South Asia. "May the Devil take you! What brings you here?" demanded a Muslim merchant on seeing the Portuguese ıips. "We have come in search of Christians and spices," one of da ama's men replied.

A few years earlier, Portuguese explorers had led Europeans to frica's west coast. Da Gama had taken the next step. He opened the ay for Europeans eager to trade with Asia. Soon ships from Spain, ance, England, and the Netherlands were in Asian waters.

KEY IDEAS

- In an age of imperialism, Great Britain gained control of India.
- Mohandas Gandhi spurred Indian nationalists to win freedom through nonviolence.
- Independence for India meant the division of the subcontinent into several nations.

KEY TERMS

nonviolent resistance
partition

ıdia and Imperialism

Western Europeans reached South ıia's coast when the Islamic Mughal npire was at its height. In the 1500s, the ughals had united most of the bcontinent for the first time in 1,000 ars. At first, these rich and powerful uth Asian leaders limited what ıropeans might do. European merchants ere permitted to build trading posts on dia's coasts. Few Europeans were lowed inside South Asia. By the 1700s, ughal rule had weakened. Europeans en gained more power.

The East India Company was a private British trading company that had become a dominant force in India. The company drew criticism in the United Kingdom and India. British adventurers who had joined the company and gone to India often grew rich at the expense of Indians. The British Parliament began to control the company when stories about such greed and corruption reached them in London.

South Asians still became angry with the East India Company's interference in their affairs. The company removed Muslim officials from power and had its own private army. Sometimes the British tried to change ancient Hindu customs.

The India Gate in New Delhi is a monument built by the British to honor Indians killed in World War I. **What are other examples of the British impact on India?**

OBJECTIVES: 4.01, 8.01, 11.04

Discussion Questions

1 How did Vasco da Gama change the course of world history?

2 Is there a business in our community that has been responsible for the development of the community?

Caption Answer

Some examples are the use of the English language, government reforms, the modern legal system, schools, the telegraph, the railroad, expansion in irrigation, and improved medical care.

Research Activity

Mughal Rule

OBJECTIVES: 4.02, 7.01, 7.02, 8.01

Have students research the expansion of Islam in the Indian subcontinent to determine who were the major rulers and how these rulers from a different faith affected the lives of Indians.

Map Activity

Mapping Investigation

NATIONAL GEOGRAPHY STANDARDS: 1, 9, 12
GEOGRAPHIC THEMES: Movement
OBJECTIVES: 8.01

Have students investigate da Gama's voyage. Using a map, have them plot da Gama's course around Africa and into Asia. What was significant about his journey? Discuss.

Teacher Notes

Indian Fabric

Some fabrics, particularly cottons, are associated and named for South Asian locations:

- madras plaid: Chennai was called Madras by the British
- calico with small print designs: Calcutta (now Kolkata)
- dungaree: canvas-like material originally produced in Dungri

Discussion Questions

1 What mistakes did Great Britain make in its relationship with South Asia?

2 Why is it so important to understand a culture before visiting it?

3 What would someone need to be aware of when visiting the United States in general and our community in particular?

4 What were some of the positive aspects of British rule? negative aspects?

5 Is the attitude of the United States toward other cultures similar to the British attitude of superiority toward India?

When South Asians rose up against the policies of the East India Company in the Sepoy Mutiny, the British crushed the rebellion and made India a colony.

Divali Festival

OBJECTIVES: 11.01, 12.02

One of the most favorite holidays in India is Divali (dee·WAH·lee), also called the Festival of Lights or the Hindu New Year. It follows the monsoon season and takes place between October and November. During this celebration, gifts are given and special foods are eaten. Fireworks are displayed. People prepare for this holiday by placing oil lamps in the windows, painting red handprints on the doorways to keep away evil spirits, and hanging leaves in doorways to announce that something special is happening in the house. Chirags (sure·oggs) are also floated down the holy rivers. Chirags are oil wicks on plantain leaves surrounded by flowers. If the chirags float out of sight, it is a sign of good luck to be brought by the goddess of the holiday, Laskhimi.

Have students prepare the room for Divali. Cover the door with banner paper for them to paint their hand prints on or have them cut out a tracing of their hands on red construction paper to place on the door. Have students trace leaves to cut out and hang from the doorway of your room. Students can also create their own chirags out of construction paper.

Becoming a Colony

South Asian discontent with the British exploded in the 1857 Sepoy Mutiny. Sepoys were Indian soldiers serving in the East India Company's army. They included both Hindus and Muslims who were outraged when they were given new cartridges for their guns. The troops heard that the cartridges had been greased with pig and beef fat. The Indians were upset because Muslims were forbidden to touch pork, and cows were sacred to Hindus.

The British crushed the revolt. Then Parliament decided that the British government must assume control from the East India Company. In 1858, Britain made India a colony. In the West, India became a symbol of British power, its "jewel in the crown."

British Rule

British colonial rule has been praised and condemned. On the one hand, the British reorganized Indian government and set up a modern legal system. British engineers built a huge network of railroads and telegraph lines. They opened schools to train Indians as government clerks. They expanded and repaired irrigation systems. Christian missionaries worked to improve medical care and help the poor. The English language helped uni the subcontinent. The British ended such practices as *sati*, widow burning, and female infanticide.

Critics, on the other hand, point out that British policies were designed to mal India a profitable colony. Railroads linke the interior to the coast to bring farm goods and minerals to ports for export. They could also move troops to trouble spots. In school, boys received a Western education with British, not Indian, history

As in Africa, colonial rule changed the traditional economy. Peasant farmers had to pay taxes in money, not crops. To earn money, they grew cash crops such as jute, instead of food. Colonial rule also hurt village industries. Villagers had grown cotton, spun it into thread, and made clot Under British rule, cotton was exported to the United Kingdom. British factories mac textiles to sell in India. South Asian textile producers were forced out of business.

The European House in Chapra, India, was built for the British East India Company. **How did the company's activities help lead to the British colonization of India?**

The East India Company

OBJECTIVES: 4.02, 7.01, 9.01

Have students research the private English trading company that controlled India. Students should determine what resources or crops were taken by the company and the means the company employed to control India. They should write a short paragraph describing their findings.

)emands or Independence

The British set up schools to educate)ung Indians in Western ways. Their goal as to change South Asians into "brown ıglishmen," a British official said. utwardly, some educated Indians did come British in taste and opinion. They udied in the United Kingdom and lopted Western customs.

Yet many inwardly resented British le. From the West, they learned about dependence. Before long, an increasing ımber dreamed of winning freedom. any of these Indians formed the Indian ational Congress in 1885. Its members cluded educated people from all ligions and language groups. At first, eir goal was self-rule within the British npire. Later, it was independence.

Under growing pressure, the British ve Indians some self-rule. The change to eater Indian authority was not easy. any Indians died during riots. Others ere jailed for protesting British rule.

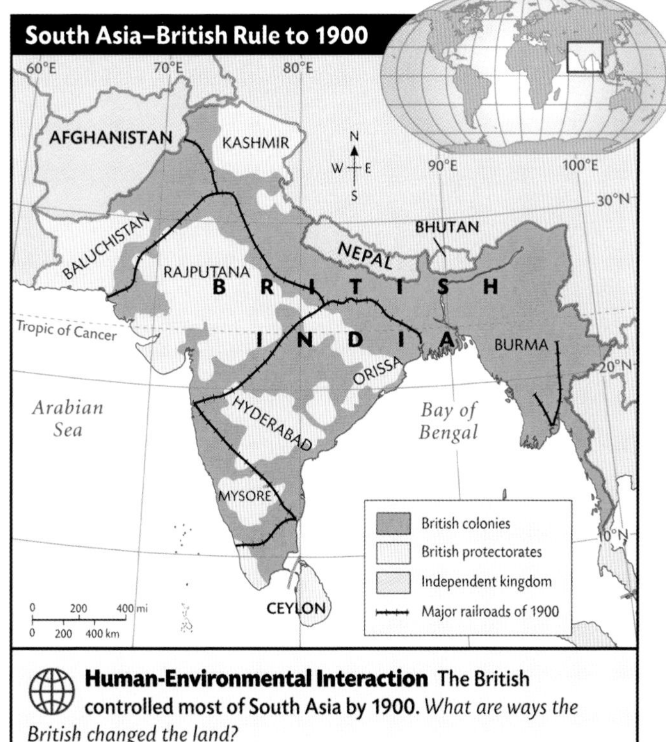

Human-Environmental Interaction The British controlled most of South Asia by 1900. *What are ways the British changed the land?*

1ohandas Gandhi

Mohandas Gandhi became the leader the struggle for independence by the 20s. As a young man, Gandhi had udied law in England. He migrated to uth Africa where he saw how white uth Africans used harsh racial laws ainst blacks and Indians. Many Indians orked in South African mines, railroads, d factories. Gandhi helped them fight scrimination. He taught peaceful, nviolent ways of protest called ***onviolent resistance.*** These ways flected Hindu and Buddhist teachings out nonviolence and Christian teachings out love and sacrifice.

After Gandhi returned to India, he plied his ideas to the struggle against itish rule. Gandhi believed the injustice colonial rule would be exposed by splays of Indian sacrifice. Gandhi's llowers would not physically attack British authorities. Rather, they would engage in nonviolent resistance. Gandhi called such a protest "a method of securing rights by personal suffering. It is the reverse of resistance by arms." His famous Salt March (see next page) was an example of nonviolent resistance.

Gandhi rallied South Asians of all religions and classes. His followers called him Mahatma, or Great Soul. British authorities often arrested Gandhi for leading nonviolent protests. Gandhi never tried to escape or to fight his jail sentences. While in jail, he refused to eat. Newspapers all over the world printed stories about Gandhi's suffering. The publicity brought worldwide support for his cause. Gandhi embarrassed the British, because they were proud of their democratic traditions. His demonstrations forced the British to recognize their denial of democracy to India.

Imperialism Compare and Contrast

OBJECTIVES: 9.01, 10.01

Compare and contrast the role of British imperialism in South Asia to that of British and European imperialism in Africa. Was the legacy of imperialism the same or different in the two regions?

Discussion Questions

1 How do the goals of the Indian National Congress compare to those of the African National Congress?

2 How successful was each?

3 Do you think Gandhi's legal background was necessary for his effectiveness?

4 How has Gandhi's philosophy influenced the United States?

5 Who in our community or country would deserve the name "Great Soul"?

They built railroads, expanded irrigation, and forced the cultivation of cash crops.

Jewel of the British Empire

NATIONAL GEOGRAPHY STANDARDS: 1, 4, 11, 12, 17

GEOGRAPHIC THEMES: Location, Place, Movement, Human-environmental Interaction, Region

OBJECTIVES: 3.03, 4.02, 5.01, 5.03

Note that the British ruled parts of South and Southeast Asia for 90 years (1857–1947) until the middle of the twentieth century (some reinforcement of what constitutes a century in year-dates may be necessary).

Using historical maps, have small groups of students identify major cites, ports, and points on the major rail lines the British built in South Asia and Southeast Asia. Have students analyze how and why this railroad network became known as the best in the British Empire (fourth largest in the world today). Explain that India's industrialization was helped by this major infrastructure advantage. Settlements founded by Britain developed into major cities and important ports. Bombay (Mumbai), Calcutta (Kolkata), and Madras (Chennai) are still three of India's largest urban centers. The ability to export raw materials and import manufactured goods, mainly from Europe, changed the pattern of India's economy. It also improved India's governability. How?

Activity

Colonial Role Play

OBJECTIVES: 9.02, 11.04, 12.01

Distribute the following scenarios to groups to present (role playing, visual arts, performing arts, diary entries):

1. British viceroy attempting to honor long list of treaties signed by the East India Company. This viceroy has British governors or commissioners from Punjab, Bengal, and Assam reporting to him, and he must report to the British Parliament and the monarch of Britain in London. His main goal is to keep India the "jewel of the British crown."
2. Maharaja of Hyderabad who is educated in Britain, returns to his homeland offering his subjects hope for democracy he saw in England. His main goal is to protect his family's heritage.
3. Muslim activist living in Kashmir (one of 562 Indian states at the time of independence) not wanting Hinduism to dominate lifestyles and seeking independence from Britain as strongly as any South Asian. Ultimately, Kashmir does not want to be part of India or Pakistan. Its main goal is to not align with any nation.
4. King of Nepal determined to keep his mountain kingdom Hindu while blending Buddhism in his country. Religious festivals draw the subsistence farming communities into celebrations while some want a more representative form of government. His main goal is to improve the living standards of his people.
5. Buddhist-Sinhalese teenage girl from Ceylon living on a tea plantation whose best friend is a Hindu-Tamil living on a neighboring rice plantation. She is trying to help her family accept her friendship with a darker-skinned, minority acquaintance—while the British seem to help the rice plantations with irrigation systems her family does not understand. Her main goal is to lessen her family's biases.

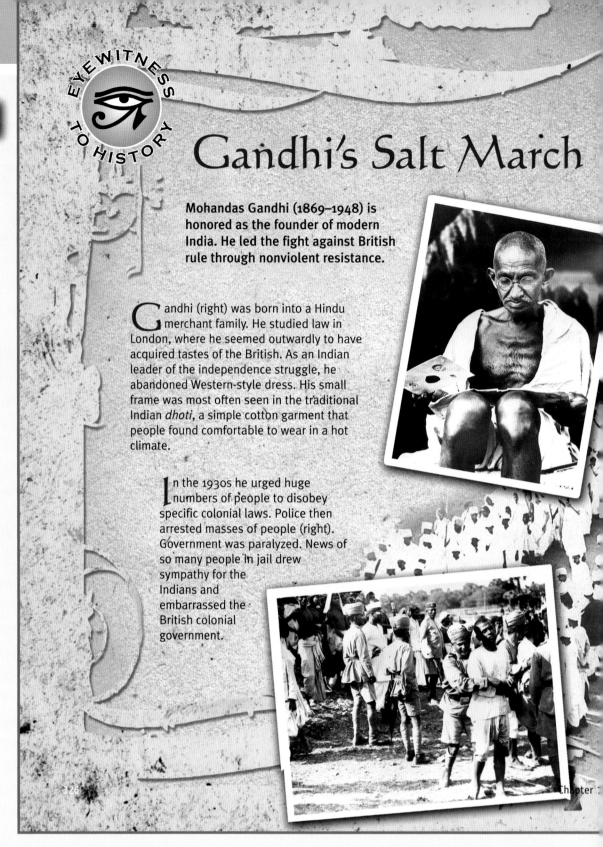

EYEWITNESS TO HISTORY

Gandhi's Salt March

Mohandas Gandhi (1869–1948) is honored as the founder of modern India. He led the fight against British rule through nonviolent resistance.

Gandhi (right) was born into a Hindu merchant family. He studied law in London, where he seemed outwardly to have acquired tastes of the British. As an Indian leader of the independence struggle, he abandoned Western-style dress. His small frame was most often seen in the traditional Indian *dhoti*, a simple cotton garment that people found comfortable to wear in a hot climate.

In the 1930s he urged huge numbers of people to disobey specific colonial laws. Police then arrested masses of people (right). Government was paralyzed. News of so many people in jail drew sympathy for the Indians and embarrassed the British colonial government.

Gandhi became the leader of the Indian National Congress, a group dedicated to gaining independence. His first step was to urge his countrymen to resist British colonialism through a *boycott*, a campaign to stop the purchase of British-made goods.

Gandhi tested this idea in 1930 by bringing together thousands of people to protest against an unpopular tax on salt. He led a march to the sea where the seawater was evaporated and salt was made (above).

Indians march to protest the salt tax

The march drew worldwide attention. About 60,000 people—including women—were arrested in the first six months of the movement. India's demand for independence had made world headlines.

Eyewitness Activity

Gandhi's Salt March

OBJECTIVES: 8.01, 13.02

In order to help students gain a better understanding of the life of Gandhi, show the movie *Gandhi*, starring Ben Kingsley.

After a discussion of boycott, have students brainstorm examples of boycotts in the United States. Examples might include the Boston Tea Party or the Greensboro lunch counter sit-in.

After students read about Gandhi in the Eyewitness, present material about Martin Luther King, Jr., and Mother Teresa to the students and ask them to identify similarities and differences in a graphic organizer. Graphic organizers in the Teacher's Resource Guide will be useful for this assignment.

Background Information

The Kashmir Conflict

In 1947, when India and Pakistan accepted partition, they also agreed that Kashmir, a small state bordering northern India and Pakistan, could choose to become part of India or Pakistan. Kashmir had a Hindu ruler, Hari Singh, but a Muslim majority. When Singh delayed making a choice, hoping to keep Kashmir independent, Pakistan acted. It considered Kashmir a natural extension of its own territory and encouraged Pathan tribesmen to invade Kashmir. When they did so, Singh fled to India and agreed to make Kashmir part of India in return for Indian military aid. Both nations sent in troops and fighting continued until 1949 when a United Nations cease-fire gave two thirds of Kashmir to India and the rest to Pakistan. Kashmir remains a source of tension between the two nations today.

Discussion Questions

1 Why do you think people of different faiths have so much trouble getting along?

2 Why would this plan for two Pakistans fail?

Caption Answer

Pakistan

Activity

Interview

OBJECTIVES: 8.01, 13.02

Divide class into groups of three. In each group, one person should research Gandhi and one Martin Luther King, Jr. The third person should study proper interviewing skills. Students should dress as a character and stage a role play of a present-day reporter interviewing Gandhi and Martin Luther King, Jr. Students could do a live or taped production. Classroom could be arranged like the set of a news program.

Muslim refugees stand in line for water outside the Purana Qila Fort in New Delhi. They had fled religious rioting in 1947 after the United Kingdom had agreed to partition India. **What Muslim nation was created out of India?**

Toward Independence and Partition

By 1945, the United Kingdom realized that it could no longer hold on to India. Within two years, South Asians would win independence.

South Asian spirits were lifted by the coming end of British rule. Yet, as independence approached, Hindu-Muslim relations became more tense. Gandhi believed that all South Asians could live together peacefully. Muslims disagreed. As a minority in a Hindu-dominated country, Muslims feared that Hindus would take advantage of them.

Years earlier, Indian Muslims had formed the Muslim League led by Muhammad Ali Jinnah. The league wante the British to form an independent Muslin nation. Muslims called it Pakistan, meanin Land of the Pure.

As Hindu-Muslim violence increased, the British agreed to ***partition,*** or divide, the subcontinent. India would occupy mos of the subcontinent. Pakistan would incluc two areas of Muslim territory. The area around the Indus Valley would be West Pakistan. The delta of the Ganges and Brahmaputra Rivers would become East Pakistan. These two areas were separated 1,000 miles of Indian territory.

This plan for a divided Pakistan later failed. In 1971, East Pakistan broke away and became the independent nation of Bangladesh. But in 1947, problems betwee West and East Pakistan were not a major concern. The partition of South Asia set of the largest migration in history.

Millions of Muslims in India fled toward Pakistan while Hindus in Pakistan escaped into India. Sadly, extremists on bo sides slaughtered hundreds of thousands o fleeing people. The British could not stop the massacres. Nor could Gandhi.

In 1948, Gandhi also fell victim to violence. A Hindu fanatic shot and killed the Mahatma. "The light has gone out of our lives," declared a longtime friend. "There is darkness everywhere." As India and Pakistan celebrated independence, bot were haunted by the killings.

LESSON 3 REVIEW

Fact Follow-Up

1. Describe early European contacts with India. What led European explorers to India?
2. What were some positive and negative results of British rule in India?
3. What tactics did Mohandas Gandhi use to challenge British rule in India?
4. What was partition, and why did the British believe it was necessary in 1947?

Talk About It

1. India was called the "jewel in the crown" of the British Empire. Was the description accurate? Explain.
2. Had you been living in India at the time, would you have been a follower of Gandhi? Explain your answer.
3. Was partitioning India and Pakistan a good thing to do? Why or why not?

LESSON 3 REVIEW

Fact Follow-Up Answers

1. Western European contact with India came through trade. At first, European merchants were allowed to build trading posts only on the coasts. Later, after Mughal rule weakened, Europeans gained more power. They had come looking, one sailor said, for "Christians and spices."
2. The British built telegraph systems and railroads, improved irrigation, modernized government and law, built schools, and improved medical care. However, the railroads were used for British trade and control of India, the schools taught only British, not Indian, history, and the British changed the traditional economy to benefit themselves.
3. Gandhi used methods of peaceful nonviolent resistance, including marches, boycotts, and fasting.
4. Partition was a division of the subcontinent into India, a predominantly Hindu nation, and Pakistan, a Muslim nation. The British believed it would end the violence between Hindus and Muslims.

Talk About It Answers

1. Important points: Students should state whether the description was accurate and explain why. Note: India had been the goal of Europeans since the Middle Ages, and possession of it was considered a great prize because of its resources. India was by far the single most valuable of the British imperial possessions.
2. Important points: Encourage students to state solid reasons for the position they take. Being a follower of Gandhi was difficult and dangerous, requiring great courage and patience.
3. Important points: Encourage students to justify either position they take. Remind them that it is easy to criticize decisions after they have been made. Note: Partition was supposed to be an answer to a dangerous situation. But the violence continued, and the nation of Pakistan ultimately broke into two countries: Pakistan to the west and Bangladesh to the east.

SKILL GOALS NORTH CAROLINA SOCIAL STUDIES

skill

Applying, Decision-Making and Problem-Solving Techniques to World Issues

Change Through Nonviolent Resistance

One of the teachers at a Methodist missionary school near Nagpur, India, rushed outside to investigate a bellowing noise that had pierced the early morning stillness. In the hut next door, he found his colleague James Lawson still in a fit of shouting and clapping and foot-stomping. Even after Theopolis burst through the door, Lawson was still dancing and could only point to a story in the English edition of the Nagpur Times *about how thousands of Negroes were refusing to ride segregated buses in a small American city.*

The year was 1955, the "small American city" was Birmingham, Alabama, and the news story reported the bus boycott that would end segregated seating on city-owned buses. The Reverend Martin Luther King, Jr., had helped organize the boycott. Lawson had gone halfway round the world to study Gandhi's principles. He was overwhelmed to read that Dr. King was following Gandhi back home in the American South.

Gandhi was the leader of Indian people without political rights or power. His acts of nonviolent resistance had challenged the British rulers and contributed to Indian independence.

Dr. King had studied Gandhi's beliefs while a seminary student. King, a Baptist preacher, led a movement that challenged legal segregation in the American South.

Gandhi believed that his actions were the only effective means powerless people had to force political change. So did Dr. King.

For Gandhi and his followers, nonviolent resistance to unjust power was an effective social activity. Both Gandhi and King understood that deliberately resisting laws they felt were unjust might result in thousands being jailed. The American civil rights movement, patterned after Gandhi's examples, resulted in changes in voting laws, education, and access to buses, trains, hotels, and restaurants.

To evaluate whether these activities were effective, ask yourself some questions:

- Could other actions have been just as effective?
- If these actions were illegal, were those who took them willing to be punished for breaking the law?
- What risks came from taking these actions?
- Were the objectives more important than the risks?

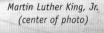

Martin Luther King, Jr. (center of photo)

Skill Lesson Review

1. Was the civil disobedience of the Reverend Martin Luther King, Jr., effective? appropriate? Explain. *Important points: Students should speculate on the effectiveness, appropriateness of the actions, giving reasons. There is no hard evidence of effectiveness. Appropriateness is a matter for discussion.*
2. Under what circumstances should nonviolent resistance to laws be used? What are some consequences? *The skill lesson sketches out the criteria for judging when nonviolent resistance should be used. Important points: Encourage students to focus on being aware of consequences and willing to take them.*
3. Is it ever right to break the law? Explain your answer. *Important points: In the discussion, emphasize that both King and Gandhi understood the consequences of lawbreaking; both spent considerable time in jail.*

Teaching This Skill Lesson

Materials Needed Textbooks. If desired, other information about King and Gandhi. The video series "Eyes on the Prize," which contains black and white footage of civil rights events, may be available in your school. Excerpts from one of the videos could be used to begin the lesson. Students are familiar with the King holiday but probably have never seen news clips of the civil rights marches of the 1960s.

Classroom Organization whole class, small groups

Beginning the Lesson Discuss the Martin Luther King holiday with students. Ask questions such as Why is the holiday celebrated? What is important about the life of Dr. King? What kinds of civil rights activities did Dr. King lead? (If it is available, show footage of marches, arrests from the *Eyes on the Prize* series.) As students suggest them, record on the chalkboard the strategies Dr. King used. If students do not mention it, lead them to list going to jail or willingness to go to jail as a strategy. Make sure they understand such terms as "nonviolent resistance" or "passive resistance."

Lesson Development Break class into smaller groups and refer them to the "Eyewitness" feature on pages 326–27. Each group is to use information from the feature to compare strategies of Gandhi and King. Allow each group to report its findings and list them on the chalkboard or overhead. Then refer students to the four questions on page 329. They are to discuss and answer these questions considering both King and Gandhi.

Conclusion Have students discuss or write a paragraph on "Indian Contributions to the American Civil Rights Movement." This might be a homework assignment.

Extension An optional activity could engage students in comparing strategies used by Gandhi and King with those used by Nelson Mandela.

Talk About It

1. Since most of India is affected by monsoons, there are alternating cycles of rain and drought. India has deserts, high mountains, hill regions, land at lower elevations, great rivers, and a long seacoast. Villages are located on all these landforms. A typical village is surrounded by fields, where small plots of land are worked by hand. Villagers live in small houses with few windows. Walls are made of packed earth or sun-baked bricks. Older children might attend a primary school. The men and boys work in the fields, and the women and girls carry water and wood and prepare food. People work most of the day.
2. Important points: Encourage students to choose one religion in each case and explain why they chose it. Note: About 80 percent of Indians are Hindus, and Hinduism influenced the caste system. Buddhism and Islam also have influenced the history of the nation. For about 500 years, Muslims ruled India.
3. Important points: Students should make a choice and explain it. Note: The caste system may have given organization to a large and diverse population. India's progress has been affected by a caste system that keeps opportunity from many people.
4. Important points: Students should give reasons for any answer they choose. Note: One important consideration would be whether or not the young woman could achieve her goals in India. Point out that life is changing in India and that the caste system is losing some of its importance.
5. Important points: Encourage students to speculate, giving reasons for their ideas. Note: The textile industry would have continued to develop; there is no way of knowing what other industries might have developed. European law and government might not have been introduced. There might still be tension between Hindus and Muslims.
6. Important points: Both Hinduism and Islam are religions that affect every aspect of life.
7. Important points: Encourage students to explore the difficulties of nonviolent resistance. Note: Injury and being jailed were very real possibilities. It would require a great deal of courage and patience.

CHAPTER 16 REVIEW

Lessons Learned

LESSON 1
History's Impact on South Asia
Important features of modern-day South Asia are directly linked to its history. The division of the subcontinent into several nations, the mix of languages, and the different religions are rooted in the region's ancient past. The Hindu faith also stands in sharp contrast to another important South Asian religion, Islam. A third important religion—Buddhism—evolved from Hinduism. Buddhism eventually faded away in India.

LESSON 2
Family and Village Life
Hinduism and traditions of rural villages combine to give India ways of life different from those of other nations. Hinduism provides foundations for the caste system in everyday life.

LESSON 3
South Asia Divided
Except for Afghanistan and Nepal, modern-day South Asian nations emerged from British colonial rule. South Asia's march toward independence was led by Mohandas Gandhi. The division of South Asia between Hindus and Muslims was marked by widespread violence.

Talk About It

1. Using the geographic theme of place, describe the physical and cultural characteristics of Indian villages.
2. Which of the three great religions—Hinduism, Buddhism, or Islam—do you think has influenced India most? least? Explain why.
3. Has the caste system been more of a benefit or a burden for India? Explain your answer.
4. Imagine that you are a young woman in India with a university education. Would you leave your homeland, or would you stay? Give reasons for your answer.
5. Suppose there never had been British colonial rule in South Asia. How might the region have been different? How would the region be unchanged? Give reasons for your answer.
6. Why do you think religious beliefs and practices have divided rather than unified people living in South Asia? Explain your answer.
7. Do you think nonviolent resistance would be easy or difficult? Why?

Mastering Mapwork

PLACE
Use the map on page 313 to answer these questions:

1. Describe the relative location of the regions in which major spoken languages come from the Dravidian family.
2. Describe the relative location of the region in which languages from the Sino-Tibetan family are spoken.
3. What is the largest language region of South Asia?
4. What are the smallest language regions of South Asia?
5. Locate the Tamil language region.

Mastering Mapwork

1. Languages from the Dravidian family are spoken along the border of Afghanistan and Pakistan and in the southeastern region of India and half of Sri Lanka.
2. Languages from the Sino-Tibetan family are spoken along the northern border of India and Pakistan and in what are now the nations of Tibet, Nepal, and Bhutan. These languages are also spoken along the northern and eastern borders of Bangladesh.
3. The Indo-European is the largest language region of South Asia.
4. The smallest language regions of South Asia are those in which languages from the Austro-Asiatic family are spoken.
5. Tamil is spoken in extreme southern India and on the island of Sri Lanka.

Go to the Source

Understanding Protest Movements

Read the passage below from Mohandas K. Gandhi's speech to the All-India Congress. Answer the questions below using specific references to the document. Gandhi gave this speech on August 7, 1942.

There are people who have hatred in their hearts for the British. I have heard of people saying that they are disgusted with them. The common people's mind does not differentiate between a Britisher and the imperialist form of their government. To them both are the same. There are people who do not mind the advent of the Japanese. To them, perhaps, it would mean a change of masters.

But it is a dangerous thing. You must remove it from your minds. This is a crucial hour. If we keep quiet and do not play our part, it will not be right.

If it is only Britain and the United States who fight this war, and if our part is only to give momentary help, whether given willingly or taken from us unwillingly, it is not a very happy proposition. But we can show our real grit and valor only when it becomes our own fight. Then every child will be brave. We shall get our freedom by fighting. It cannot fall from the skies.

I know full well that the British will have to give us our freedom when we have made sufficient sacrifices and proven our strength. We must remove the hatred for the British from our hearts. At least, in my heart there is no such hatred. As a matter of fact, I am a greater friend of the British now than I ever was.

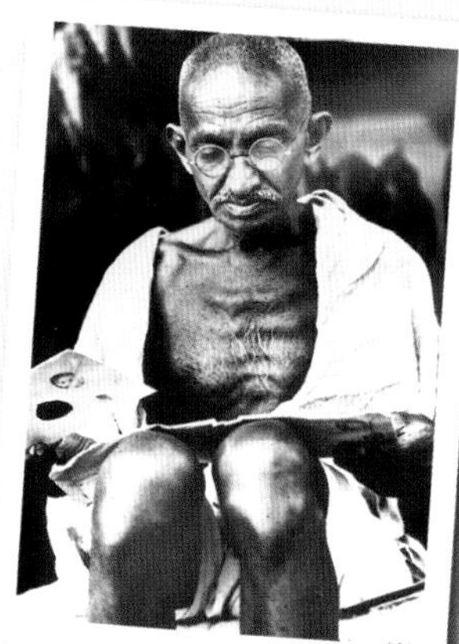

At the time when I am about to launch the biggest front in my life, there can be no hatred for the British in my heart. The thought that, because they are in difficulties, I should give them a push is totally absent from my mind. It has never been there. It may be that, in a moment of anger, they might do things that might provoke you. Nevertheless, you should not resort to violence; that would put non-violence to shame.

When such things happen, you may take it that you will not find me alive, wherever I may be. Their blood will be on your head. If you do not understand this, it will be better if you reject this resolution. It will redound to your credit.

Questions

1. What is the time period that this speech was given?
2. Who is the audience? How do you know?
3. What does Gandhi mean when he refers to "...the advent of the Japanese..."?
4. How does Gandhi view the British in his statements?
5. What approach to protesting British rule and oppression is Gandhi advocating?

Go to the Source

Go to the Source

OBJECTIVES: 4.03, 7.01, 7.02, 8.01, 8.02, 9(all), 10(all), 11.02, 11.04, 12(all) Skills 1.03, 1.04, 1.08, 2.01, 2.02

Gandhi's approach to have the powerless gain power and non-violent protest methods were emulated by others around the world, most notably by Dr. Martin Luther King, Jr.

Mohandas K. Gandhi's Speech to the All-India Congress, Bombay, August 7, 1942. Visit **NCJourneys.com** for a link to this speech.

ANSWERS

1. Students should connect that the speech was given after World War II had begun and before the bombing of Pearl Harbor.
2. Gandhi is speaking to the All-India Congress, his fellow Indians. Students should note that you could tell it is not the British because of how he uses words such as "we" and "the British."
3. Gandhi is referring to the rise in power of the Japanese in Asia during the outset of World War II. He comments on how some in India may welcome the Japanese taking over India, although he warns against it.
4. He views them as a friend, with no hatred in his heart.
5. Gandhi is advocating non-violent protests.

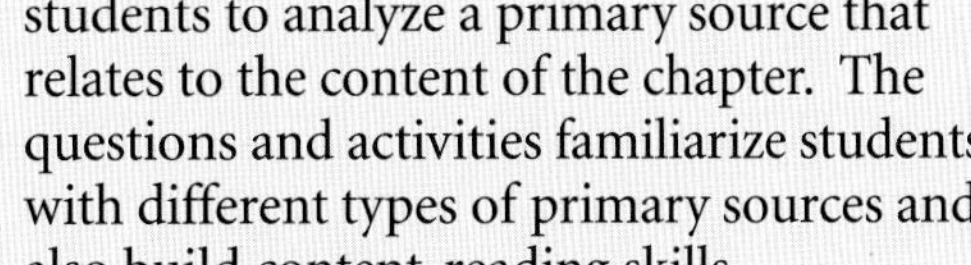

How to Use the Chapter Review

There are three sections in the Chapter Review: Talk About It, Mastering Mapwork, and Go to the Source. Use the Vocabulary Worksheets and the Chapter Review Worksheet in the Teacher's Resource Guide for additional reinforcement and preparation for the Chapter Assessments. The chapter and lesson reviews and the Chapter Review Worksheets are the basis of the assessment for each chapter.

Talk About It questions encourage students to speculate about the content of the chapter and are suitable for class or small-group discussion. They are not intended to be assigned for homework.

Mastering Mapwork has students apply one or more of the Five Themes of Geography to maps within the chapter.

Go to the Source activities allow students to analyze a primary source that relates to the content of the chapter. The questions and activities familiarize students with different types of primary sources and also build content-reading skills.

Modern India

Social Studies Strands

Government and Active Citizenship
Democracy

Economics and Development

Cultures and Diversity

Global Connections

Technological Influences

North Carolina Standard Course of Study

Goal 6 The learner will recognize the relationship between economic activity and the quality of life in Africa, Asia, and Australia.

Goal 9 The learner will analyze the different forms of government developed in Africa, Asia, and Australia.

Goal 10 The learner will compare the rights and civic responsibilities of individuals in political structures in Africa, Asia, and Australia.

Goal 12 The learner will assess the influence of major religions, ethical beliefs, and values on cultures in Africa, Asia, and Australia.

Teaching & Assessment

- English Language Learner Modified Lesson Plans for this chapter are found in the Teacher Resource Guide.
- *ExamView® Assessment Suite* is provided at **NCJourneys.com.** It includes customizable assessments for all chapters. Paper tests are also available in the Teacher Resource Guide. See pages T16–T17 for information about how to use the assessments and the Scoring Guide.

Worksheets

Worksheets and answer keys are found both in the Teacher Resource Guide and at **NCJourneys.com**, including Reading Guides, Reading Strategies, Chapter Reviews, English Language Learner and others.

ACTIVITIES AND INTEGRATIONS

SOCIAL STUDIES
● South Asian Body Language Customs, p. 332B
● What Is India Like Today?, p. 333
Sources of Conflict, p. 335
★ India Dominates South Asia's Economic Development, p. 339
Indian Culture Day, p. 345
India Food, p. 347
Skill Lesson: Planning Improvements in India, p. 349

READING/LANGUAGE ARTS	READING/LANGUAGE ARTS OBJECTIVES
★ Travel Brochure, p. 332B	2.02
Analogies, p. 332B	2.01
▲ Activator: *Our Most Dear Friend,* p. 332	2.01
Writing Prompt, India's Challenges, p. 332	3.01
ABC Book, p. 334	2.02
Central Economic Planning Outline, p. 338	1.01
India's Railway's Activities, p. 340	2.01
Matrimonial Advertisement, p. 343	2.02
★ Write a Storybook, p. 348	6.01
Go to the Source: Identifying Point-of-View, p. 351	2.01, 3.01, 4.01, 4.02, 5.03

MATHEMATICS	MATHEMATICS OBJECTIVES
● Putting an End To Poverty, p. 341	1.01, 1.02, 1.03
▲ ■ Electricity Pie Graph, p. 348	4.01

TECHNOLOGY	TECHNOLOGY OBJECTIVES
★ India's Economic Activities, p. 337	3.01, 3.11
Living in Modern India, p. 346	3.01, 3.07
Electricity Pie Graph, p. 348	2.02, 3.05

VISUAL ARTS	VISUAL ARTS OBJECTIVES
▲ ■ Paper Mosaics, p. 332B	1.02, 2.04
● ▲ ■ Flag, p. 334	2.04, 4.04
★ ▲ Batik, p. 344	2.04, 5.02
▲ ■ Design a Sari, p. 342	4.01, 6.01

CHARACTER AND VALUES EDUCATION	TRAITS
Writing Prompt, India's Challenges, p. 332	good judgment, respect
What Would You Do?, p. 343	integrity, kindness

● Basic Activities ★ Challenging Activities ▲ English Language Learner Novice ■ English Language Learner Intermediate

Chapter Activities

Introductory Activity

South Asian Body Language Customs

OBJECTIVES: 11.03, 12.01, 12.02, 12.05

Read the customs in It's a Fact on page 340 in the Teacher's Edition aloud to the class. Have students itemize any other Indian cultural customs in the textbook. Ask students what customs and traditions exist in this country. What customs and traditions exist in their families? Have students list customs and traditions that take place in their school.

Have small groups of students practice each of the South Asian samples of body language. Then they are to describe in written composition how it felt performing these gestures.

Culminating Activity

Travel Brochure

OBJECTIVES: 11.01, 11.02, 11.03

Make a travel brochure depicting a vacation in India. Be sure to include information about foods, clothing, art and architecture, means of transportation, seasons, special holidays and customs, and recreation. Be sure to explain how you would get to India and the accommodations you would enjoy when you arrive.

Extension For novice ELL students, model and provide additional explanations.

Art Activity

Paper Mosiacs

OBJECTIVES: 12.02, 12.03, 13.02

Materials construction paper 9-inch by 12-inch sheets, pencils, many different colors of construction paper cut into ¾-inch by ¾-inch squares, glue, places for drying

Review the mosaic art form by rereading "Connections" on pages 278. True mosaics should be based on the repetition of geometric patterns, but many seventh graders have difficulty with this abstraction. Have students page through their textbook to find other examples of mosaics. Note the countries where the examples were found and review the geographic theme of movement.

Hand out construction paper sheets. Have students draw a design that will incorporate three or four different colors of construction paper pieces. Once the students are satisfied with their designs, they can glue the pieces into place. Mosaics will need to lie flat to dry.

These mosaics make wonderful bulletin board displays.

Analogies

OBJECTIVES: 1.03

Analogies are useful to help students make associations with prior knowledge. They can be used as an instructional strategy to help students better understand new materials. They are not intended to be definitions or test items.

Read the analogies aloud and ask students to identify the relationship between the terms. As an extension, ask students to write their own analogies using key terms or places discussed in the chapter.

nonalignment : alignment :: unattached : attached :: crooked teeth : straight teeth (opposites)

Golden Temple : Sikhs :: Kaaba : Muslims (is holy site of)

nationalized : government :: privatized : private owners (run by)

cottage industry : home :: industrial centers : factory (workplace in)

rail system : India :: interstate highways : United States (backbone of transportation in)

class system : United States :: caste system : India (social stratification in)

Taj Mahal : India :: Statue of Liberty : United States :: Eiffel Tower : France (landmark of)

Bangalore : India :: Silicon Valley : United States (computer industry center in)

Teaching Strategies

This chapter provides an excellent opportunity for an "India Culture Day," where students may sample the sights, sounds, and tastes of India. This type of hands-on activity can be used as a culminating project for the unit after Chapter 18 has been concluded.

Activator

 **OBJECTIVES:** 12.01, 12.02, 13.02

Activators are great tools to use in order to "hook" the attention of the students.

Our Most Dear Friend: Bhagavad-Gita for Children, by Vishaka. (Torchlight Pub., 1996. ISBN 1887089047.)

OR

OBJECTIVES: 10.03, 11.01

Preamble
Provide each student with a copy of the Preamble to the United States Constitution and a copy of the Indian preamble found on page 334. Have students work with a partner to highlight words that they do not know in one color. Instruct them to try to define the new words using the context or a dictionary. Then, using a separate color, have them highlight words that are the same in both preambles. Ask students to analyze how the two preambles are similar, and follow up to their work with a group discussion.

Extension Novice and intermediate ELL students should choose one word in each document they do not know and define it using their native-language dictionary. Do not expect ELLs to participate in the discussion.

Writing Prompt

OBJECTIVES: 11.01, 11.02, 12.02

Evaluative
What do you think is the greatest challenge India faces in becoming a united country?
As you write your paper, remember to:
- clearly state your position.
- give at least three reasons and explain your reasons fully.
- give examples to support your reasons.
- write in complete sentences and paragraph form.
- organize your ideas and include an introduction and a conclusion.
- use good grammar, spelling, punctuation, and capitalization.

CHAPTER 17

Modern India

Crowds chanted with joy "Jai Hind! Victory to India!" as India's new flag was raised on August 15, 1947. The flag has three bands: saffron (orange-yellow), white, and dark green. In the center of the white band is a dark blue wheel, an ancient Buddhist symbol that stands for the wheel of law. The wheel also symbolizes for Hindus the endless cycle of life, death, and rebirth.

India's flag is a powerful symbol. It helps unite Indians. It symbolizes their ancient heritage and hopes for the future.

Chapter Preview

Lesson 1
Government and Politics
India has a constitutional government that ensures democratic rights.

Lesson 2
Economic Development
India has industry and commerce. Still, nearly half the people are poor.

Lesson 3
Society and Culture
India is a leader in modern entertainment. Yet traditional entertainment and foods remain popular.

Elephants march in a parade celebrating India's fiftieth anniversary of Independence in 1997.

332

Chapter Resources

Print Resources

Fiction

Vishaka. *Our Most Dear Friend: Bhagavad-Gita for Children.* Torchlight Pub., 1996. ISBN 1887089047.

Nonfiction

Kalman, Bobbie. *India: The Culture.* Crabtree, 2001. ISBN 0778793834.

__. *India: The People.* Crabtree, 2001. ISBN 0778793826.

__. *India: The Land.* Crabtree, 2001. ISBN 0778793818.

Back issues of magazines

India. Cobblestone Publishing Company. ISBN 0382405633.

Sikhs. Cobblestone Publishing Company. ISBN 0382445880.

Audiovisual

Images of India: The Land and the People. Cambridge Educational. Video, 35 minutes.

Video Visits India: Land of Spirit and Mystique. 1988. ISBN 0929756010. Good travelogue.

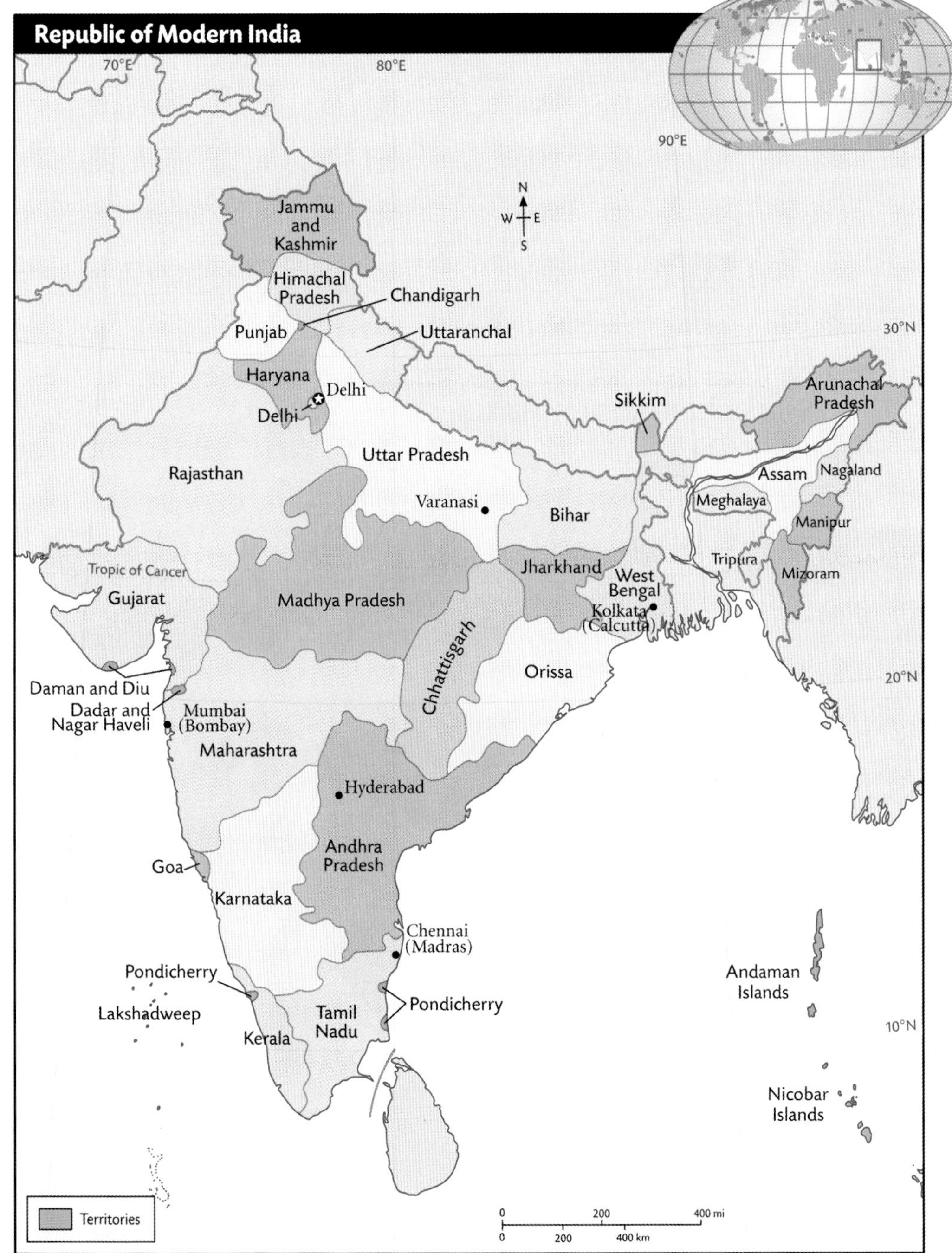

Teacher Notes

Indian States

According to the CIA World Factbook, **http://www.cia.gov/cia/publications/factbook/geos/in.html**, India had 28 states and seven territories in 2001.

Map Activity

What Is India Like Today?

NATIONAL GEOGRAPHY STANDARDS: 1, 3, 5, 9

GEOGRAPHIC THEMES: Location, Place, Region

OBJECTIVES: 1.02, 1.03

India is the world's most populous and complex federal state. It has 28 self-governing states and seven territories. Using the language map on page 313, note with students that a substantial degree of coincidence between linguistic and state boundaries exists. The most populous Indian states are Uttar Pradesh, Bihar, and Maharashtra. Have students locate and point out these three states. Discuss that the first two are located on the populated Ganges River plain. The third includes Mumbai, the world's second-largest city. Have students identify the location of this river and city.

Locate and identify some of the better-known Indian states included in Chapter 17:

- Haryana (with Delhi, capital)
- Punjab (with Amritsar)
- Guajarat
- Tamil Nadu (with Chennai)
- Kashmir
- West Bengal (with Kolkata)
- Maharashtra (with Mumbai)
- Rajasthan (with Jaipur)
- Kerala (with Kathakali dancer)
- Uttar Pradesh (with Agra and the Taj Mahal)
- Karnataka (with Bengaluru)

Show that two Indias fit comfortably within the 48 contiguous states of the United States. Coincidentally, India has about half as many states as the United States.

(India=1,266,595 sq. mi./
3,293,147sq. km.
U.S. 48 states=2,962,031 sq. mi./
7,701,281 sq. km.)

Web Sites

Go to **NCJourneys.com** for links to the following Web sites:

- BollywoodWorld
- Cultural India
- Culture of India
- India Government
- IndoLink: Kids Stories
- South Asia Culture, UCLA

 **OBJECTIVES:** 9.01, 10.01, 10.02

 Caption Answer

India is a republic with a constitutional government.

 Art Activity

Flag

OBJECTIVES: 7.02, 8.01

Draw a picture of the flag of India. It has three bands: saffron (orange-yellow), white, and dark green. In the center of the white band is a dark blue wheel. The wheel is an ancient Buddhist symbol for the wheel of law. The wheel can also symbolize power or the endless cycle of life, death, and rebirth. What do you think the designers of the flag had in mind for each element? Using the information from Chapter 17 on modern India, draw a new flag for modern India. What does each element stand for?

Extension Assign novice and intermediate ELL students to draw but not to analyze.

 Activity

ABC Book

OBJECTIVES: 11.01, 11.03, 12.03

Have students design and create an ABC book for India. Include a different Indian term, definition, and picture for each Indian word students choose. Terms can include foods, spices, crops, animals, geographical features, or other facts about India (they must have one term for each letter of the alphabet). This may also be done as a PowerPoint presentation, Web page, or digital story.

LESSON  Government and Politics

KEY IDEAS

- India has preserved its democratic government despite many obstacles.
- India's great size and diversity pose problems for the nation.
- Tensions between India and Pakistan have continued since partition. India tried to keep friendly relations with the Soviet Union and the United States during the Cold War.

KEY TERMS

federal system
nonalignment
Sikhs

> We the people of India, having solemnly resolved to constitute India into a Sovereign, Democratic Republic and to secure to all its citizens—justice, liberty, equality, fraternity—do hereby adopt, enact and give to ourselves this Constitution.

Those lines come from the preamble, or introduction, to India's constitution. Like the preamble to our own Constitution, they set high goals for the nation.

Democracy Amid Diversity

In 1947, India became an independent republic. Since then, it has built a tradition of democratic government. Its constitution set goals of justice, liberty, equality, and fraternity (brotherhood). Election campaigns in India are competitive. Voters elect candidates to local, state, and national office.

India has a parliamentary system of government. The parliament includes two houses: the Lok Sabha (lowk SAH•BAH), or House of the People, and the Rajya (RAH•jah) Sabha, or Council of States. The government is headed by a prime minister. He or she is the head of the political party that has won the most seats in parliament. The prime minister appoints a cabinet. The members lead such departments as justice or defense.

Elections in 1999 drew millions of voters in New Delhi and throughout India. **What kind of government does India have?**

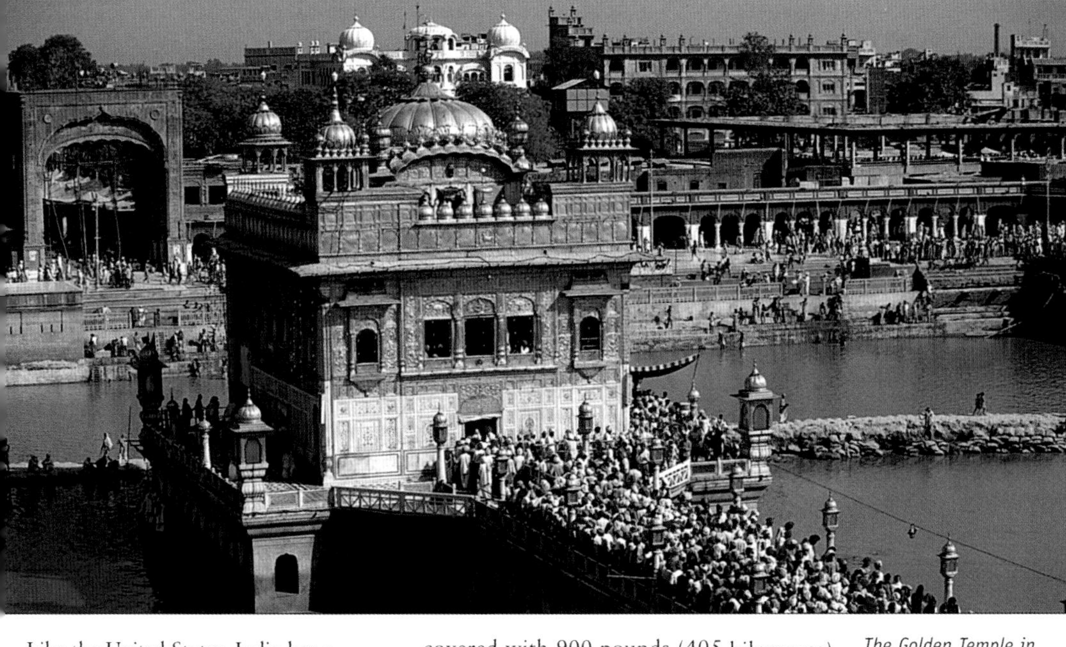

The Golden Temple in Amritsar surrounded by Sikhs, an Indian religious group. **How do India's many religious and ethnic groups challenge the nation's unity?**

Like the United States, India has a *ederal system:* power is divided between e national, or federal, government and the ates. In 2007, India had 28 states and 7 rritories (see map, page 333). Many states ave borders that bring together people who eak the same language.

Challenges to Unity

India's unity has faced severe tests. All India has rarely in its history been unified nder one government. In addition to many nguages, other forces threaten to tear dia apart. They include religious conflict, gional differences, and demands by groups ho want independence. "There is no such ing as an Indian," said Jawaharlal Nehru, dia's first prime minister. "One is either a njabi, a Gujarati, a Tamil, or a Kashmiri, nd then an Indian."

Nehru meant that Indians identify first ith their region, not with their nation. dia still struggles with this conflict.

truggle at the Golden Temple

The Golden Temple in Amritsar hm·RIT·sahr) is the holiest shrine of e *Sikhs* (seeks). Its outer walls, covered with 900 pounds (405 kilograms) of gold leaf, shimmer in the sunlight. Inside the temple are beautiful wall paintings and fine glasswork. Amritsar lies in Punjab, one of the richest states in India. Many Punjabis are Sikhs.

Sikhism blended Hindu and Muslim beliefs. It was meant to bridge the religions, but instead Sikhs faced persecution.

Today, some Sikhs want to break away from India and set up an independent country, called Khalistan. In 1984, Sikh radicals occupied the Golden Temple, where they had stored weapons. They refused to leave until India gave in to their demands. Prime Minister Indira Gandhi (no relation to the Mahatma) sent the Indian army to Amritsar. Many Sikhs were killed. The temple's interior was destroyed.

Four months later, the prime minister was killed by her Sikh bodyguards. That set off more violence. Crying "blood for blood," Hindu mobs murdered any Sikhs they saw. Order was finally restored. But the struggle has left a legacy of anger, fear, and mistrust.

Discussion Questions

1 Why do most people in North Carolina identify first as an American and then as a North Carolinian?

2 How does this affect the way our government in Washington functions?

3 Why have Sikhs been persecuted?

4 What is Khalistan?

5 Are there buildings in the United States or our community that are as important to us as the Golden Temple is in India?

Caption Answer

Indians identify first with their region, not with their nation.

Research Activity

Sources of Conflict

OBJECTIVES: 1.03, 5.01, 7.02

Using the map of India on page 333, assign each student one Indian state or territory to research. Students should determine the ethnic groups, religions, and languages found in each state as well as major economic activities (mineral resources, crops, industries, and so forth) that might be a source of conflict. After all students have had an opportunity to present their findings, brainstorm possible solutions of conflict.

Extension Research Sikhism. How does it attempt to blend Hindu and Muslim beliefs?

Background Information

Jawaharlal Nehru

Nehru, India's first prime minister, was also the father of Indira Gandhi and the grandfather of Rajiv Gandhi. Educated in England and trained as a lawyer, Nehru was one of Mahatma Gandhi's key lieutenants in the fight for Indian independence. During the 25-year struggle, he went to prison many times, spending more than nine years in jail. After Gandhi died, the public saw Nehru as his natural successor. As prime minister, Nehru worked to foster respect for democratic values and was particularly proud of reforming the ancient Hindu civil code to give Hindu widows the same inheritance and property rights as men.

Discussion Questions

1 What was the Cold War?

2 Is nonalignment a good policy? What would be the pros and cons of such a policy?

Caption Answer

Nehru worked to balance the needs and demands of many groups.

ELL Teaching Tips

Learn That Name Correctly!

Saying the name right isn't always easy, but it's important. Many Hispanic and Asian names have multiple parts, so getting them correct is important. Also, make sure you practice the correct pronunciation. Avoid Anglicizing a name; it robs your students of their identities.

Jawaharlal Nehru was India's first prime minister. **How did he work to unify India?**

Working for Unity

In 1947, many observers doubted democracy could succeed in India. Strong leaders like Jawaharlal Nehru helped bind the country together. Nehru worked to balance the needs and demands of many groups. The national government has promoted unity since independence to avoid such events as the Golden Temple fighting.

Hindu nationalism is increasing its influence in Indian politics. Some Hindu fundamentalism stems from opposition to reform of the caste system and to other religious minorities, especially Muslims. Violence and riots sometimes tinge the great progress that Indian democracy has made.

India and the World

India won independence just as the Cold War conflict between Western democracies and the Soviet Union began. India did not want to line up with either the United States or the Soviet Union, because it had just freed itself from British rule. So Prime Minister Nehru adopted a policy of ***nonalignment.*** That meant India would not become an ally of either superpower. India became a leader of nonaligned nations.

Border disputes with neighbors China and Pakistan kept India from gaining peac[e]. In 1962, China crossed India's mountain borders. China later withdrew its forces, b[ut] tensions continued for more than 30 years. India and Pakistan have fought three wars since partition. Some of their disputes have been settled through peaceful means. Whe[n] Hindu-Muslim violence occurs in India, tensions still rise between the two nations.

To protect its borders, India has spent heavily on defense. In 1974, it successfully tested an atomic bomb. India claimed it wanted to develop nuclear power for peaceful purposes. But it has refused to sig[n] a treaty that bans the spread of nuclear weapons. India claims it is unfair for the United States or Russia to keep weapons while other countries "watch with empty hands."

Word Origins

Travelers have used the **Khyber Pass** through the Hindu Kush for thousands of years. Khyber (KAI·ber) comes from a Greek word meaning "navigate." The word ***cyberspace*** has the same root as khyber. It is a computer term that describes the space you use to move around or navigate among computer programs, systems, and networks.

LESSON 1 REVIEW

Fact Follow-Up

1. Compare the forms of government in the United States and India.
2. What was the importance of the struggle at the Golden Temple in Amritsar?
3. What is the policy of nonalignment?
4. What have been the sources of rivalry between India and Pakistan since partition?

Talk About It

1. Why has unifying its people been such a difficult challenge for India?
2. Has the policy of nonalignment hurt or helped India? Explain.
3. What has been the role of religion in India's domestic and border conflicts?
4. Why does Hindu fundamentalism exist?

LESSON 1 REVIEW

Fact Follow-Up Answers

1. Both have constitutions that ensure democratic rights. India has a parliamentary system with two legislative houses, similar to our House of Representatives and Senate. India has a prime minister, whereas we have a president. India and the United States both have a federal system, in which power is shared between the national government and the state governments.
2. The struggle at the Golden Temple occurred because Sikhs were demanding independence. Four months later the prime minister of India was killed by her Sikh bodyguards. The Golden Temple tragedy has left a legacy of anger, fear, and mistrust.
3. A foreign policy whereby India avoided alliances with either the United States or the Soviet Union during the Cold War.
4. India and Pakistan have fought three wars since partition over border disputes.

Talk About It Answers

1. Important points: Encourage students to list examples of diversity and explain why each might challenge national unity. Note: different languages, religious conflict, regional groups, and demands for independence
2. Important points: Students should take a position and give reasons for it. Note: Recent independence may have encouraged India not to accept the "control" of either the United States or the Soviet Union.
3. India is largely Hindu, and Pakistan is Muslim. Turmoil within India often spills over into international disputes, and vice versa. Recent examples of domestic disturbances include Sikh independence movements such as the Golden Temple incidents.
4. Hindu fundamentalism stems from opposition to reform of the caste system and to opposition to other religious minorities, especially Muslims.

LESSON 2 Economic Development

What do a computer engineer and a camel-riding postman have in common? Both are part of India's economy. India contains contrasting modern and traditional ways. In the 'har Desert, Shanker Lal Joshi is a one-man mobile post office. Riding on camel, he braves sandstorms to carry mail to desert herders.

In the southern city of Bangalore, computer programmers are linked lectronically to colleagues around the world. Even within Bangalore, the ontrasts are vivid. Oxcarts and horse carriages rumble past research labs nd computer manufacturers.

At independence, India set ambitious economic goals. It has made great ains. It has one of the world's largest and fastest growing middle lasses—about 700 million people in 2003. Yet it has fallen short in many reas. High population growth and other problems pose obstacles to conomic progress.

KEY IDEAS

- Reforms in India have encouraged economic growth.
- Despite progress, India is still a country of contrasts between modern industrial centers and subsistence farmers.
- Caste is an obstacle to economic change, but efforts to ease caste restrictions face protests.

Economic Growth

"We feel the time is right for India to ke off," said an Indian business leader. By e mid-1990s, many Indians living abroad ere returning home or were investing in dia's businesses.

In earlier years, millions of Indians had ***migrated,*** or moved away. They looked r a better life in Britain, South Africa, the nited States, Hong Kong, and Southwest sia. Many succeeded in businesses. Now any successful Indians are returning home. thers are investing ***capital,*** or money, in dian ventures that will help the country's evelopment. India's middle class offers a ge new market.

India has a mixed economy that mbines government-run industries and rivate enterprise. After independence, ehru wanted to make India self-sufficient d raise the standard of living for all dians. He hoped to build industries so at India would not have to import anufactured goods. To do this, he used ***entral economic planning,*** which meant at the government set goals for industry d agriculture.

The government also ***nationalized,*** or took over, the ownership of some industries. It built and ran its own factories. To protect Indian industries from foreign competition, the government restricted imports. It also limited foreign investment. Privately owned factories were allowed, but they had to meet government regulations.

Zubin Mehta, a native of Mumbai, has conducted symphony orchestras all over the world. **Why are many Indians who moved away beginning to move back home?**

KEY TERMS

capital
central economic planning
cottage industries
emigrated
nationalized
privatized

odern India 337

OBJECTIVES: 4.01, 5.01, 6.01

Discussion Questions

1 Why was nonalignment a wise policy for India to pursue?

2 How will people who are returning to India from overseas affect the values and traditions of India?

3 What is the difference between "emigrated" and "immigrated"?

4 What is another definition for "capital"?

5 Why is a strong middle class necessary for a healthy economy?

6 Is it a good idea for governments to set goals for industry and agriculture? What problems could result?

7 What would be a problem if industries were nationalized? What would be the benefits?

Caption Answer

Economic progress is bringing them back.

Map Activity

India's Economic Activities

NATIONAL GEOGRAPHY STANDARDS: 1, 2, 11, 14, 16

GEOGRAPHIC THEMES: Human-Environmental Interaction

OBJECTIVES: 5.01, 5.03

Using atlases and other reference sources and blank political maps showing India's states and territories, have students create an economic activity map of India. Students should create their own map legends that include agricultural resources, mineral resources, and major industries and color or label their maps accordingly. When students have completed their maps, they should identify areas that appear to have little economic resources.

Extension ELL students should use an ELL-friendly Web site for research.

Discussion Questions

1 Why would privatization of industry work better?

Caption Answer

India's economy includes manufacturing of jute, cotton, and steel. India also produces many movies. Sri Lanka produces tea. Pakistan produces textiles.

Math Activity

Central Economic Planning Outline

OBJECTIVES: 4.03, 5.02, 5,03, 8.01

Nehru wanted to raise the standard of living in India using Central Economic Planning. Have students outline the goals he set for industry and agriculture. Show the results of his efforts.

Industry—Regulations

1. Government took over some industries.
2. Factories produced products and consumer goods.
3. Government restricted foreign imports.
4. Government limited foreign investments.
5. Privately owned factories and industries had to meet government regulations.

Industry—Results

1. Industry expanded.
2. Factories produced products and consumer goods.
3. Coal and steel production rose.
4. As time went by, progress was too slow and inefficient, so government cut back regulations and privatized.

Agriculture—Regulations

1. Green Revolution—increased farm production.
2. More food by cultivation.

Agriculture—Results

1. Prices in crops have decreased over time.
2. Farms too small to buy needed machinery.
3. Population increases have caused farmland to decrease as more houses must be built on acreage.

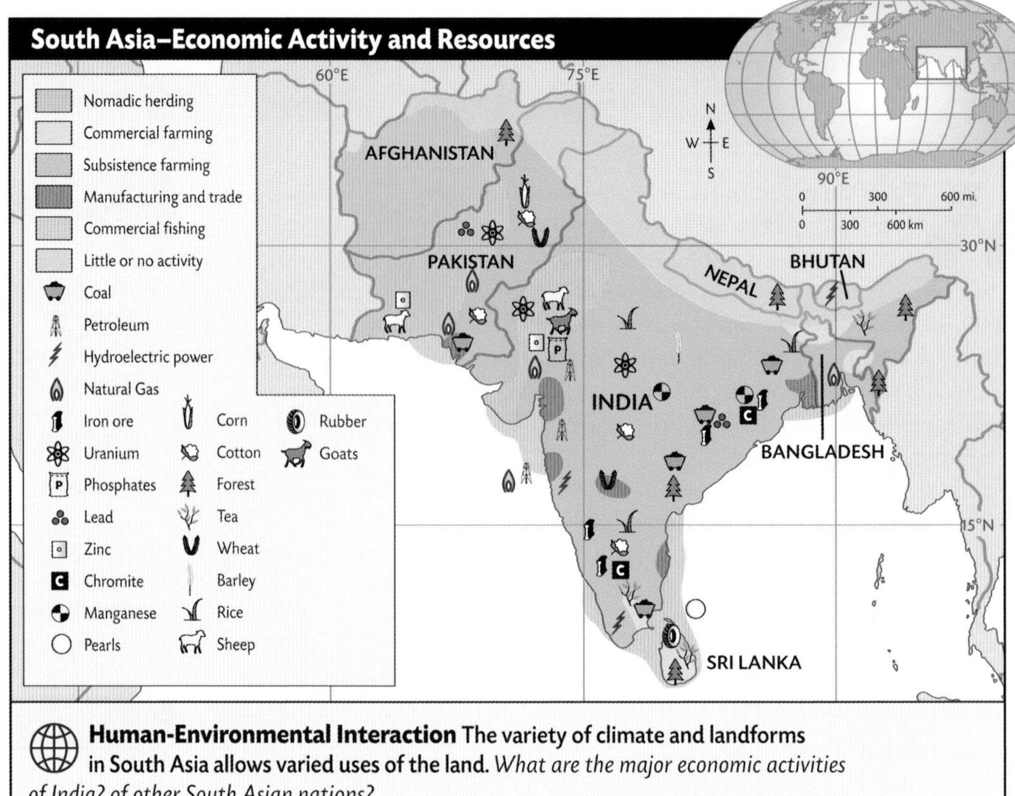

Human-Environmental Interaction The variety of climate and landforms in South Asia allows varied uses of the land. *What are the major economic activities of India? of other South Asian nations?*

In the 1950s, India's economy made big gains. Industries expanded. Factories turned out trucks, bulldozers, and chemicals along with consumer goods such as televisions. Coal and steel production rose.

Central economic planning was often slow and inefficient with many rules and regulations. By the 1980s, India's economy was not growing. So the government turned to economic reforms. It cut back on its regulations. It ***privatized,*** or sold to private owners, government-run industries. It welcomed foreign investors and supported businesses in which Indians worked with Americans, Japanese, or other foreigners. Today, India ranks among the world's leading industrial nations.

Agriculture has had some success, but less than industry. As you have read, the Green Revolution helped boost farm output. Improved seeds and farming methods produced more food than ever before. After these early successes, agricultural production leveled off. Mos Indian farmers are poor. They cannot afford the new seeds or expensive chemical fertilizers of the Green Revolution. Also, since their plots of land are small, they can neither afford nor use costly farm machinery.

Industry

India is a nation of contrasts. Small businesses thrive in villages. In other places, huge manufacturing centers make steel and other products.

Cottage Industries As her child watches, a mother works a hand-operated loom. Her long-practiced movements mak traditional patterns on a carpet. Across India, craftworkers make goods by hand.

It's a Fact

India's Industries

- The Bihar-West Bengal states (including Kolkata in West Bengal) is the center of India's eastern industrial region. Jute is most important here, but also engineering, chemical, and cotton industries exist.
- The western industrial regions are around Mumbai in the state of Maharashtra and Ahmadabad in the state of Gujarat. Both regions specialize in cotton and chemicals, with some engineering and food processing.
- The southern industrial region is around Chennai in Tamil Nadu, where textile production, light engineering, and computer technology are found.
- The states of Uttar Pradesh and Bihar have most of India's coalfields.
- Jamshedpur in West Bengal is India's leading steelmaking and metals-fabrication center. Its steel industry is growing.
- India's iron ores in Bihar and Karnataka states are believed to be some of the largest in the world.
- India exports iron ore.
- The 1984 Bhopal gas leak at Union

University students gather around a microscope in a botany class (left). A woman spins wool for carpets in Jaipur, India (below). **How do craftspeople and college-educated people both contribute to India's economy?**

These small family businesses are alled *cottage industries* because goods re made in the home. Weavers make silk r cotton goods on handlooms. Other killed workers create brass, silver, or opper goods to export. Because such oods are in demand, India's cottage ndustries are valuable to the nation's conomy.

Manufacturing and Technology

Iuge industrial centers are also nportant to India. Industry spreads out rom India's leading cities. Three large nanufacturing areas are centered around Colkata, Mumbai, and Chennai.

If you visited Kolkata in eastern ndia, you would find great jute actories. Jute is a plant used to make urlap and twine. Kolkata also contains nany cotton mills. India has exported otton goods since ancient times. Today, t outranks the United Kingdom in its olume of cotton exports. Kolkata is lso a steel hub. Everyday, trains and rucks unload tons of coal and iron ore rought from nearby mines.

If you flew west across the ubcontinent to coastal Mumbai, you vould find factories producing chemicals nd textiles or processing foods. Mumbai's power supply comes from ydroelectric plants in the Western Ghats.

Factories in the southern city of Madras turn out textiles and consumer goods. Many engineers and computer specialists live in this region, which has become a center for high technology.

Good transportation has speeded India's development. Airlines connect key cities. Its rivers provide 5,000 miles (8,050 km) of waterways. Rail transport is the most important. India has one of the world's largest rail systems.

Carbide's pesticide plant killed more than 3,400 and injured about 200,000 Indians; this is in the state of Madhya Pradesh.

■ Between 1990 and 2005, industry's contribution to the economy only grew from 25 percent to 27 percent. In the same period, the share of services leapt from 37 percent to 52 percent.

■ In the next ten years, companies in the United States, Japan, and Europe will outsource manufacturing to India, including auto parts, telecom equipmen, pharmaceuticals, fabricated metal products, high-end chemicals, consumer electronics, and computer hardware.

Discussion Questions

1 Do we have "cottage industries" in our community? What are some examples?

2 What industrial centers do we have in North Carolina? What are our state's major products?

Caption Answer

Craftspeople create fine goods that are in demand overseas. College-educated people work in high technology and other industries.

Map Activity

India Dominates South Asia's Economic Development

NATIONAL GEOGRAPHY STANDARDS: 1, 4, 16

GEOGRAPHIC THEMES: Location, Place, Human-Environmental Interaction, Region

OBJECTIVES: 5.01, 5.03, 5.04

Students should use the Republic of Modern India map on page 333 with this economic resources map.

Assign students to answer the following using textbook and above description:

1. What is the main type of farming in South Asia? *subsistence*
2. Where does most of South Asia's nomadic herding occur? *Afghanistan, Pakistan, and Great Indian/Thar Desert south to Gulf of Khambhat*
3. Where does most of South Asia's commercial farming occur? *southern three fourths of Sri Lanka; India in south-central Tamil Nadu state, north-central West Bengal state, western Meghalaya state, Tripura state; northern and east-central Bangladesh*
4. Which South Asian countries are impacted by commercial fishing? *Pakistan, India, Bangladesh, Sri Lanka*
5. Why would Bhutan, Nepal, northern India and Pakistan, as well as portions of Afghanistan have little or no farming or fishing? *highland climates, and desert in Afghanistan, with altitudes not adaptable to these economic activities*

Eyewitness Activity

India's Railways Activities

OBJECTIVES: 4.01, 6.02, 7.01, 8.03

Ask students to brainstorm what they know about train travel and railways in the United States. Ask them what kinds of goods are transported by railway. They might suggest cars, circus animals, people, coal, and so on. After brainstorming, have them read the Eyewitness to History on pages 340–41 about India's railways. Have students compare India's railways with American railways.

If possible, show the excerpt from the movie *Gandhi,* starring Ben Kingsley, where Gandhi travels around India by train. This excerpt integrates well with the text. After reading the Eyewitness and viewing the excerpt from the movie, students can describe scenes from an Indian train.

Draw the chart below on the overhead or board. Ask students to write a paragraph about India's railways using the terms the chart.

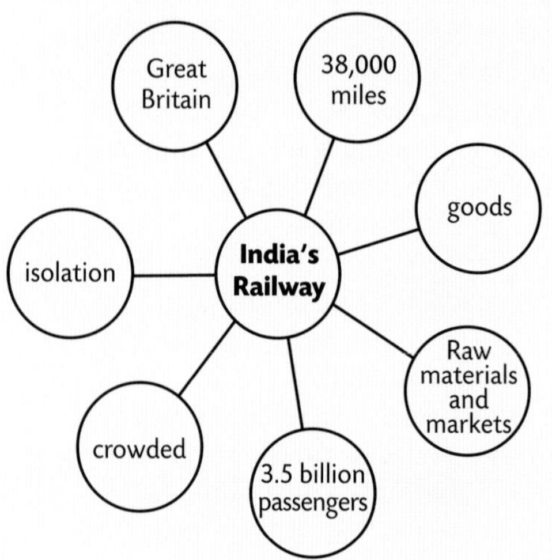

EYEWITNESS TO HISTORY

India's Railways

For centuries, elephants and pack animals carried people and trade goods across India (bottom left). In the middle of the 1800s, a different kind of beast—the railroad—took over that job.

India's railways today are built on foundations laid by the United Kingdom's colonial government. The British saw trains as a way of keeping its officials in touch with the people of a huge colony. The British also saw railways as a means for reaching India's raw materials and markets.

India has expanded the rail system built by the British and installed as much new equipment as it can afford. It depends heavily on its more than 38,000 miles (61,180 km) of track to transport people and freight across the country (below). The use of automobiles and trucks has been rapidly increasing. Yet highways crossing long distances are not common.

It's a Fact

South Asian Body Language

- The dot worn on the forehead is called a "bindi" or "Kumkum." In southern India, girls choose to wear a bindi. In other parts of India it is the prerogative of the married woman.
- Pink is the color of welcome.
- To refuse food is considered an insult.
- Pulling one's ears is a gesture of sincerity.
- Tossing one's head backward slightly is a "yes" response.
- Fingers and palms of both hands placed together with third fingers toward chin or nose and a nod of the head is the namaste. A popular greeting in South Asia, particularly in India and Sri Lanka with religious believers, it is also used to say good-bye.
- Men should not touch a woman nor speak to a lone woman in public.
- Men shake hands when meeting or leaving another man, but men and women do not shake hands.
- One uses only the right hand when passing or accepting food.
- Removing one's shoes before entering an Indian home is expected.
- When given a garland of flowers upon

oday, rail travel figures reach 5 billion passengers a year. Trains e always very crowded (right and low). Some adventurous travelers en try riding the roofs of passenger rs. Inside the cars, there are several asses of accommodations. Lowest res are for seats on hard wooden nches.

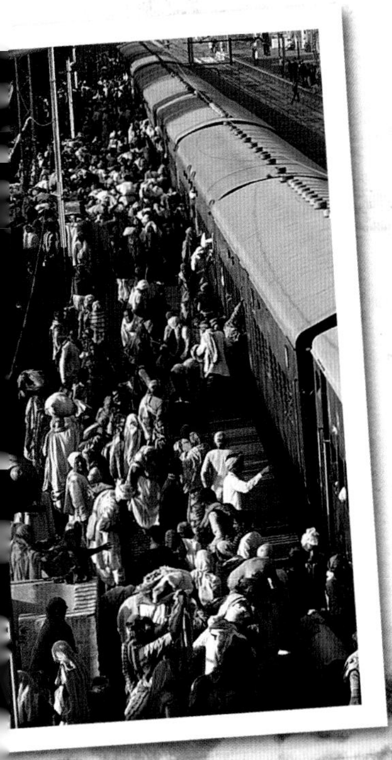

Railway expansion has broken the isolation of many villages. Tracks have been built into areas that were difficult to reach. On the route into the Himalayan foothills, engineers conquered a steep grade by building track that looped over itself in a figure eight pattern.

arriving at an Indian home, one removes the garland immediately as a sign of humility.

- By grasping your ear you either mean "I'm sorry" or "honestly." Many do this when scolded.
- If someone smiles and jerks his head backward, it can mean "yes." In southern India, if someone moves his head quickly back and forth it means "yes, I understand what you are saying."
- The head is considered sacred, so one does not touch an older person's head or pat a young person on his or her head.
- It is impolite to show the soles of your feet or point a foot while sitting on the floor (as it is in much of the Muslim world) because this part of the body is considered the lowest and dirtiest.
- Whistling in public is quite impolite.
- Use the full hand, or possibly the thumb or chin, to point. Never use any single finger—it is only used with inferiors; never point with the chin to people who are considered superior.

Math Activity

Putting an End to Poverty

OBJECTIVES: 5.03, 6.01

Using the economic activity map from page 338, form a student group for each economically depressed area identified. Each group will be given $10 million to spend to improve the standard of living for as many people as possible. Money can be spent on education, factories, health care, transportation, and utilities. Each group will use the following cost list to complete a "Standard of Living Improvement Budget" for a town or city in their area. Any factories students decide to build should reflect the limited economic activities that are close by their area. Consideration must also be given to the movement of goods.

Standard of Living Improvement Costs
coal-fired electric plant—$4 million; water treatment plant—$1.5 million; 12-bed clinic—$250 thousand; 45-bed hospital with one operating room—$1 million; each nurse—$7.5 thousand; each doctor—$20 thousand; each surgeon—$45 thousand; elementary school—$200 thousand; high school—$500 thousand; technical school—$1 million; each elementary and high school teacher—$7.5 thousand; each technical school instructor—$10 thousand; agricultural or food processing factory, employing 45 people—$1.5 million; mineral resources processing factory employing 65 people—$2.5 million; small appliances or consumer goods factory employing 80 people—$3 million; 50 miles of railroad track—$1 million; freight airport—$2.5 million.

Each student group will present their budgets to the class. Presentations should include the name of the town or city and state. All budget items and total cost must be included in the budget. After all groups have presented their budgets, the class may vote on which group appears to raise the standard of living for the most people.

Discussion Questions

1 How would Hinduism explain the "two faces" of India?

2 What challenges does India still face?

Art Activity

Design a Sari

OBJECTIVES: 4.03, 12.02, 12.03

Research the traditional style of dress, the sari worn by women and girls, and the dhoti worn by men and boys in India. Design and make a traditional sari or dhoti to wear as a costume. Another option for this project is to design and make an Indian doll wearing either a sari with jewelry or a dhoti and turban.

Extension This is a good opportunity for ELL student/parent involvement. Ask a parent or student from India to bring one in to show the class.

Caption Answer

Even though the caste system is slowly breaking down, the thousands-of-years-old system is still part of Indian society.

Two Faces of India

India's development is impressive. Only a minority, however, share the wealth India has produced. Randhir Singh is the son of a rajah, or Indian prince. He lives with his wife and children in a large house with eight servants. He owns three cars. His children wear uniforms to school, where students have their own books. Family members who become sick receive care at a nearby hospital.

In contrast, a man selling used goods in Kolkata just manages to support his wife and children. His family lives in a single room. None of his family can read or write. His wife sews to make extra money. The family cannot afford medical care. If either parent is seriously hurt or falls ill, the family may lose all that it has.

Even more desperate are the many homeless people in the cities. Many of these have fled from India's villages. These poor live on the sidewalk at night. At dawn they gather up their few belongings and look for work. Children dig through garbage to find items their parents can sell to recyclers. They may earn enough to buy their next meal. There is little hope for more.

Education and employment opportunities are two factors separating India's middle and lower classes. **Why is it hard for lower classes to move into the middle class?**

Despite government efforts to improve life for the poor, their numbers in the cities keep growing. Twenty-five percent of Indians live in poverty. More than a third of the nation is too poor to afford an adequate diet.

Great wealth and great poverty are a terrible contrast in today's India. The rich and the large middle class enjoy a high standard of living. The city poor and subsistence farmers face challenges simply survive, but the standard of living has increased for nearly everyone.

Caste

Newspapers in India regularly car ads like this one:

Handsome, well-educated Brahmin, age 25, earning good income. Seeks bride age 18 to 23, employed and educated. Caste no barrier.

You read earlier how a villager objecte to his son's drinking from a lower caste well. In village India, marriage across cas lines would be unthinkable. People fro different castes are mixing in India's lar cities.

This breakdown of the thousands-of-years-old caste system is a sweeping chang in Indian law. Under the constitution, anyone can become a doctor or lawyer, an there are penalties for discrimination. As people move to other cities, different caste mingle in the workplace, at eating stands, and on buses. Young people especially support these new ways. They think that t constitution is right.

Many business leaders agree. They often find that the caste system makes running a business difficult. Some factory owners, for example, hire people from only one caste to avoid such problems as having to provide separate eating areas. Other business leaders insist that this creates too much expense. These leader say that if people want jobs, they must forget their traditional status. Yet the caste system still has many supporters.

Caste has traditionally determined every Hindu's place in society. Hindus

…ill say that caste gives them a sense of …entity. It offers them protection and a …twork to call on for jobs or help. …ose who benefit from the caste system …ork to preserve it. Muslims, who do …t acknowledge caste, have become like …caste to many Hindus.

The debate continues. Efforts to do …way with the system are having an effect. …t eliminating attitudes that segregate …indus by caste is likely to take many …nerations.

What would YOU do?

Imagine that you know a villager of a low caste who had moved to Mumbai. She found a job in a department store where she worked with several women from higher castes. You also know these higher caste women. You could tell these higher caste women what you know about the new employee. What would you do?

Great wealth, an expanding middle class, and extreme poverty, such as these Dalit men, are all part of modern India. **How do India's poor people survive?**

LESSON 2 REVIEW

Fact Follow-Up

1. Describe India's mixed economy.
2. Why did the Indian government first nationalize and later privatize certain industries?
3. Where are some of India's industrial centers, and what are their products?
4. Compare living conditions of wealthy and poor people living in an Indian city.

Talk About It

1. What do you think is the greatest problem facing India today? Explain why.
2. How has the modern Indian economy changed the caste system?
3. If you were an advisor to the Indian government, what agricultural policies would you suggest? Explain your answer.

Discussion Questions

1 What can be done to eliminate attitudes brought about by the caste system?

2 If you were an employer, what qualifications would you look for before hiring someone? Would you consider the person's social class?

Caption Answer

The lower classes have a difficult time just making ends meet. Many cannot read or write.

Writing Activity

Matrimonial Advertisement

OBJECTIVES: 10.3, 10.4, 11.01, 12.01

Students will write their own matrimonial advertisement. Advise them to keep the information simple. In 35 words or less, they should write an ad that presents the characteristics about themselves that would prompt someone to choose them as their marriage partner. In addition, have students write in 35 words or less an ad explaining characteristics they look for in a potential marriage partner. The teacher can gather them and read them out loud for the students to figure out to whom the ad refers. (Ask if there is anyone who would not want his or hers read aloud.) This activity can be used in conjunction with a discussion or debate about arranged marriages. You can also bring up the fact that people in our society submit personal advertisements in the newspaper to find perspective partners.

LESSON 2 REVIEW

Fact Follow-Up Answers

1. India's mixed economy combines government-run industries and private enterprise. Following independence in 1947 there was a great deal of central economic planning. Since the 1980s, however, India has cut back on its ownership of businesses, encouraged privatization, and welcomed foreign investment.
2. The government nationalized industry as part of central economic planning in the hope of making India self-sufficient. Later, when central economic planning proved slow and inefficient, the government privatized industries to make them more productive.
3. Kolkata produces cotton goods and steel. Mumbai's factories make chemicals, textiles, and processed food. Chennai turns out textiles and consumer goods and is also home to many high-technology industries.
4. Wealthy people live in large houses with servants and own several cars. The children go to a private school and the family gets medical care whenever they need it. The poor live on the street and hope to make enough to buy a meal by working or selling used goods found in the garbage. They have no schooling and no medical care.

Talk About It Answers

1. Important points: Encourage students to focus on one problem and explain why that problem is the most important one. Note: Poverty is a problem that causes suffering among many people.
2. In modern work situations in the cities of India, people of different castes now mingle, though the caste system remains strong in villages. Though many support the caste system, some business leaders believe the system makes industry less productive.
3. Important points: Encourage students to suggest and explain a number of policies. Note: Loans to farmers for seeds, chemical fertilizers, and community-owned machinery to increase production.

OBJECTIVES: 11.01, 12.01, 12.02

Discussion Questions

1 What is good about diversity? What can be some of the drawbacks?

2 What are some examples of diversity in our community?

Caption Answer

They tell tales of gods and heroes from the Hindu tradition.

Art Activity

Batik

OBJECTIVES: 4.03, 12.02, 12.03, 13.02

Materials white construction paper, crayons, black watercolor paint, brush, water and water container, iron

Provide a variety of art samples from India. The students may also study pictures in their book found on pages 290-91, 319, 340, 344, and 345. You may also use illustrations from picture books to help give ideas. Instruct students to draw a picture depicting a scene from India or an animal using lots of color. They should also color very darkly with the crayons so that they use a lot of wax. Once their picture is complete, have them crumble up their picture so that the crayon wax crumbles on the paper. Once the picture is crunched, students should paint over it with black watercolor paint. Wipe off the excess paint and then have them bring the picture to you to iron. After ironing the picture, let the picture dry and then display. Ironing exposes the watercolor paint in the cracks. Students have now completed a Batik. Explain that Batik is an art form popular in India usually performed on cotton or silk material.

LESSON 3 Society and Culture

KEY IDEAS

- India has rich and varied traditions in dance and music.
- Two epic poems, the *Ramayana* and the *Mahabharata*, reflect the influence of Hindu culture.
- Even as India modernizes, its ancient tastes and culture remain vivid and alive.

KEY TERMS

Bhagavad-Gita
epic poem
Mahabharata
Ramayana

You read how Mark Twain called India the "Land of Wonders." He spoke of its diversity. India's diversity is even greater today making it difficult to make general statements about India. Even its main religion, Hinduism, is practiced in hundreds of ways. Today, there are great contrasts in India between urban and rural life and between rich and poor. Some groups of people still live by hunting and food gathering. Elsewhere, engineers design computers. India's diversity has both advantages and disadvantages. Among its benefits a[re] its rich traditions in the arts.

Dance and Music

Drums chatter and thunder across the fields. They promise an exciting performance of Kathakali (kath·ah·kah·LEE), or dance-drama. After dark, men, women, and children follow the drummers to a public space. Drummers work in relays as firelight glistens off their faces.

At midnight, performers appear dressed in fantastic costumes. They will dance all night, acting tales from Hindu tradition. Older villagers know the thrilling stories of gods and heroes. Masks and colorful makeup of green, red, white, and black show whether the dancer is a hero, god, demon, or animal. Bells on their ankles rattle as they stamp their feet.

Kathakali is performed only by boys and men. The complex dance steps take years to learn. So do the hand and eye movements. There are 24 positions of the hands that can be combined to convey more than 600 words.

Kathakali is one of many dance traditions. Each belongs to a particular region. Kathakali comes from Kerala in the southwest. Dance is always tied to music, and both are linked to Hinduism. In fact, the Hindu god Shiva (SHEE·vah) often appears as the Lord of the Dance, Nataraja (nah·tah·BAH·jah) (see photo, page 316).

A Kathakali dancer performs in Kerala Province, India. **What kinds of tales are told in this tradition of dance-drama?**

344

Chapter

Background Information

Parsis of Bombay

A tiny religious minority, known as the Parsis, have unique burial customs. They are followers of the ancient prophet Zoraster. Since the 1600s, Parsis in Bombay have carried their dead up to Malabar Hill, a 50-acre (20 sq-hm) forest in the city. There, mourners lay the corpse on one of the Towers of Silence to be picked clean by vultures. Today this burial ritual is in danger of extinction because India's vultures are disappearing. After looking at such causes as pollution and pesticide use, scientists decided an infectious disease may be the cause. The Bombay Parsi council hopes to keep this ritual alive by building an aviary where disease-free birds can be bred in captivity.

The Hindu god Krishna battles a demon in a watercolor from the Mahabharata. **What is the *Bhagavad-Gita?***

tories for All Time

Arjuna (are·JU·nah) stands in his ariot waiting for the ram's horn to sound. will signal the start of battle. Arjuna is a ave and noble warrior, but he confides to chariot driver, Krishna (KREESH·nah), at he dreads this battle. Krishna, who is lly a god in disguise, tells Arjuna that has no choice. As a warrior, it is juna's duty to fight. His wishes are important. "There is more joy in doing e's duty badly," says Krishna, "than in ing another man's duty well."

This story is part of a religious poem own to hundreds of millions of Hindus. is called the ***Bhagavad-Gita*** ah·gah·vahd-GEE·tah), or "The Song of od." From childhood, Indians hear such es that were written down in two great ic poems. An ***epic poem*** is a long poem out the deeds of heroes. The Bhagavad-ta is part of India's great epic, the ***ahabharata*** (MAH·ah·BAH·rah·tah). dians call their country "Bharat" from e story's title. Maha means "great."

This epic is one of the world's longest ems with more than 100,000 verses. rt of the poem describes how rulers ould govern, tell ancient legends, and ach about religion.

India's other great epic is the ***Ramayana*** (rah·MAH·yah·nah). It tells the story of Rama, the ideal son and warrior-king. Rama is married to the beautiful Sita, the perfect Hindu wife—loyal, obedient, and faithful. When the demon-king kidnaps Sita, Rama sets out to find her. As he roams across India, he has many adventures. Finally, helped by Hanuman, the monkey general, he finds and frees Sita.

Both the *Mahabharata* and the *Ramayana* grew out of India's cultural traditions. Both epics help keep those traditions alive. When an actor playing the god Krishna tells Arjuna that he must do his duty by going into battle, he reminds the audience of a basic Hindu belief. Other values, especially compassion and loyalty to the family, are passed along by the constant retelling of these ancient stories.

Movies and television plays are based on epics. Holidays are linked to events in the *Ramayana*. One celebration, *Dussehra* (DOO·say·rah) recalls Rama's rescue of his wife, Sita. Soon after comes *Diwali* (DEE·wah·lee), a festival celebrating the Hindu goddess of wealth and beauty. Diwali means "the garland of lights." People display lights to show Rama and Sita the way home.

Teacher Notes

India's Names

India has three names: India, Bharat and Hindustan. They are all commonly and officially used and have historical or cultural significance. The first Article of the Constitution of India states that "India, that is Bharat, shall be a union of states." Therefore, India and Bharat are official short names for the Republic of India. Hindustan, or HInd, is considered a historical name, especially India. "India" is derived from the name of the Indus River.

Discussion Questions

1 What are some stories we have that teach a lesson?

2 What are these stories called?

3 What would be considered characteristics of the perfect wife? Would "obedient" be one?

4 How do we pass along traditions and values?

Caption Answer

It is a religious poem known to hundreds of millions of Hindus. Its name means "The Song of God."

Activity

Indian Culture Day

 **OBJECTIVES:** 4.03, 12.01, 12.02, 12.03

The following activities can be combined and presented on one day as a celebration of Indian culture. Activities can be completed by cooperative groups or by individuals based on your discretion.

Student Projects

Research foods from India and find a recipe. If ingredients are available in your area, try cooking the dish for your classmates.

After studying the different styles of dress from India, design your own costume to be worn in class on Indian Culture Day. Make sure you know what region your clothing represents. (Optional: Make a doll dressed in traditional Indian clothing.)

Study different pieces and styles of artwork from India. Using available materials, create a copy of one of the pieces of art you study.

Study the music native to India and try to find an example to play for your classmates to enjoy.

Research examples of Indian literature. Read it and present to class through drama, illustrations, video, song, poster, or other presentations.

Extension ELL students should do the first three parts only. An added dimension to Culture Day can include speakers, artists, and dancers native to India or knowledgeable of the area.

Discussion Questions

1 How has the media affected tradition and values?

Living in Modern India

OBJECTIVES: 13.03

SAS Institute is the largest privately held software company in the world. It is headquartered in Cary, North Carolina. It was founded in 1976 and serves more than 35,000 business, government, and university sites in 110 countries.

SAS has locations in Europe, North America, South America, Asia, and Australia. SAS has three sites in India. They are located in Mumbai, Delhi, and Bagalore—the "Silicon Valley of India."

Have students log on to the SAS Web site **www.sas.com** and read more about SAS. Create a Web scavenger hunt for your students to complete using the SAS site. Or have each student choose a nation from the 110 and complete a mini-report on SAS's presence in that nation.

Extension Access the Web site using the **www.worldlingo.com** URL translator to increase comprehension for most ELL students. Do not assign novice and intermediate ELL students the report accompanying this activity.

Mumbai: India's Moviemaking Capital

With an evil sneer, the villain leers at the lovely young heroine draped in a dazzling costume. The figures appear on a huge billboard in Mumbai. It advertises a new adventure movie.

Called Bombay by the British, Mumbai is nicknamed Bollywood, the "Hollywood of India." Half of India's movies are made there.

India is the world's largest movie producer. It turns out 800 full-length movies a year in 12 languages, plus many documentaries and short films. Many plots come from stories in the ep poems.

Like Hollywood filmmakers, Indian moviemakers create celebrities. Audienc idolize movie stars, giving them the virtues of the heroes they play. Because their popularity, some movie stars have won election to political office.

A Journey to Modern India

India's Information Technology Industry

Education for the wealthy has been a tradition in India since the beginnings of its civilization. Great Buddhist universities at Nalanda and Taxila were famous far beyond India's borders. Today, India's educated workforce attracts investment from around the world.

India's education system has benefited from the government's socialist policies. Tuition at the majority of India's top universities does not exceed $500 annually. The Indian Institute of Technology (IIT) charges less than $100 per year in tuition. Quality education is available to a wide range of people.

India's advantage lies in its vast resource of skilled computer personnel. Engineers must attend a four-year college before they are certified. Software programmers are certified at software training institutes that require a high school diploma. These graduates are in high demand around the globe. Many computer professionals move to the United States or Persian Gulf states to work. About 30 percent of IIT graduates leave the country every year. There are also good jobs for those who choose to stay in India.

Software Technology Parks (STP) have been set up in many cities. The STPs contain centralized computing facilities along with satellite links. The southern city of Bengaluru (Bangalore) is known as the Silicon Valley of India.

In 1986, Texas Instruments opened a subsidiary there. All the software, designs, and data produced there are sent to Texas Instruments' American offices via satellite. The United States is India's largest consumer of exported software, followed by Western Europe. Many American companies have sent some or all of their information technology work to India. In developed countries, technical support is labor intensive and requires highly skilled computer personnel. Indian companies provide more cost-effective technical support than Western companies.

Indian stock brokers

346 Chapter

Background Information

Bangalore in Cyberspace

The city of Bangalore has become the center of India's growing information technology industry. Today technology parks ring this crowded city of 6 million people. Companies there provide everything from customer service centers and insurance claims processors to software developers, Web site designers, and animation artists for companies around the world. To support the sector's economic growth, the Indian government has exempted technology firms from many export restrictions that other industries face. This policy seems to be working. India's technology exports grew from $150 million in 1990 to $4 billion in 2000.

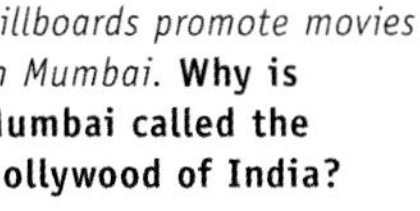

Billboards promote movies in Mumbai. **Why is Mumbai called the Hollywood of India?**

Discussion Questions

1 What foods are special to different regions in our community or region?

2 What do foods and recipes tell about communities?

3 What are some regional differences in food in the United States or North Carolina? How are these regional differences changing?

Caption Answer

Half of India's movies are made in Mumbai.

Ihe Flavor ɔf Daily Life

Have you tasted curry? Our word ırry comes from *kari*, an Indian word ıeaning "a spice sauce." Curries are ɔmmon in Indian cooking. Fish, meat, ıd vegetables are cooked in spice sauces.

Yet Indian cooking is a lot more than ırry. Dishes vary widely across India. ven curries differ. Cooks can choose from ıore than 30 different spices to make ıeir curries.

Millions of Hindus and Buddhists are ɛgetarians, people who eat no meat. So ıdians have invented many tasty meatless ishes. Although Hindus eat no beef and ʼIuslims are forbidden to touch pork, ɔme people of both faiths eat goat or .mb. These meat dishes include kabobs, ıeat grilled on skewers, and *kooftah* (KOF· ıh), meatballs cooked with spices.

India is so large, each subregion has eveloped its own dishes based on local ɔods and spices. In northern India, where wheat crops are numerous on the broad plain, people grind grain to make breads. Southern Indians eat more rice. Northerners enjoy rich foods cooked in *ghee* (guh·EE), a kind of butter, and spicy meats. Southerners tend to be vegetarians. Their dishes are lighter, but their curries are often hot. Side dishes of *raita* (RAY·tah), or yogurt, and coconut milk soothe the effects of fiery curries.

Customs

In India, as elsewhere, spring festivals are related to religions. A Hindu spring festival called *Holi* offers Indians a chance for fun and seriousness. Young people splash one another with colored water and dyes. They play tricks and practical jokes on one another. Holi honors the Hindu god Krishna, who is often portrayed as a playful child.

Activity

Indian Food

OBJECTIVES: 12.03, 13.02

In some ways, America owes the discovery of the New World to the European desire to use spices in their cooking. Access to Indian spices was one of the reasons Europeans sought a convenient route to Asia. Curry means spice sauce. Fish, poultry, meat, and vegetables all have special blends of spices in their curries. Each recipe calls for the roasting and grinding of different proportions of spices such as coriander, cumin, turmeric, and dried red chilis. A chicken recipe might call for cinnamon, cloves, and ginger as well. Fish and vegetable dishes call for less strong seasoning.

Secure a menu from a local restaurant specializing in North Indian cuisine. Distribute copies to the class. Have each student elect a meal for himself/herself and vegetarian companion.

	Yourself	Vegetarian friend
Appetizer		
Bread		
Main entree		
Beverage		

Using the United States' recommended food pyramid in the seventh grade health unit on nutrition, identify the food groups represented in your meal.

Extension This is a good activity to involve ELL students and their parents in the classroom.

Discussion Questions

1 What does the typical United States meal include? Why are these particular elements included?

Caption Answer

There is usually a selection of dishes with rice or bread. Indians also include many different flavors in their meals.

Writing Activity

Write a Storybook

OBJECTIVES: 11.01, 11.02, 12,02

After reading Lesson 3, have students use their knowledge of India to write and illustrate a child's storybook about India. The book should include a decorated cover with the student as the author and illustrator, a title page, and the story complete with text and illustrations.

Math Activity

Electricity Pie Graph

OBJECTIVES: 1.01, 3.03

Create a pie graph to show the data for production of electricity in India. Use an almanac or the CIA World Factbook to find this data. Use a spreadsheet to create the graph.

Extension Novice and intermediate ELL students should use ELL-friendly Web sites to find data. Assign peer tutors to assist with the spreadsheet and graph.

Traditional serving bowls and a Muslim bread seller display the popular foods of India. **What are some common features of Indian meals?**

Despite regional differences, Indian meals have some common features. A typical dinner includes a selection of dishes served with various breads and rice. The bread may be rolled into the shape of a scoop and used as a spoon for eating the meal.

Indians believe that a meal should include six flavors: sweet, salty, bitter, astringent, sour, and pungent. Each flavor, they claim, has a health benefit.

Like other aspects of Indian culture, tastes in food and cooking have evolved over more than 4,000 years. Today, som Indians prepare traditional foods with modern appliances. Their respect for flavors remains unchanged.

LESSON 3 REVIEW

Fact Follow-Up

1. What is Kathakali? Why are it and other dances important to Hinduism?
2. How do the *Bhagavad-Gita* and the *Mahabharata* reinforce Hindu values?
3. What are some common features of Indian cooking? What are some evidences of regional diversity in foods?
4. Why is Mumbai called the Hollywood of India?

Talk About It

1. Why is computer science education important in India? Should Indians with technology degrees stay in India or work in other countries?
2. Why do you think Indian civilizations created epic poetry? Why do Indian people still value the art form?
3. Why do you think India is the world's largest movie producer?

LESSON 3 REVIEW

Fact Follow-Up Answers

1. It is a dance-drama telling the stories of gods and heroes from the Hindu tradition. Historically, religious dance is linked to Hinduism in India. The Hindu god Shiva often appears as the Lord of the Dance.
2. The themes of the poems celebrate duty, compassion, and loyalty to family.
3. There is usually a selection of dishes with rice or bread. Indians also include many different flavors in their meals. Northerners eat more bread, while southerners serve more rice. Northerners also enjoy spicy meats, but most southerners are vegetarians.
4. Half of India's films are made in Mumbai.

Talk About It Answers

1. India's economy is changing to one based upon technology. Western companies provide jobs for Indians with computer skills. Important points: Encourage students to explore the costs and benefits to Indians with computer skills staying in India to work.
2. Important points: Encourage students to suggest a variety of reasons. Note: Epic poetry was an expression of religious feeling; the stories of gods and goddesses were a way of entertaining people and at the same time instilling religious and cultural values.
3. India produces movies to entertain people of many different languages and customs. It would be difficult to make one film that would appeal to all Indian people.

Applying Decision-Making and Problem-Solving Techniques to World Issues

Planning Improvements in India

Two sentences from Chapter 17 signal great challenges facing the Indian government and Indian people:

India contains contrasting modern and traditional ways.

Great riches and great poverty are an uncomfortable contrast in today's India.

As you have read, the Indian government's experiment with both nationalization and privatization has had mixed results.

Nationalization of industries is not now a government priority, but the Indian government still tries to make the nation's economy more productive. With greater productivity and more wealth, the government hopes to lift its poorest people to better lives.

To make the economy more productive, what projects should the Indian government support? Skim this chapter and Chapter 15 and make a list of projects the government has supported in the past. Can you suggest other projects that might help end poverty or lessen the number of people in poverty? When you have completed your list, compare it with a classmate's and add additional projects if you wish.

Next, cut your list to four or five projects that you think have the most promise for helping eliminate poverty while increasing economic productivity. When you have a shorter list, evaluate each project using the decision-making chart on this page. This sample chart has been completed, and you will need to sketch others to use for the projects you will consider.

This chart ought to help you make the best decision possible because it asks you to consider at least four—more, if you can think of them—possible consequences of the decision you make. Notice on the sample chart below that you will list both positive and negative consequences of the proposed project.

Once you have completed a decision-making chart for each proposed project, you should be able to decide which project you think is best: the one with the most positive consequences and the fewest negative consequences.

Planning to Help India's Government

Negative Consequences		Positive Consequences
Initial cost will be very high	**Proposed Project:** To extend electricity to all villages	Will encourage industries in rural areas
Maintenance will be expensive		Will enable people to use modern machinery
Industries might not move to rural areas		Will encourage villagers to be better informed
Could possibly encourage population growth		Will make life easier for many people

Teaching This Skill Lesson

Materials Needed pencils, paper, textbooks, other available resources

Classroom Organization whole class, small groups

Beginning the Lesson Read the two italicized statements on page 349 to the class. Ask students what India might do to lessen poverty and make the nation's economy more productive. Write responses on the chalkboard.

Lesson Development Ask students to skim Chapters 15 and 18 to add to the list of responses. Lead class to eliminate all but four or five of the most thoughtful and practical suggestions. Introduce the graphic organizer on page 349. Divide the class into four or five groups. Assign one suggestion to each group. As a homework assignment each member of each group is to complete a graphic organizer on the suggestion assigned to the group.

Conclusion Give groups time to compare individual work and come up with a group product. Each group is to present its work using the overhead projector or chalkboard. The class will then put the suggested projects into priority order.

Skill Lesson Review

1. Which project did you conclude to be the best one? Why was this one better than the others? *Students might debate in small groups.*
2. How helpful was the decision-making chart you used? *If made carefully and thoughtfully, the chart should be helpful.*
3. What are some other procedures you could have used for reaching this decision? Would they have been better than the decision-making chart? *Important points: Encourage students to suggest other ways of making decisions about a course of action.*
4. How important is it to consider positive and negative consequences in making a decision? *Very important. If both are not seriously considered, the action taken could be useless or even harmful.*
5. Would a decision-making chart like this one be useful in making a personal decision such as deciding which sport to try out for? *A chart of this kind encourages thoughtful, careful choice making, and so it is helpful in many situations.*

Talk About It

1. Important points: Encourage students to suggest a variety of possible actions and give reasons for each. Caution students that some actions might not be practical.
2. Important points: Students should take a position and explain it. Note: The period of nonalignment might have been a crucial time for India to learn to act independently.
3. Important points: Encourage students to come up with a variety of reasons and solutions. Note: Agricultural productivity has not grown to meet population needs. The government-sponsored expansion of agriculture might help. Continuing efforts to slow population growth might help.
4. Important points: Encourage all students to offer questions, leading them to select a few that they think are most important for their understanding of India.
5. Important points: Encourage students to make a variety of comparisons. Students should note that the class system in America is not a rigid part of society or religion as in India.
6. Positive: More jobs are available for Indians. Indians provide cost-effective technical support to American companies. Negative: Many American companies outsource jobs to Indian workers who are paid lower wages than Americans.

CHAPTER 17 REVIEW

Lessons Learned

LESSON 1
Government and Politics
After independence, India adopted a constitution establishing a constitutional democracy. This government has survived many tests. During the early years of independence, India and China quarreled over their high mountain borders. India and Pakistan have fought three times since 1947. Serious tensions between the two countries continue. During the Cold War, India refused to align itself with with either the United States or the Soviet Union.

LESSON 2
Economic Development
India's economic development has been uneven. By 2000, the nation's industry was rapidly building on earlier government efforts to promote industry. Agriculture, however, did not continue the expansion started by the Green Revolution. As a result, India's population became increasingly divided between the rich-to-moderately wealthy and large numbers of desperately poor.

LESSON 3
Society and Culture
Despite the growth of cities and changes in the nation's economy, traditional stories, music, and dance remain popular. Even India's booming filmmaking industry uses these traditions in many modern-day movies. The food eaten daily throughout the nation also continues to be influenced by tradition.

Talk About It

1. What do you think the Indian government might do to decrease religious tensions? Give reasons for your answers.
2. Are the policies of nonalignment a good idea or not? Explain.
3. Why is there such poverty in India? How might this problem be solved?
4. Why do you think stories, like epic poems or movies, are important in India's culture?
5. Compare and contrast the class structure in India to classes of the United States as you know them. How are they alike and different?
6. What are some positive and negative aspects of American companies moving technology jobs to India?

Mastering Mapwork

REGION

Use the map on page 338 to answer these questions:

1. Describe the relative location of the regions of little or no economic activity.
2. Describe the relative location of the iron- and coal-producing region of South Asia.
3. What South Asian country has the largest region of nomadic herding?
4. Describe the relative location of the gold mining region of South Asia.

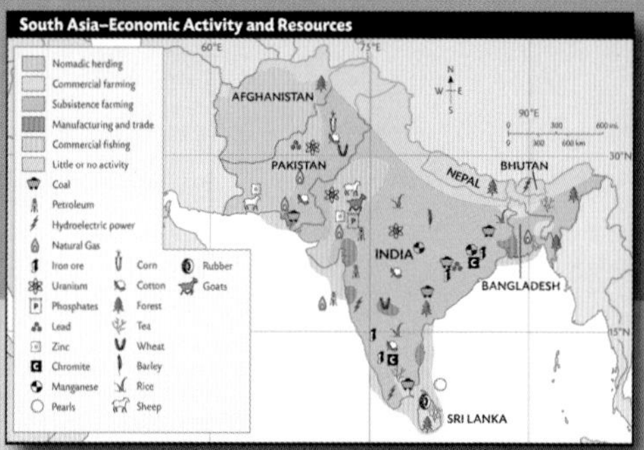

Mastering Mapwork

1. The regions of little or no economic activity are in the high mountain regions lying on the northern borders of the subcontinent. There are also smaller regions of little or no economic activity in Afghanistan, located on the north-western corner of the subcontinent.
2. The iron- and coal-producing region lies along the southeastern coast of India.
3. Afghanistan has the largest region of nomadic herding.
4. The gold mining region of South Asia is located in southern India, roughly midway between the coasts of the Arabian Sea and the Bay of Bengal.

Identifying Point-of-View

Read the excerpt below from "Indian Customs and Manners" from the Indian History Sourcebook *(1840), by Montstuart Elphinstone. Answer the questions using specific references to the document.*

The caution used against eating out of dishes or on carpets defiled by other castes gives rise to some curious customs. At a great Bramin [sic] dinner, where twenty or thirty different dishes and condiments are placed before each individual, all are served in vessels made of leaves sewed together. These are placed on the bare floor, which, as a substitute for a tablecloth, is decorated for a certain distance in front of the guests with patterns of flowers, etc., very prettily laid out in lively-colored sorts of sand, spread through frames in which the patterns are cut, and swept away after dinner. The inferior castes of Hindus eat meat, and care less for their vessels; metal, especially, can always be purified by scouring. In all classes, however, the difference of caste leads to a want of sociability. A soldier, or any one away from his family, cooks his solitary meal for himself, and finishes it without a companion, or any of the pleasures of the table, but those derived from taking the necessary supply of food. All eat with their fingers, and scrupulously wash before and after meals.

Though they have chess, a game played with tables and dice as backgammon is, and cards (which are circular, in many suits, and painted with Hindu gods, etc., instead of kings, queens, and knaves), yet the great indoor amusement is to listen to singing interspersed with slow movements which can scarcely be called dancing. The attitudes are not ungraceful, and the songs are pleasing; but it is, after all, a languid and monotonous entertainment; and it is astonishing to see the delight that all ranks take in it; the lower orders, in particular, often standing for whole nights to enjoy this unvaried amusement. These exhibitions are now often illuminated, when in rooms, by English chandeliers; but the true Hindu way of lighting them up is by torches held by men, who feed the flame with oil from a sort of bottle constructed for the purpose. For ordinary household purposes they use lamps of earthenware or metal.

In the houses of the rich, the doorways are hung with quilted silk curtains; and the doors, the arches, and other woodwork in the rooms are highly carved. The floor is entirely covered with a thin mattress of cotton over which is spread a clean white cloth to sit on; but there is no other furniture of any description. Equals sit in opposite rows down the room. A prince or great chief has a seat at the head of the room between the rows very slightly raised by an additional mattress, and covered with a small carpet of embroidered silk. This, with a high round embroidered bolster behind, forms what is called a masnad or gadi, and serves as a throne for sovereigns under the rank of king.

Questions

1. Who is the audience for Elphinstone's observations? How do you know?
2. What is Elphinstone describing in his observations?
3. What are some of the "curious" practices when eating a meal mentioned by Elphinstone?
4. What does Elphinstone's comments tell us or show us about the caste system in India?
5. Is Elphinstone showing bias in his observations? If so, what is the evidence?

Go to the Source

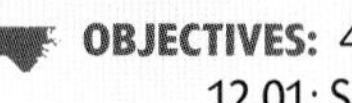

Go to the Source

OBJECTIVES: 4.03, 10.04, 11.01, 11.04, 12.01; Skills 2.02, 3.05, 4.03, 4.03

Mountstuart Elphinstone:
Indian Customs and Manners, 1840

Mountstuart Elphinstone (1779-1859) was a Scottish statesman and historian. He became the Governor of Bombay (Mumbai). Besides being a respected government leader, he wrote books on India and Afghanistan. His *History of India* of (1841) is still considered to be an important observation of Indian life and culture at that time.

ANSWERS:

1. British citizens back home. Probably a non-Indian audience since he is describing Indian customs.
2. Elphinstone is describing eating customs in some castes as well as descriptions of interiors of wealthy homes, leisure activities, games, music, and dance.
3. Elphinstone speaks of how food is served on leaves, how rooms are decorated for meals, and the lack of socializing during meals for some groups.
4. Great care is taken in maintaining certain practices depending on the castes.
5. He is basically describing his observations for his audience. Other than his comments on the "languid and monotonous" dance and music, he is relatively neutral in his comments.

How to Use the Chapter Review

There are three sections in the Chapter Review: Talk About It, Mastering Mapwork, and Go to the Source. Use the Vocabulary Worksheets and the Chapter Review Worksheet in the Teacher's Resource Guide for additional reinforcement and preparation for the Chapter Assessments. The chapter and lesson reviews and the Chapter Review Worksheets are the basis of the assessment for each chapter.

Talk About It questions encourage students to speculate about the content of the chapter and are suitable for class or small-group discussion. They are not intended to be assigned for homework.

Mastering Mapwork has students apply one or more of the Five Themes of Geography to maps within the chapter.

Go to the Source activities allow students to analyze a primary source that relates to the content of the chapter. The questions and activities familiarize students with different types of primary sources and also build content-reading skills.

Other Nations of South Asia

Social Studies Strands

Geographic Relationships

Cultures and Diversity
Religion

Economics and Development

Government and Active Citizenship

Global Connections

North Carolina Standard Course of Study Goals

Goal 2 The learner will assess the relationship between physical environment and cultural characteristics of selected societies and regions of Africa, Asia, and Australia.

Goal 3 The learner will analyze the impact of interactions between humans and their physical environments in Africa, Asia, and Australia.

Goal 5 The learner will evaluate the varied ways people of Africa, Asia, and Australia make decisions about the allocation and use of economic resources.

Goal 10 The learner will compare the rights and civic responsibilities of individuals in political structures in Africa, Asia, and Australia.

Teaching & Assessment

- English Language Learner Modified Lesson Plans for this chapter are found in the Teacher Resource Guide.
- *ExamView® Assessment Suite* is provided at **NCJourneys.com.** It includes customizable assessments for all chapters. Paper tests are also available in the Teacher Resource Guide. See pages T16–T17 for information about how to use the assessments and the Scoring Guide.

Worksheets

Worksheets and answer keys are found both in the Teacher Resource Guide and at **NCJourneys.com**, including Reading Guides, Reading Strategies, Chapter Reviews, English Language Learner and others.

ACTIVITIES AND INTEGRATIONS

SOCIAL STUDIES
● Travel Through Six South Asia Nations, p. 353
● Life Amid the Hustle and Bustle Think-Pair-Share, p. 358
★ Rhombus–Other Nations of South Asia, p. 362
Flag, p. 363
● Growing Tea in Sri Lanka, p. 365
Outline Map, p. 366
★ Skill Lesson: Comparing Nations in South Asia, p. 369

READING/LANGUAGE ARTS	READING/LANGUAGE ARTS OBJECTIVES
Developed/Developing, p. 352B	2.01
Analogies, p. 352B	
▲ ■ Activator: Family Jobs, p. 352	2.01
Writing Prompt: Female President?, p. 352	
Acrostic, p. 353	6.01
Go to the Source: Understanding Press Conferences, p. 371	2.01, 3.01, 4.01, 4.02, 5.01

MATHEMATICS	MATHEMATICS OBJECTIVES
Samosas, p. 356	2.08
▲ ■ Mango and Coconut Chutney, p. 358	2.08
Burfi, p. 359	2.08
● ▲ ■ Tea-Tasting, p. 364	4.01

SCIENCE	SCIENCE OBJECTIVES
★ Interpreting Facts on Endangered Species, p. 360	3.05
The Indian Ocean and the Mountains, p. 364	3.05

TECHNOLOGY	TECHNOLOGY OBJECTIVES
● Creating a Collage, p. 352B	3.01, 3.08

VISUAL ARTS	VISUAL ARTS OBJECTIVES
▲ ■ The Creation of the Bodhisattva Avalokiteshvara, p. 352B	2.01, 4.04
★ Designing Postcards, p. 367	4.01, 6.01

CHARACTER AND VALUES EDUCATION	TRAITS
Writing Prompt: Female President? p. 352	fairness, citizenship
What Would You Do?, p. 366	good judgement

● Basic Activities ★ Challenging Activities ▲ English Language Learner Novice ■ English Language Learner Intermediate

Chapter Activities

Introductory Activity

Developed/Developing

OBJECTIVES: 5.03, 6.01

Divide the class into groups. Ask each group to list at least five criteria used to determine if a country is developed or developing. Discuss as a class which criteria might be most helpful. List the criteria on the board.

Assign each group a South Asian nation. The students will research their country, listing the criteria and data they have found on a large index card or paste it electronically into a spreadsheet.

Using the same criteria, list the United States' statistics on one edge of the blackboard. Label this as representative of a developed nation. Draw a line across the board. Label the other edge as developing nations.

Have a student from each group come up and position themselves along the developed to developing continuum. They should justify their position. As the students hear others present, they may chose to move to another point along the continuum. Ask them to justify why they repositioned themselves.

Discuss as a class the following questions: Is there one universal definition of development? What are some obstacles of development that South Asian nations face? What are some steps these nations might take to promote development in their countries?

Culminating Activity

Creating a Collage

OBJECTIVES: 1.03, 3.01, 4.03, 11.01

Divide the class into six groups, one per country studied in Chapter 18. Have each group contact their respective embassy in Washington, D.C., and request information. Each group should then review what they receive as well as magazines, brochures, and Web sites to locate pictures depicting life in their country. They should make a collage or Web site showing its people, daily life, products, and physical and cultural characteristics.

After completing their collage, each group should show their collage to the class and explain the significance of their pictures.

Art Activity

The Creation of the Bodhisattva Avalokiteshvara

OBJECTIVES: 8.01, 12.01

This multi-armed Buddhist symbol of great Compassion is believed to lead all sentient beings away from evil and toward salvation and enlightenment.

Materials pencils, colored pencils, scissors, glue, card stock or heavy paper, magazines

Option 1: Drawing
Have students write a list of attributes or qualities that represent themselves. They should draw simple symbols that represent ten of their positive qualities. On a heavy card stock, they should draw the shape of a body with no arms and cut it out. On heavy card stock, they should draw the shape of arms with symbols in each of the hands. Size: The body should be no smaller than 11 inches tall and 5 inches wide. The arms should be about 6 inches in length. Draw straight and bent arms or create a stencil of one arm and trace it ten times. Color arms and body before gluing together. Glue the arms on the front and back of the torso. To have moving arms, use metal brads instead of glue. Incorporate the brads into the colorful designs.

Option 2: Collage
From magazines, have students cut out the torso of a body and arms from photographs. Look for arms that are in proportion to the body. Cut out symbols that represent themselves. Arrange parts, then glue.

Extension Assign intermediate ELL students Option 2 only.

Analogies

OBJECTIVES: 1.03

Analogies are useful to help students make associations with prior knowledge. Read the analogies aloud and ask students to identify the relationship between the terms. As an extension, ask students to write their own analogies using key terms or places discussed in the chapter.

Mohenjo-Daro : Indus Valley :: Sumer : Mesopotamia (ancient site in)

Indus River : Pakistan :: Mississippi River : United States (divides in half)

Benazir Bhutto : Pakistan :: Indira Gandhi : India :: Hasina Wazed : Bangladesh :: Margaret Thatcher : United Kingdom (female prime minister of)

cyclone : Indian Ocean region :: hurricane : Atlantic :: typhoon : West Pacific Ocean (fierce tropical storms in)

Bangladesh : low relief :: North Pakistan : high relief (topography)

chador : Iran :: burka : Pakistan and Bangladesh (conservative outer dress for women)

Sri Lanka : tear drop :: India : funnel (is shaped like)

tea : Sri Lanka :: coffee : Kenya :: tobacco : North Carolina (is grown in)

Teaching Strategies

In order to cover this chapter quickly, divide the class into groups of two or three students. Assign each group with a separate country and topic, for example, Pakistan: Government; Pakistan: Major Religions; Bangladesh: Government; or Bangladesh: Geography.

Each group should read the section on their country and fill in a graphic organizer comparing their topic with that of India. Each group should write a list of five questions for the class based on their findings. Groups will present their information to the class and ask the class their questions.

Activator

 **OBJECTIVES:** .03, 6.01, 7.02, 9.03, 10.04

Ask students to list things that they do to help their families. In addition, ask them if they have ever had a job and if so, what was it. After discussing the various ways students help their families, ask them to read "Obstacles to Progress" on pages 356–357. Move the discussion into child labor practices and elaborate on reasons why this practice continues to be common throughout the world. You might mention that child labor was also quite common in the United States. through the great depression. Although certainly less prevalent in heavy industry today, child labor remains an important issue—particularly in light of the millions of United States teenagers employed in the food service sector.

Writing Prompt

OBJECTIVES: 9.04, 10.01

Evaluative

Israel, the United Kingdom, Bangladesh, India, and Pakistan have each had a female leader. The United States, on the other hand, has not had a female president. Do you think a female would make a good president of the United States? Write a speech and argue your point of view in your classroom. As you write your speech, remember to:

- clearly state your position.
- give at least three reasons and explain your reasons fully.
- give examples to support your reasons.
- write in complete sentences and paragraph form.
- organize your ideas and include an introduction and a conclusion.
- use good grammar, spelling, punctuation, and capitalization.

CHAPTER 18

Statue from a Buddhist shrine in Katmandu, Nepal

Chapter Preview

LESSON 1
Pakistan
Pakistan is South Asia's second-largest nation. It is a developing nation with a largely Muslim population.

LESSON 2
Bangladesh: A Fertile Land Battered by Nature
Bangladesh is an Islamic nation with rich agricultural resources. Bangladesh faces environmental challenges.

LESSON 3
Island and Mountain Nations of South Asia
Four small nations are located on the rim of South Asia.

Other Nations of South Asia

"Better than a thousand words is one word that brings peace."

This message is from Buddha. The religion founded on his teachings, Buddhism, was born in India but now is more common in other parts of Asia and the smaller nations of South Asia.

India is the giant of South Asia. Six other nations—Pakistan, Bangladesh, Sri Lanka, Afghanistan, Nepal, and Bhutan—are also part of South Asia. All except Afghanistan live in India's shadow. Each has a unique landscape, history, and culture. It is a region striving for peace.

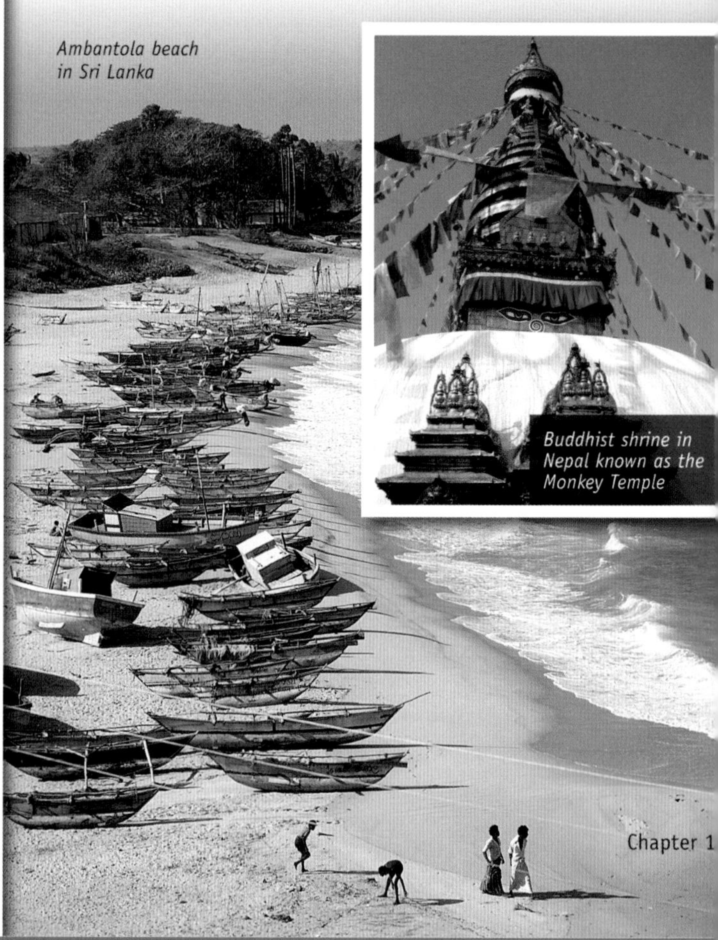

Ambantola beach in Sri Lanka

Buddhist shrine in Nepal known as the Monkey Temple

352

Chapter 1

Chapter Resources

Print Resources

Nonfiction

Ali, Sharifah. *Afghanistan* (Cultures of the World series). Marshall Cavenish, 1995. ISBN 0761401776.

Heinrichs, Ann. *Nepal* (Enchantment of the World series). Children's Press, 1996. ISBN 0516026429.

Kuklin, Susan. *Iqbal Masih and the Crusaders Against Child Slavery.* Henry Holt, 1998. ISBN 0805054596. An account of the former Pakistani child labor activist.

Reynolds, Jan. *Himalayas: Vanishing Cultures.* Harcourt Brace, 1991. ISBN 0152344659. Describes the customs of a family living in the Himalayas.

Sheehan, Sean. *Pakistan* (Cultures of the World series). Marshall Cavendish, 1996. ISBN 185435583X.

Wanasundera, Nanda P. *Sri Lanka* (Cultures of the World series). Marshall Cavendish, 1994. ISBN 1854353985.

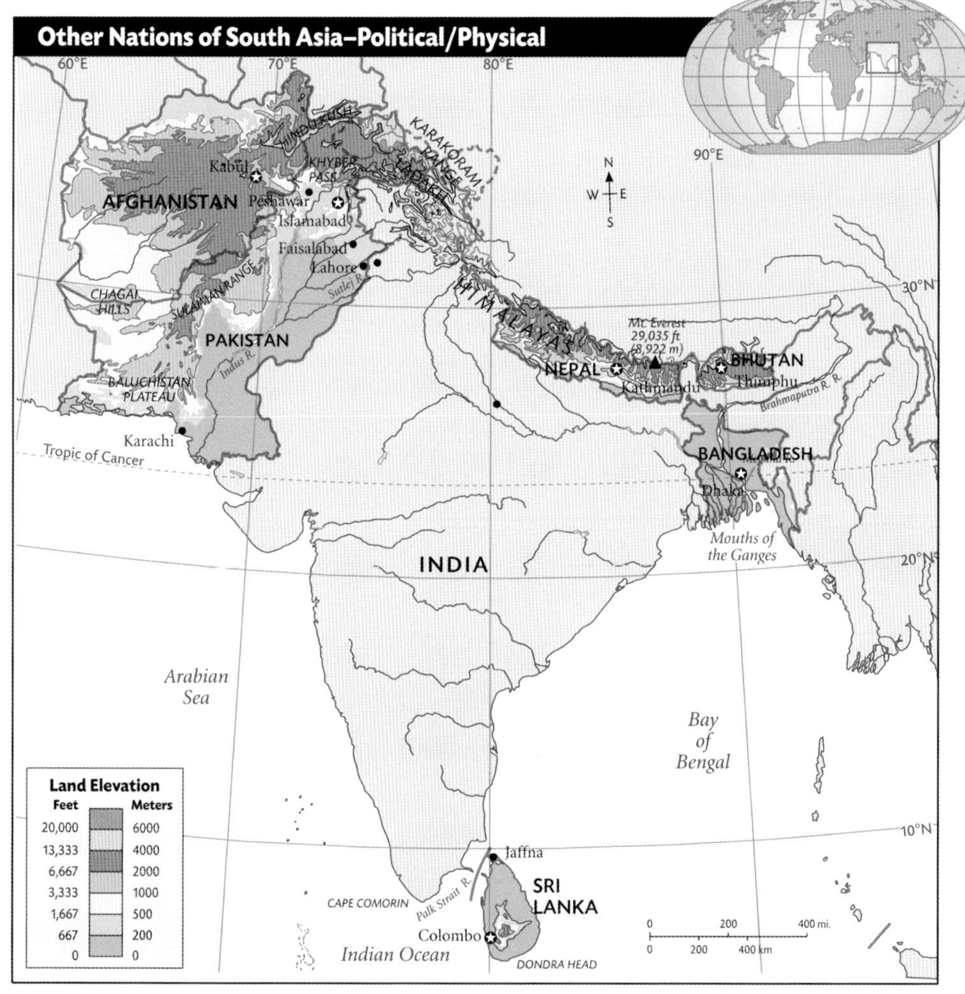

Map Activity

Travel Through Six South Asian Nations

NATIONAL GEOGRAPHY STANDARDS: 1, 4

GEOGRAPHIC THEMES: Location, Place

OBJECTIVES: 1.02, 2.01

Assign students to complete the following travelogue using only the map on page 353.

1. We start our journey in the most northwestern, landlocked country of South Asia, ___. *Afghanistan*
2. ___, the capital of Afghanistan, is our first city on this trip. *Kabul*
3. We take the ___ in the Hindu Kush passing from Afghanistan into Pakistan. *Khyber Pass*
4. The first major Pakistani city we get to is ___ at the foot of the Khyber Pass. *Peshawar*
5. From Peshawar we travel east to Pakistan's capital, ___. *Islamabad*
6. We leave this capital traveling southeast. We are on Pakistan's border with India in ___, Pakistan's second biggest city. *Lahore*
7. We fly into Nepal. We land in the capital, ___. *Katmandu*
8. Some of us hire a Sherpa guide and climb the lower elevation of Mount Everest. We are now on Nepal's border with ___. *China/Tibet*
9. Returning to Katmandu we fly once again into Thimphu, the capital of ___. *Bhutan*
10. Flying from Thimphu, we land next in Dhaka, capital of ___. *Bangladesh*
11. The final leg of our flight on this journey brings us to the island of ____, formerly called Ceylon. *Sri Lanka*

Whyte, Mariam. *Bangladesh* (Cultures of the World series). Marshall Cavendish, 1999. ISBN 076140869X.

Back issues of magazines

Himalayas. Cobblestone Publishing Company. ISBN 0382405137.

Audiovisual

Destination: Nepal. Peace Corps, 1996. ISBN 0160633982. (10 min.)

Destination: Sri Lanka. Peace Corps, 1996. ISBN 0160634016. (15 min.)

Web Sites

Go to **NCJourneys.com** for links to the following Web sites:

- Bangladesh.com
- Bangla2000
- National Fund for Cultural Heritage, Pakistan
- Nepal.com
- Tea Culture in Sri Lanka and Britain

OBJECTIVES: 2.01, 3.01, 5.01

Discussion Questions

1 What is a gorge?

2 How does the road in the picture compare with major roads in our area?

Caption Answer

For thousands of years, travelers, traders, and invaders have passed through it to reach the subcontinent.

ELL Teaching Tips

Check for Comprehension

Effective communication with ELLs requires that teachers check periodically for comprehension. A common mistake is to simply ask the student "Do you understand?" in front of the entire class. The flaw in this method is that students will say "yes" even if they don't truly comprehend the lesson. Ask them questions at their level to assess their level of comprehension.

Teacher Notes

Toponymy

Toponymy is the study of place names that reveal the history of a region and the values of the people. Pakistan's capital of Islamabad (translated as "the place of Islam") is an example of Muslim religious values evident in that South Asian country.

LESSON 1 Pakistan

KEY IDEAS

- Pakistan shares India's long history.
- A dry climate and limited resources affect Pakistan's economy. The government has tried to improve agriculture and expand industry.
- Muslims have shaped the country's culture and government.

KEY TERMS

coup
regime

The train slowly gathers steam as it rolls out of the station. Its driver, Muhammad Salim Khan, is making the weekly run from Peshawar, Pakistan, through the Khyber Pass (KAI·ber) to the border of Afghanistan. The Khyber Pass is a famous route. For thousands of years, travelers, traders, and invaders have passed throug this gap high in the Hindu Kush to reach the South Asian subcontinen

The 32-mile (52-km) run takes three hours. It is an exciting and dangerous journey. The tracks skirt rugged peaks. Trains climb and descend in snakelike loops through narrow gorges.

The British colonial government mapped the rail route through the Khyber Pass. South Asians laid the rails. Today, roads and airplanes al are part of Pakistan's transportation network.

A New Nation with a Long History

Pakistan is the second-largest South Asian country. It occupies a key location because it shares borders with India, China, Afghanistan, and Iran.

Pakistan celebrated its 60th birthday in 2007. Yet the country has an ancient history through its link to India. In Chapter 16, you read how Muslims in India wanted a homeland where they—and not Hindus—would be in the majority. So Pakistan was created in 194 as an Islamic country. Before that, it was part of India. Therefore, it shares India's long history.

In fact, the Indus River Valley in Pakistan was the site of one of the world first civilizations. The 4,500-year-old rui at Mohenjo-Daro are evidence of that early culture.

The Khyber Pass leads from Afghanistan to Pakistan through the Hindu Kush. **What is important about this opening in the mountains?**

It's a Fact

Pakistan

■ Pakistan's capital, Islamabad, was created in the 1960s as a means to relieve the overcrowding in Karachi.
■ Much of the rural transportation is still by donkey or horse-drawn cart.
■ The government of Pakistan tested their newly developed nuclear devices in 1998.
■ School attendance is not required. The literacy rate is 38 percent, the same as India's.

.andforms

High mountains cover much of ›rthern Pakistan. The Hindu Kush, imalayas, and Karakoram ah·rah·KO·ram) meet there. This region sometimes called "the roof of the orld."

The Indus River divides southern kistan in half (see map, page 353). To e west, the dry Baluchistan (bah·LOO· ey·stan) plateau receives less than 6 ches (15 cm) of rain a year. Its pulation is small. Most people are rders. A few are farmers.

Most Pakistanis live around the Indus, the Punjab and Sind. Punjab extends to India. Over the past 35 years, the infall in Punjab has varied greatly year to ar, between 19.7 to 39.4 inches (50 to)0 cm) per year. This variation is strongly fected by monsoons. Monsoons start in ne and end in September, bringing 70 rcent of the season's rainfall.

Along the southern coast of Pakistan e hot, dry deserts. Few people live there. nly the port city of Karachi (kah·RAH· ee), cooled by sea breezes, has a large pulation.

A Pakistani village hugs the slopes of the Karakoram Mountains. **What mountain ranges meet in Pakistan?**

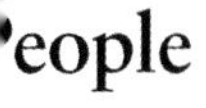

'eople

Pakistan has about 158 illion people, making it one the most populous nations the world. Although most kistanis are Muslim, they e diverse in language and lture.

Urdu is the official nguage. Many educated kistanis also speak English. ople speak other languages, ch as Punjabi, Pashto, luchi, and Sindhi.

Word Origins

The origin of the name **Pakistan** is not certain. In Urdu, the main language of Pakistan, Pakistan means "land of the pure." The name was first used in the 1930s. Some people claim that the letters stand for areas Muslims wanted to make part of their nation: P for Punjab, A for Afghania, K for Kashmir, S for Sind, and TAN for Baluchistan. Stan also means "country."

This man lives in Pakistan. **Where do most Pakistanis live?**

Discussion Questions

1 Why would most people in the Baluchistan Plateau herd?

2 How would life in the Punjab be different without irrigation?

3 What are the three major regions in Pakistan?

4 What is the climate like in the regions?

5 Should a foreign language be required in our schools? What does it say about a society that encourages a second language?

Caption Answer

The Hindu Kush and the Himalayas

Activity

Acrostic

 **OBJECTIVES:** 1.01, 1.03

As you have read in the text, some believe Pakistan was named for Punjab, Afghania, Kashmir, Sindh, and Baluchistan. Take the names of the other South Asian nations and based on what you have read, make an acrostic by spelling out the name of each country down the left-hand column of the page and then find related words that begin with each letter.

Examples

Independent
Nehru
Deccan Plateau
Islam and Hindu
Arabian Sea

Spices, Sinhalese, slash—and—burn agriculture
Rubber, Rice
Indian Ocean, Island
Lush vegetation
A lot of tea
Nice climate
Kool beaches
Animals

Discussion Questions

1 What has been the role of irrigation in human history?

2 What are some of Pakistan's industries?

Caption Answer

Textiles is Pakistan's major industry.

Activity

Samosas

OBJECTIVES: 11.01, 12,02, 12.03

Samosas are vegetable fritters. Spring roll wrappers or egg roll wrappers can be purchased in grocery stores to save time.

Wrapper
¾ cup self-rising flour
½ teaspoon salt
3 tablespoons butter, cut in small pieces
4 tablespoons water

Sift flour and salt into large mixing bowl. Add butter and rub it into flour until mixture resembles fine breadcrumbs. Pour in water and mix with fork to form dough. Pat dough into ball and knead for 5 minutes, or until dough is smooth. Add a little flour if dough is sticky. Cover and set aside to rise. After dough has risen, break small balls off the dough and roll each out very thinly to form round wrapper. Cut wrappers in half, dampen edges, and shape into cones. Fill cones with a little of potato mixture; dampen top and bottom edges, pinch together to seal. Set aside.

Filling
2 tablespoons vegetable oil
1 finely chopped onion
1 tablespoon fresh, chopped ginger root
1 finely chopped garlic clove
1 tablespoon curry powder
salt to taste
1½ cups frozen peas, thawed with liquid retained
4 medium-size, cooked potatoes, diced
¼ cup fresh, chopped coriander

Heat oil in deep skillet. Add onions, ginger and garlic. Cook a few minutes without browning. Add curry and salt. Cook 30–60 seconds. Add thawed peas and potatoes. Heat mixture thoroughly; combining well. Add coriander but do not cook. Cool completely.

Place tablespoon of filling on wrapper. Dampen edges with egg or water. Fold wrapper over filling into cone/triangular shape. Set aside each wrapper filled samosa. Heat 1 inch of oil in deep skillet/pan. Cook samosas in batches few minutes on each side until golden and crisp. Drain on rack or paper towels. Makes approximately 24 samosas.

Serving suggestion: Serve with chutney as dip, see recipe, page 358.

A stonemason chisels stone near the Badshahi mosque in Lahore, Pakistan. **What is Pakistans's major industry?**

Economic Development

Like other developing countries, Pakistan has worked to improve agriculture. A dry climate means that crops need irrigation. Pakistan has built many new irrigation projects to increase food production. Larger farms have benefited from the Green Revolution's chemical fertilizers and modern machines. Food production has kept up with Pakistan's growing population, but only barely.

Agriculture

Pakistan earns money from selling farm products abroad. Its export crops are cotton, sugarcane, and tobacco. The warm climate lets Pakistani farmers plant and harvest two crops a year. Between June and October, they might grow rice, cotto sugarcane, or maize. A second crop of tobacco or wheat is planted and harveste between November and April.

Industry

When Pakistan became independent, had few factories and little money. Its economy had been tied to that of India. There were few trained technicians and skilled workers. So Pakistan had to build from the ground up. Its leaders worked t set up banks, businesses, and factories.

Pakistan has made good progress. In 1947, Pakistan contained 17 cotton texti mills. Today, there are more than 390. Textiles is Pakistan's major industry. One in four factory workers has a job in this area. Textile mills make fabrics for clothes, towels, and much more.

Pakistan has developed a variety of other industries. It produces goods rangi from vegetable oil to cement, fertilizers, and steel. Recently, the government has tried to attract foreigners to invest mone in factories and industries. Like other developing nations, Pakistan has moved away from government control of industry. It encourages privately owned businesses.

Pakistan has tried to expand its energ sources that are needed for industry. Pakistan has some natural gas. It might also have some oil that has yet to be explored. Pakistani engineers have developed nuclear power. Pakistan has at least two nuclear reactors. They also hav built dams to provide hydroelectric powe

Obstacles to Progress

In a bicycle factory, a boy works at a old machine, turning out tire valves. In a village textile workshop, young girls wor at looms. In a Karachi brick factory, a te year-old boy pushes heavy loads of clay and sand. These children earn very little, but even their tiny wages are needed by their families.

This situation is common to most developing economies. They rely on low-paid workers, often children, to turn out goods by hand or with simple machines. Switching to machinery has high costs fo ctory owners. Better machinery is more .pensive than the low wages paid to ·ople who work by hand. Also, using achines would put many people out of ork, creating large-scale unemployment.

Many factors have slowed economic owth in Pakistan. Population growth is a g obstacle. As it increases, less resources e available to provide basic services. ırthermore, the nation's wealth and land e in the hands of a few. Large landowners ıd rich business people have political ›wer. They oppose reforms that might nit or reduce their wealth.

Geography has created other obstacles. kistan has to spend large sums to irrigate rmland because of the low rainfall the untry receives.

Outside events also pose problems. uring the 1980s, a civil war raged in fghanistan, Pakistan's neighbor. Millions Afghans fled to refugee camps in kistan. Pakistan then had to house and ed the newcomers. Many Afghans fled ;ain in 2001 when the United States vaded Afghanistan to oust the Taliban *gime,* or government leaders.

Many Pakistanis have gone abroad to ork, especially to Southwest Asia. They nd money home. Those funds are ıportant to the economy. During the rsian Gulf War in 1990–1991, many kistanis had to leave Kuwait. Their milies and country suffered.

;overnment

Like India, Pakistan is a republic. Its nstitution supports "the principles of mocracy, freedom, equality, tolerance, ıd social justice." Its first leader, uhammad Ali Jinnah (JEE·nah), favored eping religion and government separate.

But democracy has had a rocky ride. In)99, Pakistan had a fourth military keover, or ***coup.*** The Army Chief of aff, General Pervez Musharraf, suspended e constitution. Pakistan's supreme court ›held the coup in 2000.

After winning a controversial election 2002, Musharraf was "deemed to be ected" by Pakistan's electoral college. He lls his leadership, "Enlightened Moderation." This program is designed to bridge the gap between the West and the Islamic world. Under his leadership, Pakistan has usually cooperated with America in fighting the War on Terror.

Islam has helped shape Pakistan. At independence, Pakistan built its government on Islamic principles. In the 1980s, Pakistan's leaders backed Islamization. As in other Muslim countries, Islamists have tried to erase what they call dangerous Western influences. The press was strictly censored. Women lost some hard-won rights.

Yet in the 1980s and 1990s, Pakistan, Bangladesh, and India had female prime ministers. Former Prime Minister Benazir Bhutto (ben·ah·ZEER BOO·toe) was widely regarded as an able leader of Pakistan before losing an election in 1996, although her government was tainted by corruption. Her father also had been prime minister before he was executed by a military regime.

A Pakistani child works in a brick factory. Child labor is only one obstacle to economic progress in Pakistan. **What are others?**

Benazir Bhutto was the prime minister of Pakistan. **Why would it be unusual for a woman to be the leader of Pakistan?**

Discussion Questions

1 What do you think is the biggest obstacle to Pakistani development?

2 How would families and traditions be impacted if people had to find work beyond the borders of their communities?

3 Why do you think India has had a more stable democracy than Pakistan?

4 What problems could result if a government tried to include religion?

Others include the population boom, desert that needs irrigation, the fact that most of the wealth is in the hands of a few people, and international crises.

Islamic law limits the public role of women.

Activity

Mango and Coconut Chutney

OBJECTIVES: 11.01, 12,02, 12.03

1 medium mango
1 tablespoon finely chopped ginger
½ teaspoon salt
½ teaspoon red pepper flakes
¼ cup finely chopped coriander (cilantro)
½ cup shredded coconut

Cut mango into chunks. Put all ingredients in bowl and toss gently until completely mixed. Refrigerate for at least 1 hour before serving.

Activity

Life Amid the Hustle and Bustle Think-Pair-Share

 **OBJECTIVES:** 4.01, 4.02, 4.03

Living in Karachi can be used to review the theme of movement (goods, ideas, and people) from the Five Themes of Geography. Have students do a think-pair-share. First, have the students individually look at the picture on page 358 and think about ways they see move ment of people, goods, and ideas. Next, have them read the "Living In Karachi" feature and list the ways people, ideas, and goods are moved there. Have students discuss this information and compare their lists with their partner's. Finally, have students share their responses with the class.

A Journey to KARACHI

Life Amid the Hustle and Bustle

If you flew over Karachi, you would see large ships moving in and out of the harbor. Office buildings and skyscrapers hug the skyline. Yet you would have to walk or ride through the streets to get a feel for the hustle and bustle of this busy seaport, financial center, and ethnic melting pot.

Karachi is Pakistan's largest city. It has 12 million people. For a time, it was the nation's capital. Then in 1961, Pakistan built a new capital city, Islamabad.

Karachi continued to grow. Like other South Asian cities, its streets today are packed with people. Crowded bazaars—markets—spill from one street into the next. Merchants sell a large variety of goods from outdoor stalls. In one alley, they sell brass goods. In others, they sell jewelry, spices, or radios. Food vendors offer tasty snacks of shish kebab (meat on a stick) or spicy samosas (vegetable fritters).

Trucks, bicycles, motorbikes, and brightly painted buses compete for space on the streets. When buses are too full, passengers climb onto the roof. A motorbike edges along with an entire family aboard—parents and children. Motor vehicles roar by *tongas*—horse-drawn taxis—donkeys, and pedestrians. Amid the congestion, car horns blare and donkeys bray. Loudspeakers add to the noise as they blast popular songs.

Most families are crowded into tiny spaces. Often a family has nine or ten members sharing two rooms. In poor areas, families share a bathroom and courtyard with their neighbors. Parents sleep in a bed while the children lie on floor mats.

Most families have few possessions. A table, some chairs, perhaps a fan, a clock, and a tape player. A refrigerator or TV is found in some homes.

A woman cooks for her large family in a small kitchen with only a burner and sink. Few homes have running water. Each morning, the family collects water from a nearby well.

LESSON 1 REVIEW

Fact Follow-Up

1. Describe the landforms of Pakistan.
2. What are some agricultural products of Pakistan?
3. What factors have contributed to the slow economic progress of Pakistan?
4. What is the importance of Islam in the government of Pakistan?

Talk About It

1. If you were an economic advisor to the government of Pakistan, what agricultural policies would you suggest? Why?
2. Should Pakistan have stayed a part of India? Give reasons for your answer.
3. Why has democracy been difficult to maintain in Pakistan?

LESSON 1 REVIEW

Fact Follow-Up Answers

1. Mountains cover most of the North, the Indus River divides the country in half, and the West and South are desert. To the east of the Indus lies the fertile land.
2. They include cotton, sugarcane, tobacco, rice, and maize.
3. At independence, Pakistan had few trained workers and has had to educate people from its beginning. The population boom, dry lands needing irrigation, inadequate machinery, international crises, and the fact that wealth is in the hands of only a few people are other obstacles to progress.
4. Islam has helped shape Pakistan. At independence, Pakistan built its government on Islamic principles. In the 1980s, Pakistan's leaders introduced a stronger role for Islamic law and custom in the nation's laws.

Talk About It Answers

1. Important answers: Encourage students to suggest various policies and explain why. Note: Irrigation and the growing of more crops for food are both important and necessary.
2. Important points: Before reaching a decision, encourage students to suggest reasons for and against remaining a part of India. After reaching a decision, they should then support that decision with reasons. Note: Pakistan lags behind India in industry, but partition may have prevented some of the continuing disputes over religion.
3. Islam has helped shape Pakistan. Its first leader, Muhammad Ali Jinnah, favored the separation of church and state, but in the 1980s leaders backed Islamization and tried to erase what they called dangerous Western influences. The press has faced strict censorship. Military leaders have also forced government takeovers.

ESSON 2 Bangladesh: A Fertile Land Battered by Nature

Bangladesh's land is mostly flat and low-lying. The monsoon that blows from the Bay of Bengal brings high tides that flood the delta region. At times, ***cyclones***, or fierce tropical storms with rong winds, trigger monster waves. They damage crops and kill many eople. These natural disasters shape the way the world sees angladesh. Yet it is also a land rich with natural resources and culture.

ocation

Bangladesh is about the size of North arolina. With more than 129 million ople, it ranks among the world's 10 ost populous nations. Its huge opulation occupies every inch of land.

The country lies at the mouth of the anges and Brahmaputra Rivers. angladesh's flat delta makes it defenseless ainst storms and flooding. Every year, oodwaters deposit fertile soil on the ain. Over the centuries, many people ttled there to farm.

Bangladesh hugs the northern shore of e Bay of Bengal. Notice on the map on age 353 how it is almost surrounded by powerful neighbor, India.

The present-day country of Bangladesh was part of India until 1947. Many Bengalis, as the people were called, were Muslim. When India was partitioned, they formed the East Pakistan part of Pakistan. The people of present-day Pakistan lived in West Pakistan.

The two regions had little in common besides religion. They were separated by 1,000 miles (1,610 km) of Indian territory. Bengali Muslims in East Pakistan felt that West Pakistan took advantage of them. In 1970, that feeling led to revolt. After a brief and bloody civil war, East Pakistan won independence in 1971 and became Bangladesh, which means "the land of the Bengal."

KEY IDEAS

- Bangladesh is a small, mostly Muslim nation on South Asia's northeastern coast.
- Fertile soil and a favorable climate support a huge population.
- Bangladesh has suffered from political turmoil, deep poverty, and natural disasters.
- As in Pakistan, women are valued for their contributions to families, but most are restricted in what they can do outside their family circle.

KEY TERMS

cyclones
purdah

Farmland near Dhaka, Bangladesh, is nearly submerged by the Ganges and Brahmaputra Rivers. **Why is the nation often flooded?**

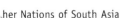

It's a Fact

Bangladesh

- Bangladesh—about the size of Wisconsin—is a low, flat plain with an average elevation of 30 feet. It experiences severe flooding yearly. The confluence of three major rivers, monsoons, cyclones, and tidal waves all contribute to high weather-related death tolls.
- The average farm size is 3 acres.
- While Bangladesh law requires children from the ages of six to eleven to attend school, the law is rarely enforced. Consequently, the literacy rate is a low 38 percent.

OBJECTIVES: 2.01, 2.02, 3.01, 3.04, 5.01, 10.04

Discussion Questions

1 To increase the standard of living, how can the government help people deal with the problems of geography?

2 Do you think that areas subject to floods should be developed?

3 Do you think the government should help people who live in flood-prone areas rebuild after a disaster?

4 How do people who live along rivers and the coast deal with the possibility of flooding?

Caption Answer

Bangladesh lies at the mouth of the Ganges and Brahmaputra Rivers. Every year the monsoon causes the rivers to flood.

Activity

Burfi

OBJECTIVES: 11.01, 12.03

Ingredients:
1 cup butter
1½ cups sugar
1 cup evaporated milk
2–3 cups powdered milk
½ cup slivered almonds or pistachios
2 teaspoons fresh ground cardamom
powdered sugar

Melt butter in large saucepan, add sugar. Add evaporated milk, stir mixture, and bring to gentle boil. Once mixture has boiled, lower heat. Continue stirring, adding powdered milk a bit at a time. Add nuts and cardamom. When mixture is very thick, spoon onto large, oiled cookie sheet. Pat mixture until flat. Refrigerate burfi two hours (or cool six hours). Cut into squares. Dust with powdered sugar.

Discussion Questions

1 Do wealthy countries have a responsibility to help countries such as Bangladesh become self-sufficient?

By building more jute manufacturing plants

The flood waters deposit fertile soil each year on the plain.

Interpreting Facts on Threatened Species

OBJECTIVES: 2.03, 3.02

Pakistan
Punjab, meaning "five rivers," is the large central plain. The Indus River and its four main tributaries, the Chenab, Jhelum, Ravi, and Sutlej, flow across the Punjab. An endangered mammal, the Indus dolphin, is vanishing because dams on the Indus have divided its breeding and fishing grounds.

Bangladesh
The world's largest delta covers much of this low-lying nation. From the Ganges and Jamuma Rivers the endangered gharial is taken. A gharial is a relative of the crocodile hunted for its skin (to make leather goods such as shoes or bags). Its eggs are also taken for food.

India
Tropical forests, mainly on the Malabar Coast, from the subcontinent's western side are home to the Indian python. This reptile is threatened by hunters for its skin. The patterned skin is made into bags, belts, shoes, and wallets.

Directions Have students choose one of these endangered species to research further. They should plan an alternative course of action to protect the animal. They will present their plan with a graphic and handout to inspire their classmates to follow their conservation strategies

This burlap sack is made of jute. **How could Bangladesh make more money from this crop?**

Agriculture

Tens of millions of people farm small plots of rice or jute in Bangladesh. Most just manage to support themselves and their extended families. Developing and improving agriculture is a major goal of the government.

For years, Bangladesh has relied heavily on help from other countries. Japan, the United States, India, Pakistan, and the United Nations give money to Bangladesh. The country has made progress, but it remains one of the poorest in the world.

Industry

After independence, Bangladesh had to send its jute to India to be milled into burlap because it lacked factories. Today, Bangladesh has some jute manufacturing plants, but much of its jute is still exported to India. India sells the finished goods, and makes a greater profit than Bangladesh, which sells only the raw material. Bangladesh's textile industry, however, is growing rapidly.

Bangladesh has water resources. Fishing is a major export industry. The land is too flat to produce much hydroelectric power. Bangladesh often has too much water. Because the water is uncontrollabl it creates destructive floods.

Government

As in Pakistan, army leaders have seized power in Bangladesh. Sometimes the military has stepped in to end unrest. At other times, it has taken steps to end corruption.

Both countries have restored democratic rule but with limited success. The military remains a powerful force. In Bangladesh, political conflict—especially at election time—has sometimes led to bloodshed.

Like Pakistan, Bangladesh has had female prime ministers. Khaleda Zia won election to parliament and served as prim minister after her husband's death. Hasin Wazed succeeded Zia in 1996. Zia was reelected in 2001. Both women have had to work with the powerful military and have faced stiff opposition from rival parties.

Agriculture is the chief economic activity of Bangladesh. **What makes the country's soil so fertile?**

360 Chapter

Background Information

Hopeful Signs for Bangladesh

Although Bangladesh still ranks as one of the world's poorest countries, there are hopeful signs. Dhaka, the nation's capital, has a growing number of garment factories that employ many hundreds of Bangladeshi women. Textiles and clothing are key exports. Living in one of the world's most densely populated countries, the nation's 129 million people are packed into an area the size of Wisconsin, but its population growth rate has slowed. Government programs have helped lower the birth rate, improve health care, and reduce infant mortality. Despite serious flooding, the nation is headed toward food self-sufficiency. Food imports are down from 10 million to 2.5 million tons a year. Finally, innovative literacy programs provide food for students and pay small stipends to parents who keep their girls in school.

Bangladeshi women march in support of a strike called by the opposition parties in 1999. **What is the traditional role of women in South Asia?**

Women of South Asia

Although South Asian nations have ad female prime ministers, women in ch public roles are quite unusual. In angladesh and Pakistan, few women are ucated for work outside the family. nly about 36 percent of Pakistani omen are literate. The literacy level for omen in Bangladesh is slightly lower at .8 percent. Both rates are slowly rising.

A Bangladeshi social worker explained ow poverty limits the opportunities for ucation and employment. "Jobs seem so r away," she said. "Women are still ncerned about survival, making sure at their families eat. After that comes ucation. And, only then, employment."

However, in both Pakistan and Bangladesh, women now have more educational choices. A number of young women are studying for degrees in business management at Lahore University in Pakistan.

Most women in Pakistan and Bangladesh conform to Muslim traditions. Some village women live in ***purdah***, or strict seclusion. They rarely leave the house. If they must, they wear a *burka*, a head-to-toe covering. This strict interpretation of Islam is heavily influenced by local custom. They believe this shows their modesty and value within the family. Many women, however, do not follow these traditions.

LESSON 2 REVIEW

Fact Follow-Up

1. Describe the physical characteristics of place in Bangladesh.
2. What are the major products of Bangladesh?
3. Describe the role of women in Bangladesh.
4. What have been some challenges faced by the government of Bangladesh?
5. How does poverty limit opportunities for jobs?

Talk About It

1. Do you think Bangladesh should have remained a part of Pakistan? Explain.
2. How has nature been both a blessing and a disaster for Bangladesh?
3. Imagine that you are an economic advisor to the government of Bangladesh. What advice would you give? Why?

Discussion Questions

1. When compared to women in South Asia, what do you think has provided the greatest opportunity for women in the United States?
2. Where are there still areas that need improvement?
3. How have the opportunities women now have impacted society?

Most South Asian women are not educated for work outside the home. Many Muslim women observe strict *purdah.*

LESSON 2 REVIEW

Fact Follow-Up Answers

1. Bangladesh is low and flat, its deltas lying at the mouth of the Ganges and Brahmaputra Rivers. Because of its location, Bangladesh is defenseless against storms and flooding.
2. Jute and rice are the major products of Bangladesh.
3. Most women are poor and illiterate. They are most concerned with helping their families survive. Many Muslim women live in *purdah*, or seclusion.
4. Military takeovers and corruption have been a problem in Bangladesh's government. Any government there faces challenges of floods and typhoons.
5. First, people must be concerned about survival. After that comes education. Without an education, job opportunites are limited.

Talk About It Answers

1. Important points: Encourage students to state a position and explain it. Note: There is a great distance between Bangladesh and Pakistan, and Pakistan is better off economically than Bangladesh.
2. The flat, fertile land is well watered by two rivers, and floods deposit fertile soil for agriculture on the plain, but floods often bring disaster.
3. Important points: Students should suggest several policies and give reasons for their suggestions. Note: Education, careful study of flood control are important.

OBJECTIVES: 3.02, 10.02

Discussion Questions

1 How have people in North Carolina changed the environment in order to make the most of the land?

2 Compare the environmental concerns and resources of Sri Lanka with North Carolina.

3 What happens if a country's (or state's) economy depends on one crop?

Caption Answer

It has a warm tropical climate, with a wet monsoon season followed by a dry season.

Art Activity

Rhombus—Other Nations of South Asia

NATIONAL GEOGRAPHY STANDARDS: 4, 9

GEOGRAPHIC THEMES: Location, Place, Human-Environmental Interaction, Region

OBJECTIVES: 1.01, 11.02, 11.03

Materials rhombus pattern from the Teacher's Resource Guide; colored pencils, markers, or crayons; scissors; rulers; glue/glue stick or transparent tape

Brainstorm with students what a rhombus looks like. Distribute rhombus pattern and assign students to illustrate in words and drawings/charts/graphs each of the six "other" South Asian nations (one on each side of the rhombus). When students are ready to cut and assemble the rhombus, remind them that this is an unusual three-dimensional shape (as compared to a cube). Students should cut out the rhombus pattern and glue tabs on inside of rhombus (students will need to be patient with themselves and careful in forming this shape). Discuss with students that this shape allows all six nations illustrated to be considered equally and from different perspectives.

LESSON  Island and Mountain Nations of South Asi

KEY IDEAS

- Sri Lanka is a tiny island-nation off the southern tip of India. It has rich agricultural resources but has been torn by ethnic fighting.
- Afghanistan, too, has suffered from a long civil war. It is a landlocked country in the Hindu Kush.
- Nepal and Bhutan are in the Himalayas. Most of their people are subsistence farmers.

KEY TERMS

truce accord

Four small mountain and island nations are located around the edges of South Asia. None covers much territory or has many people. Mountains affect life in these countries. Yet Sri Lanka, Afghanistan, Nepal, and Bhutan differ from one another.

Sri Lanka

The island nation of Sri Lanka looks like a teardrop. It sits just 22 miles (35 km) off the coast of India. This lush land is bathed by the Indian Ocean and the Bay of Bengal. It has a warm tropical climate, with a wet monsoon season followed by a dry season.

Sri Lanka was once known as Ceylon. It was long a destination for traders who valued its cinnamon. Hills and mountains fill the island's center. Rivers cut through valleys to coastal plains and the sea.

In southern Sri Lanka, farmers grow tea, rubber, and coconuts on terraced hillsides. Tea accounts for two-thirds of the island's exports. Farmers grow rice on small farms throughout the country.

Monsoons bring less rain to northern Sri Lanka. This area often suffers drough conditions. Irrigation projects built in the 1960s have provided enough water.

As it is throughout South Asia, the chief environmental concern is deforestation. Loggers and farmers have cleared the land of trees. Wildlife preserv protect jungle and forest woodlands and such animals as elephants, leopards, crocodiles, and peacocks.

Sri Lanka attracts visitors because of gemstones. A blue star sapphire, the Star of India, on display at the American Museum of Natural History, was found i Sri Lanka. Tourists also love its beaches.

The island was often influenced by India. It also developed its own culture. I the time of Asoka, a Buddhist emperor of

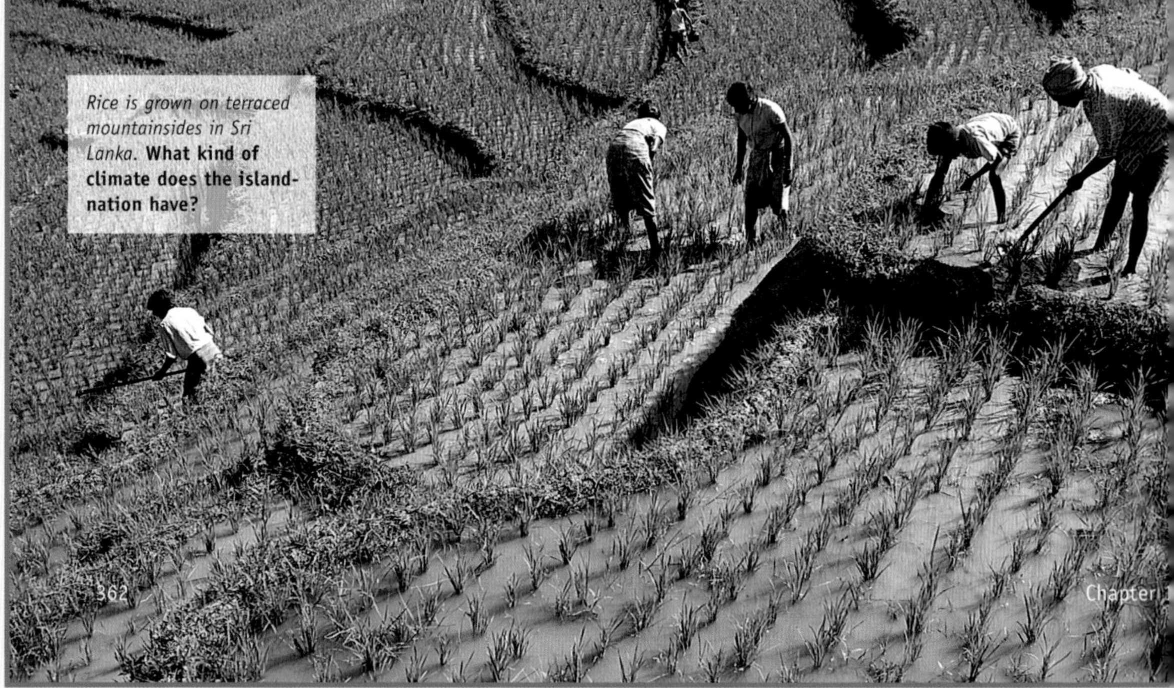

Rice is grown on terraced mountainsides in Sri Lanka. **What kind of climate does the island-nation have?**

362 Chapter 1

dia more than 2,100 years ago, uddhism reached the island. It has mained its chief religion.

People from many lands have settled the island. It is a diverse nation today. lmost three fourths of the 20.7 million eople speak Sinhalese (seen·hah·LEES) and e Buddhists. About 5 percent are Tamil-eaking Hindus. Other groups include luslims from Arab lands, Malays, and uropeans.

Sri Lanka's flag reflects its diversity. A ellow lion standing on a red background mbolizes the Sinhalese. Four yellow aves and a yellow border represent uddhism. A saffron stripe and a green ripe stand for the island's Hindu and luslim minorities.

Violence has disturbed this once eaceful island. After becoming dependent in 1948, the Sinhalese ajority ran Sri Lanka. The minority amils (tah·MEELS) tried to protect their ght. Some wanted to form their own ation. In the 1980s, extremists on both des began fighting. The conflict hurt the onomy. A ***truce accord,*** an agreement stop the fighting, was signed in 2002. eace is difficult to maintain.

fghanistan

Afghanistan is a landlocked nation out the size of Texas and almost mpletely covered by the Hindu Kush on e northwestern edge of South Asia.

Several rivers carved narrow valleys rough the mountains. These valleys and small central plateau can be farmed. otatoes, corn, rice, barley, and sugarcane e grown for the Afghans. Cotton, nuts, heat, and fruits are grown for export. fghanistan's largest (and illegal) cash op is poppies. The poppies are used to ake opiate drugs, such as morphine and eroine.

Many Afghans are herders. About half the land is used for grazing animals, pecially sheep. Until recently, sheep utnumbered Afghanistan's 29.9 million eople. Afghans also raise goats, cattle, orses, donkeys, and camels. Hides and ool provide additional exports.

Afghanistan is poor, with little industry. It has some resources, such as natural gas, coal, and iron, but only natural gas has been developed. Most industrial workers are in textile manufacturing. Others process food, build furniture, or make cement. Cottage workshops produce hand-woven fabrics, embroidery, hand-tooled metal, pottery, and guns.

Afghanistan has been long torn by war. For centuries, foreign armies swept through its mountain passes. In the 1980s, Afghan Mujahideen (moo·JA·hah·deen), Islamic fighters funded by Saudi Arabia, armed by the United states, and trained in Pakistan, defeated Soviet invaders.

By 1998, the Islamist militia, the Taliban, had gained control of most of the country. They established an Islamic fundamentalist regime that was extremely restrictive and harbored terrorists, including al-Qaeda leader Osama Bin Laden. The United States brought the Taliban down in 2001 and established a democratic government. It is struggling to take hold.

The Blue Mosque is a vivid sign of Islam in Afghanistan. **What is the most notable feature of this nation's physical characteristics?**

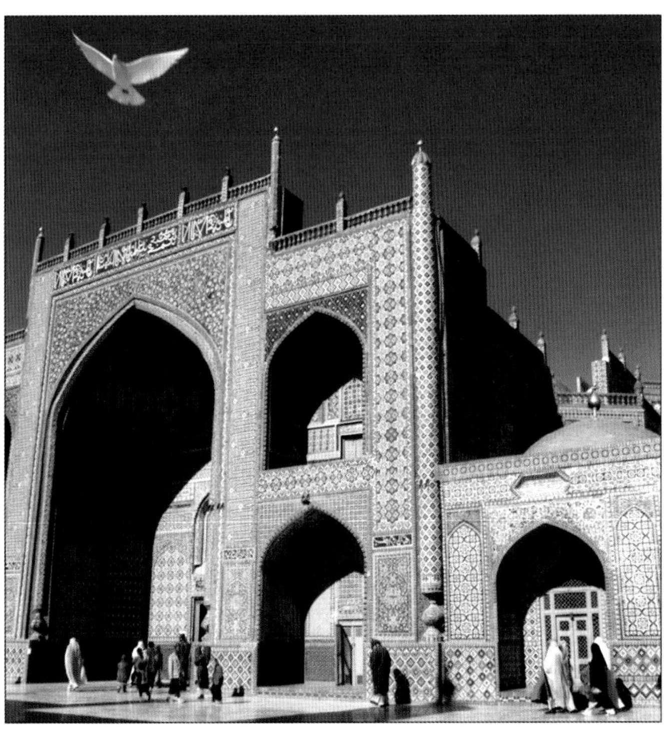

Discussion Questions

1 What is "landlocked"?

2 How have the mountains affected Afghanistan?

The mountains almost completely cover the land.

Flag

OBJECTIVES: 12.01, 12.02

Using the description in the second full paragraph on page 363, have students draw the flag of Sri Lanka.

They should explain what each element on the flag stands for. Do not show them a real flag until they are finished.

Meaning: yellow lion on red background represents Sinhalese, four yellow leaves and yellow border represent Buddhism, saffron stripe and green stripe represent Hindu and Muslim minorities.

Teacher Notes

Taliban

The Taliban took control of most of Afghanistan in 1996, removing the Shiite Communist Confederation from power. The name Taliban means "God's students." The founders of the party were students who studied Islam at religious schools.

The goal of the Taliban government was to create the world's most pure Islamic state. Many Afghans stood behind this new government because they were unhappy with the previous government. Afghanistan had experienced many years of war and economic hardship. People were seeking peace and security. Many Afghans believed the Shiite government was corrupt and welcomed the Taliban. They rallied behind the Taliban's claims of returning to a truer and purer Islam. Other Afghans and many outsiders felt that the Taliban's interpretation of Islam was too strict.

The Taliban government was only recognized by Saudi Arabia, Pakistan, and the United Arab Emirates. The rest of the world condemned this Afghan government, citing its human rights violations and support of terrorism. The United Nations leveled sanctions against Afghanistan for these same reasons.

The Taliban stripped women of their rights, including those guaranteed under the laws of Islam. Women in Afghanistan were forced to practice purdah, or seclusion. They could not work outside of the home.

The Taliban also protected Usama bin Laden, a known terrorist. Bin Laden was wanted for bombing United States embassies in Africa, as well as for the destruction of New York's World Trade Center and the attack on the Pentagon in September 2001. The United Nations condemned the Taliban for these abuses.

Research Activity

Tea-Tasting

OBJECTIVES: 4.02, 5.04, 13.03

Have students research five different teas grown from around the world and bring in samples for classmates to try. Survey classmates to see which tea is most popular and make a bar graph from the results. Students should write a summary of their conclusions. Were any of the teas grown in South Asia?

Science Activity

The Indian Ocean and the Mountains

OBJECTIVES: 1.01, 2.01

Have students study the effects of the Indian Ocean and the Himalaya and Hindu Kush Mountains have on the region's Climate. Working in small groups, students should use the Internet to identify the role the Indian Ocean plays in the monsoon winds and also the humidity of the region. How do the Mountains affect rainfall? Is there a rain shadow effect at work?

Each group should create a model showing how weather and climate patterns are affected by these natural features. The group should explain their model to the class.

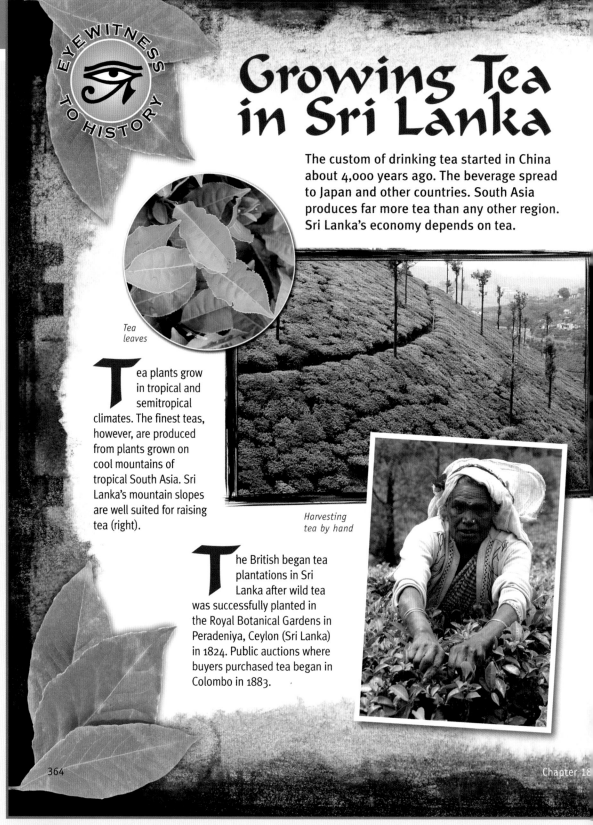

EYEWITNESS TO HISTORY

Growing Tea in Sri Lanka

The custom of drinking tea started in China about 4,000 years ago. The beverage spread to Japan and other countries. South Asia produces far more tea than any other region. Sri Lanka's economy depends on tea.

Tea leaves

Tea plants grow in tropical and semitropical climates. The finest teas, however, are produced from plants grown on cool mountains of tropical South Asia. Sri Lanka's mountain slopes are well suited for raising tea (right).

Harvesting tea by hand

The British began tea plantations in Sri Lanka after wild tea was successfully planted in the Royal Botanical Gardens in Peradeniya, Ceylon (Sri Lanka) in 1824. Public auctions where buyers purchased tea began in Colombo in 1883.

364 Chapter 18

Background Information

Sri Lanka's Political Family

Sirimavo Bandaranaike of Sri Lanka was the first woman in the world to serve as prime minister. Her political career began in 1960, one year after her husband Solomon, then prime minister, was assassinated. She became head of the political party her husband founded. Her daughter Chandrika Kumaratunga succeeded her as head of the Sri Lanka Freedom Party and has served as the country's president since 1994. Her daughter has moved the country away from a centralized, state-dominated economy to a more open, market-oriented one. She has also tried to end the two decades of ethnic violence between the Buddhist Sinhalese majority and the mostly Hindu Tamil minority. Together father, mother, and daughter have led Sri Lanka for almost half of its more than fifty years as an independent nation. Sirimaro Bandaranaike died in 2000 at the age of 84.

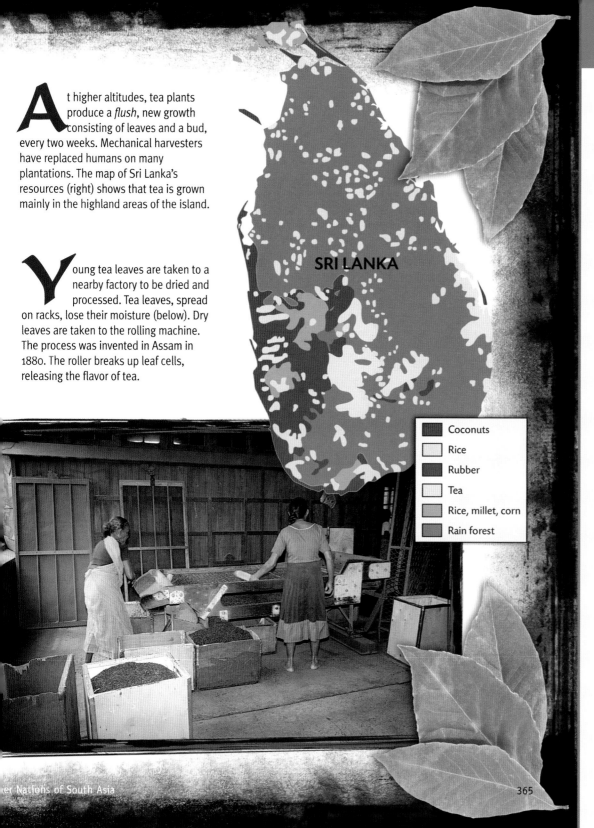

At higher altitudes, tea plants produce a *flush*, new growth consisting of leaves and a bud, every two weeks. Mechanical harvesters have replaced humans on many plantations. The map of Sri Lanka's resources (right) shows that tea is grown mainly in the highland areas of the island.

Young tea leaves are taken to a nearby factory to be dried and processed. Tea leaves, spread on racks, lose their moisture (below). Dry leaves are taken to the rolling machine. The process was invented in Assam in 1880. The roller breaks up leaf cells, releasing the flavor of tea.

SRI LANKA

Coconuts
Rice
Rubber
Tea
Rice, millet, corn
Rain forest

Growing Tea in Sri Lanka

NATIONAL GEOGRAPHY STANDARDS: 1, 4, 16

GEOGRAPHIC THEMES: Location, Place, Human-Environmental Interaction

OBJECTIVES: 3.02, 4.02, 5.01, 6.03

Using the map on this page, have students identify the six main crops raised on Sri Lanka. Ask students to identify the three chief crops of Sri Lanka listed in an almanac (tea, coconuts, and rice). (Note: Depending on the world market, supply and demand, even a given year's harvest, chief crops can fluctuate.)

Point out that rubber is usually listed as a resource in reference sources, often as "other resource," and is not always considered a crop. Mention that Sri Lanka raises sugar also. Sugar is listed in many resources as a chief crop. Have students note that rain forests cover the majority of Sri Lanka's territory. Discuss with students that forests are usually given as "other resource" in reference sources along with rubber.

Lead students to the conclusion that all of these products—coconuts, rice, rubber, tea, millet, corn, forests, and sugarcane/beets—grow and are harvested from the earth. More than one third of Sri Lanka's labor force is engaged in agriculture. Note that approximately 35 percent of Sri Lanka is forested (and suffering deforestation), thus green-key color on this map. Also, note that approximately 29 percent of Sri Lanka is arable or under cultivation (with about 7 percent in meadows and pastures). In conclusion, remind students that tea is the main export crop (two thirds) for Sri Lanka, earning 11.7 percent of the country's total value of exports.

This is a perfect time to sample Ceylon/Sri Lankan tea with students

It's a Fact

Sri Lanka

- There are two interesting myths regarding landforms of Sri Lanka. The first is that a chain of coral islands in the Palk Strait, Adam's Bridge, was said to have been built by Rama, hero of the *Ramayana*, as a means to rescue his wife, Sita, who was being held hostage. The second is a Muslim legend that explains a 5-foot hollow that looks like a footprint—Dam's Footprint—"Adam was forced to stand on one foot for a thousand years as penance for being thrown out of Paradise."
- Sri Lanka has the highest literacy rate in South Asia at 92 percent. Consequently, it also has the highest GDP per capita.
- Elephant racing is quite popular during New Year's celebration.

Discussion Questions

1 What advice would you give Nepal as it attempts to modernize?

2 What threats does modernization pose to long-held traditions?

Many want to see the Buddhist temple at Kathmandu. Mountain climbers are attracted by nearby Mount Everest.

Outline Map

NATIONAL GEOGRAPHY STANDARDS: 1, 2, 3, 12, 15

GEOGRAPHIC THEMES: Place, Location

OBJECTIVES: 1.02, 2.01, 2.02, 3.01

Using the outline map of South Asia in the Teacher's Resource Guide, have students locate Nepal, Bhutan, Sri Lanka, and Afghanistan. Place the mountains in the countries as accurately as possible using the physical map on page 353. Draw the wet monsoons in, showing them blowing from the south.

Ask students: How would rainfall in northern Sri Lanka be affected by its mountains? *There would be less rain because the wet monsoons are blocked by the mountains.*

Have students compare their maps with a population density map and physical map of South Asia. Ask them to write a paragraph making inferences about physical geography in determining where and how people live.

Nepal

As day breaks, sounds of monks chanting prayers echo from Kathmandu's Buddhist temple. Kathmandu (cat·man·DOO) is the capital of tiny Nepal. Nepal lies on the southern slopes of the Himalayas between India and China.

The city sits in a valley close to the towering Himalayas. At dawn, villagers take their yaks—large, longhaired oxen—to graze. Storekeepers set up shop, often selling goods from mats on the ground. They might offer fruit or vegetables, brassware, or carved wooden masks of gods and goddesses.

Nepal is a poor, developing country. Among its 27.1 million people are ethnic groups with their own language and traditions. Most people in Nepal are small farmers, growing food in the lower, fertile land along India's border. They trade their goods at local markets.

Nepal has many fast-running mountain streams that can be used to produce hydroelectric power. The mountains and forested foothills also provide wood products from stands of spruce, birch, juniper, fir, and cypress.

Today, change is coming to Nepal as tourists flock to Kathmandu. Tourism boosts Nepal's economy. New jobs are created in hotels and restaurants built to accomodate mountain climbers. Mount Everest lies across Nepal's northern border.

What would YOU do?

High in the mountains of Nepal there is a story about a *yeti*, also called the abominable snowman. Sometimes villagers say they hear the creature howling from the high peaks. Some claim to have glimpsed it. If you heard the story, would you believe it? Would you repeat it?

The Indrachowk market in Kathmandu, Nepal, is crowded with people buying and selling. **Why are more tourists from the West attracted to Nepal?**

Bhutan

Bhutan is one of the most difficult countries in the world to reach. A thick, semitropical forest in the south and the peaks of the Himalayas in the north have kept Bhutan isolated.

A high fertile plain lies between the high mountains and the steamy rain fores[t]. Most of the 2.2 million Bhutanese live on the plain.

Like other mountain nations of South Asia, Bhutan is a country of small farmer[s] who grow mainly rice, corn, and potatoes. Herders raise yaks and sheep in higher elevations. In the temperate and rainy south, fruit orchards produce apricots, apples, oranges, pears, peaches, plums, and walnuts.

Industry in Bhutan includes food processing, timber, and weaving. Cottage industries make matches, candles, soap, textiles, and carpets. Tourism is another important industry. Bhutan attracts visitors wanting to trek through the Himalayas or see the wildlife sanctuary in the jungle.

Because there is so little land suitable for farming in the mountainous countries, they have small populations. The mountainous hillsides are suitable for growing the most desirable types of tea. There are large tea plantations in Sri Lanka. Mountain climbing by tourists is a major part of the economy of Nepal. Half of Afghanistan is used for grazing. In Bhutan most people are farmers on its high fertile plain.

Extension Assign novice and intermediate ELL students the map only for this activity.

It's a Fact

Nepal and Bhutan

- Nepal is home to the only nonrectangular flag in the world. Health care is so severely limited outside the cities that many Nepalese still consult local shamans when sick.
- Bhutan is landlocked, and only about one third the size of North Carolina. "The Land of the Thunder Dragon" is only 2 percent arable. Even with that small amount of farmable land, Bhutan is self-sufficient in food.

Besides Bhutan's challenging landforms, [o]her circumstances have kept the nation [ou]t of world affairs. The country did not [w]elcome tourists until 1974. Telephone [se]rvice is limited, although wireless phone [se]rvices came to Bhutan in 2003. Transpor[ta]tion by pack animals is still common, [es]pecially on difficult mountain roads.

Tibet lies north of Bhutan. Most [Bh]utanese share ancestry, language, and [re]ligion with Tibet. Many speak a Tibetan [di]alect and practice a special form of [Bu]ddhism unique to the region.

Bhutan is separated from Nepal only [by] a thin strip of land belonging to India. [N]epalese settled in southern Bhutan. They [pr]actice Hinduism—as do most people in [N]epal—and speak Nepali.

Despite these links with Tibet and [N]epal, Bhutan is strengthening its ties to [In]dia, which influences Bhutan's foreign [po]licy and provides financial aid to the [go]vernment.

Bhutan's government is ruled by a [m]onarch who leads a National Assembly. [Tw]o-thirds of its members are elected.

Customs

Bhutanese call their country the "Land of the Thunder Dragon." The kings of Bhutan are crowned with the title "Druk Gyalpo," which means "Precious ruler of the Dragon People." The king's birthday and the anniversary of his coronation are national holidays.

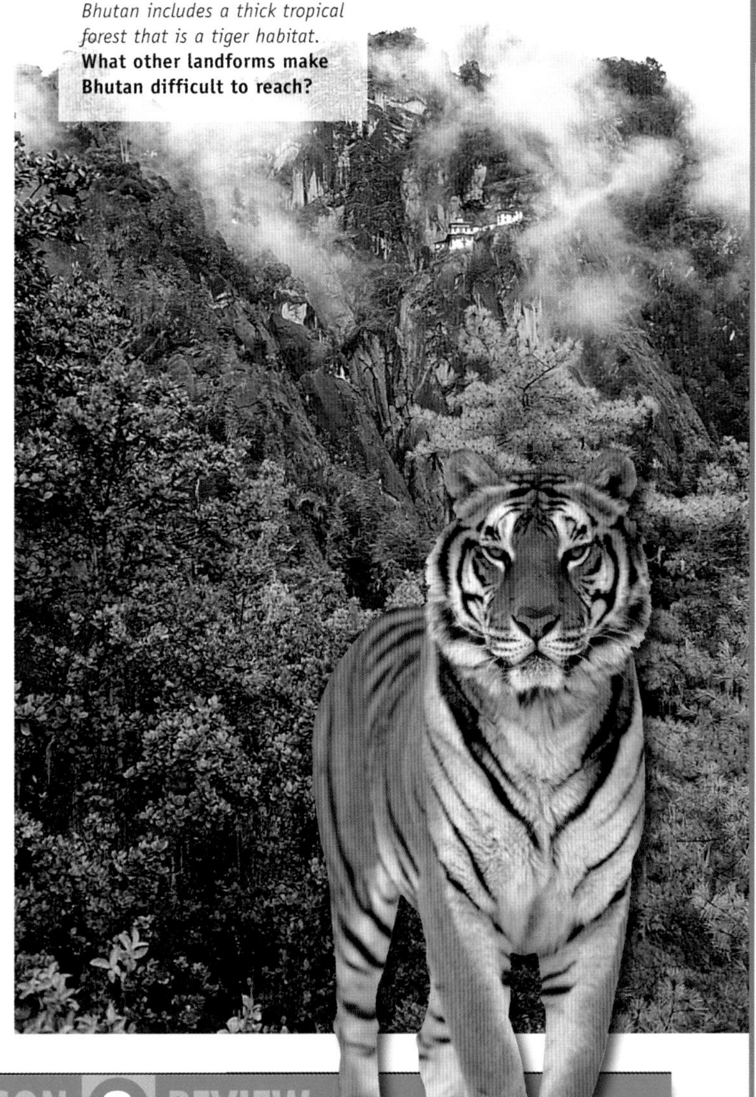

Bhutan includes a thick tropical forest that is a tiger habitat. **What other landforms make Bhutan difficult to reach?**

LESSON 3 REVIEW

Fact Follow-Up

1. Describe the physical characteristics of place in Sri Lanka and Bhutan.
2. How has their mountainous terrain affected the economies of Nepal and Afghanistan?
3. What are the major agricultural products of the four nations?
4. Describe industry in these nations.

Talk About It

1. Which of the four nations would you most like to visit? Explain your choice.
2. Describe the roles of religion in these nations.
3. Which nation has been given the most beneficial gifts of nature? the least? Explain.

Discussion Questions

1 What characteristics have made Bhutan seem to be one of the most stable countries of South Asia?

2 How do the other mountain countries of South Asia differ from Afghanistan?

Caption Answer

The Himalayas also block movement.

Art Activity

Designing Postcards

OBJECTIVES: 1.01, 2.01

Give each student six index cards to use to design a post card for each of the countries listed in Chapter 18. The students must draw a scene characteristic of that country on one side of the card. On the other side, they will write a brief description about what they may have seen or experienced if they had visited it.

LESSON 3 REVIEW

Fact Follow-Up Answers

1. Sri Lanka is an island with hills and mountains at its center. It has lush vegetation and a warm tropical climate. Bhutan is isolated by forests to the south and mountains to the north. Most people live on the central plain.
2. The mountains impede access to both countries. Nepal's nearby mountains have brought money from tourists eager to climb Mount Everest. The Afghans use their mountains to herd sheep.
3. Sri Lanka produces tea, rubber, coconuts, and rice. Afghanistan's farmers grow potatoes, corn, rice, barley, sugarcane, cotton, nuts, wheat, and fruit. Herders raise sheep, goats, and cattle. Nepal's farmers produce small amounts of fruit and vegetables and herd yaks. Bhutan produces rice, corn, potatoes, fruit, nuts, yaks, and sheep.
4. Sri Lanka depends on agriculture and tourism. Afghanistan has textile manufacturing and cottage industries. Nepal is finding that tourism is helping its economy. Bhutan's industry includes food processing, timber, and weaving.

Talk About It Answers

1. Important points: Students should choose one nation and explain their choice. Note: If there is peace, Sri Lanka's future looks bright. Nepal's new tourism industry and the promise offered by potential hydroelectric power may make a big difference for that nation.
2. Sri Lanka, Nepal, and Bhutan are predominantly Buddhist, and Afghanistan is predominantly Muslim. All four nations have experienced religious conflicts, and religious practices and traditions are powerful influences on their societies.
3. Important points: Students should choose one nation in each category and explain that choice. Note: Sri Lanka has fertile land and good location. Afghanistan is landlocked, mountainous, and has only a few resources.

Chapter 18 Skill Lesson

Teaching This Skill Lesson

Materials Needed textbooks, pencils, large sheets of paper, other reference books

Classroom Organization whole class, individual, small group

Beginning the Lesson Ask students to give you a list of some current favorites among one of the following (or another, more appropriate to your class): CDs, video games, athletic shoes, rock stars, TV programs. As students respond, list responses on the chalkboard. Ask how items on the list can be compared. (You are looking here for students to respond with attributes or criteria. One way to approach this topic is to ask, "Why is Michael Jordan called the greatest basketball player who ever lived?")

Lesson Development Remind students of the nations of South Asia they have learned about in Chapter 18. Ask questions such as these: Which one is most modern? Are most bound by tradition? Tell students they will be comparing these nations and it will be their job to come up with the criteria or attributes by which they will be compared. Make certain that students understand what criteria are. Have students copy the chart on page 368, cautioning them to leave plenty of room. Circulate and observe as students list their criteria, coaching as necessary. Students can complete the charts as a homework assignment.

Conclusion Post students' charts and have them comment on the charts. If desired, place students in small groups to compare charts and then have a general classroom discussion.

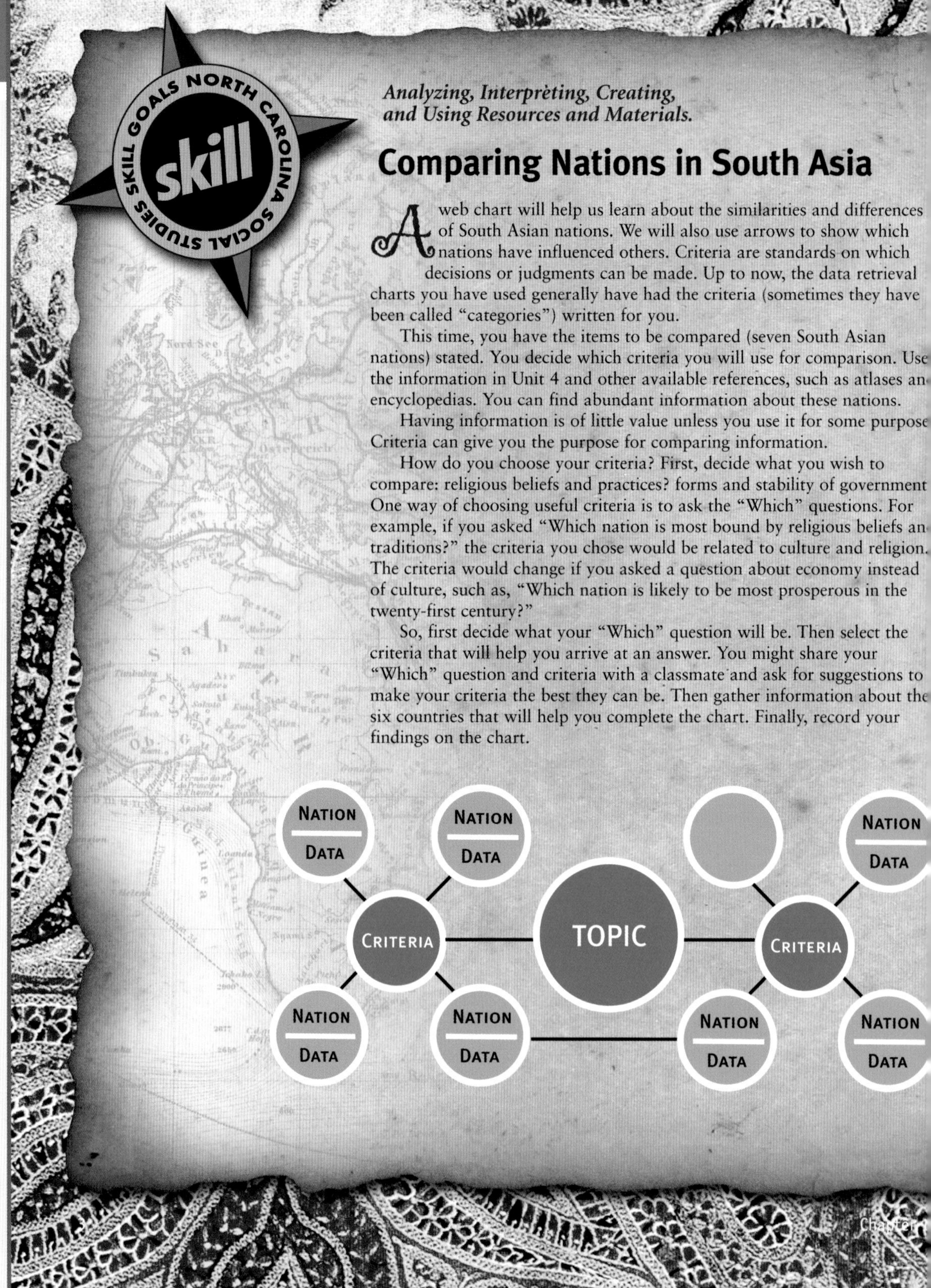

Analyzing, Interpreting, Creating, and Using Resources and Materials.

Comparing Nations in South Asia

A web chart will help us learn about the similarities and differences of South Asian nations. We will also use arrows to show which nations have influenced others. Criteria are standards on which decisions or judgments can be made. Up to now, the data retrieval charts you have used generally have had the criteria (sometimes they have been called "categories") written for you.

This time, you have the items to be compared (seven South Asian nations) stated. You decide which criteria you will use for comparison. Use the information in Unit 4 and other available references, such as atlases an encyclopedias. You can find abundant information about these nations.

Having information is of little value unless you use it for some purpose Criteria can give you the purpose for comparing information.

How do you choose your criteria? First, decide what you wish to compare: religious beliefs and practices? forms and stability of government One way of choosing useful criteria is to ask the "Which" questions. For example, if you asked "Which nation is most bound by religious beliefs an traditions?" the criteria you chose would be related to culture and religion. The criteria would change if you asked a question about economy instead of culture, such as, "Which nation is likely to be most prosperous in the twenty-first century?"

So, first decide what your "Which" question will be. Then select the criteria that will help you arrive at an answer. You might share your "Which" question and criteria with a classmate and ask for suggestions to make your criteria the best they can be. Then gather information about the six countries that will help you complete the chart. Finally, record your findings on the chart.

A Buddhist temple in Sri Lanka

Skill Lesson Review

1. What "Which" question did you ask? Why? *You might ask students if they changed their questions at any point, and why.*
2. How well did the criteria you selected help answer your "Which" question? *Students might exchange ideas about developing criteria.*
3. Suppose you were to ask, "Which South Asian nation is most like India?" What criteria would you use to compare the nations? *Population, religion, industry, resources, landforms, and types of government are possibilities.*
4. What criteria would you use to compare the nations if you asked another question: "Which South Asian nation has the most serious environmental problems?" *In answering this question, students might concentrate on pollution industries, the cutting forests, and contaminated water.*
5. In what other areas of your life could you use criteria to help make decisions? *In discussion, lead students to state that having criteria helps in making a choice among several options.*

Talk About It

1. Important points: Caution students that India is so much larger that it is best to concentrate on whether any of these nations has a mixed economy like India's. Pakistan is the closest in level of economic development.
2. Important points: Students should choose one nation and explain why that nation faces the greatest political challenges. Note: Both Sri Lanka and Afghanistan have been torn by wars and Pakistan is fighting corruption and military takeovers.
3. Important points: Encourage students' suggestions; urge them to explain these suggestions. Note: Pakistan was founded on Islamic principles. Sri Lanka has recently suffered a civil war along religious lines.
4. Important points: Caution students to include both economy and government in responding to this question. Pakistan is improving its economy and is likely to remain stable.
5. Important points: Students should give a reasoned explanation for whatever nation is chosen.
6. Important points: Students should choose one nation and explain why. Note: Pakistan probably offers the most freedom and opportunity for women at the present time.
7. People in South Asia weave and make crafts to sell at market, and they buy what they cannot grow. Cottage production, carried out in the home, encourages traditional family arrangements and values at the same time they bring added income to families.

CHAPTER 18 REVIEW

Lessons Learned

LESSON 1
Pakistan
Pakistan and Bangladesh are new nations. Yet both have been part of South Asia's development since earliest times. Pakistan has been a Muslim-led nation since independence in 1947. Islam exercises a major influence on daily life and government. Although the nation's agricultural and industrial resources are limited, Pakistan has enjoyed success in economic development.

LESSON 2
Bangladesh: A Fertile Land Battered by Nature
Bangladesh was separated from India in 1947. It was at first linked to Pakistan, but it won independence in a war. The country's major resource is rich agricultural land. This resource, however, must support an enormous population. The nation suffers from political difficulties and deep poverty. Frequent natural disasters, especially flooding, add to its woes. Islamic women in Bangladesh, as in Pakistan, are generally limited in what they can do outside family circles. Yet women have led both countries.

LESSON 3
Island and Mountain Nations of South Asia
Four small nations line the South Asian continent's rim—Sri Lanka, a mountainous island southeast of India, and Afghanistan, Nepal, and Bhutan in South Asia's northern mountains. Bhutan has strong cultural links to Tibet. All are poor. Sri Lanka and Afghanistan have suffered through recent civil wars.

Talk About It

1. Which of these six nations is most like India economically? Explain.
2. Which of these nations faces the greatest political challenges? Explain.
3. In which nation is religion the most unifying force? the most divisive? Explain.
4. Which of the nations do you think is most likely to establish a stable economy and government? Explain.
5. Which nation would you most like to visit? Explain why.
6. In which of the nations would a young woman's future be brightest? Explain why.
7. How are cottage industries important?

Mastering Mapwork

PLACE

Use the map on page 353 to answer these questions:

1. Using only the information on this map, describe the physical characteristics in Kabul, the capital of Afghanistan.
2. What other national capitals in South Asia have similar physical characteristics?
3. Using only the information on this map, describe the physical characteristics of Dhaka, the capital of Bangladesh.
4. Compare physical characteristics in Bhutan and Sri Lanka.
5. Compare the physical characteristics in Dhaka and Karachi.

370 Chapter

Mastering Mapwork

1. Kabul is located in a region of high mountains far from the ocean or any major river. Because of its elevation, it is likely to have cool temperatures.
2. Kathmandu in Nepal and Thimphu in Bhutan share similar physical characteristics of place.
3. Dhaka lies on flat land on the delta of the Ganges and Brahmaputra Rivers near the northern reaches of the Bay of Bengal. Because of the physical characteristics of this place, Dhaka is likely to experience flooding.
4. Bhutan is more mountainous than Sri Lanka and is located at higher latitudes. Thus it is likely to be considerably cooler than Sri Lanka.
5. Both are located in low-lying areas just north of the Tropic of Cancer. Dhaka lies at the mouths of the Ganges just north of the Bay of Bengal. Karachi lies on the Arabian Sea. Because of its location relative to the Ganges, Dhaka is likely to experience frequent flooding.

Go to the Source

Understanding Press Conferences

Read the excerpt below from Pakistan President Musharraf's "Remarks to the Press" with President George W. Bush on September 22, 2006. Answer the questions using specific references to the document. A press conference is when leaders meet with reporters to make announcements and answer questions about government policies and events.

On the regional side, in our region, we also discussed the rapprochement [peace talks] going on between Pakistan and India. And I proudly told the President [George W. Bush] that . . . I had an excellent meeting with Prime Minister Manmohan Singh in Havana. And it was a step forward towards resolution of disputes between India and Pakistan. . . .

. . . On the other side, we had an in-depth discussion on what is happening in Afghanistan and our tribal agency. . . . I explained to him what . . . we are doing in the form of the peace treaty that we have just signed through a grand jirga, which is an assembly of elders.

This treaty is not to deal with the Taliban. It is actually to fight the Taliban. The misperception in the media, I did clarify to the President. And may I very briefly say—and what I explained to the President— that this is a holistic approach that we are taking to fighting terrorism in Pakistan, in the tribal agencies of Pakistan. This is a political site of the holistic strategy—the holistic strategy being the military arm being used, a political element, an administrative element, and a reconstruction element.

We want to move on all these aspects forward . . . This deal is not at all with the Taliban . . . this is against the Taliban . . . This deal is with the tribal elders of north Waziristan agency. And the deal has three bottom lines . . . which I explained to the President.

Number one, there will be no al Qaeda activity in our tribal agency or across the border in Afghanistan. There will be no Taliban activity in our tribal agency or across in Afghanistan. There will be no Talibanization . . .—no Talibanization. All these three have been agreed by the tribal elders who signed that deal. And when they signed the deal, they are honor-bound, and they have already strict honor code to not only abide by it, but also that whoever violates it, they'll move against them.

So this is, in brief, the deal which I explained to the President. And I know that he's satisfied with that deal. And maybe this shows the light or the way forward for bringing peace to the region.

Questions

1. Who is the intended audience?
2. What tone is President Musharraf using?
3. What is the purpose of President Musharraf's remarks?
4. What is the "treaty" that President Musharraf mentions?
5. Why does President Musharrraf repeatedly say that the deal is not with the Taliban but against it?

Go to the Source

Go to the Source

OBJECTIVES: 7.01, 7.02, 8.02, 10.01, 10.02, 10.04, 12.01; Skills 1.03, 1.03, 1.04, 1.05, 2.02, 3.05, 4.02

In the War on Terror in Afghanistan, Pakistan is an important ally. But prior to September 11, 2001, Pakistan had recognized the Taliban government. Many Pakistanis are sympathetic to Osama Bin Laden's views as well. This puts the Leader of Pakistan, President Musharraf, in a difficult position, which he tries to mitigate in this press conference. A link to the full press statement can be found at **NCJourneys.com**.

ANSWERS

1. The speech was made at a press conference. The audience is the media and the viewers of the media.
2. He is trying to clarify and defend his positions to the media while reassuring his commitment to dealing with terrorist groups such as the Taliban and al Qaeda.
3. To inform the media as well as to clarify "the misconception in the media" of his country's treaties and efforts to combat terrorism.
4. The treaty is with tribal groups in Pakistan and Afghanistan to limit or end the influence of the Taliban and al Qaeda in those tribes.
5. He wants to reemphasize his points and clarify them. He believes that the media has some "misconceptions" about the treaty.

How to Use the Chapter Review

There are three sections in the Chapter Review: Talk About It, Mastering Mapwork, and Go to the Source. Use the Vocabulary Worksheets and the Chapter Review Worksheet in the Teacher's Resource Guide for additional reinforcement and preparation for the Chapter Assessments. The chapter and lesson reviews and the Chapter Review Worksheets are the basis of the assessment for each chapter.

Talk About It questions encourage students to speculate about the content of the chapter and are suitable for class or small-group discussion. They are not intended to be assigned for homework.

Mastering Mapwork has students apply one or more of the Five Themes of Geography to maps within the chapter.

Go to the Source activities allow students to analyze a primary source that relates to the content of the chapter. The questions and activities familiarize students with different types of primary sources and also build content-reading skills.

Unit 5 East Asia and Southeast Asia

The unit opens with a view of Mount Fuji, a symbol for Japanese of deeply held traditions and values. Throughout the unit, your students will discover the interplay of ancient and modern that shapes the regions of East Asia and Southeast Asia. Certainly since World War II, the entire region has been transformed by various economic and political relations with the West—and the United States in particular. China continues to be the major influence over the entire region. Despite this dominance, each country has managed to retain its identity and ancient traditions. Korea is now a divided nation. Vietnam, once divided, is now united. Japan, Taiwan, and Malaysia have all experienced remarkable economic growth over the past few decades.

UNIT LESSON PLAN				
	LESSON 1	LESSON 2	LESSON 3	LESSON 4
CHAPTER 19 Lands and People of East Asia and Southeast Asia	East Asia and Southeast Asia are distinct regions that share some cultural features. **Essential Question:** What cultural features are shared by the varied regions in East Asia and Southeast Asia? **Suggested time:** 1 day	Monsoons affect the climates and the economies of East Asia and Southeast Asia. **Essential Question:** How do monsoons affect the climate and economies of East Asia and Southeast Asia? **Suggested time:** 1 day	The people of East Asia and Southeast Asia belong to diverse ethnic groups and speak hundreds of languages. **Essential Question:** What are the diverse ethnic groups and languages there? **Suggested time:** 1 day	
CHAPTER 20 China's Enduring Traditions	Confucian, Daoist, and Buddhist ideas helped shape Chinese beliefs and traditions. **Essential Question:** How have Confucian, Daoist, and Buddhist ideas influenced Chinese beliefs and customs? **Suggested Time:** 2 days	China is one of the world's oldest civilizations with achievements in the arts, science, and agriculture. **Essential Question:** What are some achievements of the ancient Chinese civilizations? **Suggested Time:** 1 day	Foreign imperialism, civil wars, and invasion weakened China. In 1949, the Chinese Communists won power. **Essential Question:** What factors contributed to the rise of communism in China? **Suggested Time:** 1 day	
CHAPTER 21 China Today	China today mixes private enterprise with government ownership, but its government remains a dictatorship. **Essential Question:** How does China mix private enterprise with a Communist economy? **Suggested Time:** 1 day	China is reshaping its environment as its population grows and its economy develops. **Essential Question:** How is China reshaping its environment as its population grows and its economy develops? **Suggested Time:** 1 day	Although communism changed much in China, many traditions have survived. **Essential Question:** What Chinese traditions have survived even though communism has changed the way of life in China? **Suggested Time:** 1 day	
CHAPTER 22 Korea	Korea's location on the edge of Asia has affected its history and culture. **Essential Question:** How has Korea's location affected its history and culture? **Suggested Time:** 1 day	Each of the two Koreas, North Korea and South Korea, has its own government and economic programs. **Essential Question:** What are the differences between North and South Korea? **Suggested Time:** 1 day	As Korea has modernized, its traditions and culture have come under pressure to change. **Essential Question:** How has modernization affected the traditions and culture of Korea? **Suggested Time:** 1 day	
CHAPTER 23 Japan's Enduring Traditions	During its long history, Japan has adopted ideas from other cultures and preserved its own traditions. **Essential Question:** How has Japan preserved its own traditions while adopting ideas from other regions? **Suggested Time:** 2 days	Japan's landforms and climates have shaped national traditions. **Essential Question:** How has Japan's geographical features influenced its national traditions? **Suggested Time:** 1 day	The Japanese have worked together to make full use of their limited natural resources. **Essential Question:** How have the Japanese worked to make full use of their limited resources? **Suggested Time:** 1 day	
CHAPTER 24 Modern Japan	Japan is a democratic constitutional monarchy. **Essential Question:** What is Japan's form of government and how does it operate? **Suggested Time:** 1 day	After World War II, Japan built a strong economy that competes with other industrial powers. **Essential Question:** How did Japan rebuild its economy after its destruction in World War II? **Suggested Time:** 1 day	Japan has an urban society that blends old traditions and Western influences. **Essential Question:** How does Japan's urban society blend old traditions with Western influences? **Suggested Time:** 1 day	
CHAPTER 25 Southeast Asia	The languages and cultures of Asian and Western nations are reflected in modern Southeast Asia. **Essential Question:** Why is Southeast Asia known as a land of many different people? **Suggested Time:** 1 day	Southeast Asia's importance comes from its location on major trade routes and from its exports to the world. **Essential Question:** How is Southeast Asia affected by its location on major trade routes? **Suggested Time:** 1 day	Most Southeast Asian governments are authoritarian. The region's economy is growing. **Essential Question:** How are Southeast Asia's economies and governments changing? **Suggested Time:** 1 day	As Southeast Asia becomes more urban and industrial, centuries-old traditions are changing. **Essential Question:** How are Southeast Asian traditions changing as a result of its modernization? **Suggested Time:** 1 day

Unit Planner

Preparing the Unit

- Worksheets, assessments, and reproducibles for this unit are found in the Teacher's Resource Guide.
- See the list of Cultural Resources in the Teacher's Edition.
- Display the student work produced in Unit 5 to decorate your room.
- Review the resource list and collect as many of the suggested resources as possible for a classroom resource center.
- Share the suggested art and music activities with your cultural arts teachers so that they may help you integrate the curriculum.
- Review the suggested activities and select the ones that are most appropriate for your classroom. Plan ahead by collecting the materials for the activities.
- As you prepare your daily lessons, refer to the suggested goals listed in the chapter plan for selecting the specific objective(s) that you plan to cover in each lesson. Refer to the North Carolina Standard Course of Study for the specific objectives covered under each goal.

Unit Teaching Strategy

- Before you begin your study of East Asia and Southeast Asia, decorate your classroom with pictures and posters from this region. A party store may have items for "Chinese New Year" that will make decorating easy.
- Set up a resource area with books, pictures, and artifacts from East Asia and Southeast Asia.
- Make arrangements for a field trip to a local Chinese, Korean, Thai, or Japanese restaurant or have them come to you.
- Use the ideas in the wrap-around as suggestions to help differentiate your instruction. Please consider that there is a lot of material to be covered and you must pace yourself and activities in order to complete the seventh grade curriculum. Use these activities to best enhance your instruction. Do not feel that you should implement them all.
- Invite speakers who have a connection to East Asia and Southeast Asia to make presentations.
- Check the **NCJourneys.com** Web site for updates and materials.

Unit Projects

Students will have seven days to complete their project. They have the option of choosing from five different projects and should choose only one of the five. The five choices offer a lot of variety because students can select the project that best suits their taste. Suggested report format: two pages in length, typed, and double-spaced.

PROJECT CHOICES

OBJECTIVES: 1.02, 8.01, 9.01, 10.01

Illustrated Time Line

Have students research the different dynasties of China (*China, Then and Now* by Susan Finney [Good Apple, Good Apple, 1988. ISBN 086653458] is a good source). For the time line, include the names and dates of each dynasty and one or two important contributions from them to illustrate.

Extension ELL students should use an ELL-friendly Web site for research.

Museum Exhibit

Have students design a museum exhibit about East Asia. Students should include drawings, paintings, statues, designs of inventions, and pottery. Label each artifact with the dynasty and time period along with a brief description. Make a display and present the exhibit to the class.

Political Cartoons

Students will create a booklet of political cartoons, including cartoons on: China's Open Door Policy (1899–1900), the rise of Mao Zedong and communism, China's one child per family policy, Korean reunification, and the United States treaty to reestablish trade with Vietnam, with a short analysis of each.

Mobile with Attitude

Students will design and create a mobile illustrating influential people from the region. Mobile attachments should be cut in the shape of people and include their names. An attachment from each person should include biographical information and contributions.

Extension For ELL students, the biographical information could be copied from ELL-friendly Web sites instead of summarized in their own words.

Resource Map

Students will draw a map of East and Southeast Asia on a new shower curtain liner. Create a key of the resources found in this part of the world and include it in the bottom left corner of the curtain. Label the map using the key. Be certain to include both natural resources and important crops. An alternative to drawing on the map: Use Velcro strips to attach either the real product or cut-out designs of the product to the map. (This could also be a matching game.)

Bulletin Board Ideas

Mount Fuji

Use the facts about Mount Fuji and a picture as the centerpiece for your bulletin board. Around it have large pieces of tag board or laminated paper cut in cloud shapes. Write about the different ways the people of Japan use and think of this symbolic mountain.

Explorers

Have students recreate Marco Polo's exploration route for a bulletin board display. Use a large map of the world. Have students mark the route with arrows. They can include a drawing of the type of ship he used.

Silk

Using the Geography and Science Connection, have students bring in samples of silk, show illustrations of silk worms at work, or trace the Silk Road on a map.

Unit Activities

Introductory Activity

Room with a View

OBJECTIVES: 1.02, 1.1, 3.1, 7.1

From such resources as the student's text, the Internet, *National Geographic,* overhead transparencies of Asia, or film and videos, view various scenes of East Asia and Southeast Asia. Have students write a paragraph about what they might expect to find in a country with scenes such as these. Ways to get students started would be to direct their attention to the climate, vegetation, landforms, foods, and clothing styles of the people.

Culminating Activity

Building a Newspaper

OBJECTIVES: 1.01, 2.01

Students will create a newspaper about a country from the region studied in this unit, as they did in Unit 1. This will be issue number four of their newspaper.

Refer to the Unit 1 Culminating Activity on page 14C in the Teacher's Edition for specific directions and references on how to create and organize the newspaper. Remind students that the newspaper should feature two articles on the front. The back of the newspaper should include a map, a box displaying vital statistics, an article about something special or current events, and a puzzle. The students should use their newspapers from the previous unit as a model, and thus the students should be able to complete it in similar or slightly less time.

Have students share the newspapers with others in the class. They should keep each of their newspapers. At the end of the year, bind each student's newspapers together so each will have a volume of newspapers covering the regions studied throughout the year. Use copies of all students newspapers to organize a class volume according to region.

Technology Activity

Computer-aided Presentations

OBJECTIVES: 1.01, 4.03

Assign an Internet research project for this unit. Suggested topics include East Asian Cuisine; Southeast Asian Art, Then and Now; Regional Writing Systems; the Cultural Revolution; Dragons in Chinese Culture; Role of Women in Southeast Asia; Future of Human Rights in China.

To focus the assignment, have students develop a 3 to 5 minute presentation or digital story to share with the class. These projects can be done individually or in small groups. Presentations can be done as PowerPoint, Web quests, or hyper-studio presentations, if the students are capable. Enlist the aid of a school technology teacher.

Extension ELL students should use an ELL-friendly Web site for research. Assign peer tutors with good computer skills to assist with technology.

Science Activity

Effects of Atomic Bombs

OBJECTIVES: 8.03

Introduce such books as *Sadako and the 1,000 Papercranes* by Eleanor Coerr and *Hiroshima No Pika* by Toshi Maruki by reading one or many of them to the class. Discuss some of the environmental and biological side effects of the atomic bomb in Japan. Have students research more carefully the health hazards the people of this area endured at the time of bomb was dropped and many years after the historic event.

Extension ELL students should use an ELL-friendly Web site for researching the atomic bomb. Alternate ELL Activity: Have an Asian ELL student teach the class to make origami paper cranes, then turn your room into the "Room of 1000 Cranes."

Math Activity

Abacus versus the Calculator

OBJECTIVES: 8.03

Assign the class to find out as much information as possible about the abacus. Suggest that they consider things such as its history, how it's made, who uses it, and so forth. Mention that they might learn about the famous contest in 1946 between an abacus operator and an electronic adding machine in which the abacus won. Have the students report their findings.

Unit Resources

Fiction

China

Alexander, Lloyd. *The Remarkable Journey of Prince Jen.* Walker, 1991. ISBN 0525448268.

Bosse, Malcolm. *The Examination.* Farrar, Straus, and Giroux, 1994 . ISBN 0374322341.

Fritz, Jean. *Homesick, My Own Story.* Cornerstone Books, 1987. ISBN 1557360707.

Jagendorf, M.A., and Virginia Weng. *The Magic Boat and Other Chinese Folk Stories.* New York: The Vanguard Press, 1980. ISBN 0814908233.

Lewis, Elizabeth, *Young Fu of the Upper Yangtza.* Henry Holt, 1995. ISBN 0805005498.

Paterson, Katherine. *Rebels of the Heavenly Kingdom.* Puffin, 1995. ISBN 0140376100.

Yep, Lawrence. *Rainbow People.* Harper-Collins, 1989. ISBN 0833585541.

—. *Serpent Children.* HarperCollins, 1998. ISBN 0064406458.

China/America

Yep, Lawrence. *Child of the Owl.* Harper-Trophy, 1990. ISBN 006440336X .

—. *Dragon's Gate.* HarperTrophy, 1995. ISBN 0064404897.

—. *Dragonwings.* HarperTrophy, 1989. ISBN 0064400859.

Cambodia

Crew, Linda. *Children of the River.* Delacorte, 1989. ISBN 0385296908.

Ho, Minforg. *The Clay Marble.* Farrar, Straus, Giroux, 1991. ISBN 0374313407.

Vietnam

Garland, Sherry. *Shadow of the Dragon.* Harcourt, 2001. ISBN 0152242007.

—. *Song of the Buffalo Boy.* Harcourt Brace Jovanovich, 1992. ISBN 0152771077.

Nhoung, Huynhm. *The Land I Lost.* Harper Row, 1982. ISBN 084466586X.

Wartski, Maureen. *A Boat to Nowhere.* Westminster Press, 1980. ISBN 0664326617.

Wealan, Gloria. *Goodbye Vietnam.* Knopf, 1992. ISBN 0679822631.

Southeast Asia

Coburn, Jewell Rienhart. *Encircled Kingdom: Legends and Folktales of Laos.* Thousand Oaks, California: Burn, Hart, and Company, 1979. ISBN 0918060036.

DeSpain, Pleasant. *Thirty-Three Multi-cultural Tales to Tell.* Little Rock, Arkansas: August House, 1993. ISBN 0874832659.

Sierra, Judy. *Cinderella.* (The Oryx Multicultural Folktale series.) Phoenix, Arizona: The Oryx Press, 1992. ISBN 0897747275.

Nonfiction - Regional

Unitedn Nations World Population Fund. State of the World Population 2006: A Passage to Hope, Women and International Migration with Youth Supplement.UNFPA, 2006.

Garland, Sherry. *Vietnam: Rebuilding a Nation.* Minneapolis: Dillon, 1990. ISBN 0875184227.

Rau, Margaret. *Holding Up the Sky: Young People in China.* New York: Dutton, Lodestar, 1983. ISBN 0525667180.

Thompson, Peggy. *City Kids in China.* New York: HarperCollins, 1991. ISBN 0060216549.

Williams, Suzanne. *Made in China: Ideas and Inventions from Ancient China.* Berkeley, California: Pacific View Press, 1996. ISBN 1881896145.

Other Resources

Kamishibai for Kids (Traditional story-boards used in Japan. Cathedral Station, P.O. Box 629, New York, NY 10025, (800) 772-1228, **www.kamishibai.com**

Audiovisual

Dreams of Tibet, Frontline. 1997. PBS Video.

Web Sites

Go to **NCJourneys.com** for links to the following Web sites:

- Dreams of Tibet companion Web site
- Modern Mongolia: Reclaiming Genghis Khan

See also Unit 4 Resources for additional materials on Asia (continent-wide).

Paideia Seminar

Haiku Poetry

OBJECTIVES: 1.02, 3.01

A Paideia seminar is a formal discussion based on a text. The teacher asks only open-ended questions. Students must read and study the text, listen to other students' comments, think critically, and respond with their thoughts and with responses to the thoughts of others. Higher order thinking is evident because students are required to summarize, analyze, synthesize, compare and contrast, and use logic to defend and challenge ideas.

Three Haiku by Basho

Waterjar cracks:
I lie awake
This icy night.

Lightning:
Heron's cry
Stabs the darkness.

Sick on a journey:
Over parched fields
Dreams wander on.

Opening Questions

- What do the first two haiku have in common?
- What titles would you give to these three haiku?

Core Questions

- How is a heron's cry like lightning?
- How might dreams wander on?
- What is the connection between a waterjar cracking and an icy night?
- How does the first haiku relate to the last?
- What tensions do you notice in the text?
- How does the image of Asia or Japan contribute to your reading of the poem?

Closing Questions

- How can the images and meaning of the peoms help us understand Asia?
- How can you apply these peoms to your/our current situation?
- What action, if any, do the poems ask of the reader? What would happen if readers complied with that request?

Map Activity

Far East Mental Mapping

NATIONAL GEOGRAPHY STANDARDS: 2

GEOGRAPHIC THEMES: Location

OBJECTIVES: 1.02

This locator map is a Robinson projection with approximately 12 percent distortion of earth. As a class discuss why this area was called the "Far East." Why is it often one of the most distorted areas on a Robinson projection (it is closer to the outer edge of this type of equal-area map projection where the distortion becomes greater the farther away from center of the map).

Some visualize the red highlighted area as a person blowing from his/her mouth with the islands of Southeast Asia being particles coming from the Asian-mainland person's head (Japan is usually identified as perspiration coming from the brow of this mainland person.) Note with students that to see this mental image one must have an Eurocentric orientation—facing east just as any one does when they use the term "Far East."

Unit 5 East Asia and Southeast Asia

To Japanese, Mount Fuji is more than a beautiful mountain peak. Fujisan, as they call it, is linked to ancient beliefs about a sun goddess. It reminds them of deeply held traditions and values. Every summer thousands climb to the 12,388-foot (3,716-m) peak.

Millions visit East Asia and Southeast Asia every year to see such wonders. The world's business and political leaders are also regular visitors because Asia's modern nations play key roles in world affairs.

Mount Fuji reflected in Lake Yamanaka, Japan

Career Feature

Social Studies at Work

Academic Administrator

An academic administrator is someone who manages the business affairs of a college, university, or school.

Meet Francis Moyer, executive director of the Japan Center at North Carolina State University.

Growing up as the son of an Air Force officer, Francis "Tony" Moyer had the opportunity to see much of the world. His family lived in both Japan and England and several places in the United States.

Even though he was only nine when his family lived in Japan, something sparked a lifetime interest in other cultures and languages. Moyer remembers being fascinated with the Japanese language, especially the Japanese writing system. He learned Japanese characters for numbers by keeping track of the score during televised baseball games.

When it came time to attend college, Moyer choose to pursue a degree in East Asia studies. During his studies he lived in Japan two different times. Including these long-term stays, his years as a child in Japan, and several years as the employee of an American company operating in Japan, Moyer has lived in Japan 14 years.

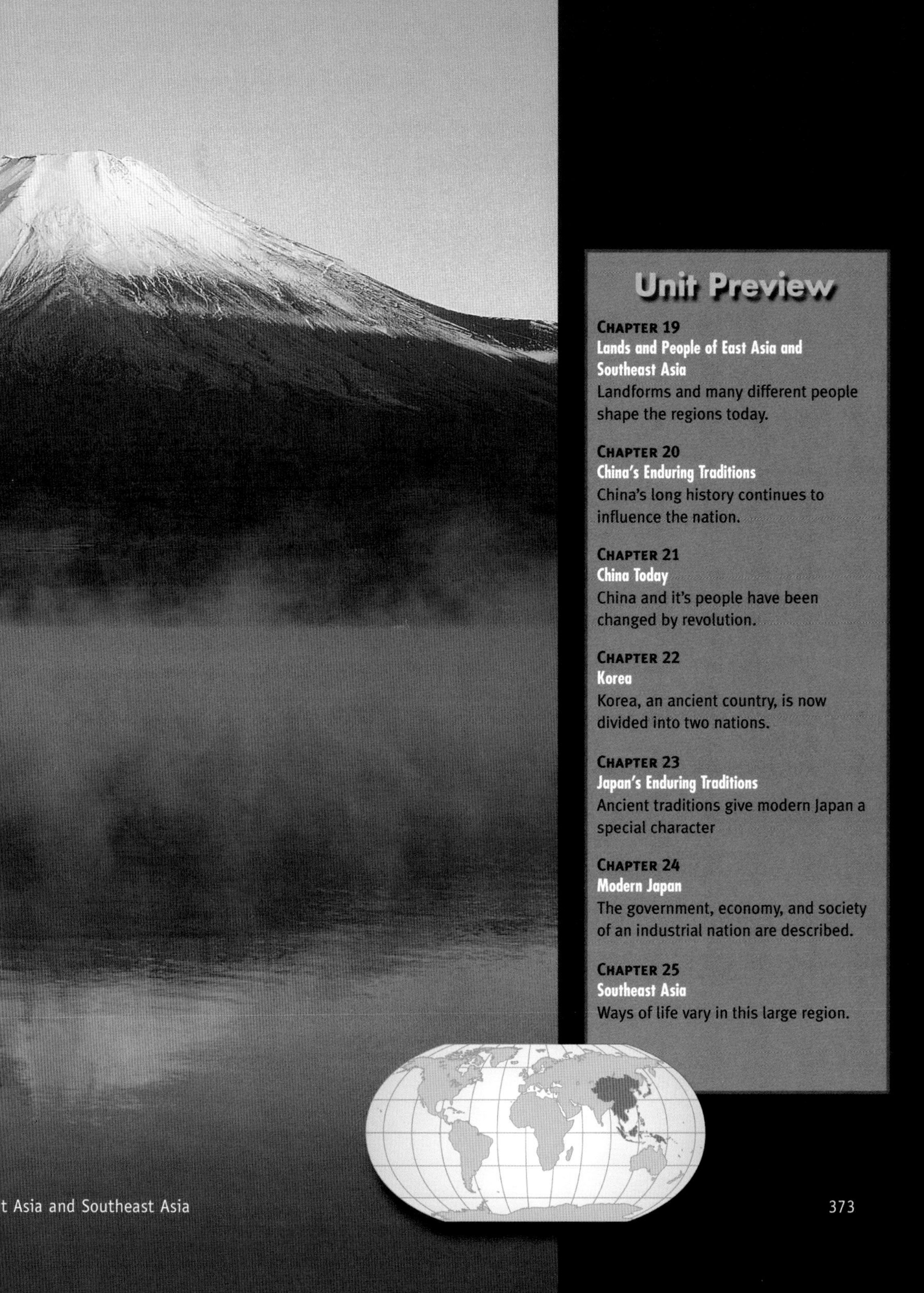

As it turns out, it was the perfect training for his current position as executive director of the Japan Center. It is his responsibility to develop academic, technological, commercial, and cultural links between North Carolina and Japan.

One service that the Japan Center provides is brochures written in Japanese that explain how to get a driver's license. New Japanese residents in North Carolina also need to learn how to handle their finances since checkbooks aren't used in Japan the way they are here. Because Moyer has spent so much time in Japan, he understands the sometimes subtle differences between the cultures and can help make the transition easier.

Academic Administrator for a Day

Imagine that a group of exchange students from Nagoya, Japan, will be attending your school next semester. Write a brochure to explain what someone from another country might need to know. Include information about the daily schedule, the food served in the cafeteria, the dress code, and any other things the Japanese students might need to know to feel comfortable.

Find Out More

Visit **NCJourneys.com** for links to the North Carolina Japan Center.

Lands and People of East Asia and Southeast Asia

Social Studies Strands

Geographic Relationships
Climate
Resources

Cultures and Diversity
Language
Education

North Carolina Standard Course of Study

Goal 2 The learner will assess the relationship between physical environment and cultural characteristics of selected societies and regions of Africa, Asia, and Australia.

Goal 3 The learner will analyze the impact of interactions between humans and their physical environments in Africa, Asia, and Australia.

Goal 5 The learner will evaluate the varied ways people of Africa, Asia, and Australia make decisions abut the allocation and use of economic resources.

Goal 11 The learner will recognize the common characteristics of different cultures in Africa, Asia, and Australia.

Teaching & Assessment

- English Language Learner Modified Lesson Plans for this chapter are found in the Teacher's Resource Guide.

- *ExamView® Assessment Suite* is provided at **NCJourneys.com.** It includes customizable assessments for all chapters. Paper tests are also available in the Teacher's Resource Guide. See pages T16–T17 for information about how to use the assessments and the Scoring Guide.

Worksheets

Worksheets and answer keys are found both in the Teacher's Resource Guide and at **NCJourneys.com**, including Reading Guides, Reading Strategies, Chapter Reviews, English Language Learner and others.

ACTIVITIES AND INTEGRATIONS

SOCIAL STUDIES
Made in Asia, p. 374B
● Travels with Marco Polo, p. 375
Comparing China, p. 376
● Digging to China, p. 379
★ Map—Political and Physical Features, p. 380
Skill Lesson: Locating a Factory in Asia, p. 391

READING/LANGUAGE ARTS	READING/LANGUAGE ARTS OBJECTIVES
Enticing Tourists, p. 374B	2.02
Analogies, p. 374B	2.01
Activator: *Lon Po Po*, p. 374B	1.03
Writing Prompt: Population, p. 374	3.01
★ ■ Silk and Silk Road, p. 384	2.01
Sell Your Country, p. 386	2.02
● What's in a Name?, p. 387	6.01
■ Lion City–One of Asia's Four Tigers, p. 389	6.01
Go to the Source: Understanding Account of Historic Events p. 393	2.01, 4.01, 5.01, 5.02

SCIENCE	SCIENCE OBJECTIVES
★ ■ Climate, p. 382	1.05, 1.08

MATHEMATICS	MATHEMATICS OBJECTIVES
★ Bar Graph, p. 385	4.01, 4.05
Word Problem, p. 390	1.02

TECHNOLOGY	TECHNOLOGY OBJECTIVES
Demographic Chart, p. 381	3.01, 3.03
■ Asian Festival, p. 386	3.01, 3.08

VISUAL ARTS	VISUAL ARTS OBJECTIVES
● ▲ ■ Design a Chinese Scroll, p. 374B	2.04, 5.01
▲ ■ East and Southeast Diorama, p. 378	2.04, 4.04

CHARACTER AND VALUES EDUCATION	TRAITS
Writing Prompt: Population, p. 374	fairness, responsibility
What Would You Do?, p. 383	responsibility
Character Education, p. 383	respect

● Basic Activities ★ Challenging Activities ▲ English Language Learner Novice ■ English Language Learner Intermediate

Chapter Activities

Made in Asia

OBJECTIVES: 4.02, 5.04, 13.03

Have students go through the labels of their clothing looking for the country of origin. List all the items from Asian nations. Similarly, have them go through items in the home, especially electronics. Work with the lists until all items are put into categories. Divide the class into groups. Give the lists to each group or give a different category to each group.

Have them consider the future of industrial development for Asia. You might phrase your question this way: Based on the large number of items from Asia, make predictions about the industrial development of Asia. Will it continue? Will all countries receive equal benefit? Will some countries receive more work and income than others?

Extension Have students brainstorm as to why so many items are made in Asia.

Novice and intermediate ELL students do not have the language ability to make the comparisons asked for in this activity, but could participate as part of a group.

Enticing Tourists

OBJECTIVES: 1.01, 2.01, 3.01

East Asian and Southeast Asian countries often depend on tourist dollars for income. This activity will help students see how tourist bureaus try to make people want to visit their country.

Prior to studying a region or subregion, have cooperative groups of two or three find the address of embassies of the countries to be studied. Have students write or e-mail their chosen embassies requesting information. Embassy addresses are given in the last entry for each nation in the World Almanac Nations section or online through the Department of State (link found at NCJourneys.com under Chapter 1 Resources). Have students use their school address.

Students will use the information from the embassies to create a tourism promotional brochure.

The task is to sell the country to potential tourists by accentuating the positive. Have students make their country as attractive and appealing as possible. Present this in the form of a tri-fold travel brochure. Grade students on creativity, accuracy, and appeal.

Extension Make lists of the items left off the brochure. Have students discuss why those things were not included.

Make sure ELL students' cooperative groups are with strong students who can act as peer tutors. Students can research on ELL-friendly Web sites to increase their comprehension. The role of the ELL student in the group should be focused on non verbal participation with limited writing.

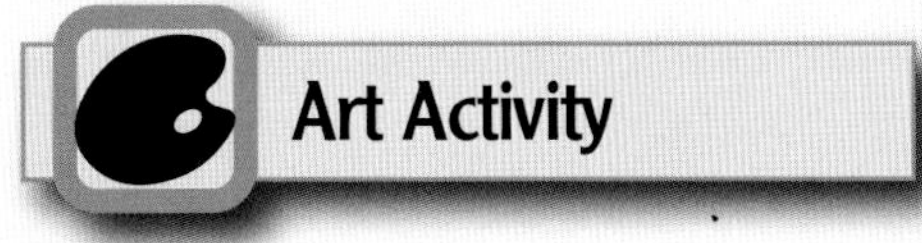

Design a Chinese Scroll

OBJECTIVES: 4.03, 12.02

Materials paper (newsprint works well), two dowel of the same length (must be as long or longer than the paper), string, tape, watercolor paints, paint brush, scissors

Directions Study pictures of traditional Chinese landscapes. Have students use the art supplies to paint their own Chinese landscape on the paper. They should leave a margin at the top and the bottom of the picture to tape it to the sticks.

Once the picture is dry, attach each end of the scroll to the dowel with tape.

Tie a length of string on each end of the dowel for a hanger.

Display the scrolls.

Analogies

OBJECTIVES: 1.02, 2.02, 3.02

Analogies are useful to help students make associations with prior knowledge. Read the analogies aloud and ask students to identify the relationship between the terms. As an extension, ask students to write their own analogies using key terms or places discussed in the chapter.

Korea : East Asia :: Italy : Europe (is a peninsula in)

Thailand : SE Asia :: Ethiopia : Africa (never under colonial rule in)

Asian Pacific Rim : Ring of Fire :: North Carolina : Tarheel State (is also known as)

Beijing, China : Philadelphia :: Shanghai, China : Savannah :: Tokyo, Japan : Raleigh (is at the same latitude as)

wheat: North China :: rice : South China (is major grain in)

deforestation : erosion of topsoil :: mining : depletion of natural resources (causes)

homogeneous : heterogeneous :: one : many (antonyms)

characters : symbols :: alphabet : sounds (represent)

Teaching Strategy

Use this chapter as a quick introduction to the landforms and physical features in East Asia and Southeast Asia. When you study individual countries in later chapters, you may want to review the geography of each country, focusing on that country's physical features and landforms.

Activator

 **OBJECTIVES:** 12.02

Activators are great tools to use in order to "hook" the attention of the students. Reading picture books or stories is an excellent way to build interest in the subject and is also a great way to integrate language arts into the social studies curriculum.

Lon Po Po—A Red-Riding Hood Story from China, translated and illustrated by Ed Young. (Putnam, 1996. ISBN 0698113829.)

Writing Prompt

OBJECTIVES: 10.03, 10.04, 11.03

Evaluative

The world's population is now more than 6.6 billion. The earth can only support a finite number. More than 1.3 billion people live in China. In an effort to control its population, China has enacted a one-child-per-family policy. Do you think this is a policy that should be adopted by countries throughout the world? Write a position paper giving your opinion and explain why you think it should or should not be adopted worldwide.

As you write or word process your paper, remember to:

- clearly state your position.
- give at least three reasons and explain your reasons fully.
- give examples to support your reasons.
- write in complete sentences and paragraph form.
- organize your ideas and include an introduction and a conclusion.
- use good grammar, spelling, punctuation, and capitalization.

CHAPTER 19

Lands and People of East Asia and Southeast Asia

Marco Polo

Marco Polo returned to Venice, Italy, in 1295 after a 26-year journey across Asia. He had seen Persia, Tibet, Mongolia, China, Burma (today's Myanmar), and Siam (today's Thailand). He had spent 17 years at the court of the Chinese Emperor Kublai Khan. In his Travels of Marco Polo, *he told of China's civilization. Europeans dismissed his stories as lies, because they could not imagine a place so different from their own. Yet Polo's travels spurred European interest in Asia. Explorers sailed southward around Africa and across the Indian Ocean. They were searching for the best route to the lands we know today as East Asia and Southeast Asia.*

Kublai Khan presents his golden seal to Marco Polo.

Chapter Preview

LESSON 1
Location and Landforms
East Asia and Southeast Asia are varied regions that share some cultural features. China has long influenced the cultures of these regions.

LESSON 2
Climates and Resources
Monsoons affect the climates and the economics of East Asia and Southeast Asia.

LESSON 3
People and Their Environment
The people of East Asia and Southeast Asia belong to diverse ethnic groups and speak hundreds of languages.

374

Chapter 1

Chapter Resources

Print Resources

Nonfiction

Forbes, Evan D., ed. *World Geography Series: Asia.* Teacher Created, 1995. Materials, Inc.

Hancock, Lisa and Sue Sutton, eds. *100 Reproducible Activities: Asia.* Instructional Fair, Inc. MI., 1996.

Kalman, Bobbie. *Tibet.* Crabtree, 1990. ISBN 0865052131.

Moore, Jo Ellen, *Asia Geography Unit.* Evan-Moor, CA, 1992.

Major, John S. *The Silk Route—7,000 Miles of History.* HarperCollins, 1995. ISBN 0064434680.

Reynolds, Jan. *Mongolia: Vanishing Cultures.* Harcourt Brace, 1994. ISBN 0152553134.

Steele, Philip. *Journey Through China.* Troll Associates,1991. ISBN 0816721130.

Yan, Martin, *Martin Yan's Asia: Favorite Recipes from Hong Kong, Singapore, Malaysia, the Philippines, and Japan.* Bay Books, 1997. ISBN 0912333642.

Back issues of magazines

Rice. Cobblestone Publishing Company. ISBN 0382407822.

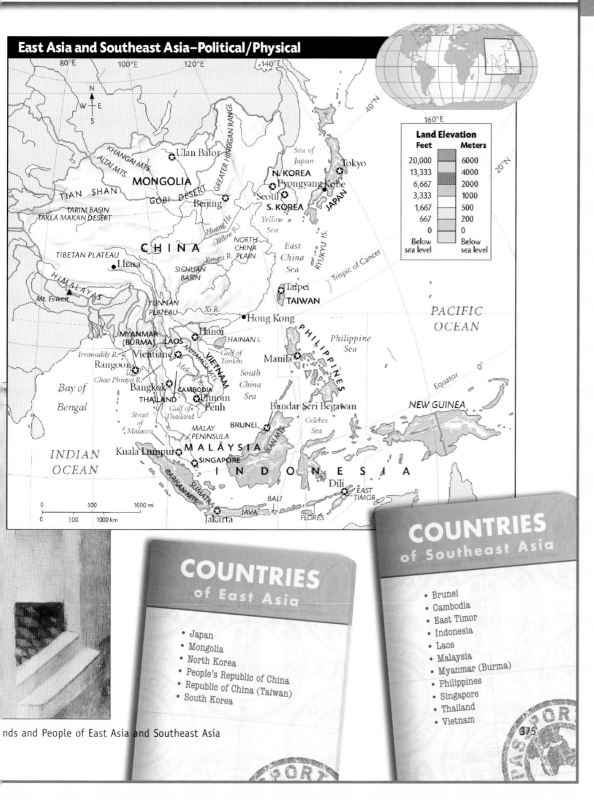

East Asia and Southeast Asia–Political/Physical

COUNTRIES of East Asia

- Japan
- Mongolia
- North Korea
- People's Republic of China
- Republic of China (Taiwan)
- South Korea

COUNTRIES of Southeast Asia

- Brunei
- Cambodia
- East Timor
- Indonesia
- Laos
- Malaysia
- Myanmar (Burma)
- Philippines
- Singapore
- Thailand
- Vietnam

nds and People of East Asia and Southeast Asia 375

Map Activity

Travels with Marco Polo

NATIONAL GEOGRAPHY STANDARDS: 1, 4, 5
GEOGRAPHIC THEMES: Place, Region
OBJECTIVES: 1.02

Marco Polo made several excursions into East and Southeast Asia during the thirteenth century by both land and water routes. Have students locate and point out these geographical features.

The most western and northern points on this map are in what country? *People's Republic of China*

The most eastern and southern points on this map are in what country? *Indonesia*

What nation is crossed by the Equator? *Indonesia*

What is the great desert that crosses China and Mongolia? *Gobi*

How many China Seas are there? *two: East, South*

How many Southeast Asian nations are on the Asian mainland? *five: Myanmar, Thailand, Laos, Vietnam, Cambodia*

What body of water separates China from Korea? *Yellow Sea*

What body of water separates Korea from Japan? *Sea of Japan*

What country is on the southern tip of the Malay Peninsula? *Singapore*

What nation shares an island with Malaysia and Indonesia? *Brunei*

What country is not a part of East Asia or Southeast Asia but shares an island with Indonesia? *Papua New Guinea*

Which oceans border East Asia and Southeast Asia? *Indian, Pacific*

What is the only landlocked East Asian nation? *Mongolia*

Which is the only Southeast Asian country that is landlocked? *Laos*

What are the archipelagos found in East and Southeast Asia? *Japan, Philippines, Indonesia*

How has China been physically cut off from the rest of Asia? *Gobi Desert, Tian Shan Mountains, Himalayas*

Maps

National Geographic Society
Available as uncirculated back issues with supplement map. Contact: *National Geographic* Back Issues (800) 777-2800, Fax: (813) 979-6685 Cost: between $5 and $10 (shipping included)
July 1980—China (political/peoples of China)
December 1996—Mongol Khans
July 1991—China (political map/historical, land use, population distribution)
November 1989—Asia-Pacific, political map and economics of the Pacific Rim
June 1984—Japan (political/historical)

Audiovisual

Dreams of Tibet, Frontline. 1997. PBS Video.

Web Sites

Go to **NCJourneys.com** for links to the following Web sites:

- Dreams of Tibet companion Web site
- Modern Mongolia: Reclaiming Genghis Khan

OBJECTIVES: 2.01, 3.01, 5.04, 11.01

Discussion Questions

1 What are the five countries of East Asia?

2 What is Eurasia?

3 How does the Republic of China differ from the People's Republic of China?

4 What features have set East Asia apart from the remainder of Eurasia?

Caption Answer

They isolated East Asia from the rest of Asia. East Asian people long ago developed their own societies.

Activity

Comparing China

NATIONAL GEOGRAPHY STANDARDS: 1, 4, 12

GEOGRAPHIC THEMES: Location, Place, Human-Environmental Interaction

OBJECTIVES: 1.02, 1.03

Show the transparency titled "East Asia and Southeast Asia—Political/Physical" found in the Teacher's Resource Guide.

Ask how the United States compares in size. Point out that given the same land area, China has four times the population of the United States.

Have students name each of the surrounding nations. Practice using relative location by phrasing questions such as "Which nation is located southwest of China?"

Point out the four major rivers of China. Explain that China has other rivers as well. Note that the Amur River is noted mostly because it forms the border between China and Russia. Try to be consistent in Chinese place names. Yellow and Yangzi are still commonly used in describing Chinese rivers, but you should use the terms in the textbook. Have the students tell you in which direction the rivers flow. Remind students of areas studied where there were early civilizations along rivers (Tigris-Euphrates, Nile, Ganges). Hypothesize where the early Chinese settlements might have been located.

Have students observe that the earliest settlements were along the Huang He (Yellow) and Yangzi Rivers. Do countries always have the same borders? Make an analogy to the United States mountains and deserts—Relate climate to landforms—milder near coast, Qinling mountains block cold Arctic air, warmer to the south, drier north of the Himalayan Mountains, and so forth. China has been isolated historically from the north by the desert, from the east by the sea, from the west by the Himalayan Mountains, and from the south by dense rain forests.

Conclusion Hand out student map. Ask students to begin by filling in the name of China's neighbors and the four major rivers. They should use their textbook as a resource to fill in countries with information from the chapter.

LESSON 1 Location and Landforms

KEY IDEAS

- East Asia and Southeast Asia are large and diverse regions.
- For many centuries, Chinese civilization greatly influenced the people of these regions.
- China is a huge country with varied landforms but limited farmland. Areas along two great rivers are densely populated.

KEY TERMS

archipelago
Asian Pacific Rim
typhoons

"Too little land, too many people," says a Chinese proverb. The Chinese have always worried about producing enough food. It is a concern that shows up in their language. Americans often greet friends by asking "How are you doing?" A common greeting in China is "Have you eaten?"

China is the third-largest country in the world in land area after Russia and Canada. So how can it have too little land? Why does it have a hard time feeding its people? The answers lie in part with the geography of East Asia.

Locating Regions: East Asia

East Asia is set off from the rest of the Eurasian landmass by high mountains, rugged plateaus, and wide deserts. Isolated behind these barriers, East Asian people long ago developed their own societies.

Today, East Asia includes five countries—China, Mongolia, North Korea, South Korea, and Japan (see map page 375). Japan, South Korea, and Nor Korea are among the world's smallest nations.

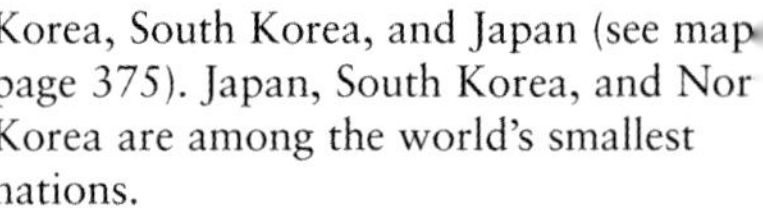

Mainland China is governed by the Communist-controlled People's Republic of China. This government rules 98 percent of China's people and almost all of its land. A rival government, the Republic of China, has built a powerful economic base on the island of Taiwan. Mainland China considers Taiwan a rebe province. However, Taiwan's governmen considers their relationship to be nation-to-nation. The tiny island of Hong Kong was under British rule until 1997, when was returned to China. Portuguese-ruled Macao was returned to China in 1999. Both areas are now special parts of Chin

Korea is a peninsula on the eastern edge of East Asia. Two rival government known as North Korea and South Korea each claim to be the legitimate governme of the peninsula.

Japan is an ***archipelago*** or chain of islands. The nation has four main island and thousands of smaller ones lying off the coast of East Asia.

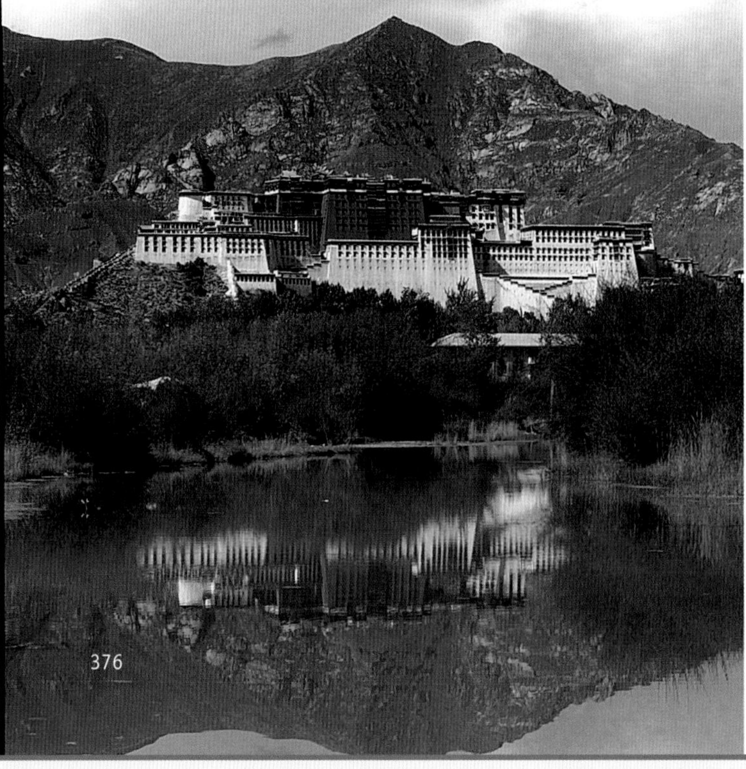

A Buddhist monastery at Lhasa, Tibet, in western China is reflected in a mountain lake. **How did high mountains affect East Asia?**

ocating Regions: outheast Asia

The giant peninsula of Southeast Asia es south of China and east of India. The gion also includes thousands of islands etween the Indian Ocean and the South hina Sea. Southeast Asia has 11 nations: lyanmar (Burma), Thailand, Laos, ambodia, Vietnam, Singapore, Indonesia, lalaysia, the Philippines, East Timor, and runei.

hared Experiences

East Asian and Southeast Asian ations differ from one another in size, conomic development, living standards, nd forms of government. Yet they share ome features.

China's influence reached nations of outheast Asia and East Asia long ago. ietnam had close links to China more an 2,000 years ago. Southeast Asia ceived many Chinese immigrants. Other vilizations influenced the region. Both uddhism and Hinduism came to the gion from India. Muslim merchants troduced Islam to Indonesia and other arts of Southeast Asia.

Korea and Japan also have long lived China's shadow. They have cultural links to China and have been greatly influenced by Chinese technology, art, writing, architecture, and belief systems.

In the 1800s and 1900s, most nations of both regions were affected by Western imperialism. Except for Thailand, all of Southeast Asia came under colonial rule. Even China was almost divided among foreign powers. Japan worried that it might fall under foreign rule. Japan did almost suffer the same fate, but its leaders strengthened Japan and turned it into a modern nation. Late in the 1800s, Japan joined Western nations in the scramble for colonies. It conquered Taiwan and Korea.

Eventually, the people of East Asia and Southeast Asia threw off foreign rule. Today, nationalism is a strong force in both regions. Most nations in these regions are experiencing rapid economic growth. South Korea, Taiwan, and Singapore have had economic booms. Japan is an economic superpower. China's economy now rivals those of the rich industrial nations.

These nations, along with Australia and New Zealand, are part of the ***Asian Pacific Rim,*** a region of nations bordering the Pacific Ocean. Experts predict it will be a growth region in this century. Many nations of the Asian Pacific Rim trade with the Americas.

Rice farmers tend their terraced paddies on the island of Bali in the nation of Indonesia. **How does the location of Indonesia allow for growing rice?**

Discussion Questions

1 Why is the name Burma in parentheses?

2 What characteristics do East Asia and Southeast Asia have in common?

3 Which Southeast Asian country did not fall under colonial rule?

4 Which religions are found in this part of Asia?

5 In what regions has China spread its influence?

6 What is nationalism?

7 What is the Pacific Rim?

8 What are some natural borders we have in our county? state? nation?

Caption Answer

As the southernmost of the Southeast Asian nations, Indonesia's climate is tropical. It is also directly in line with the monsoons, so it receives plentiful rainfall.

ELL Teaching Tips

BICS and CALP

BICS (Basic Interpersonal Communication Skills) may take up to two years to develop, whereas CALP (Cognitive Academic Language Proficiency) may take five to ten years. Avoid the common mistake of assuming that a student who speaks English is able to work academically in English.

It's a Fact

Mongolia

- Mongolia is the least densely populated country on earth. Population density is four people per square mile. Livestock outnumber people 12 to one.
- Only 1 percent of Mongolia is arable. Mongolia has a fairly high elevation: from a low of 1,800 feet to 14,000 feet in the Altai Mountains.
- Gobi (Desert) is Mongolian for gravel and rock debris.
- Mongolia was named after thirteenth-century people who created the largest land empire in history: from East Asia to Western Europe.

Caption Answer

In the highlands of Southern China

Art Activity

East and Southeast Asia Diorama

OBJECTIVES: 1.01

Materials two same-size boxes (cereal, shirt-size or small gift); four sheets of 12-inch by 24-inch construction paper (light colors or white preferably); 6-inch by 12-inch strip of construction paper (light colors or white); handout of diorama page pattern from the Teacher's Resource Guide; construction paper scraps in variety of colors; scissors; transparent tape; glue/glue stick; colored pencils, markers, crayons; various other art/found art materials

Have students design diorama boxes illustrating East Asia and Southeast Asia. Tops and bottoms of both boxes must be cut off. Cut down the vertical center of one side of each box if necessary to open both boxes so they lie flat. Both sides of each box must be covered with construction paper. Reform/refold boxes and stand them side by side. Tape the boxes together at the spine. Cover the spine with the paper strips, trimming strips to fit as necessary. Glue the strip in place completely covering the taped area. Using construction-paper scraps and various other art materials (yarn, tissue paper, foil, clear plastic wrap, acetate film—clear and colors, glue with glitter, colored sands, twigs, leaves, chalk, stickers, and so on) students are to create 3-D scenes on these two regions with each scene covering two facing panels in the diorama. Brief descriptions of each scene must be included on the panels. The cover must be illustrated and can include brief summary of diorama's contents.

Extension ELL students can make the diorama but will need to include descriptions that are very simple.

Highlands and Plains

Much of East Asia and Southeast Asia is mountainous. Use the map on page 375 to find the major mountain ranges that reach into western China and Mongolia. Notice that the Himalayas and other high mountains form the western and southern borders of China. Mountains also divide China from Southeast Asia.

Still other mountain ranges form some of Southeast Asia's borders. Mountains in western Myanmar (Burma) separate that country from India. Another range extending southward from China divides Vietnam from Southeast Asian nations lying to the west.

Because of its highlands, China tilts steeply from the western interior toward the ocean. This pattern of interior highlands tilting toward coastlines is repeated throughout the two regions. Southeast Asia's highlands border China. Rivers run from these highlands toward the sea along the continent's southern edge. High, steep mountains also fill most of the islands—the Indonesian and Japanese archipelagoes—off the coast.

The mountain areas of East Asia and Southeast Asia are thinly populated. Only a small percentage of China's more than 1.32 billion people inhabit the country's western mountains. Most Chinese are crowded into river valleys and on the fertile plains in the eastern third of the country. Southeast Asian populations also are found in river valleys and coastal plains. As on the mainlands, East Asian and Southeast Asian island populations are settled mostly on small coastal plains.

Natural forces often threaten both the islands and coasts of East Asia and Southeast Asia. Powerful typhoons destroy property and take lives along the coasts. ***Typhoons*** are wind and rain storms that strike with the force of hurricanes. The two regions are equally at risk from explosive volcanic eruptions and severe earthquakes. The regions are part of a "Ring of Fire" that runs along the eastern and western shores of the Pacific Ocean.

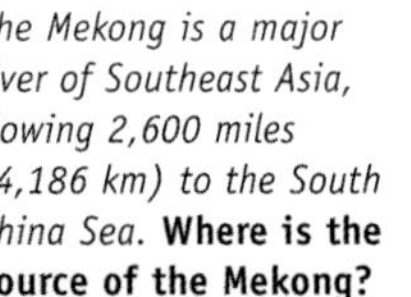

The Mekong is a major river of Southeast Asia, flowing 2,600 miles (4,186 km) to the South China Sea. **Where is the source of the Mekong?**

378 Chapter

Background Information

China High and Low

The Himalayas form a natural border between southwestern China and the Indian subcontinent to the south. With more than 110 peaks rising to 24,000 feet (7,200 m) or more above sea level, they are the highest mountain ranges in the world. One of these peaks, Mount Everest, is the world's highest at 29,035 feet (8,711 m) above sea level. The mountain chain's name comes from the Sanskrit *hima,* for "snow" and *alaya,* "abode." China's lowest point is the Turfan Depression which is 505 (152 m) feet below sea level. It experiences great extremes in temperature, holding China's record for highest temperature, 118° F (48° C) in summer. In winter nearby Fu-yan has China's lowest recorded temperature –62° F (–52° C).

Largest and Most Deadly Earthquakes, 2000–2006

Year	Magnitude	Deaths	Location
2006	8.3	0	Kuril Islands, Russia
	6.3	5,749	Java, Indonesia
2005	8.7	1,313	Northern Sumatra, Indonesia
	7.6	80,361	Pakistan
2004	9.1	283,106	Off west coast of Northern Sumatra
2003	8.3	0	Hokkaido, Japan region
	6.6	31,000	Southeastern Iran
2002	7.9	0	Central Alaska
	6.1	1,000	Hindua Kush region, Afghanistan
2001	8.5	138	Near coast of Peru
	7.7	20,023	India
2000	8.0	2	New Ireland region, Papua New Guinea
	7.9	102	Southern Sumatera, Indonesia

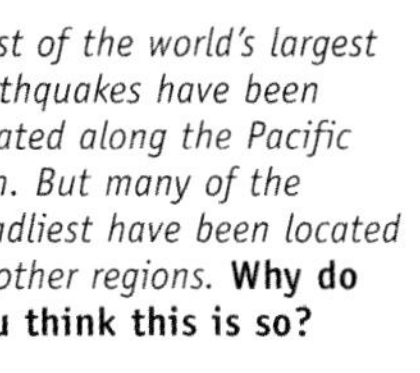

ɔst of the world's largest rthquakes have been cated along the Pacific m. But many of the adliest have been located other regions. **Why do u think this is so?**

The earthquake that struck Kobe, Japan, in 1995 twisted railroad tracks and killed 5,502 people. ***Why are the regions of East Asia and Southeast Asia vulnerable to earthquakes and volcanoes?***

LESSON 1 REVIEW

Fact Follow-Up

1. What are the nations of East Asia?
2. What are the nations of Southeast Asia?
3. What physical characteristics of place are shared by East Asia and Southeast Asia?
4. On what type of landform do most of the people of East Asia and Southeast Asia live?

Talk About It

1. What country dominates both East Asia and Southeast Asia? Why?
2. What natural forces act upon the land and people of East Asia and Southeast Asia? How do you think they affect the lives of the people?

Discussion Questions

1 Describe China's population distribution.

2 What are typhoons?

Caption Answer

Students should develop a hypothesis. Perhaps people in the "Ring of Fire" region are more prepared for earthquakes.

Caption Answer

The regions are part of a "Ring of Fire" that runs along the eastern and western shores of the Pacific Ocean.

Map Activity

Digging to China

NATIONAL GEOGRAPHY STANDARDS: 1, 3

GEOGRAPHIC THEMES: Location

OBJECTIVES: 1.02, 2.01, 2.02

Show a transparency of China on the overhead. Ask students to use the maps in their textbooks to find out if this is true: "If you dug a hole from North Carolina through the center of the earth you would surface in China on the other side of the world." In actuality you'd be in the Indian Ocean between the tip of Africa and Australia (36°N, 79°W) = (36°S, 101°E). Use a globe to locate China's location. Have students decide in which hemisphere China is located. Note that both China and the United States are at roughly the same latitude.

LESSON 1 REVIEW

Fact Follow-Up Answers

1. The nations of East Asia are Japan, Mongolia, North Korea, the People's Republic of China, the Republic of China (Taiwan), and South Korea.
2. The nations of Southeast Asia are Brunei, Cambodia, Indonesia, Laos, Malaysia, Myanmar (Burma), the Philippines, Singapore, Thailand, and Vietnam.
3. Much of East Asia and Southeast Asia is mountainous. Both regions also have a pattern of interior highlands tilting toward coastlines.
4. Most people live in the river valleys and on the coastal plains.

Talk About It Answers

1. China. China's cultural influence reached nations of Southeast Asia and East Asia long ago. It continues to be the largest and most populous nation in the regions.
2. Typhoons, volcanoes, and earthquakes occur in East Asia and Southeast Asia. Important points: Students should describe the ways they think people's lives are affected. People understand that disasters will occur, but it is difficult to prepare for them. When they do happen, people experience great upheaval.

OBJECTIVES: 2.01, 2.03, 3.01, 5.01

Discussion Questions

1 What is the difference between a typhoon and a cyclone?

2 What allows the monsoons to occur?

3 What is climate?

Caption Answer

Monsoons can bring flooding.

Map Activity

Map—Political and Physical Features

NATIONAL GEOGRAPHY STANDARDS: 1, 4, 5

GEOGRAPHIC THEMES: Region, Place

OBJECTIVES: 1.01, 1.02

Using a blank outline map of East Asia in the Teacher's Resource Guide, have students label the following political and physical features:

Countries

Japan	Mongolia
People's Republic of China	Republic of China (Taiwan)
South Korea	North Korea

Cities

Hong Kong	Beijing
Seoul	Tokyo
Tianjin	Shanghai
Whan	Taipei
Shenyang	Ulan Bator
Osaka	Yokohama
Pyongyang	Guangzhou (Canton)

Physical features

Gobi Desert	Khangai Mountains
Takla	Makan Desert
Tibetan Plateau	Himalayas
Tian Shan	North China Plain
Sichuan Basin	Greater Hinggan Range

Rivers

Huang (Yellow)	Chang
Yangzi	Mekong

Bodies of Water

East China Sea	Pacific Ocean
Gulf of Tonkin	Yellow Sea
Sea of Japan	South China Sea

Ask students:

1. How has China been physically cut off from the rest of Asia? *Gobi Desert; Tian Shan Mountains; Himalayas*
2. Where are the major cities located? Why? *east; access to water and better climate*

LESSON 2 Climates and Resources

KEY IDEAS

- Monsoons affect the climates of East Asia and Southeast Asia.
- Climates vary across these regions, depending on nearness to the sea and elevation. The climates of North China and South China differ.
- East Asia and Southeast Asia have many resources, but they are not evenly distributed.

KEY TERMS

arid China
humid China

The hurricane season in North America is in late summer and early fall. If you live in coastal North Carolina, for example, yo watch weather reports that track these violent storms. In East Asia and Southeast Asia, the summer can bring terrible typhoons. In fact, the word typhoon comes from the Chinese words *tai fong*, meanin "great wind." These same hurricane-like storms in South Asia are callec cyclones (see page 359).

Like hurricanes, typhoons can cause much damage to coastal areas. They affect Asian lands from Japan and China to the Philippines, Vietnam, and Indonesia.

Despite typhoons, many people live in coastal areas. Fertile soil for farming and offshore fishing are just two reasons why people risk nature's fury (see the climate map of Asia in the appendix).

The Monsoon in Asia

You have read how seasonal winds, called monsoons, influence climate in South Asia. The monsoon plays a large role elsewhere in Asia. Shifts in the winds, which blow either from land to sea or from sea to land, create monsoons.

In summer, the air over the interior of Asia heats up and rises. As it does, moist air flows in from the ocean. It drops moisture as rain on coastal areas. Most rain in East Asia falls during the warm summer months. Rain and warm temperatures are good for farming. In parts of East Asia and Southeast Asia, farmers grow two crops of rice a year.

Rescuers search for residents in Tienliao, Taiwan, after Typhoon Bilis crossed the island in August 2000. **What other extremes of climate threaten the people of East Asia and Southeast Asia?**

Varied Climates

Climates vary dramatically across Eas Asia and Southeast Asia. China has the most variety because it covers such a hug area. It stretches from the hot, tropical south to the colder, humid continental north.

Beijing, China's capital, is at the same latitude as Philadelphia, Pennsylvania. It has similar warm summer temperatures, but its winters are colder. Shanghai, China's busy seaport, is at the same latitude as Savannah, Georgia. Guangzho (Canton) in the far south is on the same parallel as Havana, Cuba, and has a subtropical climate.

Western China is dry. In the mountains, temperatures are colder at higher elevations (see map on page 381).

Japan's islands stretch across a great distance. If placed on a map of the easter United States, they would reach from southern Maine to northern Florida.

'okyo, Japan's capital, lies at about the ame latitude as Raleigh, North Carolina. t has a humid subtropical climate of mild vinters and warm summers. Japan eceives more snow and rain than North 'arolina does because of its high levations.

Most of Southeast Asia lies in the Tropics. Local climates vary, however. The islands of the region, Malaysia, and southern Vietnam have a tropical wet climate. The rest of the mainland has wet and dry seasons. Elevation and nearness to the sea also affect climates.

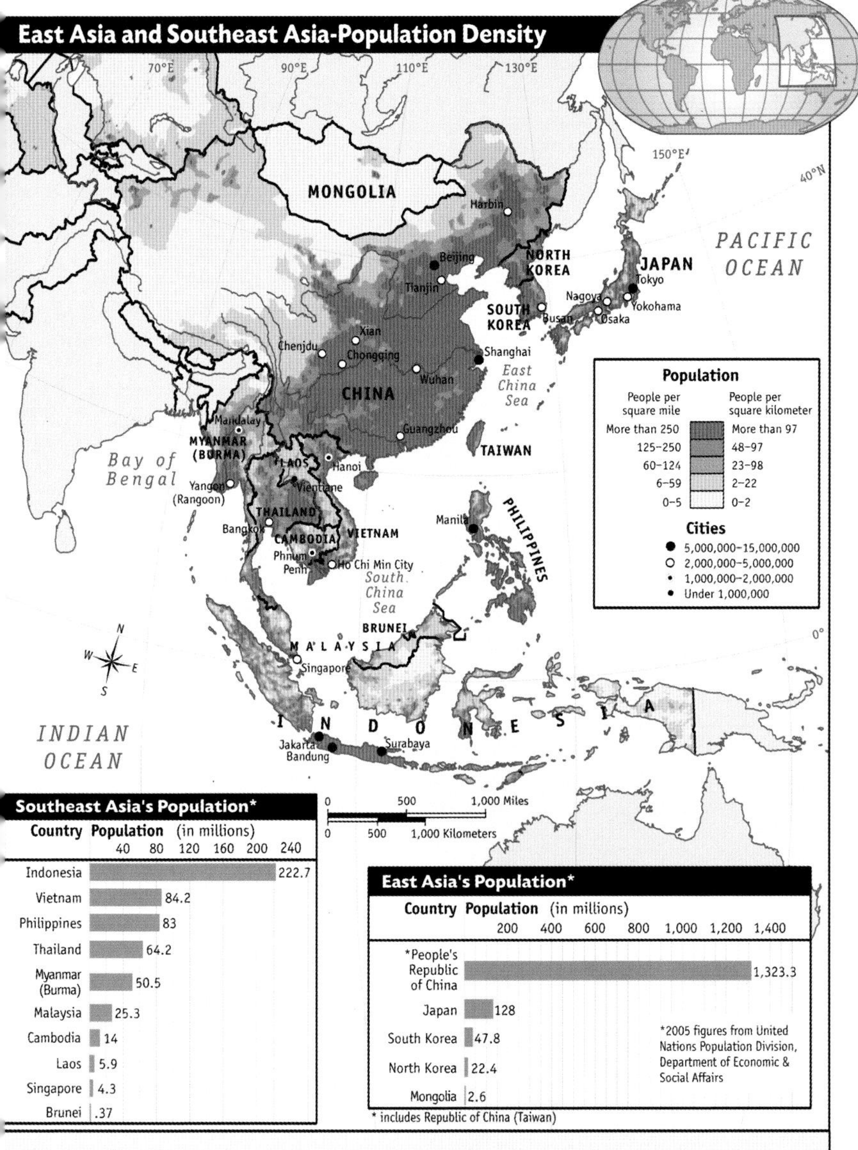

Location China is the world's most populated nation. Compare this map to the one on page 369. *Which landforms support most of China's population? What other countries in East Asia and Southeast Asia have a high population density?*

Most Chinese live in the river valleys and on the plains. Other densely populated nations include Japan, South Korea, North Korea, the Philippines, Vietnam, and Indonesia.

Demographic Chart

OBJECTIVES: 1.01

Have students use a recent almanac or the Internet to complete a chart like the one below. Students should compare and contrast these nations based on the information they find.

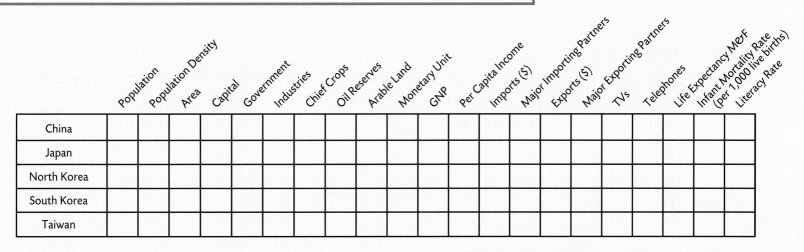

	Population	Population Density	Area	Capital	Government	Industries	Chief Crops	Oil Reserves	Arable Land	Monetary Unit	GNP	Per Capita Income	Imports ($)	Major Importing Partners	Exports ($)	Major Exporting Partners	TVs	Telephones	Life Expectancy M&F	Infant Mortality Rate (per 1,000 live births)	Literacy Rate
China																					
Japan																					
North Korea																					
South Korea																					
Taiwan																					

Discussion Questions

1 What does "arid" mean? Which context clues helped you?

2 Why does arid China have fewer people?

3 What is the other name for humid China?

4 Why would caves make comfortable homes in arid China?

5 Why would crops requiring irrigation not be grown in North China?

6 Why is South China called China's "rice bowl"?

Caption Answer

Arid China is a high, barren plateau. Some people farm at lower elevations or in oases, and nomads graze sheep, goats, and yaks on the grasslands.

Map Activity

Climate

 **OBJECTIVES:** 2.01

Review with students the factors that affect climate: latitude, elevation, nearness to large body of water, ocean currents, winds. Provide students with maps that show those features. Divide class into three groups: China, Mongolia, and Korea; Southeast Asia; and Japan.

Using maps, students will analyze factors that affect climate for their assigned country/region. They will make a list and present it to the class in the form of a TV weather report. Here's a sample:

Arid China

Imagine a diagonal line that runs across China. It connects northeastern Manchuria to eastern Tibet (see maps, pages 375 and 381). It would divide China into two climate regions—arid and humid. ***Arid China*** lies north and west of the line and is very dry. Less than 20 inches (51 cm) of rain falls each year. ***Humid China,*** to the south and east of the line, has at least 20 inches of rain a year.

Arid China includes Tibet, Xinjiang, and Inner Mongolia. Much of it is high, barren plateau, that lies almost 3 miles (4.8 km) above sea level. Arid China has limited farmland. Some people farm at lower elevations, raising barley or potatoes. Nomads graze sheep, goats, and yaks on grasslands. Elsewhere in arid China, farmers grow crops in desert oases. Arid China is thinly populated.

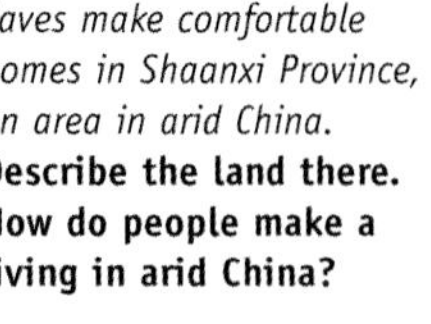

Caves make comfortable homes in Shaanxi Province, an area in arid China. **Describe the land there. How do people make a living in arid China?**

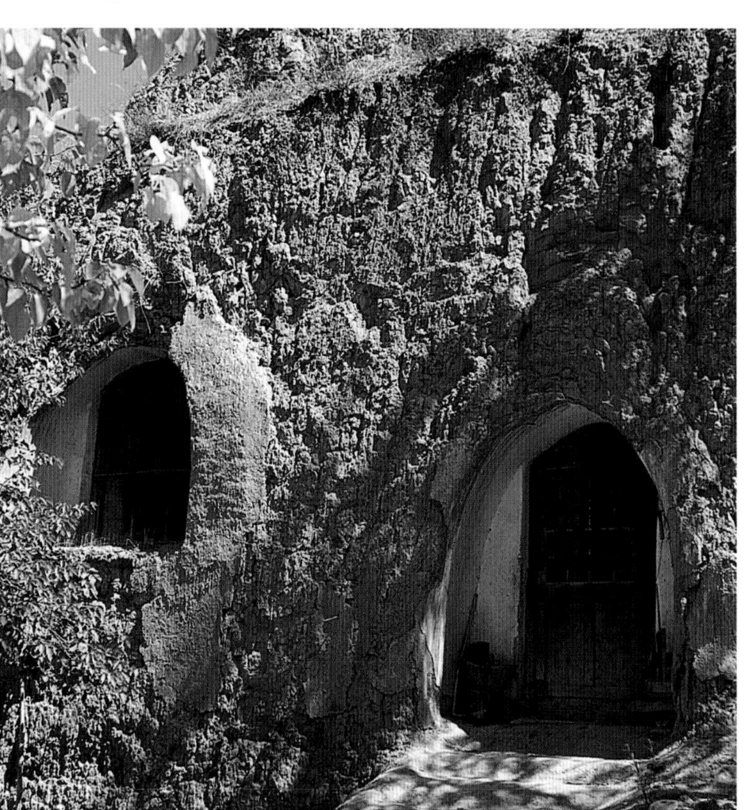

Humid China

Humid China is also called monsoon China because its moisture comes from th summer monsoons. It is densely settled. Humid China itself has two distinct regions—North China and South China. Their climates and cultures differ.

North China North China has a humid continental climate of warm summers and cold winters. Parts of the northern areas are dry, with unreliable rainfall. Farming is difficult, but North China has level, fertile land. Farmers grow such crops as millet, wheat, and sorghum. Rice and other crops requiring irrigation are not grown.

South China South China has a humid subtropical climate of hot, humid summers and cool, damp winters. South China is greener and more hilly than North China. Water buffaloes—rather than mules or donkeys—work in the hot, muddy rice fields of South China. The region is often called China's rice bowl.

Rain can come at any time, but monsoons arrive in spring and early summer. South China receives plenty of rain. It floods often. Farmers there have healthy harvests, including corn, even wit less fertile soil than North China. Almost 40 percent of the Chinese live along the Yangzi River in South China.

Customs

Feng Shui (fung schway), meaning wind and water, is the Chinese art of improving one' surroundings to enhance well-being. Some believe the proper placement of buildings and objects brings harmony with the natural world. Feng Shui's Five Elements–wood, fire, earth, metal, and water–express the rhythm of the universe. The elements should balance each other in a room's design.

Feng Shui is popular in America. People hire Feng Shui experts to arrange rooms so tha the best of luck is ensured.

Japan

Latitude—Japan stretches from latitudes as far north as southern Maine to as far south as Florida. Therefore, the climate will be from cool to warm as you travel south.

Elevation—Japan is mountainous. Therefore you will find cooler temperatures in the mountains.

Nearness to large bodies of water— Japan is made up of four main islands, and therefore coastal areas would be more temperate than other locations at the same latitude.

Ocean currents—Japan's coasts are subjected to cold and warm ocean currents. Therefore, the west coast of Honshu should be cooler than the east coast.

Winds—The mountains of Japan block prevailing winds, causing more moderate climate on the leeward side. Also typhoons off the Pacific Ocean affect the east coast of Japan.

Conclusion Students will present their findings to the class. You and/or class will modify, expand, or correct the conclusions.

A Malaysian plantation worker slashes the bark of a rubber tree to tap rubber. **What climate does Malaysia have that supports the growth of thick vegetation?**

Rich Resources

East Asia and Southeast Asia have ıineral and energy resources, but they are ınevenly distributed. China is rich in ıinerals. Korea has some natural esources. Japan has few (see maps on ›ages 415, 435, 477 and 497).

China has abundant coal and iron ore. ıost coal fields are in the north or in the ıortheast. The northeast also has iron. Vith coal and iron ore, China has the esources to become a major steel ›roducer. South China has many minerals, ncluding lead, mercury, tungsten, gold, ıranium, copper, and silver. China is lrawing on these resources to become a ıajor industrial power.

China is thought to have huge oil eserves. Other East Asian nations, ıowever, have little oil. Japan needs oil for ndustry, so it must import oil from outhwest Asia. The Southeast Asian ations of Malaysia, Indonesia, and 3runei produce oil.

Most nations use water as an energy resource. China has built hydroelectric plants along its great rivers and smaller waterways. The plants provide power for factories and villages. Japan, too, has used its rivers to develop hydroelectric power.

Southeast Asia is a source of tin and rubber, especially in Malaysia and the Philippines. Malaysia produces half of Asia's tin exports. Rubber comes from trees grown on large plantations throughout Southeast Asia.

What would YOU do?

Large, beautiful and shy, only about 1,600 giant pandas survive. They eat wild bamboo, a food source that is disappearing as forests are cut and people move onto the land. Disease also has killed bamboo forests. Without a change in environmental practices, the panda will become extinct. Yet farming and manufacturing require land. What would you recommend to help pandas?

Discussion Questions

1 How are natural resources distributed throughout East Asia and Southeast Asia?

2 Which of these countries would you expect to have the highest standard of living?

Tropical wet

Character Education

OBJECTIVES: 1.02, 3.02

To build on the "What Would You Do?" feature in the Pupil's Edition, brainstorm and discuss as a class what can be done to protect the 1,600 giant pandas that survive. Contact environmental protection agencies to see what can be done. The class can also contact the North Carolina Zoo (see Cultural Resources in the Teacher's Edition) to see what connections they have for protecting giant pandas. As a class raise money to send to a protection agency for giant pandas. If this is not a possibility, students can design posters or pamphlets to educate the school community about the endangered pandas. To differentiate, the strong writers in the class can write a letter to their school or local newspaper to educate the public about ways the giant pandas can be protected.

Extension ELL students could do poster or collage to help educate the school about endangered species.

Climate Map

Have students refer to the Asia climate map in the Atlas of the textbook's Appendix.

Activity

Silk and Silk Road

OBJECTIVES: 3.01, 4.02, 5.01

Have your students learn more about the importance of silk to China with the resources below.

The Empress and the Silkworm by Lily Toy Hong. (Albert Whitman & Co., 1995. ISBN 0807520098.)

Visit **NCJourneys.com** for a link to a Silk Road mapping activity.

Students should take notes using a graphic organizer. Discuss the importance of silk as a class.

Extension Have ELL students use the **Worldlingo** URL translator to view the Web sites. Assign peer tutors to assist as needed.

Teacher Notes

Myanmar vs. Burma

In 1989 the military junta government in Burma claimed a new name, Myanmar, for their nation. This decision was not approved by any sitting legislature in Burma, and therefore the United States government did not adopt the name. Myanmar is the common short form of Pyidaungzu Myanma Naingngandaw, translated by the United States government as Union of Myanma and by the Burmese as Union of Myanma.

As a result, some organizations have switched to Myanmar, while others still use Burma, and yet others use both.

CONNECTIONS • GEOGRAPHY & SCIENCE •

Silk

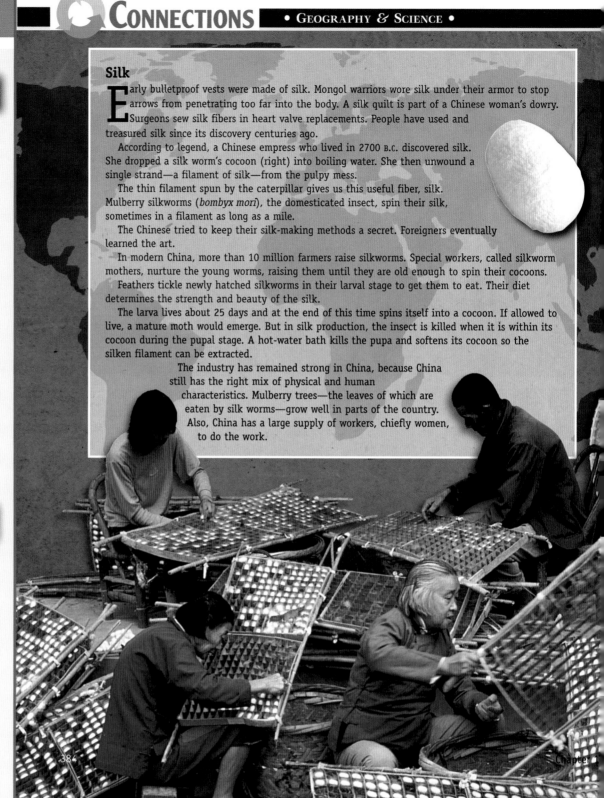

Early bulletproof vests were made of silk. Mongol warriors wore silk under their armor to stop arrows from penetrating too far into the body. A silk quilt is part of a Chinese woman's dowry. Surgeons sew silk fibers in heart valve replacements. People have used and treasured silk since its discovery centuries ago.

According to legend, a Chinese empress who lived in 2700 B.C. discovered silk. She dropped a silk worm's cocoon (right) into boiling water. She then unwound a single strand—a filament of silk—from the pulpy mess.

The thin filament spun by the caterpillar gives us this useful fiber, silk. Mulberry silkworms (*bombyx mori*), the domesticated insect, spin their silk, sometimes in a filament as long as a mile.

The Chinese tried to keep their silk-making methods a secret. Foreigners eventually learned the art.

In modern China, more than 10 million farmers raise silkworms. Special workers, called silkworm mothers, nurture the young worms, raising them until they are old enough to spin their cocoons.

Feathers tickle newly hatched silkworms in their larval stage to get them to eat. Their diet determines the strength and beauty of the silk.

The larva lives about 25 days and at the end of this time spins itself into a cocoon. If allowed to live, a mature moth would emerge. But in silk production, the insect is killed when it is within its cocoon during the pupal stage. A hot-water bath kills the pupa and softens its cocoon so the silken filament can be extracted.

The industry has remained strong in China, because China still has the right mix of physical and human characteristics. Mulberry trees—the leaves of which are eaten by silk worms—grow well in parts of the country. Also, China has a large supply of workers, chiefly women, to do the work.

Background Information

Myanmar Teak

Forests in Myanmar, formerly Burma, contain much of the world's teak. Commercial logging of teak is a key industry and export for Myanmar. This wood is highly prized in warm climates for its great durability. In India and Myanmar, teak beams have been found in good condition in buildings many centuries old. Palaces and temples with teak beams have lasted more than 1,000 years. Teak is also largely termite resistant. Craftspeople and factories use teak to make ships, fine furniture, door and window frames, bridges, flooring, paneling, railway cars, and Venetian blinds. In Myanmar and parts of Southeast Asia, illegal logging of teak is a growing concern.

Teak logs cut down in Myanmar will be shipped to Thailand. **What other forest resources exist in Southeast Asia?**

Forest Resources

Forests once covered much of East
sia. Today, large parts of China have few
ees. Bare hills stand where trees once
rew long ago. Deforestation hurts the
nd. Without roots to hold the soil in
lace, rains run off quickly and erode, or
ash away, the soil. The Chinese
overnment has set up programs to
eplant forests. Real change will take
any years of work.

Japan uses its forests to produce
mber. The government controls timber cutting and requires replanting of trees.

Parts of Southeast Asia still have huge forests. Some forests remain almost untouched because they are hard to reach. Rubber, palm oil, teak, and bamboo forests are harvested. Teak from Myanmar, Thailand, and Malaysia is highly valued.

Myanmar, China, Japan, Cambodia, and other Asian lands have bamboo forests. Hollow-stemmed bamboo is used for building or furniture products. Some tender shoots are used for food.

LESSON 2 REVIEW

Fact Follow-Up

1. How does the monsoon affect climate in East Asia and Southeast Asia?
2. Besides the climate itself, what are some differences between arid China and humid China?
3. In each region, which country has the most valuable natural resources?
4. What are the resources of Southeast Asia?

Talk About It

1. Why do Japan and China have such a variety of climates?
2. Why is South China one of the most populous areas of China?
3. What would occur if Japan's forests were not managed?
4. Compare the Population Density map on page 381 to the map on page 375. What physical features explain the population patterns of the region?

Discussion Questions

1. What is deforestation?
2. How important are timber resources?
3. What have we learned about managing our timberlands in North Carolina?

Rubber, palm oil, and bamboo

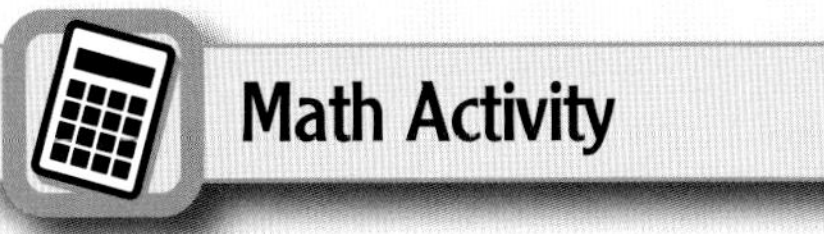

Bar Graph

OBJECTIVES: 1.01, 1.03, 7.01

Have students make a bar graph of East Asian and Southeast Asian nations. Label the vertical axis per capita GDP/GNP and list the countries on the horizontal axis. Ask: Why do you think the per capita GDP/GNP is so low for Vietnam, Laos, and Cambodia? (*war*) for Myanmar? (*civil unrest due to military dictatorship*) so high for Brunei? (*oil*), for Singapore, Malaysia, and Indonesia? (*exporting raw materials and developing industry*).

Extension ELL students will need a peer tutor to help them find information in the text to make the graph.

LESSON 2 REVIEW

Fact Follow-Up Answers

1. The monsoon brings abundant rain during the summer months. Farmers in parts of East Asia and Southeast Asia affected by the monsoon are able to grow two crops of rice a year.
2. Arid China is at a high elevation and sparsely populated. Humid China is lower in elevation and densely settled.
3. China is rich in coal and iron, lead, mercury, tungsten, gold, uranium, copper, and silver, and is thought to have huge oil reserves. Malaysia, Indonesia, and Brunei in Southeast Asia produce oil. Malaysia and the Philippines export rubber and tin. Many nations export forest products.
4. They are oil, tin, rubber, and forest products.

Talk About It Answers

1. Both countries stretch over a wide area of latitude. Landforms and wind patterns also affect climates.
2. South China has fertile land, sufficient rain, and little flooding.
3. Deforestation would cause soil erosion.
4. Plains and river valleys are densely populated.

OBJECTIVES: 2.02, 1.02, 11.01, 12.03

Discussion Questions

1 If you were new to a culture, would you keep your own ways or try to blend in?

2 Who are the Han?

The huge population puts great pressure on the land and on the country's resources.

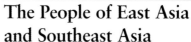

Asian Festival

OBJECTIVES: 1.01, 4.03

Divide students into cooperative groups and assign each group a specific country to research. Give each group a list of specific things to find out about their country. After researching, groups can create a booth with pictures, maps, physical objects that celebrate that country. Encourage students to dress in traditional costumes, locate music, and prepare foods to make the festival a real celebration. This activity is a great way to integrate the arts with the social studies curriculum.

Extension Asian ELL students could be a great resource for this activity. They most likely have authentic Asian cultural items/decorations at home they could bring in to share with the class. A family member may be interested in being a guest speaker as well. Use them as a resource to share whatever they are able to. ELL students of other backgrounds should use an ELL-friendly Web site for research so they can effectively participate in their groups.

LESSON 3 People and Their Environment

KEY IDEAS

- East Asia and Southeast Asia have many ethnic and language groups.
- The Chinese are mostly Han, but many national minorities also live in China.
- China has used harsh methods to control population growth.

KEY TERMS

characters
Han
homogeneous society
Mandarin

A group of foreigners stands in front of a huge poster in Beijing. Their guide translates its message. "Longer, Later, Fewer," she explains. "The government uses that slogan to limit population growth," she tells them. "It wants people to wait longer before getting married. They should have children later rather than earlier and have fewer children."

Visitors see other billboards that show smiling parents with one child. The ad campaign directs attention to a serious problem. China's population is enormous. About 1.3 billion people live there. Put another way, one in five people in the world is Chinese. Such a huge population puts great pressure on the land and on the country's resources.

The People of East Asia and Southeast Asia

Many ethnic groups live in East Asia and Southeast Asia. Each nation usually has one major ethnic group and many smaller ones. Most such small groups live in isolated or remote regions. Indonesia and the Philippines have many local groups divided by languages. Today, however, many of these ethnic groups are adopting the language and culture of the majority group within their nation.

China has the greatest ethnic diversity. It has more than 50 national minorities. Each has its own language, dress, food, customs, and beliefs. They include Zhuangs, Miaos, Huis, Yis, Manchus, Uighurs, Tibetans, Mongolians, and Koreans.

Despite China's diversity, more than 90 percent of the Chinese belong to a single group. They are ***Han*** Chinese. In ancient times, the Han expanded from the Huang He River valley into South China.

China's population includes millions of children, despite efforts to limit population growth. **Why does China want to limit that growth?**

Sell Your Country

OBJECTIVES: 1.02, 2.01, 11.02

Assign each cooperative group a country in East Asia or Southeast Asia. This may be in groups of two or three. Their task is to sell the country to someone by accentuating the positive. Make the country as attractive and appealing as possible. Present this in the form of a tri-fold travel brochure, PowerPoint Presentation, or Web page. Grade on creativity, accuracy, and appeal.

oday, Han settlers are moving north and est into regions occupied by national inorities. In some areas, they are ecoming the majority. Unlike China, orea is a ***homogeneous society.*** That is, s people belong to the same ethnic oup, speak the same language, and share e same culture. Japan, too, is a omogeneous society. The Japanese have eir own language and culture. It differs om Korean and Chinese.

anguages and Dialects

East Asia and Southeast Asia have any language families. East Asia alone as three major languages—Chinese, orean, and Japanese. Each of these three nguages differs from the others. Despite e difference between Chinese and panese, Japan uses the Chinese writing stem. Korea has developed written mbols of its own.

In ancient times, China developed a stem of writing. It used ***characters,*** nguage symbols representing objects, eas, or actions. Early writing used ctographs, or pictures of objects, like the n. In time, the characters for sun and oon were used together and came to ean "bright" or "light." The Chinese riting system became complex. Today, ere are about 50,000 characters. Each of ese can be used alone or in combination ith others. Learning to read this nguage well takes many years of hard udy. The Chinese writing system has ayed an important role in uniting the untry.

The Chinese speak dozens of regional alects. Dialects differ from one another. you lived in Beijing in the north, you ight not understand a person from uangzhou (Canton) in the south. Today, ***Iandarin,*** which is a northern Chinese alect, is China's official language. lucated Chinese from throughout China ve learned Mandarin.

Although China has many spoken alects, it has only one written language. ch written character has the same eaning to Chinese everywhere. So, in dition to speaking Mandarin, people can communicate by using their common written language.

To understand this, imagine the numbers 1 or 7. Each number is a symbol. When the number is written, it means the same thing to an American, French, or German student, even though each has a different word for it. In the same way, Chinese from different regions understand each character even though their dialects differ.

Schoolchildren practice calligraphy—writing characters—in a Shanghai, China, classroom. **Why do children begin studying writing at a young age in China?**

Some Chinese characters show how characters came out of pictographs. **How does the character for forest look like trees? Can you see the wing in the swan?**

Word Origins

The Mandarin word for "common speech" or "national language" is *putonghua*. The word **Mandarin** is a Western term first used by the Portuguese. It described the language of government officials and well-educated Chinese. It came to refer to upper-class Chinese. Mandarin became the official language because it was spoken in and around Beijing, China's capital.

Caption Answer

Learning Chinese well takes many years of hard study.

Caption Answer

Answers will vary. Trees are suggested by the vertical line and two downward strokes. The feathers of the wing could be the small strokes at the base of the character.

Discussion Questions

1 What would be the benefits of living in a homogeneous culture?

2 What would be some disadvantages?

Activity

What's in a Name?

OBJECTIVES: 4.01, 12.03

Using only the translated terms below and a physical/political map of China, have students find the meanings of the names of as many provinces, cities, and natural features as possible.

Examples:
Beijing = Northern Capital
Hainan Island = Sea _________ Island
Huanghe = Yellow _________
Nanjing = _________ Capital
Shanghai = _________

Provinces to try: Guangdong; Jiangsi; Shandong, Shanzi, Hebei, Henan, Yunnan, Sichuan.

Note: In some cases the above translations are approximations and are, as such, acceptable for the purposes of this exercise.

Pinyin (Wade-Giles)	English
zhong (chung)	middle
bei (pei)	north
hai (hai)	sea
ping (p'ing)	peace
he (ho)	river/stream
ning (ning)	peace
jiang (chiang)	river/stream
an (an)	peace
chuan (ch'uan)	river/stream
po (p'o)	slope
hu (hu)	lake
sha (sha)	sand
huang (hwang)	yellow
skhan (shan)	mountain
jing (king/ching)	capital

Pinyin (Wade-Giles)	English
shang (sheng)	above.upon
guang (kuang)	wide/broad
shen (shen)	pass
gui (kwei)	honored
xi (hsi)	west
liao (liao)	distant
si (sze/szu)	four
lin (lin)	woods
tian (tien)	heaven
ling (ling)	range
jin (tsin/chin)	ferry/ford
nan (nan)	south
dong (tung)	east
yun (yun)	clouds

Teacher Notes

Chinese Place Names in Pinyin Romanization

The following lists show the names of the provinces, autonomous regions, provincial capitals, and other major cities as they will appear in Pinyin phonetic spelling. Also included are the official abbreviations used in the People's Republic of China, based on the Pinyin spelling. Conventional or Wade-Giles spellings used heretofore appear in parenthesis.

Provinces, Autonomous Regions, Centrally-Administered Cities, and Provincial Capitals

Pinyin	Abbr.	Traditional
Anhui Prov.	AH	(Anhwei)
Beijing City	BJ	(Peking)
Fujian Prov.	FJ	(Fukien)
Gansu Prov.	GS	(Kansu)
Guangdong Prov.	GD	(Kwangtung)
Guizhou Prov.	GZ	(Kweichow)
Hebei Prov.	HEB	(Hopeh)
Heilongjiang Pv.	HB	(Heilungkiang)
Henan Prov.	HEN	(Honan)
Hubei Prov.	HB	(Hupeh)
Junan Prov.	HN	(Hunan)
Jiangsu Prov.	JS	(Kiangsu)
Jiangxi Prov.	JX	(Kiangsi)
Jilin Prov.	JL	(Kirin)
Lianoning Prov.	LN	(Liaoning)
Nei Monggol AR	NM	(Inner Mongolia)
Ningxia (Hui) AR	NX	(Ningsia)
Shanxi Prov.	SN	(Shensi)
Shandong Prov.	SD	(Shantung)
Shanghai Prov.	SD	(Shanghai)
Shanxi Prov.	SX	(Shansi)
Sichuan Prov.	SC	(Szechwan)
Tianjin City	TJ	(Tientsin)

Pinyin	Abbr.	Traditional
Xizang	XZ	(Tibet)
Yunnan Prov.	YN	(Yunnan)
Zhejiang Prov.	ZJ	(Chekiang)

Pinyin	Traditional
Hefei	(Ho-fei)
Fuzhou	(Foochow)
Lanzhou	(Lanchow)
Guangzhou	(Canton)
Guangxi	(Zhuang)
Nanning	(Nan-ning)
Guiyang	(Kweiyang)
Shijiazhuang	(Shih-chia-chuang)
Harbin	(Harbin)
Zhengzhou	(Cheng-chou)
Wuhan	(Wu-han)
Changsha	(Ch'ang-sha)

Pinyin	Traditional
Nanjing	(Nanking)
Nanchang	(Nan-ch'ang)
Shenyang	(Shenyang; Mukden)
Hohhot	(Hu-ho-hao-t'e)
Changchin	(Ch'ang-ch'un)
Yinchuan	(Yin-ch'uan)
Xi'an	(Sian)
Jinan	(Tsinon)
Taiyuan	(T'ai-yuan)
Chengdu	(Ch'eng-tu)
Xinjiang	(Uygur)
Urumqi	(Urumchi)

EYEWITNESS TO HISTORY

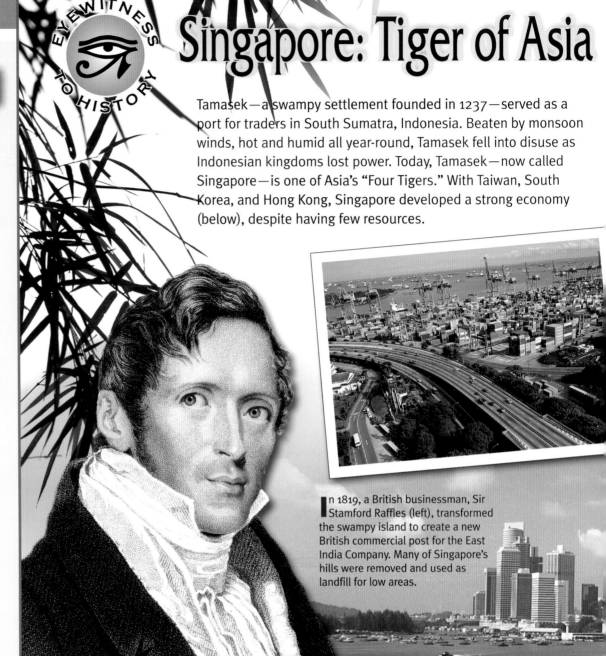

Singapore: Tiger of Asia

Tamasek—a swampy settlement founded in 1237—served as a port for traders in South Sumatra, Indonesia. Beaten by monsoon winds, hot and humid all year-round, Tamasek fell into disuse as Indonesian kingdoms lost power. Today, Tamasek—now called Singapore—is one of Asia's "Four Tigers." With Taiwan, South Korea, and Hong Kong, Singapore developed a strong economy (below), despite having few resources.

In 1819, a British businessman, Sir Stamford Raffles (left), transformed the swampy island to create a new British commercial post for the East India Company. Many of Singapore's hills were removed and used as landfill for low areas.

388 Chapter 1

ingapore, the port city and country, became a British olony about 50 years later. ingapore adopted British ustoms.

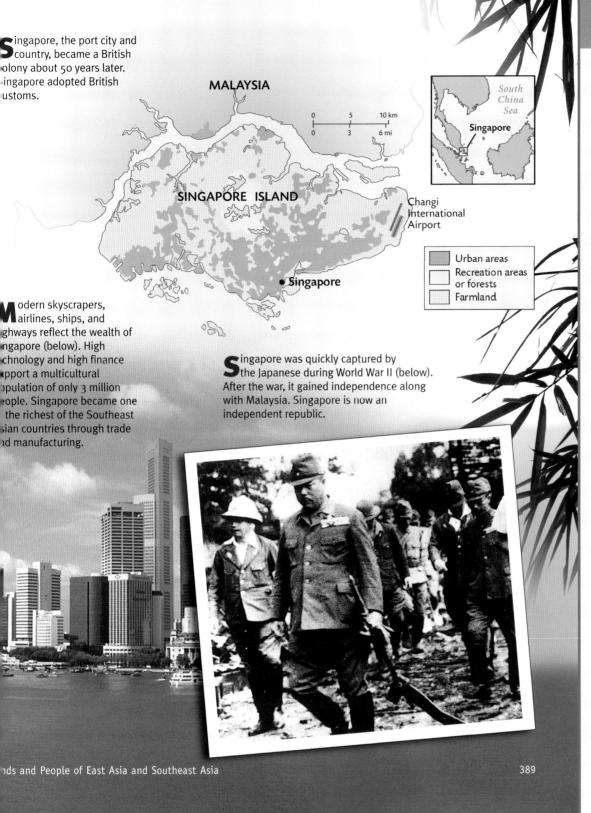

odern skyscrapers, airlines, ships, and ghways reflect the wealth of ngapore (below). High chnology and high finance pport a multicultural pulation of only 3 million ople. Singapore became one the richest of the Southeast ian countries through trade d manufacturing.

Singapore was quickly captured by the Japanese during World War II (below). After the war, it gained independence along with Malaysia. Singapore is now an independent republic.

Lion City—One of Asia's Four Tigers

OBJECTIVES: 1.03

Using the map on page 389, have students complete the following passage. ("Lion City" is Sanskrit for Singapore).

The central portion of the island of Singapore is forest with ___ areas including the Seletar and Mac Ritchie Reservoirs. (*recreation*) The highest point (177 meters) on Singapore Island is Timah in the low-lying uplands in its center.

This island city-state is smaller in both area and population than New York City. There are 40 islets included with Singapore Island totaling 250 square miles. The capital is ______. (*Singapore*) Cars carrying fewer than four people are forbidden to enter the center of this city during peak traffic hours without a special pass.

Many say the international airport, _______ ,is the best in Southeast Asia. (*Changi*) It is home to an expanding airline that has become world famous.

When the main island is divided into a northern and a southern section, the farmland is located mainly in the ______ section. (*northern*)

Most reference sources state that 100 percent of Singapore's population is urban. From this map, the majority of the urban areas are in the ___ section. (*southern*) Singapore is densely populated with almost 6,208 people living in every square kilometer. Orchard Road is a congested commercial center of hotels and duty-free shops that attract about 2 million tourists a year.

Background Information

Ancient Population Pressure

China, with about 1.3 billion people, has been the world's most populated country since records on population were first kept. In 742 during the Tang Dynasty, the country had approximately 51 million people. Five hundred years later, its population had doubled to more than 100 million. A household census in 1662 counted 111 million. In 1953, when census-taking was more accurate, the population numbered 582 million. By the 1980s it had doubled again, but the growth rate is now slowing as a result of the one-child policy. Demographers estimate China will peak at 1.49 billion in 2025, and drop back to about 1.48 billion by 2050.

Discussion Questions

1 What could be some effects of a declining population?

2 With so many people living in Asia, what trade policies would you suggest for North Carolina and the United States?

3 How is the Chinese government attempting to change people's attitude about large families?

4 Would a one-child-per-family policy be accepted in the United States? Why or why not?

5 What are some measures China can take to provide food for its growing population?

Caption Answer

The government has tried to enforce a one child per family policy. Parents who sign a one-child pledge are given privileges, but parents may be punished if they have more than one child.

Math Activity

Word Problem

 **OBJECTIVES:** 12.02

An artist is commissioned to create a mosaic. Each piece of colored tile is 1 square inch. How many tiles will be needed to cover a garden mural that is 60 inches by 48 inches?

Answer 2,880 tiles

Extension Assist ELL students by setting up the problem for them.

The Chinese government displays posters to encourage family planning. ***What other measures has it taken to control population growth?***

Population Pressures

East Asia has a population of 1.7 billion people. Southeast Asia has more than half a billion additional people. China is the world's most populated nation. Indonesia ranks fourth in population (India and the United States are second and third, respectively). About one-third of the world's population lives in East Asia and Southeast Asia.

In the late 1800s and early 1900s, Japan's population grew rapidly as the nation industrialized. That growth has now stopped. Families are having only one or two children. Due to these changes, Japan's population will begin to decline over the next ten years.

Elsewhere in East Asia and Southeast Asia, the population explosion is a major challenge.

China

China has adopted a one-child-per-family policy to limit population growth. Parents sign a "one-child" pledge. Those who have more than one child are often punished by fines or a loss of benefits.

For thousands of years, the Chinese have believed in the importance of having sons. Today, China is changing. Boys are not as necessary to support a family as they once were. Yet the tradition of havin a son—or many sons—remains strong. The government urges parents to be happ with one child, whether a boy or a girl. However, the ratio of boys to girls has changed. After more than 25 years of this policy, males outnumber females. Some men are unable to marry and have a family. The government is concerned, so i now sponsors publicity campaigns to promote the value of girls.

China's growth rate has slowed, but growth has not stopped. Its millions of young people are now marrying. Even if most of these new families have only one or two children, China's population will continue to expand well into this century.

China's concerns about its growing population are shared by most other East Asian and Southeast Asian nations. As yo have read, good farmland is limited throughout these vast regions. Leaders worry their nations may not have enough food for everyone in years to come. These leaders, like others throughout Asia and Africa, see future difficulties in providing for other basic needs—education, health care, and jobs.

LESSON 3 REVIEW

Fact Follow-Up

1. To what ethnic group do most Chinese belong?
2. What countries in Asia are the most homogeneous?
3. What do the Chinese and Japanese languages have in common?
4. What countries of the region rank in the top four in world population?

Talk About It

1. How has Chinese writing united a country of so many ethnic groups?
2. Do you agree with the Chinese methods of controlling population growth? Why or why not?
3. How is Singapore a "Tiger" of Asia?
4. Why are some nations' populations decreasing while others are increasing?

LESSON 3 REVIEW

Fact Follow-Up Answers

1. Most Chinese belong to the Han group.
2. Korea and Japan are the most homogeneous.
3. Both use characters—language symbols representing objects, ideas, or actions.
4. China is first and Indonesia is fourth.

Talk About It Answers

1. Although China has many spoken dialects, it has only one written language. People of different spoken languages can communicate by using their common written language.
2. Important points: Students should state whether they agree and support their position with explanations. Students might object to punishing families with more than one child.
3. Singapore developed a strong economy despite having few resources. Today, it is one of the richest of the Southeast Asian countries.
4. Important points: Students should come to an educated conclusion about why this is the case. Some factors influencing population growth include long-held traditions, the economy, and government policies.

Applying Decision-Making and Problem-Solving Techniques to World Issues

Locating a Factory in Asia

SKILL GOALS NORTH CAROLINA SOCIAL STUDIES skill

Imagine that you are an advisor to a furniture company. It makes inexpensive wood furniture that can be easily assembled. The design wil be simple because customers have limited incomes.

This furniture will be designed to appeal to young consumers. Therefore, locating the factory in a country with a youthful and growing population is desirable. Since the furniture will be made of wood, locating the factory in or near areas that have ample forest resources is also key. Finally, the furniture will be somewhat heavy; every effort must be made to keep shipping costs low.

The manufacturer wants to open plants in East Asia or Southeast Asia. Your task is to recommend locations in three countries. You must also identify possible target markets both in Asia and in other countries.

Electric power station

Furniture design plans

Making Your Chart

First, on a large sheet of paper, prepare a data retrieval chart that builds on the one shown below. At the top, list several nations in East Asia and Southeast Asia. On the left, list criteria that your employer may want to study—the supply of raw materials, the costs of land and factory construction, the workforce, the transportation to potential markets, and the stability of each nation's government.

Your recommendations are due when the company's executive vice president (your teacher) indicates. This will give you time to assemble data from Chapters 15–19. As you study these chapters, add data from Chapters 20–25. Your company's executive vice president also might ask you to do additional research. As data is added to your chart, eliminate countries that fail to meet the criteria that you have established.

As you add more data, you may find more than three countries that meet all of your criteria. If this happens, how do you select three to recommend? Do some meet your criteria better than others?

When you have made your decision, write a brief paragraph about each location and describe the reasons for your choices.

Locating Furniture Factories

	Nations				
Criteria	China	Japan			
Raw Materials					

Skill Lesson Review

1. How useful were the criteria you selected in helping you make a recommendation to the furniture manufacturer? *Important points: Accept student answers, encouraging them to refine their criteria. Resources and costs are very helpful in making a decision.*

2. What criteria would you use in developing recommendations for a factory that produces frozen pizza? motorcycles? *Important points: Urge students to evaluate their criteria. Skilled labor and transportation would be essential.*

Teaching This Skill Lesson

Note This lesson calls for students to examine Chapters 15 to 19 to make recommendations for three locations for manufacturing inexpensive wooden furniture. Make sure students understand that this is an extended activity. Establish a due date for their recommendations, and make a note to schedule class time to discuss their recommendations.

Materials Needed Each student will need a large sheet of posterboard or chart paper, the textbook, and pencils or markers.

Classroom Organization whole class activity, individual student work

Beginning the Lesson Tell students they will be working individually on this assignment for several weeks and that they will be responsible for independent work and for meeting deadlines. Their task is to review information from Chapters 15 to 19 in order to recommend where three factories are to be located. They will also use information from Chapters 20 to 25 as these chapters are studied.

Lesson Development Use the chart in the student lesson and the suggestions in paragraph 3, page 391, to demonstrate how students will make their charts. Make certain that students understand what criteria are and the specific criteria they will be using. Monitor as students begin to draw their charts. Remind students that they are to write a brief paragraph about each of the three locations they choose.

Conclusion On the day designated, have students display their charts; allow students to look at all charts. Compile students' recommendations on the chalkboard. Note which nations were chosen the most and least. Probe for reasons why. In general discussion, ask students if some criteria were more important than others and why or why not.

Extension For intermediate ELL students, model and provide additional explanations. Assign students to work with a partner or in groups.

Talk About It

1. Land and resources are limited. Unless population growth can be controlled, China will not be able to continue its economic progress.
2. China has many different languages and ethnic groups. A common written language gives people a way to communicate easily.
3. Important points: Encourage students to choose one hazard and explain why. Volcanoes and earthquakes can be destructive, but flooding occurs every year in some areas.
4. Important points: Students should choose one nation and explain why. China has the most resources but a huge population. Japan, among Asian nations, has the longest history of economic strength in modern times.
5. Important points: Students should take a position and explain it. There is a great diversity of climate, and mountains divide some people. Still, there are rivers and seas that offer connecting routes between people.
6. Important points: Encourage students to offer both negative and positive effects and explain them. Diversity creates a rich culture, but can make unity difficult.

CHAPTER 19 REVIEW

Lessons Learned

Lesson 1
Locations and Landforms
East Asia is a region of five nations—China, Japan, Mongolia, North Korea, and South Korea. Southeast Asia includes Myanmar (Burma), Thailand, Laos, Cambodia, Vietnam, Singapore, Indonesia, Malaysia, the Philippines, and Brunei. Most people live in the river valleys and plains of their nations.

Lesson 2
Climates and Resources
Monsoons affect climate in East Asia and Southeast Asia. Climates vary widely in East Asia, especially across China and Japan. Southeast Asia's climate is mainly tropical. China contains the regions' greatest resources.

Lesson 3
People and Their Environment
The people of East Asia and Southeast Asia belong to many ethnic groups and speak hundreds of languages. Most Chinese are Han. The Chinese and Japanese use Chinese characters in writing. Growing population is a problem in both regions, especially in China and Indonesia. Japan's population will soon begin to decline.

Talk About It

1. Why is China's large population of so much concern?
2. How is having a written language important to Chinese unity?
3. What do you think is the greatest natural hazard faced by people living in East Asia and Southeast Asia? Why?
4. Which nation of East Asia or Southeast Asia do you think has the best chances for long-term prosperity? Explain your answer.
5. Do landform and climate work more to unite or to divide nations in East Asia and Southeast Asia? Explain.
6. What effects do ethnic diversity have on a nation? Explain.

Mastering Mapwork

MOVEMENT

Use the map on page 375 to answer these questions:

1. Which national capital—Rangoon, Myanmar, or Beijing, China—has physical characteristics of place most like those of Hanoi, Vietnam?
2. In what ways are the physical characteristics of place similar in Tokyo, Japan, and Jakarta, Indonesia? How do they differ?
3. Using only the information from the map, compare the physical characteristics of place of Vientiane, Laos, to that of Manila, Philippines.
4. In what ways are the physical characteristics of place in North and South Korea similar?
5. How would you expect the physical characteristics of place to differ in Taipei, the capital of Taiwan, and Beijing, the capital of China?
6. What Chinese cities would you expect to have physical characteristics of place similar to those of Phnom Penh in Cambodia?
7. Describe the physical characteristics of place of Singapore.

392 Chapter 1

Mastering Mapwork

1. Rangoon is more like Hanoi in physical characteristics of place.
2. Both are located in hilly areas near coastal plains. Both are located on islands, though Tokyo's island is larger than Jakarta. Because of nearness to the Equator, Jakarta has a much warmer climate than does Tokyo.
3. Manila is on an island; Vientiane is located on the Southeast Asian mainland. Their altitudes differ as well. Because of its island location, Manila might be expected to be threatened from time to time by typhoons. Both are located at about the same latitude; so any great differences in temperature would be due to Manila's location on the water.
4. Both are located on a peninsula, and both have plains, hills, and mountains. The Yellow Sea borders both on the east, and both lie to the west of the Sea of Japan.
5. Taiwan is located on an island, and Beijing is on the Asian mainland. Beijing is located on the eastern edge of a desert area; the desert winds would affect Beijing. Taipei would be more affected by winds from the ocean. Beijing is farther north than Taipei and would be expected to have a cooler climate.
6. Phnom Penh is located on a coastal plain, near but not directly on the coastline, and in the Tropics. Hanoi in Vietnam, Bangkok in Thailand, and Rangoon in Myanmar (Burma) share these physical characteristics of place.
7. Singapore is located on a coastal plain, at the tip of a peninsula, and just north of the Equator. Singapore has a hot, humid climate.

Understanding Accounts of Historic Events

Sima Guang wrote Zizhi tongjian*, meaning "The Comprehensive Mirror for Aid in Government," published in 1086. This passage is from the section about the reigns of Emperor Huan and Emperor Ling in the later Han dynasty. During this time there was great unrest and conflict in the land.*

Read the excerpt below from the Zizhi tongjian*. Answer the questions using specific references to the document.*

February 2, 162–February 20, 163

In the third month, the Shendi Qiang raided Zhangye and Jiuquan. Huangfu Gui raised the tribes of the Xianlian and other Qiang people to join in a campaign west of the Long Mountain. The roads and communications, however, were under attack and broken, there was widespread sickness in the army, and three or four out of every ten died. Huangfu Gui himself took up quarters in a simple hut, and he made regular inspection of his officers and men. All the troops appreciated his concern.

Then the Eastern Qiang sent messengers, asking to surrender, and Liang province was once again in proper communication [with the rest of the empire]. Before this, the Grand Administrator of Anding, Sun Jun, had been greedy . . . the Chief Commandant of the Dependent State [of Anding] and the Imperial Clerk Commanding the Army, Li Xi and Zhang Bing, had both killed great numbers of Qiang people when they came to surrender; while Guo Hong (the Inspector of Liang province) and Zhao Xi (the Grand Administrator of Hanyang) were old and feeble and could not cope with their responsibilities. Each of them relied entirely upon the power and honour of his position, and they paid no attention to the laws or to proper principles.

When Huangfu Gui arrived, he sent in reports with detailed accounts of their crimes, and some were punished and others dismissed.

When the Qiang people heard about this, they were quite reformed, and the chieftains of the Shendi Qiang, Dianchang, Jitian and others, came once again with more than 100,000 followers to surrender to Huangfu Gui.

Questions

1. Who is the intended audience?
2. Why do you think this history of China was written?
3. What does this passage possibly tell us about the culture of China of the time?
4. As described in this passage, which leadership qualities were important to the Chinese? Which traits were frowned upon?

Go to the Source

Go to the Source

OBJECTIVES: 7.01, 9.01, 11.01; Skills 1.03, 1.08, 2.02, 3.05, 4.03

This document describes the history of the reigns of Emperor Huan and Emperor Ling from "the Chronicle of the Later Han dynasty for the years for the years 157 to 189 A.D. as recorded in Chapters 54 to 59 of the Zizhi tongjian of Sima Guang." Visit **NCJourneys.com** for a link to the document.

ANSWERS

1. Possibly the military or government leaders due to the topic being documented
2. Possibly to record major military events of the time
3. The military and its engagements are important events to note. There are also lessons to be learned concerning pride and abuse of position as stated in the latter part of the document. Leaders who abused their power and position were punished.
4. Leadership traits that were important include concern for troops, communication, and paying attention to laws and proper principles. Traits that were frowned upon include greed, killing people who are surrendering, not being able to cope with responsibilities, and misusing power.

How to Use the Chapter Review

There are three sections in the Chapter Review: Talk About It, Mastering Mapwork, and Go to the Source. Use the Vocabulary Worksheets and the Chapter Review Worksheet in the Teacher's Resource Guide for additional reinforcement and preparation for the Chapter Assessments. The chapter and lesson reviews and the Chapter Review Worksheets are the basis of the assessment for each chapter.

Talk About It questions encourage students to speculate about the content of the chapter and are suitable for class or small-group discussion. They are not intended to be assigned for homework.

Mastering Mapwork has students apply one or more of the Five Themes of Geography to maps within the chapter.

Go to the Source activities allow students to analyze a primary source that relates to the content of the chapter. The questions and activities familiarize students with different types of primary sources and also build content-reading skills.

China's Enduring Traditions

Social Studies Strands

Cultures and Diversity
Family—filial piety
Confucianism
Daoism
Ancestor worship

Historic Perspectives
Dynasty
Bureaucracy
Revolution

Government and Active Citizenship
Communism

Technological Influences and Society
Inventions

North Carolina Standard Course of Study

Goal 8 The learner will assess the influence and contributions of individuals and cultural groups in Africa, Asia, and Australia.

Goal 9 The learner will analyze the different forms of government developed in Africa, Asia, and Australia.

Goal 10 The learner will compare the rights and civic responsibilities of individuals in political structures in Africa, Asia, and Australia.

Goal 12 The learner will assess the influence of major religions, ethical beliefs, and values on cultures in Africa, Asia, and Australia.

Teaching & Assessment

- English Language Learner Modified Lesson Plans for this chapter are found in the Teacher's Resource Guide.
- *ExamView® Assessment Suite* is provided at **NCJourneys.com.** It includes customizable assessments for all chapters. Paper tests are also available in the Teacher's Resource Guide. See pages T16–T17 for information about how to use the assessments and the Scoring Guide.

Worksheets

Worksheets and answer keys are found both in the Teacher's Resource Guide and at **NCJourneys.com**, including Reading Guides, Reading Strategies, Chapter Reviews, English Language Learner and others.

ACTIVITIES AND INTEGRATIONS

SOCIAL STUDIES
● Contemporary China, p. 394
Activity for Opening Statement, p. 400
★ Shang China: Birthplace of Ancient China, p. 400
Chinese Almond Cookies, p. 401
Museum Exhibit, p. 403
● Modern China Time Line, p. 406
Who Controlled What in China?, p. 408
Skill Lesson: Comparing Obstacles to Development, p. 411

READING/LANGUAGE ARTS	READING/LANGUAGE ARTS OBJECTIVES
● Sleeping Giant, p. 394B	2.01
Radio Interviews from China's Past, p. 394B	2.01
Analogies, p. 394B	2.01
Activator: *Yeh-Shen,* p. 394	2.01
Writing Prompt: China's Contribution, p. 394	3.01
Filial Piety, p. 396	6.01
★ Myth–Legend of the Four Dragons, p. 397	2.01
★ Daoistic Beliefs, p. 402	6.01
▲ ■ Chinese Inventions, p. 403	2.02
Sun Yat Sen's Three Principles of the People, p. 408	2.01
▲ ■ Life Aboard a Junk, p. 409	3.01
Go to the Source: Interpreting Sayings, p. 413	1.02, 2.01, 4.01

MATHEMATICS	MATHEMATICS OBJECTIVES
Which is Really Larger?, p. 404	1.02, 1.03
★ Economy and Transportation, p. 405	1.02, 1.03

TECHNOLOGY	TECHNOLOGY OBJECTIVES
Traditional China's Nesting Boxes, p. 396	3.01, 3.11
State of the Art China, p. 400	3.01, 3.11

VISUAL ARTS	VISUAL ARTS OBJECTIVES
● ■ Chinese Dragon, p. 394B	2.04, 5.02
▲ ■ Traditional China's Nesting Boxes, p. 396	2.04, 5.02
Chinese Junk, p. 409	2.04, 6.01

CHARACTER AND VALUES EDUCATION	TRAITS
Writing Prompt: China's Contribution, p. 394	good judgment
What Would You Do?, p. 397	good judgment
Chinese Values, p. 398	respect, kindness

● Basic Activities ★ Challenging Activities ▲ English Language Learner Novice ■ English Language Learner Intermediate

Introductory Activity

Sleeping Giant

OBJECTIVES: 7.01

Pass out small pieces of paper or have students use scrap paper. Ask students to analyze the Chapter opener on page 394 to determine what Napoleon meant by his statement about China being a sleeping giant.

Not all students will grasp the meaning of this sentence if simply read once quickly to get to the next paragraph. Spend some time with it. You may be surprised by their analyses of the statement.

Culminating Activity

Radio Interviews from China's Past

OBJECTIVES: 8.01, 8.03

Materials textbook, reference books, pencil, paper, tape recorders and blank tapes

As a class, brainstorm a list of people who played significant roles in China's history. Some will not have names (inventors of gunpowder, block printing, the seismograph, and so on). Otherwise record names and major contributions to China on slips of paper. Place them into a hat.

Divide students into pairs: interviewer and interviewee. Two pairs will be reserved for a special assignment team (producer, director, narrator, and commercials). Each pair will pull a name from the hat to research. They will create a script using an interview technique of questions and answers. Once the script has been approved, the pair may record their interview.

The special assignment team will choose a narrator to introduce each interview, and two students will create commercials—30-second spots following each interview. The recorded commercials should deal with Chinese history or contemporary China. The producer/director is responsible for recording, keeping the dialogue flowing, and keeping the interview time under 5 minutes.

Once all the tapes have been recorded, darken the room and listen to "Radio Interviews from China's Past." Students may vote on the "Best Interview."

Art Activity

Chinese Dragon

OBJECTIVES: 4.03, 12.02

Materials construction paper 9 inches by 12 inches, scissors, pencils, glue, heavyweight paper/card stock

The Head Choose two colors of construction paper (red and black). Fold both sheets in half horizontally. Aligning the sheets back to back, draw the profile of a dragon's head, with the mouth nearest the folded edge. Cut out both sheets simultaneously. Separate the black sheet from the red and cut the red ¼ inch smaller. Align the sheets and glue the red sheet onto the black one. Use the black scraps to create designs for the head. Cut designs two at a time for symmetry.

The Tail Choose the same two colors. Repeat the instructions except fold vertically. Use extra scraps for designs.

The Body Create a truncated diamond shape on card stock 6 inches wide by 4 inches tall. This shape will be a template for students to trace. Each student should cut ten of these shapes in both colors (20 in all). Place a thin line of glue down the center of the first piece of the body. Place the next piece on top, alternating colors. Place a thin line of glue on the sides of the next piece of the body. Repeat the gluing steps until there are no more body pieces.

Connecting the Body to the Head and Tail Fold up the sides of the first section of the body. Glue to the inside of the head. Repeat for the tail. Let the dragon dry thoroughly before attempting to spring it back and forth.

Extension This is a good activity for ELL students. There may be a student (or their parent or friend) who knows how to do the Dragon (or Lion) dance to teach or demonstrate to the class.

Analogies

OBJECTIVES: 2.03, 12.01

Analogies are useful to help students make associations with prior knowledge. Read the analogies aloud and ask students to identify the relationship between the terms. As an extension, ask students to write their own analogies using key terms or places discussed in the chapter.

Pious : piety :: generous : generosity (adjective : noun)

Veneration : respect :: ridicule : disrespect (synonyms)

Shang : Huang He :: Sumerian : Tigria/Euphrates (civilization : river valley)

Terra cotta : clay :: bread : dough (is made from)

Canton : Guangzhou :: Peking : Beijing :: Mao Tse Tung : Mao Zedong (old : new transcription)

Humiliated : praised :: put-down : complimented (is the opposite of)

Teaching Strategies

Because of China's influence on other countries, spend more time on ancient China so that you can use less time for the ancient history of neighboring countries in East Asia and more time on modern culture in these countries. Lesson 3 focuses on China's Revolution, which is also a major concept that must be thoroughly understood by students.

Discussion Questions

1 Who said that China was a sleeping giant?

2 Around what year did China emerge into a modern nation?

Activator

 **OBJECTIVES:** 10.04, 12.01

Activators are great tools to use in order to "hook" the attention of the students. Reading picture books or stories is an excellent way to build interest in the subject and is also a great way to integrate language arts into the social studies curriculum.

Yeh-Shen: A Cinderella Story, retold by Ai-Ling Louie, illustrated by Ed Young. (Putnam, 1982. ISBN 039920900X.)

The Demon King and Other Festival Folktales of China, retold by Carolyn Han, illustrated by Li Ji. (University of Hawaii Press, 1995. ISBN 0824817079.)

Writing Prompt

 **OBJECTIVES:** 8.01, 8.03

Evaluative

Throughout its long history, China has made many contributions to the world. Write an article for your school newspaper identifying China's greatest contribution and explaining your choice.

As you write your article, remember to:

- clearly state your position.
- give at least three reasons and explain your reasons fully.
- give examples to support your reasons.
- write in complete sentences and paragraph form.
- organize your ideas and include an introduction and a conclusion.
- use good grammar, spelling, punctuation, and capitalization.

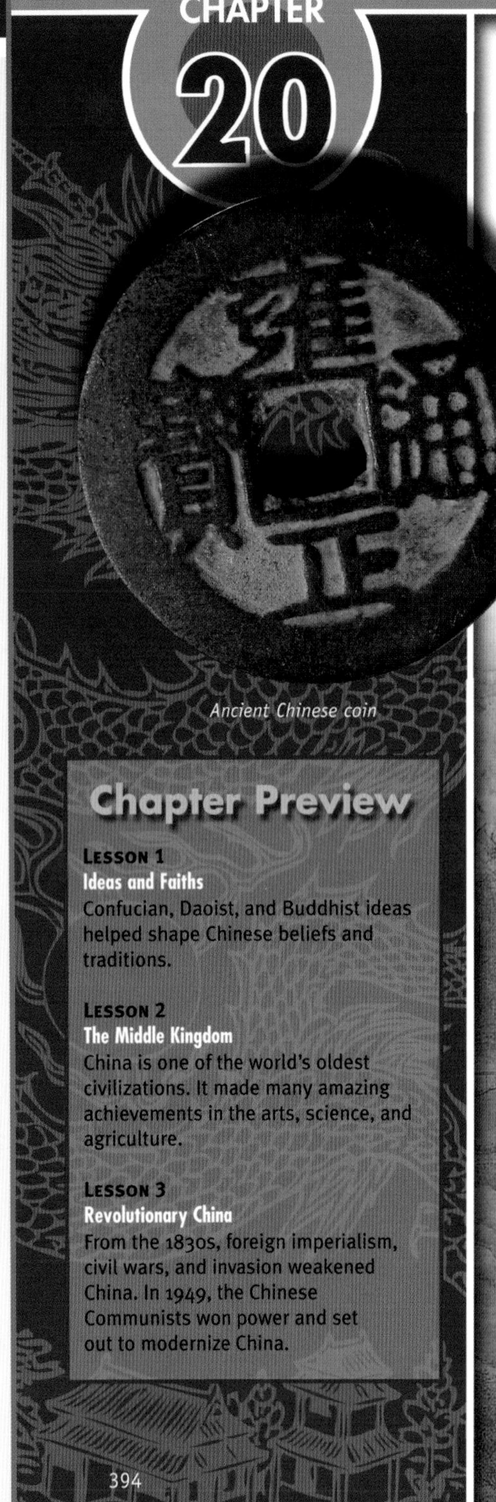

CHAPTER 20

Ancient Chinese coin

Chapter Preview

Lesson 1
Ideas and Faiths
Confucian, Daoist, and Buddhist ideas helped shape Chinese beliefs and traditions.

Lesson 2
The Middle Kingdom
China is one of the world's oldest civilizations. It made many amazing achievements in the arts, science, and agriculture.

Lesson 3
Revolutionary China
From the 1830s, foreign imperialism, civil wars, and invasion weakened China. In 1949, the Chinese Communists won power and set out to modernize China.

394

China's Enduring Traditions

In the early 1800s, the French Emperor Napoleon was asked about China. He supposedly replied: "China? There lies a sleeping giant. Let him sleep. For when he wakes he will move the world." China's civilization, already more than 4,000 years old when Napoleon spoke, had dominated East Asia and Southeast Asia. By the 1800s, however, China was weak and "sleeping."

More than a century later, China is awake. China has emerged as a giant in Asia. A tremendous revolution has created a modern nation. Yet despite far-reaching changes, many traditions survive.

Chapter 2

Chapter Resources

Print Resources

Nonfiction

Cotterell, Arthur. *Ancient China* (Eyewitness Books series). Dorling Kindersley, 2000. ISBN 078946604X.

Steele, Philip. *Chinese Empire* (Step Into series). Lorenz Books, Anness Publishing 1998. ISBN 1859677622.

Williams, Suzanne. *Made in China: Ideas and Inventions from Ancient China.* Pacific View Press, 1996. ISBN 1881896145.

Back issues of magazines

Cobblestone Publishing Company:

Confucius. ISBN 0382445120.

Daoism (Taoism). ISBN 0382445775.

Han Dynasty. ISBN 0382443896.

Ming Dynasty. ISBN 0382406079.

Shi-Huangdi, China's First Emperor. ISBN 0382408942.

Silk Road. (*Calliope* magazine 2001–02)

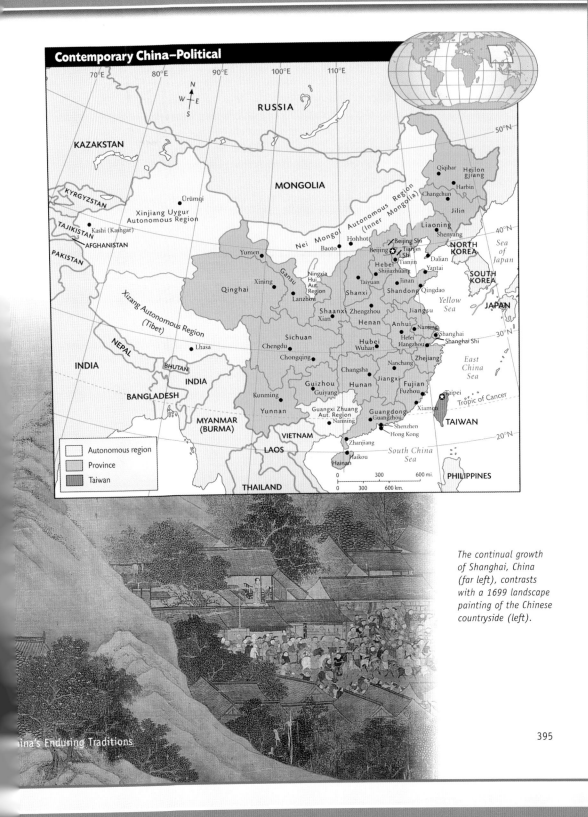

Contemporary China–Political

The continual growth of Shanghai, China (far left), contrasts with a 1699 landscape painting of the Chinese countryside (left).

Audiovisual

Sultan's Lost Treasure (shipwrecked treasures of China), Nova. 2001. PBS Video.

Web Sites

Go to **NCJourneys.com** for links to the following Web sites:

- China's Communist Revolution: A Glossary. BBC
- Exploring Ancient World Cultures: China
- History Learning Site: The Great Leap Forward
- Sultan's Lost Treasure companion Web site
- Virtual Museum of the Cultural Revolution
- UVM Asian Studies Outreach Program, Ancient China:

Map Activity

Contemporary China

NATIONAL GEOGRAPHY STANDARDS: 1

GEOGRAPHIC THEMES: Location

OBJECTIVES: 2.02, 2.03, 8.03, 10.04

Break the class into four groups. Assign each group one of the four regions of China to present to their class in 15-minute segments, using the map on page 395 and the information below.

East China is often referred to as "China Proper." This is what many consider "real" China, with its huge population centers, intensively farmed lands, numerous villages, and crowded cities. This is the location of the vast majority of the Chinese provinces and one autonomous region. China's northeast is often called Manchuria. It includes three provinces: Liaoning, Jilin, and Heilongjiang. Chinese geographers do not use the term Manchuria.

Nei Mongol is Inner Mongolia. This is a transition area between "China Proper" and the country of Mongolia. The wettest part of the Gobi desert is found here, with pasture land and spring wheat crops.

Xizang is what many call Tibet. High-altitude plateaus and tall, snow-covered mountains are situated between the Himalayas to the south and the Kunlun and Altun Mountains to the north—the roof of the world. This is the center for Tibetan Buddhism and home of the now exiled Dalai Lama.

Xinjiang is the basin region, with its two largest basins separated by the Tianshan mountain range. One basin is the Taklimakan—an interior desert. Another, the Junggar, has sizable oilfields. Islam has been an uninterrupted way of life for centuries in northwestern China.

Conclude presentations with debriefing, including the following:

Many Chinese consider Taiwan a part of China and claim it as province 23. Taiwan states there is only one China, but two political parts.

 **OBJECTIVES:** 8.01, 10.04, 12.01

1 What is filial piety?

2 "If you wish to govern the state well, first govern your family well." What does this Chinese proverb mean?

3 How many generations are included in an extended Chinese family?

4 Are children taught filial piety in our community? In what ways?

5 What is the role of the family in our community?

Caption Answer

Filial piety was the basis for family security and structure in society. Both the family and the wider society believed that individuals were not equal and that everybody must pursue their duties. Older people were respected more.

Writing Activity

Filial Piety

OBJECTIVES: 12.01

Have students write or word process their own "Filial Piety" short story. Use the story of Meng as a springboard. Length should be one to two paragraphs. Optional: Have students share their stories with the class.

Activity

Traditional China Nesting Boxes

OBJECTIVES: 4.03, 7.02

Materials handout of nesting box patterns from the Teacher's Resource Guide; blank paper (same color, style, quality
as pattern handout); colored pencils, markers, or crayons; scissors; rulers; transparent tape

Have students design three nesting boxes depicting chronological sequence of events or cultural connections from China's ideas and faiths, dynasties, inventions and achievements, or personalities. Twelve aspects will need to be selected on three related topics.

Direct students to cut out one of each cross shape so that they have three different sizes of crosses. Place each cross with the number side up; then fold up and crease the four sides to make a box shape. Do not attach the sides of the resulting three boxes until the entire project is completed. Unfold the boxes and turn each over to the back.

Number each side of the largest cross 1–4.
Number each side of the middle cross 5–8.
Number each side of the smallest cross 9–12.

Students should research findings, in sequential order, and maintain the number order on the sides. Have them decorate all three boxes using traditional Chinese designs and colors. To make a lid for each box, they can trace the bottom of the box on paper, adding tab on one side to hold it on. Decorate the three lids before cutting them out. Tape the sides of each box together.
Fold the tab of each lid on its fold line.
Tape the tab to the inside of its box and fold the lid inside its box. Put the three boxes inside each other.

LESSON  Ideas and Faiths

KEY IDEAS

- The family was at the center of society in Old China.
- Confucian ideals guided Old China.
- Confucius insisted rulers follow high moral standards.
- Daoism and Buddhism influenced Old China's beliefs.

KEY TERMS

ancestor veneration
Confucianism
Daoism
filial piety

According to an old story, a Chinese boy named Meng worried about mosquitoes swarming through his house. They bit his parents and kept them awake every night. The family was too poor to buy netting to keep the biting bugs away.

To help his parents, Meng threw his bedclothes off and whispered t the mosquitoes, "Come and bite me. I will not kill you or drive you away. Only keep away from my mother and father. They are tired and need sleep."

In Old China, people told stories like this one to their children. It taught ***filial piety,*** the respect and loyalty that children owed to their parents.

The Family Comes First

"If you wish to govern the state well, first govern your family well." This Chinese proverb describes the key role of family in Old China. Old China was the China that existed before its revolution. Children learned that helping the family was their most important duty. They knew they had to place family interests above their own.

The ideal family was an extended family of three generations. When the oldest son married, he stayed with his parents and raised his family. So grandparents, parents, and grandchildren lived together. Among some wealthy Chinese families, all the sons and their wives lived in the family home.

The Chinese family was patriarchal. This meant the oldest male made the important decisions. He might consult his wife or brothers, but he was responsible for his family's survival. Family members

One benefit of extended families are the close bonds between the elderly and the young (right). An extended family in Guangzhou, China, includes four generations (far right). **How did the values of family extend to Chinese society?**

cepted his authority. He and his wife ranged marriages for their children and andchildren. Marriages were planned to nefit the family, not any individual ember.

In Old China, the family took care of e sick and looked after the elderly. The mily was supposed to help out its embers who suffered other misfortunes. a world that was harsh and often cruel, closely knit family offered individuals eir only protection.

amily Values and Society

Within the family, a child learned oout duties, not rights. Filial piety quired a son to accept, without question, s parents' choice of a bride. When osen as a bride, a daughter had to leave ome and join her new husband's family.

Family practices and values extended to Chinese society. Older people were onsidered superior to younger ones. An derly grandmother who had lost her usband might command her sons and andsons, but usually males were placed ove females. A woman bowed early in e to her father's wishes and later to ose of her husband.

In Old China, people believed that two ideas made families work smoothly. First, individuals were *not equal*. That is, in human relationships, most dealings were between superior and inferior individuals. Second, people in these relationships must pursue their *duties*. These basic ideas shaped family life.

The head of the family might have seemed like a dictator. He was in many ways, but he was supposed to be a kindly ruler. His duties were to work in the family's interest, not his own. His conduct in his daily life was to set an example for others. The family would run smoothly only if its head attended to his duties.

These ideals were not limited to families. They also were the keys to a well-ordered society and good government.

What would YOU do?

You are a teenager in a Confucian family. Your parents have selected your future spouse, whom you have never seen, and have set the wedding date. Do you follow your parents' wishes? Why or why not?

Discussion Questions

1 In Old China, who looked after the sick and elderly?

2 In Old China, how many ideas made families work smoothly?

3 What is a right? What are some examples? What do you consider your most important right?

4 How does the Chinese attitude toward individuals differ from that of the United States? How does that affect relationships?

Activity

Myth—"Legend of the Four Dragons"

OBJECTIVES: 4.03, 13.02

Creation myths exist in most cultures of the world. Secure copies of the Chinese legend in *Dragon Tales: A Collection of Chinese Stories.* Zhang Chaoldong, ed., translated by Wa Ling. (Panda Books, Chinese Literature Press, Beijing, 1988. ISBN 08351200589.) and pass out to students. The story combines dragons and emperors with a basic geography lesson of China.

A few explanations will be needed. The Jade emperor is the ruler of the mythical heavenly court. As the story suggests, he is not the most likable of deities.

Try to find a Chinese dragon picture. They tend to be like snakes rather than dinosaurs. In China, dragons are good guys and usually associated with bringing rain and other sources of water.

Discuss this creation story with the class. Have them brainstorm a list of other creation stories from our own and other cultures.

Background Information

Confucius

For Confucius, the ideal state was not a democracy nor was it a place where all were treated equally. For his unstable times, he favored a well-ordered government in which the emperor led and the people followed. In the ideal society, the ruler's moral leadership created an environment in which people would naturally be good without coercion. The Analects put it this way: "If you use laws to direct people and punishments to control them, they will only evade the laws and develop no conscience. But if you guide them by virtue and control them by customs, they will have a conscience and a sense of what is right."

Discussion Questions

1 What are Confucian ideals?

2 Whose teaching influenced China's governmental leaders for thousands of years?

3 State Confucius's rule that was similar to the Golden Rule.

4 What different traditions did people in Old China follow?

5 State the difference between Daoism and Confucianism.

Caption Answer

Confucius saw Chinese society as one large family with the emperor as its head.

Map Activity

Chinese Values

 **OBJECTIVES:** 4.03, 12.01

Confucius developed a set of moral guidelines 2,500 years ago. How are American values similar to or different from traditional Chinese values?

Read each statement aloud. Have students write a number 1–5 according to how they respond to the statement.

1 strongly disagree
2 disagree
3 no strong feelings
4 agree
5 strongly agree

1. You should never judge others quickly.
2. Rulers should be just and fair in their decisions.
3. Parents must feed, clothe, and house their children.
4. The needs of the entire family should come before the needs and wants of any individual member of the family.
5. Rulers should help people in times of trouble.
6. You should be willing to compromise when you have conflict with others.
7. You should respect the rights of others.
8. You should pay your bills on time.
9. Society is more important than the individual.
10. Rulers should not tax the people excessively.
11. Children have a duty to obey their parents at all times.
12. You must be willing to make sacrifices for the good of the country.

Conclusion The class should tally the responses for each statement and determine the average class answer. Circle 4 (agree) for each statement scoring 4.0 or higher. Circle 2 (disagree) for each statement scoring below 3.0

What conclusions can you make about the similarities and differences between traditional Chinese values and those of your classmates?

Confucian Ideals

"Do not do to others what you do not wish yourself." That saying is similar to the Golden Rule that you might have learned. This version came from Confucius, a Chinese philosopher who lived 2,500 years ago.

Kung Fu Zu (the Master Kung) is better known in the West as Confucius. He lived in a time of disorder. He developed a set of moral guidelines that he believed would restore harmony. These teachings are called ***Confucianism.***

Confucius saw China as one large family. The emperor, much as the head of a family, could order others to do whatever he wished. Confucius taught that the good emperor must do what the head of a family should do—provide leadership that served the people's interests. A ruler, Confucius insisted, should not govern through force. People would follow a leader who set a good example. "As the wind blows," Confucius said, "so bows the grass."

Confucian teachings became the backbone of Chinese government and society. Writings on how Confucianism applied to government filled thousands of pages. To become a government official, a man had to study these writings for years and pass difficult exams.

Other Traditions

In Old China people followed different traditions. One called ***Daoism*** (DOW·ism) had many followers among Confucians. Yet some Daoist ideas contradicted those of Confucius.

The teachings of Confucius influenced government leaders for thousands of years. **How did Confucius view Chinese society?**

Daoism rejected the Confucian tradition of study and moral leadership. Good government could not come from men of learning, because no amount of study could teach what was right or wrong. Daoists did not believe government could make a better world. The best government was the one that di the least. Instead of studying and attempting to reform society, people should open themselves to nature and the wonders of the universe.

Many traditional Chinese landscape paintings reflect these ideas. Look closely at a painting on pages 394–395 to find people in it. Notice the tiny little figures blending into the natural world around them. Such a painting suggests that humans are simply part of the natural world, not the masters of it. That idea is another Daoist contribution to Chinese traditions.

Religions

Confucianism and Daoism were not religions. Both offered directions to peopl about how they should live.

However, the Chinese did have religious beliefs. They believed that they lived in a spirit-filled world. The most important spirits were those of the family ancestors. The Chinese believed their ancestors' spirits could help them. Familie set aside a space in their home for an alta a picture, or a tablet with the names of dead ancestors. There they placed offerings of food or they burned incense.

Westerners called this practice ***ancestor veneration,*** showing deep respe for one's ancestors. This respect strengthened family ties.

Later, major religions did make their way into China. Buddhism came into China from India. It contributed spiritually to Chinese life and influenced the arts, literature, music, and architecture.

By the 700s, Islam and Christianity had reached China. Islam won converts among the peoples of western China. Christian missionaries laid foundations fo modern-day Christianity in the 1800s and 1900s.

These worshippers are making offerings in a temple. **What is ancestor veneration?**

LESSON 1 REVIEW

Fact Follow-Up

1. What was the most important institution in the society of Old China?
2. Compare Confucian and Daoist views of the role of government in society.
3. What were the major religions and beliefs of Old China?

Talk About It

1. Did the ideal of filial piety affect Chinese society? Explain.
2. How were Confucianism and family relationships linked?
3. Which was more important in Old China—respect for family or spiritual beliefs? Explain.

Discussion Questions

1 What is the role of ancestors in Chinese society?

2 What is the role of ancestors in our society?

3 What are the philosophies and religions found in China today?

4 What was the Chinese religious belief?

5 What did the Westerners call the practice of religious belief?

6 How did Buddhism get into China, and what areas of life did it influence?

7 When did Christianity and Islam reach China and from where?

The honoring of and showing deep respect for one's ancestors is called ancestor veneration.

LESSON 1 REVIEW

Fact Follow-Up Answers

1. The family was the most important institution in Old China.
2. Confucian views of government envisioned China as a family with the emperor as its head. The emperor provided leadership that served the people's interest and set a good example. Unlike Confucianists, Daoists did not believe that government could make a better world. Daoists believed that the best government was the one that did the least.
3. The major religions included Buddhism, Islam, and Christianity. Confucianism and Daoism offered directions to people about how they should live. The Chinese also believed in a spirit-filled world and venerated their ancestors.

Talk About It Answers

1. Yes. Filial piety was the basis for family security and structure in society. The ideas of respect for age, the inequality of individuals, and the necessity for performing one's duties became the values of traditional Chinese society.
2. Confucius developed moral guidelines based on the principles of filial piety, and his teachings became the backbone of Chinese government and society.
3. Important points: Students should choose between the two options and explain their choice. Confucianism, a belief system, emphasized respect for family.

OBJECTIVES: 3.01, 6.02, 9.01, 10.01

Discussion Questions

1 What makes a great civilization?

2 Why is a written language a large step in developing a civilization?

3 When did King George III send an ambassador to China, and from where?

4 What did China's emperor think of Great Britain?

5 Do we think our country is the center of the civilized world?

6 From where did China's ancient civilization emerge?

7 Name four devices that China invented.

Caption Answer

The Chinese invented paper, gunpowder, block printing, and calendars.

Activity

Activity for Opening Statement

OBJECTIVES: 4.02

Have students role play with a partner the ambassador and the emperor. Have the ambassador try to convince the emperor to trade with the United Kingdom. The emperor always refuses, but he sends the ambassador away with some small presents. Then have students switch roles. Discuss the best arguments used by both sides.

Research Activity

State-of-the-Art China

OBJECTIVES: 8.03, 12.02

Have students research in the library and on the Internet what types of goods and technology the Chinese and the British had in the 1700s. They should take notes using a graphic organizer. Discuss as a class: Was the emperor's belief that China "had everything" justified?

LESSON  The Middle Kingdom

KEY IDEAS

- China's ancient civilization developed largely on its own. China had limited contacts with outsiders.
- Scholar-officials educated in Confucian teachings dominated Chinese government.
- China developed many technologies during its long history.

KEY TERMS

bureaucracy
Great Wall
Mandate of Heaven
Qin dynasty

In the 1700s, Great Britain's King George III sent an ambassador to China. His goal was to persuade the Chinese government to allow British merchants greater trading rights in China. The emperor firmly refused the king's request. He told the king that the Chinese "possess all things" and have no use "for your country's manufactures."

King George might have been surprised by the emperor's reaction. Great Britain had become a respected power in Europe. In the Chinese emperor's eyes, however, Great Britain was only a tiny country on the other side of the world. Compared to China, Great Britain was backward and lacking in civilization. China, the emperor believed, was the great Middle Kingdom, the center of the civilized world. The emperor had no interest in opening relations with a kingdom he thought was so inferior to China.

An Ancient Civilization

The emperor was proud of China's ancient civilization. It had emerged thousands of year earlier in the Huang He (Yellow River) Valley. By 3000 B.C., farmers had built villages in the fertile soil along the river. As in Sumer and Egypt, the villages grew into cities. By 1600 B.C., Chinese rulers had united these lands into strong kingdoms.

Also, as in Sumer and Egypt, the Chinese had created a written language, shaped bronze into beautiful objects, and made fine pottery. Craftspeople wove silk textiles and carved hard jade stone into ornaments. The Chinese invented many devices—from paper and gunpowder to block printing and calendars.

Chinese civilization developed largely on its own. Unlike civilizations built in Egypt, Southwest Asia, and South Asia, the Chinese had limited contact with outsiders. In general, the Chinese had more advanced technologies—or skills—than nearby neighbors. Increasingly, the Chinese saw themselves as the most advanced people in the world. It was against this background that the Chinese emperor received King George III's ambassador.

The emperor treated the ambassador as he did representatives of other small kingdoms. He sent George III presents as "evidence of his good will," but he told the British not to come again.

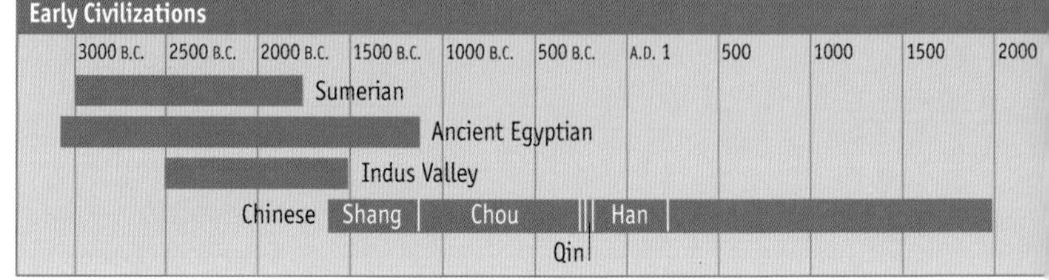

The Chinese civilization has a 3,500-year history, which began during the time of the Egyptian and Indus civilizations. **What were contributions of ancient China?**

Activity

Shang China "Birthplace of Ancient China"

NATIONAL GEOGRAPHY STANDARDS: 1, 17

GEOGRAPHIC THEMES: Location, Place, Region

OBJECTIVES: 1.02, 2.03, 8.03

Review the term confluence with the Huang He (Yellow River) and Wei He being one of four important, early cradles of civilization.

Using a large-scale Eastern Hemisphere map, have students locate three early Asian civilizations, (Mesopotamia with the Euphrates and Tigris Rivers, India with the Indus River, and China with the Huang He). Have them label rivers and major cities: Ur in Mesopotamia; Mohenjo-Daro and Harappa in India; and Anyang, Chengchow, and Loyang in China. It would be best to include Africa's Nile River civilization and locate the cities of Karnak and Memphis (reinforcing Chapter 3).

Shaping an Empire

In 221 B.C., an ambitious Chinese ruler conquered rival leaders and united much of China. He proclaimed himself to be the Emperor Qin Shi Huangdi, of the Qin (chin) *dynasty*. A dynasty is a line of rulers from the same family.

This emperor laid foundations for a system of government that lasted more than 2,000 years. He held absolute power over his subjects. To rule his empire, he created a bureaucracy that would carry out his orders. A ***bureaucracy*** is a group of specialized government agencies, such as the defense or treasury departments.

Such specialized agencies could organize people and materials to carry out large projects. The Emperor Qin ordered the building of China's ***Great Wall***. The Wall was supposed to protect China from armed invaders that sometimes rode into China from the northern plains. More than 300,000 people worked 14 years to complete it. When it was finished, the Great Wall reached 1,500 miles (2,415 km) across northern China. Chinese and foreign tourists still visit the Great Wall.

Birthplace of Ancient China

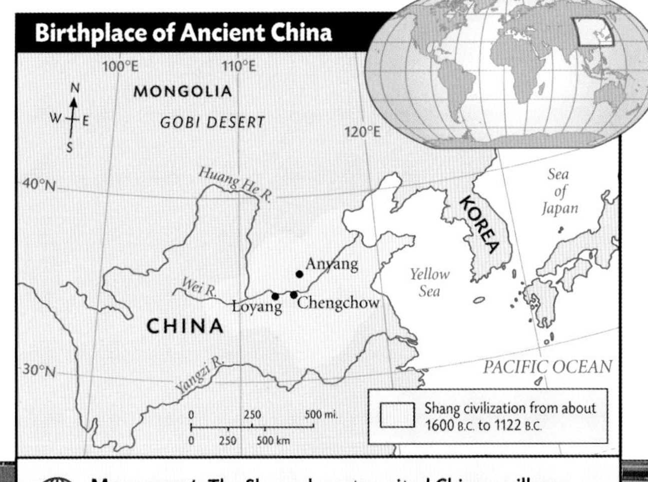

Movement The Shang dynasty united Chinese villages around 1600 B.C. *In what river valley did the dynasty begin?*

An army of terra cotta (baked clay) figures were buried at Xian, China, with Qin dynasty royalty. **How is Xian similar to other burial sites you have studied?**

A kneeling archer was part of the terra cotta army found at Xian. **What was a major success of that dynasty?**

Discussion Questions

1 Is a region's isolation helpful or harmful? What are the benefits and detriments of isolation?

2 Can you think of a time when the United States was isolationist?

3 What kind of figures were buried at Xian,China, with the Qin dynasty royalty?

4 Have we had a dynasty in the United States? What might be the benefits of one?

Caption Answer

The Shang dynasty began in the Huang He Valley.

Caption Answer

It is a royal tomb, carefully built and made to last, like the pyramids of Egypt. It contains artifacts that display how royal lives were led in both places.

Caption Answer

The Emperor Qin ordered the building of the Great Wall and developed a government bureaucracy.

Activity

Chinese Almond Cookies

 **OBJECTIVES:** 1.02

1 cup (8 oz.) lard, room temperature
1 egg
¾ teaspoon almond extract
½ cup sugar
1 cup packed brown sugar
2½ cups flour
1¼ teaspoons baking powder
50 to 55 whole blanched almonds
1 egg yolk, beaten

Preheat oven to 350°. In a bowl, beat together lard, egg, almond extract, sugar, and brown sugar until creamy. Add flour and baking powder, beat until well blended. Shape dough into 1 ¼-inch balls; place 2 inches apart on ungreased baking sheets. Press an almond in the center of each. Brush cookies with beaten egg yolk. Bake 14 to 15 minutes or until golden.

Background Information

The Qin Dynasty

The first ruler of the Qin Dynasty, Qin Shi Huangdi, ended the fighting among warring states when he seized power in 221 B.C. He created the first centralized feudal state in Chinese history. He standardized the written language, the currency, and weights and measures. In building the Great Wall, he improved communications and increased the Middle Kingdom's military capabilities. The towers spaced along the wall allowed messengers to communicate with distant villages not only on foot but by mirrors and smoke signals. The Great Wall also helped soldiers move quickly to trouble spots led by officers in horse-drawn carts.

Teacher Notes

Video Clip

If you have access to a video showing the Great Wall of China or the Terra Cotta Army, this is a good place for the class to view a brief clip.

Activity

Daoistic Beliefs

OBJECTIVES: 4.03, 7.02, 12.01

Daoists believe the human body holds two intertwining forces (ch'i)—yin and yang. The symbol for this dualistic energy is a circle with two equal teardrop shapes inside; one represents yin, the other yang. The yin teardrop has a small circle-drop of yang, and the yang has a drop of yin. Imbalance in yin and yang can cause discomfort and illness. If one is too yin or too yang, a balance is offered in food or medicine from the opposite life force. Foods fall into three categories: hot, cooling, and neutral. Cool foods include cucumbers, fruit, and watercress. Hot foods include chives, garlic, and pepper. Cool medicine is found in rhinoceros horn scrapings; hot in tifer-bone wine. The scrapings are used to cool a fever; the wine for aches and pains.

Several antonyms can be used to describe yin-ch'i and yang-ch'i:

yin	yang
passive	active
negative	positive
intuitive	intellectual
female	male
night	day
moon	sun
shady	sunny
cool/cold	warm/hot
moist/wet	arid/dry
earthly	celestial
dark	light
wood	fire
blue	red
*trigram one	*trigram eight

Early Chinese Achievements

Try to imagine the Fourth of July without fireworks. How would you survive in school without books? How did scientists measure earthquakes before electricity? Gunpowder for fireworks, a method for printing, and an ancient seismograph are examples of Chinese inventions. There are many more.

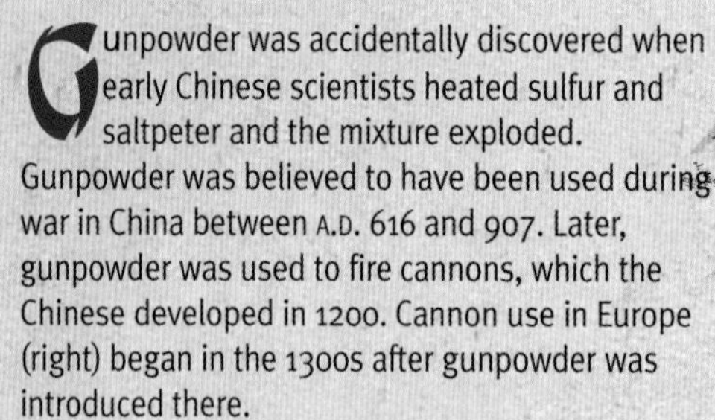

Gunpowder was accidentally discovered when early Chinese scientists heated sulfur and saltpeter and the mixture exploded. Gunpowder was believed to have been used during war in China between A.D. 616 and 907. Later, gunpowder was used to fire cannons, which the Chinese developed in 1200. Cannon use in Europe (right) began in the 1300s after gunpowder was introduced there.

Like gunpowder, paper, too, was kept a secret from Europeans. Bark, cloth, bits of netting, and pieces of hemp were boiled, rinsed, and pounded, then stretched on screens (left) to make paper—1,000 years before paper was used by Europeans. Paper was not made or used in Europe until the fourteenth century.

*A trigram consists of three lines, which can be either broken or solid; there are eight possible combinations.

Have students draw a yin/yang symbol about 6 to 8 inches in circumference. They should draw the small circle within each life force side at least 1½ inches in circumference. Using the above characteristics, list key words or write short phrases/fragments describing your yin and yang personality traits.

Tea is considered a yin beverage. Chinese drink their tea without milk or sugar. Older Chinese would not consider drinking iced tea. How is tea considered a yin drink if it is not iced?

A compass called a luopan measures the life forces of yin and yang. Have students research this, the magnetic compass (which the Chinese invented), and the color wheel to compare the similarities of these three circles.

hina led the world in producing fine pottery. Wealthy Western customers often ordered tableware with their own signs, such as this plate decorated with wers and tobacco leaves.

The ball, falling out of the dragons' jaws into the mouths of waiting frogs, enabled the Chinese to determine the direction of earthquakes. This early seismograph was invented by the Chinese 2,000 years ago.

The Great Wall of China (left) was buit by the Qin and Ming dynasties. Designed to keep out invaders, most of what remains today was built during the Ming period. The wall is the world's longest man-made structure, stretching 3,948 miles (6,352 km).

Eyewitness Activity

Chinese Inventions

OBJECTIVES: 8.03

After studying the different types of Chinese inventions, have students make a Chinese invention booklet with illustrations of the inventions and a brief summary of their uses and why they were important discoveries. The booklet should have a decorated cover with title and student's name and contain a different invention for each page.

Extension Do not assign novice and intermediate ELL students the summary. Instead, have them label the inventions and write one or two words or phrases describing what they are used for.

Activity

Museum Exhibit

OBJECTIVES: 8.03, 12.02

After reading the Eyewitness, assign students to create or bring from home artifacts to be included in a class museum exhibit on China. Students should label each item with a description of its relationship to China. Have the class organize the artifacts by criteria they determine. Invite parents to view the exhibit.

Teacher Notes

The Great Wall and the Moon

Many people claim that the Great Wall of China is the only man-made object visible from space. This, however, is a myth. In Richard Halliburton's 1938 book, *Second Book of Marvels*, he stated that the Great Wall of China is the only man-made object visible from the moon.

It is true that, from a low orbit of the earth, many artificial objects are visible on the earth (including such objects as highways, railroads, cities, crops, and even some individual buildings). At a low orbit the Great Wall of China can be seen from space, yet this is not unique.

From outside of Earth's orbit, no man-made objects are visible at all. NASA astronaut Alan Bean is quoted in Tom Burnam's book *More Misinformation*... "The only thing you can see from the moon is a beautiful sphere, mostly white (clouds), some blue (ocean), patches of yellow (deserts), and every once in a while some green vegetation. No man-made object is visible on this scale. In fact, when first leaving earth's orbit and only a few thousand miles away, no man-made object is visible at that point either."

Discussion Questions

1 What was the theory or idea of the Mandate of Heaven?

2 What happened to unjust emperors?

3 What was one area in which China led the world in production?

4 What three types of disasters showed that a dynasty had lost Heaven's favor?

5 What medical practice did the Chinese develop long ago?

6 What ideas guided all areas of government?

7 How does the size of China compare to that of the United States?

8 How many sailors, soldiers, and merchants sailed on China's expeditions?

Caption Answer

High-ranking officials surrounded the emperor in the capital while officers of lesser rank held office throughout the empire. By working together under the emperor's direction, the officials held together a vast empire.

Map Activity

Which is Really Larger?

NATIONAL GEOGRAPHY STANDARDS: 1

GEOGRAPHIC THEMES: Location

OBJECTIVES: 1.03

Have students note that, like many similar maps in the textbook, only the 48 contiguous United States are used in this comparison. Assign students to find out the land area of Alaska (*587,878 sq. mi./1,528,483 sq. km.*) and Hawaii (*6,459 sq. mi./16,793 sq. km.*). When the areas of Alaska and Hawaii are added to the contiguous 48, the total area of the United States (*3,717,796 sq. mi.*) turns out to be slightly larger than China's (*3,704,400 sq. mi.*). The difference, roughly 13,000 square miles, equals an area about twice the size of New Jersey.

Discuss how the difference in population influences the allocation of resources such as water and land for food production in each case.

Note to teacher: You may point out here that there are few dairy products available in China.

Acupuncture needles

Customs

Long ago, the Chinese developed a practice known as acupuncture, a method of inserting different-size needles into specific points of the body. The thin needles were whirled after insertion to lessen the pain or even cure disease. Today, Western medical researchers are carefully studying acupuncture and other traditional Chinese medical practices. Many of these researchers believe that the West can learn useful lessons from the Chinese.

The Mandate of Heaven

The Qin dynasty collapsed soon after the Emperor Qin died. Another ruling family took its place. This happened many times during the centuries to follow. Some dynasties were short-lived. Others survived for centuries. The Chinese explained these changes in rulers with a theory, or idea, called the ***Mandate of Heaven.***

Heaven (a force that controlled the universe) gave the emperor the mandate, or right, to rule. In exchange, the emperor had to rule wisely. He was to provide justice and protection. A wise emperor kept canals, dikes, and dams in good repair. The people were to obey emperors who gave them good government.

After dynasties had been in power for many years, emperors and their officials sometimes became dishonest and failed to provide good government. Unjust emperors lost their right to rule. Floods, droughts, civil wars, and other disasters showed a dynasty had lost Heaven's favor. People had no duty to support unjust rule. They could rebel to bring new rulers to power.

Confucian Control of the Bureaucracy

The Mandate of Heaven reflects the Confucian idea that rulers must lead the people in a moral and upright way. Confucian ideas guided all areas of government.

Soon after the Qin dynasty fell, emperors began using officials educated i[n] Confucian thought. In time, the government set up an examination syste[m]. To win a government job, young men ha[d] to study for years and then pass difficult exams. This system meant that government officials were well trained in Confucian ideas. Thus, while dynasties rose and fell, the government itself changed little. These officials followed Confucian traditions no matter who was emperor.

A Giant Empire

High-ranking Confucian officials surrounded the emperor in his capital cit[y]. Officials of lesser rank held office throughout the empire. By working together under the emperor's direction, these officials formed a government system that could hold together a vast empire.

China's Size

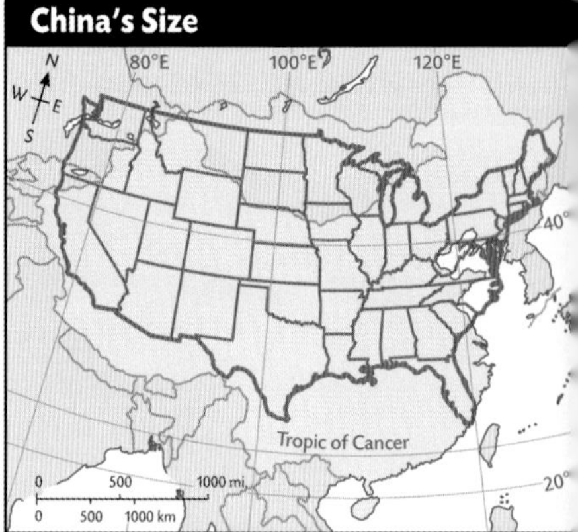

Location China is larger than the continental United States. *How did its early rulers run such a large territory?*

Teacher Notes

Acupuncture Feature

The Customs Box on page 398 provides an interesting opportunity for a guest speaker. Many chiropractors and other health care providers are licensed to practice acupuncture. Invite an acupuncturist to your class. If you are up for it, allow for a demonstration and discussion on this ancient healing art.

Bureaucracy

Point out to your class that since the Confucian-trained bureaucracy remained in place even while emperors changed, Chinese government was quite stable. Though some of your students may see this connection outright, not all will. If you have been discussing governmental stability (or lack thereof) in the non-Western world during the course of the year, this is a good example of stability.

Old China's size changed many times. Early in its history, China's empire was based in China's northern plain (see map, page 401). At other times, Chinese authority extended into modern-day Vietnam and into territory now claimed by Russia. Today, China claims borders that began to take shape in the 1600s. The map on the previous page compares the size of China to the United States.

Trade and Technology

China sent several seagoing expeditions to Southeast Asia and into the Indian Ocean in the 1400s. The largest of these boasted 62 major ships and hundreds of smaller ones. Altogether, 28,000 sailors, soldiers, and merchants sailed with the fleet.

A compass—a device that sailors were just beginning to use—guided the ships to Africa's eastern shore. There Chinese merchants traded for various African goods while zebras, giraffes, and other unusual examples of African wildlife were collected for the emperor.

This might have been for its time the largest fleet ever assembled. No other country in the world in the 1400s could have put such a fleet on the seas or have sent it so far. Yet China soon abandoned such activities. Historians think that China may have put an end to them because Chinese leaders did not think that they served any useful purpose. These leaders believed that China had everything the people needed.

They had good reasons for thinking that this was true. The country's population was growing. Between the 1300s and early 1800s, China's population increased from about 60 million to 410 million. The increase reflected a steady increase in food supply. Centuries earlier, farmers in southern China had learned how to grow two crops of rice a year. In areas where rain was scarce, farmers used advanced engineering techniques to irrigate land.

Long before railways, highways, and aircraft, China profited from a remarkable transportation system. The Yangzi River carried boats from the coast more than 1,500 miles (2,415 km) into the interior. Other rivers, canals, and coastal shipping enabled Chinese to move agricultural produce, timber, metal goods, and an enormous variety of crafts from one region to another. Before the 1800s, Old China dominated East Asia. The Middle Kingdom was large, rich in ideas, and prosperous.

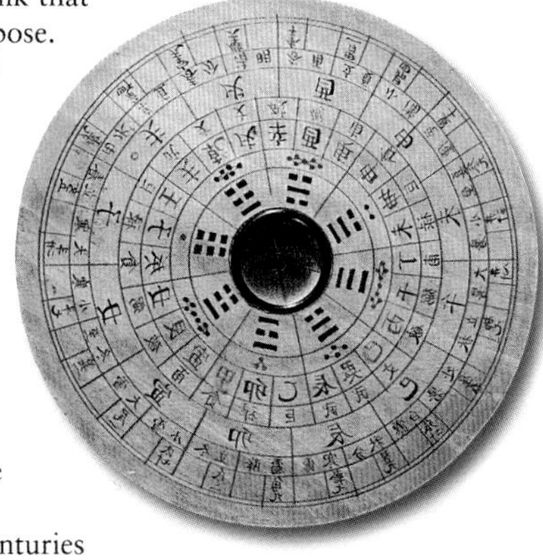

Chinese scientists used this compass to study the stars and to navigate. **Where did Chinese ships explore?**

LESSON 2 REVIEW

Fact Follow-Up

1. What was the Mandate of Heaven? How did it affect Chinese government?
2. What did the first emperor of the Qin dynasty do that affected Chinese government for thousands of years?
3. Describe China's technological achievements.
4. Why can Old China be described as "large, rich in ideas, and prosperous"?

Talk About It

1. Despite changes in dynasties, Chinese ways of governing did not change for thousands of years. Why?
2. Would the Great Wall have been built if there had not been a Chinese governmental bureaucracy? Explain.
3. Would you have supported China's decision to abandon overseas expeditions? Explain.

Discussion Questions

1. What were some of the inventions and contributions of the Chinese?
2. Do you think Middle Kingdom is an accurate description of China?
3. Where did the device [a compass] lead Chinese sailors?
4. What types of African goods were collected for the emperor?
5. In the 1400s, what was significant about China's fleet?
6. What was the increase in the size of China's population from the 1300s to the early 1800s?

Caption Answer

Southeast Asia, the Indian Ocean, and the east coast of Africa.

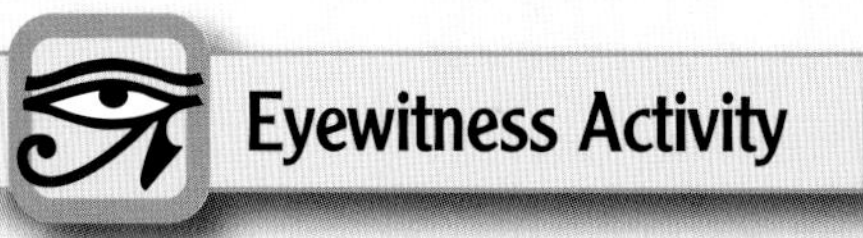

Eyewitness Activity

Economy and Transportation

NATIONAL GEOGRAPHY STANDARDS:

GEOGRAPHIC THEMES:

OBJECTIVES: 1.02, 4.02

Map Skills: Using a physical map of China, have students plot out an itinerary for a trading expedition on the Yangzi River. If you would prefer to have them create a more involved product, form groups and have them create trade companies. They should decide what types of goods or services they will trade. Have them calculate provisions for their trip, and so on. This activity can be as simple or as detailed as you wish.

LESSON 2 REVIEW

Fact Follow-Up Answers

1. The Mandate of Heaven was a theory about changes in dynasty. So long as the emperor ruled wisely, according to this idea, he would retain Heaven's permission to rule. When catastrophes (including floods, droughts, or civil war) occurred, people assumed that the dynasty had lost the Mandate of Heaven, and they rebelled or ceased to respect the government.
2. He created a government bureaucracy to carry out his orders throughout the empire.
3. The Chinese developed gunpowder, an early form of seismograph, paper, block printing, and calendars.
4. The empire was huge, its people were inventive, and the transportation system enabled China to become prosperous through trade.

Talk About It Answers

1. Confucian ideals guided all areas of government. Because of the government bureaucracy established according to these ideals, government policies and activities remained pretty much the same in spite of the rise and fall of dynasties.
2. Important points: Students should take a position and explain it. Bureaucracy made long-range planning and long-distance cooperation possible.
3. Important points: Students should choose a position and explain why. Overseas expeditions meant contact with the ideas of other cultures, as well as trade and exploration. China believed it had no need of the outside world, but it could be argued that without new ideas, there can be no growth.

OBJECTIVES: 8.01, 9.01, 10.01

Discussion Questions

1 What is a hero?

2 What qualities do you think a hero must have?

3 What was significant about China's revolutionary hero?

4 What two forces helped bring Old China down?

5 What party came to power in China in 1949?

Caption Answer

He meant that China had taken a first step toward recovery of power in the world.

Activity

Modern China Time Line

OBJECTIVES: 7.01

After completing the lesson have students review by creating a time line using this and other information.

1911: End of Qing Dynasty; a republic is established.
1927: Civil War begins between the Nationalists and the Communists.
1949: Communists take over mainland; Nationalists retreat to Taiwan.
1971: United Nations recognizes mainland China as official China.
1920: Mao Zedong begins his branch of Communist Party.
1934: Long March of 6,000 miles by nearly defeated Communists.
1936: Nationalists and Communists join together against the Japanese invaders.
1937–45: China fights Japanese as part of World War II.
1950: China joins North Koreans against United Nations forces, leading to stalemate in Korean War.
1958: China's farms are collectivized.
1960: China and Russia are no longer allies.
1962: Brief war with India.
1967: Height of the Cultural Revolution.

Assign pairs (or small groups) of students to research these events.

LESSON 3 Revolutionary China

KEY IDEAS

- Pressures from inside China and from foreign powers helped topple the Qing dynasty. Under the Nationalist Party, China tried to build a modern nation.
- In 1949, the Chinese Communists defeated the Nationalists. Under Mao Zedong and his successors, China began to build a modern economy.

KEY TERMS

Chiang Kai-shek
Mao Zedong
opium
revolution
semi-colonial status
spheres of influence
Sun Yat-sen
Three Principles of the People

China's revolutionary hero, ***Mao Zedong*** (mau zee·DUNG) stood before cheering crowds in Beijing, October 1, 1949. "The Chinese people," he declared, "one-quarter of the human race, have stood up." Mao then declared the birth of the People's Republic of China (PRC).

Unlike the emperor who had lectured King George III, Mao spoke when Old China's glory was gone. China was a weak, divided, and humiliated nation. When he proclaimed that China had "stood up," Mao meant China had taken a first step toward recovery. With the people behind him, Mao promised, China would once again be a respected power.

China's Time of Troubles

What had happened in the 1800s to bring Old China down? Some of China's troubles began because of serious problems within the country. Others came from the outside.

Troubles at Home

Early in the 1800s, Chinese officials of the Qing (ching) dynasty faced an increasingly angry people. Peasant farmer complained that they were losing ownership of their farms. To earn a living they had to rent land and pay landowner high prices. Many farmers were driven from the land and became beggars. Bandits roamed the countryside, stealing whatever they could find. People seemed to be always hungry.

These angry people began to organize into rebel armies and attacked army garrisons throughout the country. Beijing managed to crush some of these uprisings.

One uprising in central China threatened to topple the government. For several years, China lost control of part c the Yangzi River valley—one of the country's richest regions. By the time this rebellion was finally crushed, many Chinese believed the Qing dynasty had lost the Mandate of Heaven.

Mao Zedong led the Communist revolution in 1949. **What did Mao mean when he said, "The Chinese people ... have stood up."?**

China and the West

China faced threats from the outside, too. Europeans had been trading with China for 300 years. China strictly controlled foreign merchants. The foreigners had to obey Chinese rules and could trade only at Canton (present-day Guangzhou).

By the 1800s, European nations were becoming powerful. They wanted to end China's restrictions on trade. Chinese

Teacher Notes

Taiwan and China

Since 1949, Taiwan has been the base of two governments: Taiwan's provincial government operating under the Republic of China (ROC) and the ROC, a government that claims to be China's legitimate national leader, that has been temporarily displaced. The ROC and "mainland" China, called the People's Republic of China (PRC) agree that Taiwan is legitimately part of China. The two regimes have differed—and (officially) continue to disagree—on which of them is the legitimate government of both the Chinese mainland and Taiwan.

oods—silk, tea, and fine porcelain—sold or high profits in Europe. Europeans anted to expand trade to all ports along e China coast.

The British tried to increase their rofits by selling ***opium*** grown in India to e Chinese. Opium is a drug that can be sed for medicine. But in the 1800s, many hinese, as well as others, were abusing pium by smoking it.

Chinese authorities cracked down on e opium trade. The British went to war nd defeated Chinese forces. This defeat owed that China was weak.

Europe did not turn China into olonies as they did elsewhere in Asia and frica, but European nations signed eaties that gave them special rights in hina. In some regions of China, for xample, they claimed spheres of influence ee map on page 408). The ***pheres of influence*** were areas where reigners could open mines, build ailways, and conduct other business with ttle Chinese interference.

Foreigners won rights to travel and ve in China without being subject to hinese laws. Foreign nations built naval ases on Chinese soil. Foreign warships entered Chinese harbors and patrolled Chinese rivers without asking China's permission. Technically, China remained an independent nation. Yet the Chinese had turned over so many rights to foreign powers, the nation was reduced to a ***semi-colonial status.*** That is, China had given up much of its power to other nations. Increasingly, the Chinese came to resent foreigners in their land.

Word Origins

Porcelain, or chinaware as it is sometimes called, came originally from China. The word porcelain comes from porcellana, which is the name given it by Marco Polo. Porcelain, like other pottery, is made from clay. But the clay and firing methods used by Chinese to produce porcelain made it different from all other pottery. Porcelain was especially hard and, if finished with a white glaze, permitted light to pass through it.

British troops capture Chin Kiang Foo in Kiansu Province during the Opium War. **What was the result of China's defeat in that war?**

Discussion Questions

1 Based on China's experiences with the West in the late 1800s, do you think the present relationship between China and the West was inevitable?

2 "Saving face" (honor) is very important to the Chinese. What did the West do that caused the Chinese to feel as though they had "lost face"?

3 By the 1800s Europe put an end to China's what?

4 Why was there a market for opium in China?

5 What area did the British troops capture during the Opium War?

Caption Answer

Foreigners won rights to travel and live in China without being subject to Chinese law.

Teacher Notes

Health Connection—Drug Education Curriculum

Speak to a health teacher in your building. If your county has a requirement for classroom teachers to teach a certain number of lessons on drugs and alcohol, this lesson is a good starting point. Using the Opium War as an introduction, have students research the effects of the drug opium on the human body. Discuss with them the dangers of sedative, narcotic drugs. Research other narcotic drugs. You could do an interdisciplinary lesson with the health teacher on this topic.

Imperialism in China

Although the Chinese tried to avoid contact with other parts of the world, the British, French, Germans, Japanese, and Russians forced them to trade. The spheres of influence were areas where the above countries would open mines, build railways, and conduct other business with little Chinese interference. The Chinese were forced to accept Western ways. This angered the Chinese.

Background Information

Evaluating Mao Zedong

Historians continue to debate Mao's role as leader of China's Communist revolution. Some judge him harshly for the famines that caused millions of death following the 1958 Great Leap Forward. Others fault him for the chaos and devastation that accompanied the Cultural Revolution. Many others, however, argue that his faults are outweighed by the role he played in transforming China into a modern industrial nation. Book reviewer and journalist John F. Burns made this assessment: "Mao was a political and military genius who remade the most populous nation on earth and placed it…on the path to modernity. But he also devastated the lives of tens of millions of his countrymen…many of whom still struggle with the consequences."

Discussion Questions

1 What does democracy mean to you?

2 What are the three most important principles to you?

3 What were the three principles or organizing ideas for the modern Nationalist Party?

4 Who became the new leader of the modern Nationalist Party after Sun died in 1926?

Caption Answer

The Nationalist Party

Caption Answer

Semicolonial status

Activity

Sun Yat-Sen's Three Principles of the People

OBJECTIVES: 8.01, 9.02, 13.01

Hold a class discussion on nationalism, democracy, and livelihood. What do your students think about these abstractions? Do they think they were good rallying points for Sun to gain supporters? What are the connections of the Three Principles of the People to life in the United States? Start the discussion with a brainstorming activity of what these three words mean to the class. Web them out on an overhead or board. Have class recorders help out so all ideas can be listed.

Sun Yat-sen combined Western and Chinese ideas about government. **His Three Principles became the foundation for what new political party?**

China's Revolution Begins

The Qing dynasty struggled unsuccessfully to find remedies for China's problems. As troubles grew, the dynasty's support evaporated. In 1911, the Qing government collapsed, leaving China, for the next few years, without any true central authority.

Eventually, new national leaders emerged. ***Sun Yat-sen*** (soon yee·SHYAHN) became the first such leader. Sun wanted to build a strong modern nation by blending Chinese and Western ideas abou government. In his ***Three Principles of the People,*** he called for nationalism, democracy, and livelihood. Nationalism meant loyalty to China, not just to one's family or village. Democracy meant creating a representative government. Livelihood meant providing a decent standard of living for all Chinese.

Sun's Three Principles became the organizing ideas for a modern Nationalis Party. For a few years, the Nationalist Party and the Chinese Communist Party joined in an effort to regain control of China. The alliance did not last. The parties split in 1927 and became bitter enemies.

Spheres of Influence in China, 1914

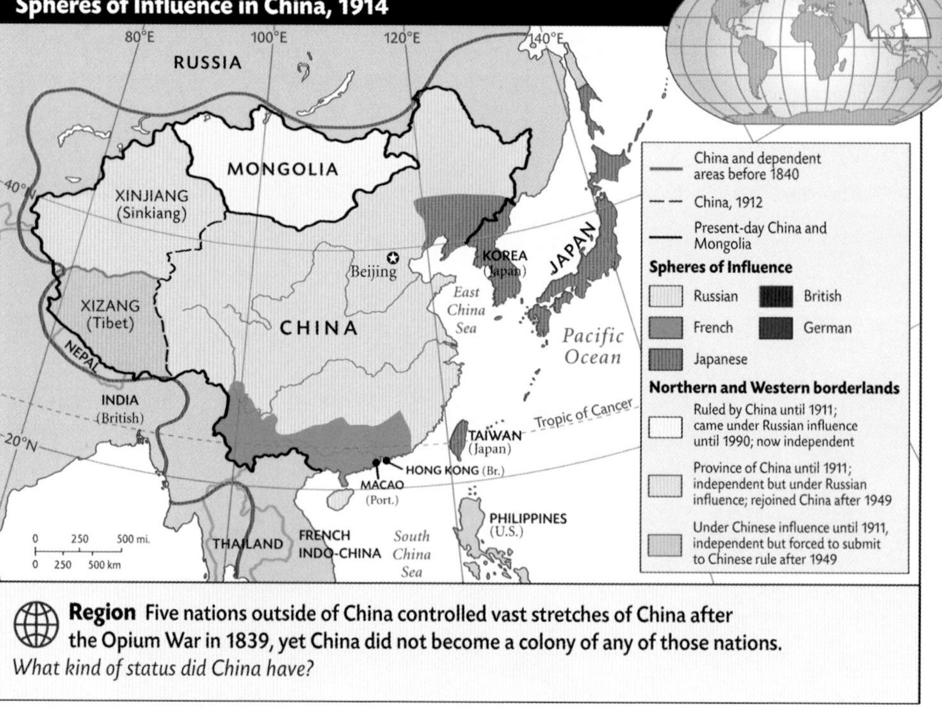

Region **Five nations outside of China controlled vast stretches of China after the Opium War in 1839, yet China did not become a colony of any of those nations.**
What kind of status did China have?

Activity

Who Controlled What in China?

NATIONAL GEOGRAPHY STANDARDS: 1, 17

GEOGRAPHIC THEMES: Location, Region

OBJECTIVES: 1.01

1. Have students identify the five nations that controlled large areas of China after the Opium War during the nineteenth century. (*Britain, France, Germany, Japan, Russia*)
2. What can you note about China and its dependent areas before 1840 compared to China today? (*area China dominated was much larger during the Ch'ing Dynasty—1644–1911—than present day China claims; Manchus ruled the Ch'ing era being the most vast of all China's dynasties, including portions of today's Russia, South and Southeast Asia*)
3. What areas of China today were not included in their territory in 1912? (*Xinjiang [Sinkiang], Xizang [Tibet]*)
4. In 1914, which nation controlled the largest area of China? (*Russia*) the territory along the Korean border? (*Japan*) much of the area along the Yangzi (*Chang Jiang*)? (*Britain*) the island of Hainan and much of the area along the South China Sea? (*France*) the smallest area of China? (*Germany*)
5. Mongolia was referred to as "Outer Mongolia" at times from 1600 to early 1900. Which sphere of influence included "Inner Mongolia"? (*Russia; just as all Mongolia—Outer and Inner—was influenced by Russia/Soviet Union until 1990*) Is Mongolia a part of China today? (*no; after the Chinese Revolu-*

Sun and his followers established a ıse in southern China and began to build ı army. After Sun died in 1926, *Chiang Kai-Shek,* the Nationalist Party's ew leader, marched his army northward ıto the Yangzi Valley and into central hina. By 1927, Chiang had gained ıough support to form a new overnment. Many rival leaders, however, pposed this government. Among the pposition leaders was Mao Zedong, a ember of the Chinese Communist Party.

For the next ten years, Chiang tried to accomplish two goals—to establish a strong foundation for his government and to destroy the Chinese Communist Party. Between 1927 and 1937, Chiang enjoyed some success in rebuilding China as an independent nation. He negotiated treaties that ended some of the special rights claimed by foreigners in China. His government regained authority in China.

A Journey to SOUTH CHINA

Life Aboard a Junk

On the south coast of China and in other coastal Southeast Asian countries, you will find families living aboard boats. Called junks, these flat-bottomed fishing vessels are where many families make their living by fishing (below).

In past years, families lived and worked aboard the boats with only sails to catch the wind and only the sky to tell them what the weather might be. Now radios broadcast the weather. Some junks have diesel engines.

The junk is a permanent home for families. Most live all their lives on the water. No living space can be wasted. Families crowd together with food, clothing, beds, fishing equipment, and the fish they catch. When they sail on rivers and bays to fish, families have to know exactly how much food is needed for each day. Only necessary amounts of food can be carried along. Even the large junks that fish in the open water have limited space for family living. Most of the space is taken up by fishing equipment or the catch.

Cooking utensils and fuel are carried along. Water for tea, cooking, and washing dishes is dipped from alongside the junk. For fishing trips in a salty sea, families bring water with them.

Huge nylon nets are used to catch eels and fish. Smaller nets are dipped into shallow waters. In southern China, large tame birds called cormorants also are used in shallow waters. The cormorants spot fish beneath the water's surface and dive to catch them. The fishermen place rings around the cormorants' necks to keep them from swallowing their catches.

Hundreds of thousands of Chinese are born, live, and die on junks that never go anywhere. They are tied together and anchored to shore in crowded ports.

tion and with Russian help Mongolia declared its independence in 1921)

6. What 1949 event made Xinjiang (Sinkiang) and Xizang (Tibet) part of China? (*Communist revolution occurred; Mao Zedong proclaimed the People's Republic of China. Also, the Soviet Union signed 30-year alliance, friendship, and mutual assistance treaty with China.*)

Teacher Notes

Mao's Legacy

Many Chinese citizens appreciate what Mao Zedong did to modernize their country. However, while they are thankful for his leadership, they do not like what happened during the Cultural Revolution. One Chinese tour guide said, "Mao Zedong is 60 percent good, 40 percent bad. We never forgive him for the Cultural Revolution but we thank him for making China a modern country."

Discussion Questions

1 What were the two goals that Chiang tried to accomplish?

2 What type of boat do some Chinese families lived on?

Activity

Life Aboard a Junk

OBJECTIVES: 3.01, 4.03, 6.01, 6.02

Ask students to draft a practice essay on the topic of junks.

Clarification: Would you like to live on a junk? Why or why not?

Point of View: People should or should not live their entire lives on junks.

Descriptive: Describe what life on a junk is like. Describe it so that someone who has never heard of a junk could picture it.

Alternate Activity Have novice and intermediate ELL students draw a picture of what they think it would be like to live aboard a junk with their family.

Activity

Chinese Junk

OBJECTIVES: 3.01

Along rivers and in harbors of Japan, China, and other Southeast Asian countries, many families live on small, lightweight fishing boats called junks. These directions are to make a junk that will float/sail.

Materials junk pattern from the Teacher's Resource Guide, scissors, wax crayons, glue

Directions

Cut out the pattern. Color the outside of the pattern with a wax crayon to waterproof it (more heavily colored—more waterproof). Crease along the dotted lines. Glue tabs to the inside of the ends of the boat. Cut a rectangular piece approximately 3-inches by 2½-inches for the cabin. Glue the ends of the rectangular ends into the inside bottom of the junk.

Discussion Questions

1 Why do you think World War II changed the balance of power between the Nationalists and the Communists?

2 For many years the United States government recognized the government on Taiwan as the legitimate one of China. What caused the United States to finally recognize the People's Republic of China as the official government?

3 What two areas did the Japanese seize in China?

4 What year did Mao's forces triumph over Japan?

5 What two areas did Mao first rebuild to start toward recovery?

Caption Answer

Mao wanted to remake Chinese political, social, and economic life through communism. He wanted to make China a modern industrial power.

ELL Teaching Tips

Print Rather Than Write in Cursive

New ELL students may know the English alphabet but will probably not be able to read cursive writing. Either print or type all notes and assignments to ensure comprehension for your ELLs.

China rebuilt after World War II. The hard work of rail building, like most labor, was done by hand. **After Mao took power, what other kinds of changes did he want to make in China?**

War with Japan

Chiang's hopes to rebuild China were destroyed by Japanese invasion. In 1931, Japan's army seized Manchuria, then marched into northern China. In 1937, Japan attacked Chinese forces along the coast. This opened a war on the Chinese mainland that lasted until 1945.

These long years of war changed the fortunes of China's two rival parties—the Nationalists and the Communists. Before the war broke out, Chiang's government clearly had been the major political force. His Nationalist forces nearly defeated the Chinese Communists. When the war ended, the Communists, now led by Mao Zedong, had won a strong following among the farmers and maintained control of northern China.

Mao's China

With Japan's surrender, Nationalist and Communist forces renewed their figh for control. By 1949, Mao's forces had won the ***revolution***, or overthrow of an existing government by those subject to i Some of Chiang's forces escaped to the island of Taiwan. Chiang reestablished hi government on Taiwan. He still hoped to again rule all of China.

Meanwhile, Mao Zedong declared th birth of the People's Republic of China (see map, page 395). To revolutionize China, the government had to rebuild after the war's destruction. Mao first concentrated on repairing railways and factories. These efforts brought substanti recovery.

Above all, Mao wanted to remake Chinese political, social, and economic lif through communism. He wanted to mak China a modern industrial nation that could join the ranks of world powers.

Mao proposed that China make a "great leap forward" in 1958. The plan called for the Chinese to build new factories and change the agriculture system. But Mao did not trust experts, so did not listen to their advice. The steel factories based on his ideas failed. The new farming techniques failed as well. China could not grow enough food to fee its people. A massive famine in 1960 and 1961 killed 20 million Chinese.

Although Mao stirred China's revolutionary spirit, the Great Leap Forward is seen as one of his failures.

LESSON 3 REVIEW

Fact Follow-Up

1. How did internal changes and foreign pressure cause the Qing dynasty to lose the Mandate of Heaven?
2. What occurred to reduce China to semicolonial status?
3. What were Sun's Three Principles of the People? What did they mean?

Talk About It

1. Chinese resentment of foreigners became one reason Chiang and Mao could rally popular support. Explain why this happened.
2. Describe Chiang Kai-shek's efforts to rebuild China.

LESSON 3 REVIEW

Fact Follow-Up Answers

1. Rebellion in the countryside led by beggars and farmers who feared losing their land threatened to topple the government. Foreign (European) nations wanting to expand trade with China on their own terms made threats and ultimately carved out spheres of influence in the nation. The dynasty's support evaporated, and the government collapsed.
2. Determined to expand trade, the British began selling Indian opium in China. When Chinese authorities cracked down on the trade, the British fought Chinese forces over the right to sell opium in China. As a result of the British victory, European nations won special rights in China. China was reduced to semicolonial status.
3. The Three Principles of the People were nationalism, democracy, and livelihood. Nationalism meant loyalty to China, not just to one's family or village. Democracy meant creating a representative government. Livelihood meant providing a decent standard of living for all Chinese.
4. Chiang wanted to rebuild China as an independent nation. Chiang negotiated treaties that ended some of the special rights claimed by foreigners in China. His government also regained authority in China. Chiang's hopes to rebuild China were destroyed by Japanese expansion and the growing strength of the Chinese Communist Party.

Talk About It Answers

1. Resentment of foreigners was linked to disapproval of the Qing government and led to its collapse. During the time China was without a true central authority, Chiang and Mao rallied popular support and established their bases of support for a new government.

Analyzing, Interpreting, Creating, and Using Resources and Materials

Obstacles to Development

In previous units you have learned about the variety of religions throughout Africa, South Asia, and Southwest Asia. In the unit on South Asia you read about the differences among Hinduism, Islam, and Buddhism. In the unit on Southwest Asia you saw how Christianity, Islam, and Judaism compared. You read about traditional religious practices in the units on Africa.

In this chapter you learned about Confucianism and Daoism. They were described as belief systems, and not religions. What is the difference? To discover the answer, it might be helpful to chart the characteristics of the religions and belief systems.

Here is an explanation of each category used to compare religions and belief systems:

Beliefs—What are the key beliefs of the religion or belief system?

Rules for Life—How are believers supposed to apply morality to their lives?

Duty to convert?—Are followers expected to convince other people to join their religion or belief system?

Supreme Being?—What does the religion or belief system teach about the existence of a Supreme Being?

Ceremonies—How do believers express their beliefs in public?

Status of women—What does the religion or belief system teach about the standing of women?

Create a graphic organizer similar to the one below. Your text contains information to complete the table (see index to find information), but you might need to do additional research.

Confucianism and Daoism give moral guidelines to their followers. Religions also give moral directions to their faithful. But there are differences.

What characteristics are shared by religions and belief systems? Does your completed graphic organizer help you see the difference between belief systems and religions?

Comparing Belief Systems and Religions

	Belief Systems		Religions		
	Confucianism	Daoism	Buddhism	Hinduism	Traditional religions
Beliefs					
Rules for Life					
Duty to convert?					
Supreme Being?					
Ceremonies					
Status of women					

Skill Lesson Review

1. What did you find to be the most significant difference between religions and belief systems? Why? *Answers will vary. Religions identify people culturally and gather them together in ritual. Belief systems operate as an ethical framework in society.*
2. What information in your graphic organizer most helped you reach your conclusion? Why? *Answers will vary. Beliefs and rules for life might resemble each other in both religions and belief systems, but ceremonies and the questions of conversion would be different.*
3. What other kinds of information would you have wanted to help you reach a clear understanding of the differences? *Answers will vary. Discuss as a class.*

Teaching This Skill Lesson

Materials Needed textbooks, large sheets of paper, pencils, rulers

Classroom Organization whole class, small groups

Beginning the Lesson Ask students what a religion or a religious group is. Accept all answers, recording them on the chalkboard. Encourage students to respond beyond their own religious orientation, mentioning Buddhism, Hinduism, and other religious groups. Then ask what a belief system is, mentioning Confucianism and Daoism. Help students see some differences between religions and belief systems. Have students look at the data retrieval chart on page 411. Make sure they understand the criteria on the chart.

Lesson Development Students may complete their charts in class or as a homework assignment.

Conclusion When students return with completed charts, place them in small groups to compare and "polish" their charts. Ask: What are differences between religions and belief systems? What are similarities?

Extension Assign peer tutors to assist intermediate ELL students as needed.

Talk About It

1. These principles of filial piety became the basis for family security and structure in society. Both the family and the wider society believed that individuals were not equal and that everybody must pursue their duties. Later, Confucian ideas of government further developed these ideals.
2. Confucius believed in leadership through example ("As the wind blows, so bows the grass"). The Mandate of Heaven reflects the Confucian idea that rulers must lead the people in a moral and upright way for the well-being of the nation. If calamities occur, therefore, it must be because the leader is unworthy.
3. Daoists believed in restraint in government. A Confucian might believe that government must be moral and also believe it must be limited if that was best for the people.
4. Confucian scholars were trained in ethics and morality. They could advise the emperor in important decisions that might affect the emperor's ability to continue to lead his people.
5. Important points: Students should state whether this was a wise decision and explain it. Note: The exchange of ideas often helps to refine them. Diverse cultures and new ideas are useful for any society, however advanced, to continue improving.
6. Important points: Students should state which pressure was, in their opinion, more important and explain why. Foreign interference reduced the power of the government, but internal struggles had already weakened it.

CHAPTER 20 REVIEW

Lessons Learned

LESSON 1
Ideas and Faiths
In Old China, filial piety, the respect owed one's family, was the basis for family security and structure in society. Confucius taught moral directions that brought family values into society. The emperor was to act as a good father. Daoism and a variety of religions also affected Chinese society.

LESSON 2
The Middle Kingdom
Chinese civilization began early through the development of cities, writing, arts, crafts, and science. The Qin dynasty began a bureaucracy which later was controlled by Confucian beliefs that lasted through many dynasties for more than 2,000 years. The bureaucracy helped make possible advances in technology unmatched at that time by any place in the world.

LESSON 3
Revolutionary China
Discontent among the people and pressure from Europeans to end trade restrictions ended the Qing dynasty. Sun Yat-sen's Three Principles of the People laid down basic ideas for modern China. Chiang Kai-shek was the first leader to attempt to build a modern government. His efforts were interrupted by Japanese invaders. After war with Japan, the Chinese Communists, led by Mao Zedong, defeated Chiang Kai-shek.

Talk About It

1. How did the two ideals of family—unequal relationships and duties—affect society in Old China? Explain.
2. Confucius said "As the wind blows, so bows the grass." How does this description of leadership help with an understanding of the Mandate of Heaven?
3. How could followers of Confucius also follow the Daoist philosophies of government?
4. Why did Chinese emperors believe they needed Confucian scholars to maintain the Mandate of Heaven?
5. Historians think that China dropped overseas expeditions because the world had nothing China needed. If this is true, was this a wise decision? Explain.
6. The Qing dynasty's collapse in 1911 came from internal and foreign pressures on the government. Which of these pressures—internal or external—was most important?

Mastering Mapwork

LOCATION

Use the map on page 395 to answer these questions:

1. What large city is located near 40°N?
2. Through what autonomous region does the Tropic of Cancer pass?
3. What provincial city is located nearest 30°N, 120°E?
4. What is the relative location of Shanghai?
5. Describe the relative location of Qinghai province.

412 Chapter 2

Mastering Mapwork

1. Beijing is at this location.
2. The Tropic of Cancer passes through Guangxi Zhuang Autonomous Region.
3. Hangzhou is at this location.
4. Shanghai is located on the east coast of China on a peninsula reaching into the East China Sea, roughly midway between Beijing in the north and Guangzhou in the south.
5. Qinghai province is located in the interior of China south of Mongolia. It is bounded on the west and northwest by the Xinjiaing Autonomous Region and on the southwest by the Xizang Autonomous Region, by Sichuan province on the southeast, and by Gansu province on the east and northeast. It lies on a line directly north of Myanmur (Burma).

Interpreting Sayings

Read the selected sayings attributed to Confucius from The Analects *below. Answer the questions using specific references to the sayings.* The Analects *is a collection of the words and acts of Confucius and his followers. His teachings value morality, honor in relationships, justice, and sincerity.*

The Master said, "It is only the truly virtuous man, who can love, or who can hate, others."

The Master said, "If the will be set on virtue, there will be no practice of wickedness."

The Master said, "Riches and honors are what men desire. If they cannot be obtained in the proper way, they should not be held. Poverty and meanness are what men dislike. If they cannot be avoided in the proper way, they should not be avoided.

"If a superior man abandon virtue, how can he fulfill the requirements of that name?"

The Master said, "The superior man, in the world, does not set his mind either for anything, or against anything; what is right he will follow."

The Master said, "The superior man thinks of virtue; the small man thinks of comfort. The superior man thinks of the sanctions of law; the small man thinks of favors which he may receive."

The Master said: "He who acts with a constant view to his own advantage will be much murmured against."

The Master said, "A man should say, I am not concerned that I have no place, I am concerned how I may fit myself for one. I am not concerned that I am not known, I seek to be worthy to be known."

The Master said, "The mind of the superior man is conversant with righteousness; the mind of the mean man is conversant with gain."

The Master said, "When we see men of worth, we should think of equaling them; when we see men of a contrary character, we should turn inwards and examine ourselves."

The Master said, "The cautious seldom err." The Master said, "The superior man wishes to be slow in his speech and earnest in his conduct."

The Master said, "Virtue is not left to stand alone. He who practices it will have neighbors."

Questions

1. What can you tell about Confucius and his beliefs?
2. What is the common theme in these selected sayings attributed to Confucius?
3. What do you think Confucius means when he says, "If [riches and honors] cannot be obtained in the proper way, they should not be held."?

Go to the Source

Go to the Source

OBJECTIVES: 8.01, 10.02, 10.04, 11.02
Skills 2.02, 3.05, 4.06

Confucious' teachings are not strictly religious. Instead, they offer a practical guide to promoting social harmony. They also serve as moral guidlines between people and social systems. The analects was published after his death. Over time, the sayings have been added to. Therefore, many sayings attributed to him are probably only loosely based on his teachings.

For a link to these and other sayings, visit **NCJourneys.com.**

ANSWERS

1. Confucius is concerned about virtuous behavior and about behaving in ethical and wise ways.
2. Truth, virtuous behavior, and wisdom from truthfulness are important themes presented.
3. He possibly means that if people want riches and honor they should obtain those things through honest and truthful practices. Dishonest people do not deserve riches and honor.

How to Use the Chapter Review

There are three sections in the Chapter Review: Talk About It, Mastering Mapwork, and Go to the Source. Use the Vocabulary Worksheets and the Chapter Review Worksheet in the Teacher's Resource Guide for additional reinforcement and preparation for the Chapter Assessments. The chapter and lesson reviews and the Chapter Review Worksheets are the basis of the assessment for each chapter.

Talk About It questions encourage students to speculate about the content of the chapter and are suitable for class or small-group discussion. They are not intended to be assigned for homework.

Mastering Mapwork has students apply one or more of the Five Themes of Geography to maps within the chapter.

Go to the Source activities allow students to analyze a primary source that relates to the content of the chapter. The questions and activities familiarize students with different types of primary sources and also build content-reading skills.

China Today

Social Studies Strands

Economic Development
- Industry and technology
- Economic growth
- Environment
- Intensive farming
- Double cropping

Cultures and Diversity
- Cultural arts

Global Connections

North Carolina Standard Course of Study

Goal 3 The learner will analyze the impact of interactions between humans and their physical environments in Africa, Asia, and Australia.

Goal 6 The learner will recognize the relationship between economic activity and the quality of life in Africa, Asia, and Australia.

Goal 10 The learner will compare the rights and civic responsibilities of individuals in political structures in Africa, Asia, and Australia.

Goal 12 The learner will assess the influence of major religions, ethical beliefs, and values on cultures in Africa, Asia, and Australia.

Teaching & Assessment

- English Language Learner Modified Lesson Plans for this chapter are found in the Teacher's Resource Guide.
- *ExamView® Assessment Suite* is provided at **NCJourneys.com.** It includes customizable assessments for all chapters. Paper tests are also available in the Teacher's Resource Guide. See pages T16–T17 for information about how to use the assessments and the Scoring Guide.

Worksheets

Worksheets and answer keys are found both in the Teacher's Resource Guide and at **NCJourneys.com**, including Reading Guides, Reading Strategies, Chapter Reviews, English Language Learner and others.

ACTIVITIES AND INTEGRATIONS

SOCIAL STUDIES
▲ Made In China, p. 414B
■ Commune "Sandwich", p. 416
● Cultural Connection: Restaurants in China, p. 417
★ Hong Kong, p. 419
Three Gorges Dam, p.424
● Chinese Names, p. 425
▲ World Superstitions, p. 427
● Personality Traits, p. 428
▲ Chinese Recipes, p. 429
Skill Lesson: Achieving Democracy in China, p. 431

READING/LANGUAGE ARTS	READING/LANGUAGE ARTS OBJECTIVES
Family Life, p. 414B	1.01
Analogies, p. 414B	2.01
● Activator: *Dragon Parade*, p. 414	2.01
★ 2049–Will China Achieve Economically Advanced Nation Status?, P. 415	2.01
Writing Prompt: Chinese Character Ed., p. 414	3.03
Compare/Contrast SEZ, p. 418	2.02
Governmental Control, p. 418	2.01
Tienanmen Role Play, p. 421	1.03
Map Activity, Three Gorges Dam, p. 424	2.01
★ Chinese Proverbs, p. 427	2.01
Chinese School System, p. 429	6.01
Go to the Source: Comparing National Symbols, p. 433	2.01, 4.01, 4.02

SCIENCE	SCIENCE OBJECTIVES
■ Silt and the Huang He River, p. 423	1.04
Pollution and China's Economy, p. 426	3.05

TECHNOLOGY	TECHNOLOGY OBJECTIVES
■ Propaganda, p. 420	3.01, 3.08
Research the Dam, p. 422	3.01, 3.07
■ Three Gorges Dam Projects, p. 422	3.01, 3.11
Chinese Architecture, p. 430	3.01, 3.08

VISUAL ARTS	VISUAL ARTS OBJECTIVES
Architecture Drawing: One Point Perspective, p. 414B	1.01, 3.02
Propaganda, p. 420	2.01, 2.04
Pentagon Pyramid, p. 420	2.04, 4.01

CHARACTER AND VALUES EDUCATION	TRAITS
Writing Prompt: Chinese Character Ed., p. 414	respect, kindness, self discipline, responsibility
What Would You Do? p.421	Respect, Responsibility, Fairness
Tiananmen Role Play, p. 421	Courage

● Basic Activities ★ Challenging Activities ▲ English Language Learner Novice ■ English Language Learner Intermediate

Chapter Activities

Made in China

OBJECTIVES: 6.02, 8.03

Have students check items in their house to see if any were made in Hong Kong or China. If so, what are the items? They should make a list of the items and share them with a partner, comparing the items found at home. What conclusions can they make about industry in Hong Kong? in China?

Extension ELL students should write a list only.

Family Life

OBJECTIVES: 11.01, 10.04

Have students pretend they are citizens of China. They should pick a city to live in along with their family. Decide on a name, the numbers of family members, work, foods they eat, beliefs, transportation, hopes and dreams for the family. Have students write a journal entry describing a typical day in China for their situation.

Extension If you have Chinese ELL students, ask them to describe what life was like for them in China.

Architecture Drawing: One-Point Perspective

OBJECTIVES: 4.03

Materials 12-inch by 18-inch heavy white paper, 8½-inch by 11-inch paper for practice drawing, pencils, colored pencils, rulers, erasers, pictures of pagodas

One-Point Perspective Practice drawing the cube (use practice paper):

Turn page sideways. Draw a 3-inch square near the bottom of the page at least an inch up from the bottom. Draw a horizontal line across page at least 2 inches from the top of the page. This will be the simulated horizon. Draw a point on the horizon line. This will be the vanishing point.

Using a ruler, lightly draw a line from each corner of the square to the vanishing point. These are the vanishing lines. (Note: Do not draw a line from a corner if you have to draw across the square.) Choose a spot on the middle vanishing line. Lightly draw a line from that point parallel to the top of the square. Stop when you reach the other vanishing line. Starting at the same point, lightly draw a line parallel to the side of the square. Stop when you reach the lower vanishing line. Darken all lines of your cube. Erase excess vanishing lines. Do not move on unless the above steps are fully understood.

One-Point Perspective Architecture (use 12-inch by 18-inch paper)

Lightly draw the front of the building. Use traditional and/or modern buildings as a guide. Keep it simple at first. (The paper can be turned in either direction.) Draw horizon line and vanishing point. Draw vanishing lines from each of the corners. (make sure not to draw vanishing lines across front of building.)

Choose a spot on a vanishing line and draw a line parallel to the side of the building. Stop when the next vanishing line is reached. Repeat for all sides and top of building. Darken lines of building. Erase excess vanishing lines. Color building and background.

Extension Novice and intermediate ELL students can do this activity if each step is modeled carefully by the teacher or a peer tutor.

OBJECTIVES: 5.04, 6.0, 10.01

Analogies are useful to help students make associations with prior knowledge. Read the analogies aloud and ask students to identify the relationship between the terms. As an extension, ask students to write their own analogies using key terms or places discussed in the chapter.

commune : China :: kibbutz : Israel (a type of community in)

Special Economic Zone (SEZ) : China :: Research Triangle Park (RTP) : North Carolina (government-initiated economic zones in)

efficiency : high performance/production :: inefficiency : low performance/production (results in)

Tienanmen Square : China :: Bastille : France :: Berlin Wall : Germany (site of democratic rebellion in)

Hong Kong : United Kingdom :: Panama Canal Zone : United States :: Macao : Portugal (formerly ruled by)

aquaculture : water :: agriculture : field/farming (relates to)

Three Gorges Dam : Yangzi :: Aswan Dam : Nile (is on)

dragons : China :: shamrocks : Ireland (sign of good luck in)

Teaching Strategies

In this chapter, students will study modern China and will be able to see how government affects daily living in China. Lead students to an understanding of the role of China's economy in the world.

Activator

OBJECTIVES: 11.01

Activators are great tools to use in order to "hook" the attention of the students. Reading picture books or stories is an excellent way to build interest in the subject and is also a great way to integrate language arts into the social studies curriculum.

Dragon Parade. Edited by Steven A. Chin and Alex Haley. (Raintree, 1993. ISBN 0811472159.)

Writing Prompt

OBJECTIVES: 4.03

Evaluative

Not only do Chinese students have a rigorous academic curriculum, but they also receive daily instruction in "politeness, discipline, and respect." Imagine that next month your school will begin taking 15 minutes each day for this type of instruction. Write or word process a letter to your principal of your school explaining why you believe that this should or should not be done.

As your write your letter remember to:

- clearly state your position.
- give at least three reasons and explain your reasons fully.
- give examples to support your reasons.
- write in complete sentences and paragraph form.
- organize your ideas and include an introduction and a conclusion.
- use good grammar, spelling, punctuation, and capitalization.

CHAPTER 21

China Today

Shanghai today?" says ninety-year-old Qi Qang (chi chang). "Everyone is making money, and I don't know if that's good or bad." Qi Qang has seen it all. Before 1949, crime was widespread. People starved to death on the streets. Foreigners controlled important parts of the city.

Mao's Communist revolution changed Shanghai—and all of China. Today's Shanghai is booming. The Chinese are firmly in control of their country even with the return of foreign businesses. China is a powerful, modern nation.

Ceremonial dragon head

Chapter Preview

LESSON 1
Economy and Government
China today mixes private enterprise with government ownership, but its government remains a dictatorship.

LESSON 2
People in a Changing Environment
China is reshaping its environment as its population grows and economy develops.

LESSON 3
Society and Culture
Although communism changed much in China, many traditions have survived.

414

Chapter Resources

Print Resources

Nonfiction

Baldwin, Robert F. *Daily Life in Ancient and Modern Beijing.* Runestone Press, 1999. ISBN 082253214X.

Burckhardt, Ann. *The People of China and Their Food.* Capstone Press, 1996. ISBN 1560654333.

Higgonbottom, Trevor. *China* (Enchantment of the World series). Children's Press, 1999. ISBN 1588101908.

Kagda, Falaq. *Hong Kong* (Cultures of the World series). Marshall Cavendish, 1997. ISBN 0761406921.

Kalman, Bobbie. *China: The Land.* Crabtree, 2001. ISBN 0778793788.

—. *China: The People.* Crabtree, 2001. ISBN 0778793766.

Back issues of magazines

Growing Up In China. Cobblestone Publishing Company. ISBN 0382407547.

Hong Kong. Cobblestone Publishing Company. ISBN 0382409108.

China–Economic Activity and Resources

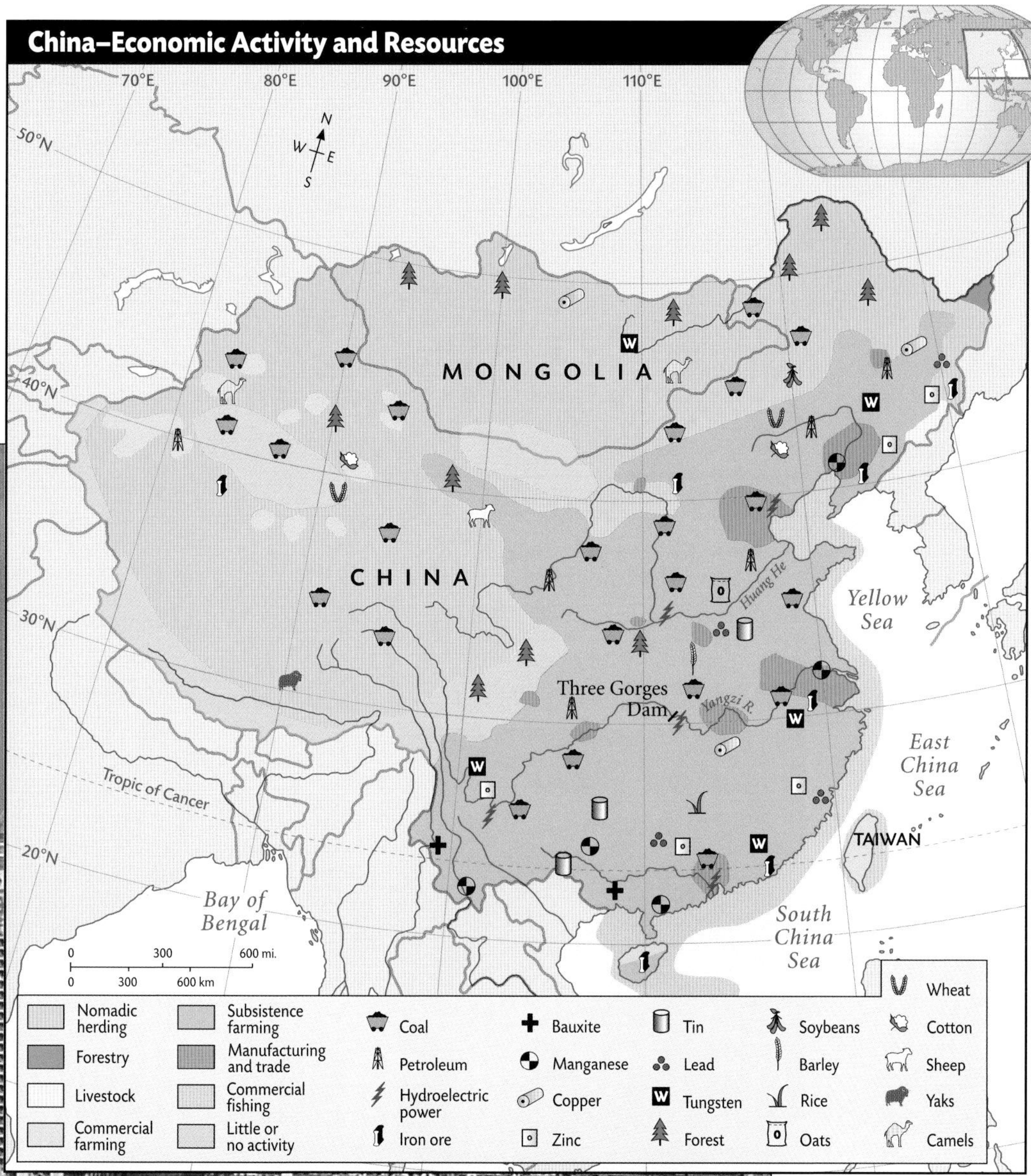

MONGOLIA

CHINA

Yellow Sea

East China Sea

South China Sea

Bay of Bengal

TAIWAN

Three Gorges Dam

Huang He

Yangzi R.

Tropic of Cancer

70°E 80°E 90°E 100°E 110°E

50°N 40°N 30°N 20°N

0 300 600 mi.

0 300 600 km

Nomadic herding
Forestry
Livestock
Commercial farming
Subsistence farming
Manufacturing and trade
Commercial fishing
Little or no activity
Coal
Petroleum
Hydroelectric power
Iron ore
Bauxite
Manganese
Copper
Zinc
Tin
Lead
Tungsten
Forest
Soybeans
Barley
Rice
Oats
Wheat
Cotton
Sheep
Yaks
Camels

Shanghai today (left) and in 1938 (far left)

415

Map Activity

2049—Will China Achieve Economically Advanced Nation Status?

NATIONAL GEOGRAPHY STANDARDS: 1, 16

GEOGRAPHIC THEMES: Location, Human-Environmental Interaction

OBJECTIVES: 3.01, 1.02, 6.01

Note with students red highlighted area on small-scale world map projection being distorted compared to large-scale China map on this page.

Answer with students:

1. When China is divided into west and east, what economic activity prevails in eastern China? *subsistence farming*
2. When China is divided into north and south, what economic activity dominates in northern China? *nomadic herding*
3. Where is livestock the main economic activity in China? *in the northeast along part of the border with North Korea*
4. What waters have most of the commercial fishing in China's area of East Asia? *Yellow Sea, East China Sea, South China Sea*
5. On Taiwan, what are the two main economic activities? *commercial and subsistence farming*
6. Which fossil fuel, coal or petroleum, is more prominent in China? *petroleum*
7. Which is more widespread across China, iron or lead deposits? *lead*
8. What resource is found at the mouth of the Huang He? *petroleum*
9. Which mineral resources are found on Taiwan? *none*
10. What economic activity and/or resources are influenced by the location of the Three Gorges Dam? *farming, mining, hydroelectric power*

Audiovisual:

China: Beyond the Clouds. National Geographic, 1994. Two 120 min. videos.

China is Changing Series (World Geography series). Benchmark Media, 569 North State Road, Briarcliff Manor, NY 10510. (800) 438-5564.

The Gate of Heavenly Peace (1989 Tiananmen protests), Frontline. 1998. PBS Video.

Great Wall Across the Yangtze, PBS Video.

In Search of China, PBS Videos

The Tank Man, Frontline. 2006. (90 mins.) PBS Video.

Web Sites

Visit **NCJourneys.com** for links:

- China the Beautiful—Chinese Art and Literature
- The Gate of Heavenly Peace Web site
- Great Wall Across the Yangtze Web site
- Illicit: How Smugglers, Traffickers, and Copycats are Hijacking the Global Economy, Carnegie Endowment for International Peace
- The Tank Man companion Web site
- Virtual China

OBJECTIVES: 5.02, 5.04, 6.01, 6.02, 8.01, 10.04, 13.03

Discussion Questions

1 How was Deng's approach toward leadership different from Mao's?

2 What is a mixed economy?

Caption Answer

He introduced modernization and allowed a mixed economy.

Activity

Commune "Sandwich"

OBJECTIVES: 10.04, 11.01

Materials handouts of sandwich patterns from the Teacher's Resource Guide, copied on to colored paper (optional: paper plate, handouts of chips, apple, beverage in glass patterns on colored paper) and glue/glue stick

The class will be a commune assigned to create a sandwich. Provide various materials and patterns of sandwich ingredients, even paper plate, to every student to work as a "commune" to create a lunch sandwich. Handout patterns, listed below, should be given to students one per color; one student should be given scissors and another student the glue/glue stick, and one student can be given a paper plate. Ensuring that every student has some material can make several sandwiches necessary.

white paper=two bread and one condiment (mayonnaise)
buff/brown paper=two meat and two strips of bacon
green paper=one lettuce and three pickles as group
pink/red paper=one tomato and one condiment (catsup)
yellow paper=two cheese and one condiment (mustard)

The commune's assignment is to build a sandwich in a designated amount of time. In presenting the sandwich to class each student must specify his or her part in the making of the sandwich (his or her part in the commune). Cut the sandwich into equal portions, giving a portion to each student in that commune. Students should open their sandwich, describing what their portion includes and which member of the commune contributed what to the sandwich. Debriefing must follow to discuss with students the costs and benefits of communes and how a communal economy does not meet all the needs of the Chinese citizens or its government.

Extended Adaptation Pattern handouts can be provided for chips, apple, and beverage in glass if additional items are needed to accommodate class size.

Extension Assign intermediate ELL students to work in groups. Review the basic vocabulary of sandwich making: bread, peanut butter, jelly, ham, cheese, mustard, mayonnaise.

LESSON  Economy and Government

KEY IDEAS

- In the 1980s, economic reforms spurred China's rapid growth.
- The Chinese Communist Party holds all real political power in China.
- All the world—and especially Taiwan—is watching how China treats Hong Kong.

KEY TERMS

commune
ideology
Special Administrative Regions
Special Economic Zones
tariff
World Trade Organization

Mao Zedong died in 1976. Millions remembered him as an heroic leader, a man who had saved the Chinese Communis Party from destruction and fought Japanese invaders. On th other hand, Mao's successor, Deng Xiaoping (duhng syow·PING), thought that Mao had tried to change the nation too quickly. "A donk is certainly slow," Deng said, "but at least it rarely has an accident."

Deng also thought Mao should not have launched his "Great Le Forward" and "Cultural Revolution." These had been campaigns change China by inspiring revolutionary spirit, but they had destroy more than they built. Deng was interested in practical results, n revolutionary spirit. "It does not matter if a cat is white or black," De said, "as long as it catches mice."

Deng's Modernizations

When Deng came to power, he launched reforms to modernize China. These reforms were (1) expanding agricultural output, (2) developing modern industry, and (3) improving Chinese science and technology.

Deng Xiaoping succeeded Mao Zedong. He was leader of China and the Communist Party until his death in 1997. **How did he try to change China's economy?**

To achieve these goals, Deng moved away from Mao's programs requiring complete government control of the economy. Instead, he allowed a mixed economy in which private businesses and government-owned enterprises operated side by side. Under Deng, therefore, Chinese gained some freedom to set up their own businesses.

Expanding Agricultural Output

Under Mao, the government had taken over all farmland and turned priva farms into communes. In a ***commune,*** village farmers worked together and shared equally what they produced. In theory, this would increase crop output, but communes were not efficient. Becaus farmers did not keep their crops, they dic not work any harder than they had to.

To improve farm production, Deng gave up the communes. The land was stil government-owned, but farm families leased the land. They made the decisions about what to grow and how much to sell. They paid part of each harvest as taxes, but they were free to do what they wished with the rest of their crop. With their profits, they bought bicycles, sewing machines, or even TVs. Some replaced ol mud huts with houses built of brick and tile.

China has many factories producing high-tech equipment for a world market. **How has the People's Republic of China improved its technology?**

eveloping Modern Industry

Deng also forced government ctories to become more efficient. anagers became responsible for oducing quality goods and for making profit. The government also allowed nall, private businesses to open. ısinessmen started barber shops, staurants, and even night clubs.

Mao had prohibited foreign businesses China. Under Deng, they were invited return. China permitted Chinese and reign experts to work together. Foreign vestors opened factories, hotels, and her businesses.

nproving Science nd Technology

Deng set aside some areas as *pecial Economic Zones* (SEZ). In Special conomic Zones, foreign investors could ın factories with little government gulation. The SEZ provided jobs and troduced Chinese to advanced science ıd technology.

Deng did not stop there. He sent thousands of students abroad to study. His efforts produced results. China today is becoming a technologically advanced nation.

Economic Growth vs. Party Leadership

Many Chinese, especially the well-educated, hoped that Deng's modernizations would bring political change. Deng, however, did not want political freedoms to spread.

China's Communist government is similar in ways to the Confucian system in Old China. In Old China, the government was run according to Confucian ideals. Since 1949, the government has relied on Communist ***ideology,*** or body of thought or theories about a culture. But both forms of government closely controlled the people. In both systems, the ideal has been to provide for the people's needs and to ensure peace and order. Yet both Confucian and Communist governments have also been brutally cruel.

Discussion Questions

1 How did Deng change communes?

2 What is the inherent strengths/weakness of the commune system?

3 How would you react if no matter how long or hard you worked you received the same share as everyone else? For example, what if each student in the class received the average of all their classmates' grades rather than their individual grade?

4 How did China's Communist government incorporate Confucian ideals?

5 Who do you think did more to bring China into the twentieth century, Mao or Deng?

Caption Answer

It has opened Special Economic Zones, where foreign investors offer jobs that introduce the Chinese to advanced science and technology. China also sends thousands of students abroad to study. Hong Kong and Macao have a large number of foreign companies working in these Special Administrative Regions.

Activity

Cultural Connection: Restaurants in China

OBJECTIVES: 1.02, 4.03, 11.01

In Chinese cities there are many restaurants. In many of these restaurants customers sit at a round table with a lazy-susan located in the middle of the table. During the meal, food servers bring many bowls of different Chinese foods and place them on the lazy-susan. Once the food arrives, customers serve themselves and spin the lazy Susan around the table so that each guest may partake in the different foods. For dessert, the Chinese prefer fresh fruit such as watermelon.

Enrichment Bring Chinese cuisine into your class by hosting a Chinese luncheon buffet. Instruct students to research the foods of China and have them prepare a dish for the students to sample. Another option for your feast is to bring in take-out from a local Chinese restaurant. Ask a local Chinese restaurant owner to speak about China's cuisine and ingredients.

Background Information

A Painful Transition to a Modern Economy

China's push to become a modern, more open economy has been difficult for millions of Chinese workers. Under Communist rule, factory workers were once secure in the knowledge that they had lifetime employment, but this is no longer the case. In the past decade the government has ordered many formerly state-owned factories to become economically self-sufficient. In Tianjin over a 10-year period, one factory moved from a state-owned company making pipes to a beverage packaging firm jointly owned by the Chinese and an American corporation. In 2000, the factory became wholly owned by its American partner. The new owners laid off workers and moved the factory to a new SEZ 30 miles outside Tianjin. In China few laid-off workers have pensions or health care benefits to ease their retirement.

Teacher Notes

Hong Kong

Find out if there is a businessperson in your community who has traveled to Hong Kong and ask him or her to make a presentation to the class.

Activity

Compare/Contrast SEZs and Spheres of Influence

 **OBJECTIVES:** 1.02, 1.03

Using a graphic organizer, such as a double bubble map or a Venn Diagram, list the similarities and differences between the SEZ and the Sphere of Influence. Discuss which gave more strength to China and which to foreign investors.

Activity

Governmental Control

 **OBJECTIVES:** 2.03, 5.01, 9.04

Read aloud the excerpt from a letter written in 1990 by a Canadian teacher working in Suzhou, China. Discuss how this description differs from the onset of winter in our country. What are the advantages or disadvantages of a government policy that ensures everyone gets equal treatment? This is an example of how a government makes decisions about distribution of resources. Have the students look through Chapter 21 for other examples of China's control of resources or people. Compare these examples to the United States.

Examples from Chapter 21:
- government leases land to farmers
- government runs factories
- government controls newspapers, radios, television
- government tells people what to think
- government tells people where their children go to school

other more positive controls:
- government ended old class system
- government gave women equal rights
- government provides free university education to top students

Excerpt from letter by a teacher at Suzhou Railway Teachers' College in Jiangsu Province, P. R. China:

A line from today's paper could sum up one of the main differences between society in China and Canada: "Many Beijingers enjoy a comfortable temperature at home and in offices in winter as the city switched on winter heating on November 15." Can you imagine how a northern city of seven million manages to switch on the heat in one day? The mind boggles at the number of boilers needed! But at least it is implementing the policy of ensuring that everybody gets it. Apparently there is an imaginary line between north and south China. Since Suzhou is in south China, there are no facilities for heating because it is supposed to be at 0°C. So our students wear many layers of clothes at all classrooms. I don't have to worry about being too hot in these classrooms. My nose is always cold. But they do provide the less hardy foreign teacher with a small portable radiator in her room. It reminds me of Star Wars' little robot, R2-D2.

Extension Assign peer tutors to assist ELL students as needed.

Hong Kong

Hong Kong, or Fragrant Harbor as it was called by the Chinese, once was the home of pirates and drug smugglers. A mere 6,000 people lived on the rocky island. How did it turn into a city of more than 7 million?

After the Opium Wars of 1839-1842, the Chinese government had to cede (transfer) the island of Hong Kong and the Kowloon peninsula to the United Kingdom. An area of 305 square miles (793 sq km) called the New Territories was leased to the British. The British returned it to China in 1997.

Vendors at the HongLok street market

Mending nets on a junk

Trade, manufacturing, and hardworking people helped Hong Kong develop into a busy, beautiful modern city. Constantly tearing old buildings down to build skyscrapers, Hong Kong keeps renewing itself. Yet there are reflections of the past.

Neon signs in Hong Kong

Making television sets

Hong Kong business leaders stay alert to changes in world needs. Moving from manufacturing simple transistor radios to manufacturing computer parts is one example of how Hong Kong industry flourishes. From a rocky pirate's den to an energetic city, Hong Kong is still making its future.

Inside the factories, now governed by China, modern technology aids the production of millions of goods shipped from Hong Kong each year. From flashlights to dolls and wool carpets to blue jeans, Hong Kong's workers keep the flow of goods moving out of the harbor and into the world.

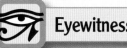

Eyewitness Activity

Hong Kong

NATIONAL GEOGRAPHY STANDARDS: 1, 17, 18

GEOGRAPHIC THEMES: Location, Place

OBJECTIVES: 1.02, 2.01

Review with students that Hong Kong is a Special Administrative Region of the People's Republic of China as of 1997. Using the map on page 389, remind students that this is part of Guangdong Province. It is about half the size of Rhode Island. Have students identify

- the four main areas of Hong Kong. *New Territories, Kowloon Peninsula, Lantau Island, and Hong Kong Island (Note that there are also two hundred smaller islands.)*
- the difference between land that is ceded and land that is leased. *The Chinese ceded or transferred Hong Kong Island (following the Opium War in 1842) and Kowloon Peninsula (following the Arrow War in 1860) to the United Kingdom; the British leased or paid to have and use the New Territories and Lantau Island for 99 years beginning in 1898.*
- the location of Victoria, the capital of this region. *Hong Kong Island*

ELL Teaching Tips

Help ELLs Interact with English-Speaking Peers

Provide ELLs with opportunities for interacting in a meaningful way with peers who speak English. This will help develop social vocabulary and acceptance as well as academic understanding. This type of exchange provides second language learners with feedback and knowledge about how to correctly communicate their ideas in English.

Discussion Questions

1 What do you think the Statue of Liberty symbolized to the Chinese students at Tiananmen Square?

2 If Mao had been a student in 1989, how do you think he would have responded to the events at Tiananmen?

Caption Answer

The government ordered protesters to leave, then sent in tanks and troops. They arrested thousands of demonstrators and wounded or killed many others. Chinese leaders said their actions were justified because the protesters posed a threat to law and order.

Activity

Propaganda

OBJECTIVES: 4.03, 9.03

Have students design and create a billboard which would be similar to that used in China to promote a Communist program. They should research and study propaganda used by the Communists to convey their programs.

Examples: one-child families, double-cropping, aquaculture, remaining in the countryside

Extension Assign peer tutors to assist ELL students as needed.

Activity

Pentagon Pyramid

OBJECTIVES: 1.01

Materials handout of the pentagon pyramid from the Teacher's Resource Guide; colored pencils, markers, crayons; rulers; scissors; glue/glue sticks

Using the pentagon pyramid pattern in the Teacher's Resource Guide, have students illustrate each of the Five Themes of Geography on a triangular side of this geometric shape. The pentagon base should be used to identify China today as this shape's topic.

No Room for Democracy

As China's economy improved, students and others demanded more political freedom. In the spring of 1989, they held rallies in Beijing, China's capital, as well as other cities. Students in Beijing set up the *Goddess of Liberty*, a statue that was inspired by our own Statue of Liberty. Crowds flocked to Tienanmen Square in the heart of Beijing. There they called for freedom and democratic reforms in China's government.

Government officials ordered the crowd to leave the square. When the demonstrators refused, troops and tanks moved in. Thousands of pro-democracy supporters were arrested. Many others were wounded or killed. The Tienanmen Square Massacre, as it was called, was filmed and reported live by international news agencies. People around the world condemned China's government. Chinese leaders declared that their actions were justified because the protesters posed a threat to law and order.

China's dictators had no intention of giving up any political power. Since 1989 many Chinese human rights activists have received long prison sentences. Although Deng encouraged free enterprise, he opposed political reforms until the end of his life in 1997.

Deng's reforms produced remarkable economic results. China today is an economic superpower and one of the United States' largest trading partners. The United States Congress voted in 2000 to establish "permanent normal trade relations" with China beginning when it joined the ***World Trade Organization.*** (WTO). China became a member of the WTO in December, 2001. As a member, China gets the same low-tariff trade status of other major trade partners. A ***tariff*** is a tax on goods or services being imported into a country. China's status is no longer subject to an annual congressional review of its human rights record. China is now more market-economy oriented. It has surpassed the United Kingdom as the world's fourth largest economy.

In 1989, thousands demonstrated for freedom and democracy in Beijing's Tienanmen Square (right). The "tank man" (above) was saved when friends pulled him out of the way of the tanks. **How did the government react? Why?**

Name Origin

China Named after the first emperor of the Tshin Dynasty

Beijing Northern Capital (Southern Capital—Nanjing)

Hangchow Mouth of the Han River

Kowloon Hong Kong, the "Nine Rivers"

Manchuria Named for the Manchus

Shanghai "Above the sea"

Yellow Sea The banks of the river are a muddy yellow color

Yangzi "Long river," third-longest river in the world—3,960 miles

Tien Shan "Celestial mountains"

Taiwan "Terraced bay." Mountain slopes are terraced for agriculture and housing.

Hong Kong "Fragrant harbor"; the incense trade was important when the port in Hong Kong was being developed.

Iong Kong
nd Taiwan

China's tough stand against democracy orried many people in Hong Kong and iwan. Dicky Yip is a Hong Kong banker. No one really knows what is going to ppen," he said.

As you read in the "Eyewitness to istory," Hong Kong has developed a oming economy. Hong Kong and Macao e two ***Special Administrative egions*** created as part of the deals to turn the cities to China. China promised at under its "one country, two systems" licy, China's socialist system will not be acticed in either area until at least 2047.

Taiwan's leaders are closely watching hina's treatment of Hong Kong. Taiwan as been transformed since 1949, when hiang Kai-shek and the remains of his my took refuge there. Despite sharp nsions with Beijing, Taiwan (with onomic assistance from the United States) gan modernizing its agriculture and nstructing new manufacturing centers. day, it boasts of having one of the orld's strongest economies, with high andards of living for its people.

What would YOU do?

me American companies have made profits China. Others want to start businesses there. ina resents criticism of its violations of man rights. Beijing says that it will not mit American businesses if the criticism ntinues. How would you resolve the problem?

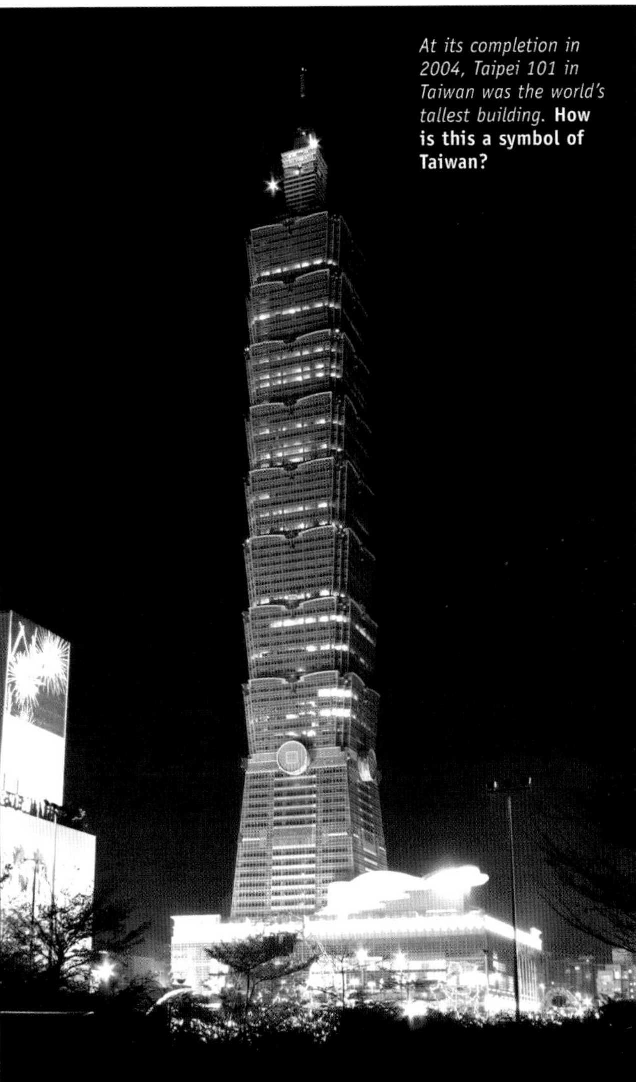

At its completion in 2004, Taipei 101 in Taiwan was the world's tallest building. **How is this a symbol of Taiwan?**

LESSON 1 REVIEW

Fact Follow-Up

1. What were Deng Xiaoping's criticisms of Mao Zedong?
2. How did agriculture change under Deng Xiaoping?
3. What did the Tienanmen Square Massacre reveal about government leadership in China?

Talk About It

1. Is China's communist leadership similar to Confucian leadership? Explain.
2. Why is China considered one of the world's economic superpowers?
3. Why would the people of Taiwan be interested in what happens to Hong Kong?

Discussion Questions

1 Do you think the United States should use military force to protect Taiwan from China?

2 Why do you think the economic successes in Taiwan and Hong Kong have differed from China's?

Activity

Tiananmen Role Play

OBJECTIVES: 7.02, 9.03

Have students research the background and events in Tiananmen Square. When research is complete, they should assume identities of participants (witness, activist, Communist, official, soldier, American reporter, or others) and present a role play depicting the events of the day.

Extension Students could write point-of-view papers, editorials, or diary entries about those days of hope and tension.

LESSON 1 REVIEW

Fact Follow-Up Answers

1. Deng thought Mao had tried to change the nation too quickly. Deng favored practical results over revolutionary spirit.
2. To increase farm production, Deng gave up direct government ownership and control of the agricultural communes and leased the land to farm families. Individual farmers decided what to grow and how much to sell. They kept their profits after paying taxes.
3. It showed that China's dictators had no intention of giving up any political power.

Think These Through Answers

4. Important points: Students should state whether it is similar and explain why. Note: Both forms of leadership are based on ideals, and both use their power to control people. Confucian ideals emphasized filial piety and responsibility to the family; communism does not.
5. Its huge population and resources make it an enormous producer and consumer of goods.
6. Like Hong Kong, Taiwan might profit from a closer economic connection to China, but the Taiwanese are watching to see if China will preserve democracy in Hong Kong.

OBJECTIVES: 2.02, 2.03, 3.01, 3.03

Discussion Questions

1 How would it feel to live in an area that is always at risk of a natural disaster? How would it change your attitude toward life?

2 China is building the Three Gorges Dam as a way of both controlling flooding and bringing hydroelectric power to China. It is being done at the expense of many homes and villages. Do you think a government has the right to take personal property to benefit the good of many?

Caption Answer

China's rivers provide a vast transportation and communication network. They also provide irrigation for cropland and are a resource that can be used to generate hydro electric power.

LESSON 2 People in a Changing Environment

KEY IDEAS

- Modern engineering and technology are helping China solve many problems of an increasingly crowded society.
- Because good farmland is scarce, the Chinese use intensive farming.
- China's huge population puts great pressure on its resources.

KEY TERMS

aquaculture
double cropping
intensive farming

Liu Ruyun is an engineer. Her job is to check for flooding along the Huang He (HWAHNG huh). The flood season lasts from July to September. "I don't get much sleep then," she says. "I spend hours talking to peasants who spot early signs of trouble." They report holes in dikes or weakened stonework.

The Chinese have struggled to control floods on the Huang He fo more than 4,000 years. Today, engineers still must work hard to contro nature's destructive force.

The Importance of China's Rivers

Millions of Chinese live along the Huang He. The river carries tons of soil that have been washed or blown into the river. This silt fills up the riverbed. "We raise the dikes as the riverbed rises," says Liu, "but we can't keep on like that." In places, the riverbanks are already 10 to 30 feet (3 to 10 m) above nearby land.

The Huang He and China's other rivers have brought floods that cause tremendous damage, but they have also brought great benefits. The Yangzi and its tributaries, for example, have provided China with about 35,000 miles (56,350 km) of navigable waterways. Boats can carry people and freight 1,700 miles (2,737 km) into the interior. Small craft can navigate streams and canals north anc south of the Yangzi—about 300 miles on either side of the river.

Old China's internal transportation system had much to do with its development and stability as an empire. The rivers' importance continues to grow. China needs water, electricity, and the ability to move people and goods in the most cost-effective way. It is building the world's most powerful hydroelectric dam on the Yangzi River. This dam will also control floods and assist in river navigation.

Farmer's fields run alongside the Yellow River. **Why are rivers important in China?**

Research Activity

Three Gorges Dam Projects

OBJECTIVES: 1.02, 3.03, 6.01

Using various Web sites (links found at **NCJourneys.com**), have students research information to criticize and defend various issues relating to the Three Gorges Dam.

Multiple Intelligences Topics:

Verbal/linguistic: Research investment banks, mainly Morgan Stanley Dean Witter, that are responsible for financing the Three Gorges Dam and how their involvement is received worldwide. Prepare a news release reporting the findings.

Musical/rhythmic: Compose lyrics and/or score, sound effects, or background music for rap, one-act play, or comedy routine on human interest topic relating to the dam.

Logical/mathematical: Prepare time line giving all major events from 1919 to 2009 as visual display (be sure to estimate events placement within display).

Visual/spatial: Create a creature or new plant specie that will evolve and live in the lake constructed on the Yangzi, and build a model.

Bodily/kinesthetic: Choose ten terms depicting the dam to present as charades or a sign language game for classmates to guess the vocabulary.

Naturalist: As the Yangzi Riverkeeper, prepare an interactive museum exhibit that can include hydrology, geology, flora, and fauna of this habitat.

Intrapersonal: Reflect on the natural environment of the Three Gorges Dam region and design a relaxation exercise (can include physical exercise, mental-visual

Jsing the Land—North and South

If you flew over the North China ain, you would see why controlling the uang He is so important. Below, the lds of yellow-brown soil seem to stretch rever. Every half-mile or so are small lages. Farmers tend crops in the fields ar the river. Farmers in northern China ise grains such as wheat, sorghum, corn, millet. Some fields have cotton, getables, or fruit trees. No one can unt the number of times these fields ve been covered by the Huang He's ods.

If you flew over southeast China, you ould have a different view. Here you ould see hills and mountains. Land is a illiant green because the climate is armer and the rainfall is more abundant. t in southern China, too, not an inch of nd is wasted. Terraces create level land hillsides.

Western China, you will recall, is too y to support much farming. Few people e in its mountains, plateaus, and deserts. ose who do are nomadic herders. rmers plant crops in sheltered valleys or nong scattered oases.

Most Chinese—almost 90 percent— e crowded into eastern China where ost farming occurs (see map, page 415). rtile land is valued because it is so nited. A large population needs large nounts of food. The government watches rming closely to avoid the terrible mines of the past.

The Chinese make the best use of their nited farmland through ***intensive rming*** —using all available fertile land r agriculture. In the south, where the owing season is long, they practice ***ouble cropping.*** This means planting a cond crop between rows of the first. The cond crop has already begun to grow by e time the first one is harvested.

The Chinese continue to create new nd by terracing hillsides and draining vamps. With irrigation, they have turned me desert land into usable, or arable, rmland.

A family of nomads moves its belongings by camel across the Mongolian steppes (top). A one-child family works in its field in southeast China. **How do both families show differing uses of the land?**

A small-size tractor nicknamed "the grasshopper" speeds the work. It is small enough to plow narrow terraces and other plots. Farmers adopt other technological improvements, such as improved seeds and chemicals, to control pests and plant diseases.

Villagers have dug artificial ponds to keep fish, another source of food. Raising food products in water is called ***aquaculture.*** Chinese farmers run a never-ending race. Almost every year they produce more food through intensive farming, double cropping, technology, and aquaculture. Yet the population is increasing at the rate of 8.6 million people a year.

imagery/meditation, and environmental stimulation w/music, sound effects).

Interpersonal: Choose related cases (Ataturk, Colorado, Grand Canal, Mekong) and prepare video, letters, or Web site to inform international organizations how the Three Gorges Dam is a major construction project.

Discussion Questions

1 What are terraces? How do they increase the amount of land used for farming?

2 What are some of the methods the Chinese use to increase food production?

3 How do these methods compare to methods used in our community?

The nomads move constantly in search of water and pasture land. The farm family stays in one place and cultivates the land to produce food.

Science Link—Silt and the Huang He River

OBJECTIVES: 1.02, 3.01

Set up an experiment where students can view a mock river with silt—a low flow of water and silt and a high flow of water. Allow students to see the affect that water volume has on silt movement. Discuss as a class whether bringing water from the Yangzi to the Huang He will make flooding more or less likely. You may want to enlist the aid of a science teacher for this lesson and work as an interdisciplinary team.

Research the Dam

OBJECTIVES: 1.02, 3.01

Have students research the progress on the conversion of the Three Gorges of the Yangzi to "Lake Yangzi." How far along is the project? What are the environmental issues? What is the government doing about the 10 million people who will have to be moved? What about ancient artifacts that will be covered up? Will the benefits of hydroelectric power outweigh all the emotional and monetary costs of the project?

Map Activity

Three Gorges Dam

NATIONAL GEOGRAPHY STANDARDS: 1, 3, 7, 14

GEOGRAPHIC THEMES: Location, Place, Human-Environmental Interaction, Movement, Region

OBJECTIVES: 1.02, 3.01

Have students answer the following questions using the map on this page:

1. Which Chinese city is closest to the Three Gorges Dam? *Yichang (note that this is sometimes labeled as Sandouping)*
2. What tributary of the Yangzi River has its confluence at Chongqing? *Jialing River*
3. How could silt close the inland harbor at Chongqing? *Silt deposits could clog or possibly close the channel that allows ships to travel so far inland from the Yellow Sea; dredging to keep this deepwater channel open might be necessary.*
4. Speculate what will happen around Yichang once this dam is completed. *Probably much of this city's area will be completely under water in the reservoir created at the Gorges.*
5. If the Dam's reservoir is to be 390 miles long (in 2009), estimate the western location of this reservoir. *approximately Chongqing, north and south between Yichang and Chongqing*
6. The mouth of the Yangzi River is where? *Yellow Sea*
7. On what bank of the Yangzi is Shanghai located? *south side, or Right Bank*
8. A large dam is defined as higher than 15 meters (taller than a four-story building). China has 19,000 large dams. The Three Gorges Dam is to be 185 meters high. Will this make it the highest dam in the world when completed in 2009? *No, there will be at least two other dams in the world also 185 meters high (Mossyrock in Cowlitz, Washington, United States, and Oymopinar in Manavgat, Turkey) as well as 42 others worldwide higher than this one (world's highest is currently 335 meters in Tajikistan; China has Ertan at 240 meters already on Yangzi/Yalong completed in 1999).*

CONNECTIONS • GEOGRAPHY & SCIENCE •

The Three Gorges Dam

The Three Gorges Dam (below) on the Yangzi River is China's largest construction project since the Great Wall. Blocking the river below the Three Gorges (see map below) has been an ambition of its leadership since Sun Yat-Sen dreamed about it in 1919. Mao Zedong pushed the idea in the 1950s, writing in a poem about the "lake within the Gorges."

Planning for the new dam began in the early 1990s. It will cost 25 billion dollars, creating a reservoir 390 miles (628 km) long when completed in 2009. The dam will span 1.44 miles, stand nearly 600 feet (180 m) high, and boast 26 supersized generators. Its hydroelectric power plant will generate more than 18,000 megawatts of clean power, which will be distributed to users throughout densely populated central China.

The dam is engineered to control the flooding on the Yangzi and to enhance navigation. It also will allow for better irrigation of farmland.

There has been much opposition to the project—both within China and from abroad. About 1.3 million people are being removed from their homes because the waters filling the reservoir are flooding not just villages but entire cities. Eight thousand cultural sites will be submerged.

Some critics say that the project's goals are incompatible. To generate power, the dam's operators might keep the reservoir at higher levels, which may interfere with flood-control operations. Opponents also argue that it may generate a great deal of silt, virtually closing Chongqing's harbor (China's biggest inland city). Finally, they claim China has a poor record of safety in building dams. Two dams collapsed on the Huai River in 1975, leading to the deaths of between 30,000 and 100,000 people. The Three Gorges Dam, however, is being built to higher standards.

Three Gorges Dam

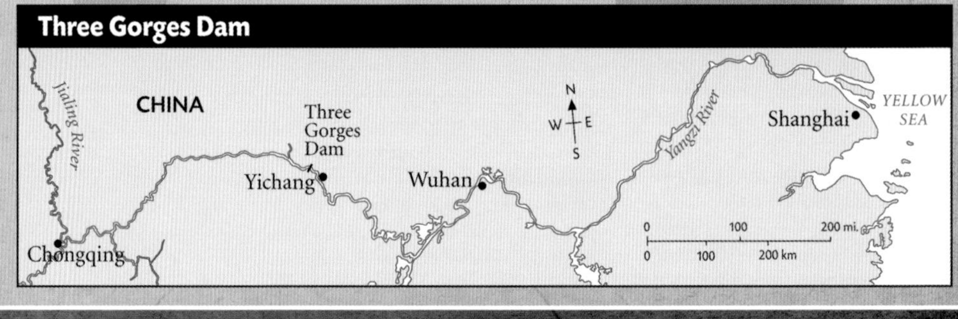

Background Information

Three Gorges Dam

The Three Gorges Dam has been called the largest construction project in China since the Great Wall. It rises more than 600 feet (180m) high and creates a reservoir nearly 390 miles (644 km) long. Supporters see it as a key source of hydroelectricity for the industrializing nation. They believe it will stop the flooding of the Yangzi that has claimed more than 1 million lives over the past century. The dam's critics fear that damming the river will cause pollution from industrial and residential areas to concentrate in the river rather than flow into the sea. Others worry about where people from the more than 1,200 villages and two major towns that have been submerged will go.

Beijing has more bikes than cars. **Why?**

?eople Rush to Cities

"It is always rush hour," says a Beijing raffic officer. Beijing, with more than 11 nillion people, always has thousands of icycles and pedestrians on its streets. Beijing, Shanghai, and other Chinese cities ave more bicycles than cars.

As in other developing countries, China's cities grow rapidly. The governnent has been trying to keep villagers rom moving to the cities. Only those with ermits may rent apartments. Newcomers nove anyway and stay without ermission.

Most large cities are in the East. There amilies crowd into tiny two-room apartnents. Often, two or more families share kitchen and bathroom. The government s tearing down older buildings and utting up concrete apartment houses. Still, cities like Beijing never have enough housing.

Despite overcrowding and lack of housing, cities continue to draw new residents every day. They have a variety of jobs, better schools, and a wider choice of activities than rural villages. These attractions outweigh the disadvantages, especially for China's young people.

China continues to be a land of farmers but this will change over the next 10 years. About 62 percent of the people lived in rural areas in 2005, down from about 70 percent in 2000. China's population will soon be evenly divided between cities and villages. Village and farm life offer more income than in the past. Housing also has improved. Rural people are less isolated than they were a few years ago. People have more consumer goods, such as TVs, bicycles, watches, and radios.

Discussion Questions

1 How is our community changing?

2 How are our challenges the same as China's? How are they different?

3 How are the changes occurring in China going to affect its involvement with the rest of the world?

Activity

Chinese Names

OBJECTIVES: 4.03, 10.04

Chinese write addresses on an envelope opposite from the Western way. The country is put first and the individual last. China on the top line, below it the province, the city neighborhood, the parents' work unit, and the apartment building, and at the bottom one's name—family name first, the generation name, then the given name. A Chinese woman keeps her own family name when she marries. Children take the name of the father. Generation names are now less common as parents often have only one child. Most children today just have a surname and the given name.

Have students address an envelope to themselves—or someone in their family —using the Chinese style. They can design their family tree using the Chinese-naming method. How similar/different is the American-naming method to the Chinese? What do many Americans call one's surname? One's given name?

Teacher Notes

Math and Social Studies

Use the population figures on the map on page 381 and the percentages given here in the text on urbanization (page 425) to create math word problems. Discussions of population growth, rates of urbanization, and other statistics are excellent opportunities to integrate percentages, statistics, graphing, estimating, and other math skills. Have students create their own math word problems to trade with other students.

It's a Fact

;hina borders 14 countries.
;rand Canal is an inland waterway iecting the Yangzi to Huang He. Begun in ;00s, it was connected to Beijing by late)s and used as major transportation ·m until early 1900s, when railroads ime more economical. Still used as a local sportation system and market place.
;hina has the largest standing army in vorld: more than 2.5 million, with her 5 million in reserve.
;reat Leap Forward was an economic ;ram designed to increase factory and crop production. Its slogan was: "more, faster, better, cheaper." Its agriculture program resulted in widespread famine.
■ The Cultural Revolution was a political program designed to create a culture based solely on Communist ideas. The Red Guard (mostly teenagers) arrested, tortured, and killed all those who disagreed with Mao's policies. They also destroyed art, books, temples, or anything seen as anti-Communist. A generation of scientists, artists, and teachers were unable to spread knowledge until after Mao's death in 1976.

Caption Answer

China's main source of energy is coal. Coal smoke from homes and factories pollutes the air.

Science Activity

Pollution and China's Economy

OBJECTIVES: 2.03, 3.02

The environmental impact of China's air pollution goes beyond its borders. Sulfur emissions from burning coal cause acid rain, which falls in neighboring countries and harms ecosystems. At the global level, emissions of carbon dioxide from the burning of fossil fuels enhance the greenhouse effect and contribute to global warming.

China's government is considering these policies to implement in order to greatly reduce pollution while not harming the growing economy: 1. Green Pricing); 2. Pollution Levy Systems (PLS); 3. Concentration-Based Emissions Standards; 4. Total Emissions Control (TEC); and 5. Emissions Trading (ET)

Divide the class into five groups. Assign each a policy. Students should research to define these policy options, the science that supports these initiatives, and the potential costs and benefits to China's economy. Have each group present their findings to the class. Each group should make a recommendation as to whether they think China should adopt the policy they researched.

Hebei, China, is polluted by factory smokestacks. **What source of energy pollutes so much of China?**

Environmental Impact

China industrializes. Its population grows. Farmers use more chemicals to increase crop yields. All these place more stress on China's environment.

Clouds of polluted air hang over China's cities. Its main source of energy is coal (see map, page 415). Coal smoke billows into the sky, blanketing the countryside with foul air. China is second only to the United States in the emission of greenhouse gases.

The government has not enforced rules against pollution. Factories and people dump untreated wastes into nearby streams or rivers.

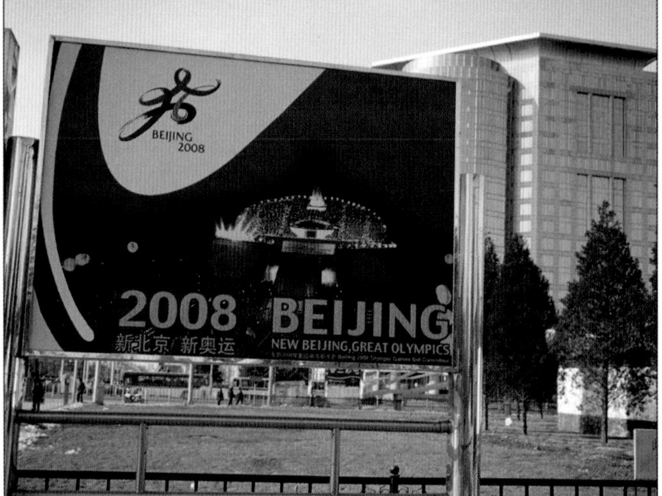

Showcasing China to the World

In 2008, China will hold the Summer Olympics in Beijing. China wants to use this to show its progress. It also wants to place the Tienanmen Square protests firmly in the past.

China's future holds many possibilities. It is becoming a major industrial and political power in the world. How it will use this power remain to be seen.

China won the bid for the 2008 Summer Olympics. **Why was this important to China's government?**

LESSON 2 REVIEW

Fact Follow-Up

1. How do Chinese make the best use of a limited amount of farmland?
2. How will the Three Gorges Dam benefit China?
3. How have changes in industry and agriculture affected China?

Talk About It

1. Why is it important to control China's rivers?
2. Why are most of China's large cities located in eastern China?
3. Using your knowledge of China's landforms, climate, and distribution of population, explain why population is unevenly distributed.

LESSON 2 REVIEW

Fact Follow-Up Answers

1. The Chinese use intensive farming, double cropping, technology, and aquaculture to produce food on a limited amount of farmland.
2. The dam should produce electrical power for central China. It is also engineered to control the flooding of the Yangzi River and to allow for better irrigation of farmland.
3. Changes in industry and agriculture have stimulated population growth. Farmers use more chemicals to increase crops and factories burn more polluting coal. The environment is under great stress.

Talk About It Answers

1. Flooding endangers people, homes, factories, and even entire cities. It also washes away the fertile topsoil. With its large population and small area of flat, fertile, well-watered soil, China's remaining land often floods.
2. The east has enough fertile land and rainfall to produce food for a large population. Cities grew here, and have grown steadily larger. Western regions of China have arid land and terrain that is often unsuitable for growing crops.
3. Low-lying, fertile, temperate areas in the east with sufficient rainfall to support crops are densely populated. Few people choose to live in the deserts, arid plateaus, and mountains.

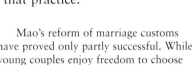

LESSON 3 Society and Culture

A young woman chooses to marry on May 18. "Everyone knows what today is!" she exclaims on her wedding morning. "I will get rich!"

In Chinese, "five one eight" is "*wu yao ba.*" That phrase sounds lmost like "*wo yao fa,*" which means "I will get rich." So marrying in he 5th month on the 18th day is considered lucky.

Chinese tradition required that marriages take place on "lucky" ays. Calendars listing lucky and unlucky days were always consulted. he Communists tried to stop the practice, calling it only superstition. oday, many Chinese are returning to that practice.

KEY IDEAS

- Despite the Communist revolution, old ways survive. Chinese life today often blends old and new ways.
- In the arts and cooking, modern China has built on traditions.
- China has made progress in educating its huge population.

KEY TERMS

Cultural Revolution

A Mix of New and Old

In 1949, the Communists replaced onfucian ideas with Communist eachings and the ideas of Mao Zedong. hey destroyed the old social order that laced some people above others. Loyalty o communism was considered more nportant than filial piety.

Communism changed family life in ther ways. "Women hold up half the ky," Mao once said. He had called for quality for women long before 1949. nce in power, the Communists declared hat women and men were equal. Women nd men were given freedom of choice in narriage. A man no longer ruled the ousehold. Women today attend niversities and hold high-level jobs.

Though both women and men work utside the home, old customs survive. Vomen do most of the housework, ooking, sewing, and childcare. A randmother will look after her randchild. A grandfather is more likely to e drinking tea and chatting with his iends.

Mao's reform of marriage customs have proved only partly successful. While young couples enjoy freedom to choose their own partners, they still ask their elders for advice. Despite Communist campaigns against expensive weddings, they are reappearing.

A woman welds at the Nanchang Metallurgical and Mining manufacturing plant. **How did Mao change the roles of women in China?**

Activity

World Superstitions

OBJECTIVES: 1.01

This lesson begins with an anecdote about a Chinese superstition. Have students research some superstitions from around the world. They should find one from each continent studied—Africa, Asia, and Australia—or allow them to choose a designated number. They can word process and illustrate them. Display the "Superstitions of the World" on a bulletin board.

OBJECTIVES: 6.02, 10.01, 11.04, 12.02

Discussion Questions

1 Explain what Deng Xiaoping was saying about Mao when he made these two statements: "A donkey is certainly slow, but at least it rarely has an accident" and "It does not matter if a cat is white or black as long as it catches mice."

2 What is a superstition? Why is it so hard to stop a person from believing in them?

3 What effect did communism have on the lives of women in China? Do you think the effects were positive or negative?

Caption Answer

Women gained political equality and began to work outside the home.

Activity

Chinese Proverbs

OBJECTIVES: 4.03

Chinese use proverbs of "literary expressions" in conversations. Many are similar to common English proverbs or sayings. Have students see if they can find an English equivalent for the following:

When hungry, one is not too fussy about what to eat.
When you are born, you don't bring it with you; when you die, you don't take it with you.
Trouble does not come singly.
When one enters a place, one should follow the customs of the place.
To lose a lot by coveting a little.
If one plants melons, one gets melons.
There are no waves if there is no wind.
To pick a needle from the bottom of the sea.
Without experiencing a thing, one does not gain knowledge of it.
For those with a will, the thing will be completed.
Ability acquired through practice produces fine performance.
Together in sweetness, together in bitterness.
The fast foot climbs to the top first.
An inch of time is an inch of gold.
The cat crying for the mouse.

Discussion Questions

1 How do the new forms of art differ from the more traditional?

Painting, literature, and theater

Possible answer: It shows that people are a part of nature but do not dominate it.

Personality Traits

OBJECTIVES: 4.03

Legend states that on his deathbed the Buddha summoned all the animals of the kingdom to his bedside. Only 12 turned up, so in order of their appearance, he dedicated a year to each of them:

Ox 1985, 1997; bright, dependable, inspiring, methodical, patient, steadfast
Tiger 1986, 1998; courageous, dynamic, a leader, open, sensitive, sincere, warm
Rabbit 1987, 1999; artistic, clearsighted, humble, lucky, peace seeking, talented
Dragon 1988, 2000; complex, flamboyant, healthy, imaginative, lucky, passionate
Snake 1989, 2001; discreet, high-spirited, intelligent, refined, sensual, wise
Horse 1990, 2002; competitive, impatient, popular, sociable, stubborn
Sheep 1991, 2003; artistic, creative, elegant, fastidious, indecisive, private
Monkey 1992, 2004; enthusiastic, good-humored, intelligent, popular, versatile, witty
Rooster 1993, 2005; aggressive, alert, eager to learn, perfectionist, pioneering
Dog 1994, 2006; conservative, generous, honest, loyal, stubborn, sympathetic
Pig 1995, 2007; caring, feisty, a friend for life, home-loving, industrious, noble
Rat 1996, 2008; ambitious, bright, charming, creative, free-spending, fun-loving

The Chinese assign these same animals to the hours of the day. The time at which one is born determines which animal's qualities one will inherit:

11 P.M.–1 A.M.	Hours of the Rat
1–3 A.M.	Hours of the Ox
3–5 A.M.	Hours of the Tiger
5–7 A.M.	Hours of the Rabbit
7–9 A.M.	Hours of the Dragon
9–11 A.M.	Hours of the Snake
11 A.M.–1 P.M.	Hours of the Horse
1–3 P.M.	Hours of the Sheep
3–5 P.M.	Hours of the Monkey
5–7 P.M.	Hours of the Rooster
7–9 P.M.	Hours of the Dog
9–11 P.M.	Hours of the Pig

Have students identify which animal(s) describe(s) them according to their date and time of birth. Are the year and the hour the same animal? Do the traits accurately describe them? Have students write a tanka or cinquain poem using the traits that best describe themselves in a personal poem.

This carved figure of royalty represents only one of China's art forms. **What are the others?**

Art and Culture

Museums around the world proudly display Chinese works of art. These include Chinese bronze objects more than 4,000 years old, handpainted scrolls of great beauty, or elegant porcelain vases. China's arts include sculpture, painting, literature, and theater.

Chinese artists developed unique ways of painting landscapes. In a single work, they captured both high mountains and people at work or play in nature. Most paintings have writing on them; a picture was not complete until the painter had briefly noted the ideas behind the work and added his seal.

The Cultural Revolution

The Communists dismissed the arts of Old China as useless. Mao proclaimed a ***Cultural Revolution*** to attack the Four Olds: old ideas, old culture, old customs, and old habits and to bring education, art, and literature in line with communism. Art must "serve the people," Mao said.

During the Cultural Revolution thousands of ancient works of art, books, and temples were destroyed. More than a million Chinese were killed. China's entire society was affected.

Under communism, artists made posters glorifying workers and farmers. New operas were written that recalled the hardships and heroes of the civil war. Books praised workers who sacrificed themselves for new China. These art forms broke away from Chinese tradition.

Today, artists respect old traditions and use methods of the great masters. Yet they may choose more modern subjects.

Customs

In China, dragons are a symbol of good luck, prosperity, and health. An emperor adopted the dragon as a royal emblem in ancient China. No one was allowed to wear clothes with the dragon symbol. Today, as in the past, Chinese celebrate their New Year with a dragon dance. A group puts on a long dragon costume (below) and parades through the streets.

This fifteenth-century Chinese painting shows people in the mountains. **How does this show the connection between people and nature?**

Word Origins

Ancient pagodas still stand in China (right). **Pagoda** comes from the Portuguese ***pagode***, which probably came from the Persian word ***butkada***, meaning "idol temple." A pagoda is a temple with many tiered roofs. Each roof gets progressively smaller. All are decorated with carvings and color.

Dish a Day or Twenty Years

Chinese food is popular around the orld. An expert on Chinese cooking has id that "if you ate a different Chinese sh [type of food] every day for 20 years, u would not exhaust all the choices."

China's geography and climate affect hat is grown and eaten in each region. In e North, people grow wheat and barley. ere, noodles and steamed buns are mmon. The South is more tropical, so eals include rice. Seafood is an portant part of the diet in eastern hina, near the Yellow Sea, East China a, and South China Sea.

Western China features hot and spicy ods. Sichuan Province alone has 2,000 shes. Some spicy Sichuan dishes can set ur tongue on fire.

The Chinese have learned to make a tle meat (or protein) stretch a long way. ey mix small amounts of meat or fish th vegetables, rice, or noodles. Because ood for cooking has been scarce for any centuries, the Chinese have veloped a method of cooking called stir-ying. They cut food into small pieces and ok them quickly in oil over a hot fire.

The Communists frowned on the vish banquets that the rich had once joyed. Today, however, successful hinese businesspeople are again ordering nquets. Brides and grooms entertain mily and friends with dozens expensive dishes.

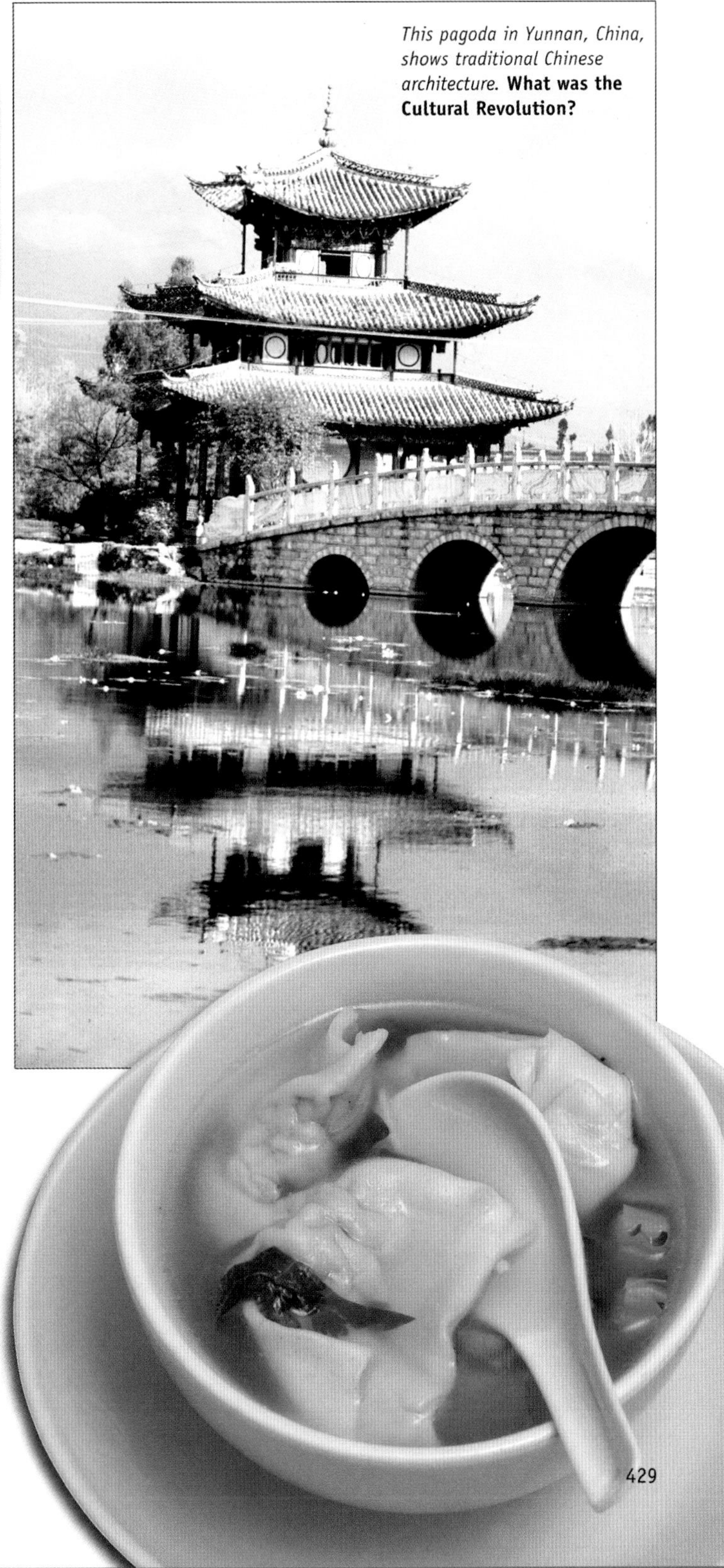

This pagoda in Yunnan, China, shows traditional Chinese architecture. **What was the Cultural Revolution?**

Americans enjoy eating many kinds of Chinese foods. **How does the environment affect the foods Chinese people eat?**

Discussion Questions

1 What are some foods we like to eat? Which of these foods would you usually find in our region?

2 Do you agree with the statement, "Until you can read, you can't learn anything"?

Caption Answer

The Cultural Revolution was Mao's program to bring art and culture in line with Communist ideals. It attacked the "old" ways of doing things.

Caption Answer

The foods of each region feature local agricultural products.

Activity

Chinese School System

 **OBJECTIVES:** 4.03

After studying about China's school system, have students read and research the school system in Japan. They should compare and contrast schools in North Carolina with those in China and Japan in an essay or a few paragraphs.

Activity

Chinese Recipes

 **OBJECTIVES:** 1.01, 4.03

Chinese restaurants are popular, but are all the foods served in these restaurants authentic? In cooperative groups, research Chinese cuisine. What foods are traditional and typical? How are these prepared? What herbs and spices do they use?

Have each group select and prepare a dish to share with the class. Students should present the dish to the class and explain the results of their research.

Extension This is a good opportunity to include your Chinese ELL students. Novice and intermediate ELL students can do this in a group with stronger students using an ELL-friendly Web site for research.

Background Information

An Ancient Pastime

In China, cricket-fighting has been popular for at least 1,000 years. The crickets, no more than 1½ inches long, battle each other in an 8-inch (20.3 cm) arena. In Beijing, Shanghai, and a few other Chinese cities, serious fans belong to associations that hold national championships each October. The Beijing Cricket Society has about 20 members, all men in their forties or older. Some who participate in the sport are serious gamblers who bet thousands of dollars at secret, illegal matches, but most are hobbyists. By tradition, Shandong Province in eastern China is the best place to buy cricket fighters. Thousands of men from all over China travel there in August and September to choose their champions.

Discussion Questions

1 Why do you think Chinese students seem to be more motivated to learn than students in the United States, and yet only about a third of them graduate from high school?

2 What would your reaction be if our government assigned you your job after you graduated?

3 What would this say about the role of the government in the lives of citizens?

Caption Answer

Chinese students learn reading, arithmetic, science, politeness, discipline, and respect.

Caption Answer

The symbol for mouth is part of the symbol for words (things coming "up out of the mouth"). The symbol for words is part of the symbol for speech. Telephone is a combination of electricity and speech, or electric speech.

Activity

Chinese Architecture

 **OBJECTIVES:** 4.03

Have students study and research traditional Chinese architecture. They can make a model of a pagoda to display in the classroom using the materials of their choice.

Kindergarten children line up before school. Chinese attend school five and a half days a week. **What do they study?**

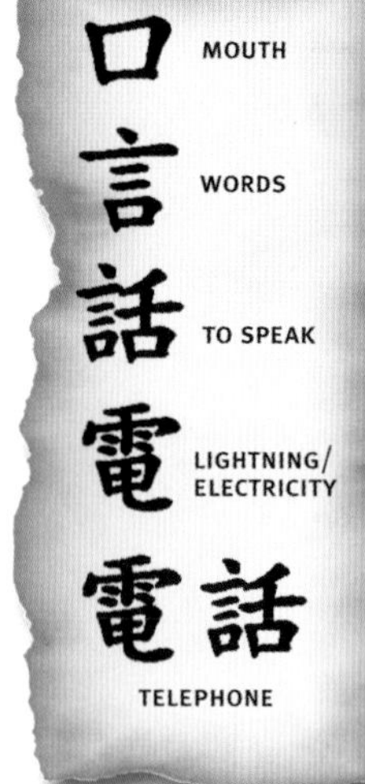

Chinese characters are pictographs that are combined with other pictographs to create words. **How are these pictographs combined to create the character for telephone?**

Education

Since 1949, China has made progress toward increasing literacy. Most young Chinese attend primary school. Children begin school at age six. Many primary schools are crowded with as many as 50 students to a class.

Students face an uphill struggle to learn to read and write thousands of Chinese characters. The government has simplified many characters. It has also introduced the roman (Western) alphabet. "Until you can read, you can't learn anything," said one young student. "So we begin with Chinese written in the roman alphabet. Then we can build up the words as American children do.... You need about 2,000 Chinese characters to understand most subjects at primary school, and it often takes four years of schooling to learn so many."

Chinese students seem motivated to learn. Children attend school Monday through Friday and on Saturday mornin[g]. Besides reading, arithmetic, and science, they learn politeness, discipline, and respect.

Only about a third of all students complete high school. Gaining acceptanc[e] to a university is hard. Students have to pass stiff three-day exams similar to thos[e] government officials once had to take.

China is trying to make higher education more available. By 2010, there will be 15 percent more university slots, room for about 18 million students. Eve[n] with this expansion, only about 20 percent of China's young people will be able to attend college.

After completing university courses, the government assigns the graduates to jobs. Today, many prefer to begin workin[g] in private business.

LESSON 3 REVIEW

Fact Follow-Up

1. Describe a Chinese tradition that is a part of modern life.
2. How have the arts changed in China?
3. Describe education in today's China.
4. What was the Cultural Revolution?
5. Why are dragons important symbols in China?

Talk About It

1. Under Chinese law, women now have the same rights as men. Has this change in law changed women's lives? Explain.
2. How does Chinese cooking reflect the geography of China? Explain.
3. How has China's change from a Confucian to a modern society changed education?

LESSON 3 REVIEW

Fact Follow-Up Answers

1. Although young people have the right to choose their own partners, they still ask their elders for advice. The wedding may be elaborate and expensive and perhaps take place on a traditional "lucky day." Other surviving traditions include the persistence of traditional roles for men and women, "lucky" days, art forms, and Chinese cooking.
2. Today, artists respect old traditions and use methods of the great masters, but they may choose more modern subjects, such as farmers, factory workers, or China's national minorities.
3. Chinese students attend school Monday through Friday and on Saturday morning. They study reading, arithmetic, politeness, discipline, and respect. Most Chinese attend primary school, but only about a third of all students complete high school. Gaining admittance to a technical school or university is difficult because there are few available positions and many applicants. However, China is trying to make higher education more available.
4. The Cultural Revolution came about because the Communists dismissed the arts of Old China as useless. Art must "serve the people," Mao said. During the Cultural Revolution, thousands of ancient works of art, books, and temples were destroyed.
5. This royal emblem brings good luck, prosperity, and wealth.

Talk About It Answers

1. Answers will vary. Although they are likely to work outside the home, women still are responsible for childcare, cooking, and cleaning.
2. In the North, where people grow wheat and barley, there are more noodles and steamed buns used in cooking. In the more tropical South, more rice is included in meals.
3. The government has introduced simplified characters and the Roman (Western) alphabet to make learning to read easier. Students still face stiff examinations, as in Confucian times, but now many choose private business as well as government employment.

Applying Decision-Making and Problem-Solving Techniques in World Issues

Achieving Democracy in China

Wu Enlai was three years old when the demonstrations for democracy took place in Tienanmen Square. Now a university student, he has heard about older brothers and sisters of his classmates who occupied the square and built the liberty statue. He has an uncle who was killed when Chinese soldiers stopped the demonstrations.

Wu and his friends want more freedoms than the Communist government allows. In small gatherings in apartments near the university, he and his friends talk about ways to increase democracy in China.

They want all the benefits of democracy: free elections, freedom of speech, freedom of religion, freedom of assembly, and a free press. Such freedoms are important to them as individuals. They also believe that China cannot become a great nation unless people have freedom to think and speak out.

Yet Wu and his friends remember how the government's forces cracked down on students in Tienanmen Square. So they must think seriously about their plans.

What can Wu and his friends do to increase democracy? What might be the consequences of their actions? What course of action would you recommend so they could be successful in making China more democratic?

To answer these questions, a consequences chart can help you organize your thoughts. Work in small groups to come up with two or three suggestions to increase democracy in China.

For each suggestion, complete a chart similar to the one on the right. Write the suggested course of action in the proposal box. List possible negative consequences in the boxes under that category on the left. List positive consequences on the right.

What proposal will do more than any other to increase democracy in China? Why? Write a paragraph explaining your best proposal. Give the reasons you think that proposal will work.

What proposal had more negative consequences than positive consequences? Was the chart helpful in making a decision?

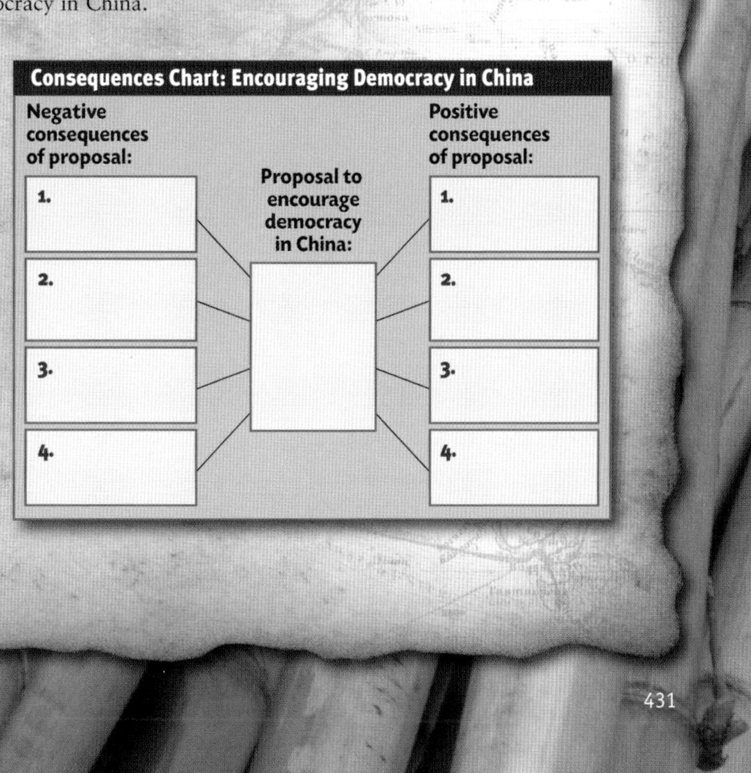

Teaching This Skill Lesson

Materials Needed textbooks, paper, pencils

Classroom Organization whole class, small groups, individual

Beginning the Lesson Tell the class the story of Wu Enlai on page 423 or relate something from your own memory about the Tienanmen Square Massacre. If appropriate, tie this student-led protest to the American civil rights movement or the work of Gandhi in India, drawing comparisons.

Lesson Development Ask what Wu Enlai and his friends might be able to do to bring more democracy to China. Accept student responses and list them on the chalkboard. Help students narrow their suggestions to four or five. Caution students that any actions the Chinese students might take will have both negative and positive consequences. Place students in small groups, assign each group one of the suggestions, and introduce the consequences chart on page 423. For a homework assignment, direct each student in a group to complete the chart.

Conclusion When students return to class, allow groups to work together to produce a group chart. Have each group explain its proposal and argue whether it should be followed. If appropriate, have students select one proposal as best.

Extension If desired, students might write letters to their United States senators and representatives suggesting that our government encourage the proposal they have selected.

Skill Lesson Review

1. What were some of the suggested proposals to increase democracy in China? *Answers will vary. A possibility is to write and publish an independent newspaper.*

2. Did any proposal produce more negative consequences than positive consequences? If so, why? If not, why not? *Answers will vary. Violent revolution would certainly lead to widespread bloodshed.*

Talk About It

1. Hong Kong has developed a booming economy and is located next to Shenzhen, a SEZ. With Hong Kong now under Chinese control, this may become one of the world's great business centers.
2. Mao emphasized political and revolutionary zeal. Deng was more practical.
3. Deng ended government controls over agricultural communes and let farmers lease the land and decide what to grow and sell.
4. Foreign investors in a SEZ provide jobs and training in advanced science and technology. Foreign investors have also opened factories and other businesses that contribute to the Chinese economy.
5. Political change might end the possibility for foreign investment. China is being influenced by Western ideas and culture through foreign investment. The economy depends on money and jobs brought by foreign investment. It is difficult for the Chinese to accept some Western ideas and not others; ideas bring the possibility that Chinese demands for more political freedoms will continue.
6. People condemned the government's action, because the students were demonstrating peacefully for reform.
7. Young people have freedom of choice in marriage. Women can work and go to school outside the home. Yet people's daily lives are still highly controlled.
8. Important points: Students should give reasons. Chinese farmers are doing what they can to use farmland and other food supplies wisely. Expanded irrigation could open up new land to cultivation.
9. Important points: The choice is between the freedom to decide on a career (with the risk of failure) and the security of an assured profession (with the risk of disappointment or boredom).
10. Both closely controlled people; both have had the ideal of providing for people's needs and ensuring peace and order, and both have been brutally cruel.
11. Important points: Students should take a position and support it with explanations. Cities are already overcrowded and have inadequate housing. Cities also offer better schools, a wider choice of activities, and a variety of jobs. Students might also mention the importance of being allowed to move freely.

CHAPTER 21 REVIEW

Lessons Learned

LESSON 1
Economy and Government
Deng Xiaoping became the new leader of the Communist Party and of China after Mao Zedong died. Deng introduced an economic reform plan. Special Economic Zones have increased foreign investment. Deng achieved much more than Mao in promoting China's economic development.

LESSON 2
People in a Changing Environment
Chinese farmers know how to make the most of their land. The Chinese have long relied on their vast network of rivers for transportation, water, and power. Southern China is hilly and mountainous, so farmers cultivate on terraces. Western China is mostly too dry to farm. Eastern China has limited land because of its large and densely settled population. People continue to move to cities.

LESSON 3
Society and Culture
Chinese pottery and paintings reflect the Chinese love of beauty. Chinese cooking reflects its geography. Families mix old and new traditions in daily life. Chinese children receive a basic education, but students have limited chances for high school and college.

Talk About It

1. Why is Hong Kong important to China?
2. Compare the leadership of Mao Zedong and Deng Xiaoping.
3. How did Deng improve agricultural production?
4. Why are foreign investors important in China?
5. What might be the risks for the foreign investors in China? For China in accepting large foreign investments?
6. What was world reaction to China's treatment of demonstrators in the 1989 student rebellion? Why?
7. How has the Communist government affected the daily lives of the Chinese?
8. Can farmers solve the problem of limited farmland? Explain your answer.
9. Would you prefer a government-assigned job such as a Chinese college graduate receives? What are the benefits? What are the risks?
10. In what ways has China's Communist government been similar to the Confucian system in Old China?
11. Should the government limit people moving into cities? Explain.

Mastering Mapwork

HUMAN-ENVIRONMENTAL INTERACTION
Use the map on page 415 to answer these questions:

1. In which areas would you expect to find the least evidence of humans interacting with the environment?
2. Locate the intersection of 30°N and 100 °E. Describe the evidence of human-environmental interaction you would expect to observe in this place.
3. Locate the intersection of 40°N and 90°E. Describe the evidence of human-environmental interaction you would expect to observe in this place.
4. Locate the intersection of 30°N and 120°E. Describe the evidence of human-environmental interaction you would expect to observe in this place.
5. Where is forestry practiced?

432

Chapter

Mastering Mapwork

1. Southern and southwest China in the areas bordering the Himalayas show areas of little or no economic activity, an indication of little human-environmental interaction. There are also areas like this in northern and northwestern China.
2. Because this is an area of little or no economic activity, one would expect to find little evidence of human-environmental interaction. Any evidence would likely be that of the environment limiting the actions of people.
3. In this place one would expect to see people engaging in nomadic herding, their animals moving about in search of grass and drinking water. If there were too many animals or too little water, the environment would be harmed.
4. Because of subsistence farming, the nearness of an area of manufacturing and trade, and the presence of nearby lead mining and hydroelectric power, one would expect to observe that humans have greatly changed the natural environment.
5. Forestry is practiced in a small area of extreme northeastern China.

Go to the Source

Comparing National Symbols

China's national anthem, "the March of the Volunteers," was first promoted secretly as part of the anti-Japanese resistance in the 1930s. It was banned during the Cultural Revolution and later restored as the national anthem in 1982. Taiwan's national anthem describes the vision and hopes of its people. The Three Principles of the People are generally described as nationalism, democracy, and the people's livelihood.

Read the national anthems of China and Taiwan below. Answer the questions using specific references to the songs.

China's National Anthem
"March of the Volunteers" (Yiyongjun Jinxingqu)

Arise,
Ye who refuse to be slaves!
With our very flesh and blood,
Let us build our new Great Wall!
The peoples of China are in the most critical time,
Everybody must roar his defiance.
Arise!
Arise!
Arise!
Millions of hearts with one mind,
Brave the enemy's gunfire, March on!
Brave the enemy's gunfire, March on!
March on!
March on!
On!

Lyrics: Tian Han
Music: Nieh Erh
Composed: 1932

Taiwan's National Anthem
"San Min Chu I" (Three Principles of the People)

"San min chu I", our aim shall be,
To found a free land, world peace be our stand.
Lead on comrades, vanguards ye are,
Hold fast your aim, by sun and star,
Be earnest and brave, your country to save,
One heart, one soul, one mind, one goal!

Lyrics: Tai Chuan-hsien, from a speech by Sun Yat Sen
Music: Cheng Mao-Yun
Adopted: 1930

Questions

1. What are these two documents?
2. In "March of the Volunteers" what do you think is meant by, "Let us build our new Great Wall?
3. Who do you think is the "enemy" referred to in the last line of China's national anthem?
4. Based on the line " 'San min chu I', our aim shall be," what do you think "San min chu I" is?
5. What are the similarities in the two anthems?
6. What are the differences in the two anthems?

Go to the Source

hina Today 434

Go to the Source

OBJECTIVES: 7.01, 7.02, 8.01, 9.01, 10.01, 10.03, 12.01 Skills 2.01, 2.02, 3.05, 4.02

National anthems, like flags, seals, and other symbols of a nation, are chosen to represent the nation's identity. Depending on the type of society or government a nation has, the leaders in power chose symbols that represent the values of the people or what they want the people to respect and follow.

Visit **NCJourneys.com** for links to these national anthems.

ANSWERS

1. The national anthems of the People's Republic of China and the Republic of China (Taiwan)
2. The reference is to the Great Wall of China that was built to protect China from invaders. This reference is possibly meaning that China needs to become strong to protect itself from modern enemies.
3. Possibly enemies of their government or way of life within their country, or possibly enemies in other countries or other countries themselves.
4. It is a goal for the country. San min chu I is actually a political philosophy of nationalism, democracy, and socialism (social welfare/people's liveilhood). Encourage students to find the meaning on the Internet or other source.
5. Both anthems are asking for the people to be brave and unite to reach the goals.
6. China's anthem is more defensive and militaristic with words such as "build our new Great Wall," "refuse to be slaves," and "roar his defiance." Taiwan's anthem is focused on peace and freedom, "To found a free land, world peace be our stand."

How to Use the Chapter Review

There are three sections in the Chapter Review: Talk About It, Mastering Mapwork, and Go to the Source. Use the Vocabulary Worksheets and the Chapter Review Worksheet in the Teacher's Resource Guide for additional reinforcement and preparation for the Chapter Assessments. The chapter and lesson reviews and the Chapter Review Worksheets are the basis of the assessment for each chapter.

Talk About It questions encourage students to speculate about the content of the chapter and are suitable for class or small-group discussion. They are not intended to be assigned for homework.

Mastering Mapwork has students apply one or more of the Five Themes of Geography to maps within the chapter.

Go to the Source activities allow students to analyze a primary source that relates to the content of the chapter. The questions and activities familiarize students with different types of primary sources and also build content-reading skills.

Korea

Social Studies Strands

Geographic Relationships
Division

Cultures and Diversity

Historic Perspectives

Global Connections

Economics and Development

Government and Active Citizenship

Worksheets

Worksheets and answer keys are found both in the Teacher's Resource Guide and at **NCJourneys.com**, including Reading Guides, Reading Strategies, Chapter Reviews, English Language Learner and others.

North Carolina Standard Course of Study

Goal 2 The learner will assess the relationship between physical environment and cultural characteristics of selected societies and regions of Africa, Asia, and Australia.

Goal 6 The learner will recognize the relationship between economic activity and the quality of life in Africa, Asia, and Australia.

Goal 9 The learner will analyze the different forms of government developed in Africa, Asia, and Australia.

Goal 10 The learner will compare the rights and civic responsibilities of individuals in political structures in Africa, Asia, and Australia.

Goal 11 The learner will recognize the common characteristics of different cultures in Africa, Asia, and Australia.eas over time and place in Africa, Asia, and Australia.

Goal 12 The learner will assess the influence of major religions, ethical beliefs, and values on cultures in Africa, Asia, and Australia.

Teaching & Assessment

- English Language Learner Modified Lesson Plans for this chapter are found in the Teacher's Resource Guide.
- *ExamView® Assessment Suite* is provided at **NCJourneys.com.** It includes customizable assessments for all chapters. Paper tests are also available in the Teacher's Resource Guide. See pages T16–T17 for information about how to use the assessments and the Scoring Guide.

ACTIVITIES AND INTEGRATIONS

SOCIAL STUDIES
● Mealtime, p. 434B
Some Korean Peninsula Economic Features, p. 437
★ ▲ ■ Korea, the Cultural Bridge, p. 425
● Daoism, p. 438
Korean Resources, p. 439
The Korean War, p. 443
Scavenger Hunt, p. 444
▲ ■ The Korean Wheel, p. 448
Po-Pawi-Kawi Game, p. 449
Skill Lesson: Perspectives on Living in a Divided Nation, p. 451

READING/LANGUAGE ARTS	READING/LANGUAGE ARTS OBJECTIVES
A Divided Nation, p. 434B	1.03
Analogies, p. 434B	1.02
Activator: *So Far From the Bamboo Grove,* p. 434	1.02
Writing Prompt: Divided Korea, p. 434	3.01
■ Korean Peninsula, p. 435	2.01
Korea, p. 442	2.01
● Women of the Sea: Compare and Contrast, p. 449	1.02
Go to the Source: Understanding Context, p. 453	1.02, 2.01, 3.01, 4.01

MATHEMATICS	MATHEMATICS OBJECTIVES
★ ■ GNP Bar Graph, p. 444	4.01, 4.05
Currency Exchange, p. 446	1.01, 1.02
Korean Kimchi, p. 447	1.01

TECHNOLOGY	TECHNOLOGY OBJECTIVES
■ A Divided Nation, p. 434B	3.01, 3.08
Mealtime in Korea, p. 437	3.01, 3.08
★ United Nations Peacekeeping, p. 440	3.01, 3.05
▲ Life in the DMZ, p. 440	
Korea, p. 442	3.01, 3.08
Korean Postage Stamps, p. 448	3.01, 3.11
★ Women of the Sea (research), p. 449	3.01, 3.07

VISUAL ARTS	VISUAL ARTS OBJECTIVES
● Korean Folding Fans, p. 434B	2.04, 5.02
Mask Dance and Drama, p. 446	4.01, 5.03

CHARACTER AND VALUES EDUCATION	TRAITS
Writing Prompt: Divided Korea, p. 434	good judgment, respect
What Would You Do?, p. 446	good judgment

● Basic Activities ★ Challenging Activities ▲ English Language Learner Novice ■ English Language Learner Intermediate

Chapter Activities

Introductory Activity

Mealtime

OBJECTIVES: 11.01, 11.02

In Korea, especially in the past, mealtime looked different than mealtime in the United States. If you can, bring in Asian food, specifically Korean food if you can find it (rice, tea, and fish are more available choices). Tell students that they are going to experience mealtime as it was in Korea. Students can remove their shoes and put them under their desks. Everyone will wash their hands carefully. Have students clear a place on the floor to sit. You might wish to put down a sheet on the floor for this.

Have the youngest females (ask birth dates) and all the males sit in a circle. The youngest females represent the children of a family. The rest of the female students will be the preparers and servers of the meal. They are to take the food to the circle, make a small bow, present the dish, and then put the plate down and leave. After all the men and children have been served, the female students may eat standing up in their section of the room.

After everything is cleaned up and the room restored to normal, have students write a journal entry on their feelings. Tell the class that on the next day, they will be asked to share those entries if they wish. Next day: Let those who want to share their journal entries do so. Then arrange the students in small groups to discuss the experience. Let them use these questions as guidelines: How did it feel to wait on someone? Were they comfortable? uncomfortable? How did it feel to be served? Who serves the food when your family eats together? Why do you think that Korean families served meals this way?

Extension This is a good activity to involve the Korean ELL students in your class. Ask them to share recipes and customs for traditional meals at their house. For novice ELL students, substitute drawing a picture(s) for the journal writing. Intermediate ELL students should write a few simple sentences. Do not expect the ELL students to participate in the discussion.

Culminating Activity

A Divided Nation

OBJECTIVES: 9.02, 11.03

Based on what has been studied, have a class debate about whether or how North and South Korea should reunite. Put students in groups of four or five. Have at least two students from each group go online for information about Korea. Mention to students that United States relations with South Korea are a part of the debate. Have teams debate one another on the issue. Make sure all teams use the facts for their basic arguments. Refer to the Guide to Student Debates in the front of the Teacher's Edition.

Art Activity

Korean Folding Fans

OBJECTIVES: 12.02

Materials heavy white 18-inch by 9-inch construction paper, watercolor paint, paintbrushes, newspapers, cups for water, drawing paper, pencils, BBQ skewers

On drawing paper practice drawing a scene or designs (scenes may be thematic based on what is being studied about Korea). On a large white sheet of paper, lightly draw the scene or designs; fill the entire sheet. Use watercolors to paint the design. When the painting is dry, measure every half inch along the bottom and top of the paper (the 18-inch side). Measure on the back of the paper to avoid placing marks on the painting. Carefully fold on each of the marks. Change the direction of each fold to create the fan. Place the skewers in the fold at either end of the fan for rigidity. The skewers should stick out and meet 2 to 3 inches below the fan.

Analogies

OBJECTIVES: 9.02, 10.04

Analogies are useful to help students make associations with prior knowledge. Read the analogies aloud and ask students to identify the relationship between the terms. As an extension, ask students to write their own analogies using key terms or places discussed in the chapter.

absorb : assimilate/incorporate :: expel : remove (synonyms)

annex : take over :: abandon : relinquish/give up (synonyms)

civilians : noncombatants :: military : combatants (synonyms)

armistice : truce :: declaration of war : battle (synonyms)

reunification : unification :: rerun : run :: retake : take (is to do again)

Koreans : bow :: Americans : handshake (greet with a)

mudang : Korea :: traditional healer : Africa (is a spiritual advisor in)

Teaching Strategies

Be sure to stress the importance of the influence of Japan and China on Korea. The Korean War is found in Lesson 2. Allocate adequate time to this important event.

Activator

OBJECTIVES: 11.02, 12.02

Activators are great tools to use in order to "hook" the attention of the students. Reading picture books or stories is an excellent way to build interest in the subject and is also a great way to integrate language arts into the social studies curriculum.

So Far From the Bamboo Grove by Yoko Kawashima Watkins. (Mass Market Paperback, Morrow, William & Co., 1994. ISBN 068813158.) This is a chapter book and not a storybook. It could be suggested as an integration between language arts and social studies.

Korean Cinderella by Shirley Climo, (Harper Collins, 1993. ISBN 006020432X.)

Tales from the Bamboo Grove by Yoko Kawashima Watkins. (Bradbury Press, 1992. ISBN 0027925250.)

Writing Prompt

OBJECTIVES: 5.03, 9.02, 10.01

Evaluative

Korea is a divided country. Write or word process an essay explaining whether you think the people of North and South Korea have more differences than they have things in common. Use facts from Chapter 22 to support your opinion.

As you write your essay, remember to:

- clearly state your position.
- give at least three reasons and explain your reasons fully.
- give examples to support your reasons.
- write in complete sentences and paragraph form.
- organize your ideas and include an introduction and a conclusion.
- use good grammar, spelling, punctuation, and capitalization.

CHAPTER 22

Korea

"The ties that bind us to Paektu Mountain are truly hard to break," said Korean writer Yuktan Ch'oe Nam-son. "The mountain and the people," he wrote, "are of a single origin, not two."

Yet Korea is divided into two rival governments—North Korea and South Korea. South Korea's national anthem mentions Mount Paektu, which lies across the border in North Korea. The hope of a united nation was symbolized in the opening ceremonies of the 2000 Summer Olympics. South Koreans and North Koreans walked together for the first time in 50 years under a fla featuring the shape of the Korean peninsula.

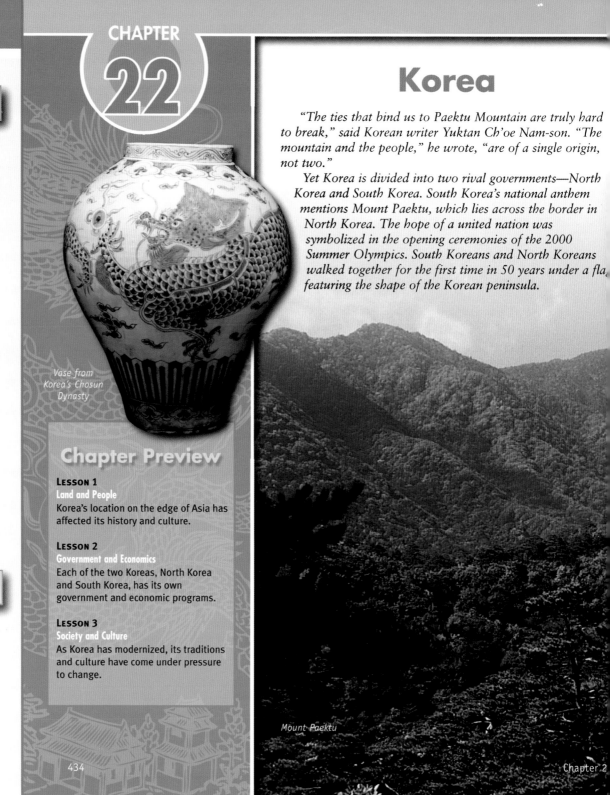

Vase from Korea's Chosun Dynasty

Chapter Preview

Lesson 1
Land and People
Korea's location on the edge of Asia has affected its history and culture.

Lesson 2
Government and Economics
Each of the two Koreas, North Korea and South Korea, has its own government and economic programs.

Lesson 3
Society and Culture
As Korea has modernized, its traditions and culture have come under pressure to change.

Mount Paektu

434

Chapter 2

Chapter Resources

Print Resources

Fiction

Choi, Sook Nyul. *Echoes of the White Giraffe.* Houghton Mifflin, 1993. ISBN 0395647215.

__. *The Year of Impossible Goodbyes.* Houghton Mifflin, 1991. ISBN 0395574196.

Lee, Marie. *If It Hadn't Been for Yoon Jur.* Houghton Mifflin, 1993. ISBN 0395629411.

Okimoto, Jean. *Molly by Any Other Name.* Scholastic, 1991. ISBN 0590429930.

Watkins, Yoko. *So Far From the Bamboo Grove.* Lothrop, Lee & Shepard, 1986. ISBN 0688061109.

Nonfiction

Kwek, Karen, Johanna Masse, Melvin Neo, Dorothy L. Gibbs. *Welcome to South Korea* (Welcome to My Country). Gareth Stevens Publishing, 2003. ISBN 0836825535.

Nash, Amy K. *North Korea* (Modern World Nations series). Chelsea House, 1999. ISBN 0791047466.

North and South Korea– Political/Physical

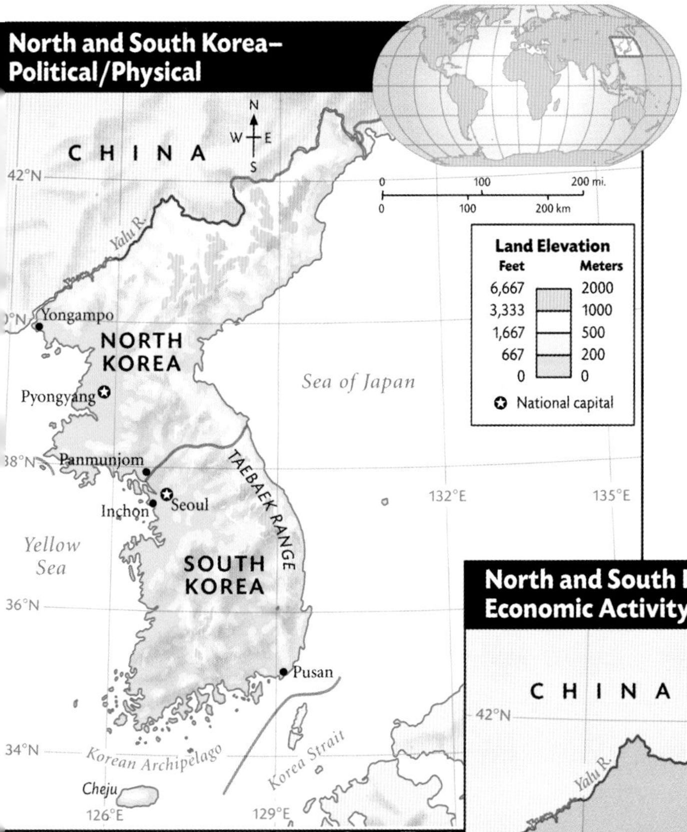

Land Elevation

Feet	Meters
6,667	2000
3,333	1000
1,667	500
667	200
0	0

National capital

Korean athletes march in the opening ceremonies of the 2000 Summer Olympics.

North and South Korea– Economic Activity and Resources

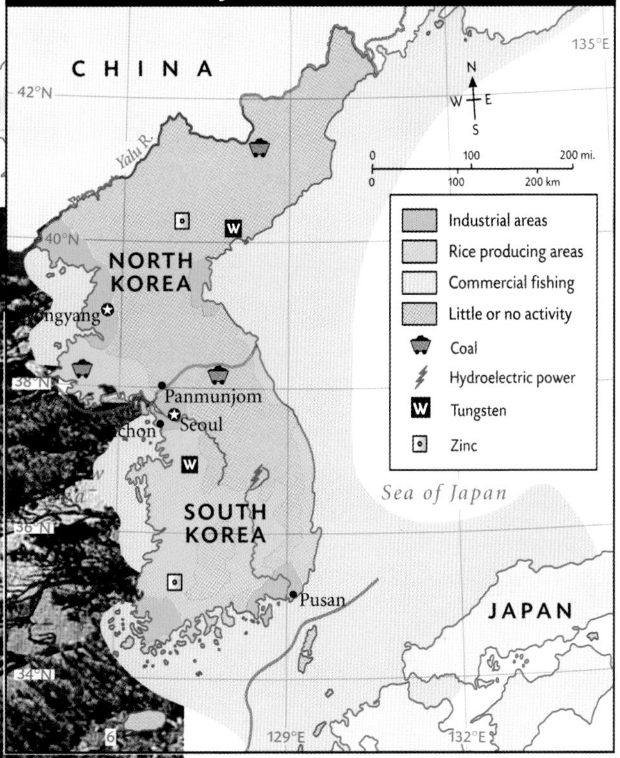

Industrial areas
Rice producing areas
Commercial fishing
Little or no activity
Coal
Hydroelectric power
Tungsten
Zinc

435

Map Activity

Korean Peninsula

NATIONAL GEOGRAPHY STANDARDS: 1, 4, 17

GEOGRAPHIC THEMES: Location, Place, Movement, Region

OBJECTIVES: 1.03, 2.02, 3.01

Students are to answer the following questions:

1. On what type of landform are North and South Korea located? *peninsula*
2. Identify the river that forms the boundary between North Korea and China. *Yalu River*
3. Name the mountain range found in eastern South Korea. *Taebaek Range*
4. What three bodies of water touch the Korean Peninsula? *Yellow Sea, Sea of Japan, Korea Strait*
5. What physical feature(s) are found in the southern part of South Korea? *archipelago/islands*
6. What line of latitude is often associated with the boundary between North Korea and South Korea? *38°N*
7. What city is often used by both Korean governments and world leaders when political discussions are held on this peninsula? *Panmunjom* Why? *It is along the Demilitarized Zone/DMZ—armistice line—established after the war in 1953*
8. Which Korea hosted the 1998 Summer Olympic Games? *South Korea*
9. At what elevation is Yongampo located? *0–667 feet/0–200 meters*
10. To what meridian of longitude is the capital of North Korea closest— 126°E or 38°N? *126°E*
11. What is the approximate latitude of Pusan? *35°N*
12. Is Inchon on the Yellow Sea or Sea of Japan? *Yellow Sea*
13. How far is Cheju from the Korean Peninsula? *approximately 61 miles (100 km)*
14. Why is Korea often seen as a connection between China and Japan? *This peninsula is located between the two nations which have used Korea as a bridge.*

Shepheard, Patricia. *South Korea* (Modern World Nations series). Chelsea House, 1999. ISBN 079104985X.

Back Issues of Magazines

Korea. Cobblestone Publishing Company. ISBN 038240789X.

Audiovisual

Hidden Korea. PBS Video.

Web Sites

Go to **NCJourneys.com** for links to the following Web sites:

- Hidden Korea companion Web site
- Korea.net
- Korean Cultural Service
- Life in Korea Cultural Spotlight

OBJECTIVES: 2.01, 2.03, 11.01, 12.03

Discussion Questions

1 Why is "bando" an appropriate description for Korea?

2 What cultures have influenced life where you live?

Caption Answer

The mountains and the sea have partly isolated Korea from its neighbors.

Activity

Korea, the Cultural Bridge

OBJECTIVES: 11.01, 12.03

Review the Chinese influence on Korean cultural development and the movement of these influences to Japan.

Divide students into groups. Design a poster that illustrates the movement of ideas from China to Korea and from Korea to Japan. Students should design two bridges that link the three countries. Develop symbols to depict each idea as it moves across each bridge. For example, a people cut-out chain depicting cultural influences could stretch across each bridge.

ELL Teaching Tips

Promote versus Prohibit Native Language Interaction

Provide periods that allow new ELLs to spend time each day speaking with others of the same native language. Everyone needs "downtime" once in a while.

LESSON 1 Land and People

KEY IDEAS

- Korea is located on a peninsula surrounded by three major powers: China, Japan, and Russia. It has served as a bridge between China and Japan.
- Much of Korea is mountainous. Mountains have been a barrier against invaders but have made farming difficult.
- Despite political divisions today, Koreans share the same language, history, culture, and ethnic background.

KEY TERMS

han' gul

Bando is the Korean word for peninsula. It means "half-island." The word describes Korea perfectly. Korea is a peninsula 600 miles (966 km) long. It is about the size of Utah, with more than 5,500 miles (8,855 km) of coastline.

Korea is connected to China—and East Asia—in the north. Yet it is cut off from mainland Asia by rugged mountains. Like an island, it is partly isolated by its location.

On the Edge of Asia

Look at the map locating Korea in East Asia (page 375). Think about why Koreans sometimes compare it to a rabbit. In the north, the rabbit's ears touch China and bump against a corner of Russia. In the west, the rabbit's whiskers dip into Korea Bay. Its paws paddle in the Yellow Sea. In the east, its backbone is the T'aebaek Range, which curves along the Sea of Japan.

Comparing Korea to a rabbit works in another way. Korea is a small country surrounded by major powers—China, Russia, and Japan. Korea has never tried to conquer these other lands, but it often has been invaded.

Early on, Korea developed its own culture. Because of its nearness to China, it absorbed ideas from that neighbor. Koreans made their own uses of Chinese arts, architecture, belief systems, and medicine.

Korea then served as a cultural bridge. It passed Chinese influences on to Japan. For more than 1,000 years, Korea provided a peaceful link between China and Japan.

Buddhist temples are found high in the mountains of Korea. **How have the mountains and sea affected Korea?**

436 Chapter 2

It's a Fact

Korea

- The first armored vessel, in 1592, was used by Korea against Japan's invasion. It was called the Turtle Ship.
- Korean Peninsula is the length of Florida. North Korea is slightly smaller than Mississippi. South Korea is slightly larger than Indiana.
- Self-reliance (juche) has been the emphasis of the North Korean government since 1953.
- Species of animals once thought to be bordering on the brink of extinction have flourished in the DMZ.
- There is a 20- to 25-year difference in the life expectancy between the populations of North and South Korea.
- A peace treaty ending the war between North and South Korea was never signed.

A woman weeds rice in a paddy near Seoul, South Korea. **What part of the peninsula has the most fertile farmland?**

Mountainous Terrain

Visitors to Korea must be in good ıape to reach its most famous Buddhist mples and shrines. Many are found high the mountains. Mountains cover more ıan 70 percent of Korea. Most run north south or northeast to southeast.

The largest chain is the T'aebaek ange. It runs along the entire east coast. he lashing tides of the Sea of Japan have ırved out sheer cliffs along the coastal ınge.

Mountains have made life rough, especially in more mountainous North Korea. The rugged land has made farming nearly impossible and movement difficult. "Over the mountains, more mountains" is a Korean proverb that describes Korea's landforms. The saying also suggests that Koreans have overcome one obstacle only to meet another.

Korea's south and west coasts consist of coastal plains and low hills. The best farmland is found on southern coastal plains. Most people live there, too.

Customs

Kimchi, a spicy dish served with most every meal, reflects differences between Korean foods and those of China and Japan. Cabbage is chopped, mixed with salt, garlic, hot red peppers, and equally hot ground ginger. It is then stored in large earthenware jars until the cabbage is pickled. Tradition says that every family needs 50 heads of cabbage for a year's supply.

Climate

Like much of East Asia, monsoons influence the climate of Korea. The summer monsoon brings rains that let Koreans grow rice, a major food crop. The moist, tropical summers are balanced by cold, dry winters that last from November to April.

The climate varies somewhat from north to south. Winters are harsh in the North with heavy snows and bitter winds. Farmers there can harvest only one crop a year. The climate of the South is milder and offers a longer growing season. Some South Korean farmers can grow two crops a year.

Discussion Questions

1 Why do you think Buddhist temples and shrines are built high on the mountains? Wouldn't you expect them to be located so people can reach them more easily?

2 What are some of the obstacles Korea has had to overcome?

3 The climate of Korea is most like the climate of which region in North Carolina?

Caption Answer

The best farmland is found on the southern coastal plains.

Activity

Mealtime in Korea

OBJECTIVES: 4.03, 11.01

Have students research Korean foods. On a bulletin board, draw an outline map. Label areas that could be sources for foods.

Seas: fish, eel, squid, seaweed, shellfish

Highlands: mushrooms, roots, greens, such fruit as apples, pears, plums

Lowlands: vegetables such as cabbages, radishes, carrots, peppers, onions, beans, cucumbers

Generally meals include rice, kimchi, soup, vegetable, fruit, sometimes fish or meat

Plan and prepare a meal at school. Students may sit on floor in family groupings with food on a cloth in center.

Practice some Korean table manners:

- It is impolite to eat before elders start.
- Only spoons or chopsticks may be used to pick up food—no fingers.
- Leave a small amount of food on plate when finished, to show there was enough to eat.
- Talking or making noises while eating is considered impolite.
- Jokes about food are impolite.

Extension Novice and intermediate ELL students should use an ELL-friendly Web site for research. A peer tutor or group help may be needed to complete the activity.

Map Activity

Some Korean Peninsula Economic Features (page 435)

NATIONAL GEOGRAPHY STANDARDS: 1, 4, 16

GEOGRAPHIC THEMES: Location, Place, Human-Environmental Interaction, Region

OBJECTIVES: 1.02, 2.01

Have students answer the following:

1. Which economic activity has the greatest area of influence? *commercial fishing*
2. What economic activity is found around Pyongyang, North Korea? *industrial areas*
3. Are there more rice-producing areas in North Korea or South Korea? *South Korea*
4. What resource is found in northern North Korea? *coal*
5. Which of the Korean countries uses hydroelectric power according to this map? *South Korea*
6. Is tungsten found in both North Korea and South Korea? *yes*
7. In which Korea are zinc deposits noted on this map? *both North Korea and South Korea*

Discussion Questions

1 Though there are few natural resources in Korea, the people of Korea are fortunate and have made amazing economic progress. How is this possible?

2 What important factors unite the Korean people?

3 How was Korea influenced by Chinese civilization?

Caption Answer

Koreans adopted Buddhism but then mixed it with Confucian teachings. In the 1440s, King Sejong replaced the Chinese writing system with a simpler one based on the way Koreans spoke. Koreans also made their own uses of Chinese arts, architecture, belief systems, and medicine.

Activity

Daoism

OBJECTIVES: 11.03, 12.01

T'au Chi is the symbol of Daoism. This symbol represents Yin and Yang, which are both compatible and opposing forces of nature—such as light and dark, male and female, right and wrong. When these forces are in balance there is harmony.

Find a picture of the flag of South Korea. Draw it and color it.

1. Why do you think these symbols are used on the South Korean flag? *Korea was the gateway through which Daoism passed from China to Japan. Daoism is still actively practiced in Korea.*
2. Why might these symbols be a representation of Korean unity? *The Yin and Yang symbol might be viewed as a representation of a divided Korea. With North Korea (Red) and South Korea (Blue) at the top and bottom, Korea's division into North and South may be seen.*

Making the Most of a Little

Only about 25 percent of Korea is suitable for farming. Koreans have made successful use of their limited farmland. Korea, especially the South, has been called a "rice bowl" of Asia. It also produces grains and such vegetables as barley, corn, potatoes, and cabbage.

Koreans turn to the sea for most of their diet. Korea has one of the world's largest fishing industries. Fish make up nearly all of the animal protein consumed by Koreans.

Korea has limited natural resources (see map, page 435). It does, however, have rivers. The Yalu River in the North divides the Korean peninsula from the Asian mainland. The rivers form rich deltas at their mouths. The deltas and river valleys are good for growing rice.

North Korea has mineral resources. Its mountains are mined for coal, iron, lead, copper, silver, and gold. Its racing rivers can provide hydroelectric power. In recent years North Korea has suffered terrible food shortages.

Korea's most important resource is its people. Both North and South Korea have been successful at building industries. Their successes are due in large part to a highly educated and hardworking people.

A United People

Koreans have a long history as a united people. More than 5,000 years ago, people from Siberia migrated into the Korean Peninsula. They were the ancestors of today's Koreans. Korea was first united in A.D. 668 by the Silla dynasty. It would remain a united land until 1945.

The Koreans preserved their unique language and culture through many years of isolation. Mountains and seas could no keep invaders away. Yet Koreans' fierce attachment to tradition protected their ways of life. Now, although divided by politics, the Koreans are still one ethnic group, united by language and culture.

Chinese Influences on Korean Dynasties

Early on, Korea was strongly influenced by Chinese civilization. Buddhist monks went to Korea from China. Soon after, Koreans built their ow beautiful Buddhist temples. Their workshops produced the *Tripitaka*, a complete set of Buddhist scriptures. It wa carved onto 81,258 wood blocks and printed as a book.

Koreans made fine porcelain like the Chinese. They perfected their own style, producing celadon, a highly-prized green porcelain.

A Celadon porcelain vase is an example of Koreans using Chinese influence to create thei own style. **What other Chinese ideas have been adopted and changed by Korea?**

Word Origins

General Yi Song-gye overthrew the Koryo dynasty in 1389 and set up his own ruling house. He called his kingdom *Choson*, meaning "Land of the Morning Calm." That is a name people sometimes call Korea. **Korea**, however, is named for the Koryo dynasty. The word means "high and clear." The name captures the country's high mountains, clear skies, and tumbling streams.

Background Information

Han'gul

During his reign from 1419 through 1450, Sejong, the fourth king of the Yi dynasty, created Han'gul, a phonetic system for writing the Korean language. The alphabet consists of 24 letters, including 10 vowel sound (compared to 6 in English). King Sejong issued a decree in the mid-1440s making Han'gul the official writing system for Korea. Although it was far better than using Chinese characters to represent Korean sounds, Korean scholars refused to use it. A committee of scholars explained that "the use of letters for phonetic values violates ancient practice and has no valid ground. If this becomes known to China, it would disgrace our policy of respecting China." Han'gul was not widely used in Korea until after World War II ended.

In the 1300 and 1400s, Confucian ·achings from China joined Buddhism to ›rm Korea's belief system. Confucian leas took deep root.

Koreans sometimes rejected elements f Chinese culture. In the 1440s, King ejong decided that Koreans needed a ew, simpler method of writing based on ne way Koreans spoke. Until then, orean scholars had used a form of hinese writing. Students had to learn 0,000 characters to read and write. King ejong's scholars developed ***han'gul,*** a orean alphabet. Easier to learn, *han'gul* elped increase literacy.

nvaders of Korea

The Chinese, Mongols, and Russians epeatedly threatened Korea. Constant utside interference fed Korean distrust of ›reigners. In the 1600s, Korea cut itself ff from the outside world and remained olated for almost 200 years.

In the late 1800s, Europeans were ›mpeting for colonies. Japan joined the ace for colonies and forced Korea to open s ports to trade. Western nations emanded the same rights. Before long, ıpan, China, and Russia were all ruggling to control Korea. Japan efeated its rivals. By 1910, it had nnexed, or taken, Korea as a colony.

Imagine going to class one day and aving your teacher tell you to change your last name, stop speaking English, and use a new language. The Koreans experienced this when Japan took over their country. The Japanese wanted to make Korea Japanese. Koreans had to take Japanese last names and speak mainly Japanese.

Japan also wanted to make Korea a profitable colony. They seized Korean businesses and forced Koreans to build factories, roads, and railroads to benefit Japan. Koreans were forced to fight for Japan during World War II. It was a bitter time for Koreans. Yet their culture and national pride survived.

Japanese policemen in Korea pose for a picture in 1910 soon after Japan had made Korea a colony. **How did Japan try to change Korea?**

LESSON 1 REVIEW

Fact Follow-Up

1. What is the relative location of Korea?
2. How has the location of Korea influenced its culture?
3. How much of Korea is suitable for farming? Where is the farming area?
4. Where do the majority of Korean people live?

Talk About It

1. Explain how Koreans are unified by culture, despite living in two nations with different governments.
2. Explain this statement: "Korea served as a cultural bridge."
3. What might Korea be like today if the writing system had not been changed? Why?

Discussion Questions

1 How many characters did you have to learn to be able to read and write?

2 How did Korea's isolation cause it harm?

3 What changes were made in Korea after Japan made it one of its colonies?

Caption Answer

Japan forced Korea to open its ports to trade. The Japanese also forced Koreans to take Japanese last names and speak only Japanese. They made Koreans build factories, roads, and railroads to benefit Japan, and forced Koreans to fight for Japan during World War II.

Activity

Korean Resources

OBJECTIVES: 2.03, 3.01

Pass out copies of the black line map of Korea found in the Teacher's Resource Guide. Have students make a list of agricultural and natural resources that are found on the Korean peninsula. They will design a symbol for each of the resources and place on the map. They should make a map key and use color on the map and research the uses for each resource and then make a chart showing resource and uses.

Extension Assign peer tutors to assist ELL students as needed.

LESSON 1 REVIEW

Fact Follow-Up Answers

1. Korea is south of China, east of the Yellow Sea, west of the Sea of Japan, and northwest of Japan.
2. Because of its nearness to China, Korea absorbed ideas from that neighbor. Korea's location on a peninsula has meant that because of oceangoing trade it has both influenced and been influenced by other societies.
3. Only about 25 percent of Korea is suitable for farming. The best farmland is found on the southern coastal plains.
4. Most people live on the southern coastal plains.

Talk About It Answers

1. More than 5,000 years ago, people from Siberia migrated into the Korean peninsula. Today's Koreans are their descendants. Although divided by politics, the Koreans are still one ethnic group, united by language and culture.
2. Because China borders Korea, Chinese ideas came into Korea. Korea passed these ideas to the neighboring archipelago of Japan.
3. Important points: Encourage students to speculate and give reasons for their suggestions. Since the older writing system was difficult, literacy might have suffered. A high literacy rate may well have encouraged economic development.

OBJECTIVES: 6.02, 7.02, 9.01, 10.04

Discussion Questions

1 Why would a DMZ be created? What purpose would it serve?

2 How would you feel if you had been separated from your family members for 50 years?

3 What do you think are some of the political and economic problems that Korea faced as a divided nation?

Caption Answer

American soldiers guard the South Korean side of the demilitarized zone (DMZ).

Activity

United Nations Peacekeeping

OBJECTIVES: 9.02, 11.03

Have students research the United Nations' attempts to maintain peace since its creation in 1945. Divide students into groups to present a short synopsis on each peacekeeping mission.

Teacher Notes

Life in the DMZ

Until recently, little human activity has occurred in the 487 square miles that make up the demilitarized zone. Although there are many land mines there, for more than 50 years animals have been free from hunting or habitat destruction. With free passage through the DMZ or the eventual removal of the physical barriers, some species could once again be on the endangered species list. The Asiatic black bear and the Siberian tiger are two such animals.

LESSON 2 Government and Economics

KEY IDEAS

- North Korea and South Korea have followed very different paths toward economic development.
- South Korea's economic success was built on trade. North Korea has isolated itself from most of the world.
- Koreans want to reunite their divided land, but political and economic differences make that unlikely to happen soon.

KEY TERMS

armistice
DMZ
Juche
stalemate

An eerie calm has hung over the border between North Korea and South Korea for more than 50 years. Called the ***DMZ,*** or demilitarized zone, no armed forces or fortifications are allowed within the zone along the 38th parallel North.

In theory, the DMZ has been a peace zone. But, as one American soldier guarding the South Korean's side of the DMZ said, "There ain't no 'D' in the DMZ." One and a half million heavily armed troops face each other along the DMZ.

Some of the tension disappeared briefly in 2000 and 2001. Some North and South Koreans were allowed to visit family members on the other side of the border. Mail was exchanged between the two nations for the first time in the spring of 2001. However, tensions remain high today.

A Divided Country

When Japan was defeated in 1945, Koreans expected to rule themselves again. Yet Korea was soon caught up in the Cold War struggles between the United States and the Soviet Union. The two powers had agreed to a temporary division of Korea when the Japanese left. Soviet troops moved into the north and American troops landed in the south.

In the north, the Russians put Korean Communists in charge. Anti-Communist leaders were brought in by the Americans in the south. Then the two sides plunged into a bitter war involving the Americans, Russians, Chinese, and United Nations forces. When the war ended in 1953, Korea was still divided. Both sides faced huge political and economic problems. The two Koreas followed different paths toward development and economic growth.

Two American soldiers are among the 37,000 troops stationed in South Korea. **Why are United States troops in South Korea?**

North Korea

In the 1980s, Dr. Ronald K. Chung visited his boyhood home in North Korea. Chung had moved to Los Angeles many years before. "The main thing that struck me," said Chung, as he rode through the clean, wide avenues of Pyongyang, "was the oppressive feeling of isolation from m fellow human beings. We saw few pedestrians and very few other cars." Dr. Chung had a rare view of North Korea, one of the most closed countries in the world.

Like other Communist governments, North Korea is a one-party dictatorship. The Korean Workers Party controls all

Writing Activity

Life in the DMZ

OBJECTIVES: 2.02, 3.02

Have students research animals indigenous to the Korean peninsula and create a short report complete with pictures. Students should determine which animals might be endangered by the removal of the DMZ.

Alternate Activity

ELL students should use an ELL-friendly Web site to research animals and make a poster or booklet of some of the animals they find. Novice ELL students should label the names of animals. Intermediate ELL students should write one or two simple sentences describing these animals.

A huge mural dedicated to Kim Il Sung hangs in Pyongyang, the capital of North Korea. **Who was Kim Il Sung? Why was he honored by North Korea? Who is Kim Jong Il (below)?**

Kim Jong Il

pects of life. It and the nation were ruled · one man, Kim Il Sung, for 48 years.

Kim was an all-powerful dictator. He ·mmanded respect and obedience rough fear and unending propaganda. orth Koreans were taught to obey "Our reat Leader." Workers sang his praises ery day. His image appeared all over the untry. Government-owned radio and levision stations glorified him. If people estioned Kim or the party, they were verely punished.

Kim closed North Korea to all outside fluences. He preached the idea of ***juche,*** self-reliance. During the 1960s, Kim led e country to an impressive recovery om the Korean War. North Korea rebuilt anufacturing and chemical industries at had been set up by the Japanese years rlier. Power plants were built along orth Korean rivers. Collective farms oduced food.

By the 1990s, North Korea's economy d stopped growing. When communism llapsed in Eastern Europe, North Korea came more isolated. Kim died in 1994. s son, Kim Jong Il, replaced him as ctator. Many factories have closed. Power shortages are common, and many people have been starving.

To solve these problems, North Korea began to open itself to the outside world. It renewed contact with China and South Korea and accepted food aid. However, the development of a nuclear weapons program shows that its intent may not be peaceful. Missile tests in 2006 sparked talks between North Korea, South Korea, Japan, Russia, and the United States. The talks are trying to resolve the ***stalemate,*** or deadlock, over North Korea's nuclear disarmament. South Korea worries about the possibility of a nuclear-armed North.

Even though the 2006 missle test failed, North Korea still poses a potential danger to the entire region of East Asia, as well as Russia and the United States. This issue has isolated North Korea even more.

South Korean soldiers patrol the DMZ in the snow. **What is the DMZ? Why does the military guard it?**

Discussion Questions

1 What do you think it would be like to live in a country where a person ruled for 48 years?

2 What is propaganda? How did it help Kim Il Sung remain in power?

3 What are some examples of propaganda that we see in our lives?

4 What has happened to the North Korean economy since Kim Jong Il has taken over?

5 In what ways will the Korean government need to change in order for the economy to thrive again?

6 What are the benefits of our form of government in which voters get to select the next leader?

Caption Answer

Kim was the all-powerful dictator of North Korea for 48 years. During the 1960s, Kim led the country to an impressive recovery from the Korean War.

Caption Answer

The DMZ is the demilitarized zone on the border of North Korea and South Korea. No armed forces or fortifications are allowed within the zone.

Teacher Notes

North Korea's Nuclear Program

On October 16, 2006, North Korea conducted an underground nuclear explosive test. The yield of the test was estimated to be less than one kiloton.

In a breakthrough February 13, 2007 agreement through the Six-Party Talks, in return for 50,000 metric tons of oil, North Korea agreed with South Korea, the United States, and three other countries to shut down its nuclear facilities and allow inspectors into the country. Further steps to completely "disable" its nuclear weapons program will give North Korea another 950,000 metric tons of oil or other aid.

A major concern of the United States has been the possibility of North Korea exporting nuclear weapons, fuels, or technology to other rogue states or third parties, such as Al-Qaida or other terrorist organizations.

Eyewitness Activity

Korea

OBJECTIVES: 7.01, 7.02

Resources

The Korean War: "The Forgotten War" by R. Conrad Stein. (Enslow Pub., 2000. ISBN 076601729X.)

The Korean War by Tom McGowen. (Watts Franklin, 1993. ISBN 0531156559.)

Have students research the activities of the United Nations to see if it is involved in any modern-day activities similar to that of the Korean War.

Alternate Activity On each of several large sheets of construction paper, write a different topic about the Korean War. Divide the class into small groups and give each group one of the topics. Instruct students to find out as much information about their topic as possible and list their findings on the construction paper. After a designated time for research is up, ask students to share their information with the rest of the class. This type of activity gives students a chance to practice their verbal skills by presenting to the class. If time permits, each group can prepare a presentation in the form of a skit, song, cheer, talk show, or story.

Possible Topics: United Nations, Douglas MacArthur, *M*A*S*H*, DMZ

Extension Novice and intermediate ELL students should use an ELL-friendly Web site for research and participate in nonverbal ways in the presentation.

EYEWITNESS TO HISTORY
The Korean War
In 1950, Communist North Korea invaded South Korea. Its leaders wanted to u
Korea under Communist rule. Harry Truman, the president of the United State
on the United Nations to send troops to help South Korea. Douglas MacArthu
(below), an American general, was given command of the United Nations troo
The Korean War left the peninsula in ruins
page, top right). More than 5 million peo
killed. About 3.5 million were civilians, peo
were not in the military. Most villages were
So were Pyongyang, capital of North Korea,
Seoul, capital of South Korea.
United States troops head for the battleground as Koreans flee their homes.
442
Chapter 2

A Korean family amid the remains of their bombed home

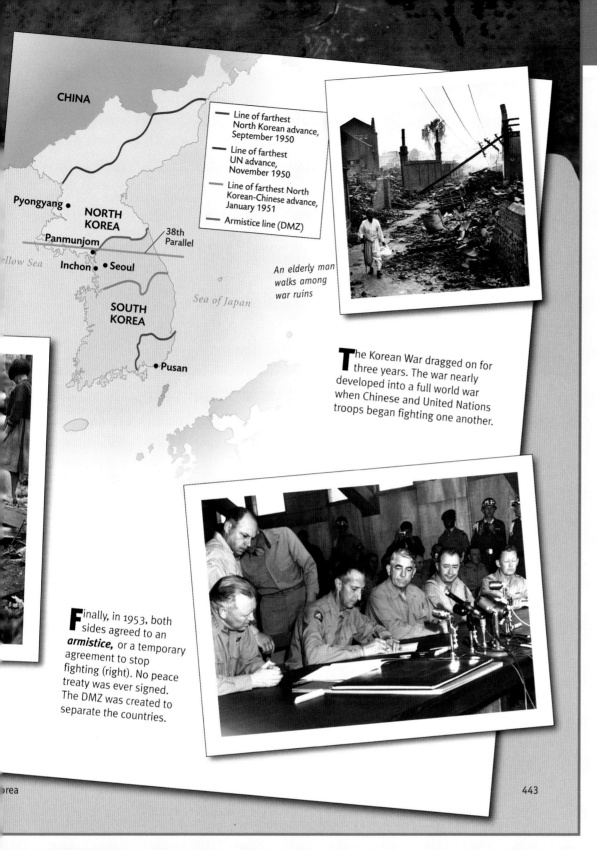

An elderly man walks among war ruins

The Korean War dragged on for three years. The war nearly developed into a full world war when Chinese and United Nations troops began fighting one another.

Finally, in 1953, both sides agreed to an ***armistice,*** or a temporary agreement to stop fighting (right). No peace treaty was ever signed. The DMZ was created to separate the countries.

rea 443

Map Activity

The Korean War

NATIONAL GEOGRAPHY STANDARDS: 1, 17, 18

GEOGRAPHIC THEMES: Location

OBJECTIVES: 1.02, 7.01

Discuss and answer with students:

1. In what century did the Korean War take place? *twentieth century*
2. What line of latitude is the division between North and South Korea mostly associated? *38°N*
3. Did North Korea totally invade and dominate South Korea in the 1950s? *No; area around Pusan, South Korea, in the southeast never fell to the Communists.*
4. Did United Nations troops led by General Douglas MacArthur invade and dominate all of North Korea? *No; from area north of Pyongyang across northern North Korea to the Chinese border was never under United Nations control.*
5. What is the armistice line today? *demilitarized zone (DMZ) border between North Korea and South Korea, world's most heavily armed area*

Teacher Notes

The Korean War

President Harry S. Truman did not ask Congress for a declaration of war, knowing that days of debate would be necessary. Therefore, the United States involvement in Korea was considered a "police action." Truman always referred to the fighting as "the Korean Conflict."

The newly formed United Nations declared the North Korean invasion of South Korea "a war against the United Nations" and requested member nations to help restore international peace. Fifteen members responded to the July 7, 1950, Security Council Resolution and joined the United States armed forces: Australia, Belgium, Canada, Columbia, Ethiopia, France, Great Britain, Greece, Luxembourg, The Netherlands, New Zealand, the Philippines, Thailand, Turkey, and the Union of South Africa. Other member nations with strong neutrality policies sent humanitarian aid: Denmark, Germany, Italy, Liberia, Norway, Pakistan, Sweden, and Venezuela.

Women formed their own army, the Korean Women's Army, and fought along with their brothers, fathers, and husbands on combat front lines.

Many North Korean troops surrendered to United Nations member armies rather than face capture by force. Following the 1953 armistice, nearly 23,000 United Nations prisoners refused repatriation to North Korea. Member nations of the United Nations that had remained neutral during the conflict took custody of the prisoners, providing them with a new country to call home.

Discussion Questions

1 What factors do you think have contributed to South Korea's economic success?

2 Why do you think the "Four Tigers" had such rapid growth after the 1960s?

Caption Answer

South Korea has few natural resources, but it has built a strong export economy with American aid and hard work.

Math Activity

GNP Bar Graph

OBJECTIVES: 5.02, 5.03, 6.02

Have students research the GNP or GDP for both North Korea and South Korea from 1950–95. Enter this into a spead-sheet. Use this data to create a double bar graph to illustrate the rise (and fall) of the two Korean economies.

Extension ELL students should use an ELL-friendly Web site for research. Assign peer tutors as needed to help with the graphing.

Activity

Scavenger Hunt

OBJECTIVES: 4.02, 5.04

Korea in our lives: To demonstrate South Korea's export economy, assign students to look for items (clothing tags, appliances, toys) that were made in South Korea. Make a class list of items as they are identified.

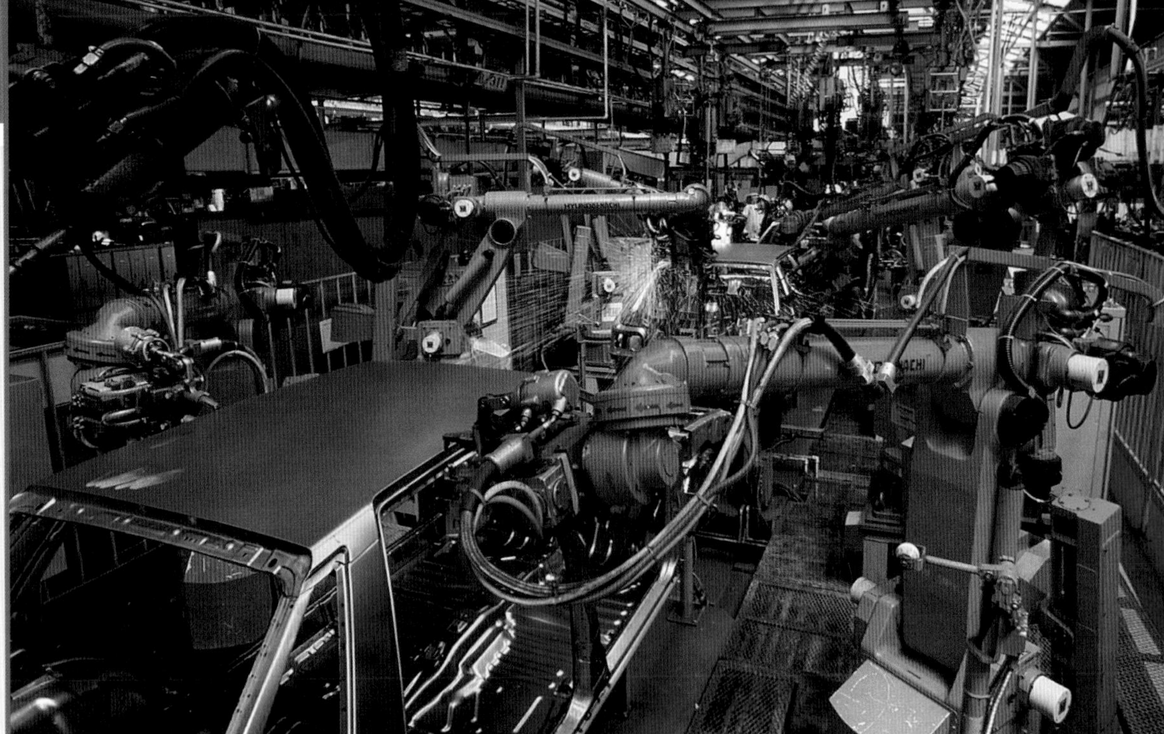

Robots assemble autos at a Hyundai factory in Ulsan, South Korea. **How is exporting cars tied to South Korea's economic success?**

South Korea

In 1988, world attention focused on the Summer Olympics in Seoul, South Korea. For South Koreans, the event was a showcase for their economic success. Foreigners drove around the city in Korean-made cars. They stayed in Korean-owned luxury hotels. They made telephone calls on Korean-made phones and watched replays of events on Korean-made televisions. People the world over saw Seoul as a bustling, modern city.

South Korea had come a long way since its destruction in the 1950s. In 1970, South Korea's gross domestic product (GDP) was about $249 per person, per year in United States dollars. By 1985, it was more than $2,000 per person per year. By 2002, it was almost $17,000. In the 1960s, few people had telephones or televisions. By the 1980s, most had those items, plus CD players, computers, and VCRs.

Economists have called South Korea one of Asia's "Four Tigers." South Korea had joined three other small Asian places—Hong Kong, Singapore, and Taiwan—in achieving remarkable economic growth. Despite their size, each ranks high on the world's list of influential, newly industrialized countries

A country with few natural resources achieved this economic miracle by building a strong export economy. With American aid, South Korea bought raw materials and equipment to begin manufacturing. Its workforce was motivated and well educated. At first, it exported textiles and electronic devices. Later, it built cars and heavier equipment using the most up-to-date technology, including robotics. Export became a patriotic duty. South Koreans celebrate November 30 as National Export Day.

There was a grim side to South Korea's economic miracle. It took place under harsh military dictators. The government banned free speech. Workers had few rights. Many worked more than 50 hours a week for low pay. As the economy grew and people became better educated, they demanded more rights. Th government crushed protests by workers and students.

Background Information

Kim Dae Jung Works for Reunification

In 2000, South Korea's President Kim Dae Jung won the Nobel Peace Prize for his efforts to make peace between the two Koreas. Because of his work, the leaders of the two countries held their first summit in Pyongyang, the North Korean capital, in June of that year. At the awards ceremony in Stockholm, Sweden, Kim was cited for his contribution to "democracy and human rights in South Korea and in East Asia in general and for peace and reconciliation with North Korea in particular." He was elected president of South Korea in 1997 for a five-year term.

Under pressure, the government finally oved toward democratic reforms. In 988, South Korea held its first free ections. South Korea has since aintained its commitment to democracy.

Two issues now loom over South orea. One is industrialization's effect on e environment. Seoul is among the orld's most polluted cities. Business and overnment will have to cooperate to save e environment. The second issue is orth Korea.

eunification: Iopes for the Future

The governments of North Korea and outh Korea hold opposing political and onomic beliefs. North Korea's Commu-ist dictatorship exercises tight control ver the economy. South Korea rejects ommunism and thrives on a free nterprise economy.

The people of Korea on both sides of e DMZ hope for reunification. North nd South Koreans remember that they are the same language, history, and hnic heritage. "Unification will be fficult, and require us to divert a large mount of our resources," says Chun oon-mok, a South Korean businessman. But the yearning for unity is not about onomic gain or access to markets. It's ecause they are our brothers. We are the ame people."

In 2000, the first summit between the leaders of North and South Korea brought hopes of reunification and international praise. Reunification would be a slow process, however. The countries remain technically at war because no formal peace treaty ending the Korean War was ever signed. North Korea has a history of terrorism, infiltration, and provocations against South Korea. There is distrust on both sides, now complicated by the nuclear issue.

Reunification would be expensive. As was the case with German reunification, the more wealthy capitalist state would have to pay most of the costs. North Korea lacks the infrastructure, technology, and resources of South Korea. The future of reunification is uncertain.

In August of 2000, the North and South Korean governments allowed some families to be reunited for four days. This mother and son had not seen each other in 50 years. **Why do Koreans want to reunify their peninsula?**

LESSON 2 REVIEW

Fact Follow-Up

1. What is the DMZ? Where is it?
2. Who divided Korea and why?
3. What have been the economic problems in North Korea?
4. What have been the economic problems in South Korea?

Talk About It

1. Two issues loom over Korea today: reunification and the environment. Of the two, which do you think will be solved more easily? Explain.
2. How might the political and economic differences between North and South Korea be solved?

Discussion Questions

1 What do you think is the connection between education and the demand for more rights?

2 How do you think South Korea's government can solve the problems of pollution and reunification?

3 What part did the United States play in South Korea's successful economy? Do you think the United States had a responsibility in making certain South Korea was strong?

4 Why does the United States continue to send troops to South Korea to patrol the DMZ?

5 After more than 50 years, why is it so important to Koreans that they be reunited?

3 Do you think it is possible for the differences between North and South Korea to be resolved, and if so, how?

Koreans are the same people. They share the same language, history, and ethnic heritage. Families were split by the DMZ.

LESSON 2 REVIEW

Fact Follow-Up Answers

1. The DMZ is the demilitarized zone on the border between North Korea and South Korea. It is located at the 38th parallel North.
2. When the Japanese left Korea after World War II, the United States and the Soviet Union agreed on a temporary division of the nation. Russian forces put Korean Communists in charge in the North. Anti-Communist leaders were brought in by the Americans in the South. This led to a war between Communist forces in the North led by Russia and then by China and by United Nations forces in the South led first by the United States. Korea is still divided.
3. North Korea has been economically isolated, a condition that has worsened with the collapse of communism in Eastern Europe. North Korea suffers from food shortages as well. Because of these problems North Korea has renewed contact with China and South Korea and accepted food aid. North Korea has also begun to talk to Japan and the United States.
4. Formerly, workers had few rights in South Korea. Now pollution is causing serious problems.

Talk About It Answers

1. Important points: Students should choose one issue and give reasons why it will be more easily solved. Both will be expensive. Because Koreans share a history and culture, reunification may be a more attractive investment.
2. Important points: Encourage students to make suggestions and explain why they are feasible. Negotiation and cooperation are essential.

OBJECTIVES: 4.03, 10.02, 11.01

Discussion Questions

1 What are some signs of disrespect for elders in the United States?

2 What are some signs of respect for elders in the United States?

Caption Answer

Answers will vary.

Art Activity

Mask Dance and Drama

OBJECTIVES: 12.01

Mask dramas have been performed by Koreans for hundreds of years. Popular themes often satirized daily life: a wayward Buddhist priest being eaten by a lion; common people making fun of noblemen; husband and wife problems with each other or with a mother-in-law. Students might dramatize a Korean folktale and choreograph a mask dance as part of their presentation. "The Magic Mallet" is a folktale that could easily be adapted to a mask dance performance.

Sun and Moon: Fairy Tales from Korea by Kathleen Seros (Elizabeth NJ: Hollym International Corp., 1987. ISBN 0930878256.)

LESSON 3 Society and Culture

KEY IDEAS

- Long ago, Koreans adopted Confucian values. Yet modernization and urbanization are changing traditional ways.
- South Koreans value education and put much pressure on students to do well in school.
- Koreans accept the existence of spirits as part of their ancient religious beliefs.

KEY TERMS

mudang

In mid-September, South Koreans celebrate Ch'usok, the autumn harvest festival. Roads leaving Seoul for the countryside are clogged with cars. Trains and buses going to rural villages are packed. During Ch'usok, people visit the graves of their ancestors to pray and pay their respects. The movement of people from cities to the countryside at Ch'usok shows how the nation has changed.

As South Korea's economy has shifted from farming to industry, people have moved to the cities. Today, 80 percent of South Koreans live in cities. Seoul contains 21 percent of the nation's population.

The move to the cities has happened in a short time. It has had a major impact on Korean life. Old ways are disappearing in the face of modern, urban life.

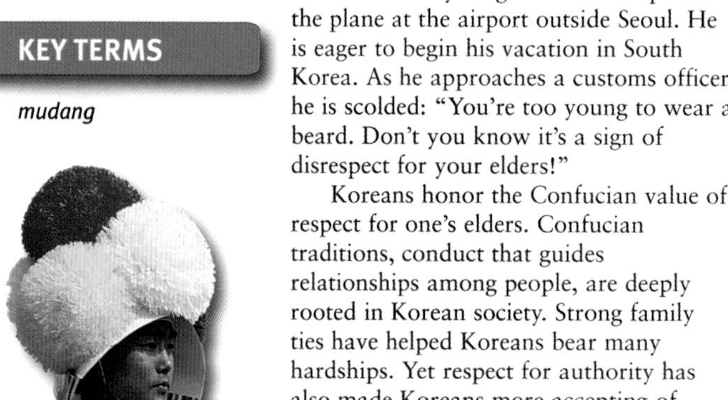

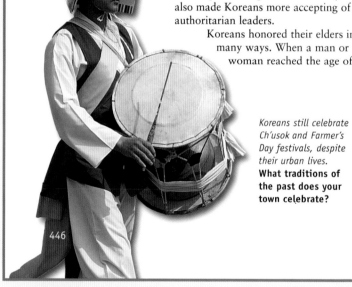

Koreans still celebrate Ch'usok and Farmer's Day festivals, despite their urban lives. **What traditions of the past does your town celebrate?**

Family Ties

A bearded young American steps off the plane at the airport outside Seoul. He is eager to begin his vacation in South Korea. As he approaches a customs officer, he is scolded: "You're too young to wear a beard. Don't you know it's a sign of disrespect for your elders!"

Koreans honor the Confucian value of respect for one's elders. Confucian traditions, conduct that guides relationships among people, are deeply rooted in Korean society. Strong family ties have helped Koreans bear many hardships. Yet respect for authority has also made Koreans more accepting of authoritarian leaders.

Koreans honored their elders in many ways. When a man or woman reached the age of sixty, the family held a big celebration, called *Hwan'gap*. The extended family gathered to honor the sixty-year-old. After turning sixty, parents could expect their children to take care of them.

In Korea, the father—or oldest male—traditionally ruled the family. When he died, his oldest son inherited that role. Years ago, women were considered inferior to men. After a woman married, she lived with her husband's family. Her mother-in-law could make life difficult for her. According to a Korean saying, a new bride must be "three years deaf, three years dumb, and three years blind."

For centuries, women were confined to their homes. They could not own property or seek an education. In 1948, women finally gained voting rights and educational rights.

What would YOU do?

In Korea, as in many societies, children are expected to look after their aging parents. Yet in Seoul many families live in tiny apartments. Both husband and wife work long hours. They may have children. Imagine that you are in this situation. How would you care for your parents?

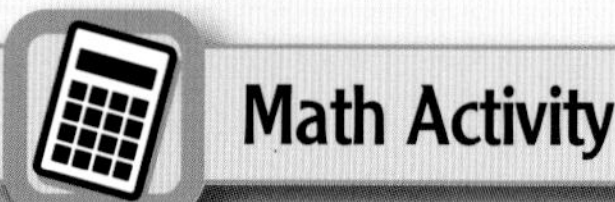

Math Activity

Currency Exchange Problem

OBJECTIVES: 5.04, 6.01

Korea is a major market for the United States. Convert the dollar price, given below, to the Korean price for the items. Use the newspaper or Internet to find the current exchange rate.

1 liter cola	1.09
chocolate bar	0.33
bicycle	250.00

Extension Assist novice and inter-mediate ELL students by setting up the problem.

Confucian Values in an Urban Society

As Koreans move to the cities, Confucian traditions change. In the past, extended families lived together in a cluster of houses. Village life hardly changed. Traditions of filial piety were closely observed.

Families were separated as some members moved to cities. As Korea rebuilt its economy after the war, women in cities took jobs. There they could move about more freely than women in villages. Many women attended universities and started careers. In Seoul, women in designer dresses shop in fashionable stores. Young women in jeans carry their book bags into libraries. Women in gray uniforms board buses at dawn to ride to their factories.

Some old traditions remain. Women are expected to marry, and they walk a step or two behind their husbands. Women leave their jobs to raise their children. Well-educated Korean women often have lower-level jobs than men with similar educations. In North Korea, which has a shortage of labor, women are more likely to hold the same jobs as men.

City life forces other changes in the Confucian values of order and harmony. City apartments are usually much too small for an entire family to gather. Today, *Hwan'gap* celebrations are often held in rented halls. In a giant city like Seoul, people sometimes fight in public. Students protest in the streets. Some talk back to their parents, which perhaps reflects the influence of Western movies and TV.

These changes upset Koreans. Yet visitors see Koreans as polite and respectful. They bow to each other when they meet. Through bowing, Koreans follow traditional rules for greeting people by their rank or family status. A deeper bow is required, for example, for one's employer than for one's coworker.

South Koreans have more freedom. Today, their nation is a modern democracy. South Korea has built one of the world's strongest economies. The people of that country are enjoying a rising standard of living. Unlike the people of North Korea, South Koreans are not faced with serious food shortages.

South Korean women are no longer forced to remain home to work. **What other changes have they experienced?**

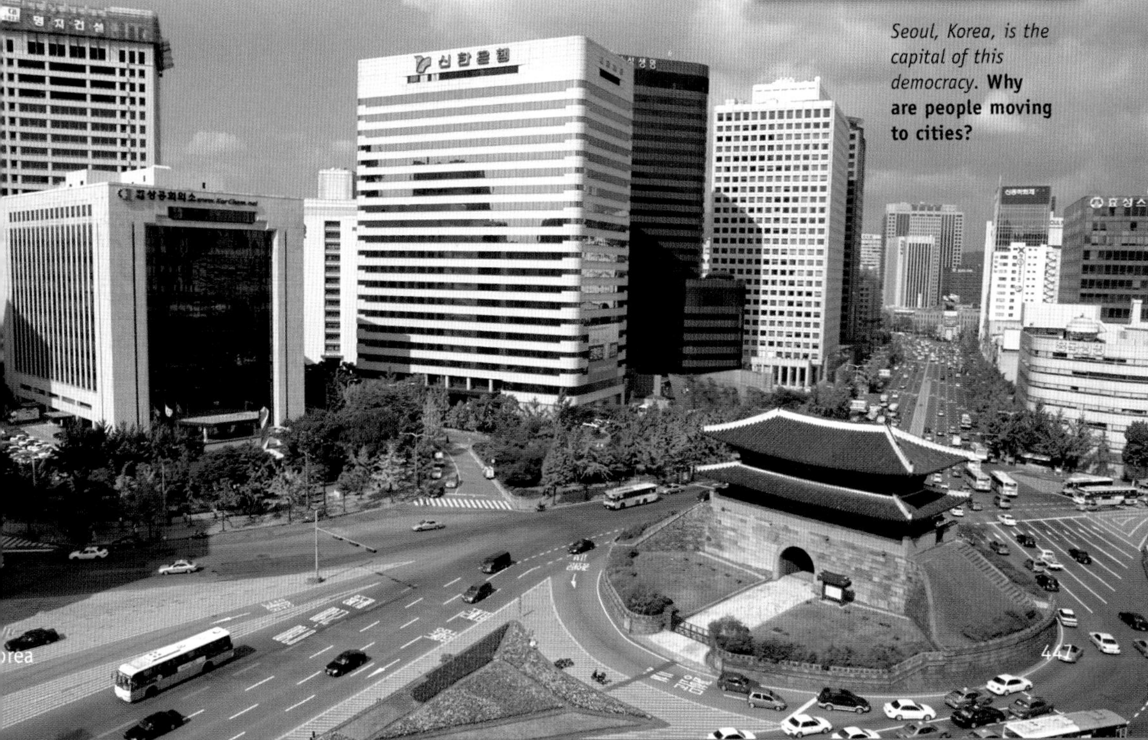

Seoul, Korea, is the capital of this democracy. **Why are people moving to cities?**

Background Information

Hopes for Better Relations

North Korea has been one of the world's-most closed and isolated nations. North Korea's authoritarian leaders have greatly limited contact between its people and the South Koreans, whose society is far more prosperous and democratic. In North Korea, all TVs and radios must be registered with the government. The only programs broadcast are government-sponsored shows. Most describe leader Kim Jong Il 's activities. However, cooperation between the two Koreas may one day lead to greater openness in the North. In 2000 the nations agreed to build a railway across the DMZ to link their capitals for the first time in 50 years. South Korea also began work on a four-lane highway to connect with expressways in North Korea. Both sides hope the new transportation links will boost trade. But North Korea continues to stall, using the project as a way to try to obtain more aid from the South.

Discussion Questions

1 What basic Confucian values are followed in Korea?

2 How does city life challenge Confucian values?

3 If you were a female, would you rather live in North Korea or South Korea? Why?

Caption Answer

Women also have gained voting rights and access to education.

Caption Answer

People move to cities for jobs and education opportunities.

Activity

Korean Kimchi

 **OBJECTIVES:** 11.02

Kimchi, or pickled cabbage, is a special dish for Koreans and is usually served at every meal. During the Korean War, Korean soldiers took tins of kimchi into battle with them. During a late autumn ritual, Korean families chop cabbage and pack pickle pots, making kimchi for winter.

Kimchi

2 cups Chinese cabbage
1 cup carrots, finely shredded
Napa cabbage, chopped
1 tablespoon fresh ginger, peeled and finely chopped
½ cup coarse or kosher salt
3 garlic cloves, finely chopped
4 green onions, finely chopped
3 tablespoons dried red pepper flakes

In a large mixing bowl, toss the cabbage with the salt. Set aside for 30 minutes. Toss the mixture every 10 minutes. Transfer the cabbage to a colander and rinse under cold water. Drain well. Return cabbage to the large bowl. Add green onions, carrots, ginger, garlic, sugar, and red pepper flakes. Mix well. Pack the mixture in a clean jar and cover. Keep the jar at room temperature for about two days, then refrigerate (serves 8). Serve as a side dish with a meal.

Divide class into three or more groups to prepare this Kimchi recipe.

Discussion Questions

1 What kinds of comparisons can you make between this and other cultures that have similar beliefs?

2 Would you consider Korea to be a religious country?

3 What are some symbols or actions used to show respect in our culture?

Caption Answer

Other religious traditions are Confucianism, Daoism, Christianity, and spirit worship.

Art Activity

Korean Postage Stamps

OBJECTIVES: 5.01, 6.01, 11.03

Review the purpose of postage stamps and the information they contain. Divide class into two groups, one representing North Korea, the other South Korea. Subdivide each group into the following categories:

A. Landforms
B. Climate
C. Government
D. Economy and Resources
E. History
F. Chinese Influence
G. Culture Today

After researching their category, each group should design two or three postage stamps. Each group will make a presentation to the class. Stamps can be displayed on the bulletin board with a 3-inch by 5-inch index card to explain the significance of stamps.

Extension Do not assign the presentation portion of this activity to novice and intermediate ELL students.

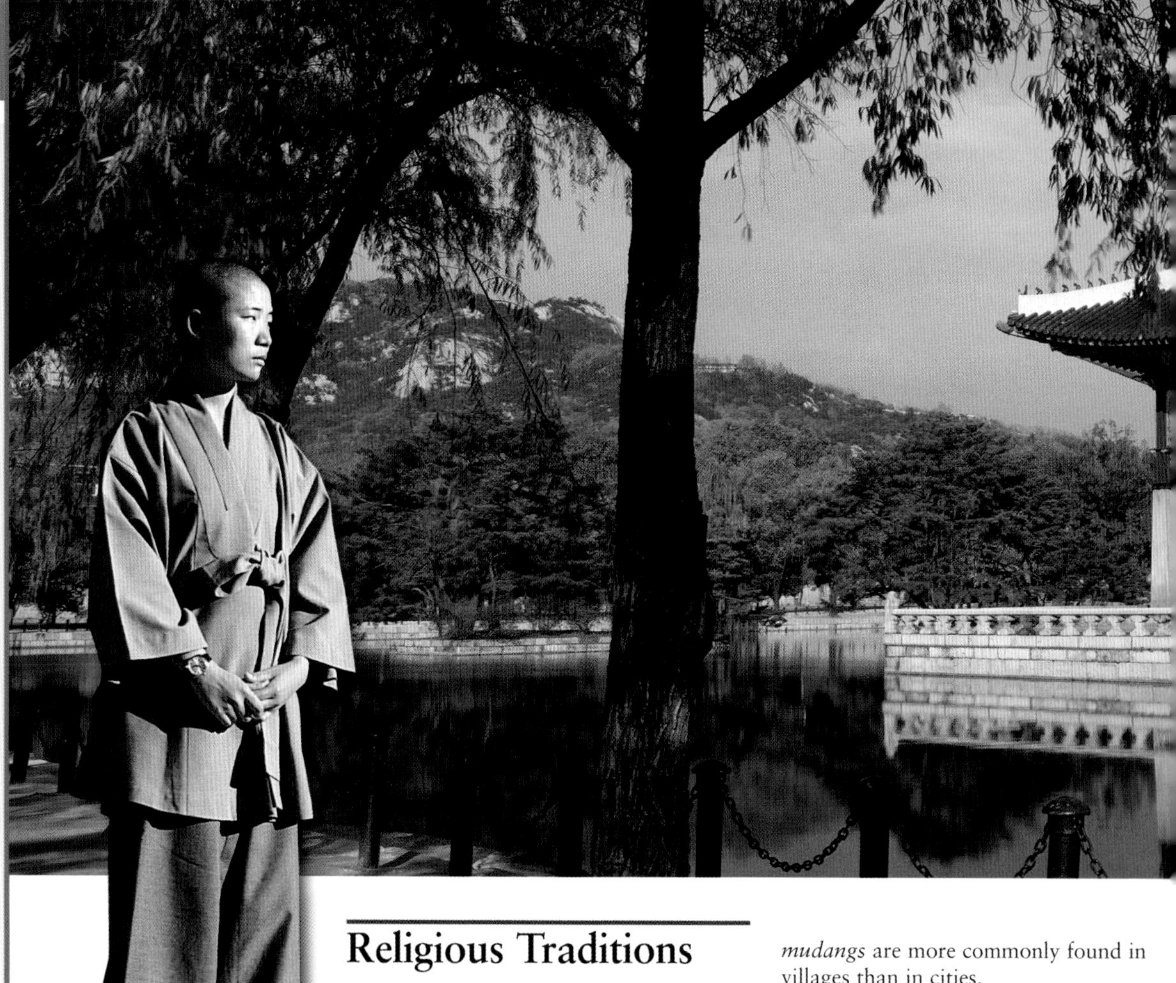

A Buddhist nun is one image of religion in Korea. **What other religious traditions guide Koreans?**

Religious Traditions

Su-na O is a young woman in her early twenties. She goes to meet with a ***mudang***, a spiritual medium. O has recently met a young accountant whom she likes a lot. The *mudang* promises O she can convince him of O's beauty.

Spirit worship is Korea's oldest religion. It is based on the belief that all things have spirits. By pleasing certain spirits, people can ensure good luck, avoid bad luck, or cure illnesses.

In Korea, a *mudang* is thought to have special powers to "speak" to the spirit world. A *mudang* is always a woman. Often she inherits her job from her mother. Unlike other Korean women, *mudangs* earn their own living and move about freely in society. These days, *mudangs* are more commonly found in villages than in cities.

Elements of Korean spirit worship have often been woven into other belief systems and religions. Most Koreans, especially in South Korea, think of themselves as Confucianists, Daoists, Christians, or Buddhists. A Buddhist, however, probably would not be surprise[d] to find in his temple a shrine to a mountain spirit.

Many Koreans believe in some form o[f] spirits. Some think that household spirits hover above the *kimchi* jars or under wood beams on the ceiling. To please these spirits, Koreans offer them special rice cakes with pine needles. Other signs of respect for the spirits are symbols of long life or good luck drawn on roof tiles, doorways, or dinner plates.

448 Chapter 2

Activity

The Korean Wheel

OBJECTIVES: 11.02, 12.03

Distribute fact wheels found in the Teacher's Resource Guide to students. Using the text, atlas, Internet, and other available resources, have students complete each section of the fact wheel with specific examples and influences. Distribute the cover wheel to each student. Have students cut out one sixth of the wheel. Illustrate facts on the cover wheel. Then students can attatch the cover to the fact wheel with a brass fastener. Have students share their Korean wheels. Write a descriptive paragraph about the Korean peninsula.

Extension ELL students should use an ELL-friendly Web site and their textbook for research.

The Kyonghoeru Pavillion in the Kyungbok Palace in Seoul, South Korea, was a feasting hall for gatherings of Korea's royal ministers and diplomats. **How do Koreans blend old ways with the new?**

A Journey to CHEJU DO

Women of the Sea

Cheju Do is a volcanic island about sixty miles (97 km) off the southern tip of Korea. The mild climate makes it a favorite spot for honeymooners. It is also famous for the lava cone of Mount Halla.

The shiny black figures diving offshore, however, are the island's most unusual feature. At first glance, they might look like seals or mermaids. In fact, they are the *haen-yo*, women divers.

No one knows exactly how Cheju Do's small fishing villages came to be run by women. The women divers range from age 10 to 60. In summer and winter, they harvest shellfish from the ocean floor. They collect abalone, octopus, and sea cucumbers. The men stay home. They cook and take care of the young children. In their spare time, the men chat and tend the ancestors' graves.

After their dives, the women change out of their wet suits into market clothes. "Bad day," says one. "Only 4 kilos of shells and the water is so cold." In winter, the divers do not stay underwater as long as they do in summer.

Haen-yo often dive as deep as 60 feet. Some can stay underwater for up to 4 minutes. A shivering visitor to the islands shouts to the women: "Why do you dive in the winter?"

"The money," they yell back. They are as rugged as a crew of construction workers. "How do you think we live if we don't work?"

Activity

Women of the Sea: Compare and Contrast

OBJECTIVES: 11.04

The role of women in Korea highlighted in this feature is unique. Have students research other unique occupations of women in the world. Also, compare and contrast the role of the haen-yo of Cheju Do to the other roles of women in the Korean society in the present and the past. Discuss as a class how the women must dive during the winter months as well as the summer months out of necessity. Students can also speculate why women's bodies might be better suited to this job than men's. Perhaps since their hands are smaller, they can reach more shellfish on the ocean floor. Or perhaps it is because women have more body fat and are able to stay warmer in the water during the winter.

Research Activity

Women of the Sea

OBJECTIVES: 3.01, 5.01

In groups, have students research the abalone, octopus, sea cucumber, and sea anemones found off the coast of Cheju Do. Students can discover the habitat, predators, and unique characteristics of these sea creatures. Students can find out from their research the ways these creatures are used by people in Korea, including interesting recipes.

Alternate Activity

Novice and intermediate ELL students should use an ELL-friendly Web site for research. They should create a diorama of the habitat of the area around Cheju Do. Novice ELL students should label some of the plants and animals. Intermediate ELL students should write one or two sentences about what is unique to this area.

Activity

Po-Pawi-Kawi Game

 **OBJECTIVES:** 11.01

Known to children in the United States as "rock-paper-scissors," the game po-pawi-kawi is often played by Korean school children while walking home from school, and the loser carries all the school bags for his or her friends. Po-pawi-kawi is played with each player facing another with one hand outstretched while saying "po, pawi, kawi." On the last word, each player makes one of three signs with her or his hand: palms up=po (paper), clenched fists=pawi (rock), index and middle fingers extended=kawi (scissors). The winner is decided by formula: kawi cuts po, po covers pawi, pawi breaks kawi. If two players make the same sign, they repeat the game. Who carries the school bags?

Discussion Questions

1 What are some examples that education is valued in Korea?

2 Contrast that with the United States.

3 The more difficult a goal is to achieve, the more valued it is. How does this pertain to education in Korea?

4 What does a literacy rate of 95 percent mean? What does it mean to the overall standard of living in a country?

5 Do young people in the United States have the same desire to please their parents? Do they have the same motives?

Caption Answer

Students study 14 hours a day and work with tutors hired by their parents.

Teacher Notes

Shh! Testing!

The college entrance exam in South Korea is so important that the government requires businesses to reschedule the workday so students do not have to fight rush hour traffic. Even the stock-market opens late and closes early.

Police ask people not to honk car horns near schools. People volunteer to direct traffic. Airline flights to Seoul arc re-routed. The United States military halts live-fire training and grounds airplanes to keep it quiet for the test-takers.

Respect for Education

Cho Hyang Soon waits nervously outside Yonsei University. Inside, her son is taking an all-day exam. This exam determines whether he is admitted into the university's mathematics department. Everything is in Buddha's hands, she tells herself. Like so many other mothers, she has left rice cakes for Buddha on the university steps.

Mrs. Cho's son is taking South Korea's national exam. Every December, more than 600,000 Korean high school students take the examination that decides their futures.

Students in Pusan, South Korea, pose for a class photo. **What must a student do to prepare for the national university entrance examination?**

Children and parents often make grea[t] sacrifices. Students study 14 hours a day. Parents hire special tutors. A boy's sister might work long hours in a factory to help pay for her brother's education.

Newspapers report success stories. Th[e] top scorer for a Seoul university one year was a nineteen-year-old boy. His father had lived on the streets, and his mother worked as a maid. The boy slept only 4 hours a night for an entire year. He attended "cramming institutes" with money his parents earned making envelopes at night.

Respect for education is rooted in Confucian traditions. In the past, only th[e] sons of wealthy families received an education. By the 1950s and 1960s, Koreans realized that everyone needed an education.

South Korea saw dramatic changes. I[n] 1965, only 35 percent of children were enrolled in secondary schools. In 2005, 9[7] percent of Koreans between the ages of twenty-five and thirty-four had graduated high school. This is the highest graduatio[n] rate in the world. The literacy rate in South Korea is 98 percent.

Korean students feel enormous pressure to please their parents by doing well in school. "I know that my parents wanted me to be an engineer," says Eugene Kim. "To impress and please them I followed their thoughtful suggestion."

LESSON 3 REVIEW

Fact Follow-Up

1. What basic Confucian beliefs do Koreans follow?
2. By what percentage did school enrollment rise in South Korean between 1965 and 1999?
3. Why do Korean students take an all-day exam?
4. Describe the work of a *mudang*.

Talk About It

1. How does city life challenge Confucian values in Korea? How have these traditions changed?
2. How do Koreans express their beliefs in spirit worship?
3. How are the women divers of Cheju Do unusual for Korean society?

450 Chapter 2[2]

LESSON 3 REVIEW

Fact Follow-Up Answers

1. Koreans honor the Confucian value of respect for elders. They continue to have strong family ties.
2. School enrollment increased by 63 percent.
3. It is a national exam that decides who will be accepted into the universities. Of 800,000 students who take the exam, only 300,000 will gain entrance.
4. A mudang is a spiritual medium who is thought to have special powers to "speak" to the spirit world. She acts as a connection between people and the spirits they wish to contact or influence. Unlike many other Korean women in villages, a mudang earns her own living and moves about freely in society.

Talk About It Answers

1. Apartments are small, and so extended families rarely live together. When they gather for special occasions, families often have to rent a hall.
2. Koreans contact a mudang to ensure luck. They also offer household spirits rice cakes with pine needles and draw symbols on the roof tiles, doorways, or dinner plates to show respect.
3. The women work harvesting shellfish while their husbands stay home to cook and take care of the children.

Analyzing, Interpreting, Creating, and Using Resources and Materials

Perspectives on Living in a Divided Nation

Korea has been split since 1945. Korea north of the 38th parallel was occupied by Soviet troops after World War II. American forces occupied Korea south of that line of latitude. In 1948, the South Koreans formed the Republic of Korea. The two Koreas fought each other from 1950 to 1953.

People who live in North Korea live under Communist rule. Their activities are closely controlled. The country had purposely isolated itself from the world for many years.

South Koreans have more freedom. South Korea has built one of the world's strongest economies. The people of that country are enjoying a rising standard of living. Unlike the people of North Korea, South Koreans are not faced with food shortages.

Many years have passed since the two countries were one. Koreans under age fifty-five cannot remember a united Korea. Yet if Korea were to unite again, North Koreans and South Koreans would need to understand the experiences of one another.

Glance back through the chapter and record information about everyday life in North Korea and South Korea. Make two lists: one listing characteristics of life in North Korea, and the other listing characteristics of life in South Korea.

After your lists are complete, write two letters. In one letter, write as if you are a South Korean explaining to someone in North Korea how you feel about your way of life. Explain the good and not-so-good aspects of life there.

Then write a letter from the perspective of a North Korean. Try to explain your ways of life to a South Korean and how you feel about being a resident of North Korea.

Which letter was easier to write? Which perspective was easier to express? After looking at life from both sides, do you understand more fully how people with much in common may have different perspectives?

Characteristics of Life in North Korea
1.
2.
3.
4.
5.
6.
7.
8.

Characteristics of Life in South Korea
1.
2.
3.
4.
5.
6.
7.
8.

orea 451

Skill Lesson Review

1. Why is it important to take notes about the characteristics of a place before you can decide your perspective of that place? *Answers will vary. You may see characteristics at first that you might not see after you form an opinion.*
2. Why do feelings have so much to do with your perspective of a place? *Answers will vary. Emotions can color our perception of reality.*
3. Is it possible to have a perspective about a place without having visited it? Explain. *Answers will vary. Perspective can come from what we have heard or read about a place.*
4. What is it about the Communist system that would make it difficult for a North Korean to write accurately about his or her country? *Fear of arrest or punishment might make it difficult.*
5. What aspects of South Korean life might interfere with an accurate portrayal of that country? *Family pressure might interfere.*

Teaching This Skill Lesson

Note If desired, students may go online to get information about life in North Korea, since life inside that country is not detailed in the textbook. If you wish to use this strategy, you will need to make arrangements for students to have access to computers and will want to choose sites beforehand that you will have your students use.

Materials Needed textbooks, paper, pencils, references including online

Classroom Organization whole class, individual, pairs

Beginning the Lesson Ask students to imagine that they have just learned that they have family members they never knew they had, that these relatives have not heard from their family members for more than 50 years. (Note: This scenario is very real. With international Internet access, families all over the world are finding relatives they never knew they had.) Your students have been asked to write letters to their newly found relatives telling what their lives are like. What should they include in these letters?

Lesson Development Tell students that in the spring of 2001, for the first time in nearly 50 years, North and South Korean family members were allowed to exchange letters and photographs. Ask how they, if they were South Koreans, would describe their lives to someone in North Korea and vice versa. Tell them they will be writing such letters. Direct them to look at the note-making charts on page 443 and use the textbook to note characteristics of life in North and South Korea that they might write about. If you plan to use online reference materials, this is an appropriate time. When students have made their notes for both North and South Korea, they may write the actual letters as a homework assignment.

Conclusion Pair students so they can read their letters to each other. Have them reflect on which letters were easier to write.

Extension Intermediate ELL students should write the list only.

Talk About It

1. The climate supports more agriculture in the South. North Korea has built industrially but still suffers from food shortages.
2. Important points: Students should choose a position and give reasons for it. The Japanese ordered the building of factories, roads, and railroads that have helped Korea industrialize.
3. Important points: Students should take a position and explain it. Family ties remain strong; Koreans feel themselves to be one people. Economic problems in North Korea might lead them to wish for reunification as a way to a better life.
4. Important points: Problems might include food shortages, the cost of rebuilding North Korea's economy, and creating a unified government that would unite the nation. Benefits would include the reunification of families, the possibility of a stronger nation in the future, and lessening of tensions in this area of the world.
5. American aid, a well-educated and motivated workforce, and a strong government all contributed to South Korea's development. Other world areas have had strong governments and American aid and yet have not had strong economic development. A well-educated and motivated workforce may be the key.
6. South Korea has relied on imported raw materials because it has few natural resources, has used those raw materials to produce more valuable manufactured products, and has exported its goods to the world. South Korea has also invested in education and has a highly qualified work force.
7. Important points: Environmental damage may save costs in the short run, but ultimately it is expensive in reconstruction costs and damage to health. Lead students to understand that South Korea did not deliberately set out to damage the environment.

CHAPTER 22 REVIEW

Lessons Learned

LESSON 1
Land and People
Korea is a 600-mile-long peninsula with 5,500 miles of coastline. Mountains are Korea's major landform. Good farmland is limited. South Korea and North Korea have similar climates. Major powers have always taken an interest in Korea. Culturally and politically it has been influenced by other Asian countries.

LESSON 2
Government and Economics
Korea has suffered through many wars, including occupation by Japan. Now it is divided into North and South Korea. North Korea practices communism. South Korea has a democratic government. Many Koreans hope for the reunification of their nation, but tensions remain.

LESSON 3
Society and Culture
Traditions have changed in Korea. Women have more open roles in the family and in work. More people have moved to the cities. These changes have affected the families of Korea. Korean students face hard examinations to enter universities. Their families make many sacrifices so that their sons and daughters can succeed.

Talk About It

1. How do the differences in climate affect the economy of northern and southern Korea?
2. Did Japanese colonial rule do anything to help the Koreans? Explain your answer.
3. Given the sharp differences in today's North Korea and South Korea, do you think that they can unite? Explain your thinking.
4. If Korea reunites, what might be some problems? What might be some benefits?
5. List factors that have contributed to South Korea's economic development. Which factors seem most important? Why?
6. Why is South Korea so economically healthy?
7. Should South Korea have damaged its environment to become economically successful? Explain your answer.

Mastering Mapwork

MOVEMENT

Use the map on page 435 to answer these questions:

1. Locate the DMZ, the line dividing North from South Korea. Which movement—of people, goods, or ideas—would be most difficult across this line? least difficult? Explain why.
2. Study the physical map of Korea. What physical features discourage the movement of people, goods, and ideas?
3. In what areas of Korea is the movement of people and goods easiest?
4. In what ways would the reunification of Korea improve the movement of people, goods, and ideas?
5. What physical features of Korea encourage the movement of people, goods, and ideas?

452 Chapter 2

Mastering Mapwork

1. The movement of people and goods would be most difficult because the border is heavily guarded. Ideas, however, can move by radio and television signals and could move more easily across this border.
2. Historically, the mountain range along the east coast of the peninsula has discouraged the movement of people, goods, and ideas.
3. The movement of people and goods is easiest along the west coast of the peninsula.
4. Reunification would make movement easier along the entire west coast of the peninsula. In addition, roads and rail lines could be built to connect the entire country.
5. The fact that Korea is a peninsula, surrounded on three sides by water, encourages the movement of people, goods, and ideas by water.

Go to the Source

Understanding Context

Read the "Statement of the Government of the Republic of Korea" (South Korea) on the North Korean Nuclear Test, October 9, 2006, below. Answer the questions using specific references to the document. This was issued the same day that the nuclear test in North Korea was detected.

On October 9, the [South] Korean Government detected signs suspected of a nuclear test in the Hamgyongbuk-do . . . region in North Korea, and the President presided over an emergency meeting of the security related ministers in the morning. While the meeting was going on, North Korea announced that it had successfully conducted a nuclear test, and the meeting was turned into a National Security Council meeting accordingly. The Government has decided to make public its official stance as follows.

1. Despite the repeated warnings from the ROK [Republic of Korea (South Korea)] Government and the international community, North Korea announced that it conducted a nuclear test today. The Government will resolutely respond to the situation in accordance with the principle that it will not tolerate North Korea's possession of nuclear weapons.

2. This action taken by North Korea poses a grave threat that undermines stability and peace on the Korean Peninsula as well as in Northeast Asia. It is also an act of trampling on the hope of the international community to resolve the North Korean nuclear issue peacefully through dialogue in its quest for the denuclearization of the Korean Peninsula.

3. North Korea's conduct also constitutes a failure to meet its obligations under the September 19, 2005 Joint Statement, on which all parties of the Six-Party Talks concurred, and is in outright defiance of the UN Security Council Resolution 1695 adopted earlier on July 15. This is a provocative act that can never be condoned.

4. At the same time . . . North Korea has unilaterally breached and annulled the Joint Declaration of the Denuclearization of the Korean Peninsula that it signed with the Republic of Korea in 1991. . . .

5. We urge North Korea to immediately abandon any nuclear weapons and related programs, to return to the Nuclear Nonproliferation Treaty (NPT) system, and to faithfully comply with international norms as a responsible member of the international community.

6. Based on the ROK-U.S. alliance, our Armed Forces are fully prepared and equipped to thwart any provocation from North Korea. We warn the North to have a forthright recognition of this fact and refrain from making a misjudgment under any circumstances.

7. The Government is closely consulting with the international community . . . and supports . . . the immediate discussion of this issue by the UN Security Council. . . . the Government will seek broad views on the situation from the leaders of the ruling and opposition parties as well as the opinion leaders. It will continue to coordinate countermeasures domestically and internationally and take actions in cool-headed and resolute manner.

Questions

1. Who is the intended audience of this document? Who is the author?
2. What is the occasion on which this document was created?
3. What is the tone of this document?
4. What is the problem presented by this document?
5. What are the possible solutions to the problems as presented by the document?
6. What is the United States' role as presented in this document?

Go to the Source

Go to the Source

OBJECTIVES: 7.01, 7.02, 8.01, 8.03, 9.01, 9.02, 9.03; Skills 2.01, 2.02 3.05, 4.02

Statement of the Government of the Republic of Korea on the North Korean Nuclear Test, October 9, 2006

On April 24, 2003, in discussions with the United States and China in Beijing, North Korean officials admitted for the first time that they had developed nuclear weapons. North Korean officials also claim to have reprocessed spent fuel rods. They threatened to begin exporting nuclear materials unless the United States agreed to one-on-one talks with North Korea, which the United States refused to do.

Visit **NCJourneys.com** for a link to this document.

ANSWERS

1. North Korea and the world community are the audience. The Government of the Republic of Korea (South Korea) is the author.
2. This statement was in response to North Korea's suspected test of a nuclear weapon.
3. The tone is one of great concern over North Korea's actions.
4. North Korea has tested a nuclear device despite warnings from South Korea and the world community in the months and years leading up to the test. Nuclear weapons proliferation is a concern of the world community.
5. South Korea urges North Korea to abandon its nuclear program, encourages North Korea to return to the Nuclear Nonproliferation Treaty, it warns that the United States will assist South Korea to defend itself, and that South Korea will consult with the world community for possible solutions to the issue.
6. The United States is defined as a strong ally with South Korea.

How to Use the Chapter Review

There are three sections in the Chapter Review: Talk About It, Mastering Mapwork, and Go to the Source. Use the Vocabulary Worksheets and the Chapter Review Worksheet in the Teacher's Resource Guide for additional reinforcement and preparation for the Chapter Assessments. The chapter and lesson reviews and the Chapter Review Worksheets are the basis of the assessment for each chapter.

Talk About It questions encourage students to speculate about the content of the chapter and are suitable for class or small-group discussion. They are not intended to be assigned for homework.

Mastering Mapwork has students apply one or more of the Five Themes of Geography to maps within the chapter.

Go to the Source activities allow students to analyze a primary source that relates to the content of the chapter. The questions and activities familiarize students with different types of primary sources and also build content-reading skills.

Japan's Enduring Tradition

Social Studies Strands

Geographic Relationships
Physical features
Absolute and relative location
Climate and vegetation

Cultures and Diversity

North Carolina Standard Course of Study

Goal 2 The learner will assess the relationship between physical environment and cultural characteristics of selected societies and regions of Africa, Asia, and Australia.

Goal 3 The learner will analyze the impact of interactions between humans and their physical environments in Africa, Asia, and Australia.

Goal 7 The learner will assess the connections between historical events and contemporary issues in Africa, Asia, and Australia.

Goal 11 The learner will recognize the common characteristics of different cultures in Africa, Asia, and Australia.

Goal 12 The learner will assess the influence of major religions, ethical beliefs, and values on cultures in Africa, Asia, and Australia.

Teaching & Assessment

- English Language Learner Modified Lesson Plans for this chapter are found in the Teacher's Resource Guide.
- *ExamView® Assessment Suite* is provided at **NCJourneys.com.** It includes customizable assessments for all chapters. Paper tests are also available in the Teacher's Resource Guide. See pages T16–T17 for information about how to use the assessments and the Scoring Guide.

Worksheets

Worksheets and answer keys are found both in the Teacher's Resource Guide and at **NCJourneys.com,** including Reading Guides, Reading Strategies, Chapter Reviews, English Language Learner and others.

ACTIVITIES AND INTEGRATIONS

SOCIAL STUDIES
Archipelago Japan "Japan–Political/Physical", p. 455
Time Line, p. 457
▲ ■ Resources for a Hungry Nation, p. 459
Japan's Empire?, p. 462
Cartography, p. 463
▲ ■ Satellite Image of Japan, p. 463
● Think-Pair-Share with a Partner, p. 468
Skill Lesson: Planning With Population Profiles, p. 473

READING/LANGUAGE ARTS	READING/LANGUAGE ARTS OBJECTIVES
● Symbols and Their Meaning, p. 454B	2.01
Analogies, p. 454B	2.01
★ New Versus Tradition, p. 454B	1.03
Activator: *The Bicycle Man*, p. 454	2.01
Writing Prompt: Japanese Exchange Student, p. 454	3.03
★ Dropping the Bomb, p. 460	3.01
Stories of Hiroshima Survivors, p. 461	1.01
■ Japanese Language, p. 470	6.01
Go to the Source: Understanding Culture Through Ceremonies, p. 475	1.02, 2.01, 5.01

MATHEMATICS	MATHEMATICS OBJECTIVES
★ Climate Graphs, p. 464	1.03, 3.05

SCIENCE	SCIENCE OBJECTIVES
Climate Graphs, p. 464	1.03, 3.05

TECHNOLOGY	TECHNOLOGY OBJECTIVES
● Rock Gardens, p. 466	3.01, 3.11

VISUAL ARTS	VISUAL ARTS OBJECTIVES
● Cherry Blossom Trees, p. 454B	2.04, 4.01
Kojiki by Kitaro, p. 456	4.01, 7.01
Japanese Symbolism, p. 458	4.06, 6.01
▲ Country Wheel: Japan, p. 464	2.04, 4.01
▲ ■ Watercolor and Haiku, p. 465	2.04, 7.01
★ Origami, p. 469	2.04, 5.03

CHARACTER AND VALUES EDUCATION	TRAITS
Writing Prompt: Japanese Exchange Student, p. 454	respect, responsibility, kindness, integrity
What Would You Do?, p. 457	self discipline

● Basic Activities ★ Challenging Activities ▲ English Language Learner Novice ■ English Language Learner Intermediate

Chapter Activities

Introductory Activity

Symbols and Their Meaning

OBJECTIVES: 4.03, 12.01

Nations use symbols to represent their land, their people, and the spirit of their country. In Japan, the sun is used to represent the country. The use of the sun as a symbol comes from ancient Japanese myths concerning the ruling families of Japan.

Have students work in cooperative groups. Have them compare various symbols and their messages. Have students list the symbols they are discussing. Then have them write two or three descriptive sentences about each symbol, including what type of message that symbol conveys and why. Some suggestions for symbols might come from advertising or the local, state, and national governments.

Extend the lesson with focus on the symbol of the sun in ancient Greek and Roman myths and Japanese culture. This would involve additional research in the media center to locate the myths and their meaning. Students might then compare the different myths about the sun.

Culminating Activity

New Versus Tradition

OBJECTIVES: 4.03, 11.02, 12.02

Ancient Japanese teachings show that the Japanese believed that spirits lived in natural objects. They created shrines to worship these spirits (see page 455, text).

Form two debate teams of four students each. Have a moderator and a timekeeper. One debate team will take the role of a Japanese citizen of ancient times who worshiped spirits. The other side will reflect the views of executives of a modern Japanese business who want to develop the land now used for shrines. Have the teams research the beliefs around the Shinto shrines. Have each debate team research Japan's gross national product, employment figures, land use, and profitable businesses. Have teams debate the issues. Then have students switch roles and take different sides.

Art Activity

Cherry Blossom Trees

OBJECTIVES: 2.01

Background Use this simple art activity to create a "Japanese" climate in your classroom. Students may work individually or in pairs to create these trees.

Materials container such as a flower pot or can, small twig or a small branch of a tree, pink tissue paper, glue, scissors, dirt or rocks

Directions

1. Stand your twig or small branch in your selected container. Surround your twig or branch with dirt or rocks so that it will stand up by itself.
2. Cut small circles out of the tissue paper.
3. Pinch the center of your tissue paper circles and twist each one so that it looks like a flower blossom.
4. Glue the blossoms on the branches of your "tree."
5. Display your trees around the room so that you bring Japan to your classroom.

The size of your twig or branch will determine the size of the pot that you will need.

Analogies

OBJECTIVES: 2.01, 11.01, 12.01

Analogies are useful to help students make associations with prior knowledge. Read the analogies aloud and ask students to identify the relationship between the terms. As an extension, ask students to write their own analogies using key terms or places discussed in the chapter.

samurai : medieval Japan :: knight : medieval Europe (was warrior in)

kami : Japan :: orisha : Yoruba (Nigeria) (spirits in natural objects in)

Mount Fuji : Japan :: pyramids : Egypt :: Cape Hatteras Lighthouse : North Carolina (landmark of)

Hokkeido : New England :: Kyushu/Shikoku : Southeastern United States (has a similar latitude to)

Ainu : Japan :: Native Americans : United States (original people of)

kimono : Japan :: sari : India (is the traditional women's dress of)

Teaching Strategies

- Stress the importance of tradition in Japanese culture.
- Students should understand how the Japanese rebuilt after WWII as well as how they have adapted to their limited resources.

Activator

OBJECTIVES: 4.03, 12.01

Activators are great tools to use in order to "hook" the attention of the students. Reading picture books or stories is an excellent way to build interest in the subject and is also a great way to integrate language arts into the social studies curriculum.

The Bicycle Man by Allen Say. (Parnassus Press, 1982. ISBN AAX-3977.)

Lily and the Wooden Bowl by Alan Schroeder, illustrated by Yoriko Ito. (New York: Doubleday Book for Young Readers, 1994. ISBN 0385307926.)

Writing Prompt

OBJECTIVES: 11.01

Evaluative

Imagine your family has decided to host a Japanese exchange student. During his or her first week at your house, you have been asked to take your guest around the community. What are the most important things you can show him or her to make sure the visit is a safe and enjoyable one? Explain your choices.

As you write or word process your paper, remember to:

- clearly identify the things you will show your guest.
- give at least things and explain your reasons fully.
- give examples to support your reasons.
- write in complete sentences and paragraph form.
- organize your ideas and include an introduction and a conclusion.
- use good grammar, spelling, punctuation, and capitalization.

CHAPTER 23

Japan's Enduring Traditions

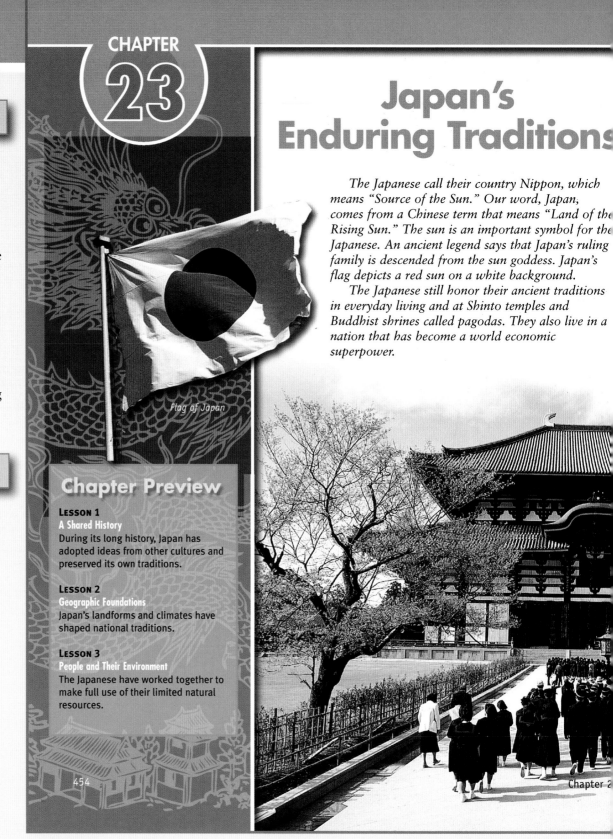

The Japanese call their country Nippon, which means "Source of the Sun." Our word, Japan, comes from a Chinese term that means "Land of the Rising Sun." The sun is an important symbol for the Japanese. An ancient legend says that Japan's ruling family is descended from the sun goddess. Japan's flag depicts a red sun on a white background.

The Japanese still honor their ancient traditions in everyday living and at Shinto temples and Buddhist shrines called pagodas. They also live in a nation that has become a world economic superpower.

Flag of Japan

Chapter Preview

LESSON 1
A Shared History
During its long history, Japan has adopted ideas from other cultures and preserved its own traditions.

LESSON 2
Geographic Foundations
Japan's landforms and climates have shaped national traditions.

LESSON 3
People and Their Environment
The Japanese have worked together to make full use of their limited natural resources.

454

Chapter 2

Chapter Resources

Print Resources

Fiction

Haugaard, Erik Christian. *The Samurai's Tale.* Houghton Mifflin, 1984. ISBN 0395345596.

Hersey, John. *Hiroshima.* Bantam, 1975.

Houston, Jeanne. *Farewell to Manzanar.* Houghton Mifflin, 1973. ISBN 0913374040.

___. *The Invisible Thread.* Atheneum, 1981. ISBN 0689502109.

___. *A Jar of Dreams.* Beech Tree Books, 1995. ISBN 0688137032.

Mori, Kyoko. *Shizuko's Daughter.* Fawcett Juniper, 1994. ISBN 0449704335.

___. *Of Nightingales that Weep.* Avon, 1980. ISBN 038051110X.

Paterson, Katherine. *The Master Puppeteer.* Crowell, 1975. ISBN 0690009135.

Salisbury, Graham. *Under the Blood-Red Sun.* Delacorte, 1994. ISBN 038532099X.

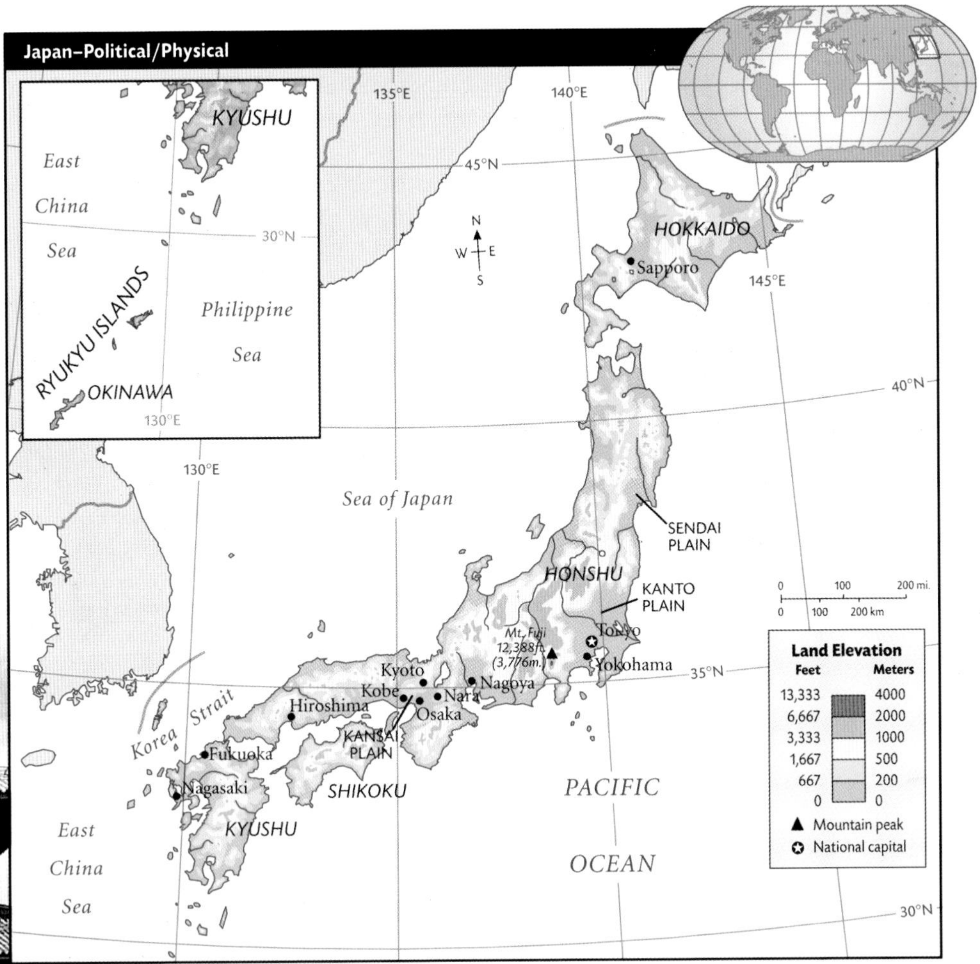

Japan–Political/Physical

Todai-ji Temple in Nara, Japan (far left); Golden Pavilion in Kyoto (left)

Map Activity

Archipelago Japan "Japan–Political/Physical"

NATIONAL GEOGRAPHY STANDARDS: 1, 4

GEOGRAPHIC THEMES: Location, Place

OBJECTIVES: 1.02, 2.01, 3.04

Note with students the small, red highlighted area on the small-scale world map projection that creates the large-scale map of Japan. Discuss with students that this highlighted area is one good example of the 12-percent distortion on any equal-area (Robinson) map projection.

Discuss with students what an archipelago is. (See the "Dictionary of Geographic Terms," page 576) Note with students that Japan is an archipelago just smaller than Montana in land area.

Have students complete the following:

1. Identify the four main islands of Japan. *Hokkaido, Honshu, Shikoku, Kyushu*
2. What islands, that include Okinawa, are also a part of Japan? *Ryukyu Islands*
3. Which is Japan's northernmost island, where the Winter Olympics were held in 1972? *Hokkaido*
4. What is the name of the largest Japanese island also known for the 1995 earthquake in and around Kobe that killed more than 5,000 people? *Honshu*
5. Which is Japan's smallest island, separated from Honshu by the Inland Sea? *Shikoku*
6. Of Japan's four main islands, which is the most southern, known for its rapidly declining coal fields? *Kyushu*
7. Name the five bodies of water surrounding Japan. *Pacific Ocean, Sea of Japan, East China Sea, Philippine Sea, Korea Strait*
8. Mount Fuji at 12,388 feet (3,716 m) above sea level on which island is Japan's highest peak? *Honshu*
9. The Kanto Plain, a primary region in Japan known for its urban, industrial and agricultural focus, is located on which island? *Honshu*
10. Which Japanese city—Hiroshima or Nagasaki—is located closest to the Equator? *Nagasaki*

Say, Allen. *The Ink-Keepers Apprentice.* Houghton Mifflin, 1997. ISBN 039585895X.

—. *The Sign of the Chrysanthemum.* Avon, 1980. ISBN 0380492881.

Uchida, Yoshiko. *The Best Bad Thing.* Alladin, 1986. ISBN 0689710690.

Audiovisual

Japan: Memoirs of a Secret Empire. 2004. PBS Video.

Web Sites

Go to **NCJourneys.com** for links to the following Web sites:

- Ancient Japan
- Japan: Memoirs of a Secret Empire companion Web site
- Museums of Japan Links

OOBJECTIVES: 7.02, 11.04, 12.03

Discussion Questions

1 What did the Emperor Meiji mean when he said, "Be not inferior"?

2 Why do you think Japan looked to China for ideas early in its history?

3 What would have been some examples of technology during that time?

Caption Answer

China was a powerful empire, and Japan wanted to learn from its advanced civilization.

Activity

Kojiki by Kitaro

OBJECTIVES: 2.01, 12.02

Kojiki is a musical interpretation of the creation myth of Japan. Kitaro, a Japanese musician, took the creation myth of Japan and broke it into chapters. Each chapter is a music track.

Materials creation myth of Japan (also found in the jacket of the CD); Kitaro's *Kojiki* (1997)cassette or CD; CD or cassette player; 24-inch by 24-inch off-white, ivory or cream paper for each student; black watercolor or tempera paint; brushes; pictures of Japan; Japanese/Chinese paintings with horizontal/vertical strokes to reflect calligraphy; *A Young Painter: The Life and Paintings of Wang Yani, China's Extraordinary Young Artist* by Zheng Zhensun and Alice Low. (Houghton Mifflin, 1995. ISBN 0395732689.)

Distribute copies of Kojiko. Read myth aloud, pointing out chapters and headings. Stop after each chapter. Have students write a one- or two-sentence summary of chapter. Read each chapter again. Ask students to listen for physical features and natural objects. Write on the board:

Chapter	Features
1	water, mud, shoots
2	mud, islands
3	god of fire-islands
4	mountains and valleys
5	celestial rock cave
6	cave—rock
7	flowers

Pass out paint, brushes, and paper. Have students fold paper in half, then in half again, and once more (create eight squares). Students will paint one chapter in each square.

Play Kitaro's Kojiki and instruct students to paint a symbol, or whatever the music moves them to paint (in calligraphy-style). Stop briefly after each chapter/CD track to give time to complete picture.

While their artwork is drying discuss the geological creation and physical features of Japan and how that relates to the myth/music. Show pictures of Japan that show those physical elements. Discuss briefly the Japanese reverence for natural beauty.

When student artwork is dry instruct students to write their brief chapter summaries underneath each symbol they drew.

Evaluation Have students write in their response journals a descriptive paragraph about what Japan might have looked like before man.

LESSON 1 A Shared History

KEY IDEAS

- Over many centuries, Japanese adapted ideas and technologies first from China and much later from the West.
- In the 1930s and 1940s, Japan tried to build an Asian empire. Its efforts led to a terrible war and Japan's defeat.
- After World War II, Japan built a democratic government and a strong economy.

KEY TERMS

samurai

In the late 1800s, the Emperor Meiji watched anxiously as Japan adopted many new ideas from Europe and the United States. He knew there were good reasons for borrowing foreign ideas. Japan needed to become as strong as the Western powers. The emperor expressed his hopes and concerns in these lines:

May our country,
Taking what is good,
And rejecting what is bad,
Be not inferior
To any other.

Early Japan

Japan was already an old country when the Emperor Meiji wrote those words. Thousands of years earlier, the ancestors of modern-day Japanese had migrated to the islands. They learned from Koreans and Chinese how to farm and to make metal tools. They no longer had to depend on hunting and gathering. They settled into communities.

Since these early times, the Japanese have often adopted ideas from outsiders. Yet they have never lost their own special character. The Japanese have always preserved their own spoken language and ancient customs.

Japanese artists used Chinese methods to make art with Japanese themes, such as this fish bowl. **Why did Japan adopt ideas from China?**

Chinese Influences

In the A.D. 600s, Japan again turned t China to learn from its advanced civilization. Japan's ruler sent students to China to study its literature, arts, and technology. Buddhist missionaries from China and Korea were welcomed to Japan. Buddhism spread through Japan.

China was a powerful empire at that time. Its capital was a rich city with stunning temples and palaces. Officials running China's huge empire were experts in Confucian teachings on government. Chinese technology led the world.

For about 300 years, Japan took man ideas from China. The Japanese had no system for writing its spoken language, so they imported the Chinese system. Japanese students brought back Confucia ideas on government. The Japanese court adopted Buddhism alongside their traditional religious beliefs. The Japanese emperor even built a new capital city that was a smaller copy of China's capital. The streets were laid out in the same way as the Chinese city, and buildings copied Chinese architectural design.

Many other new ideas took root. Yet Japan did not become just like China. Instead, Japan preserved its own special culture. It did so by sifting through what i had borrowed.

The Japanese eventually abandoned ome Chinese ideas that did not suit them. or example, the Chinese emperor ppointed men to office who had passed iff examinations in Confucianism. In pan, military leaders already held overnment offices. The emperor did not ave enough power to replace them with onfucian scholars.

The Japanese kept Chinese ways of riting, but they made changes. The panese found Chinese writing difficult to se because the Chinese and Japanese oken languages were so different. The panese solved the problem by adding mbols of their own to the Chinese stem.

apan Isolates Itself

By the 1200s, powerful military aders called ***samurai*** challenged the nperor's authority. The emperor mained on the throne, but he ruled in ame only. Meanwhile, the samurai began fight one another.

These wars finally ended after 400 ars when a powerful samurai family, the okugawa, gained power. The Tokugawa en took advantage of Japan's island cation to isolate it from the world. They led from 1603 to 1868.

Japanese farmers and fishermen ovided enough food for Japan to remain olated until the 1800s. Then one day in 853, four large ships sailed into Tokyo ay. This fleet had sailed from the United ates under the command of Commodore latthew Perry. Perry demanded that pan open its ports to trade.

The Japanese did not want to open y ports, but they did not want to risk ar. Japanese leaders knew that several uropean powers were eager to make pan part of their colonial empires. rry was given part of what he wanted ecause Japan hoped to keep peace ith Western powers. Meanwhile, pan began to search for ways to otect itself from foreigners.

What would YOU do?

Judo (JOO • doh) is a Japanese sport similar to wrestling. Students learn that skillful use of the body and mind is prized over great strength. To become an expert, a person must learn how to discipline mind and body. Would you be willing to spend years in hard training to become a judo expert?

In this wood-block print, a samurai wields a sword. **Who were the samurai?**

Discussion Questions

1 What do you think is the greatest strength of the Japanese people?

2 Why would being an island nation have its advantages?

3 Why would being an island nation have its disadvantages?

Caption Answer

The samurai were powerful military leaders who challenged the emperor's authority in the 1200s.

Activity

Time Line

OBJECTIVES: 7.01, 7.02

Construct a time line showing major events in Japan involving contact with the Western nations during the sixteenth through the twentieth centuries. Use the textbook or encyclopedia for information.

1543: Portuguese sailors became the first Europeans to reach Japan.
1638: All foreigners are expelled from the country except the Dutch.
1853: Commodore Matthew Perry arrives in Tokyo Bay and demands Japan open its ports to other nations.
1868: Matsuhito, the Emperor Meiji, decides Japan would become a modern industrial nation.
1905: Japan defeats Russia in war.
1941: Japan attacks the United States.
1945: United States drops atomic bombs on Hiroshima and Nagasaki. Japan surrenders.
1980–90s: Strong opposition to Japanese trade practices in the United States.

Write a summary showing how change takes place over time based on the time line data.

Extension ELL students should use an ELL-friendly Web site for research. Do not assign the summary portion of the activity.

Background Information

The Meiji Learn from the West

After centralizing power and creating a national government, one of the first steps Meiji leaders took on the path to modernization was to travel abroad. In 1871 about half of the most important Meiji leaders went to the United States and Europe. Their goal was to study and learn from the West. They visited parliaments, schools, and factories. The first Meiji Constitution of 1889 drew heavily on Western models. Ito Hirobumi who went abroad to shop for a constitution for the Meiji government, found Germany's conservative constitution to his liking. He convinced a German legal scholar to return with him to Japan to adapt the Prussian constitution of 1850 for Japan.

Discussion Questions

1 What are "ethics"?

2 What does the phrase "Eastern ethics and Western science" mean?

3 Who is "Eastern" and who is "Western"?

4 What effects did this trade agreement have on government and military leaders in Japan?

5 What were the reasons Japan's military leaders wanted a large empire?

Japanese fishermen helped provide enough food for Japan to remain isolated.

The Japanese did not want to risk war, and they knew that several European powers were eager to make Japan part of their colonial empires. By trading with the United States, Japan hoped to keep peace with Western powers.

Japanese Symbolism

OBJECTIVES: 4.03, 12.01

Heraldry illustrates Japanese symbolism. Heraldry is a system of hereditary identification used many years ago when societies were mainly illiterate. Heraldry is the study of the origin, development, symbols of honor, and the official regulation of their use.

Japan is the only nation outside of Europe that uses a system of heraldry. The kimono—a long, flowing robe worn with a sash—became the standard garment for both Japanese men and women. During seventeenth to nineteenth centuries, the shoguns who led Japan's government tried to restrict expensive and colorful kimonos to members of the samurai class during peacetime.

Symbols on a Japanese kimono are called "mons." These are usually circular. Symbolic patterns were also used to denote rank in the Japanese society. Every family has a mon or family insignia (called a monisuki), which is embroidered on the back of the kimono for weddings and other formal occasions. Kimonos often reflect the changing seasons in Japan's climates. A summer kimono could have a morning-glory pattern, one for the fall could have chrysanthemums or maple leaves, a winter kimono might have a snowflake pattern, and a spring kimono might be decorated with early flowers. This shows the Japanese admiration of nature. The chrysanthemum is the national flower of Japan and a symbol of long life and prosperity.

Have students design a mon for their family monisuki. Dress a paper doll or puppet in a kimono using the design.

A color wood-block print shows Japanese casting their nets into the sea. **How did fishermen help Japan remain isolated?**

Japan Turns to the West

By 1868, Japan was on its way to becoming a modern nation. The Tokugawa was overthrown. Reformers "restored" the Emperor Meiji to power. Under his leadership, Japan looked to Europe and the United States for examples of how to create a powerful national government and up-to-date industry. The reformers did *not* want to make Japan into a Western-style nation. They adopted a slogan—"Eastern ethics and Western science"—that summarized their desire to use Western ideas while maintaining Japanese culture.

Urged on by the reformers, Emperor Meiji led Japan with stunning speed through change. By 1900, Japan was an industrial power. It was the first Asian country to achieve that status.

Japan's government provided money to start key industries. Old-fashioned military forces became a modern army and navy. Railroads were built. The Japanese wrote a constitution and Western-style law codes. The old government was replaced with one much like Germany's. Schools taught science and technology.

Commodore Matthew Perry sailed into Tokyo harbor in 1853. **Why did the Japanese agree to begin trading with the United States?**

The reforms soon gave Japan some surprising successes. In 1894–1895, tiny Japan defeated giant China in a quarrel over Korea. In 1905, the Japanese navy sank two Russian fleets and the Japanese army defeated Russian troops in another war over Korea.

Japanese Imperialism

The Japanese islands had few of the resources needed by its growing industr Japan tried to solve this problem by doing what European powers had done. It would find raw materials and market by creating its own empire. It took Taiwan in 1895 and Korea in 1910. In 1931, Japanese troops seized Manchuri (today, part of northeastern China).

These conquests helped military leaders gain power. They promoted the idea of building powerful armed forces that could make Japan the leading empire in Asia. In 1937, Japan invaded China. Later, while continuing to fight i China, Japanese forces pushed into Southeast Asia. Japan needed the region's resources to keep its war machine running.

)isaster in Vorld War II

Japan's efforts to win an empire in Asia ould eventually end in disaster. Although s forces conquered most of Southeast Asia id several Pacific islands, they gained little om their victories. Like the Chinese, outheast Asians did not want to be ruled y Japan. Groups opposing Japanese rule ormed throughout Asia. Japan obtained w of the raw materials that it needed.

In a surprise attack on December 7, 941, Japanese planes bombed the United tates Pacific fleet riding at anchor at Pearl larbor, a naval base in Hawaii. Before the ttack, the United States had tried to onvince Japan to give up its dreams of an sian empire. Japan had hoped that its ttack would hit the United States so hard at the Americans would allow Japan to eep its empire in exchange for peace. istead, the attack at Pearl Harbor united e American people behind the war effort. he United States declared war the next ay. The military leaders controlling Japan ad made a costly mistake.

Japan won other battles over American nd British forces in 1942 (see map, page 62). By 1943, though, Japanese forces had egun retreating toward their home islands. Soon, Japan itself suffered from heavy bombing raids that destroyed entire cities. The Japanese people were cut off from supplies from outside the islands. In August 1945, American planes dropped atomic bombs on two Japanese cities—Hiroshima and Nagasaki. Tens of thousands were killed in those two attacks.

Japan surrendered. American forces occupied the islands and began changing Japanese traditions that had glorified the military. They also helped Japan begin to build a democratic government and to reconstruct its ruined economy.

Japan bombed Pearl Harbor on December 7, 1941. **Why?**

Japanese troops land at Yongampo, Korea, to fight Russian troops along the Yalu River. **Who won the Russo-Japanese War in 1905?**

Discussion Questions

1 Suppose you were at Pearl Harbor on December 7, 1941. What would be your thoughts and feelings? What would your first reactions be?

2 Due to the high number of casualties inflicted in the Pacific during World War II and the Japanese determination to fight to the death, President Truman and the military knew that American casualties would be extremely high if the United States invaded Japan. Thousands of caskets were ordered in preparation. Was President Truman right when he avoided invasion and ordered the dropping of the atomic bomb on Hiroshima?

3 How do you think Japanese experiences during World War II have affected their attitudes toward events (nuclear arms, United States, military defense, and so forth) in the world today?

4 Because of Pearl Harbor, many Japanese-Americans were interned at special camps in which they lost their rights and property. Was the United States government justified in doing this to United States citizens?

5 Some people will always remember what they were doing when Pearl Harbor was attacked, others will always remember what they were doing when President Kennedy was assassinated. Why?

6 What were you doing when you heard about the terrorist attack on the World Trade Center on September 11, 2001?

Caption Answer

Japan hoped that its attack would hit the United States so hard that they would be able to win the war before the United States could mount an offensive.

Caption Answer

The Japanese

Map Activity

Resources for a Hungry Nation

NATIONAL GEOGRAPHY STANDARDS: 1, 9, 11, 12

GEOGRAPHIC THEMES: Location, Place

OBJECTIVES: 1.02, 2.03, 5.03

Review the reasons for imperialism: need for raw materials, market for manufactured goods, acquisition of territory, and increased popularity at home. With few natural resources, Japan needed raw materials for its growing industrialization. Using an atlas, the map on page 462, and a blank map of East Asia, Southeast Asia, and the Pacific Islands, have students identify the countries that came under Japanese domination. Once the countries have been identified, students can create a map legend that shows the natural resources Japan took from her colonies. They should label the map using the map legend symbols or colors. Question for students: Why might Japan have taken control of areas having no identifiable natural resources?

Eyewitness Activity

Dropping the Bomb

 **OBJECTIVES:** 7.01, 7.02

Complete a T-chart about the pros and cons of the American decision to drop the atomic bomb on Japan. After the chart is completed, ask students to take a side and write a persuasive argument that the use of the atomic bomb was a good or bad decision.

Complete a cause-and-effect graphic organizer on the use of the atomic bomb by the Americans in World War II.

Teacher Notes

Pre-War and Wartime Japan

The gradual military takeover of Japan's government began in the late 1920s. Governmental officials were also military officers. As the Japanese Empire expanded so did the military control of the government. Several members of the National Diet who opposed Japan's forceful expansion were assassinated. Moderate representatives, fearing for their lives, refused to speak out against the militarists. By 1936 the constitutional monarchy with a civilian government was ineffective. In October of 1941 Emperor Hirohito, advised now only by militarists, acquiesced to the military leaders until August 15, 1945.

Early in 1945, planes from American aircraft carriers continually bombed Tokyo and other major cities. Hundreds of thousands died in the bombings. The military leaders, claiming to speak for Emperor Hirohito, refused to surrender.

Hiroshima was leveled on August 6, 1945, with the world's first atomic bomb. More than 4 square miles of the 6.9-square-mile city vanished. When Japan still refused to surrender, American planes dropped leaflets over several other Japanese cities warning the people to petition the emperor and government officials to cease military resistance or face more devastation.

On August 15, 1945, Japanese citizens heard their emperor's voice for the first time in a radio broadcast as he asked his people to "endure the unendurable and suffer the insufferable" as the only way to peace and to accept the surrender declaration.

The formal surrender was signed on September 2, 1945, aboard the USS *Missouri*, just one of several American ships in Tokyo Bay. The last time a United States fleet had visited Japan was 92 years earlier, under the command of Commodore Matthew Perry.

EYEWITNESS TO HISTORY

Dropping the Bomb

In August 1945, President Truman made the historic decision to use the atomic bomb. He hoped to end the war with Japan without an invasion of the island nation. The Allies gave Japan an ultimatum: surrender unconditionally or face "prompt and utter destruction." Japan refused. This decision not only led to the end of the war with Japan but also changed how people thought about going to war.

On August 6, 1945, at 8:15 A.M. (left), an American B-29 airplane dropped a uranium bomb on the center of the Japanese city of Hiroshima. The bomb leveled 3 square miles (7.8 sq km) of the city.

When the bomb exploded, many people were on their way to work. Out of a population of 350,000, an estimated 92,000 people died instantly from the blast, and another 100,000 died later from burns, radiation, or other wounds caused by the blast.

Within one mile from where the bomb exploded, flash burns killed people directly exposed to the heat. Radiation within a half-mile exceeded six times the dose that would cause death within a month. The blast cracked walls 12 inches (30.5 cm) thick.

Fires consumed most wooden homes and gutted concrete buildings within 2 miles (3.2 km) of the bomb's blast. Temperatures of up to 3,000 degrees caused first-degree burns and melted glass, metal, and even stones. The bomb destroyed more than 60,000 homes within 3 miles (4.8 km) of the blast. Ninety percent of Hiroshima's physicians died, preventing most victims from getting immediate medical attention.

Prefectual Industrial Promotional Hall, Hiroshima, after the blast.

Map Activity

Stories of Hiroshima Survivors

NATIONAL GEOGRAPHY STANDARDS: 1, 17

GEOGRAPHIC THEMES: Location

OBJECTIVES: 1.02, 7.01

Point out the small, red highlighted area on the inset map. That is the location of Hiroshima on the southwest side of the big island of Honshu (34°N, 132°E). Also note that the uranium bomb dropped on Hiroshima was nicknamed "Little Boy" by the scientists at Los Alamos who created it and by the crew of the Enola Gay (the B-29 that dropped this bomb on August 6, 1945). The plutonium bomb dropped on Nagasaki was nicknamed "Fat Man."

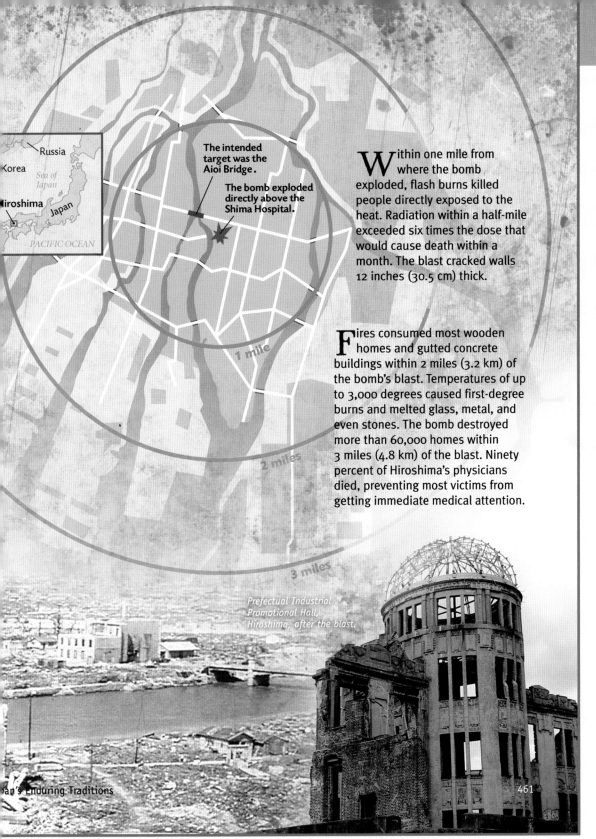

The red explosion symbol on this map is the hypocenter of "Little Boy," that hit Hiroshima. Have students estimate how far the Enola Gay was from hitting their target, the Aioi Bridge. (*approximately one-fourth of a mile southwest of intended target*)

Assign students to compose journal entries describing what happened in the 1-mile, 2-mile, and 3-mile radius of the hypocenter the morning of August 6, 1945. Note with students that there were survivors who had stories to tell.

Teacher Notes

Japan's Brutality in World War II

It is easier to understand some of the tensions and distrust between Japan and the United States and other Allied powers with additional knowledge of the brutality of the invading Japanese forces in World War II. Although Japan had not signed the Geneva Conventions (which defines war crimes), it had signed a number of other treaties and had its own laws prohibiting many of the atrocities their forces committed during the occupation of East and Southeast Asia as well as against the Allies during World War II.

The bomb exploded directly above the Shima Hospital.

All of the crimes listed here have been documented, althougth the Japanese government does not neccessarulty recognize they occured. These war crimes include: mass killings, experiments on humans, use of biological weapons, use of chemical weapons, torture of POWs, cannibalism, forced labor, forced prostitiution, and other atrocities. As many as 30 million Filipinos, Malays, Vietnamese, Cambodians, Indonesians, and Burmese, and at least 23 million ethnic Chinese were killed. The death rate for Allied POWs held by the Japanese was nearly 30 percent (as opposed to about 6 percent in the Nazi POW camps).

Caption Answer

All of Southeast Asia, all of Oceania, and eastern China

Map Activity

Japan's Empire?

NATIONAL GEOGRAPHY STANDARDS: 1, 17

GEOGRAPHIC THEMES: Location

OBJECTIVES: 1.02, 7.01

Note with students the red, highlighted area on small-scale world map projection showing Japan's empire's peak.

What occurred with Japan's empire from 1933 through 1942? *Expanded from Japan's four main islands into Taiwan, Korean peninsula, northeastern China, Kurile Islands, and Karafuto, then into eastern China and Southeast Asia as well as various Pacific Ocean islands (including Aleutian Islands, Mariana Islands, Marshall Islands, Caroline Islands, Solomon Islands).*

What occurred on December 7, 1941? *Japanese attacked Pearl Harbor. United States entered World War II.*

What occurred on August 6, 1945? *United States bombed Hiroshima, Japan, using first atomic bomb in history.*

What occurred in 1945 to reduce Japan's empire to the main islands of Hokkaido, Honshu, Shikoku, and Kyushu? *End of World War II in the Pacific (Victory in Japan [VJ] Day August 14, 1945). Japan was defeated by Allied forces and occupied militarily, mainly by the U.S. Army, until 1952.*

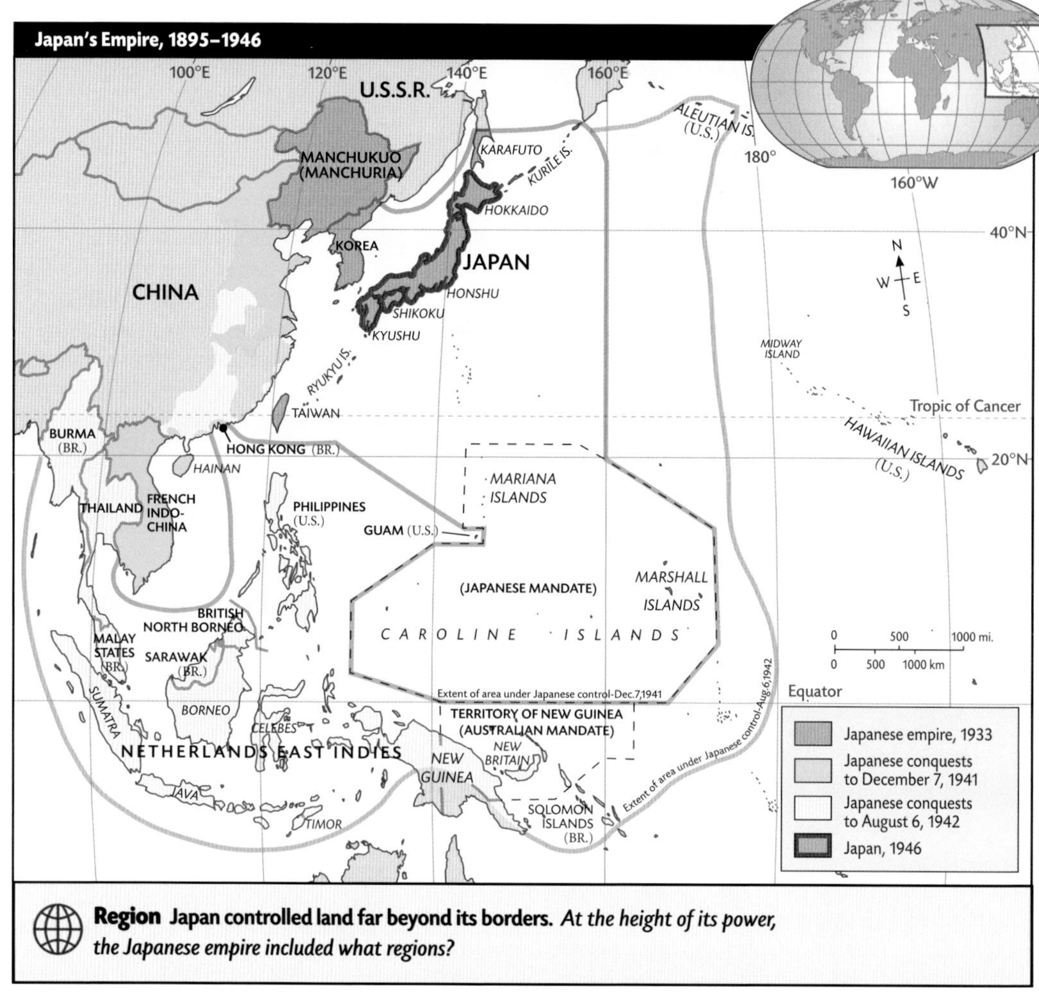

Region **Japan controlled land far beyond its borders.** *At the height of its power, the Japanese empire included what regions?*

LESSON 1 REVIEW

Fact Follow-Up

1. Early in their history, what ideas and technologies did the Japanese borrow from Korea and China?
2. Later, beginning in the 1800s, Japan borrowed from the West. What ideas and technologies interested the Japanese this time?
3. What lands were conquered by Japan during the period from 1895 to 1945?

Talk About It

1. Why do you think Japan looked to China for ideas early in its history and to the West later?
2. Did Japan's military leaders want a large empire only for economic reasons? Explain.
3. Do you believe the United States was justified in dropping the atomic bombs on Hiroshima and Nagasaki?

LESSON 1 REVIEW

Fact Follow-Up Answers

1. Early on, the Japanese learned from the Koreans and Chinese how to farm and to make metal tools. In the 600s, Japan studied Chinese literature, arts, and technology. Chinese and Korean missionaries introduced Buddhism to Japan. Later, Japan imported the Chinese writing system for use in Japanese.
2. Japan looked to Europe and the United States for examples of how to create a powerful national government and up-to-date industry. Japan started key industries, modernized the army and navy, and built railroads. They wrote a constitution and Western-style law codes, and replaced their government with one much like Germany's. Schools taught science and technology.
3. Taiwan, Korea, Manchuria, part of eastern and northeastern China, the Philippines, Indo-China, the Netherlands East Indies, and other Pacific island territories fell under Japanese control before the end of World War II in 1945.

Talk About It Answers

1. Early on, China was a great empire that led the world in learning. By the 1800s, the West was a center of technology and modernization. It seems that Japan had been interested in studying ideas of powerful civilizations and adopting or adapting them for Japanese use.
2. Important points: Encourage students to discuss whether Japan's desire for empire was purely economic in nature. Like European nations, Japan looked to support its industrialization by getting raw materials and markets through empire. And like Europe, Japan may have had other reasons, such as national pride, for expanding its influence.
2. Important points: students should support their opinion with reasons.

LESSON 2 Geographic Foundations

Thousands of Japanese climb Mount Fuji every year. They do so partly to appreciate the power and beauty of nature. Respect for nature has long shaped Japanese culture.

Early Japanese believed that ***kami,*** or spirits, lived in natural objects. ami inhabited beautiful rocks or weathered trees. A religion called ***hinto,*** or "the way of the gods," grew out of this reverence for nature. ollowers of Shinto built shrines, places where people might pay respect to *kami.* Honoring these spirits became part of Japanese daily life.

Shinto's customs are still followed in Japan. Shinto shrines dot the lands in peaceful settings near ancient trees or unusual rocks.

mportance of an sland Location

Twice in the 1200s, the Mongols reatened Japan. The Mongols had ized all of China, captured lands retching from Russia to Europe, and ecided to add Japan to their empire. rst, a Mongol fleet carrying 30,000 oops reached southern Japan. A phoon hit with such force that the eet was destroyed. Seven years later, a uch larger force of 140,000 soldiers nded in Japan. Another typhoon ruck, destroying the Mongol army on e Japanese coast. The Japanese called at typhoon *kamikaze,* "divine wind."

The closest Japanese island to the sian mainland, Kyushu, is about 100 iles (161 km) away. Its other main lands are Hokkaido, Honshu, and ikoku. (see map, page 455). The islands ave provided Japan with a line of efense. Until American forces occupied pan in 1945, the Japanese had prevented y successful invasion.

The islands have set Japan apart from Asia and the world. Even today, the Japanese have a sense of themselves as a people apart. They think of themselves as "We Japanese," a people who are different from foreigners.

Yet Japan has not been isolated. Japan's closeness to the Asian mainland enabled it to develop links with Korea and China. Korea was a bridge for Chinese civilization to reach Japan. In more recent times, Japan's surrounding seas have given her people easy access to the entire world.

KEY IDEAS

- Japan's island location has set it apart from other nations and has helped it develop a culture of its own.
- Mountains and frequent earthquakes have influenced Japanese life.
- Japan has few agricultural and mineral resources. As an industrial nation, Japan's well-educated people are a great resource.

KEY TERMS

kami
Shinto
tsunami

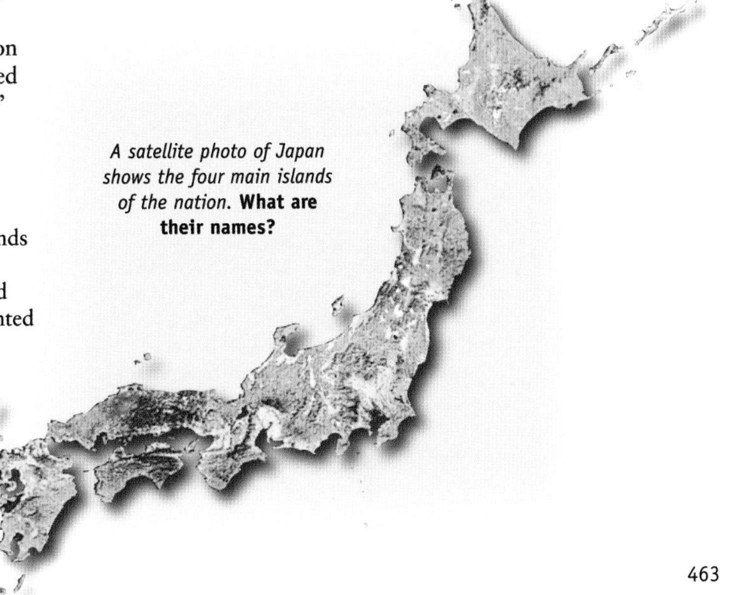

A satellite photo of Japan shows the four main islands of the nation. **What are their names?**

 **OBJECTIVES:** 2.01, 2.03, 3.01, 3.04

Discussion Questions

1. How do you think the emphasis on nature is directly related to the daily life and activities in Japan?
2. Do you think it is important in Japan to protect the environment? How do our attitudes toward the environment differ from the Japanese?
3. What is a typhoon?
4. Who were the kamikazes during World War II? How did they get this name?
5. How have the islands provided protection for Japan?

Caption Answer

Hokkaido, Honshu, Shikoku, and Kyushu

Map Activity

Cartography

NATIONAL GEOGRAPHY STANDARDS: 1
GEOGRAPHIC THEMES: Location
OBJECTIVES: 1.01, 2.01

Have students research the geography of Japan and prepare a poster-size map of Japan, including the following items in their correct location on the map:

- four main islands, capital city
- major cities, major landforms
- native animals, native vegetation
- historical sites/tourist attractions

Map Activity

Satellite Image of Japan

NATIONAL GEOGRAPHY STANDARDS: 1
GEOGRAPHIC THEMES: Location
OBJECTIVES: 1.03

Have students compare this satellite view with the map of Japan on page 447. Can students see the white dot of Mount Fuji on the south central side of Honshu?

Ask students why the yellow areas appear this color on this satellite image. *large urban/metropolitan areas*

Many refer to the overall image of Japan as a samurai sword—Hokkaido is the sword's handle with Honshu, Shikoku, and Kyushu as the blade of the long sword.

Discussion Questions

1 Why is it important for the Japanese to keep up with the most current methods in agriculture and conservation?

Caption Answer

Mountains cover about 70 percent of Japan. Few people live in the mountains, and so many Japanese are crowded into the coastal plains.

Activity

Country Wheel: Japan

OBJECTIVES: 1.02, 3.04

Materials handouts of the country wheel and cover patterns from the Teacher's Resource Guide, posterboard, pens, colored pencils, markers, crayons, scissors, glue/glue sticks, brad

Directions for Students Cut out the wheel and glue it to a piece of posterboard. Cut out the wheel again. In the outer, smaller section labeled 1, write a question on Japan. In the pie-shaped section that is numbered 1, write the answer to question 1. Continue writing ten questions and answers in this manner until the entire wheel is complete. Decorate the cover with Japanese illustrations and words. Place the cover on top of the country wheel so that the centers are aligned. Use point of scissors (or straight pin or compass point) to poke a small hole in the center of the cover and wheel. Push a brad through the pinhole to attach the cover to the wheel. Exchange your wheel with a partner to share questions and answers with one another.

Extension Assign a peer tutor or group to help the ELL students create questions.

Mount Fuji is a symbol of Japan. **How have mountains affected Japanese settlement patterns?**

Limited Land

Mount Fuji draws attention because of its spectacular beauty. It is the most photographed site in Japan. The nation also has countless other mountains to admire. Mountains—many with steep slopes—cover at least 70 percent of Japan. Hills and narrow river valleys occupy much of the remaining land. Coastal plains offer the little flat land that can be found in the islands.

There is very little living space in Japan. Few people live in the mountains. People have clustered on small coastal plains where land could be farmed or fishermen could go to sea. In recent years, cities have been built on these same coastal plains. The Kanto Plain on Honshu Island, for example, was once one of Japan's largest farming areas. Now it is filled mostly by Tokyo and surrounding urban settlements. A second important agricultural area, the Kinai Plain, is today home to Osaka and Kyoto.

The Uncertain Earth

September 1 is Disaster Prevention Day in Japan. Every year on that day, people practice survival skills. Students with wet handkerchiefs over their faces run through halls filled with smoke. Police and fire rescue squads rehearse for real disasters. Everyone takes these practices seriously. September 1 is the anniversary of the great 1923 earthquake that destroyed Tokyo.

Earthquakes and Tsunamis

Minor earthquakes shake parts of Japan almost every day. Scarcely a year passes without a serious tremor hitting some part of the islands. Japan has a set of tough

Science Activity

Climate Graphs

OBJECTIVES: 2.02

Japan nicely illustrates the effect of location on climate. Review factors that affect climate: latitude, elevation, nearness to bodies of water, ocean currents, and winds. Divide class into groups of five. Assign each person in group one of the five cities. Provide group with maps of Japan that show the cold and warm ocean currents near the coast. Students will graph temperature and precipitation for the five cities and draw conclusions after comparing completed graphs.

Extension Assign a peer tutor in the group to help the ELL student find and graph the information.

ilding codes to protect its cities during akes. All new structures now have to be ade to withstand severe earthquake ocks.

A test of these codes came in January 95 when a major earthquake hit Kobe, a ge port city. Many older homes collapsed residents. Expressways crumbled. Many the destroyed structures had been built fore the new codes became law. Most wer earthquake-resistant buildings rvived. Japan has continued to experience number of smaller earthquakes since the be earthquake.

The Japanese also watch for rthquakes occurring on the ocean floor. is will produce a small, rapidly moving ave in the ocean. As the wave moves ickly towards shore, it grows into a giant ave, called a ***tsunami*** (soo·NAH·mee). unamis flood coastal villages and sweep people off shorelines. With modern instruments, scientists can detect ocean quakes and alert coastal areas of coming dangers.

Movements deep in the earth along the Ring of Fire (see page 506) are the sources of Japan's earthquakes and volcanoes.

Mount Fuji is a dormant, or sleeping, volcanic mountain. It has not erupted since 1707. Nearby Mount Asama, however, rumbles and blows smoke. One or another of such active volcanoes can erupt every few months. Japan has 109 active volcanoes. It has around 100 dormant ones that have not erupted for a long time.

In a country as densely populated as Japan, a volcanic eruption can be deadly. Volcanoes also generate heat that warms spring water. Resort towns have sprung up in mountain areas where these natural hot tubs bubble up from beneath the ground.

A large earthquake struck Kobe, Japan, in 1995, destroying thousands of buildings. **How did some structures survive?**

Discussion Questions

1 How does the drill in the first paragraph compare to "disaster" drills we have in school?

2 What kinds of disasters can we have in our area?

3 Why does it seem that we often wait until a tragedy occurs before we implement necessary safety measures?

Caption Answer

They were newer, earthquake-resistant buildings.

Activity

Watercolor and Haiku

OBJECTIVES: 2.01, 3.04

After discussing Mount Fuji and providing visuals, give the students an opportunity to present their own watercolor drawing accompanied by an original haiku.

Extension Assign novice and intermediate ELL students the watercolor only. Intermediate ELL students can attempt haiku, but may only be able to write three words (do not worry about syllables)

Background Information

Tokyo and Earthquakes

Tokyo, a city of about 8 million people (not including the suburbs), sits atop one of the world's most complex areas of seismic faults. People there take earthquakes very seriously. All of Tokyo's tallest buildings must meet building codes that enable them to withstand an earthquake of 7.2 on the Richter scale. Tokyo's most devastating, twentieth-century earthquake, known as the Great Kanto Quake, shook the city in 1923, leaving 140,000 dead. It measured 7.9 on the Richter scale. Since that time building materials and techniques have greatly improved. Today one method of ensuring building stability is to put tanks holding at least 150 tons of water on the roofs of tall buildings. In an earthquake, architects believe that the swaying of the water will offset the swaying of the building.

Discussion Questions

1 No point in Japan is more than 80 miles from the coast. How does this affect life in Japan?

2 How do you think life in North Carolina would compare to life in Japan?

Caption Answer

Kyushu has a humid subtropical climate (hot summers/cool winters). Shikoku also has a humid subtropical climate. Northern Honshu and Hokkaido have humid continental climates (snowy winters). Southern Honshu has warm summers and cool winters.

Activity

Rock Gardens

OBJECTIVES: 2.01, 3.01

Use pictures from the book listed below to help students gain a perception of Japanese rock gardens. Once students have studied and researched different types of rock gardens, let them make their own mini-version of a Japanese rock garden using a pan, small rocks, pebbles or marbles, and small plants (live or silk).

Thousand Mountains, a Million Hills: Creating the Rock Work of Japanese Gardens by David H. Engel. (Japan Publications (U.S.A.), Inc., 1995. ISBN 0870409697.)

Cherry trees bloom on Kyushu. **What is the climate of the island? What is the climate of the other main islands of Japan?**

Climate and Resources

If you watch winter sports on television, you have seen skiers racing down steep mountain slopes or flying off into space at the end of a ski jump. The events probably happened in Europe or the United States, but they could have occurred in Japan. Skiing there has become a popular winter sport. The 1998 Winter Olympics were held in Japan.

Japan's islands occupy the same latitudes as the eastern states of the United States (left). The seasonal temperatures in these two areas are about the same. The islands stretch 1,864 miles (3,001 km) from north to south—mileage that equals the distance between southern Maine and northern Florida.

Northern Honshu and Hokkaido are far enough north to be "snow country" in winter months. They have a humid continental climate. Japan's two southern islands, Kyushu and Shikoku, have the hot summers and cool winters of a humid subtropical climate. Southern Honshu has warm summers and cool winters.

Japan's Size

Japan's length is about equal to the distance between Maine and Florida. **Which Japanese island is partly at the same latitude as North Carolina?**

Climate and rainfall make several kinds of farming possible. Throughout much of the nation's history, Japanese farmers and fishermen were able to produce enough food to feed the Japanese. However, much of the best agricultural land has been lost in recent years as cities have spread into coastal plains.

Japan has only a few resources needed by an industrial nation. The rivers rushing down its steep mountains provide a dependable source of hydroelectric power. Some of the timber that the nation needs comes from careful cutting of its heavily forested mountain

Since World War II, Japan has purchased other resources in world markets. Giant tankers bring oil from Southwest Asia. From other parts of the world come coal and iron ore, wheat, soybeans, cotton, and wool. Japan pays for these purchases by converting raw materials into high-technology products—electronic equipment, automobiles, and chemicals. Such products come from Japan's most abundant resource, its well-educated workforce.

Customs

Small gardens are found in most Japanese temples. One famous garden (below) features carefully raked white gravel that looks like ocean waves. These waves surround large dark rocks.

Other gardens have neatly trimmed trees and flowering plants near a small waterfall. The small works of beauty reflect the Japanese respect for nature and a spiritual yearning for peace.

Teacher Notes

Japanese Language

With a pronunciation similar to the Spanish pronunciation of vowels, the characters on this page represent the Japanese vowel syllables. In Japanese there are five vowel sounds (a, i, u, e, o). "Consonant" sounds may proceed them (b, d, f, g, h, j, k, m, n, p, r, s, t, z, and the blends ch, sh, and ts). There are a few other possible sounds (y, w). Japanese characters do not depict individual "consonant" sounds. They are combined with vowels.

In *hiragana,* the "cursive" Japanese script, the characters denote consonant-vowel combinations, such as "ka, ki, ku, ke, ko." These characters are adaptations of Chinese characters that have lost their meaning and are now used only for their phonetic values. In all, there are 46 of these vowels or consonant-vowel combinations in hiragana. In modern Japanese, hiragana is used for simple words. Books for beginning readers are printed completely in hiragana without any Chinese characters.

The printing script of Japanese, *katakana,* corresponds exactly to hiragana in terms of pronunciation. It, too, has 46 characters. In modern Japanese, katakana are used for words that derive from languages other than Japanese or Chinese (such as "aspirin," written as "a • su • pi • ri • n").

In addition to these phonetic characters representing vowel and vowel-consonant combinations, Japanese uses many Chinese characters, called *kanji,* to represent words. Many of these characters have retained the same or similar meaning in Japanese as they have in Chinese but are pronounced differently in each language, similar to the use of Arabic numerals in French, English, Spanish, and other Western languages.

Graduate students at the University of Tsukuba are trying out a robotic suit that can give an average person twice his or her usual strength. The suit was developed to assist the elderly in their everyday lives. **Why are Japan's people considered its most abundant resource?**

LESSON 2 REVIEW

Fact Follow-Up

1. Name Japan's four main islands. Describe their relative location.
2. Explain the effects of mountains on Japan.
3. How does the geographic theme of location help explain Japan's range of climates?
4. List Japan's major resources. Which resources are limited?

Talk About It

1. Did Japan's location help or hurt early Japanese efforts to borrow ideas from China and use them in their own society? Explain.
2. Since the late 1800s, Japan has tried to obtain resources first through imperialism and, later, through trade. Which has worked more successfully? Explain your answer.

Discussion Questions

1 Do you think it is more important to preserve good farmland for crops or for housing? What can be done to balance the need for food and the need for housing?

2 How does the Japanese attitude toward the timber industry compare to North Carolina's?

3 Much of Japan's oil comes from Southwest Asia. How do you think the Japanese view unrest there?

4 How do you think Japan has become such a strong economic power since World War II?

Honshu

Japan must import oil, coal, iron, wheat, soybeans, cotton, and wool. Japan pays for these imports by exporting high-technology products.

LESSON 2 REVIEW

Fact Follow-Up Answers

1. Kyushu is about 100 miles off the southeastern coast of Korea. Shikoku is to the northeast of Kyushu. Honshu is the central island, between the Sea of Japan and the Pacific Ocean. Hokkaido is north of Honshu.
2. Mountains cover about 70 percent of Japan. Although the mountains are beautiful, few people can live there. Most crowd into the coastal plains. Mountains have also made road-building difficult and have historically served to divide people.
3. Japan's archipelago extends a long distance from north to south and passes through many degrees of latitude. Japan's location helps explain its range of climates.
4. Japan has fishing, farmland, hydroelectric power, and timber. Farmland and mineral resources are limited.

Talk About It Answers

1. Important points: In their discussion, students should focus on Japan's location. It seems that Japan was near enough to borrow the ideas and far enough away to adopt them in their own way.
2. Important points: Students should state which—imperialism or trade—has been more successful and explain why. Trade seems to have been more successful and less destructive than war.

OBJECTIVES: 3.01, 4.01, 6.02, 12.03

Discussion Questions

1 What do you dream about becoming when you grow up? Why does this appeal to you?

Caption Answer

Between the 1860s and 1960s, the population of Japan tripled. Now it is growing slowly.

Activity

Think/Pair/Share with a Partner

OBJECTIVES: 2.02, 2.03, 3.01

While discussing the Japanese Bullet Train, refer to page 476 for more details on the crowded conditions on public transportation in Japan. Ask students to imagine being pushed onto a school bus and to think about what it would be like. They should share their thoughts with a partner.

Activity

Graham Cracker Flags

OBJECTIVES: 12.01

Materials graham crackers, canned white cake icing, red colored sugar

Directions After viewing the flag of Japan, students may make their own edible flag of Japan by spreading white icing on a graham cracker and sprinkling the red colored sugar in a circle in the middle of the graham cracker. After making the flag, they can enjoy a sweet treat.

This activity can be done for any country by changing the colors of the icing and sugar. Decorator icing may also be used to make the flag symbols.

LESSON 3 People and Their Environment

KEY IDEAS

- Unlike most African and Asian nations, Japan is urban and highly industrialized. Population growth has almost stopped.
- Japanese children have to work hard to learn their complex language.
- Japanese have invented unusual ways to make the most of their space.

KEY TERMS

Ainu
kana
kimono
origami

Like many children, Kautaro Ohishi loved trains. "As a child, I dreamt of becoming an engineer," he says. His dream came true when he got a job with the Japanese railroad. At first he worked on steam locomotives. Then he operated electric trains. His greatest moment was driving the newest, most modern *shinkansen* (sheen·KAHN·say·n), the bullet train.

This sleek silver capsule shoots across the Japanese countryside at speeds of 170 miles per hour (274 kph). Hundreds of trains a day carry riders to and from Tokyo. They cover long distances in a matter of hours. The bullet trains proved to be one of Japan's many successes. They show how Japan has applied technology to move people through a crowded land.

Population Patterns

In the 1800s and early 1900s, Japan's population growth resembled the patterns of most Asian and African nations. Between the 1860s and 1960s, population tripled. That jump made Japan one of the world's most populous nations. Today, with more than 128 million people, Japan ranks ninth in population.

Population patterns have changed dramatically in recent years. Japanese families no longer are large. Most couples have one or two children. Japan's population is projected to decrease.

As you have read, families in many Asian and African nations want several children. Japanese families once thought this way, but they no longer do. Today, medical care is excellent. Serious childhood diseases are rare. Parents today worry about having good housing, clothes, and education for their children. They do not have to think much about losing a child to an illness.

Japanese children are seldom expected to work to help support their families or even to provide themselves with spending money. From an early age children are expected to work hard at only one thing—taking advantage of every educational opportunity that comes their way.

Homes in the city of Nagasaki are crammed together. **How have Japan's population patterns changed?**

CONNECTIONS • GEOGRAPHY & LANGUAGE ARTS •

The Thousand Cranes

In Hiroshima the most powerful weapon of World War II exploded in bright blinding light, followed by shocks that rocked the ground. Swirling winds and black skies announced the destruction. Ten of thousands died immediately, and others died later of radiation poison.

Out of that day of destruction have come efforts for peace and remembrance. In *Sadako and the Thousand Cranes,* author Eleanor Coerr writes about a young girl's illness.

The story, as written in English, is fiction. It is based on Japanese stories about the life of Sadako, who was two years old when the bomb exploded in Hiroshima. She later died at the age of twelve.

While Sadako was in the hospital, a friend brought her a piece of gold paper to create ***origami*** (or·ih·GAH·mee)—artfully folded paper. Sadako's friend folded the paper over and over again until it had the shape of a crane.

Her friend told Sadako of the legend. "A crane lives a thousand years. If a sick person folds one thousand paper cranes the gods will grant her wish and make her well again."

Sadako folded 644 cranes before she died. After her death, Sadako's classmates folded the rest of the cranes for her.

Today, there is a statue of Sadako in Hiroshima Peace Park. A crane with spreading wings sits atop her shoulders. Children leave paper cranes at the statue in honor of Sadako and the children who died from the atomic blast.

...nique Challenges

Elsewhere in Asia and Africa families ...ten worry about survival. Fatal diseases ...ke lives. Families need children to help ...ovide income, therefore young people ...ake up a large percentage of the ...pulation. Governments worry about ...ople finding jobs.

In Japan, where families are smaller, officials wonder where they will find enough workers, especially for low-skilled jobs. Leaders worry about funding the pension system and the effects on Japan's educational system, society, and traditions.

But others see opportunity. A smaller population may force Japan to create innovations that keep productivity high.

Discussion Questions

1 What do you think caused the tremendous population increase between 1860 and 1960? What will cause the population decrease between now and 2025?

2 What causes population in our area to either increase or decrease? What types of problems can result because of demographic (population) changes?

3 What are some issues that concern parents in our area?

4 Why is it important to remember Sadako? Why do children still make cranes in her honor?

Art Activity

Origami

OBJECTIVES: 12.02

Read *Sadako and the Thousand Paper Cranes* by Eleanor Coerr. (Penguin Putnam, 1999. ISBN 0698118022.)

The art of paper folding, origami, is a time-honored tradition in Japan. At the 1992 World Fair in Sevilla, Spain, the Japanese pavilion featured a 30-foot display case that exhibited the diversity of the country of Japan. Each item displayed was a piece of origami—houses, people, trees, and mountains. Locate origami books in your library and have students try some of the simplest designs first. Initially, have them use plain paper and then give them special origami paper or perfect squares of high quality wrapping paper.

Resource *Origami: Japanese Paper Folding, Vol. 3* by Florence Sakade (Charles E. Tuttle Co., Inc., 1983. ISBN 0804804567.)

Extension ELL students can follow modeling from a peer, teacher, or book to participate.

Background Information

Japan's Aging Population

With 17 percent of its population over the age of 65, Japan has one of the world's fastest aging populations. Since 1945, Japan's birth rate and death rate have been declining. The nation has one of the world's lowest rates of population increase. At the same time, the Japanese on average live longer than most people, with an average life span of 77 years for men and 83 years for women. The aging population has led to severe labor shortages as well as concerns about the care of the elderly. The number of Japanese of working age peaked at 87 million in 1995 and is projected to decline by more than one third to 55 million by 2050. So far temporary foreign workers have helped Japan meet its need for low-skill workers.

Discussion Questions

1 Describe the work ethic in Japan.

2 What are the expectations in your family about your working to help support yourself?

3 What are the educational expectations in your household?

4 Who are the indigenous people in Japan?

Caption Answer

Almost all Japanese belong to the same ethnic group. They think of themselves as people who are shaped by a common heritage that no one else shares.

Activity

Japanese Language

OBJECTIVES: 12.03

Materials handout—Japanese words of possible foreign origin from the Teacher's Resource Guide

Have students list as many languages of the world as they can remember. Review their answers aloud. Locate information about language families of the world. Develop the concept that languages from similar backgrounds share more common traits than unrelated languages.

You might use the example of "mother" in several languages: mother (English), madre (Spanish), mere (French), muder (German), mater (Latin), meter (Greek), and matr (Sanskrit). Ask the class if they think Japanese would resemble English.

Review with the class some facts previously covered in this unit:

Japan is isolated geographically.

Although the Japanese use Chinese characters to write their language, the Japanese language is not a form of Chinese.

Japan isolated itself from 1603 until the nineteenth century.

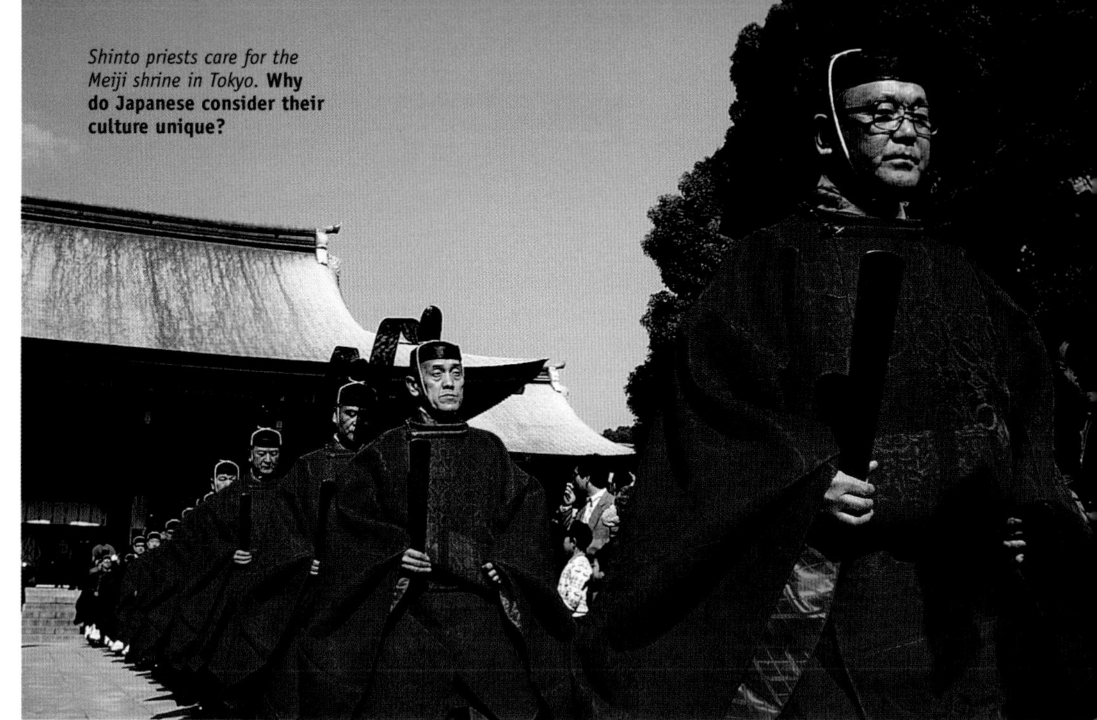

Shinto priests care for the Meiji shrine in Tokyo. **Why do Japanese consider their culture unique?**

A People Apart—"We Japanese"

Almost all Japanese belong to the same racial group. There are only a few minorities. Among them are Koreans, who were forced to come to Japan when Korea was a Japanese colony. About 20,000 ***Ainu*** (EYE·new)—descendants of the first settlers in the Japanese islands—live in northern Hokkaido. Other minorities are Chinese, Americans, and Europeans.

Word Origins

Among Japanese, a form of Buddhism called Zen became popular. Zen Buddhists gained spiritual enlightenment through quiet meditation, not through study of holy books. The word **Zen** comes from the Chinese word ***Ch'an***. Ch'an in turn comes from the Sanskrit word ***Ch'an***, which means "meditation."

Japanese believe their culture is unique. They think of themselves as people who are shaped by a common heritage. They believe that outsiders can never truly fit into their ways of life. "We Japanese," they often say when they compare their way of life to those of other people. Foreigners are warmly welcomed when visiting Japan, but they are seldom allowed to become citizens.

Language and Writing

You have read that centuries ago Japan adopted the Chinese writing system. This does not mean that the languages are alike. Spoken Japanese is completely different from—and more complex than—Chinese. Early settlers in the Japanese islands brought the language with them when they migrated from somewhere in Siberia.

Mastering Japanese is difficult because the system for writing the language is complex. Like the Chinese, students must spend hours memorizing thousands of characters—those symbols for things and ideas. In addition, Japanese must learn

Discussion If Japanese is from a different language family, why would the words on the handout appear similar to English? Lead the discussion to discover that most of these words refer to something that was not present in the Japanese culture prior to contact with the West. For example, point out English words (succotash, hurricane, moccasin, canoe) that Europeans borrowed from Native American words to describe something for which they had no word. Look carefully at the list of Japanese words. The Japanese table is much shorter than the English. For this reason they used the English word "table" to describe high tables. The bed used in Japan is a mattress (futon) on the floor, not a mattress on a raised platform (beh-oh). The Japanese eat with chopsticks, not with a knife, fork, and spoon. A shoji in Japan refers to a light sliding screen made of paper stretched over a wooden frame: a door that swings on hinges needed a new word to differentiate it from a shoji, hence doh-ah.

Ask the students if they think that the diffusion of foreign words into Japanese is a one-way street. Does it happen in most languages?

ana, a language system that is used along ith the characters. *Kana* is composed of 6 symbols.

When the spoken and written nguage systems are combined, Japanese ecomes one of the world's most difficult nguages. Language instruction takes up uch of a student's time in school, and omework assignments are heavy. Many oreigners have gained mastery of panese. Yet these foreign experts and panese agree that only those with xtensive experience using the language a Japanese social setting can truly aster it.

ity Life

At midnight, a tired Tokyo usinessman is finally ready to go to bed. e worked late. Then he joined colleagues r dinner and talk. He lives an hour and a alf away. To catch the train home and still turn for the early start of his workday is o much. So he checks in at one of okyo's "capsule hotels."

His room looks like a cupboard built into a wall with other cupboards above, below, and on either side. His space is only slightly larger than his body, but he climbs into his capsule and stretches out on his sleeping mat. The room has a television and a telephone. He is ready for a night's rest.

Capsule hotels are one way the Japanese have adapted to the demands of long work hours, long commutes, and crowded cities. Almost 80 percent of Japanese work in cities.

Downtown Tokyo looks like cities the world over. Glass, steel, and concrete buildings soar overhead. Commuters pour out of railway and subway stations. Buses, cars, and motorbikes clog the streets. Busy train stations in Tokyo handle 20 million commuters a day. Smaller towns and cities are less congested. Yet traffic is heavy everywhere.

Land is expensive, especially in and around Tokyo. The Japanese have had to adapt to crowded conditions and limited land. Companies have offered a solution

Japanese Vowels

Hiragana		Katakana	
あ	a	ア	a
い	i	イ	i
う	u	ウ	u
え	e	エ	e
お	o	オ	o

The Japanese language, like English, uses both a cursive script—hiragana—and a printing script—katakana. These are the characters for the Japanese vowel syllables, which are pronounced similarly to the vowels in Spanish. **Why is it so difficult to learn Japanese?**

A Tokyo businessman reads before going to bed in a capsule hotel cupboard. **What aspects of Japanese life make these hotels necessary?**

Discussion Questions

1 Why would the Japanese not encourage foreigners to become citizens?

2 What influences from other cultures do we find in our language?

3 How does the "capsule hotel" compare to a hotel we normally find?

Long commutes, long work hours, and crowded cities make these hotels necessary.

Japanese is difficult to learn because students must study both a Japanese character system, *kana,* and about 2,000 Chinese characters used by the Japanese.

English has a larger vocabulary than any other language in the world, primarily because it freely borrows foreign words. Ask the students to list all of the English words they can think of that might have come from Japanese. Remind them that most of these words will refer to something or some behavior that English-speaking people first observed had no existing English word in Japan.

This exercise is meant to be analytical, not definitive.

Discussion Questions

1 How have the Japanese managed to adapt to their conditions?

2 What do you think your everyday life would be like if you lived in Japan?

Caption Answer

They live in tiny apartments and houses that are about one third the size of American homes.

A Japanese woman (below) wears a traditional kimono. Rooftops (right) are used for sports, gardening, and relaxing. **How do the Japanese adapt to living on limited land?**

to city golfers and tennis players. They have built driving ranges and tennis courts on top of high-rise buildings.

Limited living space means that homes are small. Many people live in tiny apartments. Privately owned houses are about one-third the size of American homes. Finding parking space for an automobile is always a big problem.

City life is a mix of Western and traditional. Most people—men and women—dress in Western-style clothing. Some women wear the traditional ***kimono.*** It is a long robe-like garment that wraps across itself in the front. It is tied in place with a sash, or *obi,* in the back. Men wear Western-style suits to the office. At home, c for a family outing in a park, they change into the more comfortable *yukate,* a lightweight cotton robe.

LESSON 3 REVIEW

Fact Follow-Up

1. In what ways do Japan's economy and society differ from most other Asian and African nations?
2. Why do the Japanese consider themselves unique? How does that belief affect the way Japanese accept foreigners?
3. What are characteristics of city life in Japan?

Talk About It

1. How do landforms and living patterns in Japan make trains, especially the bullet train, an especially good solution to the movement of people?
2. Japanese families usually have only one or two children. Why is the number smaller than in most African and Asian families?

LESSON 3 REVIEW

Fact Follow-Up Answers

1. Japan is urbanized and industrialized. Population growth is slow.
2. Almost all Japanese belong to the same ethnic group. They think of themselves as people who are shaped by a common heritage that no one else shares. Foreign visitors are welcomed in Japan, but they are seldom allowed to become citizens.
3. Almost 90 percent of Japanese workers work in cities; so cities are crowded and traffic is heavy. Glass, steel, and concrete buildings soar overhead. Frequently their rooftops include tennis courts and golf driving ranges that could not fit anywhere else in the crowded city. Apartments and houses in and around the city are small because land is expensive. City life also mixes Western and traditional customs and clothing.

Talk About It Answers

1. Important points: Trains reduce traffic congestion, and they are a fast way to get to the outlying suburbs from the cities, where most Japanese work. The bullet trains are a rapid and efficient means of traveling throughout the archipelago.
2. Good health care in Japan has reduced the possibility of children dying from disease, so Japanese families do not have to worry as much about the survival of their children.

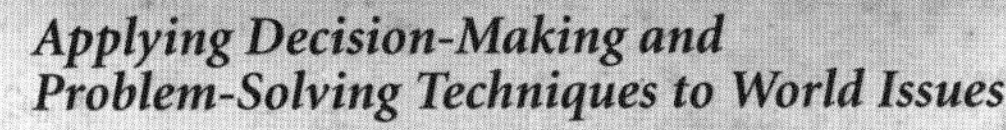

Applying Decision-Making and Problem-Solving Techniques to World Issues

Planning with Population Profiles

Imagine that you have been employed by two Asian governments—India and Japan—to help decide what kind of problems lie ahead as each tries to expand its economy. Your assignment is to provide data that will help answer these questions:

1. If the number of jobs expands, will we have people to fill them?
2. If our industries can expand the production of consumer goods, should those products be made mostly for people under forty years or for older people?
3. Should our government and people invest all available money in industry? Should we invest heavily in such services as education, medical care, or nursing homes for the elderly?

You can learn much about whether the answers are the same or different for India and Japan by studying the two population profiles below. These profiles tell you at a glance what percentage of the total population falls into each age group.

In Japan, the percentage in the birth-to-four-years age group is less than half of India's (about 3 percent female and 3 percent male). People under the age of forty in Japan make up about 60 percent of the population.

Which nation, according to the population profiles, will have the larger labor force in the future? Examine the population profiles and discuss your findings/answer to the question with another classmate.

Answer questions 2 and 3 above and compare your answers with a classmate. Are they the same or different? Would more information help you arrive at better answers? What kinds of additional information do you need?

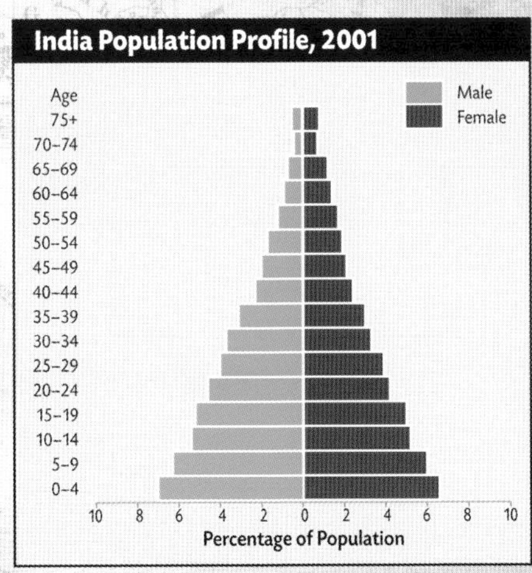

Source: 2001 Census of India; Office of the Registrar General

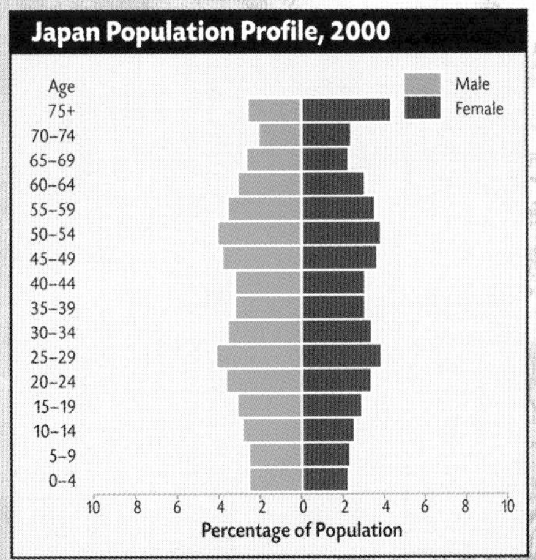

Source: 2000 Population Census of Japan; Statistics Bureau, Ministry of Internal Affairs and Communications

Skill Lesson Review

1. Which nation appears, based on the population profile, to have the brighter economic future? *India will have many more workers for an expanding economy. The question is can its economy keep pace with population growth.*
2. What other uses might population profiles have? *Answers will vary. They can be used by advertising agencies to create marketing campaigns targeted to the largest groups.*
3. India's population is much larger than Japan's. In answering the three questions in the Skill Lesson, which was more important: the numbers of people or the percentage of people in each age group? Why? *Answers will vary. Both are important. Percentages will help you plan for employment and industry, and the numbers will tell you the amount of production necessary to support the population.*

Teaching This Skill Lesson

Materials Needed textbooks, paper, pencils

Classroom Organization entire class

Beginning the Lesson If a new business has recently located in the community, ask students why they think the particular location was chosen. Accept all answers. Alternatively, if a business has recently closed, ask why and accept all answers.

Have students examine the two population profiles on page 473. Ask them to comment on differences and similarities, probing to lead them to speculate on why differences exist.

Lesson Development Ask students to use the population profiles to answer question 1. (Remind students that these figures are percentages—not actual population figures.)

Ask these questions: Which nation is more likely to have an expanding labor force in the future? What, if anything, could happen to change this answer? Direct students to look at the profile for Japan, asking how Japan might expand its workforce. Suggest—if students do not—that older workers could be used, that women could enter formerly male-dominated jobs.

Once you are confident that students can read and use the population profiles, have them work on questions 2 and 3 independently. (This could be a homework assignment.)

Conclusion Have students report on their responses to questions 2 and 3, noting responses on the chalkboard. Since the population profiles were the only sources students were to use in this assignment, ask students to support their answers with evidence from the profiles. Ask what additional information might be useful in making a final determination, cautioning that decisions such as the ones they have been making are rarely made on the basis of a single piece of information. Ask for generalizations about the usefulness of population profiles for policy makers.

Extension If desired, have students collect advertisements from newspapers and magazines or keep a log of TV commercials that seem to be directed toward a particular age group. Example: differences in commercials on network news and afternoon soap operas or sports events.

Talk About It

1. Japan is an island, relatively isolated from the cultures from which it chose to borrow. A strong cultural identity helped the Japanese make borrowed ideas their own.
2. Since other resources are limited, a highly educated workforce is an important economic resource.
3. Important points: factors include that the Japanese are mainly one ethnic group, they share a common heritage, they believe their culture is unique, and few foreigners become citizens.
4. Important points: The Japanese have adapted and used technology and inventions to overcome challenges: bullet trains speed commuters through a crowded land, capsule hotels make the best use of space, homes are small because of space, roofs are used for recretion and gardening. technology also improves the resistence of buildings to earthquakes.

Mastering Mapwork

1. Both are located either on or near water; both are either in or near mountainous areas. Because Nagasaki is considerably farther south, it has a much warmer climate than that of Sapporo.
2. Kobe lies near both water and mountains on the island of Honshu. Given its latitude and its protection by land masses, one would expect a moderate climate.
3. Tokyo is a very large city with tall buildings, busy streets, and many people. One would expect the cultural characteristics of place to influence the lives of people more than the physical characteristics of place.

CHAPTER 23 REVIEW

Lessons Learned

Lesson 1
A Shared History
Today, almost all Japanese are descended from people who migrated from Asia. Through many centuries, they have become a homogeneous people. This unity has enabled them to survive as a distinctive people through many great changes: industrialization, urbanization, empire building, a devastating defeat in World War II, and change from an authoritarian government to democracy.

Lesson 2
Geographic Foundations
Geography has played a major role in shaping Japan. The islands' location has served as a barrier to movement, protecting the Japanese from foreign invaders. The oceans also have served as highways, enabling the Japanese to import foreign ideas, technologies, and raw materials for an industrial society. The rugged mountains covering the islands have made the islands a difficult and crowded place to live.

Lesson 3
People and Their Environment
The Japanese think of themselves as a special people. Foreigners are seldom welcome to join Japanese society. The Japanese language is complex and difficult to learn. The Japanese stand apart from others in Africa and Asia by living in a highly industrialized, homogeneous, and prosperous society. The population is beginning to decline in size, but Japan remains crowded.

Talk About It

1. You have read that Japan kept its own distinctive society even though it borrowed much from others. How can this be explained?
2. How might Japan's emphasis on education be related to the nation's belief that its people are its most important resource?
3. Why do the Japanese consider themselves a special people?
4. How does Japan use technology to adapt to problems created by overcrowding and their environment?

Mastering Mapwork

PLACE

Use the map on page 455 to answer these questions:

1. Compare the physical characteristics of place you would observe in Nagasaki (on Kyushu) and Sapporo (on Hokkaido).
2. Locate Kobe (35°N and 135°E). What physical characteristics of place would you expect to observe in Kobe?
3. In Tokyo, which do you think would influence the lives of people more: the physical or cultural characteristics of place? Explain your answer.

Go to the Source

日本

Understanding Culture through Ceremonies

Read the passage outlining the "Official Duties and Public Activities in the Imperial Palace: His Majesty's [Emperor of Japan] Birthday Receptions" below. Answer the questions using specific references to the document. Each year on December 23, these functions are held in celebration of the emperor's birthday.

(1) Congratulatory Ceremony
His Majesty the Emperor receives congratulations from His Imperial Highness the Crown Prince and the rest of the Imperial Family; the Prime Minister; the Speaker of the House of Representatives and the President of the House of Councillors; and the Chief Justice of the Supreme Court.

(2) Luncheon
Their Majesties the Emperor and Empress hold a birthday luncheon and invite the Speaker and Vice-Speaker of the House of Representatives and the President and Vice-President of the House of Councillors; Diet members; the Prime Minister; Ministers of State; the Chief Justice and Justices of the Supreme Court; other government officials with Imperial attestation (Ninshokan); Administrative Vice-Ministers of Ministries and Agencies and other leading figures of legislative, executive and judicial organs; and prefectural governors and representatives from all fields and their spouses. Birthday greetings are received and His Imperial Highness the Crown Prince and the rest of the Imperial Family are also in attendance.

(3) Reception
Their Majesties the Emperor and Empress invite heads of the diplomatic missions in Japan and their spouses to a tea reception. Birthday greetings are received and His Imperial Highness the Crown Prince and the rest of the Imperial Family are also in attendance.

(4) People's visit to the Palace for His Majesty's Birthday
His Majesty the Emperor receives congratulations from the people. In the morning Their Majesties the Emperor and Empress appear together several times. His Majesty the Emperor addresses the people. Visitors enter from the Main Gate and offer their good wishes in the East Plaza of the Imperial Palace. Due to the court functions none of the members of the Imperial Family appeared in the afternoon. Visitors enter from the Sakashita-mon Gate and sign the guest books in front of the Imperial Household Agency building or submit business cards.

Questions
1. Who is the intended audience of this document?
2. What is the occasion of this document?
3. What does this document tell us about Japanese culture?
4. In what way do the Japanese view the emperor and royal family?

Go to the Source

Go to the Source

OBJECTIVES: 8.01, 9.01, 9.02, 10.01, 11.03 Skills 1.01, 1.03, 2.01, 2.02, 3.05

The birthday of the reigning emperor is a national holiday in Japan. The Imperial Palace in Tokyo is open to the public. Hundreds of thousands of Japanese wave flags in honor of the occasion. Emperor Akihito was born on December 23, 1933.

Visit **NCJourneys.com** for a link to the document.

ANSWERS:

1. The general public and those participating in the ceremonies.
2. The Japanese emperor's yearly birthday celebration.
3. One can conclude that the Japanese culture is very orderly and shows great respect for its leaders. This document also shows that Japan maintains a monarchy although the monarch or royal family has limited or no governmental powers. All levels of society are involved and invited to the ceremonies.
4. The schedule of events and the people involved shows that the Japanese have great honor and respect as well as deep traditions.

How to Use the Chapter Review

There are three sections in the Chapter Review: Talk About It, Mastering Mapwork, and Go to the Source. Use the Vocabulary Worksheets and the Chapter Review Worksheet in the Teacher's Resource Guide for additional reinforcement and preparation for the Chapter Assessments. The chapter and lesson reviews and the Chapter Review Worksheets are the basis of the assessment for each chapter.

Talk About It questions encourage students to speculate about the content of the chapter and are suitable for class or small-group discussion. They are not intended to be assigned for homework.

Mastering Mapwork has students apply one or more of the Five Themes of Geography to maps within the chapter.

Go to the Source activities allow students to analyze a primary source that relates to the content of the chapter. The questions and activities familiarize students with different types of primary sources and also build content-reading skills.

Modern Japan

Social Studies Strands

Economics and Development

Government and Active Citizenship

Technological Influences and Society

Global Connections

Cultures and Diversity

North Carolina Standard Course of Study

Goal 6 The learner will recognize the relationship between economic activity and the quality of life in Africa, Asia, and Australia.

Goal 10 The learner will compare the rights and civic responsibilities of individuals in political structures in Africa, Asia, and Australia.

Goal 12 The learner will assess the influence of major religions, ethical beliefs, and values on cultures in Africa, Asia, and Australia.

Goal 13 The learner will describe the historic, economic and cultural connections among North Carolina, the United States, Africa, Asia, and Australia.

Teaching & Assessment

- English Language Learner Modified Lesson Plans for this chapter are found in the Teacher Resource Guide.
- *ExamView® Assessment Suite* is provided at **NCJourneys.com.** It includes customizable assessments for all chapters. Paper tests are also available in the Teacher Resource Guide. See pages T16–T17 for information about how to use the assessments and the Scoring Guide.

Worksheets

Worksheets and answer keys are found both in the Teacher Resource Guide and at **NCJourneys.com**, including Reading Guides, Reading Strategies, Chapter Reviews, English Language Learner and others.

ACTIVITIES AND INTEGRATIONS

SOCIAL STUDIES
● Straight from Japan, p. 476B
▲ ■ Japan's Modern Economy, p. 477
★ Japanese Americans During World War II, p. 478
Emperor, p. 480
Japanese Succession Debate, p. 480
▲ ■ Becoming Emperor, p. 481
Japanese School Day, p. 486
Japanese Tea Ceremony Demonstration, p. 488
Skill Lesson: Cooperation with Outsiders, p. 492

READING/LANGUAGE ARTS	READING/LANGUAGE ARTS OBJECTIVES
Analogies, p. 476B	2.01
Activator: *The Tale of the Mandarin Ducks*, p. 476	2.01
Writing Prompt: Japanese Schools, p. 476	3.03
★ Debating the "No-War" Clause, p. 482	1.03
● Match and Write, p. 485	6.01
Japanese Haiku & Tanka Poetry, p. 490	5.02
Go to the Source: Analyzing Art as an Artifact, p. 495	2.01, 4.01, 4.02, 4.03

MATHEMATICS	MATHEMATICS OBJECTIVES
Japan Means Business, p. 483	4.01, 4.05
● ▲ Word Problem, p. 483	1.02, 1.03
■ Sushi Math, p. 487	1.01, 1.08

TECHNOLOGY	TECHNOLOGY OBJECTIVES
● Images of Japan, p. 476B	3.01, 3.11

FINE ARTS	FINE ARTS OBJECTIVES
Designing Japanese Wood Blocks, p. 476B	2.04, 5.03
Bracelets, p. 478	2.04, 5.03
★ Origami, p. 491	2.04, 5.01

CHARACTER AND VALUES EDUCATION	TRAITS
Writing Prompt: Japanese Schools, p. 476	Respect, responsibility, good judgment
What Would You Do?, p. 484	Respect

● Basic Activities ★ Challenging Activities ▲ English Language Learner Novice ■ English Language Learner Intermediate

Chapter Activities

Introductory Activity

Straight from Japan

OBJECTIVES: 5.02, 5.04, 6.02

This is an organizing activity. Students will name products that are from Japan. Have them use advertisements in newspapers and magazines, and have them look at the product names of items at school and home. The items might include types of cars, bicycles, electronic equipment, and foods. Have students talk about those items they found. Put students in cooperative groups and have them list the products they found. Then have them list those items in order of popularity. Have each group graph its findings. Display these graphs for comparison.

(Note: several chapters in this unit have similar activities. This repetition reinforces the concept of the United States' economic dependence on this region. As an extension, if you have done several of these activities, have the students record their findings for each activity on a graphic organizer. Then compare the findings. Which nation of East and Southeast Asia seems to make more clothing? electronics? toys? cars? and so on. Students should share and compare their findings. Do they draw the same conclusions?)

Culminating Activity

Images of Japan

OBJECTIVES: 4.03, 11.01

Have students research images of Japan. They may use their own original drawings, Japanese cartoons and cartoon films, or pictures from advertisements, news magazines, travel magazine or downloaded from the Internet (respect copyright restrictions)s. As a class, have students contribute to a collage that will reflect their study of Japan.

Display for viewing by class and others in the school. The collage should reflect the culture of Japan.

Art Activity

Designing Japanese Wood Blocks

OBJECTIVES: 12.02

Have students study and research traditional Japanese woodblock prints. Give these directions: After researching, select a design. Carefully draw the outline of your design on a piece of thick cardboard. Cut this out. Using the outlined design, make any interior cuts or etches necessary to enhance your design. Next, glue the design to a block-shaped piece of wood or cardboard. Dip the design into ink or paint and carefully press onto a piece of paper. When dry, matt and display.

Analogies

OBJECTIVES: 5.04, 9.04, 12.02

Analogies are useful to help students make associations with prior knowledge. Read the analogies aloud and ask students to identify the relationship between the terms. As an extension, ask students to write their own analogies using key terms or places discussed in the chapter.

constitutional monarchy : Japan, United Kingdom :: absolute monarchy : Saudi Arabia (kind of government in)

pacifist : peace lover :: militant : aggressor (synonym)

seibo : Japan :: Christmas : United States (a time to exchange gifts in)

Sony, Honda, Nissan : Japan :: Motorola, General Motors, Ford : United States (are major corporations of)

sumo/Greco-Roman/freestyle : wrestling :: butterfly/freestyle/breaststroke : swimming (are styles of)

ikebana : flowers :: bonsai : trees (is the artful manipulation of)

noh : ballet :: kabuki : musical :: bunraku : puppet show (is the traditional Japanese theater equivalent to)

Teaching Strategies

Students should be able to relate to modern Japan as they can compare Japan's bustling cities with those found in the United States. Students will also recognize Japanese influence on life in America through its games, electronics, and cars that are bought by American consumers. This chapter provides an excellent opportunity for an intense economic study of imports and exports.

Activator

OBJECTIVES: 4.03, 12.02

Activators are great tools to use in order to "hook" the attention of the students. Reading picture books or stories is an excellent way to build interest in the subject and is also a great way to integrate language arts into the social studies curriculum.

The Tale of the Mandarin Ducks by Katherine Paterson. (Dutton, 1990. ISBN 0525672834.)
The Bicycle Man by Allen Say. (Houghton Mifflin, 1989. ISBN 0395506522.)
Sadako and the Thousand Paper Cranes by Eleanor Coerr. (Penguin Putnam, 1999. ISBN 0698118022.)

Writing Prompt

OBJECTIVES: 11.03, 12.01

Evaluative

Schools in the United States are often compared to schools in Japan. If you were going to create the ideal system, combining features from both the Japanese and American schools, what one feature of the Japanese schools would you use? Name the feature and explain why you would select it.

As you write, remember to

- name the feature.
- give at least two reasons to support your position.
- write in complete sentences.
- use correct grammar and punctuation.

Modern Japan

Sights that bring together traditional and modern Japan often startle visitors. They can see a centuries-old temple just beyond a brightly colored sign advertising an American brand of gasoline. Tourists might photograph a sumo wrestler wearing a light robe striding through a crowd of men dressed in business suits.

The Japanese are used to the sight of a geisha (left), a traditional entertainer, walking to a train station. But the Japanese are still impressed by the bullet train and other signs of Japan's strong recovery from the ruins of war (bottom right).

Chapter Preview

Lesson 1
Government
Japan is a democratic constitutional monarchy.

Lesson 2
Economy
After World War II, Japan built a strong economy that competes with other industrial powers.

Lesson 3
Society and Culture
Japan has an urban society that blends old traditions and Western influences.

Chapter Resources

Print Resources

Galef, David. *Even Monkeys Fall from Trees; and Other Japanese Proverbs.* Tokyo and Rutland, Vt.: Charles E. Tuttle Company, 1987. ISBN 0804816255.

Heinrichs, Ann. *Japan* (Enchantment of the World series). Children's Press, 1997. ISBN 0516206494.

Jacobsen, Peter Otto, and Preben Sejer Kristensen. *A Family in Japan.* New York: The Bookwright Press, 1983. ISBN 0531038254.

Kalman, Bobbie. *Japan : The Culture.* Crabtree, 2001. ISBN 077879377.

__. *Japan: The Land.* Crabtree, 2001. ISBN 0778793753.

__. *Japan: The People.* Crabtree, 2001. ISBN 0778793761.

Kent, Deborah. *Tokyo* (Cities of the World series). Children's Press, 1996. ISBN 0516003542.

Whyte, Harlinah, and Nicole Frank. Welcome to Japan (Welcome to My Country). Gareth Stevens Publishing,1999. ISBN 0836823974.

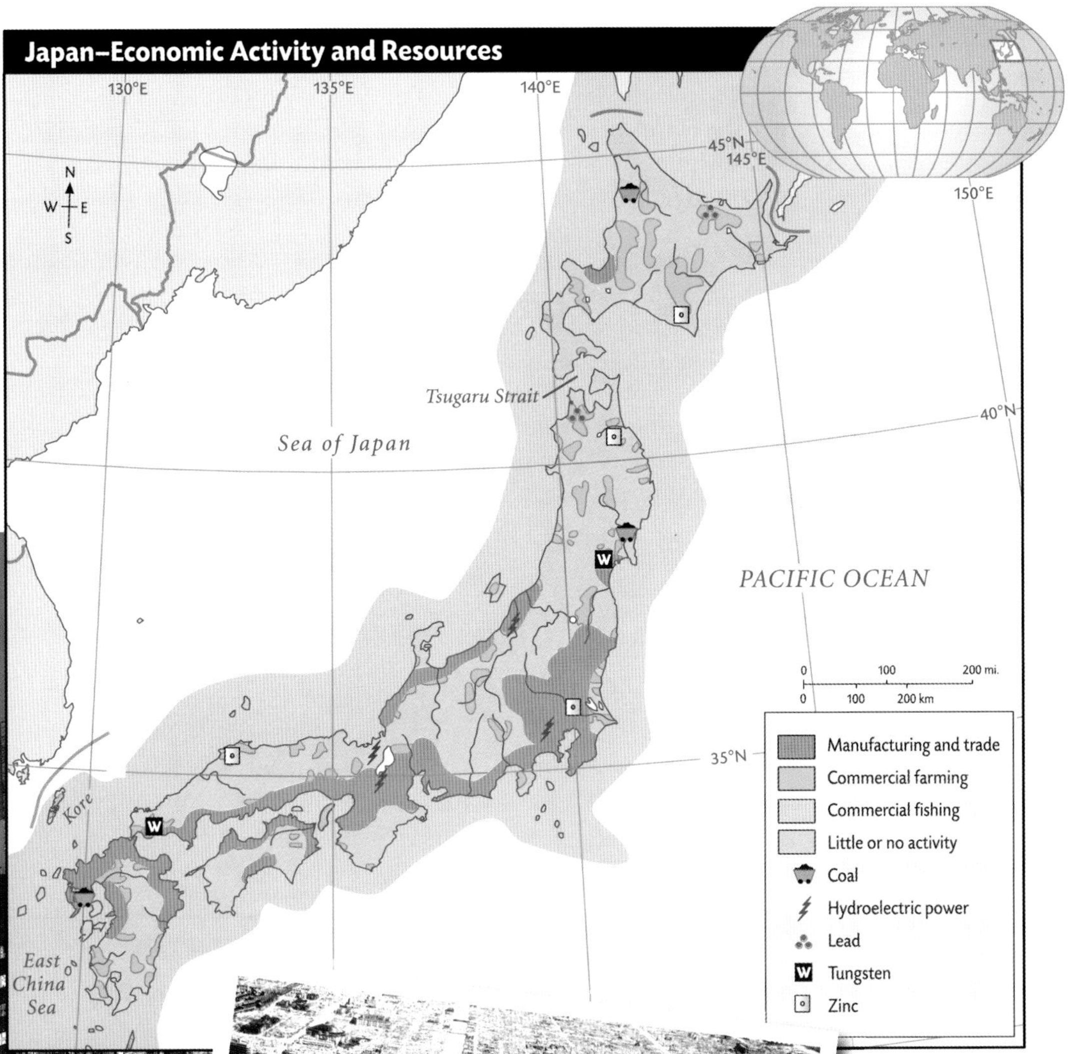

Japan–Economic Activity and Resources

Tokyo today (far left); Tokyo in 1945 (left)

odern Japan

477

Map Activity

Japan's Modern Economy

NATIONAL GEOGRAPHY STANDARDS: 1, 16

GEOGRAPHIC THEMES: Location, Human-Environmental Interaction

OBJECTIVES: 2.01, 3.01, 5.04

Discuss with students that Japan has an extensive, highly developed, efficient mass transit system including buses, high-speed trains (Shinkansen), and subways. Private cars, heavy traffic, five international airports and some of East Asia's best deepwater ports help give Japan an infrastructure rivaled by few Asian nations. Also note that Japan has limited mineral resources. In achieving modernization since World War II, Japan depends greatly on imported raw materials, including energy resources.

Teacher Notes

Japan's Powerful Economy

Although Japan's land area is relatively small, the country is an economic giant. Japan is one of the world's major industrial powers. It makes use of every resource—people, technology, land, and sea. The Fuji Bank, Ltd., is Japan's largest commercial bank, with a network of offices, affiliates, and subsidiaries in Japan and overseas.

Million, Billion, Trillion

Although Japan's currency is the yen, when we compare Japan's economy to that of the United States, we use dollars. Both nations' economies are measured in trillions of dollars. What does a trillion look like? Help your students visualize this by writing a trillion on the board.

1 trillion = 1,000,000,000,000

2006 Gross Domestic Product (GDP)
Japan: $4,220,000,000,000
United States: $12,980,000,000,000
North Carolina (2005): $346,600,000,000

ack issues of magazines

apan. Cobblestone Publishing Company. ISBN 0382405315.

udiovisual

une In Japan: Approaching Cultures through Television. Asia Society. 69 min.

une In Japan: Global Connections. Asia Society. Video, 40 min.

apan–North Carolina Connections. Humanities Extension/Publications, NCSU. 1999. 25 min.

_. *Living in 21st Century Japan.* 2001. 28 minutes.

Web Sites

Go to **NCJourneys.com** for links:

- Japan Guide
- Virtual Museum of Japanese Art
- Cultural Information, Ministry of Foreign Affairs, Japan
- Japan Information Network

OBJECTIVES: 9.04, 10.01, 10.02

Discussion Questions

1 Why has the Japanese flag sparked a national debate?

2 Do you think patriotism can be dangerous?

3 The Japanese are just now beginning to discuss the events surrounding Pearl Harbor. How do you think this is going to change their perceptions of themselves and World War II?

4 Why is it important that we know the history of our country?

Caption Answer

He lost the power to rule and became a "symbol of the state and the unity of the people."

Activity

Japanese Americans During World War II

OBJECTIVES: 7.01, 7.02, 13.01

Read aloud to the class or have students, in small groups, read the novel, *Farewell to Manzinar: A True Story of Japanese American Experience During and After the World War II Internment* by Jeanne W. and James D. Houston (Bantam, 1981. ISBN 0553272586.) Discuss the treatment of Japanese Americans by the United States government during the war. Students may explain in an essay or short story how they would have reacted to this treatment.

LESSON 1 Government

KEY IDEAS

- After World War II, Japan adopted a new constitution approved by the United States.
- The constitution changed the status of the emperor and provided for democratic government.
- Japanese have debated the wisdom of revising parts of the constitution. Japan's government, however, has been stable and democratic.

KEY TERMS

constitutional monarchy
National Diet
pacifists

Recently, Japan's Ministry of Education said all students must learn the national anthem, "The Reign of Our Emperor." The ministry also said that students must be taught to recognize the red sun flag as Japan's flag. Those instructions sparked a national debate.

Many teachers said the government had violated the constitution. They believed the ministry's order limited people's freedom by trying to shape their thoughts. The national anthem, they claimed, glorified a time when the emperor was all-powerful. The sun flag called up memories of World War II. "Never send our students to the battlefields again" became the teachers' slogan.

Despite the teachers' objections, most schools accepted the new rules. So students today sing these lines:

Ten thousand years of happy reign be thine:
Rule on, my lord, till what are pebbles now
By ages united to mighty rocks shall grow
Whose venerable sides the moss doth line.

Memories of World War II and Japan's occupation by foreign troops are still vivid. Japanese agree that heavy loss of life, destroyed cities, and defeat form a painful chapter in their proud history. The Japanese, however, sometimes have difficulty agreeing about how to solve problems the war left behind. Japan's postwar constitution is one of the sources of controversy.

The Emperor and the People

Before World War II, Japan's constitution gave the emperor great power to rule Japan. Military leaders who wanted Japan to dominate Asia went further. They claimed that the Japanese emperor was a god descended from the sun goddess Amaterasu. During the war, young Japanese were taught to sacrifice their lives for the emperor.

Some Japanese thought of Emperor Hirohito (front) as a god before World War II. **What became the role of the emperor after the war**

Activity

Bracelets

 **OBJECTIVES:** 12.02

After reading the story *The Bracelet* by Yoshiko Uchida (Putnam, 1996. ISBN 069811390X.), give students materials to make their own friendship bracelets. Cut four 24-inch strands of embroidery floss, each in a different color. Make an overhand knot 8 inches from one end and tie to the back of a chair. Assign each strand with letters A,B,C, and D. Hold A and B in your hands. Wrap A over and under B, pulling the end of A through the loop with your right hand. Holding B tight in your left hand, pull up on A, tightening it into a knot. Repeat, making a second knot with A over B. Drop B and make two knots with A over C. Drop C and make two knots with A over D. This completes one row. Make the second row by knotting B over C twice, B over D twice, and B over A twice. Continue in this way until the bracelet is the desired length; tie an overhand knot. Leave enough floss at both ends to tie the bracelet into a circle; cut away any extra.

Alternative Many of your students will know how to make their own version of a friendship bracelet. Ask them to do a demonstration of bracelet making.

After World War II, occupying ›rces—United States troops under ıe command of General Douglas IacArthur—wanted to make sure that ıpan would never again threaten world eace. The occupying forces set out to :make Japanese government and society. 'he United States hoped to erase the 'aditions that had plunged Japan into 'ar. So MacArthur pushed Japan to :form its government by taking away the mperor's power and creating a emocratic way of life.

Japan adopted a new constitution that ad been approved by the Americans. Inder the constitution, the emperor no ›nger had power to rule. He became a symbol of the state and unity of the eople." The constitution gave the ıpanese the authority to govern ıemselves.

Japan's new government was similar › that of the Netherlands and Sweden. It ; a *constitutional monarchy,* a govern-ıent with a democratic constitution eaded by a monarch as the symbolic :ader.

This change in the emperor's role roke with time-honored traditions. Yet ıere were few protests. Hirohito, the :igning emperor, helped the Japanese ccept the change. The emperor did not ublicly criticize the constitution or the mericans sponsoring the change.

Japanese newspapers customarily peak only in respectful tones about the mperor and his family. Hirohito's son, rince Akihito, was popular when he took ıe throne in 1990 after Hirohito's death. 'et some Japanese objected to part of the eremony making him emperor. The critics id not approve of the emperor's articipation in the *Daijosai* (digh·joh·GH), the Great Food Offering Rite. It ›ok place behind closed curtains late at ight. Newly harvested rice and sake SAH·kay) (rice wine) were offered to the ods. According to tradition, the emperor hen awaited the arrival of the sun oddess Amaterasu, who would change im into a "living god."

Those who criticized the ceremony vere similar to the teachers who opposed inging the national anthem and offering instruction about the flag. Both groups feared that Japan might be moving away from constitutional government. Others did not believe the ceremony threatened their democracy.

Democracy in Japan

The 1947 constitution made the emperor a symbolic leader and gave Japan a democratic system of government. It set up a legislature called the ***National Diet,*** which consists of two houses: the House of Representatives and the House of Councillors. Both houses are elected by the people. The executive branch of government is run by the cabinet, which is led by the prime minister. Usually, the prime minister comes from the political party with the most representatives in the Diet.

Japan has many political parties. Fair elections are held regularly. Candidates campaigning for office speak freely. Voter turnout is usually high.

Japan's constitution has a Bill of Rights. It protects the rights and duties of Japanese citizens. It guarantees the right to vote by secret ballot, freedom of speech and religion, and equality for all.

General Douglas MacArthur (left), the commander of United States occupying forces in Japan after World War II, is visited by Emperor Hirohito (right). **What role did the United States play in changing Japan and the emperor's role after the war?**

Discussion Questions

1 Although the Japanese get most of their oil from Southwest Asia, they refused to become involved in the Persian Gulf War in 1990–91. Do you think it was the correct decision?

2 Should the United States bear the responsibility of protecting Japan's interests?

3 How does the National Diet compare to our Congress?

Caption Answer

The United States pushed Japan to reform the government by taking away the emperor's power and creating a democratic way of life.

Teacher Notes

MacArthur

General Douglas MacArthur is best known for his participation in the Korean War, although his military service began a half-century earlier. MacArthur was the son of another famous soldier, Arthur MacArthur II, who led troops in the Civil War, the Spanish American War, and in the Philippines.

MacArthur first led troops into combat in World War I, where he earned honors for bravery and leader-ship. After the war he served as superin-tendent of West Point, as army chief of staff under Herbert Hoover and Franklin Roosevelt, and as a military adviser to the new Philippine Common-wealth.

After retiring from the U.S. Army in 1937, MacArthur went back to active duty after the Japanese attack on Pearl Harbor on December 7, 1941. As commander of American troops in the southwestern Pacific, he led much of the drive to defeat Japan's quest for domina-tion of the Asian Pacific.

Background Information

The No-War Pledge

Because Japan's constitution has a no-war clause, it has a self-defense force but no national army. In 2001, Japan's newly electe d Prime Minister Junichiro Koizumi alarmed Japan's pacifists and her neighbors by suggesting that changes be made in Japan's constitution to allow Japan's self-defense force to be reorganized as a national army. Many of Japan's neighbors recall the militant nationalism that preceded World War II and watch carefully for signs of renewed nationalism. Koizumi sought to calm fears by saying that the nation had become involved in World War II because Japan became isolated from international society. What is most impor-tant is that we do not fight a war again and do not again become internationally isolated. United States leaders and many Japanese favor a more active role for Japan in international peacekeeping operations and in resolving global conflicts.

Eyewitness Activity

Emperor

OBJECTIVES: 9.04, 10.02

Ask students to brainstorm what they know about the inauguration process of the president of the United States and then compare their information with the text on "Becoming Emperor in Japan."

List the differences between Emperor Akihito and Emperor Hirohito.

Activity

Japanese Succession Debate

OBJECTIVES: 9.04, 10.02

The succession to the imperial throne in Japan historically has always passed to descendants in male line from the imperial lineage. Generally these descendents have been males. However, seven of the more than 100 emperors have been women on nine occasions. But laws passed in 1947 under the new constitution ban females from acceding to the throne. For a brief time in the past decade or so, there was no direct male heir to the throne. The Japanese considered altering their laws to allow a female in direct line to become emperor.

Divide the class into teams of two to four students. All students should research the rules of imperial sucession for Japan. Assign half of the groups the affirmative side, and half the groups teh negative side of the following: Resolved: That femlaes should be allowed to succeed to the Chysanthemum Throne of Japan. Refer to the Guidelines for Student Debates in the front of the Teacher's Edition.

EYEWITNESS TO HISTORY

Becoming Emperor

On January 7, 1989, Akihito became Japan's 125th emperor. He followed his father's path into a tradition that, at one time, declared the ruler of Japan to be a god.

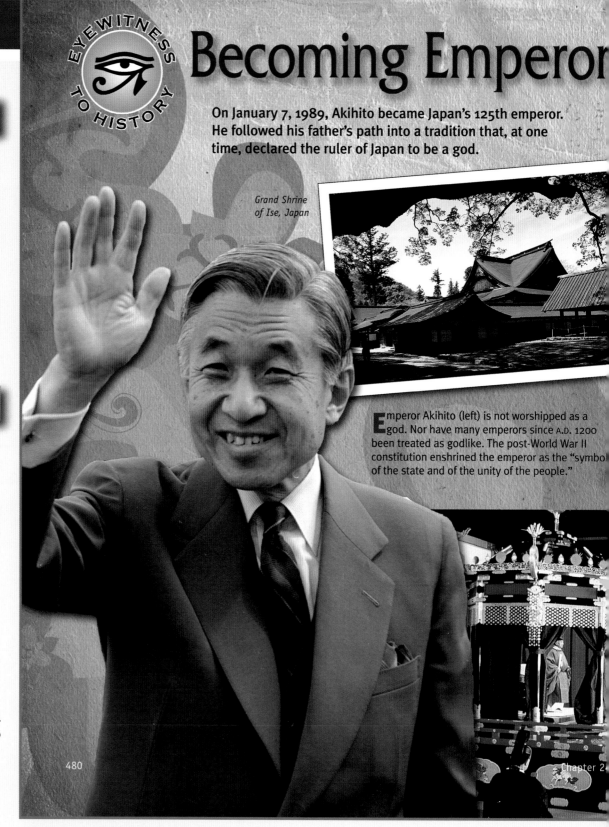

Grand Shrine of Ise, Japan

Emperor Akihito (left) is not worshipped as a god. Nor have many emperors since A.D. 1200 been treated as godlike. The post-World War II constitution enshrined the emperor as the "symbol of the state and of the unity of the people."

480

Chapter 2

Teacher Notes

Emperor Akihito

Upon the death of his father on January 7, 1989, Emperor Akihito acceded to the throne. He was formally inaugurated as Emperor of Japan on November 12, 1990.

n a place 310 miles (499 km) from Tokyo, Emperor Akihito left the present nd entered the past. As emperors have one before him, he entered the 2,000-ear-old Grand Shinto Shrine of Ise :E-say) on the Shima Peninsula.

uring his visit, Akihito dressed in silken robes made in the ighth century. After walking over he Uji Bashi (bridge), which rosses the water of the sacred suzu River, Akihito entered the aiku Inner Shrine. This shrine an be viewed only by the mperor and a few Shinto priests. ourists are allowed to go as far s the wooden walls, but there hey must stop.

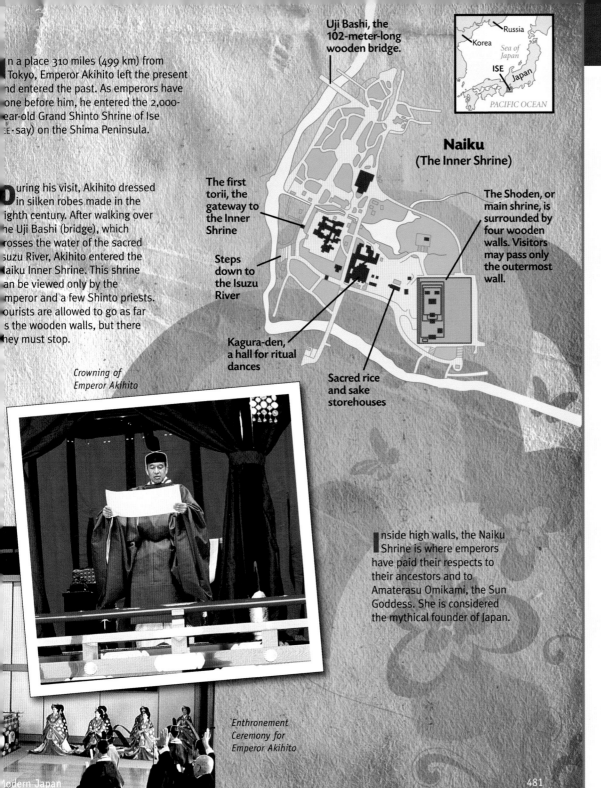

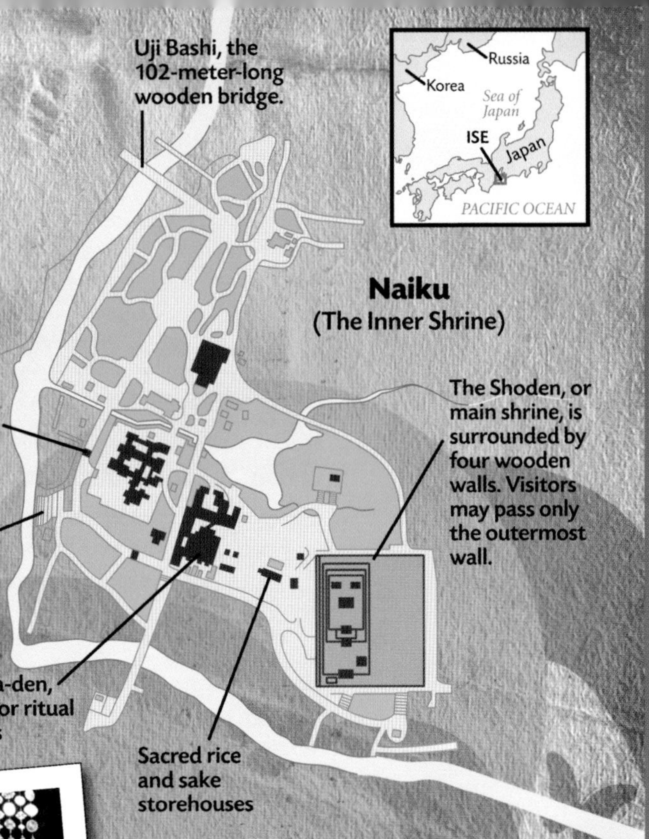

Uji Bashi, the 102-meter-long wooden bridge.

Russia

Korea

Sea of Japan

ISE

Japan

PACIFIC OCEAN

Naiku
(The Inner Shrine)

The first torii, the gateway to the Inner Shrine

The Shoden, or main shrine, is surrounded by four wooden walls. Visitors may pass only the outermost wall.

Steps down to the Isuzu River

Kagura-den, a hall for ritual dances

Sacred rice and sake storehouses

Crowning of Emperor Akihito

Inside high walls, the Naiku Shrine is where emperors have paid their respects to their ancestors and to Amaterasu Omikami, the Sun Goddess. She is considered the mythical founder of Japan.

Enthronement Ceremony for Emperor Akihito

Modern Japan 481

Discussion Questions

1 How do Japan's political parties and elections differ from ours?

2 What rights do the Japanese enjoy? What rights do we enjoy?

Map Activity

Becoming Emperor

NATIONAL GEOGRAPHY STANDARDS: 1, 17, 18

GEOGRAPHIC THEMES: Location

OBJECTIVES: 1.02

Using the inset map on page 473 and large-scale map of Japan (page 447), locate Ise and the Shima Peninsula.

Imagining the map of Naiku having a typical orientation with north at the top of this map, have students answer the following:

When Japan's emperor crosses Uji Bahi, the wooden bridge, and walks [southeast, southwest] (*southeast*) he crosses the Isuzu River. Once on Naiku, the Inner Shrineland, he walks to the first torii to the [southeast, southwest] (*southwest*). Passing by the steps on the [southeast, southwest] (*southwest*) that lead down to the sacred river, he then continues walking toward the [southeast, southwest] (*southeast*) to the inner shrine. Before entering Naiku, the emperor passes Kagura-den on the [north, south] (*north*) side of the walkway. He also sees the sacred storehouses for rice and sake on the [north, south] (*north*) side of the walkway. The actual Naiku Shrine is on the [east, west] (*west*) side of Shoden. This is where Japan's emperor honors Amaterasu Omikami, Japan's Sun Goddess.

It's a Fact

Japan

- Japan's shoguns, "supreme generals of the emperor's army," often had dictatorial powers. They controlled taxes, roads, armies, and courts of law.
- Eighty percent of the people live on the island of Honshu. The Japanese Alps were the site of the 1998 Winter Olympics.
- Japan has 150 major volcanoes, 60 of which are considered active and 19 are considered dangerous.
- Japan has the world's largest fishing industry. It is the eighth most populous nation and the second-largest garbage producer, just slightly behind the United States. Japan is the number one importer of petroleum products.
- Japan limits the height of buildings due to the frequency of earthquakes.

ELL Teaching Tips

Try to Learn Your ELL Students' Language

Attempt to learn a few words in your new ELL students' native language. When you are able to laugh at yourself for making errors in a new language, your new ELL student will become more comfortable speaking in English.

Discussion Questions

1 Did the United States have the right to put Article IX, the "no-war" clause, in Japan's constitution following WWII?

2 Why would some Japanese argue that this clause should be changed? Should this clause be changed?

The devastation of Hiroshima at the end of World War II so affected the Japanese that some wanted the government to give up the right to make war.

Debating the "No-War" Clause

OBJECTIVES: 7.02, 10.02

Using the Guidelines for Student Debates in the Teacher's Edition, arrange cooperative groups along both sides of the "no-war" clause issue: those who want to maintain the clause and have Japan continue to give up the right to make war and those who want to eliminate this clause so that Japan can develop a strong military to protect its economic interests.

More than 60,000 people attend a memorial service at the Hiroshima Peace Park. **How is Hiroshima involved with Japanese who support Article 9 in Japan's constitution?**

The "No-War Clause" —Article 9

"I was just twenty when Japan was defeated in World War II," noted Michitada Takasugi, a former member of the Diet. He saw pictures of what the atomic bombs did to Hiroshima and Nagasaki. Japan must "never repeat the mistake" of going to war, he says. "We must build a peaceful society so that we will never see nuclear weapons used."

Along with many other Japanese, Takasugi approves of Article 9, the "no-war" clause in Japan's constitution. In Article 9, Japan gave up the right to make war. It also banned armed forces that could attack another country. Japan has only a small military force. Its job is to defend Japan from attack.

Today, Japan is a major economic power. Some Japanese would like to change Article 9. They would like Japan to have armed forces so the nation could protect its worldwide economic interests. In 1992, Japan passed the International Peace Cooperation Law. This law allows Japan's small self-defense forces to participate in international peacekeeping missions around the world.

Many other Japanese oppose changing Article 9. They will always remember World War II, especially the effects of the atomic bombs. Many Japanese are ***pacifists.*** They oppose all war. They do not want Japan to become a military power.

Debate over Article 9 continues. The Japanese people are about evenly divided on the issue.

LESSON 1 REVIEW

Fact Follow-Up

1. In what ways did the American occupation forces try to change Japan's government?
2. How is the role of the emperor now defined in the constitution? In what ways is this new definition different from the past?
3. What is Article 9 in Japan's postwar constitution? Why is it important?

Talk About It

1. In the dispute over the flag and national anthem, which side would you have supported? Why?
2. Does the definition of the emperor's status as "symbol of the state and unity of the people" help strengthen democracy in Japan? Explain.

LESSON 1 REVIEW

Fact Follow-Up Answers

1. The occupying forces set out to remake Japanese government and society so that Japan could never again threaten world peace. They pushed Japan to reform its government by taking away the emperor's power and creating a democratic way of life. Japan adopted a new constitution that was approved by the Americans.
2. In the constitution, the emperor is described as a symbol of the state and the symbol of unity of the people. He no longer has the power to rule. The constitution gave the Japanese people the authority to govern themselves.
3. Article 9 is the "no-war" clause in Japan's constitution. In it, Japan gave up the right to make war and banned armed forces that might attack another country (offensive forces). Now that Japan is a major economic power, some Japanese would like to have armed forces so the nation can protect its worldwide economic interests.

Talk About It Answers

1. Important points: Students should take a side and give reasons why. The issues here involve the use of symbols to express national identity and the danger of extremism.
2. Important points: Students should state a position and explain it. Under Japan's constitution, power is in the hands of the people. The role of the emperor is clearly limited. Lead students to understand that constitutions, however, may be amended.

ESSON 2 Economy

ecember is a frantic month in most Japanese homes. It is gift-giving season, called *seibo* (SAY · bo). Giving gifts is an old tradition. You give a gift to thank people for favors or help uring the year. Companies also give presents to favored customers.

Seibo lasts from December 10 to 31. Gifts may vary in value, but ney are always beautifully wrapped. In the past, the giver delivered the ift in person. Today, few have time for that personal touch. Gifts are nailed or delivered by messenger.

In early December, husbands and wives make a list of what to buy, or whom, and how much to spend. They give gifts of special foods or hocolate to friends and their childrens' teachers. Department store ounters are stacked with elegantly wrapped gifts. Many people enjoy ending gifts from celebrated stores. Traditions such as these affect the vay people do business and how they treat one another.

Foreigners have begun to learn about Japanese gift-giving and other raditions. After all, Japan is a world economic power. If Americans nd others want to do business in Japan, they need to understand :s traditions.

KEY IDEAS

- Japan took advantage of its human resources and opportunities in world markets to rebuild rapidly after World War II.
- Japan has become an economic superpower, but its economy depends on world trade.

KEY TERMS

"economic miracle"
Group of Eight
Japan Incorporated

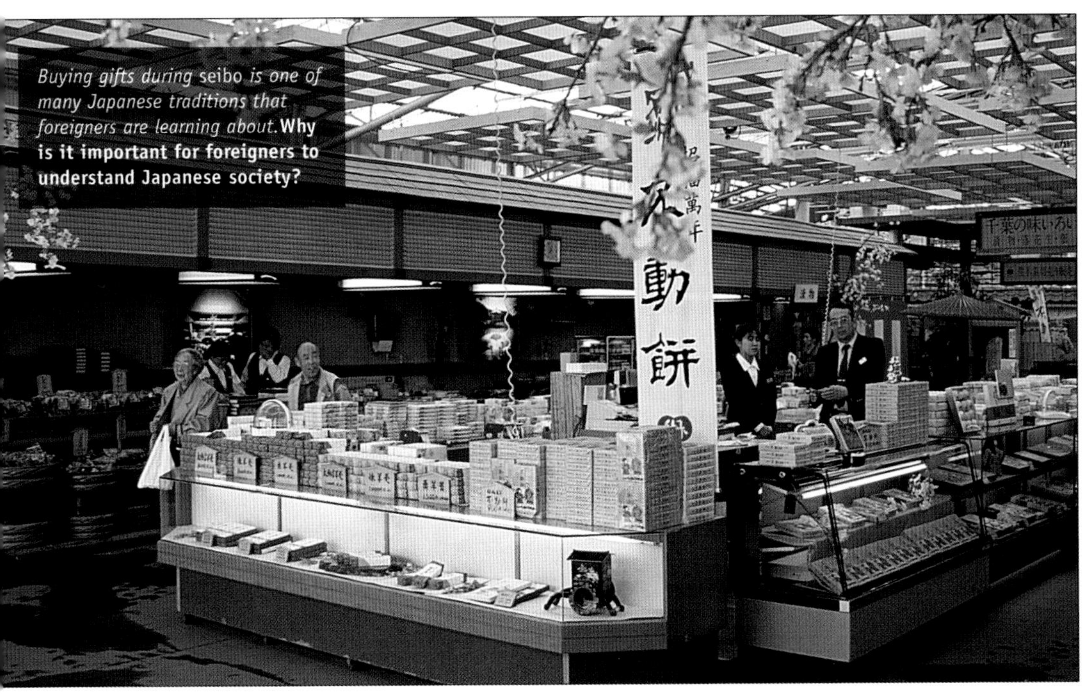

Buying gifts during seibo is one of many Japanese traditions that foreigners are learning about. **Why is it important for foreigners to understand Japanese society?**

Chapter 24, Lesson 2

OBJECTIVES: 5.04, 6.01, 6.02, 13.03

Discussion Questions

1 What are some ways we thank people and show them that we care?

2 The book tells us that the personal touch has been removed from seibo. We find the same situation in many of our holidays as well. To what do we attribute this change? Has the true meaning of the festivities changed as well?

3 Why is it becoming not only helpful but also necessary for us to learn about other cultures?

Math Activity

Japan Means Business

 **OBJECTIVES:** 5.04, 6.02, 11.03

Using the information in the table, have students create a graph showing Japan's share of world motor vehicle production using a dotted line to connect the points. They should use a dashed line to show the United States' share of the world motor vehicle production. Ask: What conclusions are you able to draw by comparing the dotted and dashed lines? Japan's production has grown from a very small percentage of world production to exceed that of the United States in the 1980s and early 1990s.

World Motor Vehicle Production, 1950–94

Year	U.S. % of World Total	Japan % of World Total
1994	24.7	21.2
1993	23.5	24.2
1992	24.5	26.2
1991	18.9	28.4
1990	20.2	27.9
1985	26.0	24.7
1980	20.8	28.7
1970	28.2	18.0
1960	47.9	2.9
1950	75.7	0.3

Source: American Automobile Manufacturers Association

Extension Assign novice and intermediate ELL students the graph, but not the conclusions.

Math Activity

Word Problem

 **OBJECTIVES:** 2.03, 4.01

Japan is an island nation with a large population. If an area has 900 people per square mile, what would the total population be in an area of 30 square miles?

Answer 27,000 people

Extension Assist ELL students by setting up the problem for them.

Caption Answer

Japan is a world economic power, and people wanting to do business there must understand its traditions.

Discussion Questions

1 Why do you think it was important for the United States to help rebuild Japan following World War II?

2 Is it possible for other countries to experience the Japanese Miracle?

3 The Cold War between the United States and the former Soviet Union is now over. Do you think the United States needs to maintain a military base on Okinawa?

4 Why do you think the United States now needs Japan as an ally?

Caption Answer

The United States provided money and technology to rebuild Japan after the war.

Teacher Notes

Japanese Holidays

New Year's day is one of Japan's most important holidays. It's a three-day celebration casting off the previous year's difficulties, disappointments, and evil spirits, and welcoming a new beginning.

Other holidays include:

Coming of Age the second Monday in January. All young people turning twenty years old are celebrated on Seijin no hi. This is a significant birthday for the Japanese. It signifies adulthood along with its privileges and responsibilities.

Doll's Festival or Girl's Festival (Hinamatsuri) is celebrated on March 3. Daughters are wished a successful and happy life, and dolls are displayed in the house along with peach blossoms. Adapted from a Chinese custom, bad fortune is transferred to a doll and then removed from the owner by abandoning the doll on a river.

Constitution Day (Kenpo kinenbi) May 3, honors the 1947 constitution celebrating the prohibition of war, human rights, and the sovereignty of the Japanese people.

Children's Day (Kodomo no hi), May 5, is also called Boy's Festival. Sons are wished good fortune and carp streamers are hung outside the home, while inside samurai dolls are displayed, symbolizing strength, power, and success in life.

The Japanese Miracle

In 1945, Japan was in ruins. Allied bombers had smashed its cities, factories, roads, and railroads. The economy was near collapse. Most people were close to starvation.

With American aid, Japan began to rebuild. In the 1950s and 1960s, it rapidly advanced on its own. Japan today is among the world's most prosperous nations. Workers earn high wages. Most enjoy a comfortable standard of living. Although Japan has some poor people, it has few slums.

Experts in other countries were amazed. They spoke of Japan's ***"economic miracle"*** and asked how Japan could have recovered so quickly. Manufacturing plants had to be rebuilt and equipped. Workers had to be trained for new jobs. Resources for industry that Japan lacked had to be shipped to Japan, and customers had to be found for the goods produced in Japan.

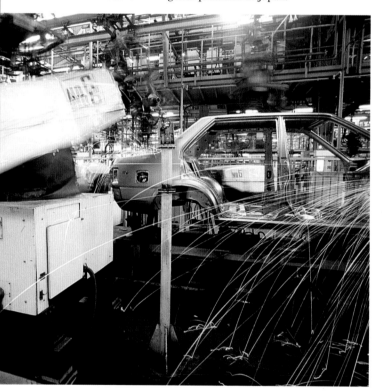

Japanese industry uses high technology to produce goods it sells around the world. **How did the United States help Japan achieve its "economic miracle"?**

The "Miracle" in World Affairs

Japan's "economic miracle" could be partly explained by the nation's quick response to the world's new economy. Japan was not the only nation to lose an empire. You have read how European nations after World War II surrendered colonies in Africa and Asia. With colonial empires gone, nations lowered trade barriers to buy raw materials and sell manufactured goods on world markets. Japan realized that it had to manufacture products that would sell in a highly competitive world market.

Japan received vital aid for this task from the United States. Soon after World War II ended, the United States discovered that it needed its former enemy as an ally. The United States gave help to several Japanese businesses. American experts in textile manufacturing were sent to Japan to provide companies with the most advanced technology. Equipped with this knowledge, Japan began making high-quality textiles that sold well around the world.

The United States wanted to help Japan rebuild its economy because of the Cold War rivalry between the United States and Communist powers in the Soviet Union and China. You have read about the Korean War and the American decision to send troops to Korea in 1950. During the war, the United States used Japan as a base for its military operations in Asia and bought military supplies from the Japanese.

What would YOU do?

In Tokyo, there are many foods to eat. Shrimp tempura, tofu (bean curd) in soy sauce, noodles with sesame seeds, rice, and sukiyaki—a one-pot meal. Your host offers you *sashimi*—fresh, raw fish wrapped around rice. You are unsure if you would enjoy eating raw fish, but to refuse your host's hospitality would be an insult. What would you do?

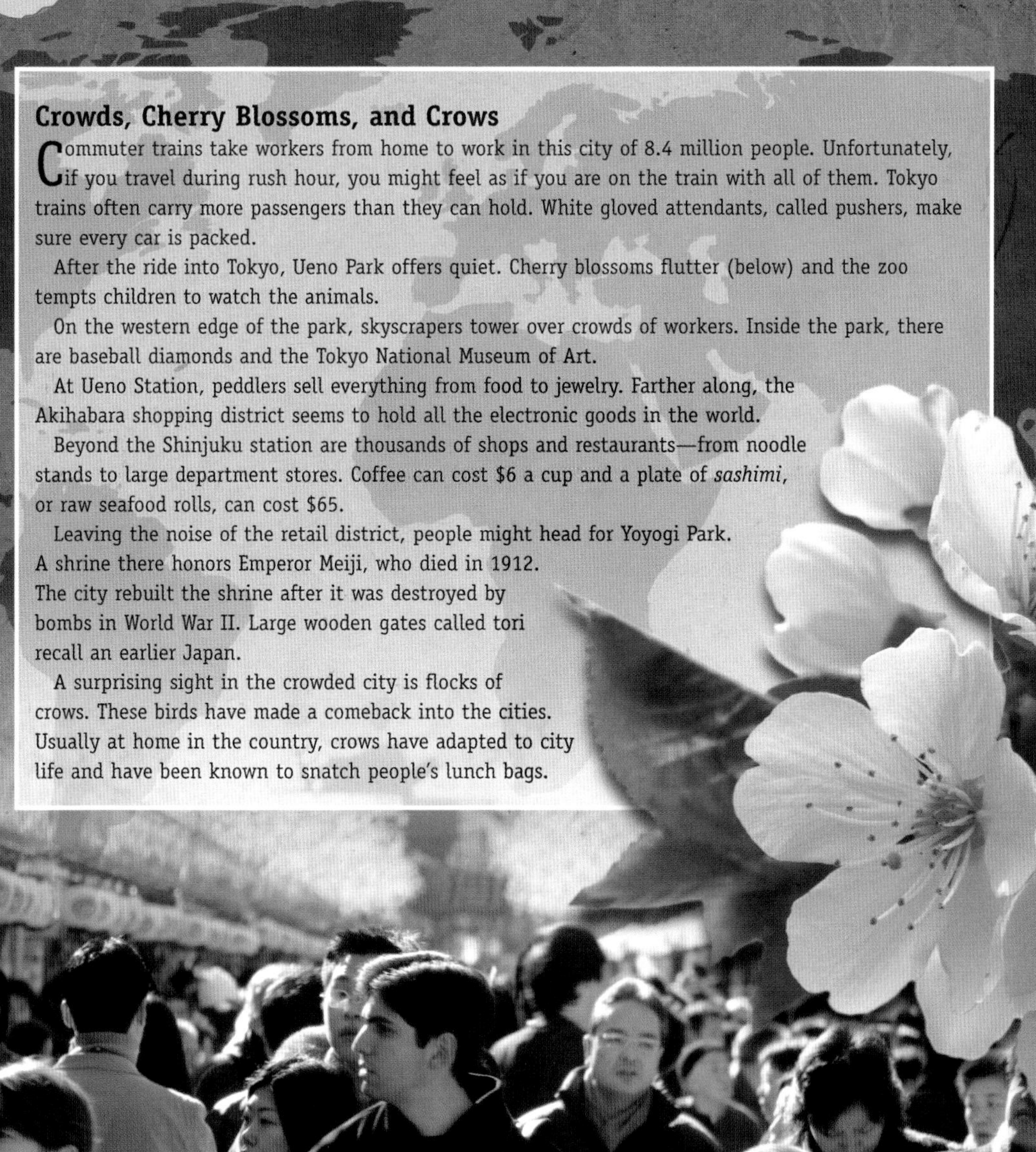

A Journey to Tokyo

Crowds, Cherry Blossoms, and Crows

Commuter trains take workers from home to work in this city of 8.4 million people. Unfortunately, if you travel during rush hour, you might feel as if you are on the train with all of them. Tokyo trains often carry more passengers than they can hold. White gloved attendants, called pushers, make sure every car is packed.

After the ride into Tokyo, Ueno Park offers quiet. Cherry blossoms flutter (below) and the zoo tempts children to watch the animals.

On the western edge of the park, skyscrapers tower over crowds of workers. Inside the park, there are baseball diamonds and the Tokyo National Museum of Art.

At Ueno Station, peddlers sell everything from food to jewelry. Farther along, the Akihabara shopping district seems to hold all the electronic goods in the world.

Beyond the Shinjuku station are thousands of shops and restaurants—from noodle stands to large department stores. Coffee can cost $6 a cup and a plate of *sashimi*, or raw seafood rolls, can cost $65.

Leaving the noise of the retail district, people might head for Yoyogi Park. A shrine there honors Emperor Meiji, who died in 1912. The city rebuilt the shrine after it was destroyed by bombs in World War II. Large wooden gates called tori recall an earlier Japan.

A surprising sight in the crowded city is flocks of crows. These birds have made a comeback into the cities. Usually at home in the country, crows have adapted to city life and have been known to snatch people's lunch bags.

odern Japan 485

Discussion Questions

1 As crowded as our halls can be in schools and on buses, how would you feel if you had to be pushed into a train?

2 What are some sights that you would see in Tokyo that you probably would not see in our own community?

Teacher Notes

D.C. Cherry Trees

The government of Japan presented thousands of Oriental and Nanking Cherry trees to the United States in 1912 as a gesture of friendship between the two nations. The trees were planted in Washington, D.C., around the Potomac Basin, along the Mall, and throughout the city. Each April, Washington, D.C., holds a Cherry Blossom Festival that includes a lengthy parade of marching bands. High school bands face tough state competition in order to represent their state at this annual event.

Activity

Match and Write

OBJECTIVES: 3.04, 11.01, 12.01

Have students match the Japanese vocabulary word to its correct definition.

tsunami, shinto, ainu, kimono, kami, kana

- spirits that live in natural objects
- "the way of the Gods"
- a long robe-like garment
- descendants of the first settlers
- giant wave created by earthquakes
- Japanese written language

Writing Integration: Story Writing Using the six vocabulary words above, have students write a story set in Japan that uses the terms in their correct context. They should use information they have learned while studying Japan to make the story realistic and accurate.

Extension Instead of writing a story, have ELL students draw a picture definition or define the words in their native language using a native language dictionary.

Background Information

Japan's Economic Woes

For more than a decade, Japan has experienced its worst economic downturn since World War II. Efforts to jump-start the economy through large public works projects failed to end the slump. The nation now faces a variety of economic problems from a shrinking labor force to low productivity, bad bank loans, and huge budget deficits. Japan's Asian neighbors from China and India to Singapore and the other little tigers are now producing the kinds of electronic goods that once made Japan prosperous. Moreover, they are doing it more quickly and more cheaply. Yet Japan's manufacturing sector remains strong. It leads the world in such industries as cars, industrial robots, and some kinds of lasers and other high-tech goods.

Discussion Questions

1 Why are the people of Japan considered its most valuable resource?

2 Is the same true for the United States?

3 Why do Japanese products have such a good reputation?

4 What does that say about the workforce?

Caption Answer

The cooperation among leaders of government, business, and labor has pulled together the talents of the nation's greatest resource, its people. Japan's people are loyal, hardworking, and well educated. The government has also helped Japanese businesses find markets throughout the world.

Activity

Japanese School Day

 **OBJECTIVES:** 4.03, 12.01

Plan a simulation of a Japanese school day for your team. Each homeroom on the team will pick a crest and create a banner to carry into the assembly on Friday. Other students will make a tissue paper carp to be carried on a stick. In Japan teachers, not students, move from room to room. Students stand, bow, and greet their teachers as they enter or exit the classroom. Throughout the week have students practice Japanese phrases and proper bowing techniques. Students in Japan wear uniforms. Give your students an incentive to wear a uniform of dark pants (jeans) and a white shirt on Friday. Plan a special menu in the cafeteria and try to invite local Japanese residents or students to join each classroom on Friday. On Friday start the day with an assembly much like the daily routine in Japan. Have the music department play both the United States and Japanese national anthems. Have homerooms march into the assembly area and maintain straight lines behind their crest banner and carp. Display the United States and Japanese flags. Have the principal address the assembled students and be sure students understand the schedule. Classes are dismissed one at a time and walk single file back to the classroom.

Each content teacher will teach a related subject in their classes: communication skills, haiku; science, earthquakes; math, abacus and tangrams; social studies, Japanese language or other topic. When the teacher enters or leaves the room a key student leads class in the bow and greeting. When students are called upon they will stand. A midday recess can be scheduled to compete in popular Japanese games.

Japan is a leading producer of calculators, video equipment, cameras, stereos, and TVs. **How has Japan Incorporated led to Japan's international economic success?**

Japan Makes the "Miracle" Happen

"Sony has grown to be a huge company," says Mikio Takahashi. In 1946, the company employed only about 20 workers. It had no research labs and made large, bulky tape recorders. In 1968, Takahashi joined the Sony Corporation in Tokyo as a designer. His work improving cassette players resulted in the Sony Walkman. By the 1980s, the Walkman was popular around the world. Sony employed more than 20,000 people who worked in factories in several countries.

Sony's story is typical of dozens of Japanese companies. Sony's technology in 1946, like that of most Japanese companies, was not advanced. That is why the American decision to share its technology was so important to Japan. In the 1950s and 1960s, Japanese manufacturers began to market products made with the latest technologies. Japan began to win a reputation for manufacturing high-quality goods and selling them for reasonable prices.

Soon Japan's industries took another step. They began to develop their own advanced technologies. In textiles, electronics, and automobile manufacturing, Japan's firms now are known as the designers and producers of advanced machinery and production methods. Sony, Honda, Nissan, and Mitsubishi have become global giants.

Japan's economic growth is also partly the product of cooperation among leaders of government, business, and labor. This combination, which has been called ***Japan Incorporated,*** has enjoyed unusual success in pulling together the talents of the nation's greatest resource—its people. Japan's corporations have benefited from the cooperation of a loyal, hardworking, and educated workforce. Government agencies have helped Japanese businesses find markets throughout the world.

Strong but Weak"

Japan is an economic giant. Its leaders ...tend meetings of the *Group of Eight,* ...8) an organization of the world's ...ading industrial nations. As a member of ...is group, Japan influences economic ...fairs. Yet the Japanese are cautious ...out the future. Some have described ...eir economy as "strong but weak."

The strengths of Japan's economy are ...pressive. Japan is the world's leading ...ipbuilder and is a major steelmaker. ...panese-built ships transport cars and ...ucks from Japanese assembly lines to ...nsumers around the world. Japan ...oduces other diverse goods—from ...actors and cranes to computers, ...levisions, and cameras. Manufacturing ...d trade industries occupy many square ...iles of land (see map, page 477).

So how can its economy be weak? ...panese leaders worry about a nation ...at depends so heavily on world trade. ...he Pacific Ocean is a highway to a world ...at provides most of what Japan needs to ...rvive. Ships bring the raw materials that ...pan's factories make into finished ...roducts and food. Japan's major ...arkets—the nations of Europe and the ...mericas—lie half a world away.

Japan's economy requires a world of peace and free trade. In the 1970s, the Japanese were shocked when Southwest Asian oil producers cut shipments. Without oil, Japanese industries could not operate. Such international trading blocs as the European Union and the North American Free Trade Association worry the Japanese. They fear that they might be isolated from their best trading partners.

Japanese-built tankers carry oil to Japan from Southwest Asia.
Why do some Japanese believe that such world trade makes Japan weak?

LESSON 2 REVIEW

Fact Follow-Up

1. In what ways did Japan's economy suffer from World War II?
2. How does Japan fit the description, "economic miracle"?
3. Despite Japan's standing as an economic giant, many Japanese say that their country is weak. Why do they say this?

Talk About It

1. The Japanese people are often said to be the nation's greatest resource. Do you agree or disagree? Explain.
2. Are the Japanese ideas of "We Japanese" and "Japan Incorporated" linked? Explain your answer.
3. Japan is described as an "economic superpower." What does this mean? Is the description accurate? Explain.

Discussion Questions

1. Why is it important for countries to diversify their economic base?
2. What is the paradox in strong but weak? How can Japan be both?
3. What could be the long-term effects of Japan's dependence on oil from other countries?
4. What would be the benefits of belonging to the Group of Eight?

Caption Answer

Because Japan imports so much food, energy, and raw materials, its economy depends on peace and free trade throughout the world. War or trade restrictions could devastate Japan's economy.

Math Activity

Sushi Math

 **OBJECTIVES:** 11.01

Japanese people like sushi. The best fish are bought at auction. If an 85 pound tuna is purchased for $1,275.00, what is the price per pound for the fish?

Answer $15 per pound

Extension Assist ELL students by setting up the problem for them.

LESSON 2 REVIEW

Fact Follow-Up Answers

1. The war had destroyed Japan's cities, factories, roads, and railroads. The economy was near collapse. Most people were close to starvation.
2. After the devastation of the war, Japan surged back economically to become one of the world's most prosperous nations.
3. Japan's industry depends on world trade. A change in trade policies or the outbreak of war could destroy Japan's economy.

Talk About It Answers

1. Important points: Students should take a position and explain it. Although Japan has few resources, Japan has a highly educated and hardworking workforce. This is a definite advantage in developing the highly technical industries for which Japan is famous.
2. Important points: Encourage students to suggest links. "We Japanese" is identified with Japan's sense of isolation and its entire national identity. The cooperative efforts of government, business, and labor are referred to as Japan Incorporated. One term thus has to do with national identity; the other has to do with Japan's way of conducting business.
3. Japan is one of the world's leading industrial nations, supplying the world market with ships, steel, cars, trucks, and electronic products. It is an economic superpower because its industrial production is enormous and reaches so much of the world market.

OBJECTIVES: 4.03, 11.01, 12.02, 12.03

Discussion Questions

1 Why do many people need to have a connection with the dead? Why do most cultures have a belief in the afterlife?

2 What changes do you think will occur in Japan with the shift from an extended to a nuclear family?

Caption Answer

The Japanese still honor family loyalty in rituals, but extended families may live apart.

Activity

Japanese Tea Ceremony Demonstration

OBJECTIVES: 11.01, 12.01

Students may gain an appreciation of the Japanese Tea Ceremony by participating in this reenactment. Note: this demonstration is designed to expose the students to the process of the ceremony. It does not replicate the elaborate steps and intricate details of an authentic Japanese Tea Ceremony.

Materials Needed
a kettle or tea pot; cups (one per student); tea leaves or bags; hot water (can be prepared in an automatic coffeepot); kimono for the host (if available); sweet candy (such as a maple hard candy or maple cookie); basin of water; towel; recording of sounds from nature, fresh flowers or plants; small gong, bell, or band triangle; and brown construction paper to be used as tatami mats, optional

Extension This is a good activity to invite Japanese ELL students to demonstrate or comment upon since they may have authentic tea ceremony materials. Assign ELL students to define terms in pictures to increase comprehension.

Vocabulary
Chado: the way of tea; Cha: tea; Tatami mats: woven mats that are used in a teahouse as floor covering.

LESSON 3 Society and Culture

KEY IDEAS

- Such values as loyalty, hard work, and filial piety remain strong in modern Japan.
- Japanese schools are highly competitive, partly because students want to enter the best universities.
- Japanese enjoy traditional sports and arts. Western sports and art are also important.

KEY TERMS

bunkaru
"cram schools"
ikebana
Kabuki
noh
sumo

"Are you going home for *Obon?*" Japanese ask their friends. *Obon* is a major festival that occurs in mid-August. Roads, trains, and buses are packed as millions of Japanese travel to their hometowns.

In their hometowns they take part in ceremonies for their ancestors. People believe that during *Obon* the souls of their ancestors return for a brief visit. To prepare for their coming, grave sites are weeded. On the 13th, people light fires to welcome the spirits back to earth. They set out barley and vegetables.

Three days later, the spirits are believed to be ready to leave. In the evening's dark, families float paper lanterns with lighted candles in lakes and streams. The lanterns drift away, returning the spirits to their own world for another year.

Obon mixes Buddhist and traditional Japanese customs. Today, *Obon* also is a kind of "old home day." It means relatives and childhood friends meet for dancing, music, and sharing memories.

Family Life

In 1945, most Japanese lived in small wooden houses. Rooms were separated by paper screens that could be moved to change the size and shape of rooms. Men worked on family-owned land or in famil[y] businesses. Women accepted traditional roles as wives and mothers.

Today, most Japanese live in or near cities. For many, home is an apartment in a high-rise building. Although screens are still sometimes used to reshape rooms, homes are very different. Families have appliances, computers, and televisions. They drive cars. Some take vacations overseas in the United States or Europe.

Families once included three generations. Today, many number just three people—mother, father, and child. Men once dominated the household. Women now have more freedom. Some work outside the home.

Men still work long hours, but employers are large companies, not family businesses. Recently, a push began for men to spend more time with their families.

Floating paper lanterns are a sign of lasting tradition in Japan. **How do the Japanese mix old traditions with urban life?**

Background Typically, tea ceremonies take place in a teahouse surrounded by a garden. They may also occur in specified areas of homes or apartments. Instruct students that they are to use their imaginations and all senses during the ceremony. It is a quiet and dignified process. They should be silent in order to appreciate the sights and sounds of nature as soon as the ceremony begins with the ringing of the gong or like sound). They will hear the sounds of nature from the recording, smell the flowers and the tea, feel the warm cup of tea in their hands, and observe the beauty of the plants or flowers.

Set Up

1. Try to go over the ceremony's steps and process with the class prior, so that they know what to expect and are familiar with what they are to do and why.
2. To lend more authenticity, arrange the room so that as students enter, they may wash their hands in a basin of water, dry them, move to a mat on the floor arranged in a circle, and sit on the mat. Once again, instruct students to enter and remain silent during the ceremony. If you prefer, you can skip this step and have students sit at their desks.

amily Values

Older Japanese talk about rapid anges. Some ways have not changed all at much. Family bonds remain strong. hildren learn early to respect their elders d the family. That respect is later tended to groups at school and at work.

In old Japan, filial piety—deep respect r one's parents—was the chief virtue. he worst criticism a person might hear as to be called disobedient. An dividual had to protect the family's good ame. The head of the family had to be beyed. He in turn was responsible for the mily's well-being.

Japan still honors such values as yalty, obedience, and hard work. Yet in day's urban setting, the family has less fluence than it once did. After children e grown, many leave home to find work. hey do not always accept their parents' ews. Fewer children grow up with their andparents in the same house.

chools: A Competitive World

"After school, more school." That ould be the motto of Japanese children. he Japanese stress education. From an rly age, students are expected to work ard to get into good universities. Success school sets them on the right path for e future.

Parents and schools encourage iscipline and hard work. These values are qually important in the workplace. arents closely monitor their children's choolwork. Failing grades hurt the entire amily. Some Japanese do not like the ompetition and anxiety of school life. Yet ost see no way to change the situation.

Public schools are free. All children ust attend school from ages six to fteen. Until recently, classes met five and half days a week. Saturday morning asses were given up only after much ebate. More than 87 percent of students omplete high school. Although Japan's opulation is declining, the number of udents who attend universities continues o grow.

Students attend a study session to prepare for university entrance exams. **Why do many Japanese go to "more school" after school?**

Admission to the top schools is competitive. Hundreds of thousands of students are tutored after school. Many go to *juku*, or ***"cram schools,"*** after the regular school day. These private schools prepare students for the entrance exams of the top universities. In cram schools, students review basic subjects. Students may also study such traditional arts as calligraphy—the art of beautiful writing—music, flower arrangement, and the tea ceremony. Some also improve skills in sports or yoga.

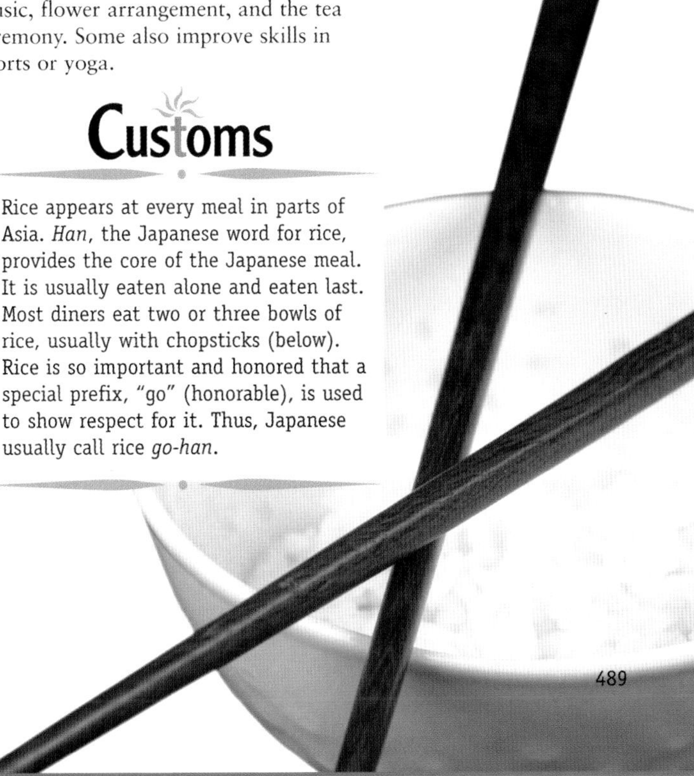

Customs

Rice appears at every meal in parts of Asia. *Han*, the Japanese word for rice, provides the core of the Japanese meal. It is usually eaten alone and eaten last. Most diners eat two or three bowls of rice, usually with chopsticks (below). Rice is so important and honored that a special prefix, "go" (honorable), is used to show respect for it. Thus, Japanese usually call rice *go-han*.

Discussion Questions

1 What is a virtue? What is an important virtue that is valued in our culture?

2 Do virtues and what is valued change over time? Should they?

3 Think of a time when you might have been disobedient. How did your parents react to it?

4 Do you think it is part of your responsibility to keep your family name in good standing?

5 What values explain why Japanese students work so hard?

6 Students in Japan attend "cram schools" after the regular school day. What are some of the things students in your area do after school each day?

They go to prepare for the entrance exams of the top universities. Success in the exams sets them on the right path for the future.

3. To save time, make the tea ahead of time in a large automatic coffeepot and have it sitting out of sight of the students.
4. Ring the gong (or bell) to begin.
5. Instruct students to observe the sights and sounds of nature.
6. Explain that authentic tea ceremonies occur in a teahouse. If you can find a picture of one, show it to the students.
7. Show the kettle or teapot to the students. You can demonstrate how the tea would have been prepared by mixing hot water and tea leaves and using a tea whisk to bring the tea to a froth. If you prefer, you can fill the teapot ahead of time from the automatic coffeepot or fill the cups directly from the coffeepot and use the teapot or kettle as a visual. Explain that the tea would have been prepared for each guest individually by you, the host.
8. Serve the tea and remind students to feel the warmth of the cup and smell the aroma of the tea before drinking.
9. After students have tasted their tea, pass out one sweet treat for them to enjoy.
10. Collect the cups and bow to the students and explain that the ceremony has concluded.

Discussion Questions

1 Why is sumo wrestling such a valued tradition in Japan?
2 Why do you think the United States has adopted martial arts traditions from Japan?
3 What Western influences have been adopted by Japan?

Caption Answer

They include the traditional dramas called noh and bunraku, martial arts like judo, kendo, and karate, and arts including the tea ceremony and flower arranging.

Activity

Japanese Haiku & Tanka Poetry

OBJECTIVES: 12.02

Students should write a poem in one of the forms of Japanese poetry. Finish final copies on half-cut construction paper. Use bright gel pens or fine-point markers. Illustrate poems (more than stick figures). Hints for great poems: Avoid rhyming; have several dictionaries and thesaurus available; model the poems for the students. This is a great time to review metaphor, simile, onomatopoeia, and personification.

Specific Topics: Christmas, End of Year, Academic Subject, People, Places, Events, Sports (Events), Animals, Seasons, Plants, Historical Events, Emotions

Haiku: 3 lines, each one based on syllables

Line One: 5 syllables
Line Two: 7 syllables
Line Three: 5 syllables

Tanka: 5 lines with a total of 31 syllables (no set format for number of syllables in each line)

Sumo (above) and Kabuki *(right) are popular forms of entertainment in Japan.* **What other traditional sports and art forms are favorites among the Japanese?**

Sports

Crowds pack Tokyo arenas to watch ***sumo***, Japanese wrestling. Top sumo wrestlers are treated like royalty. They have fan clubs and business sponsors. They get as much news coverage as Hollywood stars in the United States.

Sumo is Japan's most popular spectator sport. It is also one of the world's oldest sports. Japanese legends say that it was the sport of the gods.

Sumo has rituals that link it to Shinto and other traditions. The rules of the match are simple. A wrestler's goal is to force his opponent to touch a straw-rope circle with any part of his body except the soles of his feet. Or he tries to force his opponent out of the ring. Sumo wrestlers are large, but matches are more often wo through skill, not size.

Sports, such as sumo, have local root Others, like baseball, come from the Wes American missionaries introduced baseba to Japan. It soon became popular. The Japanese play many other Western sports including golf, bowling, tennis, soccer, basketball, and volleyball.

Japan, in turn, has exported its marti arts traditions around the world. Judo, kendo, and karate are popular in the United States and elsewhere. They are used for self-defense and sport. The martial arts are linked to samurai traditions of self-discipline and morality.

Word Origins

Samurai, like the knights of medieval Europe, were soldiers. They were honored for their military skills, bravery, and loyalty to their lords. In the 1600s, however, Japan was a united country at peace. With no wars to fight, samurai developed martial arts and led in such other arts as the tea ceremony and flower arrangement. Some became high government leaders. Later, when Japan modernized, some became businessmen.

The Arts

On Sunday afternoons in Tokyo, certain streets are closed to traffic. Rock bands set up small bandstands and electronic gear and begin to play. Large crowds—mostly teenagers in faded jeans—gather around their favorite groups. Meanwhile, others go to movies or concerts to listen to Western classical music or jazz.

The West has influenced other art forms in Japan, but traditional arts remai

Background Information

Japanese Fast Food

The Japanese have an age-old form of fast food known as *ekiben*, or station, lunches. These boxed meals are sold at stands in train stations, on platforms, and on trains. The word *ekiben* comes from *eki*, meaning station. Beginning in 1885, passengers could buy lunches in a box at Utsunomiya Station north of Tokyo. Lunches consisted of rice balls with different fillings wrapped in a bamboo leaf. Today commuters can buy many kinds of *ekiben* while the train is stopped through an open window without leaving their seats. *Ekiben* come with throw-away chopsticks. Many stations have become famous for their tasty *ekiben* using local food favorites.

›opular. The arts that Japanese have njoyed for centuries continue to have nthusiastic followings.

'raditional Art Forms

Japan developed several kinds of lrama. An early form was ***noh,*** a kind of lance drama. Actors performed on an mpty stage accompanied by singers and nusicians. By the 1700s, ***Kabuki*** theater ıad become popular. *Kabuki* means 'song, dance, act." Plays might be about ›rdinary people or nobles.

Japanese audiences have enjoyed ***Bunraku*** (boo·n·RAH·koo), or puppet ›lays, for more than 300 years. The ›uppets, almost life-size with many noving parts, each have three handlers. Ͻne puppeteer moves the head, eyes, nouth, and arm of a puppet. The other wo operate other body parts. The masked ›uppeteers dress in black. They practice 'or 30 years to become experts.

The Japanese have perfected many ›ther arts. Their pottery, swords, and acquerware are prized works. Japan leveloped ***ikebana,*** (ih·kay·BAH·nah) the ırt of flower arranging. Today, as in the ›ast, Japanese artists and craftworkers eflect traditions and values shaped by Buddhism and Shinto. These traditions equire artists to work in harmony with he materials they use.

Japan enjoys a worldwide reputation 'or excellence in the visual arts. In the 1700s, artists found ways of carving woodblocks and printing pictures in colors. Prints similar to those on pages 457 and 458 draw high prices on the world's art markets. Woodblocks are still used by artists, but their prints are less likely to feature scenes from daily life. Contemporary artists often use wood-block printing to portray the colors and shapes of abstract art.

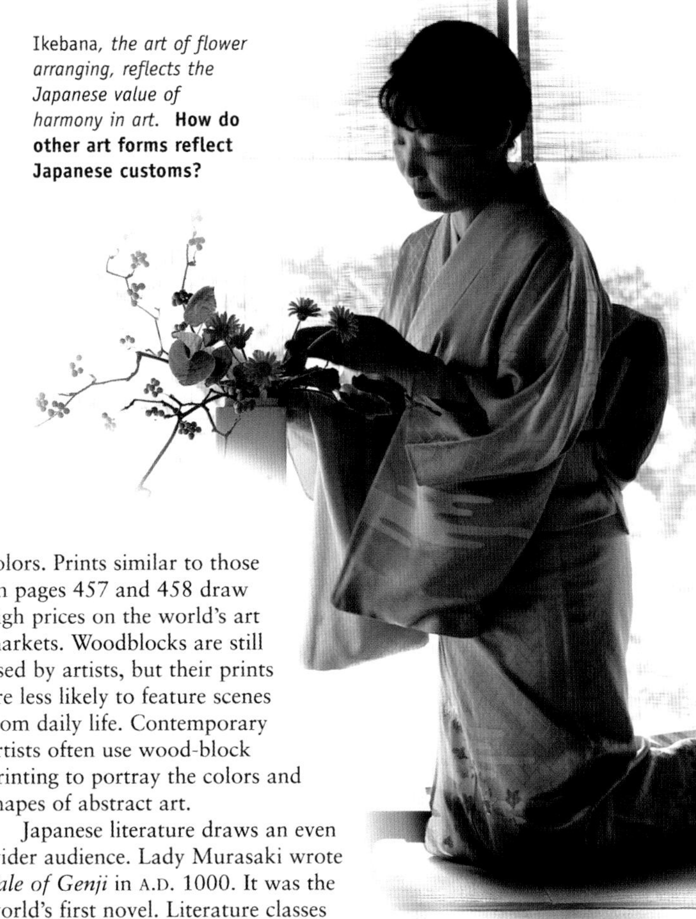

Ikebana, *the art of flower arranging, reflects the Japanese value of harmony in art.* **How do other art forms reflect Japanese customs?**

Japanese literature draws an even wider audience. Lady Murasaki wrote *Tale of Genji* in A.D. 1000. It was the world's first novel. Literature classes around the world study the book. Several modern Japanese writers have won the Nobel Prize for literature.

LESSON 3 REVIEW

Fact Follow-Up

1. In what ways has Japan's changing economy affected the ways families live?
2. What ideas—or values—have strengthened traditional families?
3. What modern or Western art forms and entertainment have become popular in Japan?

Talk About It

1. What traditional Japanese values are important in explaining why Japanese students work so hard? Explain.
2. Have changing ways of living strengthened or weakened traditional family values? Explain.
3. Choose one of Japan's traditional art forms and describe how it reflects Japan's traditional values.

LESSON 3 REVIEW

Fact Follow-Up Answers

1. Families are still close, but few households now include three generations, as in the past. Women have more freedom, and some work outside the home. The family has less influence than it once did, since many children now leave home to find work.
2. Loyalty, hard work, and the tradition of filial piety have strengthened families.
3. Rock, jazz, and Western classical music as well as baseball, golf, and bowling have become popular in Japan.

Talk About It Answers

1. Important points: Students should state the traditional values and use them to explain students' hard work. The honor of the family is affected by a student's performance. The traditional of filial piety demands that a student work hard to succeed.
2. Important points: Students should take a position and support it with reasons. City life can divide family members, but people still honor their families and maintain their bonds.
3. Important points: Students should choose one art form and describe it. Traditional art forms include theater (noh and kabuki), puppet plays, ikebana, visual arts, and literature.

Discussion Questions

1 Would you agree thatthe Japanese respect their culture, heritage, and nation? Give examples..

2 Do you think the people of the United States or North Carolina have the same passion for their heritage? Explain.

Japanese artists and craftworkers reflect traditions and values shaped by Buddhism and Shinto, requiring artists to work in harmony with their materials.

Origami

OBJECTIVES: 12.02

Have students learn origami by making a kimono doll or sumo wrestler.

Materials

6-inch square paper (white or construction paper); colored markers or crayons; tape; 6-inch by ⅜-inch strip of paper in a contrasting color from the square above for the sash; large popsicle sticks; glue; handouts from the Teacher's Resource Guide

Kimono Doll Directions Place the 6-inch square on a flat surface. Fold down the top of the square about ⅛ inch. Color this folded part with a marker. It will be the collar of the kimono. Turn the square over so that the fold is face down on the working surface. Place the popsicle stick vertically in the middle of the square and slide up so that a portion of it can be decorated as the doll's face, and secure to the paper with glue. Fold the left top corner of the paper approximately halfway down to form a triangle. Repeat the fold on the right side so that it overlaps the previous fold around the popsicle stick. To complete the kimono, fold each side vertically to cover the rest of the popsicle stick. Wrap the sash around the front and secure on the back with tape. To finish the doll, draw a face and hair on the popsicle stick. Students can also draw designs on the kimono such as cherry blossoms and birds.

Sumo Wrestler Directions See handout in the Teacher's Resource Guide.

Teaching This Skill Lesson

Materials Needed textbooks, paper, pencils

Classroom Organization whole class activity

Beginning the Lesson Ask how many students have black hair, brown hair, red hair, blond hair. Sketch a simple table on the chalkboard to record numbers. Do the same for eye color. Ask if/how the results would be different if a seventh grade class in Japan were doing the same exercise. Probe for reasons behind differences.

Lesson Development Either review with students or have them read the first four paragraphs on page 485. Tell students they will be looking for reasons why Japanese people in the past have distrusted people who are unlike them. Introduce the term ethnocentrism if students do not already know it; mention the traditional cultural isolation of the Japanese. Ask why this isolation might be a problem today and in the future for the Japanese. Have students brainstorm possible reasons (causes) for Japan's ethnocentrism. Have students consider ethnocentrism in other cultures (including that of the United States) Record these on the chalkboard. Sketch a simple Ishikawa (fishbone) diagram and lead students to place a few of the causes they have mentioned on the bones of the fish. Through discussion lead students to realize that sometimes there may be other causes behind the causes they have mentioned, attaching additional, smaller fishbones to the larger bones. Students may then construct their own Ishikawa diagrams as completely as possible. This could be a homework assignment. Students are to use their textbooks and any other available materials to do the research necessary to complete the diagrams.

Conclusion Have students display and compare the diagrams they have completed. Discuss any differences among them. Ask if the diagrams can suggest any solutions or actions the Japanese might take to improve their relationships with other people.

Analyzing, Interpreting, Creating, and Using Resources and Materials

Cooperation with Outsiders

In Chapter 23 you learned that foreign businesspeople often feel unwanted in Japan. Such ethnic minorities as the Ainu (below) and Koreans have suffered discrimination.

This chapter describes recent controversies—a requirement that students learn the national anthem, "The Reign of Our Emperor," and the Daijosia ceremony performed by Emperor Akihito when he ascended the throne. These events highlight how the Japanese often think of themselves as a people set apart.

Yet Japan and its people have special needs for cooperating with others. Japan must live in harmony with other nations because it depends on the world for raw materials and markets. As the Japanese population ages, the nation may need outsiders for labor.

Some friendly critics say that the Japanese must learn to work more easily with outsiders. They argue that Japan needs to be more open to foreign businesses. The Japanese people need to learn how to make minorities or foreigners doing business in Japan feel more comfortable.

How might this be done? In order to suggest useful solutions, it is wise to try to find the causes of problems.

The Ainu are a minority in Japan.

492 Chapter 2

Yamaha Motor Company President Takashi Kajikawa sits on a racing motorcycle at company headquarters. Yamaha Motor Company is the world's second-largest maker of motorcycles.

Take a sheet of paper and "brainstorm" possible causes of the problem. (To "brainstorm," list every idea that comes to your mind for minute or two.)

Next, sketch an Ishikawa, or "fish" diagram (invented by a Japanese engineer to help solve problems in industry). A sample diagram is shown. On the "head" of the fish, write the problem. Then, select the four causes of the problem that seem most important. List these on lines on the "body" of the fish. Add additional fishbones if you need them.

Now you are ready to suggest some possible solutions to the problems. Again, it is useful to brainstorm possible solutions. Combine or categorize them and discuss them with a classmate. What solutions did you discover?

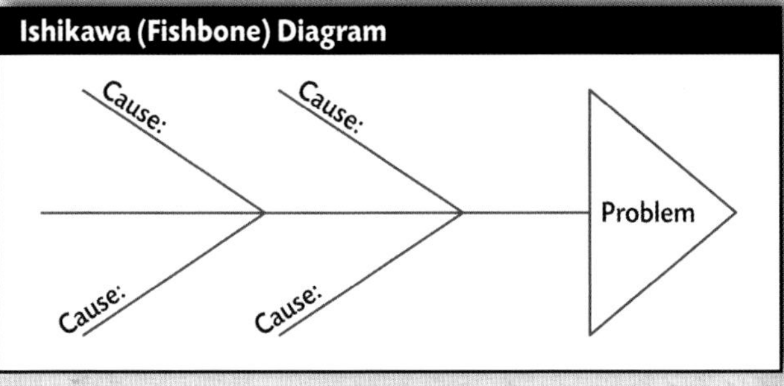

Skill Lesson Review

1. Which was easier—stating the problem or stating the causes of the problem? *Important points: Encourage students to share their opinions.*
2. Did you find that some of the causes had causes behind them? *Give students an example, such as: language might be given as a cause; one of the causes behind this cause is that the Japanese language is so difficult for non-Japanese to learn. Encourage them to offer other examples.*
3. As you worked with causes, did you find it necessary to re-state the problem? *Often, by looking at causes, the problem will need to be re-stated.*
4. Once you have stated the causes, do you think it will be easier to solve the problem by solving the causes behind the problem? *Often, this will be the case.*

Talk About It

1. Important points: Students should state agreement or disagreement and give reasons. The ceremony is a link to the older view of the emperor as an all-powerful leader of Japan, and so it worried some Japanese.
2. Free trade carries less risk and less need for control than an empire. Japan was free to concentrate on development of its economy rather than on maintaining power over conquered people.
3. Important point: Students should state whether they see a connection or not. Education prepares people for work. The better the preparation is, the more valuable the work will be.

Mastering Mapwork

1. Though a major rail line passes through this place, there is little manufacturing. Commercial farming is practiced. One would expect to find that humans have influenced the environment by building transportation systems and cutting down forests to clear fields for agriculture.
2. A major rail line passes through this place; there is commercial farming, and there is manufacturing and trade. One would expect to observe that humans have greatly influenced the environment by building transportation systems, factories, and commercial farms.
3. The greatest environmental influences on people would be observed in those areas in which neither commercial farming nor manufacturing and trade are prominent economic activities. These areas would likely be mountainous, forested areas.
4. The greatest influence of people on the environment would be found in the most densely populated areas that engage most intensively in manufacturing and trade.

CHAPTER 24 REVIEW

Lessons Learned

LESSON 1
Government
Japan's postwar constitution laid the foundation for democratic government—free speech, free elections, and representative government. Some Japanese believe that democratic reforms have gone too far and want to revise parts of the constitution, especially Article 9 (the no-war clause). However, most Japanese have accepted the changes. Democracy is working well.

LESSON 2
Economy
When World War II ended, Japan's economy seemed ruined. Its empire—an important source of industrial raw materials—was gone. The nation's factories had been destroyed. Assisted by the United States and a world eager to trade, the Japanese adopted the latest technology and worked hard. The nation became an economic superpower.

LESSON 3
Society and Culture
A visitor to Japan from Europe or the Americas will find modern cities, automobiles, and Western-style sports. These may suggest that Japanese and Western societies are much alike. Close observation shows that these Western features have been blended with age-old Japanese traditions. Japanese society is not the same as Western societies.

Talk About It

1. Why do you think some Japanese were upset by the part of the installation ceremonies that by tradition turned the new emperor into a "living god"? Would you agree or disagree with those who thought the ceremony was not important? Explain your answer.
2. Japan wanted to join European powers in building a colonial empire. An empire was supposed to be a source of strength. Yet Japan has attained greater prestige and power without an empire since World War II. Explain why Japan's fortunes have been better without an empire than with one.
3. You have read that Japanese think of their people as being the nation's most valuable resource. Do you think that there might be a connection between this belief and the nation's insistence that young people work hard in school? Explain your answer.

Mastering Mapwork

HUMAN-ENVIRONMENTAL INTERACTION

Use the map on page 477 to answer these questions:

1. Find the intersection of 40°N and 140°E. Describe the evidence of human-environmental interaction you would observe here.
2. Find the intersection of 35°N and 135°E. Describe the evidence of human-environmental interaction you would expect to observe in this place.
3. Where in Japan would you expect to observe the greatest environmental influence on the lives of people? Explain why.
4. Where in Japan would you expect to observe the greatest influence of people on the environment? Explain your answer.

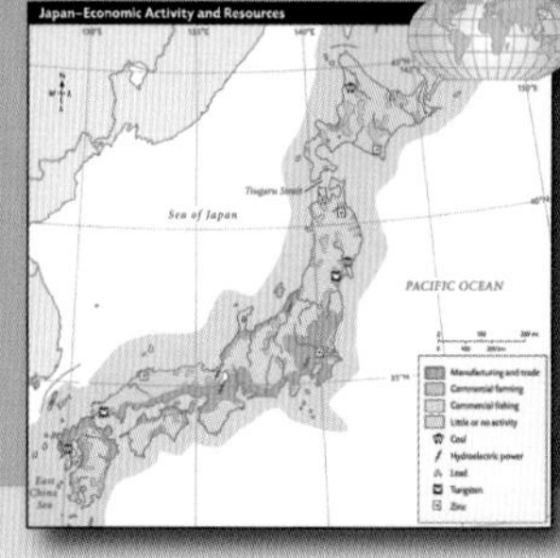

Go to the Source

Analyzing Art as an Artifact

This artwork, ink on paper, is comprised of two folding screens. It depicts two civil wars from the 1150s. The city of Kyoto, mountains, rivers, and hundreds of people are shown. Important parts of the battles are depicted in the centers of the screens.

Study The Battles of Hogen and Heiji, *painted in seventeenth century Japan, below. Answer the questions using specific references to the image.*

Go to the Source

Questions

1. What is the subject of this piece of art?
2. Why do you think it was painted?
3. How can historians use this painting to study Japan's past?

Go to the Source

OBJECTIVES: 8.01, 9.01, 9.02, 10.01, 11.03; Skills 2.01, 2.02, 3.05

The two civil wars of the Hogen and Heiji eras occurred in 1156 and 1159. In both wars, the fighting lasted only a few days. However, both are some of the most memorable battles in medival Japanese history. These battles signaled the onset of a new era. The first historical war novel of Japan, the "Hogen Monogatari" (Tale of the Hogen Incident) was based on these civil wars.

ANSWERS

1. The piece shows a military battle in Japan.
2. Answers will vary. Important points: It was possibly to commemorate an important military battle or important historical event in Japan's history. It may have been used to teach people about battles or history.
3. Historians look at the style and the subject matter of the artwork to give them clues to historic events, clothing styles, and architectural styles of the time period.

How to Use the Chapter Review

There are three sections in the Chapter Review: Talk About It, Mastering Mapwork, and Go to the Source. Use the Vocabulary Worksheets and the Chapter Review Worksheet in the Teacher's Resource Guide for additional reinforcement and preparation for the Chapter Assessments. The chapter and lesson reviews and the Chapter Review Worksheets are the basis of the assessment for each chapter.

Talk About It questions encourage students to speculate about the content of the chapter and are suitable for class or small-group discussion. They are not intended to be assigned for homework.

Mastering Mapwork has students apply one or more of the Five Themes of Geography to maps within the chapter.

Go to the Source activities allow students to analyze a primary source that relates to the content of the chapter. The questions and activities familiarize students with different types of primary sources and also build content-reading skills.

A Diversity of People and Lands

Social Studies Strands

Geographic Relationships
- Climate
- Resources

Global Connections
- Western Influence

Historic Perspectives
- Colonialism
- Vietnam War

North Carolina Standard Course of Study

Goal 3 The learner will analyze the impact of interactions between humans and their physical environments in Africa, Asia, and Australia.

Goal 6 The learner will recognize the relationship between economic activity and the quality of life in Africa, Asia, and Australia.

Goal 9 The learner will analyze the different forms of government developed in Africa, Asia, and Australia.

Goal 12 The learner will assess the influence of major religions, ethical beliefs, and values on cultures in Africa, Asia, and Australia.

Teaching & Assessment

- English Language Learner Modified Lesson Plans for this chapter are found in the Teacher Resource Guide.
- *ExamView® Assessment Suite* is provided at **NCJourneys.com.** It includes customizable assessments for all chapters. Paper tests are also available in the Teacher Resource Guide. See pages T16–T17 for information about how to use the assessments and the Scoring Guide.

Worksheets

Worksheets and answer keys are found both in the Teacher Resource Guide and at **NCJourneys.com**, including Reading Guides, Reading Strategies, Chapter Reviews, English Language Learner and others.

ACTIVITIES AND INTEGRATIONS

SOCIAL STUDIES
Activator: "Wake Up and Smell the Coffee," p. 496
▲ ■ Southeast Asia, p. 497
Economic Activity, p. 497
★ Colonial Consequences Cube, p. 499
● Country Cube, p. 499
▲ ■ Vietnam War Student Memorial, p. 501
▲ Ring of Fire, p. 506
Skill Lesson: World Influences Shaping Southeast Asia, p. 517

READING/LANGUAGE ARTS	READING/LANGUAGE ARTS OBJECTIVES
Analogies, p. 496B	2.01
Writing Prompt: Helmet Laws, p. 496	3.01
Cultural Connections, p. 498	1.03
Creation Stories, p. 504	1.01, 1.02, 2.01
● River Trip, p. 505	1.01
Panel Discussion/Debate, p. 511	1.03
Go to the Source: Analyzing Public Awareness Campaigns, p. 519	2.01, 3.01, 3.02, 4(all)

MATHEMATICS	MATH OBJECTIVES
Elephant Puzzle, p. 505	3.01
● ■ Coconut Beef Patties, p. 507	1.01
▲ Graph, p. 514	4.01, 4.05
▲ ■ Coconut Custard (Laos), p. 515	1.01

SCIENCE	SCIENCE OBJECTIVES
★ The Phillipines, p. 502	3.06
Mount Pinatubo and Other Famous Volcanoes of the World, p. 506	3.06

TECHNOLOGY	TECHNOLOGY OBJECTIVES
Rules!, p. 496B	3.01, 3.07
▲ Colonial Imprints, p. 500	3.01, 3.03
Crops Flow Chart, p. 508	3.01, 3.03
★ Endangered Orangutan, p. 509	3.01, 3.11

VISUAL ARTS	VISUAL ARTS OBJECTIVES
Sailing Down the River–Mainland Southeast Asia, p. 496B	4.01, 4.03
Buddhist Prayer Wheel, p. 496B	2.04, 5.03
War Music, p. 501	7.01, 7.03
Rice Paintings, p. 504	2.04, 4.02
● ■ Who's Who in Southeast Asia, p. 512	4.01, 4.04
■ Shadow Puppets, p. 516	4.01, 6.01

CHARACTER AND VALUES EDUCATION	TRAITS
Writing Prompt: Helmet Laws, p. 496	Citizenship/responsiblity
What Would You Do?, p. 505	Responsibility, good judgment
Consider Character Socratic Seminar, p. 510	good citizenzhip, perserverence, responsibility

● Basic Activities ★ Challenging Activities ▲ English Language Learner Novice ■ English Language Learner Intermediate

Chapter Activities

Introductory Activity

Sailing Down the River—Mainland Southeast Asia

OBJECTIVES: 1.02, 2.01, 2.02

Materials atlases, almanacs, 3-foot pieces of white bulletin board backdrop paper, crayons or markers (several colors), reference books

Divide class into five groups. Each group will represent one of the major rivers in Southeast Asia: Irrawaddy, Salween, Chao Prayha (Menam), Red, and Mekong.

Student groups should trace (map) their individual river from its source to its mouth and draw and color it in on their piece of bulletin board paper. Countries that the river runs through should be drawn in and identified. Cities along the river should be labeled. (Special attention should be paid to city names reflecting colonial rule.) Goods and crops that may be transported on these rivers should be noted in a map/legend key.

River presentations will be made at the end of the assignment. The following questions should be answered from the presentations: Without noting in presentations, is it possible to determine the colonial ruler from the names of the river cities/towns? How are the rivers important to the people who live along its banks? Can the uneven distribution of natural resources be determined from the movement of goods along the rivers? In what ways could these cities or towns improve their livelihood by living on the river?

Hang maps during the study of Southeast Asia and refer to as needed.

Extension Do not assign novice or intermediate ELL students the presentation.

Culminating Activity

Rules!

OBJECTIVES: 4.03, 9.02, 10.03

Have students read the section on Singapore again (see page 515). Tell students about an incident in 1994. An American teenager, Michael Fay, was punished by caning because he vandalized cars in Singapore. The punishment was severe by American standards. Have students look on the Internet for information about the incident. In comparison, have them then look up county and neighborhood regulations for their neighborhoods. Compare local crime statistics to those of Singapore.

Using a Venn Diagram or other graphic organizer, have students list regulations of Singapore. Have them list the regulations of their neighborhood, county, school, or classroom. Have students compare the regulations. Ask them to write a short paper on why they think Singapore's rules are more or less strict than those of their own county, neighborhood, school, or classroom. Which rules are similar? For what purpose might a nation create these rules?

Art Activity

Buddhist Prayer Wheel

OBJECTIVES: 12.01

Materials round oatmeal container, ½-inch wooden dowel, colored construction paper, markers or tempera paint, rulers, and cord, chain or thick yarn

The Buddhist Prayer Wheel is a Tibetan artifact that always includes the words "om mani padme hum," meaning "Om the Jewel in the Lotus Hum."

Punch a small hole in the lid and in the bottom of the oatmeal container. Decorate the construction paper with paint or markers (precut the paper to fit around outside of prayer wheel). Include the phrase "om mani padme hum." It is a good idea to practice the lettering prior to writing it on the final construction paper, then put designs around the words.

Cut small hole in the side of the wheel. Tie a knot on one end of cord or thick yarn and insert through hole. The knot should be large enough to prevent the cord from going through hole. Tie heavy object to a piece of cord, chain, or thick yarn (students can design and create an object). The size should be between a quarter and a half dollar. Put lid on and push dowel through bottom of oatmeal container all the way through the top.

Buddhists place holy texts inside the prayer wheels.

Analogies

OBJECTIVES: 2.01, 7.01, 8.01, 13.03

Analogies are useful to help students make associations with prior knowledge. Read the analogies aloud and ask students to identify the relationship between the terms. As an extension, ask students to write their own analogies using key terms or places discussed in the chapter.

Filipinos : Philippines :: Thais : Thailand :: Laotians : Laos (are people from)

Vietnam War : 1960s :: Korean War : 1950s :: World War II : 1940s (was fought primarily during)

Japan : SE Asia :: England : India :: Portugal : Brazil (colonized)

Strait of Malacca : Indian Ocean/South China Sea :: Hormuz Strait : Persian Gulf/Gulf of Oman (connects)

ASEAN : Southeast Asia :: European Union : Europe :: NAFTA : North America (regional economic organization in)

Aung San Suu Kyi : Myanmar :: Bishop Desmond Tutu : South Africa :: Nelson Mandela : South Africa :: Martin Luther King, Jr. : United States (Nobel Peace Prize winner from)

Teaching Strategies

While you will want to spend some time on Vietnam due to its connection with the United States, you may need to quickly cover the other countries of the region. Refer to the suggested research projects listed and use one of these ideas to help students learn about the countries of Southeast Asia

Divide the students into collaborative pairs and assign a country from Southeast Asia for students to research and complete the Country Profile project.

Activator

OBJECTIVES: 2.02, 3.01

Bring in samples of coffee, tea, cinnamon, thai peppers, and rice. Put each of the items in brown paper bags and pass around the room. Instruct students to smell and touch the items in the bag but not to look. Ask them to identify the items based on touch and smell. After participating in the activity, explain that these are items grown in Southeast Asia, the region that they will be studying (additional spices or items may be used if they are available). Refer students to page 508 for follow-up on the Spice Islands and Java Island.

Extension ELL students may not be able to identify the items in English but should still participate to get the idea. Have them define the words using their native language dictionary.

Writing Prompt

OBJECTIVES: 9.02, 10.03

Evaluative

Singapore is sometimes referred to as a 'fine place to live' because of the many fines that are imposed if someone breaks a law. North Carolina now has a law that fines individuals that do not wear a helmet when riding a bicycle. Are you in favor of this law or are you against it. Explain your answer.

As you write remember to:

- clearly state your position.
- give at least three reasons and explain your reasons fully.
- give examples to support your reasons.
- write in complete sentences and paragraph form.
- organize your ideas and include an introduction and a conclusion.
- use good grammar, spelling, punctuation, and capitalization.

CHAPTER 25

Southeast Asia

Like many of the nations of Southeast Asia, Thailand has transformed itself from an old kingdom into a rising economic giant. In Bangkok, its capital, this transition can be seen everywhere. "Old Bangkok" glitters with temples and the old palace, while "New Bangkok" is a modern city of commercial and tourist districts and large residential neighborhoods. All over Southeast Asia traditional ways of life are being adapted to the changes and challenges brought by the global economy.

A Thai monk types on a laptop in Bangkok (far left), a temple in old Bangkok in 1950 (left), Bangkok's monorail in the commercial district (below)

Chapter Preview

Lesson 1
Many Different People
The languages and cultures of Asian and Western nations are reflected in modern Southeast Asia.

Lesson 2
People and Their Environment
Southeast Asia's importance comes from its location on major trade routes and from its exports to the world.

Lesson 3
Governments and Economies
Some Southeast Asian governments are authoritarian, but the number of democracies is growing. The region is enjoying rapid economic growth.

Lesson 4
Society and Culture
As Southeast Asia becomes increasingly urban and industrial, centuries-old traditions are changing or growing weaker.

Chapter Resources

Print Resources

Nonfiction

Kalman, Bobbie. *Vietnam: The Culture.* Crabtree, 1996. ISBN 0865052255.

—. *Vietnam: The Land.* Crabtree, 1996. ISBN 0865052247.

—. *Vietnam: The People.* Crabtree, 1996. ISBN 077879380X.

McNair, Sylvia. *Thailand* (Enchantment of the World series). Children's Press, 1998. ISBN 0516211005.

__. *Bangkok* (Cities of the World series). Children's Press, 1999. ISBN 0516211951.

Cultures of the World series (Marshall Cavendish):

Mansfield, Stephen. *Laos.* 1998. ISBN 0761406891.

Seah, Audrey. *Vietnam.*1996. ISBN 1854355848.

Modern World Nation series (Chelsea House):

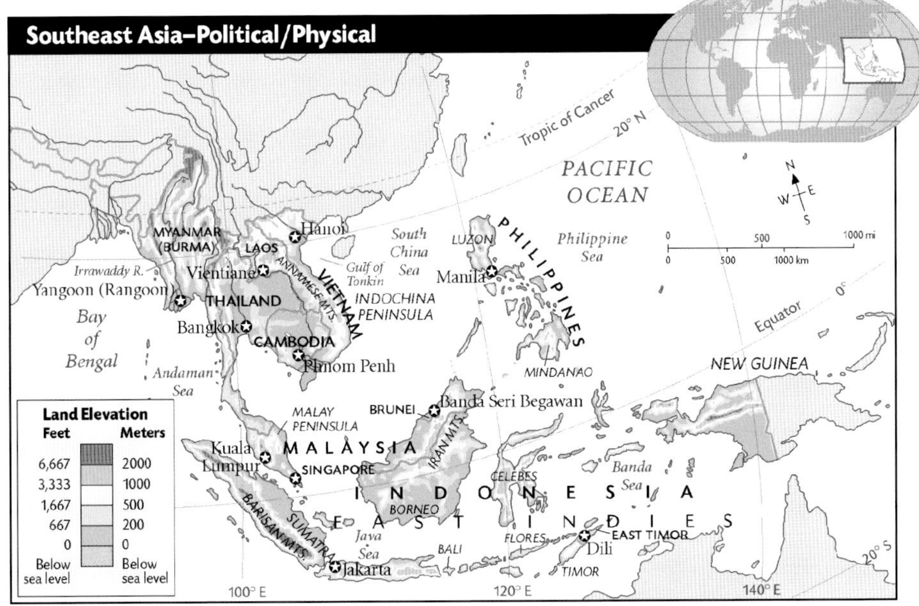

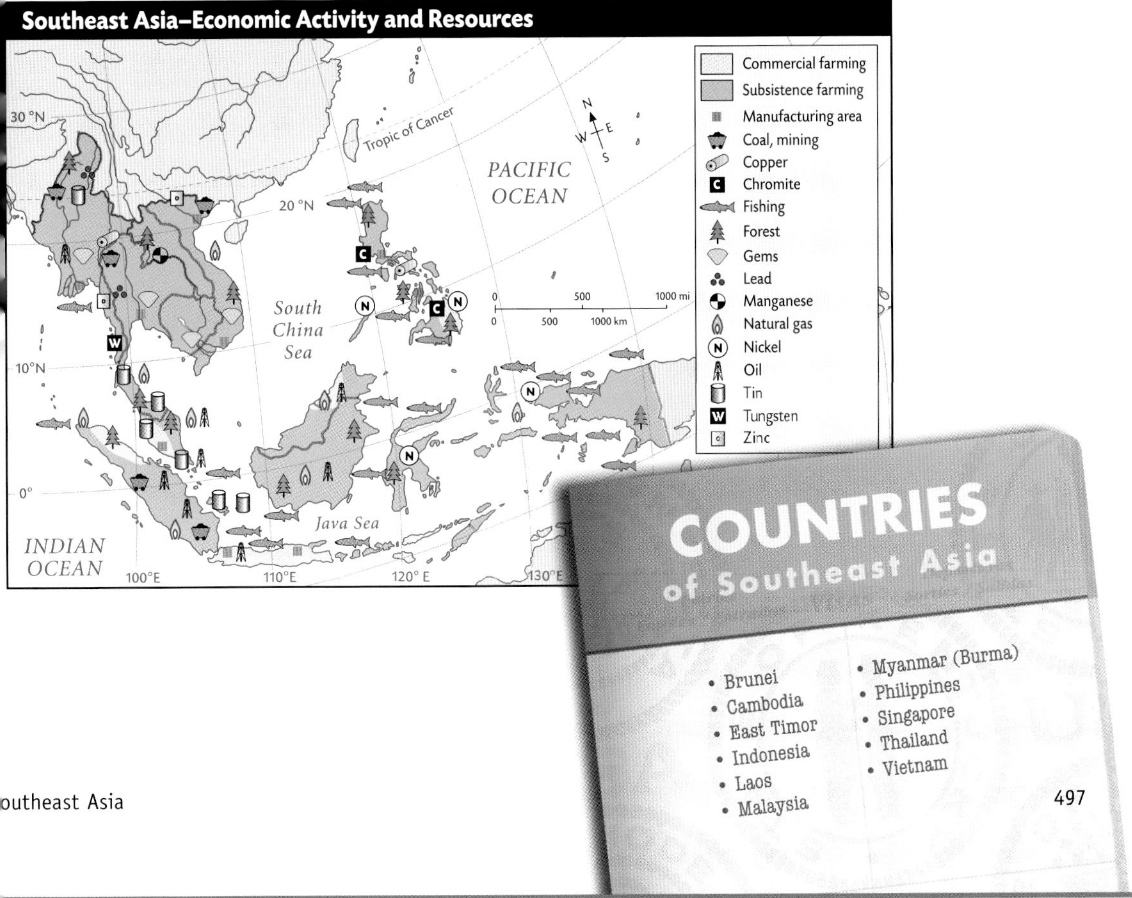

outheast Asia 497

Canesso, Claudia. *Cambodia.* 1999. ISBN 0791047326.

Wee, Jessie. *The Philippines.* 1999. ISBN 0791049841.

Welcome to My Country series (Gareth Stevens Publishing):

Mesenas, Geraldine, and Frederick Fisher. Welcome to Indonesia. ISBN 0836825179.

Ng, Yumi, and Amy Condra-Peters. Welcome to Vietnam. 2002. ISBN 0836825489.

Wynaden, Jo, Joaquin L. Gonzalez, and Alan Wachtel. Welcome to the Philippines. 2001. ISBN 0836825349.

Yong, Jui Lin. Welcome to Singapore. 2000. ISBN 0836825462.

Continued on page 500

Map Activity

Southeast Asia

NATIONAL GEOGRAPHY STANDARDS: 1, 4, 5

GEOGRAPHIC THEMES: Location, Place, Region

OBJECTIVES: 1.02, 2.01

Have students answer the following questions:

1. Identify the nations included in Southeast Asia. *Myanmar (Burma), Thailand, Laos, Cambodia, Vietnam, Philippines, Brunei, Malaysia, Singapore, Indonesia, East Timor*
2. Which of these 11 countries is located on the Asian mainland? *Myanmar (Burma), Thailand, Laos, Cambodia, Vietnam, and part of Malaysia*
3. Which of the Southeast Asian countries are located on Asian islands? *Philippines, Brunei, part of Malaysia, Singapore, Indonesia, East Timor*
4. Name eight bodies of water crucial to Southeast Asia. *Bay of Bengal, Andaman Sea, Gulf of Tonkin, South China Sea, Philippine Sea, Pacific Ocean, Java Sea, Banda Sea*

Map Activity

Economic Activity

NATIONAL GEOGRAPHY STANDARDS: 1, 4, 16

GEOGRAPHIC THEMES: Location, Place, Human-Environmental Interaction, Region

OBJECTIVES: 1.02, 2.03, 3.01, 5.01

Have students answer the following questions:

1. Name the types of economic activities found in Southeast Asia. *farming: commercial and subsistence, manufacturing, mining, fishing*
2. Which type of farming is mainly used across all countries in Southeast Asia? *subsistence*
3. Which energy source is found the most throughout Southeast Asia? *oil*
4. Are gems mined on the mainland or in the islands of Southeast Asia? *on the mainland*
5. Identify which mineral resources are found in the Philippines. *copper, chromite, nickel*

OBJECTIVES: 7.02, 9.01, 12.01

Discussion Questions

1 Imagine a world with no calendars or clocks. How would you know when to do important activities during the day and when to celebrate the important events of your lives?

2 What is the relationship between spiritual beliefs and celebrations of life?

3 Speculate about the types of problems that might arise in a region with so many diverse religions.

Caption Answer

They are not veiled or wearing restrictive clothing. Refer students to Unit 3.

Activity

Cultural Connections

OBJECTIVES: 12.03, 13.02

This can be done as a total class activity using a large world map on a bulletin board or as an individual or small-group activity. Have students identify cultural influences coming into the region by colored arrow lines (Europe, Africa, United States, Japan, China, India). Have students identify influences the region has had on other cultures (exports, ideas, vocabulary). Use different colors for these outgoing lines and arrows. Identify any connections that the region has with North Carolina in gold.

LESSON 1 Many Different People

KEY IDEAS

- Buddhism, Islam, and Christianity are the region's major religions.
- India, China, and Western colonialism have helped shape modern Southeast Asian nations.
- From the 1940s through the 1980s, World War II and the Cold War had major impacts on Southeast Asia.

KEY TERMS

Filipinos
plantations
Vietnam War

Singapore's calendar lists many festivals of different cultures—Chinese New Year, the Buddha's birthday, the Hindu Festival of Lights, Christmas, and the Islamic holy month of Ramadan.

Malaysia has a similar story. Its language, Malay, was once written in Sanskrit brought by Indian merchants. Later, Arabic script took the place of Sanskrit. In the 1900s, our Latin alphabet began to replace Arabic writing. Spoken Malay remained the same through all the writing changes.

Over thousands of years, people from India, China, Southwest Asia and Europe brought their languages, ways of life, and religions to Southeast Asia. Southeast Asia's people absorbed these outside cultures while keeping their identities.

A Cultural Crossroads

Several thousand years ago, a people known as the Malayans spread over most of the region now called Southeast Asia. They developed their own languages, beliefs, and ways of life. Yet they often felt the pull of outside influences. Armies, merchants, and missionaries representing different faiths pushed into the region.

These two Muslim women show how Islam has been adapted by Indonesians. **In what ways do they demonstrate this?**

Foundations

Indian merchants and monks brought Hinduism and Buddhism to the region. Buddhism, often mixed with Hindu ideas, had widespread influence, especially on the mainland of Southeast Asia. Today, Buddhism remains the major faith in that part of the region. Daily life there has been shaped by Buddhist values, art, and architecture.

By A.D. 1200, Muslim merchants had introduced Islam to Southeast Asia. It took root in Malaysia and Indonesia. Indonesia now has the world's largest Muslim population. Indonesian Muslims did not give up all of their ancient beliefs. Islam teaches belief in one God, but many Indonesian Muslims still honor local gods.

In China's Shadow

China has long been a powerful influence on parts of Southeast Asia. Confucian ideas about filial piety and respect for elders shaped values. China's advanced civilization impressed local rulers. They adopted many Chinese ideas about government and styles of art.

China's influence was especially strong in Vietnam. Confucian ideas influenced Vietnamese government and society. Yet the Vietnamese resented the Chinese. Today a museum in Vietnam honors the fight against Chinese domination.

Name Origin

Cambodia Named after Kamber, the legendary founder of the Khmer or Cambodian people.

East Timor "Timor" isfrom timor or timur, the word for "east" in Malay and Indonesian; it became "timor" in Portuguese.

Indonesia Greek for "Islands of the Indies"

Laos Named after the local ethnic group and language.

Malaysia Named for the people—Malays—"people of the mountains."

Myanmar from the Chinese language: mian meaning "strong" and suffix 'ma, meaning "honorable"

Philippines Named to honor Prince Philip II of Spain, who would later become king.

Singapore Singha means "lions" and pore means "city;" thus, "city of lions."

Thailand from the Thai language meaning "free"

Vietnam Chinese for "far south"

Bangkok "water flower village"

Jakarta "important city"

A plantation worker in Myanmar rakes red peppers to help them dry in the sun. **Why did plantations benefit European colonists more than local people?**

Western Expansion

In the 1500s, European explorers reached Southeast Asia. Ferdinand Magellan of Spain reached the Philippine Islands in 1521, named them for his king, and claimed them for his country. Spain ruled the Philippines until 1898. The United States then won control of the islands and governed them for nearly 50 years.

In the 1800s, the British, Dutch, and French took over much of the rest of Southeast Asia. Britain expanded from India into Myanmar (Burma). It also conquered what is today Malaysia and Singapore. France built an empire in Indochina, today's Laos, Cambodia, and Vietnam. The Dutch ruled the East Indies, now Indonesia. Only Siam, modern Thailand, remained independent.

As in Africa, colonial powers sought to make their colonies profitable. They set up *plantations* —large farms specializing in one or two crops—to export sugar, coffee, rubber, tea, and palm and coconut oils. European landowners and merchants earned profits, but local people gained few benefits. Local farmers grew less rice and other food crops because they had to produce export crops to pay taxes. Food shortages led to hunger and misery.

Westerners did introduce modern medical care and opened some schools. By the early 1900s, young students who had learned Western ideas about freedom and democracy began to protest colonial rule. Independence movements grew throughout the region during the 1930s.

Word Origins

We use the word **boondocks** to mean a remote, rural area. In fact, that word comes from the Philippines. In Tagalog, a language of the Philippines, the word bundok means a mountain or highland area. American soldiers who served in the Philippines early in the 1900s brought it back to the United States. Americans still use the word to mean a remote area.

Discussion Questions

1 How did the effects of Western imperialism result in the war in Southeast Asia?

2 During the Vietnam War period, there was a great influx of American military personnel in Saigon—which created a whole new market for South Vietnamese merchants. What effect do you think this new group of consumers had on South Vietnam?

3 Why would a country that can support itself by growing its own food choose to grow crops to export rather than to feed its own people?

Caption Answer

Plantations specialized in cash crops for export. The profits went to the European landowners and merchants. The concentration on cash crops left much less land for food crops. The food shortages led to hunger and misery.

Activity

Colonial Consequences Cube

OBJECTIVES: 12.03, 13.01

Assign students (in groups of two or three) one of the Southeast Asian countries. Give each group the task of creating a "Colonial Consequences Cube" for their country (you might use the cube pattern in the Teacher's Resource Guide to cut out or a cubic box with construction paper panels glued on). Each side of the cube is to reflect a different aspect of colonial influence on the country: name of country, flag, languages and religions, government, economy, and colonial ruler (European country of influence).

Tell students to cut along the heavy black lines. Fold on the dashed lines. Tabs can be taped or glued. Have students explain their finished products and then hang them in the room.

Activity

Country Cube

OBJECTIVES: 1.01, 2.01, 5.04, 9.02

Have students cut out a cube—each side should be about 4 inches by 4 inches or use the pattern in the Teacher's Resource Guide. Have students include tabs to ease assembly of cubes. Before assembling, each student will research a Southeast Asian country. They will then put specific information on each side of the cube with colorful illustrations, then assemble.

Teacher Notes

The Ho Chi Mihn Trail

During the Vietnam War, the Ho Chi Minh Trail was the major supply route for the North Vietnamese forces that eventually invaded and overran South Vietnam. Traffic on the trail was little affected by repeated American bombing raids. At the beginning of the conflict, the trail was not much more than a network of loosely connected jungle paths and a few dirt roads. By 1974, the trail was a well-marked series of jungle roads, many of which were paved, with underground support facilities such as hospitals, fuel-storage tanks, and weapons and supply caches.

Activity

Colonial Imprints

OBJECTIVES: 7.02, 12.03, 13.01

Have students research and prepare exhibits (shadow box, Web page, PowerPoint presentation, digital story, or poster) that show the lasting imprint of colonialism on Southeast Asia.

Possible Topics

- the French in Vietnam
- the Americans in Vietnam
- the Dutch in Indonesia
- Indian influences in the entire region
- Chinese influences in the entire region
- the British in Thailand
- the Spanish in the Philippines
- the Americans in the Philippines
- plantation economy
- export economy
- missionary influences

Extension ELL students should use an ELL-friendly Web site for research. Limit the writing for intermediate ELL students.

EYEWITNESS TO HISTORY

THE VIETNAM WAR

Vietnam had been part of a large French colony called Indochina. Ho Chi Minh (left), a Communist, was determined that the French would not return after World War II. He led the Vietnamese in this fight with assistance from Communist China and the Soviet Union. After many years of battle, the French withdrew in 1954, dividing Vietnam along the 17th parallel.

Ho Chi Minh's fierce anti-colonialism, political skills, and military leadership were never matched by the leadership in the South. Bao Dai (right) was France's choice to lead South Vietnam. Neither Bao Dai nor his successors could rally South Vietnam behind them. North Vietnam carried the war into South Vietnam.

American soldiers question a Vietnamese man during the Vietnam War

The United States entered the war as "advisors" to South Vietnam. Soon American troops were doing much of the fighting. They fought bravely but faced great difficulties. They seldom fought uniformed enemy troops. Their North Vietnamese opponents blended in with the villagers of South Vietnam. Americans often had trouble telling friend from foe.

50 Chapter 2

Chapter Resources (continued)

Back issues of magazines

Cobblestone Publishing Company.
Cambodia. ISBN 0382443780.
Indonesia. ISBN 0382405420.
Laos. ISBN 0382445872.
Philippines. ISBN 0382405587.
Thailand. ISBN 0382405714.
Vietnam. ISBN 0382409027.

Ancient Khmer Empire. Cobblestone Publishing Company. (*Calliope* magazine, 2001-02).

Audiovisual

Indonesia, a Southeast Asian Country. Humanities Extension/Publications, North Carolina State University, 1999. 19

Vietnam: A Television History. 1983. PBS Video.

Web Sites

Go to **NCJourneys.com** for links to these Web sites:

- Center for Southeast Asian Studies at Northern Illinois University
- Eggi's Village: Life Among the Minangkabau of Indonesia
- NOAA Center for Tsunami Research, December 26, 2004 Indonesia (Sumatra)
- Vietnam Online

American bombers targeted the Ho Chi Minh Trail, the road bringing supplies from the North to troops in the South. Bomb damage blocked much of the road to trucks, but thousands of Vietnamese brought tons of supplies to the South on bicycles. American planes (above) sprayed chemicals to defoliate the jungle and deprive the enemy of cover.

In the United States, the war divided the American people. President Richard Nixon decided that the United States must withdraw from the fighting. South Vietnam continued to fight, but by 1976 its forces surrendered. Vietnam was united under a Communist government. Over a million Americans served in Vietnam. More than 58,000 were killed and many others were seriously wounded. Today, thousands of Americans visit the Vietnam Veterans Memorial in Washington, D.C., to honor those who served (left).

Eyewitness Activity

War Music

OBJECTIVES: 7.01, 7.02

While studying the Vietnam War, use music from the Vietnam era to help grab students' attention and enhance their understanding of the time. Explain that much of this music was used at antiwar protests and benefits. There were also a few songs that were in support of the war. You can also find just the lyrics on the Internet and have students analyze them as poetry.

Music

Antiwar

"Blowin in the Wind" by Bob Dylan
"Live On" by Crosby, Stills, Nash, and Young; also "Ohio"
"I'm Fixing to Die Rag" by Country Joe and the Fish
"Sam Stone" by John Prine
"Give Peace a Chance" by John Lennon
"For What It's Worth" by Buffalo Springfield
"War (What is it Good for?)" by Edwin Starr

Supported the war

"The Ballad of the Green Beret" by Sergeant Barry Sadler (also a film starring John Wayne)
"The Fightin' Side Of Me" by Merle Haggard

Teacher Notes

Twenty-Sixth Constitutional Amendment

On July 1, 1971, Congress enacted the twentysixth Amendment to the United States Constitution: suffrage for all citizens eighteen years old and older. During the Vietnam War and the strong antiwar protests the government faced during the conflict, members of Congress and their constituents believed the voting age should be lowered. The theory behind this legislation was that if a young man was old enough to be drafted, he should be able to vote for or against those officials who would lead the nation into war. Because of the nineteenth amendment (Women's Suffrage) the voting age was lowered for women as well.

Activity

Vietnam War Student Memorial

OBJECTIVES: 7.01, 9.01, 13.01

Abouut 58,209 lost their lives during the Vietnam War. An additional 153,363 were wounded between August 4, 1964, and January 27, 1973. It takes almost 152 pieces of graph paper filled with 300 x's each to approximate the number of Americans who lost their lives.

Give each student at least one sheet of graph paper (½-inch works best). Every sheet of graph paper is to have 15 x's in a row on 20 rows (totaling 300 x's). Some students may do more than one sheet of graph paper (total 152 sheets). These are to be displayed on a wall to help students visualize the magnitude of the effects this war. Doing the x's in a series of red, blue, and black on white paper will allow this display to be posted on the wall in a United States flag configuration. Displaying this for Veteran's Day or Memorial Day allows students to honor veterans of this war with their own Vietnam Wall Memorial.

Discussion Questions

1 Do any of you have friends or relatives who fought in the Vietnam War? Have they shared specific incidences with you?

2 Why did the people of Southeast Asia welcome Japanese expansion?

3 Explain Japan's interest in Southeast Asia. Why was it so easy for Japan to control the region?

4 Who are the Filipinos?

5 The Philippines did not immediately gain their independence following World War II, as had been promised. The United States continues to have a military presence there, and many Filipinos want the United States out. Should the United States withdraw its military bases?

Caption Answer

Other colonial legacies include medical care, schools, and plantations of sugar, spices, and other crops.

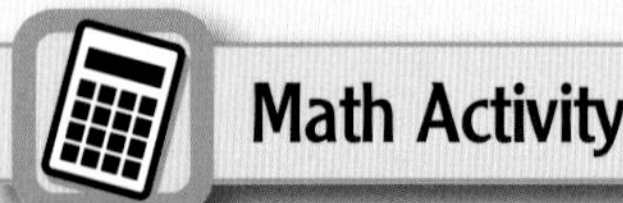

Math Activity

The Philippines

OBJECTIVES: 2.01, 3.04

The Philippines has over 7,000 islands, and only about 25 have cities.

Discuss with students that volcanology is the study of volcanoes. Note that the Philippines has more than 30 active volcanoes. Mount Pinatubo erupted in 1991 burying entire villages, killing approximately 800 people, and affecting global weather patterns for two years. Note that ash flows from this volcano still threaten fields and roads during rainy, monsoon seasons. Also, describe that in 1984 the Mayon volcano on Luzon hurled boulders as big as cars down its slopes destroying villages. Mayon erupted again in 1993. The Philippines is part of the Ring of Fire (see page 506).

The United States government started public education in the Philippines when it was the colonial power there. As a result, English is the Philippines' official language today. **What are other colonial legacies in Southeast Asia?**

Winning Independence

World War II boosted independence movements throughout Southeast Asia. Japan's armed forces swept through the region. They quickly defeated the United States and European military forces. Japanese-led governments replaced Western colonialism.

Japan's success at first excited Southeast Asian independence leaders. Japan's slogan "Asia for Asiatics" encouraged Southeast Asians to believe that the days of colonialism were over. Moreover, Japan's quick victories demonstrated that Westerners were not all-powerful.

This enthusiasm for the coming of the Japanese soon faded. Japanese leaders had wanted Southeast Asia for its raw materials. The Japanese established military governments that were far more harsh than Western colonialism. When independence leaders saw what was happening, they began to organize against Japan. By the time World War II ended, Southeast Asians were ready to resist any efforts to reestablish foreign rule.

The United States was also an imperial power in Southeast Asia. In 1898, Spain, which had ruled the Philippines since the 1500s, ceded control to the United States as part of the terms ending the Spanish-American War. ***Filipinos*** who had united their island nation in opposition to Spanish rule, demanded that the Americans abandon colonial rule. The United States promised independence would be granted when the people were better able to govern themselves. After World War II, Filipinos gained their freedom.

The Vietnam War

After the United States granted independence to the Philippines, it urged European powers to free their colonies. Europe was reluctant to let go of these valuable assets. The Dutch fought briefly in the East Indies as did the British in Malaya. The French fought to keep Indochina from 1945 to 1954. When the French withdrew they left Vietnam "temporarily" divided along the 17th parallel. Communists, led by Ho Chi Minh, ruled the North, and were assisted by communist China and the Soviet Union. Western nations, particularly the United States—which was concerned

Background Information

Continuing Human Costs of War

Another tragic legacy of the Vietnam War was the displacement of nearly 2 million people from their homes in Vietnam, Laos, and Cambodia. After 1975 many of these refugees came to camps along the Thai border. Eventually most were resettled in other countries or returned to their own countries. Among those refugees were the Hmong people. Because many Hmong men served as secret fighters for the United States, in the 20 years after the war ended, the United States government accepted 127,000 Hmong refugees. Most had been subsistence farmers who practiced shifting, slash-and-burn agriculture. Almost none could read or write and few had ever had electricity, indoor plumbing, or telephones. Most settled in California, Wisconsin, and Minnesota. Many moved to North Carolina.

bout stopping communist expansion—upported the government in the South. ʻoth of these governments pledged to eunite Vietnam. Their conflict led to the *Vietnam War.*

At first, American support was nodest. During the 1960s, the United tates' role grew. More than 7 million mericans served in Vietnam. They battled he Communist forces of Ho Chi Minh longside South Vietnamese and also ustralian forces. The United States elieved that a Communist victory in 'ietnam would encourage the expansion f communism throughout Southeast Asia. 'he idea was called the "Domino Theory."

American forces remained in Vietnam ntil 1973. Two years after the Americans vithdrew, South Vietnam collapsed in efeat to the northern government. A arsh Communist-led dictatorship was nposed on the country.

Much of Southeast Asia was hurt by he war. It spread from Vietnam into eighboring Laos and Cambodia. In 'ambodia, a brutal Communist overnment, the Khmer Rouge, came to ower. Its leaders turned on their people, illing 1 million Cambodians. Vietnam, vhose entire nation had been a attleground for 30 years, was badly amaged. At least 2 million Vietnamese ad been killed. Rebuilding the country ook years of hard work.

In the late 1980s, Vietnamese leaders ecided to reform their society and timulate economic growth. They abandoned efforts to build a fully Communist society and decided instead to build a mixed economy. Foreign investment was encouraged. Vietnam has improved its position in foreign affairs. It signed a peace agreement with Cambodia in 1991. During the 1990s, Vietnam made serious attempts to improve ties with China and the United States, which established full diplomatic relations in 1995. Like the leadership in neighboring China, Vietnamese leaders have declared their support for a policy of "economic reform, political stability."

United States forces fought in Vietnam for ten years. More than 58,000 Americans died there.
What happened to Vietnam after the war?

LESSON 1 REVIEW

Fact Follow-Up
1. What cultures have influenced Southeast Asia over the centuries?
2. How did European and United States imperialism influence the economies of Southeast Asia?
3. Why did Southeast Asians first welcome Japanese expansion?
4. What were some of the tragic results of war in Vietnam?

Talk About It
1. Which culture do you think has had the most influence on life in Southeast Asia? Explain why.
2. How did European nations benefit from colonialism in Southeast Asia? Explain your choice.
3. How has Vietnam changed since the 1980s?

Discussion Questions
1 What were some of the tragic results of the Vietnamese War?

2 What is ironic about the fact that Vietnam is in the process of changing to a mixed economy?

3 Do you think it is important for nations and citizens to forget old enmities and do what is necessary to encourage global trade?

Caption Answer

South Vietnam collapsed in defeat, and a Communist-led dictatorship took control of the country.

Teacher Notes

Agent Orange
Much of the fighting during the Vietnam War took place in the thick swamps and jungles of Vietnam. The United States used helicopters to spray Agent Orange, a mixture of herbicides, to defoliate the forest areas concealing Communist forces and to destroy crops that might feed the enemy. The chemicals in Agent Orange caused significant health problems for the Vietnamese people and American forces. More recently the United States government has recognized the special needs of veterans who were exposed to Agent Orange.

LESSON 1 REVIEW

Fact Follow-Up Answers
1. India, China, and Western nations have influenced Southeast Asia. Muslim merchants also brought Islam to the region.
2. They set up plantations to grow a few cash crops (such as sugar, coffee, rubber, tea, and palm and coconut oils) to be sold in the West. Local farmers grew less rice and other food crops.
3. Japan's slogan "Asia for Asiatics" encouraged Southeast Asians to believe that the days of colonialism were over. Southeast Asians changed their minds when they saw that Japan wanted to control the region for raw materials, just as the Europeans had done.
4. Vietnam fell under a Communist-led dictatorship. The country was badly damaged by 30 years of war. At least 2 million Vietnamese died. The nation was rebuilt only after years of hard work. The war spread into Cambodia and Laos. In Cambodia, a brutal Communist government came to power and killed 1 million Cambodians. More than 58,000 Americans were killed in the war. Many more were disabled.

Talk About It Answers
1. Important points: Students should select one culture and explain its importance. India's religious tradition of Hinduism and Buddhism greatly influenced Southeast Asia. China contributed Confucianism, ideas about government, and art. The Western nations changed the economies, brought modern medical care, and opened schools that introduced ideas about freedom and democracy but did not encourage people to practice those ideas.
2. European nations gained access to the crops and raw materials of Southeast Asia. Their landowners and merchants profited from the resources and the labor of Southeast Asians. Their national economies were enriched.
3. Vietnam now has a policy of economic reform, political stability. It has relations with the United States again.

OBJECTIVES: 2.01, 3.01, 3.02, 5.01

Discussion Questions

1 Think about other places we have studied that grow coffee. What characteristics do these regions share?

2 What role has water played in the history of Southeast Asia?

3 How has the theme of location been important to the region?

Caption Answer

The name comes from the island of Java, in Indonesia, where strong coffee is grown in rich soil.

Writing Activity

Creation Stories

OBJECTIVES: 12.01, 12.02, 12.03

After students have read the creation legend found in Tanzania, have them compare it to creation stories with which they are familiar, such as one from Native American, Greek, or Norse mythology. Students can use graphic organizers for the comparisons. As a follow-up, have students write their own creation story as to how something in nature came about.

Extension ELL students can draw an explanation instead of writing one.

LESSON 2 People and Their Environment

KEY IDEAS

- Southeast Asia's importance was established long ago by its location on key water routes.
- The world also was drawn to the region by the export crops produced in its wet tropical climate.

KEY TERMS

Spice Islands

Have you ever heard anyone say, "I'd like a cup of Java?" In the United States, "java" is slang for coffee. Java is an island, part of Indonesia. It is famous for the strong coffee grown on its rich soil. Coffee is just one of many tropical products exported from Southeast Asia.

Five hundred years ago, Indonesia was better known for its spices. In fact, the archipelago was then known as the ***Spice Islands.*** This was the place Columbus wanted to find when he set sail in 1492.

A World Crossroads

Look at the list of Southeast Asian nations on page 497. Check their relative locations to China and India on the map. Notice that the region's nations lie *south* of China and *east* of India. The mainland nations of Southeast Asia jut southward from the continent, just as India does. The remainder of the region is a cluster of islands. They are scattered from the Indian Ocean east to the South China Sea.

Southeast Asia long has been a crossroads of the world. People, goods, and ideas flowed north and south through the Malay Peninsula between China and the islands.

The most important route flowed east and west through the Strait of Malacca. This waterway was the shortest, fastest route between the Indian Ocean and South China Sea. Ships have passed through these waters for thousands of years. Today, Singapore prospers from its location on this busy shipping lane.

Workers sort coffee beans in East Java, Indonesia. **Why is coffee sometimes called java in the United States?**

Lands and Climate

Southeast Asia's mainland nations contrast with the island nations. Their differences are due to landforms and climates.

Mainland Southeast Asia

Mainland Southeast Asia is wedged between two giants, India and China. It shares landforms with these neighbors. Mountain ranges slice through the region north to south. In the past, these highlands isolated people. As a result, today's national borders follow the mountain ranges.

Rivers flow from the interior highlands to the sea. The most important rivers are the Irrawaddy and Salween in Myanmar, the Chao Phraya in Thailand, and the Mekong. The Mekong flows through Laos, Cambodia, and Vietnam. At

Activity

Rice Paintings

OBJECTIVES: 1.01, 1.03

Rice Preparation Mix four or more drops of food coloring in a tablespoon of water. Pour into a plastic bag with 2 cups of uncooked white rice. Shake until the color is blended. Spread rice on newspapers to dry overnight. For darker colors use more food coloring or less rice.

Materials several containers of different colored rice, brown rice, school glue, 5-inch by 8-inch unlined index cards or lightweight poster board, pencils, toothpicks or craft sticks, and plastic spoons

Have students work together in groups to share containers of colored rice. They should write their names on one side of the card. One the other side they should draw a picture reflecting East or Southeast Asia, or a map or flag from the regions. Students should spread a thin layer of glue over one section to be filled in with colored rice. Rice is then sprinkled over the glue and pushed into proper position with the toothpick or craft stick. Rice should be only one layer deep. Continue this step until the picture is complete, and allow pictures to dry overnight.

Variations: If a three-dimensional effect is desired, a second layer may be added after the first layer is dry. For different effects, pastas, barley, tapioca, dried beans, or seeds may be used

ir mouths, the rivers broaden into great deltas. Silt carried downstream tilizes the river valleys and deltas.

Few people live in the rugged hlands. Most live in the river valleys. e earliest civilizations of Southeast Asia w up along the rivers. These rivers still ve as highways between villages. Their ters irrigate rice paddies.

Most of mainland Southeast Asia is pical with little change in temperatures. e tropics range from warm to hot.

Rainfall is linked to the monsoon. om May to October, southern winds ow over the mainland, bringing heavy wnpours. Myanmar receives as much as 7 inches (500 cm) of rain a year. From cember to April, northern winds bring weather. So people on the Southeast ian mainland think of seasons as wet or rather than as winter and summer.

land Southeast Asia

Thousands of islands occupy this part the region. Indonesia has more than ,000 of them. The Philippines has about)00. Many of the islands are little more n rocks in the ocean. Most people live a few larger islands.

Island Southeast Asia lies along the cific Ring of Fire (see page 506). You ght think that people would live far ay from the Ring of Fire's volcanoes, t the opposite is true. Volcanic ash athers into rich, black topsoil. Volcanic ls in Java (Indonesia) and Luzon nilippines) are some of Southeast Asia's ost fertile. As a result, these islands are nsely populated. Java is smaller than orth Carolina. Yet about 124 million people, about 55 percent of Indonesia's population, live there.

The islands have a hot tropical climate. It is hot and rainy all year, with no separate wet or dry seasons.

What would YOU do?

You live on a small volcanic island. You make a good living as a farmer with land that grows enough crops to sell. Your family has farmed this land for more than 20 years. Then you are told to leave. The volcano will erupt sometime soon. No one knows exactly when. If you leave, you lose your crops. If you stay, you might lose your life. What would you do?

Mainland Southeast Asia (top, in Myanmar) and island Southeast Asia (bottom, in Java, Indonesia) are located at a world crossroads. **How does the region's name show its location?**

Discussion Questions

1 What is a monsoon?

2 What part of the United States is affected by the Ring of Fire?

Caption Answer

It is south of China and east of India.

Writing Activity

River Trip

OBJECTIVES: 1.02, 2.03, 3.01, 3.04

Rivers play extremely important roles in Southeast Asia. They are widely used as major water highways. Have students choose one of the rivers in this region: the Mekong, Irrawaddy, Salween, or the Chao Phraya. They will prepare to take a trip down the river from its source to its mouth. Have students research using the Internet the areas they will travel through. From the length of the river, estimate how many days it will take to complete the journey.

Students will keep a journal and include: type of boat traveling in; country and types of terrain river passes through; what types of crops are being grown along the river; what kind of foods they can buy or trade for along the way; the types of plant and animal life; descriptions of the people, homes, customs, religious practices; what type of currency should be taken; what problems they see: flooding, hunger, injustices, government corruption; and a comparison of cities to rural areas.

Alternate ELL Activity Instead of a journal, have novice and intermediate ELL students make a diorama or poster of the area they researched using ELL-friendly Web sites.

Art Activity

Elephant Puzzle

OBJECTIVES: 2.01, 3.04

Elephants are valuable animals that have been used in Southeast Asia, especially in Myanmar and Thailand, for hundreds of years. Have students cut the tetrahedron pattern, found in the Teacher's Resource Guide, including cutting only to the center of the hexagon portion (not all the way through). Crease along all the lines and fold the triangles into a tetrahedron. The head, body, and tail of the elephant match up and the remaining face is blank. Either the blank face can be the base upon which to sit the tetrahedron or the triangle with string attached to hand the tetrahedron. Use transparent tape to close opening sides forming this tetrahedron.

Activity

Ring of Fire

NATIONAL GEOGRAPHY STANDARDS: 1, 4, 7, 15; **GEOGRAPHIC THEMES:** Location, Place, Human-Environmental Interaction, Region

OBJECTIVES: 1.07, 2.03, 3.01, 3.04

Students are to answer the following questions:

1. Which ocean is associated with the Ring of Fire? *Pacific*
2. Which area of the Ring of Fire has more earthquakes—Southeast Asia or Australia? *Southeast Asia*
3. Estimate whether there are more earthquakes north or south of the Equator. *north* Are there more east or west of 160°E? *east*
4. Are there earthquakes on the mainland of Southeast Asia? *yes*
5. Speculate why there are areas, including circular regions off the west coast of South America and East Asia, where few earthquakes occur. *many geologists state this absence is due to the boundaries of various tectonic plates*
6. Where would you choose to live in Southeast Asia if you wanted to avoid earthquake-prone areas? *Vietnam or Cambodia*
7. Which country's territory in Southeast Asia has so many earthquake symbols that they seem to form a solid-color mass on this map? *Indonesia*
8. Why is it difficult to see all of the land for the Philippines and Japan? *green-colored countries/continents are densely covered by red dots representing earthquakes*
9. Are there earthquakes shown in North Carolina? *yes*
10. If you were a seismologist studying earthquakes, where along the Ring of Fire would you choose to conduct your research? Why? *individual answers with supporting elaboration are necessary*

CONNECTIONS • GEOGRAPHY & SCIENCE •

RING OF FIRE

Volcanoes

On August 27, 1883, a volcano on the island of Krakatau, west of Java, exploded with the force of many atomic bombs. The explosion was so loud it was heard in Australia, more than 2,000 miles (3,220 km) away. The eruption sent a 100-foot (30-m) tsunami crashing into Java, killing thousands of people.

Volcanoes, large vents or openings in the surface of the earth, allow ash and different gases to erupt. There are about 800 active volcanoes in the world today. More than 75 percent of these active volcanoes are located in the Pacific Ocean's Ring of Fire. The name comes from the concentration of volcanic and earthquake activity that rings the Pacific Ocean. Hot magma can potentially explode along the rim of the Pacific Ocean. The Ring of Fire includes the Asian islands of Japan, the Philippines, and Indonesia. It circles northward and eastward toward North America and extends southward along the western coast of the Americas.

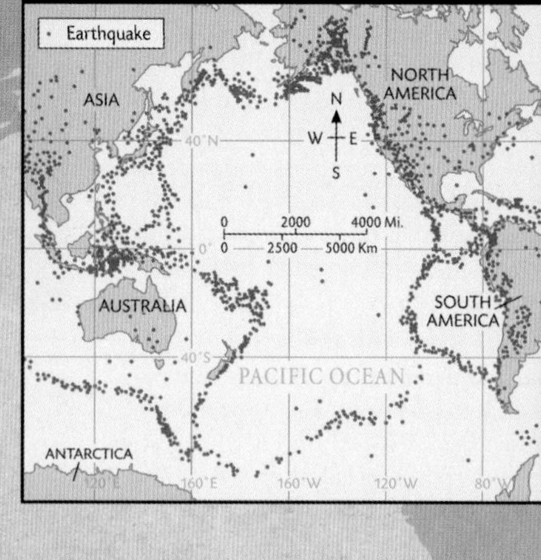

Indonesia has 70 active volcanoes. In one area of Japan, children wear hard hats because they live so close to active volcanoes.

Now people might be warned of a possible volcanic eruption and leave before it happens. In 1991, Mount Pinatubo in the Philippines erupted. Scientists had warned of the explosion, and nearly 200,000 people left the area. Lava and ash from Pinatubo buried the American naval base at Subic Bay. After the eruption, people had to wear filter masks so they could breathe without inhaling ash. Pinatubo shot so much dust into the atmosphere that, for months, sunsets all over the world took on a dusky orange hue. Volcanoes act like nature's cannons, shooting ash and gases that can harm us.

Ash from the eruption of Mount Pinatubu in the Philippines

506 Chapter 25

Activity

Mount Pinatubo and Other Famous Volcanoes of the World

OBJECTIVES: 2.01, 3.04

Ask students to name some of the world's existing volcanoes that they have heard of. Discuss the difference between inactive and active volcanoes. Have students recall what they know about Mount St. Helen's. Compare it to the Ring of Fire and Mount Pinatubo. Assign one group to investigate how volcanoes work. Assign another group to determine how volcanoes are detected and the technology involved in volcano research. Have each group present their findings to the class.

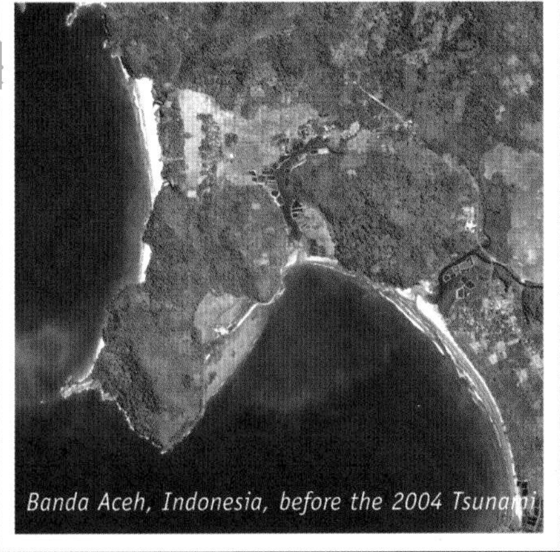

Banda Aceh, Indonesia, before the 2004 Tsunami

Banda Aceh, Indonesia, after the 2004 Tsunami

Tsunamis

Tsunamis caused by volcanic eruptions can also have devastating effects. On December 26, 2004, a massive earthquake occurred under the Indian Ocean just off the coast of the Island of Sumatra, Indonesia. The 9.1 magnitude quake created a series of tsunamis that caused great destruction and loss of life.

Within several hours of the quake, tsunamis rippled throughout the Indian Ocean. These tremendous waves devastated not only coastal areas of Indonesia but the coasts of India, Sri Lanka, the Maldives, Myanmar (Burma), and Thailand. Effects were even felt as far away as the eastern coast of Africa.

About 1.69 million people lost their homes. More than 184,000 people died; at least 45,000 others remain missing. The exact number of victims will probably never be known.

Survivors walk amid the 2004 Tsunami debris in Banda Aceh, Sumatra, Indonesia.

Discussion Questions

1 Explain why the RIng of Fire can be so deadly.

2 One of the reasons the 2004 Tsunami was so devastating was that there was no tsunami warning system in the Indian Ocean. Why do you think that was so?

Activity

Coconut Beef Patties

 **OBJECTIVES:** 3.01

Many dishes in Southeast Asia use coconut and coconut milk.

Ingredients

1 pound lean ground beef
3 3½ ounce packages (4 cups) unsweetened flaked coconut
1 egg
2 teaspoons ground coriander
2 finely chopped garlic cloves
⅛ teaspoon ground cumin
2 teaspoons salt
¼ teaspoon pepper
½ cup cooking oil

In large bowl, combine all ingredients except oil. Beat with wooden spoon until mixture is light and fluffy. Form it into patties, each about ½-inch thick. Heat oil in large skillet. Fry patties, about 8 minutes on each side, until crisp and dark brown.

Background Information

Smoke Signals

Besides deforestation, Southeast Asia has another environmental problem in its woodlands. The massive burning of forests is causing smog and other forms of air pollution. As Southeast Asian nations industrialize, more and more land is cleared. Burning is often the cheapest way to clear the land. Logging companies, small farmers, and owners of large plantations all use this method. Most Southeast Asian governments lack the money or the political will to enforce environmental laws limiting unrestricted burning. In 1996 forest fires in Indonesia caused smoke so thick in Kuala Lumpur, the Malaysian capital, that students wore surgical masks in schools. Smog blanketed six Southeast Asian countries closing airports, contributing to ship collisions, and reducing tourism.

Discussion Questions

1 What are some of the resources found in Southeast Asia?

2 Java's population is ten times more dense than that of North Carolina. If you lived in Java, how would your life be different, based on these statistics?

Caption Answer

Spices, rubber, palm and coconut oil, rice, and lumber.

Activity

Crops Flow Chart

OBJECTIVES: 5.4, 13.03

Southeast Asia grows many crops that are consumed worldwide. In groups, have students select a product and research the steps involved: growing the crop, processing it, and finally getting it to the consumer. On poster board, create a flow chart showing the steps involved.

Southeast Asian products include: rubber, tea, palm nut oil, coconuts, rice, cinnamon, pepper, coffee, and hardwoods teak, mahogany, and ebony.

Mechanical harvesters shave leaves off tea bushes, one of Southeast Asia's major export crops (right). Rice terraces cover the mountainsides in Luzon, Philippines. They are considered to be among the finest fields in the country (below). **What are the other farm products and natural resources exported by Southeast Asia?**

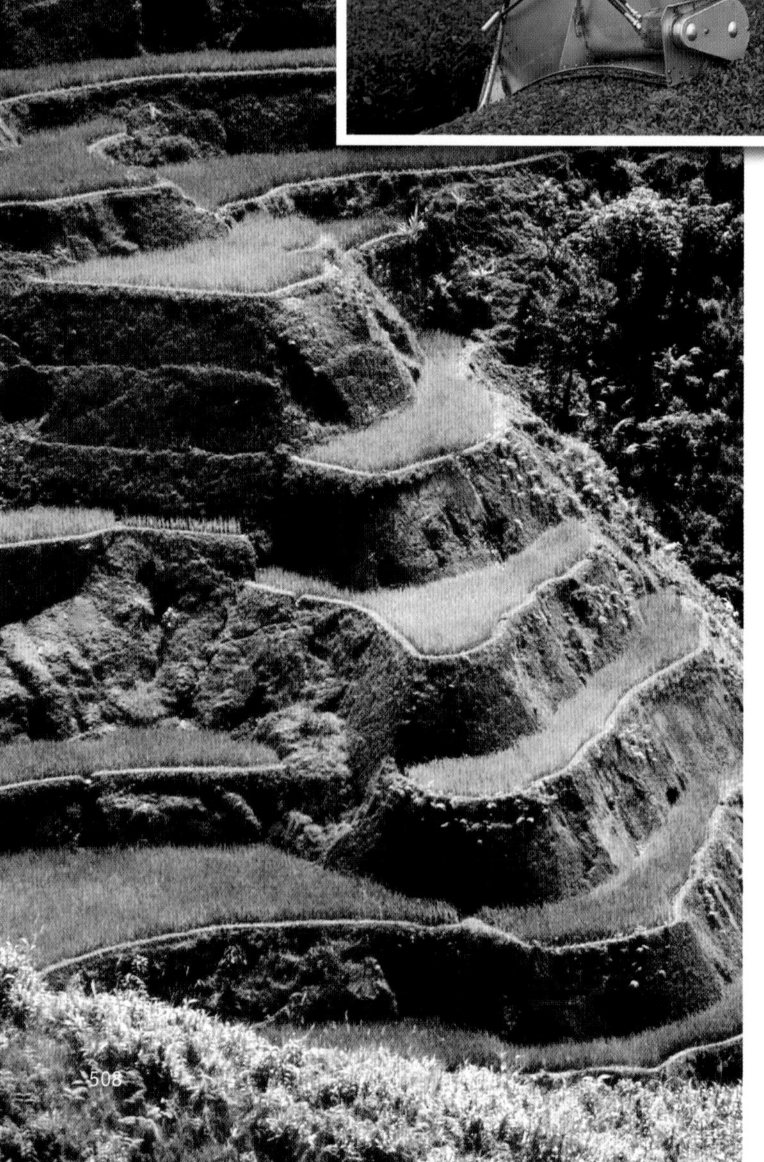

Natural Resources

Most Southeast Asians are farmers. Some countries have factories, but the region's economy is based mainly on the export of raw materials and farm products.

Spices are still an important export, but the region sells many other goods. In the 1800s, Europeans colonized the region. They brought new crops, includin rubber trees from Brazil. Today, Southeas Asia produces 80 percent of the world's natural rubber.

The Dutch set up tea plantations, still a major export for Indonesia. Palm and coconut oil are exported from the islands of Southeast Asia. These oils are used in food processing and are sold as cooking oils.

The region's warm temperatures and abundant water are ideal for growing rice Farmers have built terraces like steps climbing up steep mountainsides. These catch and hold water, so that land for growing rice has been expanded. Southeast Asia grows enough rice for its own people and for export.

Fishing, too, is a major industry. Fresl and dried fish are a major source of protein in the region's diets.

Background Information

The Sweatshop Controversy

Should Americans protest working conditions in cramped, poorly ventilated Southeast Asian factories where adults and children labor seven days a week for very low wages in largely unsafe conditions? Some Americans have written angry letters to United States companies that produce shoes, toys, and other products in such factories. However, others say that closing down these factories will hurt the very people it intends to help. They argue that the best way to improve working conditions is to buy more of the products such factories produce. They point to the experience of South Korea and Taiwan, where income from sales of products made in sweatshops generated more jobs and led eventually to higher wages, improved working conditions, and a higher standard of living.

:ndangered Forests

A century ago, Europeans admired the orests that covered plains and mountains or hundreds of miles. Tropical rain forests till blanket parts of Myanmar, Thailand, Malaysia, Indonesia, and the Philippines. .oggers, however, are rapidly cutting such ardwood trees as teak, ebony, and nahogany. These valuable woods are sent o Japan, Europe, and the Americas.

Clearing rain forests has hurt the environment. Once trees are gone, soils wash away in heavy downpours. Plant and animal life are destroyed.

Southeast Asian nations face hard choices. They need money from timber sales to develop their economies. Under pressure, some governments have taken steps to protect the rain forests. In 1989, for example, Thailand banned logging in many parts of the country.

Borneo logging operations have stripped acres of rain forest. **Why is it important to replace the forest?**

LESSON 2 REVIEW

Fact Follow-Up

1. Describe the relative location of Southeast Asia.
2. Why was Indonesia once called the Spice Islands?
3. Describe the climate of Southeast Asia.
4. What are some natural hazards to people in Southeast Asia?
5. What are the major natural products of Southeast Asia?

Talk About It

1. Why do people of island Southeast Asia live near volcanoes?
2. What is the most difficult economic challenge faced by Southeast Asian nations? Explain your choice.
3. Why is Southeast Asia a world crossroads?

Discussion Questions

1 Companies in the United States realize the importance of protecting the environment and endangered forests. Many are now refusing to sell products from these forests. What would you say to a business that continues to sell imported wood products to get them to stop?

2 What would you say to leaders of Indonesia and countries that need the income derived from the sale of valuable woods? What suggestions would you give them as to how the countries could develop their economies?

Once trees are gone, soils wash away in heavy downpours. Plant and animal life are destroyed.

Endangered Orangutan

OBJECTIVES: 3.02, 11.02

The most endangered species in Southeast Asia is the orangutan. Using the Internet, have students research orangutans: physical characteristics, diet, habitat, and range. In groups, have students devise a recovery plan that will help remove orangutans from the endangered species list. Consideration should be given to human needs. Allow each group to present its plan and then have the class vote on the "best plan."

LESSON 2 REVIEW

Fact Follow-Up Answers

1. Southeast Asia is south of China and east of India. Its mainland juts southward from the continent of Asia. The remainder of the region is a cluster of islands scattered from the Indian Ocean east to the South China Sea.
2. Indonesia was well known for the spices it produced. This was the place Columbus wanted to find when he set sail in 1492.
3. Most of mainland Southeast Asia is tropical with little change in temperatures. The Tropics range from warm to hot. Rainfall is linked to the monsoon. The months from May to October have heavy downpours; December to April is the dry season. Island Southeast Asia has a hot, tropical climate. It is hot and rainy all year, with no distinct wet or dry seasons.
4. Volcanoes, earthquakes, and tsunamis present great danger to people in Southeast Asia.
5. The major products are coffee, spices, rubber, tea, palm and coconut oil, rice, and valuable timber such as teak, ebony, and mahogany.

Talk About It Answers

1. Volcanic soil is rich and good for farming.
2. Important points: Students should choose one economic challenge and explain their choice. The region relies on money from the sale of timber, but the cutting down of the rain forest has caused environmental damage. The nations of the region must develop their economies without destroying the environment.
3. Major trade routes pass through this region. Also, world powers from both the West and East have built colonies and influenced life here.

OBJECTIVES: 6.02, 9.02, 10.02, 13.03

Discussion Questions

1 What is courage? For what would you be willing to sacrifice?

2 What role do political parties play in a democracy?

3 The United States at one time was a colony of Great Britain. Why do you suppose we were able to create a democratic government rather than an authoritarian one, such as is found in some Southeast Asian countries?

She was awarded the Nobel Peace Prize. She has lost personal freedom.

Consider Character Socratic Seminar

OBJECTIVES: 4.03

Before the seminar, chose a Southeast Asian leader, such as Aung San Suu Kyi or Corazon Aquino. Assign students to do additional research the person's life. Have students take a notes on things in the person's life that reflect the character traits of courage, good judgment, integrity, kindness, perseverance, respect, responsibility, self-discipline, and good citizenship.

Opening Question: What is it about this person's experience and character that makes/made them a strong leader?

Suggested Stem Questions:

Support

- Can you give us an example of the decisions this person made?
- Why do you think he or she might have made that decision?
- What character traits does this person demonstrate?

Cause and Effect

- Why do you think that happened?
- How could that have been prevented?
- Do you think that would happen that way again? Why?
- What are some reasons people . . .?
- Would that still happen if . . . ?
- What might have made the difference in the way things turned out?

LESSON  Governments and Economies

KEY IDEAS

- The Philippines enjoy democratic rights. Some Southeast Asian governments, however, are authoritarian.
- Several nations are undergoing rapid economic development. They are exporting agricultural and forest products and building modern industries.
- Economic development is encouraging the movement of people to cities.

KEY TERMS

ASEAN

In July 1989, police surrounded the home of Aung San Suu Kyi. She was taken by the police and forced to live under "house arrest." Her crime was trying to bring democracy to Myanmar (Burma). In 1991, she was awarded the Nobel Peace Prize for her courageous fight. The country's military rulers refused to release Kyi until 1995. The rulers then placed her under house arrest again from 2000 to 2002 and in 2005. She remains indefinitely a prisoner of the government. The rulers continue to harass and restrict her and her followers. The military has not surrendered power.

Kyi was a natural leader of the pro-democracy forces. Her father, also a nationalist leader, had helped the country win freedom from British rule. Today, Kyi still hopes that democracy will replace Myanmar's unpopular military government.

Aung San Suu Kyi is a leader of the democracy movement in Myanmar (Burma). **What has she gained for her efforts? What has she lost?**

COUNTRY	TYPE OF GOVERNMENT
BRUNEI	constitutional sultanate
CAMBODIA	multiparty democracy under a constitutional monarchy
EAST TIMOR	republic
INDONESIA	republic
LAOS	Communist state
MALAYSIA	constitutional monarchy
MYANMAR (BURMA)	military junta
PHILIPPINES	republic
SINGAPORE	parliamentary republic
THAILAND	constitutional monarchy
VIETNAM	Communist state

*Source: 2007 U.S. Central Intelligence Agency's World Factbook

Democracy Versus Authoritarian Rule

Some Southeast Asian countries have authoritarian governments. Each country has a constitution that promises citizens the right to vote. But elections—if they are held—are strictly controlled. Political parties opposed to ruling governments are usually outlawed. Freedom of speech is limited. Critics of government are often jailed for many years.

Authoritarian governments in Southeast Asia are partly the result of the region's colonial experience. European colonial powers did not permit native people to have much of a role in governmental affairs. Only the Philippines enjoyed some experience with democracy

Compare / Contrast

- How are __________ and ________ alike? Different?
- What is that similar to?

Point of View / Perspective

- How might she/he have felt . . .?
- What do you think he/she was thinking when . . .?
- Can you think of someone who has had a similar experience and made a different decision?
- Do you have a different interpretation?
- How did you arrive at your view?

Structure / Function

- If that was the goal, what do you think about . . (the action, reaction)?
- What were her/his choices of how to . . .?
- Why was she/he doing that? What do you think of that approach?
- What better choices could he/she have made?

Personal Experience

- What are some things that you wonder about?
- What would you like to know about?
- What would you do in that situation?
- Has anything like that ever happened to you?
- In what way are you alike or different from . . .?

See the Socratic Seminar Guidelines in the front of the Teacher's Edition.

nder the United States. Overall, however, emocratic government has not had much f a foundation on which to build in outheast Asia.

The Philippines has the most emocratic government in the region. Yet ven Filipinos lost their rights for years. In 965, Ferdinand Marcos was elected resident, but he led a military ictatorship for almost 20 years. Under ressure, he agreed to elections. He lost ut refused to give up power. Filipinos rotested in the streets. Faced with this people's revolution," Marcos fled. A ewly elected president, Corazon Aquino, ook office.

Economic Development

Bangkok, Thailand, is a showcase for outheast Asia's economic development. Not so long ago, it was a city of green rees and peaceful canals. Today, the anals are gone. They were filled in to viden the streets. Superhighways cross the ity. Yet traffic still grinds to a halt at rush our.

Skyscrapers dwarf Buddhist temples. "We're beginning to look like any other ity," says a Bangkok resident. "Now verybody is hurrying, hurrying, money n their minds."

Not all the old ways are gone. Even in ustling Bangkok, some Thai people try not to get irritated when stuck in a traffic am. "At such times, we meditate," one lriver explains. "It is the Buddhist way."

Southeast Asian nations have been rying to increase farm output, create nodern industries, and improve life for heir people. The Green Revolution of the 1960s gave a boost to farm output. Farmers produced larger crops with new kinds of rice.

Only farmers with money to spare could buy the fertilizers and pesticides needed to grow new crops. Many poor peasants had to sell their land. They could not compete with wealthier farmers. Some of these landless farmers stayed in their villages. They worked as hired hands. Others, especially young people, moved to cities.

These changes affect village life. Villages are less isolated than they once were. Buses and motorcycles carry people back and forth between their villages and nearby towns or cities. Many villagers now have radios and television sets that put them in touch with the larger world.

As you have read, Southeast Asian nations earn much of their income from exporting raw materials and agricultural products. They are now trying to increase wealth by developing their own industries. In the 1990s, governments looked for foreign investors. Japanese, American, and European companies set up joint projects with local businesses. With foreign capital, local business leaders built textile factories and other industries that paid low wages to workers who had few skills. Many newer industries, such as those that assemble computers, are now manufacturing high-technology products.

Corazon Aquino was elected president of the Philippines after Ferdinand Marcos gave up his office. **What kind of governments do most nations in Southeast Asia have?**

Discussion Questions

1 What is progress? Is the price sometimes paid for progress worth it?

2 Road rage and anger management are becoming more serious issues in our country. What are some ways people use to handle stress?

3 Should foreign companies invest in countries where wages are low? These developing economies need the investment, but is it taking advantage of the workers, and what does it do to the economies and workers in the home countries?

Caption Answer

Most have some form of democratic government

Activity

Panel Discussion/Debate

OBJECTIVES: 9.02, 9.04, 10.03

Have students write about one of the following topics:

- Which is more important, democratic rights or authoritarian rule?
- Discuss your preference, preserving old traditions or creating modern developments.
- Which would be more comfortable, personal freedom or orderly controls?

Have a panel discussion to allow students to discuss important positions and issues written about.

Form debate groups to allow students to verbally express their opinions, ideas, and beliefs.

After presentations or debates have been completed, the audience will discuss the most compelling arguments on each side of the debate.

1. Democratic Rights versus Authoritarian Rule
2. Preserving Old Traditions versus Creating Modern Developments
3. Personal Freedoms versus Orderly Control

It's a Fact

Southeast Asia

■ Brunei's full name is Brunei Darussalam, which means "abode of peace." Education, including attendance at foreign universities, is paid for by the government. Half of the working population is employed by the government. It has the world's largest palace—1,788 rooms, covering 50 acres. The official religion is Islam. No discos, nightclubs, or concerts are allowed. It is about the size of Delaware.

■ Cambodia's stilt houses are built in monsoon regions that can receive up to 200 inches (508 cm) of rain a year.

■ Myanmar, about the size of Texas, is the largest country on the Southeast Asian mainland. Women keep their own name after marriage and share property ownership. Colleges and universities have been closed in an effort to suppress democracy.

■ Laos is one of the world's most undeveloped countries. Eighty percent of the population is rural. Only 3 percent of land is arable. It has no railroads, and water must be boiled before drinking.

Discussion Questions

1 Would you rather live in a city or in a rural area? What would be the benefits of each? What would be the drawbacks of each?

2 Why do economic experts say that Southeast Asia is an area to watch?

Caption Answer

Southeast Asian cities are growing because of both the growth of their economies and the movement of people from the countryside to the cities.

Activity

Who's Who in Southeast Asia

OBJECTIVES: 3.01, 4.02, 9.02, 13.03

Materials posterboard or white bulletin board paper; markers; magazines/ product labels; encyclopedias/*National Geographics*/software data

Assignment Divide the class into groups of four to research a specific Southeast Asian country and produce a poster-collage addressing the following items: access (trade routes); type of government; natural resources; agricultural products; and major industries.

Each group will present their country to the class with the emphasis being placed on trying to attract foreign investors. Poster collages may be hung to create a bulletin board.

Extension ELL students should use an ELL-friendly Web site for research. Do not assign novice and intermediate the presentation.

The second-tallest buildings in the world, the twin Petronas Towers, rise above the office buildings of Kuala Lampur, Malaysia. **Why are Southeast Asian cities growing?**

The Move to Cities

Prateep lives in a crowded Bangkok slum. "My parents were fishermen on the coast," she said. One day a great storm wrecked all that they had. "So they moved here in search of opportunity." Prateep studied to become a teacher. "I worked on the docks to pay for my education," she said.

Although Prateep could leave the slums, she stayed. She opened a school and health clinic. She organized residents to push the government for water, electricity, and sewer services.

Throughout Southeast Asia, millions of people migrate each year from villages to big cities. Most arrive with little or no money. Life is hard. Yet young people hope to do better than their parents. In villages they would become rice farmers o fishermen. In the cities they have more choices.

It's a Fact

Southeast Asia

■ Thailand is a patriarchal society from the monarchy on down. The size of Texas, it is the world's largest exporter of rice and shrimp.

■ Vietnam. the size of New Mexic, has the oldest capital city in Southeast Asia, established in A.D. 1010. Only 1 percent of the population owns a car. About 27 percent of the population is under the age of 14.

■ Indonesia has 60 active volcanoes. Seven percent of the land area (island of Java) is occupied by 60 percent of Indonesia's population. Two and a half million acres of rain forest are cut down annually. It is the home of the Komodo Dragon, the world's largest lizard.

■ Philippines, the size of Nevada, has 7,100 islands, but many are uninhabitable because they lack water. Three fourths of the people live in poverty; there is a small middle class. The country averages five typhoons a year. The voting age is fifteen. Farming is still done on terraces that date back more than 2,000 years.

■ Singapore is second only to Japan in its standard of living. It is the size of New York City. Ninety percent of the population lives in the city of Singapore. All education is conducted in English.

■ Two thirds of Malaysia's land is jungle. The constitutional monarch, the "Paramount Ruler," is elected every 5 years by 13 hereditary rulers.

13th ASEAN REGIONAL FORUM
KUALA LUMPUR, MALAYSIA
28 JULY 2006

Foreign ministers from Southeast Asian nations and the United States stand together at the conclusion of an ASEAN meeting in Kuala Lumpur, Malaysia. **What are the goals of ASEAN?**

The Future

Economic experts say that Southeast Asia is a key region to watch. The economies of several countries are growing, especially in Thailand, Malaysia, Indonesia, and Singapore.

Vietnam is still ruled by a Communist government. Yet it encourages private enterprise to promote economic expansion. The government is trying to attract foreign investors to help develop factories, farms, and roads. Some businesses are willing to take the risk. "This is one of the last frontiers of the business world," said the manager of an American company investing in Vietnam.

Like many new nations in Africa, independent nations of Southeast Asia at first traded almost entirely with their former rulers. More recently, as a way of promoting economic growth, these nations have been cooperating with one another. In 1967, six nations in the region pledged to lay aside quarrels with one another. Brunei, Indonesia, Malaysia, Philippines, Singapore, and Thailand established the ***Association of Southeast Asian Nations*** (ASEAN).

The organization's goals are similar to the European Union's goals for Europe. The members are trying to resolve the region's social and economic problems by working together. ASEAN has successfully promoted good working relationships among the region's nations. Along with China, Korea, and Japan, ASEAN's members are enjoying the benefits of expanding trade on Asia's Pacific Rim.

LESSON 3 REVIEW

Fact Follow-Up

1. Describe the governments of Southeast Asian nations.
2. How has economic development affected such cities as Bangkok, Thailand?
3. Which Southeast Asian nations are most prosperous?
4. What is the Association of Southeast Asian Nations (ASEAN), and what are its goals?

Talk About It

1. How can governments have constitutions and be authoritarian?
2. What is the greatest political challenge facing Southeast Asia? Explain.
3. What do you think is the greatest economic challenge facing Southeast Asia? Explain.

 **OBJECTIVES:** 6.01, 6.02, 12.01, 12.02

Discussion Questions

1. Do you think the members of ASEAN will be more successful in working together than the European Union or a pan-African movement? Why?
2. As these countries grow in wealth, do you think their individual goals will change?

The goals of ASEAN are to resolve the region's social and economic problems by working together.

LESSON 3 REVIEW

Fact Follow-Up Answers

1. Most Southeast Asian nations no longer have authoritarian governments. Some nations are Communist, and their economies are under government control. The Philippines has the most democratic government in the region.
2. Not long ago, Bangkok was a city of green trees and peaceful canals. Now superhighways cross the city and skyscrapers dwarf Buddhist temples. It is crowded and the pace of life has become very fast.
3. The most prosperous Southeast Asian nations are Thailand, Malaysia, Indonesia, and Singapore.
4. ASEAN includes the nations of Brunei, Indonesia, Malaysia, Philippines, Singapore, and Thailand. ASEAN's goals are to promote good working relationships and economic growth among its members.

Talk About It Answers

1. Important points: Simply having a constitution does not guarantee democracy. Elections, if held, may be tightly controlled; freedom of speech may be limited. Such governments often fix elections through corruption or intimidation.
2. Important points: Students should choose one challenge and explain their choice. Democratic government is a goal in many nations. Reducing the power of authoritarian governments and assuring that written constitutions are followed in practice is another.
3. Important points: Students should choose one challenge and explain their choice. Expanding trade within the region, building productive economies without destroying the environment, developing industries that produce goods to meet the needs of their own people—all are among the challenges facing these nations.

OBJECTIVES: 6.01, 6.02, 12.01, 12.02

Discussion Questions

1 What is meant by the quote "harmony among man, earth, and heaven"? What happens when there is no longer this harmony?

2 What role does Buddhism play in the everyday lives of the people of Thailand?

3 Monasteries have many functions in Thai life. Is there a place in our community that has a function similar to that of a monastery?

Caption Answer

The monastery is a religious and cultural center. Women gather there to watch their children play. Monasteries often hold fairs that villagers enjoy. At one time, they also served as schools and hospitals.

Activity

Graph

OBJECTIVES: 1.02, 4.01, 5.03, 6.01

Divide class into pairs. Each pair should choose one item from the list below to graph. Research the information on the ten countries of Southeast Asia. Choose a bar graph, pictograph, or pie graph. When graphing is completed, rank the countries from highest to lowest. Each group will present its graph and record on the board the highest and lowest countries under each item. When all the presentations are completed, students decide if each country is developed or developing. Students should explain reasons to support their decisions and other conclusions from the graphs.

- per capita GDP
- percentage of population under age of fifteen
- literacy rate (male/female)
- percentage annual population growth
- life expectancy population density
- percentage rural/urban population
- labor force
- percentage of population > than 65
- number of physicians
- infant mortality rate
- exports/imports
- number of televisions
- number of radios
- number of telephones

Extension This activity is suitable for both novice and intermediate ELL students if the partner is a stronger/advanced student.

LESSON  Society and Culture

KEY IDEAS

- Age-old traditions and modern ways exist side by side throughout Southeast Asia.
- Buddhism, one of the region's major religions, continues to play a prominent role in daily life. Yet modern life may be weakening the faith.
- Singapore illustrates the mixing of traditional Confucian ideals with modern urban life.

The world of Wong Li is changing. Wong owns a small furniture-making business in Kuala Lumpur, the capital of Malaysia. In a workshop, his employees use hand tools to fashion chairs out of rattan. Wong keeps his accounts on an abacus, an ancient kind of calculator.

Nearby, Wong's nephew runs a large electronics store. Every day the store delivers MP3 players and DVDs. The young man uses a computer to keep track of his stock. Wong and his nephew work in the same neighborhood, but they live in different worlds.

Southeast Asians welcome new economic opportunities, but rapid change threatens long-held values. "Traditionally, there was harmony among man, earth and heaven," one Vietnamese says. To many, that harmony now seems under attack. Many wonder how to balance old and traditional with the new and modern.

A Buddhist monk begs for food in Thailand. **What role do monasteries play in village life?**

Customs

Monks are allowed to eat only between dawn and noon. They must beg for their food. The people who share food with the monks are not upset when a monk stops at their door. Buddhists believe that charity is a good deed that brings spiritual reward. So the monk is thanked at each house for accepting the food.

Every Man a Monk

Before dawn, a young man moves silently through a Thai village. He wears orange-colored robes and carries a tin "begging" bowl. At one house, a woman puts rice wrapped in a banana leaf into his bowl. Without speaking, he moves on to another house.

The young man is a Buddhist monk. He is part of a 2,000-year-old tradition. In the past, all young men spent a part of their lives as monks. Today, about half of Thailand's young men become monks. Most are monks for only a few months, often just before they marry. Becoming a monk prepares them for adulthood.

The monastery is a place for meditation. Yet it is not a place of gloomy silence. The monastery in most villages is a religious and cultural center. Women gather there to chat or watch their children play. Monasteries hold fairs that villagers enjoy. Historically, monasteries have served as schools and hospitals. Most children now attend government schools. People seek medical help elsewhere.

514 Chapter 25

)rderly Singapore

Singapore is an island, a nation, and city all at the same time. It is less than ne-fifth the size of Rhode Island and has o natural resources, except its harbor. Yet s population numbers 4.3 million people. is the richest country in the region.

Singapore is located on one of the orld's busiest shipping lanes. The cation is ideal for gathering Southeast sia's goods—oil from Indonesia or tin id rubber from Malaysia—for shipping the world's ports. Goods headed for aces in Southeast Asia usually pass rough Singapore.

Singapore became an important Asian ort during its days as a colony of the nited Kingdom. High technology helped ingapore become the busiest port in the orld in 2005. Automated equipment andles freight brought to the port in erchant vessels. Electronic devices help orkers track cargo quickly as it is moved om one ship to another. Trade has made ingapore a world leader in banking, idustry, and tourism.

Officially, Singapore is a democracy. ee Kwan Yew was the nation's first prime iinister. He ruled from 1959 until 1990, nd is still influential. Lee grew up with aditional Chinese ideals, prizing self-iscipline, hard work, and education.

Lee's strict control as prime minister shaped modern Singapore. It reflects his commitment to Confucian ethics and values. Singapore's government urges people to smile. No one should chew gum because it is impolite. Littering or jaywalking brings big fines. Homeowners are fined if they allow water puddles to stand in their yards—the puddles could become mosquito breeding grounds.

Lee's regulations have not bothered most residents. They enjoy the nation's high standard of living. Singapore also makes services available that are almost unknown in Southeast Asia. The government has built apartment houses to ease the housing shortage, provides low-cost medical care, and supports excellent schools. It has relaxed just a few social laws, since Lee left office.

Singapore is Southeast Asia's wealthiest nation. **How has its port helped Singapore gain this position?**

A transit train in Singapore is kept spotless, like all public places. **How does the nation reflect the Confucian beliefs of former Prime Minister Lee Kwan Yew?**

Discussion Questions

1 As densely populated as Singapore is, what are some possible reasons for the many fines the people have there?

2 Singapore is a thriving country, partly because of its location. If you could create the ideal country, which of the Five Themes of Geography would you consider the most important? Explain your answer.

3 People in the United States often complain that the government is too big. Would the people in Singapore think their government is too big?

Caption Answer

It is located on an important shipping lane. High-tech has helped it become the world's busiest port.

Caption Answer

Lee Kwan Yew believes in the Confucian values of self-discipline, hard work, and education. Singapore's people adhere to strict rules regarding politeness and cleanliness, and the government provides good health care, housing, and education.

Activity

Coconut Custard (Laos)

OBJECTIVES: 3.01

Ingredients

½ cup whole wheat flour
¼ teaspoon salt
½ teaspoon baking soda
¾ cup brown sugar
1½ cups canned thick coconut milk
5 eggs

Preheat oven to 350° F. In medium-size bowl, beat eggs lightly with fork. Stir in coconut milk. Set aside. In large bowl, combine flour, salt, baking soda, and brown sugar. Stir in coconut milk mixture, a little at a time, stirring well after each addition. Pour batter into shallow oven-proof baking dish. Bake for 40 minutes, or until puffy and golden brown. (You may want to put a pan of water on the lower shelf in the oven to keep the custard moist.) Serve immediately.

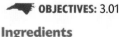

Background Information

All Wet at Thailand's Water Festival

During Thailand's annual water festival of Songkran, many families in Bangkok think the best way to celebrate is to stay off the streets. There's good reason to be home-bound for this festival. Young people roam the streets armed with water buckets, high-pressure hoses, water bombs, squirt guns, and water rifles. They ride around in pickup trucks tossing barrels of water on pedestrians or stand on corners with fire hoses squirting at buses when doors or windows open. In earlier times this festival was a time for villagers to show respect for elders by sprinkling them with a few drops of scented water. Families visited temples and ancient statues of Buddha. Today celebrants have to be prepared to give and get a good soaking.

Discussion Questions

1 Why is it so important to teach the arts and to make certain they remain alive in a culture?

2 What do the arts reflect about a culture?

3 Suppose you wanted to restrict your study of Asia to "the arts." What would you include? Do you think the definition of "art" changes from culture to culture?

Caption Answer

The puppet shows tell ancient stories about kings, heroes, and battles. Some recall Indonesia's fight for independence.

Activity

Shadow Puppets

OBJECTIVES: 11.01, 12.01, 12.02

Review with students the art of shadow puppetry. Students will do shadow plays by cutting out small characters and scenery from construction paper. Paper cutouts are attached to pencils manipulated on an overhead to present a short play. Ideas for shadow plays are skits written by students demonstrating knowledge of Asian beliefs, facts about Southeast Asian culture, or Asian folk tales.

Puppeteers move shadow puppets to embrace in midair. **How do such shows reflect the history of the region?**

Art that Entertains

From Indonesia to Thailand, puppet shows are popular as entertainment and as an art form. When puppeteers arrive in a village, everyone from old to young prepares for the show. The performance often lasts from 9:00 P.M. to 6:00 A.M., nine hours altogether. Audiences will return home exhausted but happy.

The puppeteers set up a white screen with a lamp behind. The puppets are moved about in the space between the lan and the screen. The audience sees the puppets' shadows dance across the screen The puppeteers and several singers sometimes tell ancient stories about kings, heroes, and battles. Other plays have a more modern setting. They recall Indonesia's fight for independence.

The puppets that cast the shadows are sometimes one-dimensional, flat cutouts. Others are more lifelike three-dimensional figures. Their form, however, really does not matter. Each puppet is a work of art. Most are made of leather and are painted in gold or other colors.

Puppet theater is only one of many traditional arts that the public appreciates Local audiences and tourists also enjoy the elaborate classical dance forms of Bali (an island in Indonesia). Flutes, strings, and percussion instruments create the distinctive sounds of gamelan orchestras. Batik fabric, created by an ancient wax-dy process, is a popular material for clothing, tablecloths, and banners. Some Southeast Asian governments help keep traditional arts alive by opening theaters where artists perform. Government-owned stores provi outlets for traditional crafts.

As in many countries, beautifully decorated kites are built for flying. This recreation is sometimes turned into competitive sport. Kite flyers maneuver their kites to knock an opponent's kite ou of the air.

LESSON 4 REVIEW

Fact Follow-Up

1. How does the relative location of Singapore benefit that nation?
2. How does the government of Singapore influence the everyday lives of people?
3. What are some popular art forms in Southeast Asia?
4. What does the saying "Every man a monk" mean? Is it accurate? Explain.

Talk About It

1. How does rapid economic development threaten traditional values in Southeast Asia?
2. Would Lee Kwan Yew, the former prime minister of Singapore, be as popular in the United States as he was in his own nation? Explain.
3. Which art form do you think is most useful in understanding people in Southeast Asia? Explain.

LESSON 4 REVIEW

Fact Follow-Up Answers

1. Many Southeast Asian countries have authoritarian governments. A country may have a constitution that promises citizens the right to vote, but elections, if they are held, are strictly controlled, and freedom of speech is limited. Some nations are Communist, and their economies are under government control. Other authoritarian governments support private enterprise. The Philippines has the most democratic government in the region.
2. Not long ago, Bangkok was a city of green trees and peaceful canals. Now superhighways cross the city and skyscrapers dwarf Buddhist temples. It is crowded and the pace of life has become very fast.
3. The most prosperous Southeast Asian nations are Thailand, Malaysia, Indonesia, and Singapore.
4. ASEAN includes the nations of Brunei, Indonesia, Malaysia, Philippines, Singapore, and Thailand. ASEAN's goals are to promote good working relationships and economic growth among its members.

Talk About It Answers

1. Important points: Simply having a constitution does not guarantee democracy. Elections, if held, may be tightly controlled; freedom of speech may be limited. Such governments often fix elections through corruption or intimidation.
2. Important points: Students should choose one challenge and explain their choice. Democratic government is a goal in many nations. Reducing the power of authoritarian governments and assuring that written constitutions are followed in practice is another.
3. Important points: Students should choose one challenge and explain their choice. Expanding trade within the region, building productive economies without destroying the environment, developing industries that produce goods to meet the needs of their own people—all are among the challenges facing these nations.

Applying Decision-Making and Problem-Solving Techniques in World Issues

World Influences Shaping Southeast Asia

SKILL GOALS NORTH CAROLINA SOCIAL STUDIES skill

In this chapter, Southeast Asia is described as being one of the world's great crossroads, a region that has attracted people, goods, and ideas from north, south, and the West. It is a region of exceptional diversity. A Malay people were the earliest settlers. They brought their culture into Southeast Asia. China, India, Japan, and European colonial powers have introduced other influences into the region at one time or another.

Today, the nations of the region are establishing their own identities. Influences from other regions remain. Which other cultures from the outside have had the most important influence on Southeast Asia?

To begin to answer this question, take a sheet of paper. Across the top, list the nations that have influenced Southeast Asia. You may include all Western influences under one heading. Then, using the text of Chapter 25, make notes of the influences, listing them under their origins. (For example, Hinduism and Buddhism arrived in Southeast Asia from India.) Include in your notes information about parts of Southeast Asia where an outside culture was most influential.

Once you have completed your notes, you will have considerable information about influences from other world regions on Southeast Asia. Your information is now partly organized. At this point, compare your list with a classmate's and learn from each other.

To organize your information further, a web chart like the one shown here about the Philippines is helpful. As you construct the chart, you will need to decide on the categories of information to include. To do this, return to your list of influences. Do any fit together? (Hint: one category might be "Religion." What are some others?) Pick a Southeast Asian country and record its name in the center of the chart. Enter the categories of influence around the center. Once you have done this, are you confident that you can say which other world region most influenced the country? When you have completed your web chart, discuss it with a classmate.

Now you should be ready to answer the question "Which outside culture has most influenced Southeast Asia?" Write a persuasive paragraph giving your conclusions. Remember that the first sentence should read something like this: "______________ is the culture that has most influenced Southeast Asia."

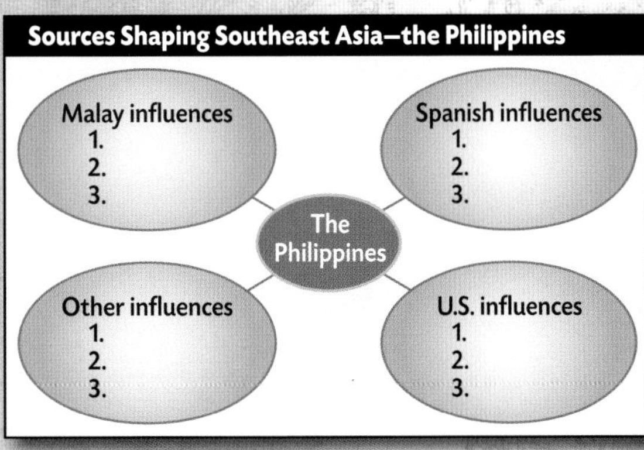

Teaching This Skill Lesson

Materials Needed textbooks, paper, pencils

Classroom Organization whole class, individual, small group

Beginning the Lesson Ask students who and what have influenced their lives. Accept answers and record them on the chalkboard. Probe for influences students might not recall (such as teachers, scoutmasters, MTV).

Lesson Development Tell students they will be looking at how outside influences have helped the Philippines. Direct them to skim Chapter 25, listing all the examples of influences they can find. Circulate, encouraging students and when necessary pointing out examples students may have missed. (It is not necessary that students complete their lists at this point; the lists may be completed as a part of the homework assignment.) Have students examine the chart on page 517. Tell them they will be completing a chart like this one as a homework assignment. Make sure students understand the relationship between the lists they are making and use of the chart to organize information.

Conclusion Place students in small groups to compare and polish their charts. Ask which influence on the Philippines was greatest, least. Post charts.

Skill Lesson Review

1. Which form of notemaking—listing or the data retrieval chart—was more helpful in organizing your thoughts? Why? *Answers will vary, depending on learning and analytical styles.*
2. What are some other ways you could have organized information to reach the same conclusion? *Answers will vary. You could organize the web around the nation by topics, such as government, language, and religion. Under each topic, you could list the nations that have influenced that part of culture. The nation most often listed would have a greater influence than others.*

Talk About It

1. Important points: Students should make a choice and explain it. European colonialism lasted longer and brought great changes in land use, economy, and government.
2. Important points: Students should choose either China or India and explain why. India's influence has been spiritual. China's influence extends into government and the arts.
3. Important points: Students should state whether economic development is a benefit or burden and explain their position. Change is always painful, but economic development brings the promise of an improved standard of living for many people.
4. Important points: Students should take a position and support that position with reasons. The two are often linked. Economic development, however, can occur under a dictatorship or in a democracy. Political stability requires the continued support of the people.
5. Important points: Students should choose one nation and explain why they chose it. Criteria might include physical and/or cultural characteristics of place or personal reasons, such as relatives may have served in the military in one of the nations or relatives might live in the region.

CHAPTER 25 REVIEW

Lessons Learned

Lesson 1
Many Different People
Southeast Asian nations reflect influences of India and China. European powers and the United States established colonies that introduced Western ideas. World War II and the Vietnam War brought destructive influences.

Lesson 2
People and their Environment
The migration of diverse people into Southeast Asia, the establishment of colonies there, and the region's involvement in world affairs has come partly from Southeast Asia's location on important trade routes.

Lesson 3
Governments and Economies
Most nations in Southeast Asia gained independence from colonial rule after World War II. The region is experiencing rapid economic and social change. Industries operate along with businesses that export crops and timber. Many people are moving into cities.

Lesson 4
Society and Culture
Crowds at shadow puppet plays and Buddhist monks stopping at homes for food show how traditions continue. Urban life is bringing change. Confucian ideals mix with and support authoritarian government in Singapore.

Talk About It

1. Which was a more important influence in Southeast Asia—European colonialism or Japanese imperialism? Explain.
2. Which has had the greater influence on life in Southeast Asia—China or India? Explain.
3. Has recent economic development in Southeast Asia been more of a benefit or more of a burden? Explain.
4. What do you think is harder to achieve: economic development or political stability? Why?
5. If you could visit one country in Southeast Asia, which one would you choose to visit? Explain why.

Mastering Mapwork

REGION
Use the map on page 497 to answer these questions:

1. Which nations in this region are located on the Asian mainland?
2. Which are island nations?
3. In which political regions are there natural gas deposits?
4. Which political region has the largest tin deposits?
5. In what ways does the Mekong River help to make Laos, Cambodia, and Vietnam a region?
6. Is Southeast Asia more a cultural or a physical region? Explain.

518 Chapter 2

Mastering Mapwork

1. Myanmar (Burma), Laos, Thailand, Cambodia, Singapore, and Vietnam are located on the Asian mainland.
2. The Philippines, Indonesia, Malaysia, East Timor, and Brunei are island nations.
3. There are natural gas deposits in Brunei, Indonesia, Sumatra, and Malaysia.
4. Malaysia has the largest tin deposits.
5. Because the Mekong winds through the three countries, all three use the river for the movement of people and goods.
6. Important points: Students should make a choice and explain that choice. Southeast Asia has both mainland and island nations, and these nations differ physically except that all are located in the Tropics. Southeast Asia lies southeast of China and east of India and has long been a crossroads with people, goods, and ideas flowing north and south along the Malay Peninsula and east and west through the Strait of Malacca linking China and India.

Go to the Source

Analyzing Public Awareness Campaigns

Read the text below and study the photograph. Answer the questions with specific references to the documents.

In Singapore, the government is concerned about people speaking non-standard English, called Singlish. The "Speak Good English Movement" is a public awareness campaign to encourage more Singaporeans to make it a habit to speak standard, or "good" English. The government believes "good English" will give Singapore a more competitive edge, especially in the service industry.

Go to the Source

Questions

1. Who is the intended audience of this campaign?
2. Why would the government of Singapore believe that it is the government's role to encourage people to speak better English?
3. What is the purpose of banners like the one shown?

Go to the Source

OBJECTIVES: 4.03, 7.02, 10.02
Skills 2.02, 3.04, 3.05, 4.06

The Speak Good English Movement campaign encourages Singaporeans to improve their use of English and to make a conscious effort to speak Standard English. The campaign uses the image of chalk on blackboards to emphasize the element of learning to speak better English.

Visit **NCJourneys.com** for a link to the Singapore "Speak Good English Movement" Web site.

ANSWERS

1. The public of Singapore who do not use Standard English is the audience.
2. The government believes "Good English" will give Singapore a more competitive edge, especially in the service industry.
3. The banners teach people the proper way in English to express what they want to say. The banner shows a phrase in Singlish and then Standard English.

How to Use the Chapter Review

There are three sections in the Chapter Review: Talk About It, Mastering Mapwork, and Go to the Source. Use the Vocabulary Worksheets and the Chapter Review Worksheet in the Teacher's Resource Guide for additional reinforcement and preparation for the Chapter Assessments. The chapter and lesson reviews and the Chapter Review Worksheets are the basis of the assessment for each chapter.

Talk About It questions encourage students to speculate about the content of the chapter and are suitable for class or small-group discussion. They are not intended to be assigned for homework.

Mastering Mapwork has students apply one or more of the Five Themes of Geography to maps within the chapter.

Go to the Source activities allow students to analyze a primary source that relates to the content of the chapter. The questions and activities familiarize students with different types of primary sources and also build content-reading skills.

Unit 6 The Pacific Realm

The unit opens with a view of the Pacific Islands, dots of land in the region known as Oceania. In this unit, your students will learn about the Pacific Realm—the mountainous islands of New Zealand, Australia, a country that is also a continent, and Oceania. The Pacific Islands groups of Melanesia, Polynesia, and Micronesia make up Oceania. Islanders preserve traditional ways of life while others have built modern cities.

UNIT LESSON PLAN

	LESSON 1	LESSON 2	LESSON 3
CHAPTER 26 Australia and New Zealand	Australia's dry climate and flat land and New Zealand's mountains caused populations there to settle on the coasts. **Essential Question:** How did the geography of Australia and New Zealand influence the population patterns? **Suggested Time:** 1 day	Settlers in Australia and New Zealand have been influenced and challenged by the environment. **Essential Question:** How did the environment influence the way of life for settlers in Australia and New Zealand? **Suggested Time:** 1 day	Australia and New Zealand offer to their citizens diverse cultures and an active, outdoor life. **Essential Question:** How do the diverse cultures of Australia and New Zealand offer an active, outdoor life? **Suggested Time:** 1 day
CHAPTER 27 Oceania	Oceania is made up of mostly small islands spread across the Pacific Ocean. The region has few people. **Essential Question:** How can you describe the region of Oceania? **Suggested Time:** 1 day	Pacific Islanders fell increasingly under the control of foreign powers. Most are now independent, but outside contacts brought economic change. **Essential Question:** How were the islands of Oceania affected by foreign powers? **Suggested Time:** 1 day	While traditional ways still command respect, increasing contact with the outside is changing life in the Pacific Islands. **Essential Question:** How is life changing in the Pacific Islands as a result of contact with the outside? **Suggested Time:** 1 day

Unit Planner

Preparing the Unit

- Worksheets, assessments, and reproducibles for this unit are found in the Teacher's Resource Guide.
- See the list of Cultural Resources in the Teacher's Edition.
- After reviewing the suggested resources list for the unit, find as many as possible and prepare a resource area for your classroom.
- Share the suggested activities with your cultural arts teachers, who may be able to integrate them into their field of study.
- Decorate your room so that it has an "island" look. Have fun with it.

Teaching the Unit

- Some teachers prefer to begin their study of Africa, Asia, and the Pacific Realm with this unit because the cultures of Australia and New Zealand have much in common with the United States and the United Kingdom (which was studied in the sixth grade). Emphasize the similarities and differences between these Western cultures.
- If you are short of time at the end of the school year to teach this as a traditional unit, break the class into three groups, and assign one group Australia, another New Zealand, and the third Oceania. Have each group prepare a class presentation on their area, using their textbook and outside resources. Have the class take notes.
- Check the **NCJourneys.com** Web site for updates and materials.

Unit Projects

Students will have seven days to complete their project. They have the option of choosing from five different projects and should choose only one of the five projects. The five choices offer a lot of variety because students can select the project that best suits their taste. Suggested report format: two pages in length, typed, and double-spaced.

PROJECT CHOICES

OBJECTIVES: 3.01, 5.01, 11.01

Pictograph and Bar Graph
Students will create two graphs showing the population of the states and territories of Australia. One graph will be a pictograph and the other will be a bar graph. Be certain to include a key for the pictograph and round the population to the nearest one hundred thousand.

Travel Brochure
Students will choose one island country to research. Create a travel brochure for that country. Include a map, flag, imaginary hotel complete with amenities, weather, medical information, currency, and tourist attractions. The brochure should be bright, colorful, and as informative as possible to entice tourists to want to travel to their country. Students will present their brochure to the class as a means of advertising their country as "the place to visit."

Wildlife ABC Book
Students will create an Illustrated ABC Book of Wildlife about animals that inhabit the region. Be certain to include the animal's habitat, food and eating habits, natural protection, and status on the endangered species list. Find a creative way to bind the book together.

Great Barrier Reef Diorama
Students will create a diorama of the Great Barrier Reef using a BIG box and fluorescent paints. Paint the background of the box as the water. Make the coral out of clay or papier mâché to give a three-dimensional effect. Paint the background and the coral using the fluorescent paint. Draw and cut out fish and other ocean life found in the reef. Suspend these from the top of the box using fishing line.

Pacific Island Journal
Students will research and create a travel journal of Oceania. Imagine being a part of Captain James Cook's expedition that set out in 1768 to find a giant continent in the Southern Hemisphere. As a part of the crew, write journal entries about the three-year journey. Entries can include descriptions and drawings of the great coral reefs, the beautiful fish, the animals, the Aborigines who inhabit the island, the volcanic eruptions, and/or the storms at sea. Present the journals to the class.

Extension Assign novice and intermediate ELL students a picture book and limit writing.

Bulletin Board Ideas

Theme of Movement of People and Ideas
Use a background map as the centerpiece. With all the water surrounding the regions, place various drawings of ships—ancient and modern—that have sailed these waters. You could note major discoveries and battles that happened on the islands or the ocean.

Art Australia-Style
Materials: paper bags, markers, tempera paint
Have some examples of Aborigine art for students to view. Give them some background information. Your media center should have some reference material. Have students paint the figures on the paper bags. After they dry, display the art on the bulletin board.

Extension Have students write a short story to go with their paintings. Display with paintings.

Australia and New Zealand Bulletin Board
Create a display (pictures, postcards, PowerPoint, or overheads) of Australia including kangaroos, kaolas, sheep, rugby, the Great Barrier Reef, gold, the Sydney Opera House, and so on, to show to the students. After the presentation, have students complete a KWHL chart on Australia and New Zealand.

Unit Activities

Introductory Activity

Pacific Realm Centers

OBJECTIVES: 2.02, 3.01, 11.02

Have students create centers about Australia by dividing them into groups and giving them a topic. Using research materials, students will come up with hands-on activities to be done at their center. The following are just ideas; students will take more of an active role if they can select their own activities. Possible list of topics for centers: music—listening to music, especially the didgeridoo and other traditional music; foods—students can research foods and make lamingtons (cubed pound cake dipped in chocolate and coated with coconut); unique animals—koala, kangaroo, kiwi, platypus; painting—Dreamtime-like "x-ray" painting; coral reef life—making a class mural or shadow boxes; storytelling—creating Dreamtime stories and sharing them; mapmaking—have students make a vegetative or precipitation chloropleth map (will show the most dramatic differences). Have group members include the following criteria in their center: a map illustrating their topic, 300- to 500-word essay on their subject, a minimum of three illustrations, hands-on activities for center visitors (with clear directions and all supplies necessary), center materials displayed on a tri-fold display board, and a short test for center visitors. After students have had the opportunity to explore the centers, create a rubric to evaluate the centers as a class. Then have each group score the other centers.

Extension For intermediate ELL students, assign partners and make sure each ELL student has input into the text.

Culminating Activity

Building a Newspaper

OBJECTIVES: 7.01, 7.02, 11.01

Students will create a newspaper about a country from the region studied in this unit, as they did in Unit 1. This will be issue number four of their newspaper.

Refer to the Unit 1 Culminating Activity on page 12C in the Teacher's Edition for specific directions and references on how to create and organize the newspaper. Remind students that the newspaper should feature two articles on the front. The back of the newspaper should include a map, a box displaying vital statistics, an article about something special or current events, and a puzzle. The students should use their newspapers from the previous unit as a model, and thus the students should be able to complete it in similar or slightly less time.

Share the newspapers with others in the class. Have the students keep each of their newspapers. At the end of the year, bind each student's newspapers together so he or she will have their own volume of newspapers covering the regions studied throughout the year. Use copies of all students newspapers to organize a class volume according to region.

Science Activity

Australian Animal Fact Card

OBJECTIVES: 2.03, 3.02

Seven families of mammals and four families of birds are classified as native to Australia. Seven of the more than 750 known species of birds have become extinct since the beginning of European settlement and another 45 species are endangered. In this activity, students will create an animal fact card on a 3-inch by 5-inch note card of an animal unique to Australia. The fact card can include such information as a photo or drawing of the animal, the scientific name, some interesting facts, the average size of the animal, the normal life span, the habitat, any predators or prey, and the typical diet. Students can also find out if their animal is endangered. Also, students may want to further research other behaviors of their animal.

Extension Ask intermediate ELL students to briefly describe any animals unique to their region of origin.

Novice ELL students should limit facts on cards to one or two words. Intermediate ELL students should write one or two sentences. Do not assign them to use their region of origin (it would most likely not be similar to Australia). Instead, let them use ELL-friendly Web sites to research the correct animals for the activity.

Technology Activity

Island Colonies

OBJECTIVES: 4.01, 7.01, 11.01

Divide students into groups for online research about the exploration of the South Pacific by Europeans and North Americans. Assign each group an island country and have them provide a brief history of its colonization(s). Students should identify what peoples inhabited the island, which explorers/settlers landed there, and the results of the interaction among the native and non-native people.

Extension This activity is suitable for novice and intermediate ELL students since they are in groups. ELL students should use an ELL-friendly Web site for research.

Math Activity

Comparing Charts

OBJECTIVES: 1.02

Using the data below, have students create two sets of charts and graphs. First, they will create pie charts for each nation. Second, they will compare data for all countries by industry sector type in three bar graphs (Service, Industry, and Agriculture). Have student determine the mean, median, mode and outliers for the data in each category. (Source: 2006 U.S. CIA World Factbook)

Data

- Australia: agriculture: 3.8%, industry: 26.2%, services: 70%
- New Zealand: agriculture: 4.3%, industry: 26.9%, services: 68.8%
- Fiji: agriculture: 8.9%, industry: 13.5%, services: 77.6%
- Palau: agriculture: 6.2%, industry: 12%, services: 81.8%
- Papua New Guinea: agriculture: 35.7%, industry: 37.1%, services: 27.2%
- Samoa (Western): agriculture: 11.4%, industry: 58.4%, services: 30.2%

Extension Have students write a brief paragraph explaining how the two different types of graphs/charts give new meaning to the same information.

Assist ELL students by assigning a partner.

Unit Resources

Print Resources

Fiction

Arnold, Caroline. *A Walk on the Great Barrier Reef*. Carolrhoda Books, 1988. ISBN 0876142854.

Savage, Deborah. *Flight of the Albatross.* Boston: Houghton Mifflin, 1989. ISBN 0395457114.

Southall, Ivan. *Josh.* New York: Macmillan, 1988. ISBN 0027862801.

Wrightson, Patricia. *Balyet.* New York: Macmillan, 1989. ISBN 0140343393.

Nonfiction

Ball, John. *We Live in New Zealand.* New York: Franklin Watts, 1982. ISBN 0531047814. Interviews with 30 New Zealanders, including Maoris, people of European descent, and Pacific Islanders.

Gunner, Emily. *A Family in Australia.* New York: The Bookwright Press, 1985. ISBN 0531038246.

Sammis, Fran. *Australia and the South Pacific.* Benchmark Books, New York 2000. ISBN 0761403736.

Twist, Clint. *James Cook: Across the Pacific to Australia* (Beyond the Horizon series). Raintree Steck-Vaughn, 1995. ISBN 0811439755.

Other Resources

Roots & Wings
P. O. Box 19678
Boulder, CO 80308-2678
(800) 833-1787
Excellent source of materials on Australia. Culture, geography, maps, Aborigines, folktales, music.

Maps

National Geographic Society
Each is available as an uncirculated back issue with supplement map.
Contact: *National Geographic* Back Issues
(800) 777-2800, Fax: (813) 979-6685
Cost: ranges between $5 and $10 (shipping included)
February 1988—Australia

Web Sites

Visit **NCJourneys.com** for links to:

- AboriginalConnections.com
- Introduction to Pacific Islands Archaeology
- Oceanic Art and Culture, The Art of the Pacific Islands, Polynesian Art: A Web Directory

Paideia Seminar

National Anthems

OBJECTIVES: 11.01, 11.03

Consider the national anthems of Australia and Tonga.

Opening Questions

- How would you compare the major themes of these two songs?
- What do these two songs tell you about the cultures they come from?

Core Questions:

- What role does "toil" have in Australia's future?
- What role does toil have in Tonga's future?

Closing Questions:

- How do these anthems compare to "The Star Spangled Banner"?
- What functions do national anthems serve?

Tonga

*****

'E 'Otua Mafimafi,
Ko ho mau 'Eiki Koe,
Ko Koe Koe fa la la 'anga,
Mo ia 'ofa ki Tonga

'Afio hifo 'emau lotu,
'Aia 'oku mau fai ni,
Mo Ke tali homau loto,
'O mala'i 'a Tupou.

TRANSLATION
Oh Almighty God above,
Thou art our Lord and sure defense,
In our goodness we do trust Thee
And our Tonga Thou dost love;

Hear our prayer, for though unseen
We know that Thou hast blessed our land;
Grant our earnest supplication,
Guard and save Tupou our King.

*****

Australia

*****

Australians all let us rejoice,
For we are young and free,
We've golden soil and wealth for toil;
Our home is girt by sea;
Our land abounds in nature's gifts
Of beauty rich and rare;
In history's page, let every stage
Advance Australia fair.

CHORUS
In joyful strains then let us sing,
"Advance Australia Fair."

Beneath our radiant Southern Cross
We'll toil with hearts and hands
To make this Commonwealth of ours
Renowned of all the lands;
For those who've come across the seas
We've boundless plains to share,
With courage let us all combine
To Advance Australia fair.

*****

Map Activity

The Australian Profile

NATIONAL GEOGRAPHY STANDARDS: 2

GEOGRAPHIC THEMES: Location

OBJECTIVES: 1.02

Using the Robinson world map projection with Australia, New Zealand, and other tiny Pacific islands highlighted in red, ask students to visualize an image or the map of this region. Turned sideways, the map may offer a human profile with Kimberley Plateau as human eye, Darwin/Arnhem Land as the nose, Gulf of Carpentaria as an open mouth, and the Cape York Peninsula as the extended lower lip and chin.

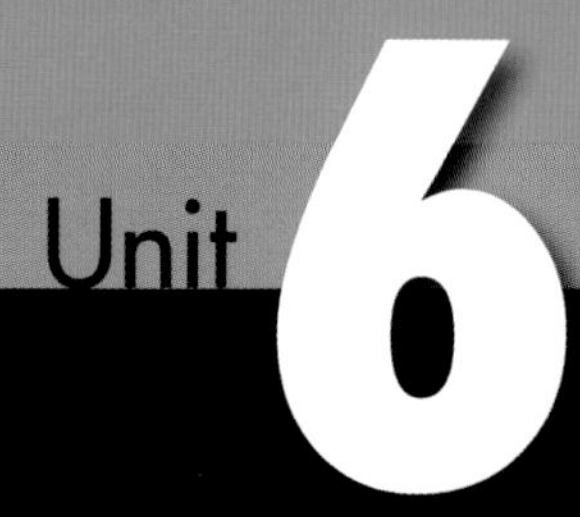

Unit 6

From an airplane, the Pacific Islands seem like twinkling dots of land in a sky-blue ocean. The watery openness of the ocean, not the land, is the first thing one notices about this part of the earth. That is why the region is called Oceania.

The people of Oceania, like the earliest settlers in Australia, lived for thousands of years in villages unseen by the rest of the world. Then, in the 1500s, European explorers appeared. Australia and New Zealand became the first areas of the Pacific Realm to be changed by colonization. Today, life in the Pacific Realm continues to change.

The Pacific Realm

Tahiti, French Polynesia

Social Studies at Work

Public Service Official

A maritime business development executive is someone responsible for generating new cargo business for the shipping industry from both local and international clients.

Meet Sarah Gaillard

Deputy executive director, North Carolina State Ports Authority.

For as long as ships have set sail, the shipping industry has been almost completely male-dominated. But with women like Sarah Gaillard on the job that's starting to change. Gaillard is one of the highest-ranking women working in the ports industry in the United States. According to Gaillard, her climb to the top has been a matter of being in the right place at the right time.

Some 25 years ago she had completed two years of college when she realized she needed to get out and start making some money. It didn't take long to land an entry-level position as a billing clerk for a shipping company in Charleston, and she's been in the maritime business ever since.

Her "big break" came when a company she was working for decided to start a new company based on a new shipping concept called intermodal service. That's when ships dock on the west coast and its contents are unloaded onto railroad

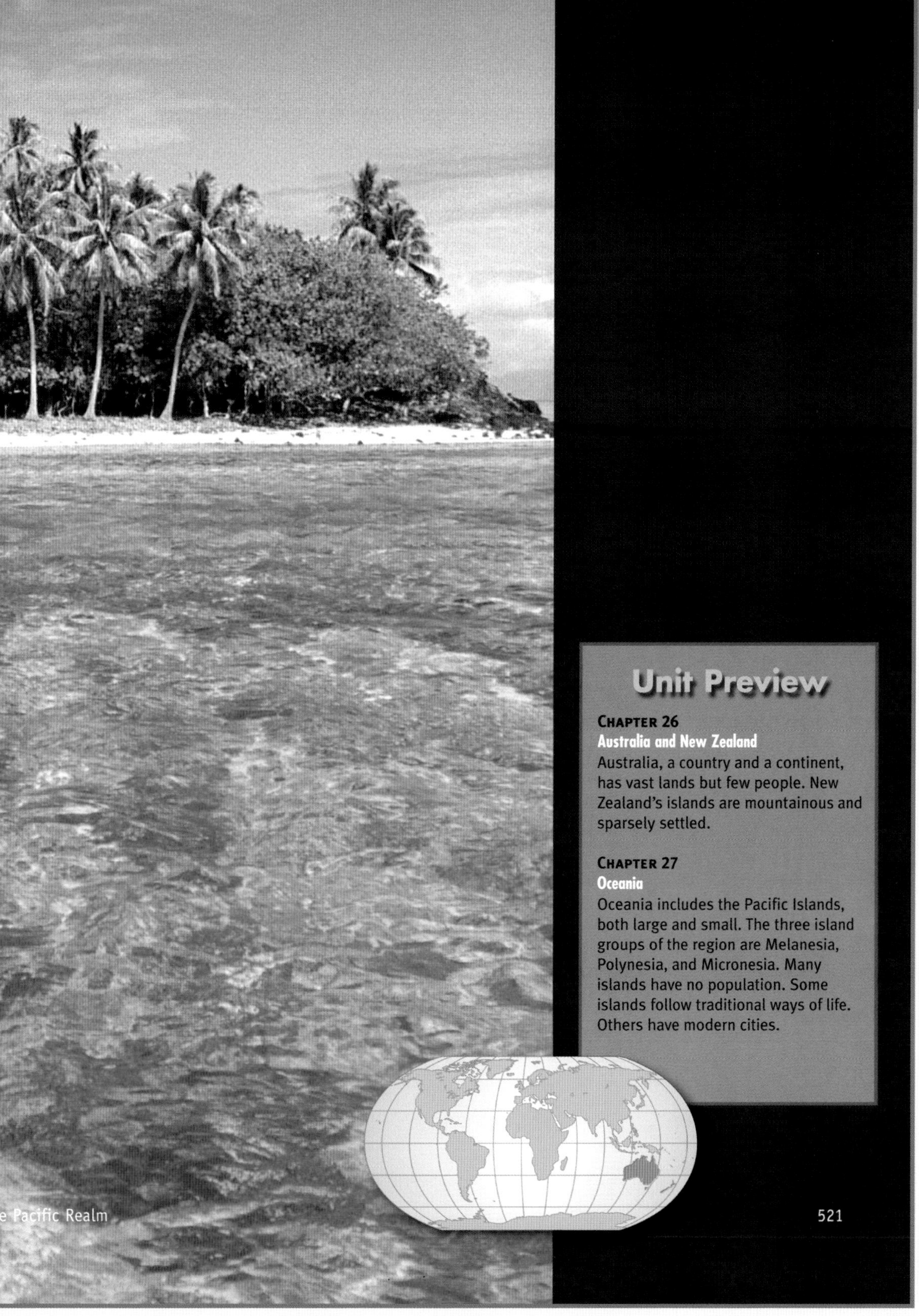

cars for shipment to the east coast. She started out as the terminal manager and was eventually elected vice president of the company. The company was unique in more ways than one in that it was run entirely by women, which made the company not only unusual but also, according to Gaillard, a lot of fun.

Unit Preview
CHAPTER 26
Australia and New Zealand
Australia, a country and a continent, has vast lands but few people. New Zealand's islands are mountainous and sparsely settled.
CHAPTER 27
Oceania
Oceania includes the Pacific Islands, both large and small. The three island groups of the region are Melanesia, Polynesia, and Micronesia. Many islands have no population. Some islands follow traditional ways of life. Others have modern cities.
e Pacific Realm
521

The job involves increasing business of the ports in Wilmington, Charlotte, Morehead City, and Greensboro. This in turn involves drumming up shipping business in five eastern states and in places all over the world. The Far East trade lanes are especially important to North Carolina, so Gaillard often finds herself meeting with corporate executives in places like Japan, Korea, Taiwan, China, and Singapore. Since the maritime industry is responsible for generating some 80,000 jobs in the state, Gaillard's success is closely linked with North Carolina's economic success.

International Shipping Executive for a Day

Say you have several truckloads of wood pulp you need to ship to the Far East as soon as possible. Go online to the North Carolina Ports Authority to check the schedules of ships leaving from Wilmington and Morehead City. Which ship will get it there quickest?

Find Out More

Visit **NCJourneys.com** for a link to North Carolina ports.

Australia and New Zealand

Social Studies Strands

Geographic Relationships

Government and Active Citizenship

Economics and Development

Culture and Diversity
- Ancestry
- Traditional ways of living

Worksheets

Worksheets and answer keys are found both in the Teacher Resource Guide and at **NCJourneys.com**, including Reading Guides, Reading Strategies, Chapter Reviews, English Language Learner and others.

North Carolina Standard Course of Study

Goal 3 The learner will analyze the impact of interactions between humans and their physical environments in Africa, Asia, and Australia.

Goal 4 The learner will identify significant patterns in the movement of people, goods and ideas over time and place in Africa, Asia, and Australia.

Goal 5 The learner will evaluate the varied ways people of Africa, Asia, and Australia make decisions about the allocation and use of economic resources.

Goal 9 The learner will analyze the different forms of government developed in Africa, Asia, and Australia.

Goal 11 The learner will recognize the common characteristics of different cultures in Africa, Asia, and Australia.

Teaching & Assessment

- English Language Learner Modified Lesson Plans for this chapter are found in the Teacher Resource Guide.
- *ExamView® Assessment Suite* is provided at **NCJourneys.com.** It includes customizable assessments for all chapters. Paper tests are also available in the Teacher Resource Guide. See pages T16–T17 for information about how to use the assessments and the Scoring Guide.

ACTIVITIES AND INTEGRATIONS

SOCIAL STUDIES
Australia/New Zealand—Political, p. 523
Australia/New Zealand—Economic and Resources, p. 523
Down Under Maps, p. 524
Australian Gold Rush, p. 529
Aussie States, p. 530
Australia/New Zealand—Population Density, p. 531
European Settlement Brought Trouble Down Under, p. 533
■ Health Slogans and Safety Programs, p. 536
★ Skill Lesson: Diversity in Australia, p. 542

READING/LANGUAGE ARTS	READING/LANGUAGE ARTS OBJECTIVES
▲ A New Life, p. 522B	1.01
● ▲ Family Work, p. 522B	2.01
Analogies, p. 522B	2.01
Activator: *Colors of Australia*, p. 522	1.03
Writing Prompt: Voting in Australia, p. 522	3.03
★ Editorial, p. 532	3.01
Fact Cards, p. 534	2.01
Australian Slang Terms, p. 540	6.01
Go to the Source: Analyzing Historic Documents, p. 545	2.01, 3.01, 4.01, 4.02

MATHEMATICS	MATHEMATICS OBJECTIVES
■ Prism of Australia, p. 535	3.01

SCIENCE	SCIENCE OBJECTIVES
Hurricanes and Typhoons, p. 525	3.05

TECHNOLOGY	TECHNOLOGY OBJECTIVES
● ▲ Great Barrier Reef, p. 525	3.01, 3.11
Land Area Map, p. 527	3.01, 3.11
■ Fact Cards, p. 534	3.01, 3.11

VISUAL ARTS	VISUAL ARTS OBJECTIVES
● Family Work, p. 522B	5.01, 5.03
★ Aboriginal Art–Illustrating a Dream, p. 522B	4.01, 5.01
Great Barrier Reef, p. 525	1.03, 4.01
Gold in 'Them Thar Hills,' p. 529	1.01, 4.01
Model Station, p. 537	2.01, 4.01
● Boomerang!, p. 539	2.01, 4.01
Australian Strips and Scrolls, p. 541	2.05, 5.01

CHARACTER AND VALUES EDUCATION	TRAITS
Writing Prompt: Voting in Australia, p. 522	Good citizenship, integrity, responsibility
What Would You Do?, p. 539	Good citizenship, integrity, perserverance

● Basic Activities ★ Challenging Activities ▲ English Language Learner Novice ■ English Language Learner Intermediate

Chapter Activities

Introductory Activity

A New Life

OBJECTIVES: 7.01, 7.02, 8.02

Australia was a penal colony for Great Britain. Criminals were sent over by ship to live out their sentences on the continent. Times were hard and treatment by soldiers was harsh. Young people, for stealing a loaf of bread or other minor crimes, were sent to Australia as criminals. If they could live through their sentence, they often made a new life for themselves.

Have your students write a short story about such a person. They might choose to write it in the first person. They might write their story as if they were a mother or father of a young person who was sent to Australia for stealing a loaf of bread to feed the family. It is documented that one young person, aged fourteen, was sentenced to Australia for stealing books. Share the stories with the class if students are comfortable with sharing their stories. You might consider making up a class book of the stories.

Family Work

OBJECTIVES: 11.01, 11.02, 12.02

This activity will be enhanced if you can bring in the art teacher to work with your students.

Have students act as if they are part of Maori society. Families are expected to train their children to be woodcarvers. Have students draw a mask to represent their family, their favorite interest, or their school. Students can draw these masks using rough brown paper and only primary colors. They may decorate them with shells, leaves, and bark if available. After the work is done, display their efforts.

Lead a discussion about who found it easy, more difficult. Ask what aspects of the work they liked better, planning or drawing. Then lead a discussion of how a young Maori who has to become a woodcarver might feel if he or she did not like to practice that art.

Art Activity

Aboriginal Art—Illustrating a Dream

OBJECTIVES: 11.02, 12.01, 12.02

Aboriginal people traditionally used the materials available to them to symbolize the Dreamtime and their world. As a result, art forms varied in different areas of Australia. In the central desert, ground drawing was an important style of art, and throughout Australia rock art as well as body painting and decoration were common. There are a wide range of traditional Aboriginal art forms and styles.

The dreaming does not fully convey the concept of the Aboriginal people, but it is the most acceptable English word because visions are often derivative from dreams. The dreaming is how the Aboriginal people explain their life, culture, and their relationship with every living creature and every feature of the landscape.

Materials pencils, drawing paper, 18-inch by 24-inch heavy paper to paint on, tempera paint, paintbrushes, cotton swabs, newspapers

Think of a dream image (animal, person, machine, or any combination—this does not necessarily have to be an image seen while sleeping—it could be a "daydream"). On practice paper, draw the image until comfortable. Keep the drawings simple. On large white paper, lightly pencil out design.

Create a 1½- to 2-inch border of geometric designs (practice designs prior to drawing the final design). Use simple repeated shapes, triangles, diamonds, etc. Draw lightly. Using a paintbrush, fill in Dream image, background, and border designs with solid colors. Use cotton swabs to dip in paint to fill the image and border designs with small circular spots. Use a variety of colors. This is not the exact tool the Aborigines would use, but it creates a nice simulation.

Analogies

OBJECTIVES: 1.03

Analogies are useful to help students make associations with prior knowledge. Read the analogies aloud and ask students to identify the relationship between the terms. As an extension, ask students to write their own analogies using key terms or places discussed in the chapter.

Outback : Australia :: Western Frontier : United States (is in)

Great Barrier Reef : coral :: forest : trees (contains)

Great Dividing Range : Australia :: Appalachian Mountains : United States (is eastern mountain chain of)

stations : Australia :: ranches : United States (are in)

Aborigines : Australia :: Maoris : New Zealand :: Native Americans : Americas (are indigenous to)

cricket : Australia :: baseball : United States (is played in)

rugby : United Kingdom :: football :: United States (is played in)

Teaching Strategies

Because of the limited amount of time in the year to cover all of the material in the book, preview the chapter and identify the most important concepts for students to learn and plan accordingly.

Activator

OBJECTIVES: 12.02, 12.03, 13.02

Activators are great tools to use in order to "hook" the attention of the students. Reading picture books or stories is an excellent way to build interest in the subject and is also a great way to integrate language arts into the social studies
curriculum.

Colors of Australia by Lynn Ainsworth Okawsky (Lerner, 1997. ISBN 157505213X.)

OR

Use some of the phrases from *Lonely Planet Australian Phrasebook* by Sue Butler and Denise Angelo (ISBN 0864425767) to grab the attention of the students. Teach them the phrases and the meanings and give them some time to practice their Australian accents.

Writing Prompt

OBJECTIVES: 10.02, 10.03, 10.04

Problem-Solution

Voting is considered so important a civic duty in Australia that citizens are actually fined for not voting. During the 2000 elections in the United States, approximately 50 percent of registered voters in North Carolina voted. Do you think voters in the United States should be fined for not voting? Explain your answer.

As you write, remember to:

- clearly state your position.
- give at least three reasons and explain your reasons fully.
- give examples to support your reasons.
- write in complete sentences and paragraph form.
- organize your ideas and include an introduction and a conclusion.
- use good grammar, spelling, punctuation, and capitalization.

CHAPTER 26

Australia and New Zealand

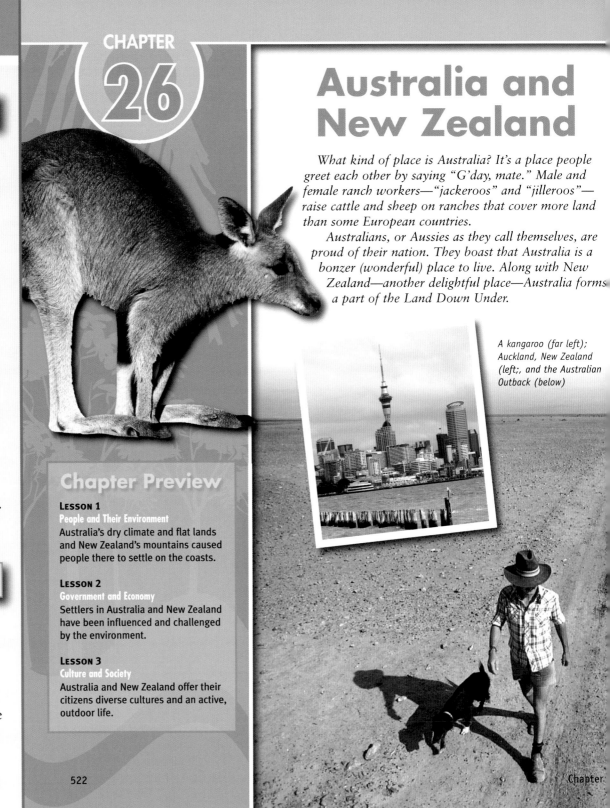

What kind of place is Australia? It's a place people greet each other by saying "G'day, mate." Male and female ranch workers—"jackeroos" and "jilleroos"—raise cattle and sheep on ranches that cover more land than some European countries.

Australians, or Aussies as they call themselves, are proud of their nation. They boast that Australia is a bonzer (wonderful) place to live. Along with New Zealand—another delightful place—Australia forms a part of the Land Down Under.

A kangaroo (far left); Auckland, New Zealand (left;, and the Australian Outback (below)

Chapter Preview

Lesson 1
People and Their Environment
Australia's dry climate and flat lands and New Zealand's mountains caused people there to settle on the coasts.

Lesson 2
Government and Economy
Settlers in Australia and New Zealand have been influenced and challenged by the environment.

Lesson 3
Culture and Society
Australia and New Zealand offer their citizens diverse cultures and an active, outdoor life.

522

Chapter

Chapter Resources

Print Resources

Fiction

Marshall, James Vance. *Walkabout.* Sundance Pub., 1984. ISBN 0887410995.

Nonfiction

Darian-Smith, Kate. *Exploration Into Australia* (Exploration Into series). Chelsea House, 2001. ISBN 0791060209.

Dolce, Laura. *Australia.* (Modern World Nation series). Chelsea House, 1999. ISBN 0791047318.

Finley, Carol. *Aboriginal Art of Australia: Exploring Cultural Traditions* (Art Around the World series). Lerner, 1999. ISBN 0822520761.

Gutnik, Martin J. *Great Barrier Reef* (Wonders of the World series). Raintree Steck-Vaughn, 1994. ISBN 0811463699.

Heinrichs, Ann. *Australia* (Enchantment of the World series). Children's Press, 1998. ISBN 0516206486.

Ryan, Pat (Patrick M.). *New Zealand.* Child'sWorld, 1999. ISBN 1567665772.

Stein, R. Conrad. *Sydney* (Cities of the World series). Children's Press, 1998. ISBN 0516205935.

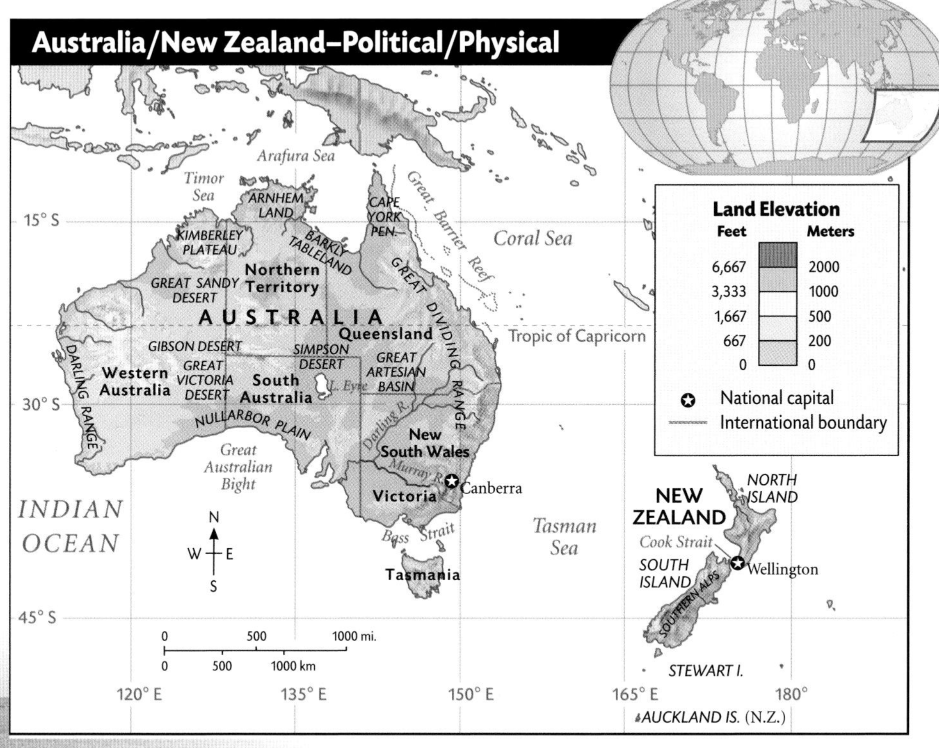

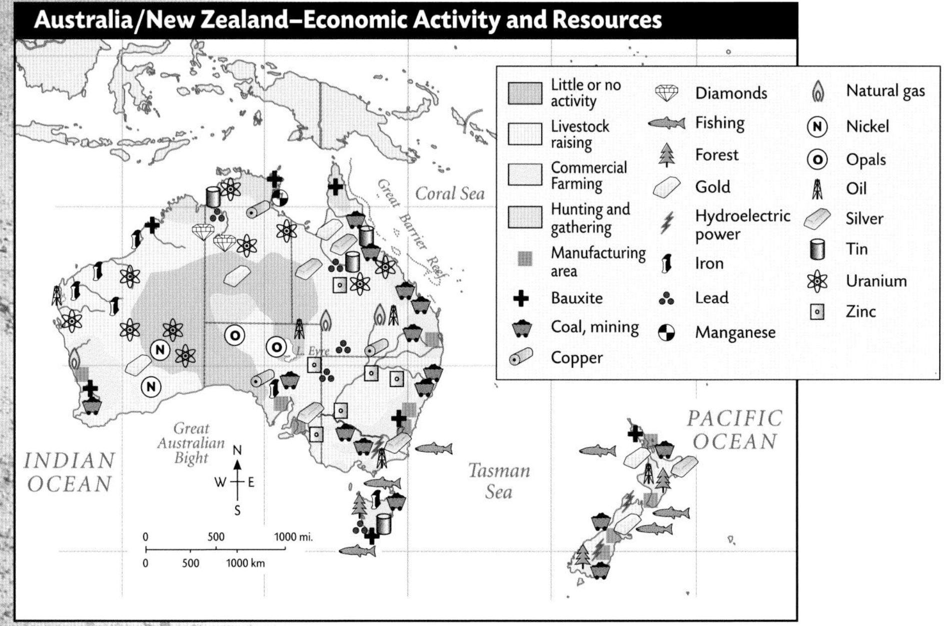

Australia and New Zealand 523

Map Activity

Australia/New Zealand–Political

NATIONAL GEOGRAPHY STANDARDS: 1, 6, 10

GEOGRAPHIC THEMES: Location, Place, Region

OBJECTIVES: 1.02, 1.03

Note with students that Australia is both a continent and an island. New Zealand is often paired with Australia in most regional studies of the Pacific Realm that is sometimes referred to as Oceania.

Map Activity

Australia/New Zealand–Economic and Resources

NATIONAL GEOGRAPHY STANDARDS: 1, 16

GEOGRAPHIC THEMES: Location, Human-Environmental Interaction

OBJECTIVES: 3.01, 5.01

Students are to answer the following questions:

1. Which economic activity covers the majority of Australia's land area? *livestock raising*
2. Where is the majority of Australia's fishing concentrated? *in the Tasman Sea off the coast of New South Wales and Victoria, Bass Strait, and south of Tasmania*
3. Which economic activity is found in Australia but not in New Zealand? *hunting and gathering*
4. Why would areas of Australia have "little or no activity" across Northern Territory, Western Australia, and South Australia? *deserts, Outback, lack of populated areas and transportation links*
5. Does Australia or New Zealand have more manufacturing areas? *Australia*
6. Which is more abundant in Australia, gold or silver? *silver*
7. Which Australian state or territory has more uranium mined? *Western Australia*
8. New Zealand has less of which energy-producing resource, coal or oil? *oil*

Back issues of magazines

Cobblestone Publishing Company.:
Australia. ISBN 038240551X.
New Zealand. ISBN 0382445902.
Voyages of Captain Cook. (CALLIOPE magazine, 2001–02).

Audiovisual

Australia's Aborigines. National Geographic, 1988. (60 minutes.)
Australia: Beyond the Fatal Shore (6-part series). 2000. PBS Video.

Web Sites

Visit **NCJourneys.com** for links to:

- Archives New Zealand
- Australia: Beyond the Fatal Shore companion Web site
- Australasia Museums
- Australia's Antiquity Museums
- National Archives of Australia
- New Zealand History. A Web Directory
- New Zealand in History

OBJECTIVES: 2.02, 4.01, 5.01

Discussion Questions

1 If New Zealand, Australia's closest neighbor, is more than 1,200 miles away, how do you think the isolation affected the development of Australia's culture?

2 How do the Appalachian Mountains in the western part of North Carolina affect the climate in our state?

3 North Carolina has several major rivers. How would our state be different if we only had one or two of them?

Caption Answer

The Great Dividing Range creates a rain shadow effect, so that the mountains keep moisture-bearing winds from reaching inland.

Map Activity

Down Under Maps

NATIONAL GEOGRAPHY STANDARDS: 1, 4

GEOGRAPHIC THEMES: Region, Place

OBJECTIVES: 1.01

Have students create a physical/political map of Australia. Using either an outline map or student-made clay maps, have students locate the following:

Great Dividing Range, Brisbane, Melbourne, Murray River, Queensland, Perth, New South Wales, Darling River, Victoria, Darwin, Northern Territory, Adelaide, South Australia, Canberra, Western Australia, Outback, Tasmania, Great Barrier Reef, Ayers Rock (Uhuru)

LESSON 1 People and Their Environment

KEY IDEAS

- Australia and New Zealand differ physically.
- Both countries are sparsely settled.

KEY TERMS

Outback
Great Barrer Reef
stations
Aborigines
exiled

To find Australia and New Zealand on a globe, look to the south. Australia is called the Land Down Under because it lies entirely within the Southern Hemisphere, as does New Zealand. Although New Zealand is almost 1,250 miles (2,013 km) southeast of Australia across the Tasman Sea, it is one of Australia's closer neighbors.

Both countries are not far from Asia. Yet New Zealand and Australia were both settled and developed by the British.

Physical Features

Australia and New Zealand are each surrounded by water. They offer vast deserts, rolling mountains, ancient forests, beautiful beaches, and active volcanoes.

Australia

Australia is the world's sixth-largest country and the smallest continent. It is the only country that is also a continent. It is also the flattest continent on earth.

Australia's Murray River is one of the continent's few rivers. **Why is water scarce in Australia's interior?**

Except for Antarctica, Australia is als the driest continent. One reason for the extreme dryness is its highest mountain range, the Great Dividing Range. Runnin along the east coast, the Great Dividing Range creates a rain shadow effect. The mountains keep moisture-bearing winds from reaching inland. Parts of the interio called the ***Outback,*** are semiarid or desert, where summer temperatures sizzle over 120° F (49° C).

Most precipitation falls on the easter side of the range along the coast. This are has rain in the summer months and heavy snowfalls in the mountains in the winter.

Australia has few major lakes or rivers. Most lakes stay dry much of the year, unless temporarily filled by an unusually heavy rainstorm.

Australia's most important rivers are the Murray and the Darling Rivers. They begin in the Great Dividing Range, then join and flow 2,300 miles (3,703 km) through southeastern Australia to the Southern Ocean. Both rivers lose some water through evaporation as they flow through the Outback.

A key physical feature of Australia lie underwater. The ***Great Barrier Reef*** extends across the northeastern coast of Australia in a 1,250-mile (2,013-km) arc. Ordinary rock would be worn down by the force of the Pacific Ocean. Yet living coral continually renews the Great Barrie Reef.

he Great Barrier Reef lies off the oast of Australia. **Why doesn't he ocean wear it away?**

Mount Ngauruhoe is an active volcano in New Zealand. **What covers most of the country?**

New Zealand

Much smaller in size and population than Australia, New Zealand consists of two large islands and many smaller islands. The two largest are North Island and South Island.

In contrast to Australia, much of New Zealand is mountainous. South Island has a snowcapped range called the Southern Alps. Its glaciers slowly slide down the mountains to the sea. North Island also has some mountains, but these are more low-lying.

Except on the mountain peaks, New Zealand's climate is mild year-round. Most areas receive ample rainfall for farming, and snow rarely falls, except in the mountains.

The Shotover River flows through the South Island of New Zealand. **What land feature dominates the nation?**

Caption Answer

Living coral constantly renews the reef.

Caption Answer

New Zealand is mountainous.

Caption Answer

The Southern Alps

Art Activity

Great Barrier Reef

OBJECTIVES: 1.01, 3.01, 3.02

The Great Barrier Reef runs for more than 1,200 miles off the northeastern coast of Australia. Build a classroom Great Barrier Reef. Research the ecosystem of the coral reef. Students may draw, color, and cut out the different life forms that exists around a coral reef. Use a large cardboard box and cut out just one side. Paint or cover with blue paper the insides of this box to simulate the water world. Use clay dough, sugar cubes, powdered sugar, and sugar paste (sugar and water) to build a reef in the bottom of the box. String life forms from the top. Glue them to the sides of the box and place them in the reef. Number each creature and post a matching index of names on the outside of "the reef." Students may design "protest" signs about the destruction of this fragile ecosystem.

Extension Assign novice and intermediate ELL students to work with a partner or in groups.

Activity

Hurricanes and Typhoons

OBJECTIVES: 2.01, 3.01

Students will be assigned a research project on typhoons and hurricanes. Break the class into cooperative learning groups. Each group should research how hurricanes and typhoons form and strengthen. Using a grpahic organizer, have students compare the similarities and the difference of the storms. Then students should use their organizers to write a paragraph comparing and contrasting the storms and learninging about their fomation.

Discussion Questions

1 How does the geography of New Zealand contrast to Australia's?

2 Would you rather live in Australia or New Zealand? Why?

3 Why would seaports play such an important role in the history and economic development of a country?

4 How does Australia's gold rush compare to the 1849 Gold Rush in California?

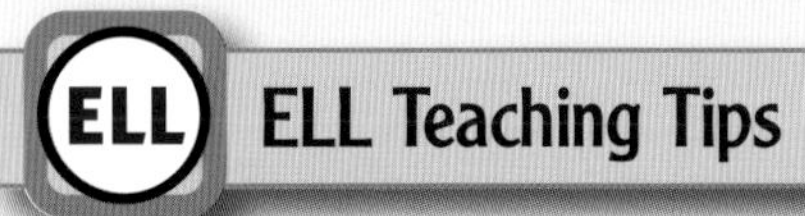

Support Native Language Development

Anything your students learn in their native languages will eventually be transferred to English. Encourage them to continue speaking, reading, and writing in that language at home.

The dry Outback is sparsely settled and has a harsh climate. Most people live in coastal cities.

A Largely Urban Population

Both Australia and New Zealand are sparsely populated. Their populations are unevenly distributed. Most people live in coastal cities, not in the countries' interiors (see map, page 531).

Australia

Although Australia is the size of the continental United States, it has only about 20 million people. Rain, or the lack of it, determines where most live. The majority live along the wetter east and southeast coasts between the Great Dividing Range and the Pacific Ocean. Settlements also exist on the southwest coast.

The dry Outback is sparsely settled because of its harsh climate. Many of the people there live on large ranches called ***stations,*** which are often hundreds of miles from the nearest city.

In the Outback, medical help comes by airplane. In home schools, children listen to lessons broadcast over short-wav radio or beamed by satellite.

Almost 93 percent of Australians live in cities. More than half the people live in Australia's five largest cities. All of Australia's major cities except one, Canberra, the nation's capital, are located on the coast. As seaports, these cities play an important economic part. Each of thes coastal cities is also the capital of one of Australia's five mainland states (see map, page 531).

New Zealand

New Zealand also is a sparsely populated country. Most of the 4 million people live along the coast because of hig mountains in the centers of both islands. As in Australia, most New Zealanders liv in cities.

North Island, which has warmer weather and flatter land, has a larger population than South Island. Two of the nation's largest cities, Auckland and Manukau, are in North Island. Wellington, the nation's capital, is also located there.

Brisbane, Australia, is the capital city of Australia's state of Queensland. It is located on the Pacific coast. **Why do most Australians live in cities?**

Word Origins

The word **Aborigine**, which comes from a Latin word meaning "from the beginning," refers to the first known inhabitants of any place or region. It also refers specifically to the first inhabitants of Australia.

An Aborigine stands in the Outback next to his work of art (left). This Maori warrior (below) is giving the traditional Maori Haka greeting. **What happened to Aborigines when Europeans came to Australia?**

First Settlers

Australia

The first people arrived in Australia more than 50,000 years ago. Scientists believe they reached the continent from Southeast Asia by raft. The descendants of these first immigrants are now called ***Aborigines*** (ab·uh·RIJ·uh·nees).

The Aborigines, who were hunter-gatherers, divided into hundreds of groups. They spoke different languages and practiced different customs. On the Cape York Peninsula, in the Northern Territory where many Aborigines lived, some 45 languages were spoken at the time the Europeans settled.

Around 300,000 Aborigines lived in Australia when the Europeans arrived. They faced severe hardships after European settlement. Many died from European diseases. Others were killed in battles or had their lands taken from them. Many moved into the Outback.

Today, Aborigines make up about 1 percent of the population. The Australian government has begun to repay Aborigines for their lost property.

New Zealand

The first settlers arrived in New Zealand much later than Australia's first settlers. About 700 to 1,000 years ago, the Maori (MAH·oh·ree) people came by canoe to New Zealand from a distant part of the South Pacific islands.

Almost 10 percent of New Zealand's population are Maori. For the past 30 years, New Zealand's government has been reviewing Maori land claims and making payments to tribes or, in some cases, returning their land to them.

Customs

The Maori tell the story of their origins in song. Kupe, a skilled navigator, set out to find an uninhabited southern land, covered with mists. After a difficult voyage, Kupe's wife saw what looked like a white cloud. It was land. The voyagers named it *Aotearoa*, "Land of the Long White Cloud." Maoris still use this name for New Zealand.

Map Activity

Land Area Map

NATIONAL GEOGRAPHY STANDARDS: 1, 5, 6, 9

GEOGRAPHIC THEMES: Region, Location, Place, Human-Environmental Interaction, Movement

OBJECTIVES: 2.03, 3.01, 4.02, 5.01

Assign each student (or group of students) one Australian state. Research land area, population, and economic resources. Look for interesting facts, personalities, or sights. Have each student (or group) find a United States region or state comparable in land area to their Australian state. Have them identify similarities and differences, focusing on population distribution and use of economic resources. Have students share their findings with the class.

Extension Novice and intermediate ELL students should do this activity in pairs or groups. ELL students should use an ELL-friendly Web site for research.

Caption Answer

Many died from diseases brought by the Europeans. Others were killed in battles or had their lands taken from them. Many moved into the Outback.

Background Information

Jandamarra: Aboriginal Hero

It's more than 100 years since he died, but a hero of the Aborigines is finally getting his due. Jandamarra, a member of the Bunuba tribe, was born in 1873 at a time when white ranchers were expanding into Western Australia. White settlers drove Aborigines from lands that had been theirs for thousands of years. At age twenty-four he was shot to death for leading a three-year, local Aboriginal movement against white settlement of Aboriginal lands. Now students across Australia are learning about Jandamarra in schools. This new interest in Janadamarra reflects the growing effort by the Australians to give Aborigines greater rights not only in education but also in other areas of national life. Recent governments have returned some tribal lands and increased funding of Aboriginal social welfare programs.

Eyewitness Activity

Australian Gold Rush Activities

OBJECTIVES: 7.01, 7.02, 13.01

After reading about the Australian gold rush, provide material to the students on the American Gold Rush and have students compare and contrast the two events. Write a paragraph explaining how the gold rush affected settlement in these areas.

Resource *Gold Fever! Tales from California Gold Rush* by Rosalyn Schanzer. National Geographic Society, 1999. ISBN 0792273036.

In order to help students organize the most important concepts about the Australian Gold Rush, ask students to complete the graphic organizer in the Teacher's Resource Guide for who, when, and other discoveries.

Research the price of gold in today's market and compare the cost of gold with prices of gold jewelry.

Extension Assign intermediate ELL students the diagram only

EYEWITNESS TO HISTORY

Australia's GOLD RUSH

In 1851, just two years after gold fever hit California, Australia had its own major gold rush. Edward Hargraves, who started Australia's great gold rush, had already tried to find gold in California. While in California, he found gold-bearing rocks that looked like rocks he had seen back home.

Hargraves (below) returned to Australia and began searching for gold in the southeast corner of the country. On a stream about 170 miles (274 km) west of the city of Sydney in New South Wales, he hit pay dirt.

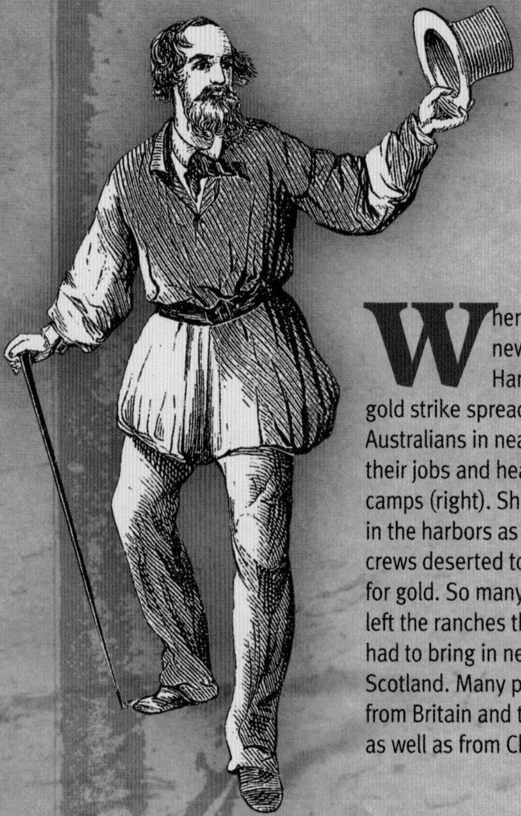

When news of Hargraves' gold strike spread, Australians in nearby cities quit their jobs and headed for mining camps (right). Ships stood empty in the harbors as captains and crews deserted to join the hunt for gold. So many sheep herders left the ranches that their owners had to bring in new workers from Scotland. Many prospectors came from Britain and the United States as well as from China.

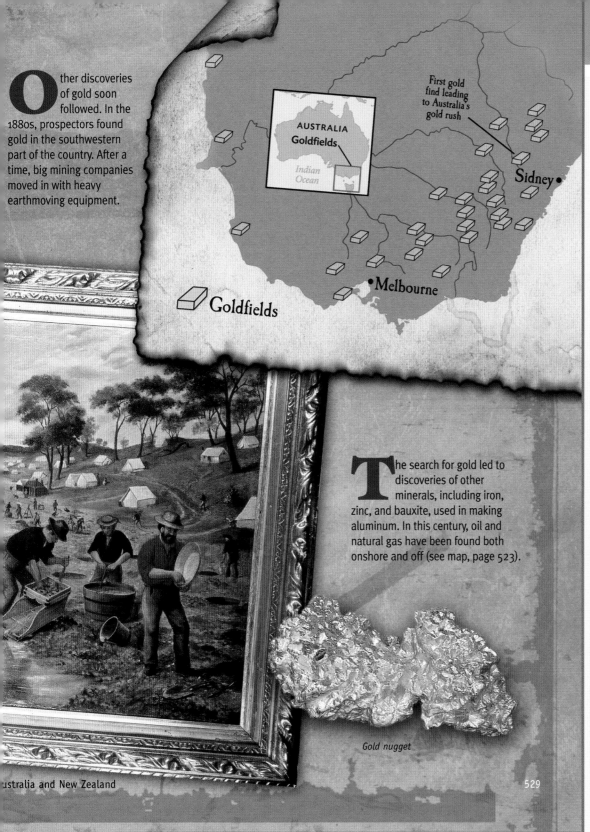

Other discoveries of gold soon followed. In the 1880s, prospectors found gold in the southwestern part of the country. After a time, big mining companies moved in with heavy earthmoving equipment.

The search for gold led to discoveries of other minerals, including iron, zinc, and bauxite, used in making aluminum. In this century, oil and natural gas have been found both onshore and off (see map, page 523).

Gold nugget

Australian Gold Rush

NATIONAL GEOGRAPHY STANDARDS: 1, 16

GEOGRAPHIC THEMES: Location, Human-Environmental Interaction

OBJECTIVES: 1.03, 2.01, 2.02, 2.03

Have students note which Australian regions are emphasized in this map displaying where the main goldfields are located. (*New South Wales, Victoria, South Australia*) Which region has the majority of Australia's goldfields? (*New South Wales*)

Discuss with students how many Australian gold mines are located near streams and rivers. (*9*)

Gold in 'Them Thar Hills'

OBJECTIVES: 1.01, 1.03, 2.02, 4.02

Materials textbook, atlases, reference books, outline maps (Africa, Australia, United States, South/Southeast/Southwest Asia), colored pencils, unlined paper, Internet access, *National Geographic* magazines.

Divide students into groups: Northern Africa, Western Africa, Southwest Asia, South/Southeast Asia, Australia and the Pacific Realm, North Carolina, California, and Alaska.

Each group should research gold in relationship to their area: locations of resources, uses, trade relationships, development of civilization. Each group will create a booklet that reflects the influence of "gold" in their specific area. Booklets will contain maps, with names of gold-related areas highlighted, and specific gold-related historical incidences. Students will share their information with the class.

Extension Limit the amount of writing novice and intermediate ELL students will need to do in this activity.

Discussion Questions

1 What happened to Native Americans when Europeans came to America?

2 Do you think the Maori in New Zealand are entitled to payments for their lands? What about the Native Americans in the United States?

3 How important do you think it was in Australia's development that its original European settlers were convicts?

4 How do you think those origins shaped the character of today's Aussies?

Caption Answer

A curtain down the center of the church separated the convicts from everyone else.

Map Activity

Aussie States

NATIONAL GEOGRAPHY STANDARDS: 1, 5

GEOGRAPHIC THEMES: Place

OBJECTIVES: 3.1, 3.2, 12.1

Enlarge an outline map of Australia that shows the states. Cut out the outline of each state and copy each one on a different color paper. Cooperative groups of three or four students should cut out and assemble a "set" of states on a poster. Glue the parts in place, outline the borders in marker, label the capitals, and add the surrounding bodies of water. Each group should include three statements about the location of the country/state.

The ruins of Port Arthur, a penal colony between 1830 and 1877, are a popular tourist attraction. **What was unusual about this church in Port Arthur? Why?**

European Settlement

Australia

In the 1830s, worshippers prayed in an unusual church in Port Arthur, Tasmania. A curtain down the center aisle separated convict worshippers from everyone else.

Australia's first European settlers came from the United Kingdom. They were convicts ***exiled*** —removed forcibly from their country—and sent to British penal, or prison, colonies in Australia as a punishment for crimes. The British called this sentence "transportation."

The first prison ships arrived in Australia in 1788. The last boatloads of prisoners landed 80 years later, in 1868. By that time, thousands of settlers had arrived during the gold rush, lured by hopes of making their fortunes.

For much of its history, Australia's immigration policies favored people from England, Ireland, and Scotland. White, English-speaking immigrants could settle Down Under, but most Asians and Africans were not allowed to move there.

After World War II, Australia first received people from Italy, Greece, and other parts of Europe. Then, in the 1970s, the government admitted Asian immigrants—many from war-torn countries in Southeast Asia. More recently, people have come from Hong Kong, China, Malaysia, and the Philippines.

New Zealand

The first European to see New Zealand was Dutch captain Abel Tasman. He arrived in 1642 and claimed the islands for the Netherlands. Dutch maps called the place New Zealand. European settlers arrived in the 1800s. Whalers and seal hunters made North Island a base for repairing and resupplying their ships. Eventually missionaries also settled there. In the 1830s, New Zealand became a British colony.

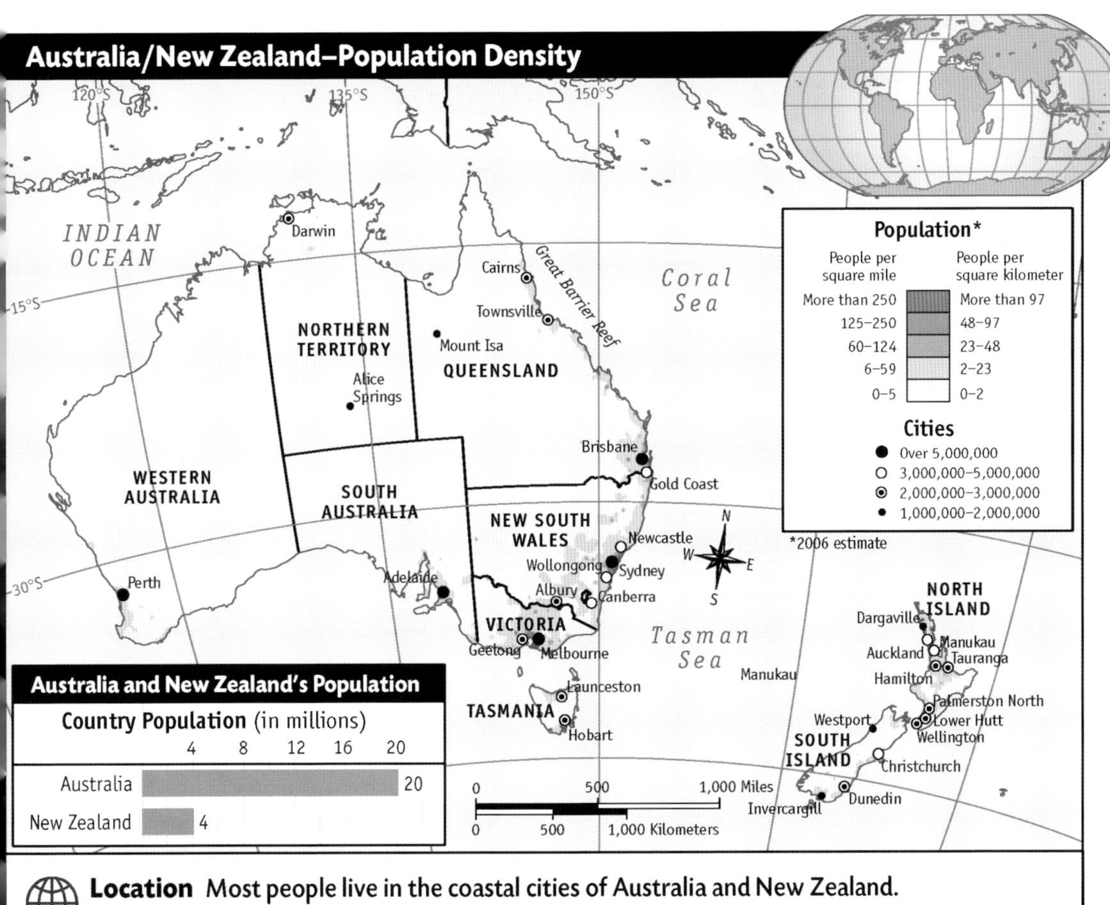

Location Most people live in the coastal cities of Australia and New Zealand. *What are the largest cities in each nation? What features of their interiors prevent many people from living there?*

LESSON 1 REVIEW

Fact Follow-Up

1. Describe the size and relative location of Australia and New Zealand.
2. What are two unique features of the Australian continent?
3. Name the islands that compose New Zealand.
4. What are two major rivers in Australia?

Talk About It

1. What would Australia be like today if the climate of the entire continent had been similar to the one settlers found on the eastern coast? Explain.
2. How are the Aborigines and Maoris like the Native American people of the Western Hemisphere? How are they different?

Caption Answer

Australia's largest cities are Perth, Adelaide, Melbourne, Sydney, and Brisbane. New Zealand's largest cities are Auckland, Manukau, and Christchurch. Australia's interior is too dry to support a large population. New Zealand's interior is mountains.

Map Activity

Australia/New Zealand–Population Density

NATIONAL GEOGRAPHY STANDARDS: 1, 9

GEOGRAPHIC THEMES: Location, Place

OBJECTIVES: 1.03, 2.02, 2.03

Have students complete the following:

1. Which Australian city has the greatest population density surrounding it? *Melbourne*
2. Which Australian cities have populations of more than 1 million. *Adelaide, Brisbane, Melbourne, Perth, Sydney*
3. Which Australian city in the Northern Territory has a population under 50,000? *Alice Springs*
4. Which Australian city is located on the Indian Ocean in the southwestern part of Western Australia? *Perth*
5. How many people live in Hobart? *50,000–250,000*
6. Which island in New Zealand has more major populated cities? *North Island*
7. Which New Zealand cities have a population of fewer than 1 million? *Auckland, Christchurch, Manukau*

LESSON 1 REVIEW

Fact Follow-Up Answers

1. Australia, an island nation, lies south of Indonesia. It is bounded by the Timor and Arafura Seas to the north, the Coral and Tasman Seas to the east, the Great Australian Bight to the south, and the Indian Ocean to the west. It is the world's sixth largest country and smallest continent. New Zealand is about 1,250 miles southeast of Australia across the Tasman Sea. It is bounded on the east by the Pacific Ocean. New Zealand is much smaller than Australia.
2. It is the flattest and smallest continent, and the only country that is also a continent.
3. The islands of New Zealand are North Island, South Island, and many smaller islands.
4. Australia's two major rivers are the Murray and the Darling.

Talk About It Answers

1. Important points: Encourage students to speculate. It might have more people and a more evenly distributed population. It is possible that it might produce more agricultural exports.
2. Important points: Students should state both likenesses and differences. Like Native Americans, many Aborigines died from diseases when the Europeans came. They also lost their land. Unlike Native Americans, the Aborigines were all hunter-gatherers. Unlike Native Americans, the Maori make up almost 15 percent of the population.

OBJECTIVES: 3.02, 7.01, 10.03, 11.03

Discussion Questions

1 Why do you think Australia has maintained ties to Great Britain?

2 Who were some of the early settlers to North Carolina?

3 What would motivate someone to move to a new land?

Caption Answer

Although she has no real decision-making power, the queen is a symbol of New Zealand's and Australia's British connection.

Writing Activity

Editorial

OBJECTIVES: 10.02, 10,03, 10.04

Over the past few decades, voter turnout in United States presidential elections is often around or less than 50 percent. The United States is a democracy, as is Australia. In both countries citizens have the right to vote. However, there is one major difference; citizens of Australia are fined if they fail to vote. Divide the class into two sides. Assign each side a different point of view on this issue. Point: Citizens in a democracy should be required to vote. Counterpoint: Citizens in a democracy should not be required to vote. Have students write or word process a newspaper editorial that includes an introductory paragraph, three supporting statements of the given point of view, and a closing paragraph. Have students brainstorm reasons for each point of view before they begin writing. Have students read editorials to class.

LESSON 2 Government and Economy

KEY IDEAS

- Australia was settled by theives and inmates from debtor's prisons.
- Both Australia and New Zealand share a common British heritage.
- Cattle, sheep, and farming are important to these two countries.

KEY TERMS

British Commonwealth of Nations
referendum

From 1788 to 1868, British prisoners, sentenced to exile in Australia, sailed 16,000 miles (25,760 km) across the Pacific Ocean to an unknown land. They worked as laborers, building roads or clearing land for farms. Most would never see their homeland again.

Most of the first European settlers had been convicted of stealing small amounts of money or property. These poor and uneducated people became the builders of a new nation. From its beginnings as a penal colony, Australia has grown into a land of stable government and strong democracy.

British Heritage

Australia

For tens of thousands of years, Australia belonged to the Aborigines. In 1770, British sea captain James Cook claimed Australia for Britain.

Eighteen years later, Britain turned the southeast corner of the continent into the penal colony of New South Wales. After the prisoners completed their sentences, many remained to make a new start in Australia. Many soldiers who moved to Australia as prison guards also stayed. Free settlers came too, attracted by gold or good grazing land. By 1859, six British colonies had been started on the continent.

In 1901, these colonies—New South Wales, Victoria, Tasmania, South Australia, Western Australia, and Queensland—formed the Commonwealth of Australia. As a former colony, Australia later joined the ***British Commonwealth of Nations,*** an association of countries that were once part of the British empire.

Britain's Queen Elizabeth II is Australia's official head of state. The British monarch has no decision-making power. This position is a symbol of Australia's British connection. A parliamentary democracy, Australian citizens elect members to parliament. The party that ha won the general election chooses the prim minister.

A ***referendum,*** or issue which is decided by all voters, to change Australia from a commonwealth headed by the British monarch to an independent republic was defeated in 1999.

Queen Elizabeth II (right) is the official head of the governments of both Australia and New Zealand. **What is her role in Australia and New Zealand?**

New Zealand

New Zealand, like Australia, was settled by the British. In 1840, as settlers sought to make New Zealand a British colony, they made an agreement with the Maori. The Maori people gave Britain's Queen Victoria the right to rule over New Zealand. In return, they received the right to keep whatever land they wished.

Europeans continued to arrive, taking Maori land without regard for the treaty. The British government did little to stop them. For several years the Maori and the British battled over land. The superiority of British weapons led to the Maori's defeat and loss of 3 million acres (1.2 million sq hm) of land.

Over the years the Maori became more outspoken about land rights. In the 1990s, they publicly protested and filed lawsuits to pressure the government to return the land more quickly. The New Zealand government began returning more land that Maori groups can prove once belonged to them. Today, many Maori are much more a part of New Zealand's economic and social life than the Aborigines in Australia.

New Zealand is a parliamentary democracy. The government has reserved four of the seats in this 95-member lawmaking body for Maori-elected officials. Like Australia, New Zealand belongs to the British Commonwealth of Nations.

Economy: Farm Products and Minerals

Australia

Once, Australia's economy "rode on the sheep's back." Today, cattle, wheat, and minerals help carry the load (see map, page 523).

Sheep, cattle, and wool are still Australia's most important farm exports. Australia produces 24 percent of all the wool in the world. The sparsely populated nation has five times as many sheep as people.

Australia leads the world in the exportation of beef. Most cattle stations lie in the Outback on the western side of the Great Dividing Range. These dry lands offer just enough grass and shrubs to provide grazing lands for millions of cattle.

To grow enough wheat for export, most farmers depend on machinery to do the work. Because most people live in cities, farm workers are scarce. Farm owners rely on huge machines to plant, weed, and harvest wheat.

Since the gold rushes of the 1850s, mining has been important to Australia's economy. Today, Australia is among the leading exporters of coal, bauxite, iron ore, uranium, lead, and zinc. Japan and China are key customers for Australia's minerals.

Australians are primarily producers of raw materials rather than makers of finished products for export. However, unlike most countries that depend on the export of raw materials, Australians have a relatively high standard of living.

Australia imports many of its manufactured goods, mainly from Japan, South Korea, Taiwan, and Hong Kong. Australian factories do produce a wide variety of products—including cars, paper, steel, and electrical equipment—but most of these goods are sold only within the country.

Maori children practice a Maori dance in front of their school. **How did New Zealand's European settlers treat the Maori?**

Discussion Questions

1 How did Europeans deal with the indigenous population in New Zealand?

2 Do you think Australia or New Zealand has a more successful relationship with the indigenous population?

3 Why do you think the Maori are more politically active than the Aborigines of Australia?

4 How do farmers in North Carolina adapt to a shortage of farm workers?

5 Why do countries that depend on the export of raw materials usually have a lower standard of living? What do you think has made the difference in Australia?

European Settlement Brought Trouble Down Under

OBJECTIVES: 3.02, 7.01, 7.02

When Europeans settled in Australia, they brought with them many species of animals. The wild descendants of these new animals created serious environmental threats. The European rabbit was brought to Australia for sporting purposes in the mid-nineteenth century. The population of this rabbit quickly escalated, to almost 500 million, because it had no natural predators. The damage this can cause includes soil erosion, native habitat destruction, and commercial production loses. Because of these damages, massive national efforts have been made to control the population of these rabbits and other animals. Students can research more about the European rabbit and how biology is used to control the population of this animal. Students can also find other animals such as foxes and cats that have caused similar problems in Australia. Students should write a summary of their findings and share them with the class.

The British made a treaty with the Maori but allowed Europeans to break it. As a result, the Maori and the British went to war, and the Maori lost 3 million acres of land.

Caption Answer

Sheep meat and wool are important exports for New Zealand.

Activity

Fact Cards

OBJECTIVES: 3.01, 5.01

Have pairs of students research from the text, or available resources, a minimum of 15 facts about agricultural (sheep or cattle) production or mineral resources in Australia or New Zealand. Have students write one question about each fact on the front side of an index card. Put the answer on the back of a different card. Have students place the question cards on a large map of Australia. Staple the answer card underneath the question card. Keep a blank sheet of paper next to the map so students can put down the question they answered.

Caption Answer

Farmers changed the name, cooks created special recipes, and new methods of refrigeration allowed the fruit to be flown anywhere without spoiling. As a result, the kiwi became a worldwide favorite.

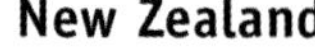

Sheep are herded in the Ben Ohau Range of South Island. **Why are sheep important to New Zealand?**

New Zealand

Like Australia, New Zealand is a supplier of meat and wool to other nations. New Zealand lamb and beef can be found on dinner tables around the world. New Zealand is second only to Australia in the export of wool.

New Zealand's mild winters, warm summers, and plentiful rainfall are ideal for raising livestock. Grass grows all year, and animals do not need to be kept inside during the winter months.

Sheep and cattle stations are much smaller than in the Australian Outback. Average stations cover around 375 acres (150 sq hm) of land. The largest stations border the slopes of the Southern Alps on South Island.

One of New Zealand's most unusual exports is a small egg-shaped fruit with a hairy brown outside and an emerald greer inside. This fruit was first called the Chinese gooseberry.

In the 1970s, demand for New Zealand's apples and peaches dropped. Shrewd farmers renamed the Chinese gooseberry the *kiwi* after the flightless bir found only in New Zealand. Cooks created special kiwi fruit recipes. New technology in refrigeration allowed kiwi t be flown anywhere without spoiling. As kiwi, the fruit became an international success. Today, the kiwi has become a worldwide favorite.

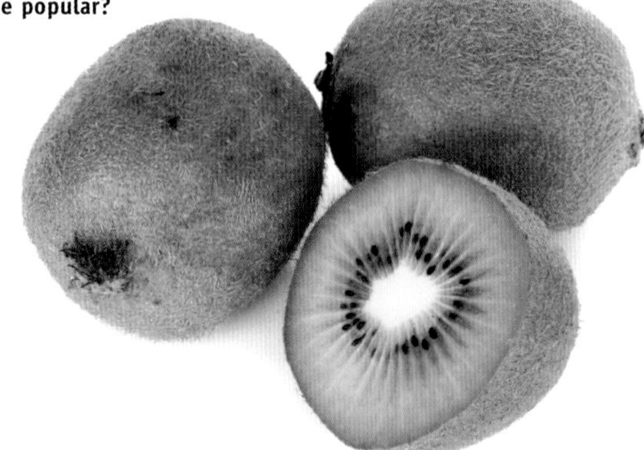

Kiwi fruit, formerly known as the Chinese gooseberry, is an international favorite. **How did kiwi become popular?**

534 Chapter 2

Background Information

New Zealand's Agriculture

In New Zealand, agriculture and food processing are key economic activities. Because of its geographic isolation, New Zealand's farms, orchards, and tree plantations have remained largely free of the pests and diseases that drive up production costs and could restrict export of New Zealand produce to other countries. However, this isolation has also left native plants and animals highly susceptible to foreign invaders such as cats, dogs, rats, and mites that have come by boat and plane. These animals and insects have multiplied rapidly in the absence of natural predators. The Australian brushtail possum, introduced to New Zealand a century ago—despite control efforts—now numbers about 70 million. Each year, New Zealand intercepts about 4,500 organisms and seizes 86,000 goods, like apples, meat, and honey, that could carry diseases. The more than 60,000 imported used cars that enter New Zealand each year are carefully checked for insect hitchhikers.

'acific Partners

In the 1970s, income from trade with ıe United Kingdom and other parts of Vestern Europe dropped for both ustralia and New Zealand. In 1973, the nited Kingdom joined the European ommon Market, now known as the uropean Union.

The European Union, a trade rganization of most of the nations of Vestern Europe, requires members to ade with other European nations first. his prompted Australia and New ealand to look for new trading partners.

The booming economies of Japan, hina, and other parts of Asia offered ew markets for products manufactured in ustralia and New Zealand. Malaysia, hina, and Japan have invested in ustralia and New Zealand. The Japanese uy more than $21 billion worth of ustralian products per year. Australia xports more to Japan than to any other ation. Australia also imports more roducts from the United States than from ny other single country. New Zealand's ading trade partner is Australia.

Today, both countries are working to uild strong ties with the Asian nations of ıe Pacific Rim—those nations that border ıe Pacific Ocean. To show goodwill oward Asian nations, Australia ended its white Australia" immigration policy. sians and Africans soon became ustralian residents.

Japanese tourists hold koala bears during a visit to Australia. **How are Australia and New Zealand building stronger ties to Asia?**

Today, Japanese is taught in hundreds of Australian schools. Thousands of Japanese tourists stream through Australia's tourist attractions, climbing Uluru (Ayers) Rock and touring Sydney's Opera House (see page 541). Window signs and restaurant menus appear in Japanese and English.

New Zealand also looked to Asia for new markets for its products and found many customers. Japan has become a key trading partner. Japanese manufacturers have built factories in Auckland to produce goods for Asian buyers. Korea has now overtaken the United Kingdom as a market for New Zealand's products. Asian immigrants, students, and tourists have helped turn New Zealand's economy toward the Pacific Rim.

LESSON 2 REVIEW

Fact Follow-Up

1. For what country did James Cook claim Australia? Who were its first settlers?
2. Who are New Zealand's native people?
3. What are Australia's important farm products? minerals?
4. What are New Zealand's important farm products?
5. What two Asian nations have become important trading partners for New Zealand?

Talk About It

1. What effect did the United Kingdom's entry into the European Union have on the economies of Australia and New Zealand? Explain.
2. Why did Australia change its immigration policy?
3. Throughout this textbook you have read about European Imperialism, especially the influence of the British Empire. Do you think British Imperialsim has done more to help or hurt the cultures it has been involved with? Explain.

Discussion Questions

1 Why are trade organizations such as the European Union good? What are some of their drawbacks?

2 Would you recommend that the United States belong to one?

3 What are some of the changes that have occurred in Australia as a result of closer trading ties with Asia?

Caption Answer

Asians can now become Australian citizens. Japanese is taught in Australian schools, and some window signs appear in English and Japanese. Both Australia and New Zealand are increasing trade with Asian nations.

Activity

Prism of Australia

OBJECTIVES: 1.03, 2.01, 3.01

Materials handouts octagonal prism pattern; pens; colored pencils, markers, crayons; scissors, transparent tape or glue/glue sticks

Using hexagonal prism pattern found in the Teacher's Resource Guide, have students illustrate the eight Australian states and territories, using one side of the prism for each (Australian Capital Territory, New South Wales, Northern Territory, Queensland, South Australia, Tasmania, Victoria, and Western Australia). One end of the prism can be used to describe Australia as a country and the opposite end used to describe Australia as a continent.

LESSON 2 REVIEW

Fact Follow-Up Answers

1. Cook claimed Australia for Britain. For tens of thousands of years, Australia had belonged to the Aborigines.
2. The Maori.
3. Australia's important farm products are sheep, cattle, and wool. Minerals include coal, bauxite, iron ore, uranium, lead, and zinc.
4. New Zealand's important farm products are sheep, farming, and kiwi fruit.
5. Japan and Korea are important trading partners for New Zealand.

Talk About It Answers

1. Important points: Student responses should focus on economic effects. Trade with Britain has dropped. Both Australia and New Zealand are looking to Pacific Rim nations for trading partners.
2. Australia needed new trading partners, so it worked to build stronger ties with Pacific Rim nations. ending the "White Australia" policy was a sign of goodwill.
3. Important points: Guide students in a discussion of the benefits brought by the British and modernization weighed against the loss of rights and culture by aboriginal/native peoples.

OBJECTIVES: 4.03, 6.01, 10.04

Discussion Questions

1 What are some expressions we have that visitors to our area might have difficulties understanding?

Caption Answer

The warm, dry climate encourages outdoor recreation. Beautiful beaches are near the cities.

Teacher Notes

Slip, Slap, Slop!

Australia leads the world in the number of cases of skin cancer reported each year. Students are required by law to wear hats when going outside for recess or physical education. In a continuing effort to protect its citizens, Australia's public health department has placed the following slogan on billboards and on radio and television public announcements: Slip, Slap, Slop!: Slip on a t-shirt, slap on a hat, and slop on the sunscreen.

Activity

Healthy Slogans and Safety Programs

OBJECTIVES: 3.01, 6.02, 11.02

Have students brainstorm slogans and programs that they are already familiar with: "Click It or Ticket," North Carolina's seatbelt slogan; "Remember, only you can prevent forest fires," promoting fire safety; DARE; MADD; SADD; and others. Next, student groups should brainstorm new slogans promoting safety or healthy habits. Once they have determined a slogan, each group should create a bumper sticker for their slogan.

LESSON 3 Culture and Society

KEY IDEAS

- Australians and New Zealanders enjoy outdoor life.
- Large isolated farms create special ways of life.
- Aborigines struggle to maintain traditional ways of life.

KEY TERMS

Dreamtime
tramping

Australians love the outdoors and the beaches in particular. One Outback town, Alice Springs, has found a way to enjoy water sports even though the ocean or even a trickle of water is hundreds of miles away. Every year, the people of Alice Springs hold a "boat race" (right) on the dusty, dry riverbed of the Todd River. Thousands of Aussies come to watch teams of people carrying bottomless boats and sprinting toward the finish line.

Outdoor People

Australians like to have fun, and they like to have their fun outdoors. In the warm, dry climate, the weather usually cooperates. If you hear someone say "Let's put a steak on the barbie," would you know that means barbecuing steak or shrimp on an outdoor grill? It is a popular way to entertain.

Windsurfing, sailing, swimming, water-skiing, and other water sports are popular along the coasts. They attract vacationers from the Outback. Australia has many beautiful beaches, and many are less than an hour from a major city.

Aussies also enjoy team sports, especially cricket, soccer, Australian Rules football, and rugby. Cricket, which came from the United Kingdom, is something like baseball. It is a summertime sport played with a ball and bat. Cricket requires considerable skill from the two teams of eleven players each.

In the winter, fast and rough Australian Rules football is a crowd pleaser. Unlike American football, players do not wear helmets or heavy padding. They can use their hands and feet to tackle their opponents and capture the ball.

Boats and seaplanes bring tourists to the Great Barrier Reef on Australia's east coast. **Why do you think many Australians prefer outdoor sports?**

536 Chapter 2

Teacher Notes

Didgeridoo

More than 1,000 years ago, Aborigines of Northern Australia created a tubelike instrument, the didjeridu, to accompany their singing and dancing in rituals and entertainment. The didgeridoo is made from an irregular eucalyptus branch. They selected branches between 3 to 5-feet long that has been hollowed out by termites. It is polished and decorated with totemic designs. At the smaller end of the tube a mouthpiece is made of beeswax. To make music with the didgeridoo, players use a technique called "circular breathing": inhaling through the nose and exhaling through the tube while loosely vibrating the lips. The pitch and texture of sound can be changed by altering lip placement, tongue placement, and diaphragm pressure. Vocal sounds are included to create buzzing, chirping, croaking, growling, and humming effects that imitate animals, birds, and insects.

In New Zealand, the favorite national game is rugby, a game similar to football. The national rugby team, the All Blacks, whose name comes from the players' black shorts and shirts, has won many international sports meets. Cricket and soccer are other popular team sports.

New Zealanders will go to almost any length for an outdoor adventure, especially on the water. They also enjoy skydiving, skiing, mountain biking, sailing, exploring caves, and rafting through caverns.

With New Zealand's many scenic mountains, it is not surprising that its people want to spend their leisure time on the slopes. New Zealanders love backpacking and hiking, which they call ***tramping.*** Many New Zealanders also enjoy mountain climbing. This outdoor activity has won New Zealand a place in sports history. New Zealander Sir Edmund Hillary led the first team of climbers ever to reach the top of Mount Everest, the world's highest mountain.

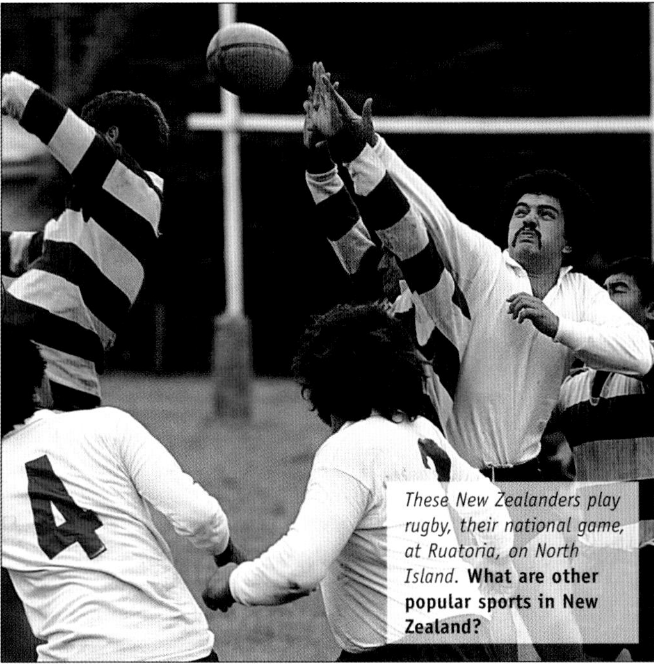

These New Zealanders play rugby, their national game, at Ruatoria, on North Island. **What are other popular sports in New Zealand?**

On a South Island Sheep Station

Sheep farmer Hamish MacArthur and his family run a sheep station on New Zealand's South Island. Like Australian sheep stations, Hamish's farm is far away from large cities. Because sheep flock together, he does not need much help tending his herd of 2,000 sheep.

August is the busiest month of the year because that is when the sheep are sheared. With the help of his two sons and their sheep dog, Hamish herds his sheep into a large fenced pasture close to the shearing shed. Hamish hires professional shearers to come to the station to shear the sheep. These shearers work swiftly using electric clippers to remove the entire fleece in one piece.

Farmworkers gather the heaps of wool and sort them according to the quality of the wool. Then the wool is bound into huge bales and shipped to market.

A sheep shearer removes wool without harming the sheep. **Why is New Zealand an ideal place to raise sheep?**

Discussion Questions

1 What are some outdoor activities people in North Carolina enjoy?

2 What is something you would like to be the "first" to accomplish?

Caption Answer

Other popular sports include skydiving, skiing, mountain biking, exploring caves, and rafting through caverns.

Caption Answer

Its climate offers mild winters, warm summers, and plentiful rainfall. Grass grows all year, and the animals do not need to be housed indoors during the winter.

Activity

Model Station

OBJECTIVES: 1.01, 1.03

Have students make a model of a sheep or cattle station in New Zealand or Australia. They should research the topic and label parts of the station. Have students attach an index card explaining the importance of sheep and cattle to either country's economy and present projects to the class.

Background Information

Changing Sydney

Sydneysiders is the name residents of Sydney, Australia's largest city, like to call themselves. Once smaller than Melbourne, its nearby sister city, Sydney is today a city of 3.6 million with a dynamic economy fueled by its global connections. Its futures exchange is the biggest in the Asian market, and its branch of the Australian Stock Exchange now ranks right behind Tokyo and Hong Kong in the Asian region. Two thirds of all international businesses choose Sydney for their Australian headquarters. Its role as host of the 2000 Summer Olympics increased its international visibility. Australian writer David Dale said of Sydney, "Fifty years ago we ate British food, read British books, lived unadventurous British lives. Then we had a boom of non-British immigrants. . . . It completely transformed Australia, especially the big cities."

Discussion Questions

1 Why are stations in the Outback so large?

2 Would you like to depend on short-wave radios for your education? What would be some of the benefits and disadvantages?

Teacher Notes

Rugby

Rugby is named for a borough of central England near Birmingham. The Rugby School is located there. The game of rugby originated at this school in 1823, when during a game of soccer a player picked up the ball and ran with it. From its origin at the Rugby School the game spread. In 1871 the rules were standardized by the English Rugby Union. Since its humble beginnings, rugby has spread all over the world and teams can be found on every continent except Antarctica. The international governing body for this sport is the International Rugby Football Board, or IRFB. The World Cup is the international championship title.

New Zealand's National Rugby Team: The All Blacks

The first rugby game was played in New Zealand on May 14, 1870. It wasn't until 1892 that the New Zealand Rugby Football Union was established to administer the game at the national level. The national team is called the All Blacks, named for their jerseys, which are all black with a silver fern on the left breast.

The All Blacks have a unique tradition. Before a rugby match the team performs a haka. Haka is a Maori word for dance. The haka is performed to intimidate the opposing team. The haka performed by the All Blacks is called "Ka Mate, Ka Mate." This haka is performed before every All Blacks game. This tradition goes all the way back to the1880s.

THE OUTBACK

Mustering Cattle on 600,000 Acres

The Koeyers family lives on a 600,000-acre (240,000 sq hm) cattle ranch in northwestern Australia. The nearest school is more than 200 miles (322 km) away in the city of Derby, Western Australia, so the Koeyers children attend the School of the Air. Classes are beamed each morning by short-wave radio from Derby. Visits from the Royal Flying Doctor Service keep their shots up to date. In the vast Outback there are even Flying Padres, priests or ministers who come by plane to perform christenings, marriages, burials, and other religious services.

The Koeyers's cattle station is small compared to some. One of the earliest cattle stations, known as Kidman's Corner, took up an area the size of Washington state. The 12,000-square-mile (31,200-sq-km) Anna Creek cattle station in South Australia is larger than either Maryland or Vermont.

Every year at roundup, called the "muster" by Australians, all the cattle at the station are collected in one place. On large stations, the muster can take three or four days to complete. When station owner John Koeyers goes out to muster the last of his cattle, he does not go by horse like the jackeroos (male station hands) of 30 or 40 years ago. He catches his stray cattle from a sturdy jeep called a bull buggy. When he sees a young cow that has strayed from the herd, he follows it in his bull buggy until he gets close enough to lasso it with a sturdy rope from the front seat of his jeep. After tying its front legs together, he waits for station hands to come and load the struggling cow onto their truck for the trip back to the station. Even this method of ranching is becoming outdated. Today, many of the large cattle stations use helicopters to bring in the stray cattle.

Cattle station, Western Queensland

538 Chapter 26

It's a Fact

Australia

■ Australia has a railroad track that runs in a straight line for 297 miles (478 km). It is call the "long straight." It is a part of the Indian Pacific railroad that runs from Sidney to Perth—from the Pacific Ocean to the Indian Ocean. It is the world's longest railroad at 2,795 miles (4,500 km).

■ Camels were brought to Australia from Afghanistan to use for exploration and to carry cargo in the desert. Wild camels are found only in Australia. Some have been exported to Arabian countries. Camel racing is popular in Alice Springs.

■ Cargo is carried largely by the truck trains (54 wheelers). These truckers drive 65-horse power, 20-gear rigs to carry essential items to the stations. Some of the truckers pull as many as six trailers along the east coast roads of Australia.

The First Australians: Yesterday and Today

Aborigines originally were hunters and atherers. Woomeras—wooden hrowers—helped them hurl spears long istances. Boomerangs—flat, curved vooden objects—stunned or killed small nimals. Aborigines also gathered plants, nushrooms, birds' eggs, caterpillars, and hellfish.

Today, few Aboriginal communities till follow traditional ways of life. Those hat do are located in the Northern erritory, the northern part of Western ustralia, and in northern Queensland. Aany Aborigines work on cattle stations n the Outback. They hold mostly low-aying, unskilled, or semiskilled jobs.

Although scattered across the ontinent, Aborigines continue to be nited by their spiritual beliefs. Aborigines ave an important uniting spiritual belief alled ***Dreamtime.*** This comes from a nystic time long ago when the "Ancients" or "Sky Heroes" created everything. The Aborigines' stories about Dreamtime xplain how animals, trees, rocks, water oles, and other parts of the natural world ame to exist.

The Aborigines believe that the Ancients made them the caretakers of the and and that the land has to be treated vith great respect. Aborigines have many acred sites associated with the deeds of he Ancients. Many of these sites have painted rocks thousands of years old. Aborigines believe that these paintings were done in Dreamtime. When the British settled Australia, they occupied many places considered sacred by the Aborigines.

The Aborigines have faced severe discrimination for much of this century. They were not allowed to vote until 1962. They were not included in the national population census until 1967. By the 1970s, Aborigine groups were working to win back land taken from them by the early settlers.

Some Aborigines have left cities and resettled on reserves in remote areas where they can practice traditional ways of living. In 1985, the Australian government began preserving places of special importance to Aborigines. The government returned Uluru Rock, also known as Ayers Rock, one of the Aborigines' most sacred sites. In turn, they agreed to lease it back to the government for 99 years as Uluru National Park.

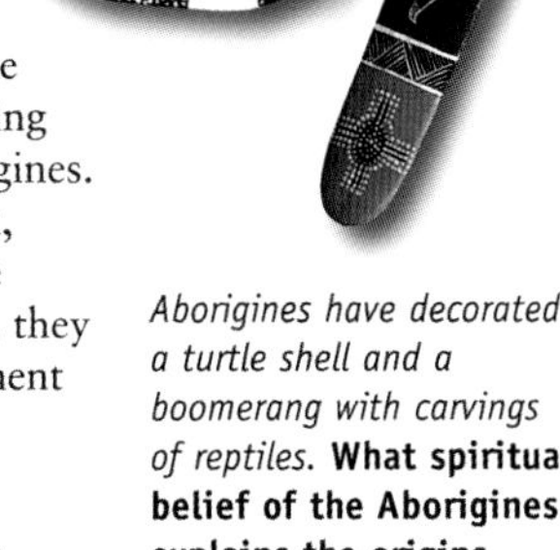

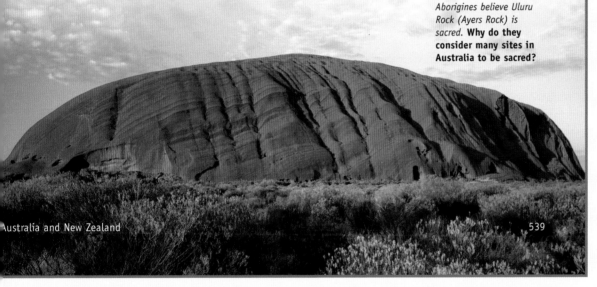

Aborigines have decorated a turtle shell and a boomerang with carvings of reptiles. **What spiritual belief of the Aborigines explains the origins of animals?**

What would YOU do?

Now that Australia has been establishing reserves for Aborigines, the descendants of these first settlers may be finding it easier to live in their traditional ways. Imagine that you are part of an Aboriginal community. Would you want to stay with the community and traditional ways? Or would you leave for a ranch or city, seeking a modern way of life?

Aborigines believe Uluru Rock (Ayers Rock) is sacred. **Why do they consider many sites in Australia to be sacred?**

■ The Tasmanian devil is a member of the marsupial family. It is actually the largest surviving carnivorous marsupial. Although only the size of a small dog, its physical features and high-pitched sounds prompted the early European settlers to name it the Devil. Its powerful jaws and teeth make it possible to completely devour prey whole. These devils once roamed the mainland of Australia, but today are found only in Tasmania. It is believed that the devils became extinct on the mainland about 600 years ago—before European settlement of the continent. Scientists believe that the dingo drove these devils from the mainland. These fierce creatures can be seen at the Asbestos Range National Park, Mountain William National Park, Cradle Mountain National Park, the Arthur River, and highland lake area.

Discussion Questions

1 Why do you think early cultures placed so much emphasis on nature?

2 How involved are Native Americans in United States culture? Why do you think there is such a movement today in preserving Native American culture?

3 Do you think the government has a responsibility in helping to preserve the indigenous culture?

4 What do you think should happen to Uluru in 99 years?

5 What are two cities or towns in North Carolina that have a friendly rivalry? How can such a rivalry be beneficial?

Caption Answer

The spiritual belief called Dreamtime explains that the Ancients created everything.

Caption Answer

Aborigines associate many sites with the deeds of the Ancients.

Math Activity

Boomerang!

OBJECTIVES: 8.03, 12.02

Boomerangs—flat, curved wooden objects—stunned or killed small animals. The Australian boomerang was a hunting tool. Have students make boomerangs using tagboard, Styrofoam, and/or balsa wood. Have students decorate boomerangs in traditional designs. Hold a boomerang race, judging most creative, greatest distance traveled, and most durable. Divide boomerangs into two categories—the nonreturning variety (heavy, less curved , used for hunting) and the returning type (lighter, smaller, and used mostly for fun and show).

Make a histogram displaying the results of throwing the nonreturning boomerangs.

Extension Novice and intermediate ELL students will need peer tutor to complete the histogram.

Discussion Questions

1 Do you think the decision to make Canberra the capital of Australia was a wise one?

2 How does that decision compare to the decision to establish a new city—Washington, D.C.—to be the capital of the United States, or the decision to make Raleigh the capital of North Carolina?

Caption Answer

Melbourne is quieter and more British than Sydney.

Activity

Australian Slang Terms

OBJECTIVES: 11.01, 12.03

Give students a list of slang terms along with their meanings and have them try to match them correctly, or read the terms aloud to students one at a time and have them guess the meaning.

biscuit = cookie
bloke = man
sheila = girl or woman
mate = friend or pal
tucker = food
tuck shop = school cafeteria
ollies = candy
footie = Australian football rules
Yankie = Australian name for all Americans
walkie = journey or just a short walk
milk bar = soda fountain
Mum = mother
lemonade = 7-Up
hard yakka = really hard work
torch = flash light
postie = mail carrier
roo = kangaroo
mozzies = mosquitoes
Oz = Australia
bloody oath! = No kidding!
fair dinkum! = For real! Or You're not kidding!

The Flinders Street Station in Melbourne shows the British influence in the city. **How is Melbourne different from Sydney?**

Rival Cities: Sydney and Melbourne

Australia's two largest cities, Sydney and Melbourne, are friendly rivals. Their citizens enjoy arguing about the merits of their hometowns. These cities hold a combined population of almost 8 million people. They are home to two out of every five Australians. Each city has developed its own identity.

Sydney is a city of beaches and lively night spots. Sydneysiders, as the people are called, love to catch the rays on nearby Bondi Beach.

Sydney grew up around the harbor, one of the largest in the world with 150 miles (242 km) of shoreline. One of Sydney's most famous landmarks is the Opera House. Its curving shapes, like billowing sails of a ship, seem to flow out across the harbor.

Multiethnic Sydney has neighborhoods of many nationalities. In the year 2000, Sydney hosted the Summer Olympic Games.

Melbourne is known as a city of parks and gardens. It is quieter and considered less flashy and more British than Sydney.

Melbournians proudly point to the carefully restored banks, train stations, office buildings, churches, theaters, and row houses that date back to the late 1800s. Green and yellow trams crisscross the city, serving commuters and tourists. At the Melbourne Cricket Grounds, 100,000 fans can watch their teams play. The Cricket Grounds were the site of the 1956 Olympic Games.

Although the rivalry between the two cities is now a friendly one, it was much more heated in 1901 when Australia's British colonies were becoming a nation. Once united, Australia needed a national capital. Both Sydney and Melbourne wanted the honor. Competition became so fierce that government leaders decided not to choose either one. Instead, they built Canberra, some distance from both cities (see map, page 531). Canberra became Australia's only large city not on the coast

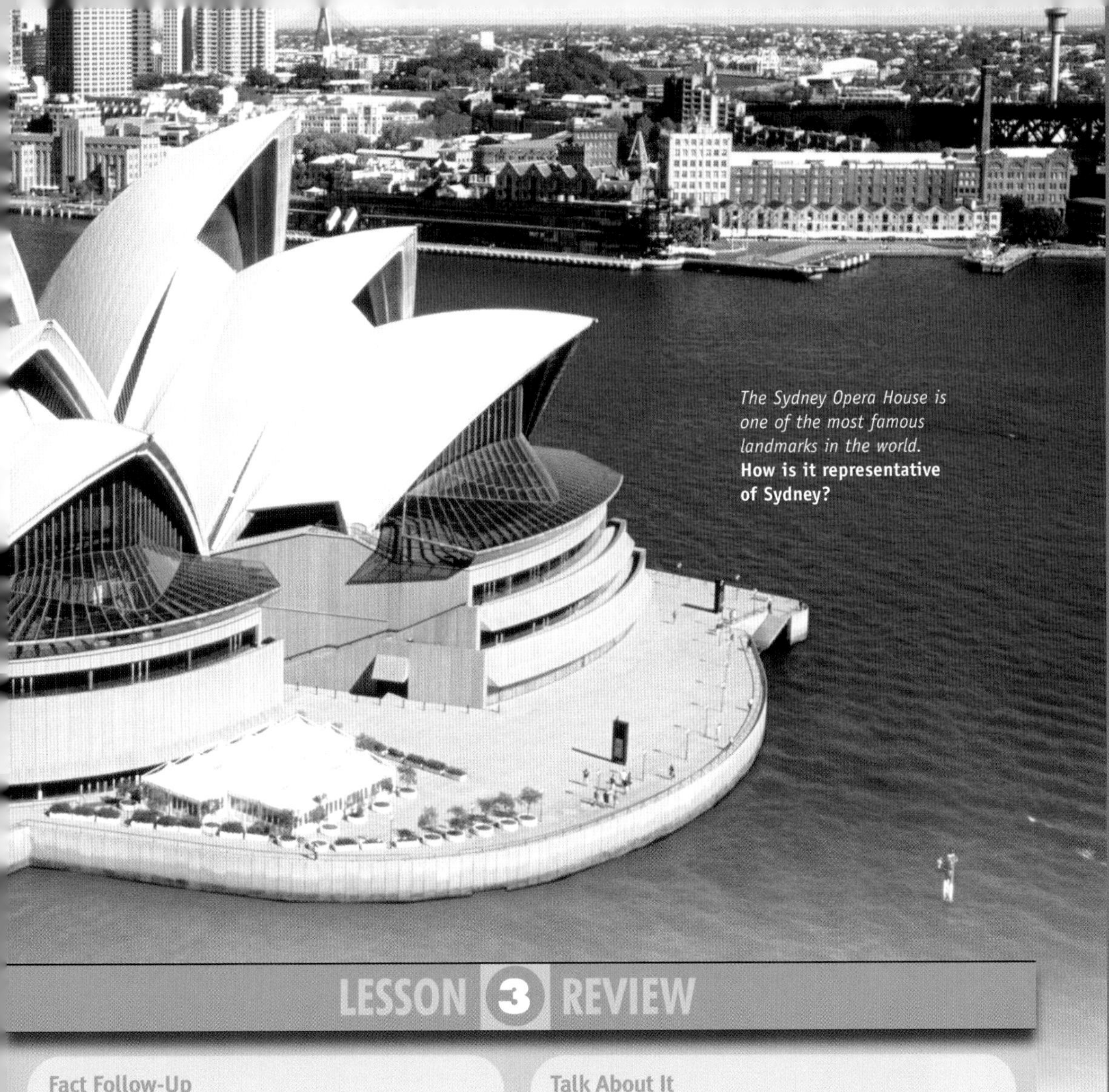

The Sydney Opera House is one of the most famous landmarks in the world. **How is it representative of Sydney?**

LESSON 3 REVIEW

Fact Follow-Up

1. What are some sports enjoyed by Australian people?
2. What is Dreamtime, and what is its importance for Aborigines and other Australians?
3. What are the two largest cities in Australia? Describe their relative location.
4. What is tramping?

Talk About It

1. Do you think that Australians were wise to establish Canberra as the capital city? Explain your answer.
2. Apply the geographic theme of human-environmental interaction to one feature of Australian life.
3. Why are Melbourne and Sydney friendly rivals? Where would you prefer to live? Why?

Caption Answer

Its curving shapes, like the billowing sails of a ship, seem to sail out across Sydney's harbor. Sydney is a port city, and its harbor is one of the largest in the world.

Activity

Australian Strips and Scrolls

OBJECTIVES: 11.01, 11.02, 11.03

Many Australian cultures and special ways of life can be illustrated using tagboard strips or scroll books. Choose a topic and illustrate traditional ways of Australian life.

Suggested topics:

- School of the Air
- Life on the Outback Mustering
- The Sheep Farms of Australia
- The Ways of Life of the Aborigine
- Hunting in the Outback
- Outdoor Sports

Extension ELL students should use an ELL-friendly Web site for research.

LESSON 3 REVIEW

Fact Follow-Up Answers

1. Water sports include windsurfing, sailing, swimming, and skiing. Other sports include cricket, soccer, Australian Rules football, and rugby.
2. Dreamtime is an ancient time when Aborigines believe the world and everything in it was created. They believe the Ancients made them caretakers of the land, which has to be treated with great respect. Europeans took over many sacred sites that only recently have begun to be returned to the Aborigines.
3. The two largest cities are Sydney and Melbourne. Sydney is on Australia's southeast coast, on the Tasman Sea. Melbourne is on the south coast, across from Tasmania.
4. New Zealanders call backpacking and hiking "tramping".

Talk About It Answers

1. Students should state an opinion and explain it. It was a way of striking a compromise between two important cities.
2. Important points: Students should choose one example and explain the human-environmental interaction in that example. Note: Aborigine feelings about the earth, the development of sheep farming, and mining are possible examples.
3. The rivalry is now a friendly one, but it was more heated at the time a decision had to be made about where the national capital would be. The rivalry was so fierce that leaders chose neither one but built Canberra instead. The two cities are relatively close but very different. This often leads to rivalry. Important points: Students should state which city they would choose and give reasons for their answer. Preferences should refer to physical and cultural characteristics of place.

Teaching This Skill Lesson

Materials textbooks, paper, pencils

Classroom Organization whole class, small group work

Beginning the Lesson Read the four questions posed in the student Skill Lesson aloud, replacing "Australia" with "the United States" or "North Carolina." (Note: Issues related to immigration can be highly inflammatory. Be sure to handle this discussion with sensitivity.) Do questions like these reflect a "real" problem in Australia, the United States, or North Carolina? Ask: How can we tell whether there is a real problem with immigration in both nations.

Lesson Development Refer students to the chart showing annual population growth. Have them compare growth (estimating actual numbers in thousands) from natural increase and net overseas migration using the information in the chart. Remind students that this is population growth, not the entire population. Ask questions such as: Does it appear that the rate of natural increase in population is rising or falling? Is the increase from immigration rising or falling? Next, refer students to the Settler's Arrivals chart in the Skill Lesson. Ask what the major sources of immigrants are? How many are of European descent?

Place students in pairs or groups of three and assign each grouping one of the five questions posed in the lesson. Ask students to imagine they are employees of the Australian government. Using the information they have, how would they answer the questions? (Allow different groups dealing with the same question to share their responses.)

Conclusion Ask: Is there a "real" problem with immigration to Australia?

Extension Have each student write a persuasive paragraph responding to one of the questions as a homework assignment. If desirable, have students visit the Web site for Australia's Department of Immigration and Multicultural Affairs to compare their own answers with those of the Australian government.

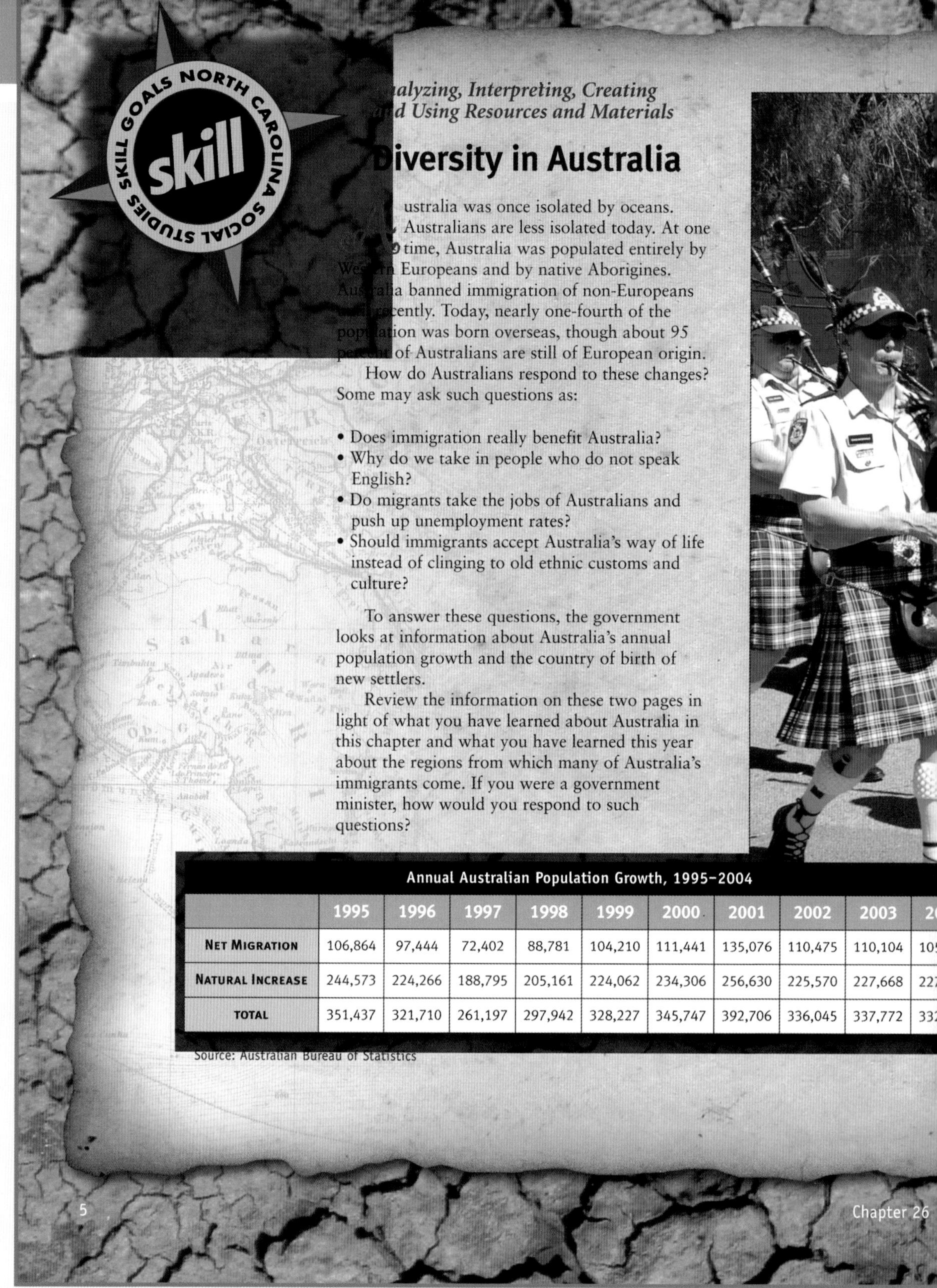

Analyzing, Interpreting, Creating and Using Resources and Materials

Diversity in Australia

Australia was once isolated by oceans. Australians are less isolated today. At one time, Australia was populated entirely by Western Europeans and by native Aborigines. Australia banned immigration of non-Europeans until recently. Today, nearly one-fourth of the population was born overseas, though about 95 percent of Australians are still of European origin.

How do Australians respond to these changes? Some may ask such questions as:

- Does immigration really benefit Australia?
- Why do we take in people who do not speak English?
- Do migrants take the jobs of Australians and push up unemployment rates?
- Should immigrants accept Australia's way of life instead of clinging to old ethnic customs and culture?

To answer these questions, the government looks at information about Australia's annual population growth and the country of birth of new settlers.

Review the information on these two pages in light of what you have learned about Australia in this chapter and what you have learned this year about the regions from which many of Australia's immigrants come. If you were a government minister, how would you respond to such questions?

Annual Australian Population Growth, 1995–2004

	1995	1996	1997	1998	1999	2000	2001	2002	2003	20
NET MIGRATION	106,864	97,444	72,402	88,781	104,210	111,441	135,076	110,475	110,104	10
NATURAL INCREASE	244,573	224,266	188,795	205,161	224,062	234,306	256,630	225,570	227,668	22
TOTAL	351,437	321,710	261,197	297,942	328,227	345,747	392,706	336,045	337,772	33

Source: Australian Bureau of Statistics

5 Chapter 26

Police bagpipers at the Perth Royal Show

Top Ten Settler Arrivals in Australia by Country of Birth, 2001

Country	Number of Settlers	Percentage of Total Settlers
New Zealand	12,275	14.9
United Kingdom	8,656	10.5
China (excludes SARs and Taiwan)	4,506	5.4
India	4,223	5.1
Malaysia	3,861	4.7
South Africa	3,684	4.4
South Korea	3,010	3.6
Singapore	2,822	3.4
Indonesia	2,753	3.3
United States	2,566	3.1

Skill Lesson Review

1. How are Australians' concerns about immigration similar to and different from concerns of people in the United States? *Important points: Students will likely see many similarities. Encourage their responses.*
2. Is immigration into Australia large enough so that Australians should be concerned? *Important points: Refer students to the tables in the skill lesson.*
3. What are some benefits for Australia that immigrants bring with them? *Important points: Encourage students to speculate on possible benefits.*

Talk About It

1. Important points: Encourage students to speculate on reasons why (1) the policy was adopted, and (2) why the policy was later changed. At one time it seemed important to Australians to keep their European cultural identity. Now the nation wants to build strong ties to neighboring Asian nations.
2. Important points: Students should be encouraged to state a position and give reasons for the position. The British had a treaty with the Maori, but they did not honor it. Possibly the superior weapons of the British encouraged them not to honor the treaty; such a situation would hardly have happened in Europe.
3. Important points: Students should choose several places they would wish to visit, what they would expect to see in these locations, and give reasons why they would choose these places over others.
4. Important points: Students should take a position and give reasons for it. It is important that students focus on both sports participation and spectator sports.

CHAPTER 26 REVIEW

Lessons Learned

LESSON 1
People and their Environment
Australia and New Zealand lie entirely within the Southern Hemisphere. Australia is south of Indonesia. New Zealand is located 1,250 miles (2,013 km) southeast of Australia. It is one of Australia's closest neighbors. The people of Australia and New Zealand live near the coasts because of the ruggedness of the countries' interiors.

LESSON 2
Government and Economy
Australia was first settled more than 50,000 years ago by Aborigines, people from Southeast Asia. New Zealand's first settlers were Maori from the Pacific Islands who arrived about 1,000 years ago. Britsh settlers claimed both territories in the eighteenth and nineteenth centuries. The United Kingdom's influence is seen in the governments and cultures of Australia and New Zealand. Both nations allowed only white people to move to their countries. After World War II, both countries changed immigration policies by removing racial barriers.

LESSON 3
Culture and Society
Australians and New Zealanders enjoy the outdoors. Farming creates special ways of life. Aborigines are scattered throughout the continent but are united by their spiritual beliefs. Many places in Australia are sacred to the Aborigine people.

Talk About It

1. Why do you think Australia adopted a policy that restricted immigration on the basis of race? Why did the nation then later remove racial barriers?
2. In the struggle between the Maori and the British, were the Maori treated as the British might have treated defeated Europeans? Explain.
3. If you were to visit Australia and New Zealand, what places would you visit, and what would you especially like to see? Give reasons for your answers.
4. Are sports more important to Australians and New Zealanders than to Americans? Explain.

Mastering Mapwork

LOCATION

Use the maps on page 523 to answer these questions:

1. Describe the relative location of iron mining regions in Australia.
2. Describe the location of New Zealand relative to the location of Australia.
3. Describe the relative location of Canberra, Australia.
4. Describe the relative location of Perth, Australia.
5. Describe the relative of location of gold mining areas in Australia.
6. Describe the relative location of coal mining areas of Australia.
7. Describe the relative location of areas of little or no economic activity in Australia.
8. Describe the relative location of Tasmania.

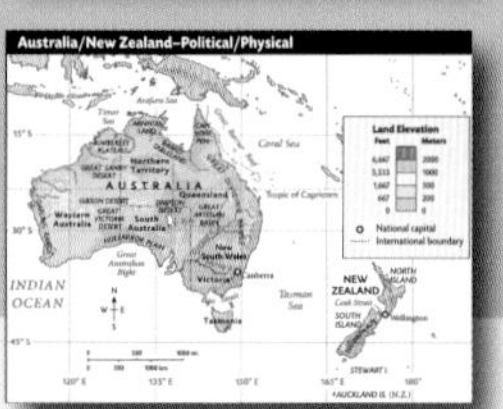

544 Chapter 26

Mastering Mapwork

1. Iron mining regions are located in northern, northwestern, western, and southern Australia. There are some iron deposits in southeastern Australia and on the island of Tasmania.
2. New Zealand is located southeast of Australia and is separated from Australia by the Tasman Sea.
3. Canberra is located roughly between Sydney to the north and Melbourne to the south along the southeast coast of Australia.
4. Perth is located on the southwestern coast of Australia.
5. Gold mining regions are, for the most part, located relatively near Australia's northeastern, southwestern, and southern coastlines.
6. Coal mining regions are located along northern, eastern, and southern coastlines, along the southwestern coast, and in Tasmania.
7. Areas of little or no economic activity are located in the center of the continent and along the south central coastline.
8. Tasmania is an island located directly south of Australia off the coast of the state of New South Wales.

Go to the Source

Analyzing Historic Documents

Read the Proclamation below issued by New South Wales Governor, Sir Richard Bourke. Answer the questions using specific references to the document.

When John Batman, a pioneer in Victoria, first settled at Port Phillip, he tried to buy the land from the Aboriginal people through a "treaty." Governor Bourke stopped the treaty with this Proclamation. Its publication in the colony meant that from then on, people found in possession of land without the authority of the government would be considered trespassers.

By His Excellency Major General Sir Richard Bourke, K.C.B. Commanding His Majesty's Forces, Captain General and Governor in Chief of the Territory of New South Wales and its Dependencies, and Vice Admiral of the same &c. &c. &c.

Whereas, it has been represented to me, that divers [various] of His Majesty's Subjects have taken possession of vacant Lands of the Crown, within the limits of this Colony, under the pretence [untruth] of a treaty, bargain, or contract, for the purchase thereof, with the Aboriginal Natives;

Now therefore, I, the Governor, in virtue and in exercise of the power and authority in me vested, do hereby proclaim and notify to all His Majesty's Subjects, and others whom it may concern, that every such treaty, bargain, and contract with the Aboriginal Natives . . . for the possession, title, or claim to any Lands lying and being within the limits of the Government of the Colony of New South Wales . . . is void and of no effect against the rights of the Crown; and that all Persons who shall be found in possession of any such Lands as aforesaid, without the license or authority of His Majesty's Government . . . will be considered as trespassers, and liable to be dealt with in like manner as other intruders upon the vacant Lands of the Crown within the said Colony.

Given under my Hand and Seal, at Government House, Sydney, this
(L.S) twenty sixth Day of August, One thousand eight hundred and thirty five.

(Signed) Alexander McLeay
God Save the King!
True Copy Deas Thomson Clk Co

(Signed) "Richard Bourke"
By His Excellency's Command

Questions

1. Who is the intended audience of this document?
2. Who are "His Majesty's Subjects"?
3. What does Richard Bourke indicate in his letter would happen to those who have made deals or may make future deals to get land from the Aboriginal natives?
4. Why do you think this document was written?
5. How do you think the Aborigines felt about the decision?
6. What is the writer's tone in this document?

Go to the Source

Go to the Source

OBJECTIVES: 4.01, 4.03, 7.01, 7.02
Skills 2.02, 3.05, 4.02, 4.03, 4.06

This document established the doctrine of "terra nullius" for British settlement, meaning that the land belonged to no one before the British Crown took possession of it. This policy robbed Aboriginal people of any rights to the land. They could not not sell or give the rights to use the land to someone. British settlers could not buy the land either. The land belonged to the British government and it was the government's privilege to distribute it.

ANSWERS

1. The intended audience are those who have made deals or intend to make deals to buy land from the Aborigines without the consent of the government.
2. British citizens or those under the control of the British
3. He declares that all deals without government approval are voided and those continuing to claim lands will be viewed as trespassers.
4. To protect the interests of the government, not necessarily the landholders or Aborigines
5. They may feel as if they are not being compensated for their land. Land was taken away from the Aborigines and they were treated poorly by the British government for much of Australia's history.
6. Bourke is exercising his and the government's power to rule. He is also giving a strong warning of what will happen to those who do not follow the decision.

How to Use the Chapter Review

There are three sections in the Chapter Review: Talk About It, Mastering Mapwork, and Go to the Source. Use the Vocabulary Worksheets and the Chapter Review Worksheet in the Teacher's Resource Guide for additional reinforcement and preparation for the Chapter Assessments. The chapter and lesson reviews and the Chapter Review Worksheets are the basis of the assessment for each chapter.

Talk About It questions encourage students to speculate about the content of the chapter and are suitable for class or small-group discussion. They are not intended to be assigned for homework.

Mastering Mapwork has students apply one or more of the Five Themes of Geography to maps within the chapter.

Go to the Source activities allow students to analyze a primary source that relates to the content of the chapter. The questions and activities familiarize students with different types of primary sources and also build content-reading skills.

Oceania

Social Studies Strands

Geographic Relationships
Trust Territories

Economics and Development
Resources
Tourism

North Carolina Standard Course of Study

Goal 3 The learner will analyze the impact of interactions between humans and their physical environments in Africa, Asia, and Australia.

Goal 4 The learner will identify significant patterns in the movement of people, goods, and ideas over time and place in Africa, Asia, and Australia.

Goal 11 The learner will recognize the common characteristics of different cultures in Africa, Asia, and Australia.

Goal 12 The learner will assess the influence of major religions, ethical beliefs, and values on cultures in Africa, Asia, and Australia.

Teaching & Assessment

- English Language Learner Modified Lesson Plans for this chapter are found in the Teacher Resource Guide.
- *ExamView® Assessment Suite* is provided at **NCJourneys.com.** It includes customizable assessments for all chapters. Paper tests are also available in the Teacher Resource Guide. See pages T16–T17 for information about how to use the assessments and the Scoring Guide.

Worksheets

Worksheets and answer keys are found both in the Teacher Resource Guide and at **NCJourneys.com**, including Reading Guides, Reading Strategies, Chapter Reviews, English Language Learner and others.

ACTIVITIES AND INTEGRATIONS

SOCIAL STUDIES
● ■ Activator: *The Island Below the Star,* p. 546
▲ The World's Water Region "Oceana–Political/Physical," p. 547
● Coconut: The Tree of Life, p. 554
▲ "Star Light Star Bright...," p. 561

READING/LANGUAGE ARTS	READING/LANGUAGE ARTS OBJECTIVES
● Island Group Names, p. 546B	6.01
▲ ■ Island Categories, p. 546B	2.01
Analogies, p. 546B	2.01
Writing Prompt: Development in Oceania, p. 546	3.02
★ The Pacific Island Travelogue/Journal, p. 548	2.02
Pacific Island Travel Brochure, p. 552	2.02
Advertisement/Postcard, p. 556	2.02
★ Nuclear Testing Debate, p. 556	3.01
■ Vignettes, p. 559	1.02
Go to the Source: Interpreting Statistics, p. 565	2.01, 2.02, 5.01

MATHEMATICS	MATHEMATICS OBJECTIVES
★ Island Population Density, p. 551	3.01

TECHNOLOGY	TECHNOLOGY OBJECTIVES
■ Pacific Islands Salt Map, p. 549	3.01, 3.11
▲ Nuts About Coconuts, p. 555	3.01, 3.11
Overview, p. 562	3.01, 3.11

VISUAL ARTS	VISUAL ARTS OBJECTIVES
Art of Oceania: Designing a Ceremonial Headdress, p. 546B	2.04, 4.01
● Life in the Pacific and the Rain Forest, p. 550	2.04, 4.01
▲ Nuts About Coconuts, p. 555	1.01, 4.04
Editorial Cartoon, p. 557	4.01
Paper Fale Activity, p. 558	2.04, 4.01
Design for Masi or Wedding Cloth (Fiji), p. 559	2.05, 5.02
Pacific Realm in Triarama, p. 560	1.02, 2.04

CHARACTER AND VALUES EDUCATION	TRAITS
Writing Prompt: Development in Oceania, p. 546	Respect, responsibility, good judgment, good citizenship
What Would You Do?, p. 557	Good judgment
Skill Lesson: The Changing Pacific Islands, p. 563	Respect

● Basic Activities ★ Challenging Activities ▲ English Language Learner Novice ■ English Language Learner Intermediate

Chapter Activities

Introductory Activity

Island Group Names

OBJECTIVES: 12.03

Using the Word Origins feature in Chapter 27, discuss with students that many words are based on Greek root words. The islands of Oceania have roots words that are traceable to Greek. Westerners named these islands with their knowledge of the Greek language. This introductory activity can lead to a conversation about other Greek root words used in our language.

Melanesia: "black island" named for inhabitants with dark hair and dark skin

Micronesia: "tiny islands"

Polynesia: "many islands"

Culminating Activity

Island Categories

OBJECTIVES: 5.02, 6.01, 12.02

Have students look at the map on page 537 of the text. Ask them to study the blocks that show the islands' areas.

Put students in cooperative learning groups. Have them divide the islands into groups (of their choosing) based on cultural geography—language, customs, foods, clothing, and religious practices.

Have them divide the islands by economic categories, whether wealthy or poor. Lastly, have them divide the islands by physical characteristics. After they have made these choices, see if they can put any group of islands together and create a new nation. Have them name their nation and create its economy and a flag.

Art Activity

Art of Oceania: Designing a Ceremonial Headdress

OBJECTIVES: 12.02

Materials newsprint, heavy 9-inch by 12-inch drawing paper, pencils, colored pencils, tempera paint, paint brushes, One-gallon milk jugs or hard plastic bottles, scissors, paper towel tubes, heavy card stock, feathers, beads, glue, small found objects, small balloons, masking tape or duct tape, wheat paste, newspaper, colored construction paper

Medium Papier-mâché

Directions On drawing paper, have students sketch small designs for a headdress. Include things that will be added onto the basic head shape. The headdress does not have to be a realistic representation. Once a quality shape is achieved draw a larger design on 9-inch by 12-inch heavy drawing paper. This drawing should include details and colors. Think about eyes, nose, mouth, ears, hair, wings, horns, jewelry, etc. Also think about how the headdress will fit. Will it come around under the chin or will it just fit on the head? Note: The final headdress does not have to look exactly like the design. The design helps the student make and correct mistakes before the construction begins on the final artwork.

Cut milk jug in half or cut a hole in the bottom big enough to fit on head. The student needs to think about how the headdress will fit. Use paper towel tubes, card stock, balloons, and tape to construct foundation for headdress. Make sure additions are well attached prior to the papier-mâché process.

Papier-mâché

Tear paper into 2-inch by 6-inch strips. Cover artwork with newspaper coated in wheat paste. Let dry and repeat until artwork is very firm with no weak spots. Add more newspaper dipped in wheat paste to weak spots. Paint white, and let dry. Paint according to design. Glue on any additions.

OR

Cover artwork with newspaper coated in wheat paste. Let dry. Cover artwork with colored construction paper coated in wheat paste. Use design as a guide. Glue on any additions such as beads.

Analogies

OBJECTIVES: 1.03

Analogies are useful to help students make associations with prior knowledge. Read the analogies aloud and ask students to identify the relationship between the terms. As an extension, ask students to write their own analogies using key terms or places discussed in the chapter.

high islands : volcanic mountains :: low islands : coral reefs (are made from)

atoll : lagoon :: iris : pupil (surrounds)

Guam : United States :: Tahiti : France (is the trust territory of)

copra : coconut palm :: palm oil : oil palm :: date : date palm (comes from)

canoeing/hiking/photography : ecotourism :: motorboats/four-wheel drives : conventional tourism (are examples of)

matai : Samoa :: mansa : ancient Mali (is a leader in)

Teaching Strategies

Plan activities that utilize research materials and the Internet to help students complete investigative projects on the islands of Oceania.

Because of the number of islands, students may be divided into groups to research different islands, with a class presentation to follow at the end of their study.

Activator

OBJECTIVES: 4.02, 13.02

Activators are great tools to use in order to "hook" the attention of the students. Reading picture books or stories is an excellent way to build interest in the subject and is also a great way to integrate language arts into the social studies curriculum.

The Island Below the Star by James Rumford (Houghton Mifflin, Boston. 1998).

OR

Bring in a coconut for students to taste. If you cannot bring in a fresh coconut, substitute flaked or coconut milk.

Writing Prompt

OBJECTIVES: 3.01, 3.02, 13.01

Problem-Solution

Oceania faces the dilemma of developing its natural resources while preserving the environment that attracts tourists. The United States is facing a similar problem. The issue facing the United States is its need for oil and the importance of preserving the Alaskan Arctic National Wildlife Refuge from exploitation. Some experts say there is only enough oil reserve in Alaska for approximately 50 years. Should the United States drill for oil in this region and put at risk this very fragile ecosystem?

As you write, remember to:

- state your position.
- give at least two reasons to support your position.
- write in complete sentences.
- use correct grammar and punctuation.

CHAPTER 27

Oceania

The Marshall Islands people have a legend about creation. At first there was only the ocean. Then the god Lowa came down, made the Marshall Islands, and went back to heaven. Then four gods came. One was the Sun, who brought light. Life brought all living things. The others were Wind and Death.

A fifth god came to arrange the islands. He placed all the islands in a basket, and then carefully placed them in the ocean. One island, Namorik, slipped out of his hand. To this day, it stands a little apart from the others.

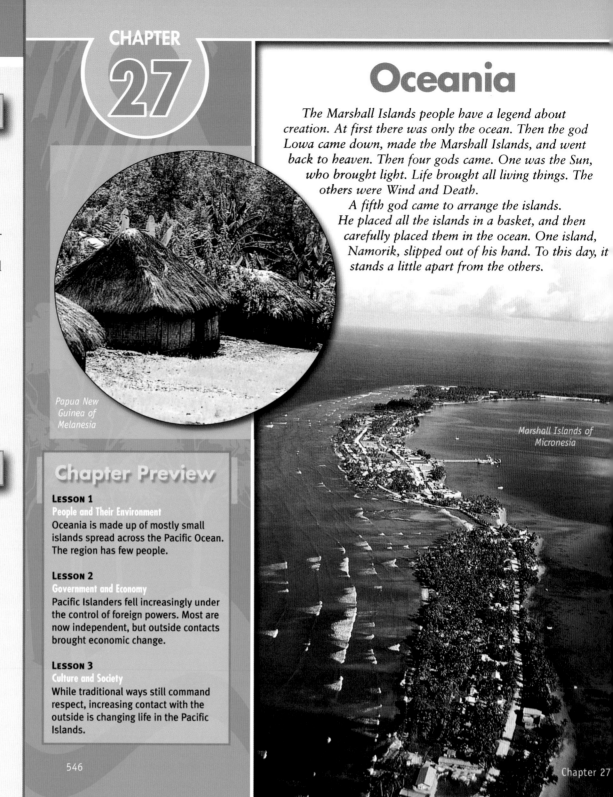

Papua New Guinea of Melanesia

Marshall Islands of Micronesia

Chapter Preview

Lesson 1
People and Their Environment
Oceania is made up of mostly small islands spread across the Pacific Ocean. The region has few people.

Lesson 2
Government and Economy
Pacific Islanders fell increasingly under the control of foreign powers. Most are now independent, but outside contacts brought economic change.

Lesson 3
Culture and Society
While traditional ways still command respect, increasing contact with the outside is changing life in the Pacific Islands.

Chapter Resources

Print Resources

Nonfiction

Coffey, Maria. *Jungle Islands: My South Sea Adventure.* Annick Press, distributed in the United States by Firefly Books, 2000. ISBN 1550375962.

Hermes, Jules. *The Children of Micronesia.* Carolrhoda Books, 1994. ISBN 0876148194.

Thompson, Kathleen. *Pacific Islands.* Raintree Steck-Vaughn, 1996. ISBN 0811473988.

Back Issues of Magazines

Samoans. Cobblestone Publishing Company (issue of *Faces* magazine in 2001–02).

Audiovisual

Destination: Marshall Islands. Peace Corps, 1996. Introduces students to the culture and geography of the Marshall Islands. (20 minutes) ISBN 0160633990.

Wayfinders: A Pacific Oddyssey. PBS Video.

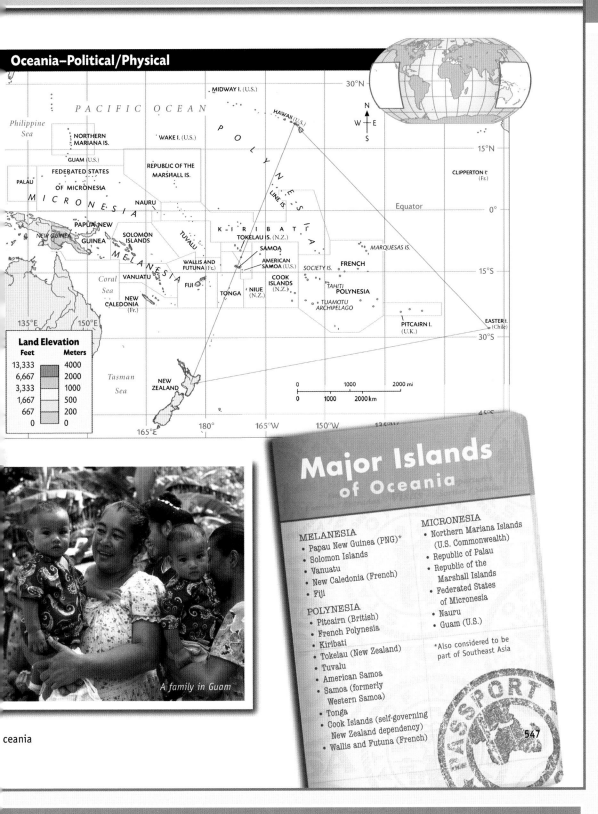

Oceania–Political/Physical

MIDWAY I. (U.S.)
PACIFIC OCEAN
HAWAII (U.S.)
Philippine Sea
NORTHERN MARIANA IS.
WAKE I. (U.S.)
POLYNESIA
GUAM (U.S.)
REPUBLIC OF THE MARSHALL IS.
FEDERATED STATES OF MICRONESIA
PALAU
MICRONESIA
NAURU
LINE IS.
CLIPPERTON I. (Fr.)
Equator
PAPUA NEW GUINEA
NEW GUINEA
SOLOMON ISLANDS
TUVALU
KIRIBATI
TOKELAU IS. (N.Z.)
SAMOA
AMERICAN SAMOA (U.S.)
MARQUESAS IS.
MELANESIA
WALLIS AND FUTUNA (Fr.)
SOCIETY IS.
FRENCH POLYNESIA
TAHITI
Coral Sea
VANUATU
FIJI
TONGA
NIUE (N.Z.)
COOK ISLANDS (N.Z.)
NEW CALEDONIA (Fr.)
TUAMOTU ARCHIPELAGO
PITCAIRN I. (U.K.)
EASTER I. (Chile)
Tasman Sea
NEW ZEALAND
30°N
15°N
0°
15°S
30°S
135°E
150°E
165°E
180°
165°W
150°W

Land Elevation

Feet	Meters
13,333	4000
6,667	2000
3,333	1000
1,667	500
667	200
0	0

0 — 1000 — 2000 mi
0 — 1000 — 2000 km

A family in Guam

Major Islands of Oceania

MELANESIA
- Papau New Guinea (PNG)*
- Solomon Islands
- Vanuatu
- New Caledonia (French)
- Fiji

POLYNESIA
- Pitcairn (British)
- French Polynesia
- Kiribati
- Tokelau (New Zealand)
- Tuvalu
- American Samoa
- Samoa (formerly Western Samoa)
- Tonga
- Cook Islands (self-governing New Zealand dependency)
- Wallis and Futuna (French)

MICRONESIA
- Northern Mariana Islands (U.S. Commonwealth)
- Republic of Palau
- Republic of the Marshall Islands
- Federated States of Micronesia
- Nauru
- Guam (U.S.)

*Also considered to be part of Southeast Asia

PASSPORT

547

ceania

Map Activity

The World's Water Region "Oceania-Political/Physical"

NATIONAL GEOGRAPHY STANDARDS: 1

GEOGRAPHIC THEMES: Location

OBJECTIVES: 1.02, 1.03

Using the world map with some of the Pacific Realm highlighted in red, discuss with students how this area would be divided. Note with students that Pacific-centered maps are designed to prevent having to divide this water realm.

Complete the following with students (may be combined with page 515 and page 521 maps):

1. In the Pacific Realm, also called Oceania, what are the five major places? *Australia, New Zealand, Melanesia, Micronesia, Polynesia*
2. The Equator crosses what portion of the Pacific west of 180° longitude? *Polynesia*
3. The 180° meridian of longitude crosses what portion of the Pacific south of the Equator? *Melanesia*
4. What Pacific island nation is located at the intersection of the Equator and 180° longitude? *Kiribati*
5. Which is the most western of the islands included in Micronesia? *Palau*
6. Which is the most eastern of the islands included in Polynesia? *Pitcairn*
7. Which is the most western of the islands included in Melanesia? *Papua New Guinea*
8. What are the two external territories the United States has north of Micronesia and Polynesia? *Midway and Wake Islands*
9. Tahiti is in which part of Polynesia? *French Polynesia*
10. Which Samoa is independent? *Western Samoa*

Web Sites

Go to **NCJourneys.com** for links to the following Web sites:

- American Samoa Historic Preservation Office
- Oceania Centre for Arts and Culture, University of the South Pacific
- Oceania Football Confederation
- Sailing the Ocean Without Map or Compass: Traditional Navigation in the Western Pacific
- Small Island Developing States Network
- Wayfinders: A Pacific Oddyssey companion Web site

OBJECTIVES: 2.01, 3.04, 12.03

Discussion Questions

1 How would the vastness of the region impact the individual nations?

Caption Answer

High islands are formed by volcanic eruptions on the ocean floor that produce volcanic mountains and surrounding land that rise above the level of the ocean. Low islands are coral reefs made from the gradual buildup of the skeletons of tiny sea creatures that live in the warm, shallow waters near the reef.

Writing Activity

The Pacific Island Travelogue/Journal

OBJECTIVES: 1.01, 1.03, 4.03, 5.01

Materials reference materials (travel books, brochures); drawing paper; poster board; 3-inch by 5-inch index cards

Directions Create a travelogue/journal of Oceania. Imagine being a part of Captain James Cook's expedition that set out in 1768 to find a giant continent in the Southern Hemisphere. As a part of the crew, write journal entries about the three-year journey. Entries can include descriptions and drawings of the great coral reefs, the beautiful fish, the animals, the Aborigines who inhabited the island, the Ring of Fire, volcanic eruptions, or storms at sea. Share travelogues and journals with the class.

Extension Assign limited writing for novice and intermediate ELL students. ELL students should use an ELL-friendly Web site to research and illustrate their journal. Novices should write one- or two-word descriptions. Intermediate students should write one- or two-sentence descriptions.

LESSON 1 People and Their Environment

KEY IDEAS

- Oceania covers one-third of the earth, but it contains little land.
- Volcanic eruptions and coral formed three island groups in Oceania—Melanesia, Micronesia, and Polynesia.
- People from Southeast Asia began settling the Pacific Islands 50,000 years ago.

KEY TERMS

atoll
high islands
low islands
pidgin

The Pacific Ocean covers one-third of the earth's surface and is bigger than all the world's continents and islands combined. In total area including both land and sea, Oceania, or the Pacific Islands region, is the largest in the world. Most of this vast region, however, is water. When only the land area is counted, Oceania is one of the world's smallest regions.

A Variety of Islands

Few of these islands have much land area. Papua New Guinea is a giant when compared to other lands in Oceania (see map, page 547). The Solomon Islands, with ten large islands and many more smaller ones, have a total land area about the size of our state of Maryland. Many islands are scarcely more than dots measuring more than a square mile (2.6 sq km).

As you read earlier, much of the Pacific Rim is a part of the Ring of Fire, where earthquakes and volcanic eruptions are common. Volcanic eruptions have produced many of the larger, more rugged islands. These ***high islands*** are the result of eruptions taking place on the ocean floor. Repeated eruptions over millions of years have produced volcanic mountains and surrounding land that rise above the level of the ocean. On high islands, the soil is generally fertile and supports tropical vegetation.

Mooréa in the Society Islands (below) is a high island. One of the small Fiji Islands (right) is a low island. **How is each type of island formed?**

Low islands are much flatter and smaller. Low islands are coral reefs made from the gradual buildup of the skeletons of tiny sea creatures that live in the warm, shallow waters near the reef. The sea creatures use the calcium in sea water to make limestone. As they die, their skeletons pile up. It takes thousands of years to form a coral base to create islands.

Low islands lack fresh water for drinking. Nearly all fresh water comes from rainfall and has to be collected in large containers. Few islands have soil in which plants can grow. Besides limestone and sand, the only other natural resources low islands offer are sea shells and palm trees. Far fewer people live on these low islands than on the high islands. Fish supply food and trade for islanders.

The most distinctive form of low island is the coral ***atoll*** (AY·toll). An atoll is a ring-shaped island with a lagoon in the center. This formation happens over a long time.

Early in its formation, the ring of coral surrounded a volcano. Over time, the volcano became extinct. Struck by wind and rain over thousands of years, the volcanic soil eroded. The volcano eventually sank below the surface. Only the coral fringe around the outside remained above sea level. In the 1950s, the United States used Bikini and Enewetak Atolls in the Marshall Islands as testing grounds for nuclear bombs.

Houses built on stilts crowd the waterfront at Port Moresby, Papua New Guinea. PNG is a high island. **Why are high islands more fertile than low islands?**

Word Origins

The islands of Oceania were named by Westerners with a knowledge of Greek. **Melanesia** comes from a Greek word meaning "black islands," a reference to the dark skin and hair of the island people. **Micronesia** is Greek for "tiny islands." **Polynesia** comes from the Greek words ***poly*** and ***nesia,*** meaning "many islands."

Background Information

Future Worries of Global Warming

Some scientists worry that global warming may one day spell disaster for some of the smaller Pacific Island nations. Global warming caused by greenhouse gas emissions has been linked to rising sea levels as glaciers and ice caps melt. Many island nations sit just a few feet above sea level and are only about a hundred yards wide. Kiribati, for example, can be three times as big at low tide as at high. Even a rise of two or three feet could wreak havoc on this tiny nation of 92,000 people. The nations most likely to be submerged by a rise in sea level would be Kiribati, the Marshall Islands, and Tuvalu. Many other nations including Tonga, Palau, Nauru, and the Federated States of Micronesia would not be totally under water but would lose much of their territory.

Discussion Questions

1 How are atolls formed?

Caption Answer

High islands contain volcanic soil, which is very rich.

Map Activity

Pacific Islands Salt Map

NATIONAL GEOGRAPHY STANDARDS: 1, 3, 7

GEOGRAPHIC THEMES: Region, Location, Place

OBJECTIVES: 1.01, 1.03

Salt Dough:
1 cup flour
½ teaspoon salt
2 teaspoons cream of tartar
1 tablespoon vegetable oil

Materials salt dough; food coloring; blue bulletin board paper; popsicle sticks/toothpicks; white paper or 3 by 5-inch cards; markers; quarter-inch 2 feet by 4 feet sheet of plywood; graph paper; Atlas, and almanacs

Directions Divide the class into three groups: Melanesia, Polynesia, and Micronesia.

Each group will research three islands in their subregion. Students will use graph paper to draw an outline map of their islands (scale determined by teacher). This is the base upon which the salt map will be constructed. Students will create their own elevation color key and build their salt map accordingly on the cardboard squares.

Flags should be drawn on strips of white paper, colored and glued to popsicle or toothpick masts to be planted on the island. The island name should be printed on cards along with any facts the group finds interesting. The capital city must be one of the facts. The capital city on the salt map should be identified by a red star. Cover the plywood with the blue bulletin board paper and draw a line to represent the Equator. Students should carefully slide their island(s) onto the "Pacific Ocean" board in the approximate location. The fact cards should be taped next to the correct island. Display in the library.

Discussion Questions

1 Why do you think the United States wants to keep Guam?

2 How do Melanesia, Micronesia, and Polynesia differ?

3 What are outrigger canoes?

Papua New Guinea, Fiji, and the Solomon Islands

Allow Time for Translation

All ELLs are busy translating the English they hear into their native language, mentally responding, and then translating that answer once again into English. Remember to be patient while they process all this information.

Life in the Pacific and the Rain Forest

OBJECTIVES: 1.01, 1.03, 2.01

Materials bulletin board paper, markers, overhead projector, colored chalk, clear transparencies, tempera paints

Directions Divide the class into two teams. Students will use reference materials and *National Geographic* to find pictures and/or ideas for the murals. Students will create a scene illustrating New Guinea's rain forest, plant and animal life, and a scene illustrating life in the Pacific Ocean (sunken warships and whales can be included). Paint the murals on bulletin board paper and display.

Three Island Groups

Geographers divide the Pacific Islands into three major groups: Melanesia, Micronesia, and Polynesia. Melanesia is the largest island group. Its islands were the first to be settled by humans.

On the map on page 534, look northeast of Australia to locate Melanesia. Papua New Guinea (often referred to as PNG) occupies part of New Guinea, the largest island in Melanesia. Other large islands in the Melanesian group include Fiji and the Solomon Islands. These islands are hot, damp, and mountainous.

The islands of Micronesia lie mostly north of the Equator, north of Melanesia, and to the east of the Philippines. Guam, a possession of the United States, is typical of most islands in this group. It is a low island and small (210 square miles or 546 sq km). The islands of Micronesia lie scattered across an ocean area the size of the continental United States. Their total land area measures roughly the same as Rhode Island's.

Polynesia spreads across a greater expanse of water than either Melanesia or Micronesia. Its ocean area forms a rough triangle. New Zealand, Easter Island, and Hawaii are the three corners.

Samoa, Tahiti, and Tonga are well-known islands in this group. Polynesia has both high and low islands. Many Polynesia high islands have ample land for farming, mining, and tourism.

Spreading Across the Pacific

Scientists believe human settlement of Oceania began about 50,000 years ago, when wandering hunter-gatherers crossed from Southeast Asia's islands into New

Mokil Atoll (below, top) is typical of Micronesia— a small and low island. Polynesia contains both high and low islands, such as Bora Bora (bottom), a high island. **What are some of the larger islands of Melanesia?**

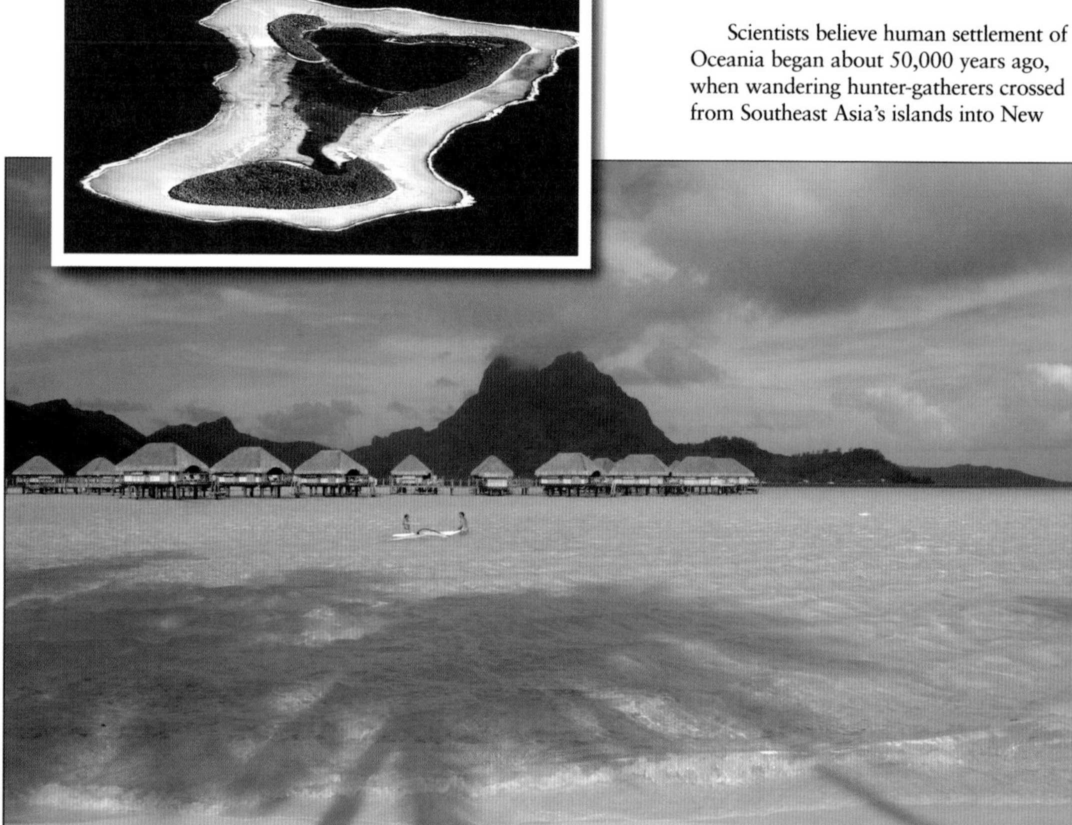

ɿuinea. From there they were able to reach ɿlands of the Melanesian group. Settlement ɿf more distant islands came much later. ɿbout 5,000 years ago, craftsmen learned to ɿuild canoes capable of going long distances ɿcross the ocean. From New Guinea, early ɿeoples fanned out across the Pacific in their ɿutrigger canoes.

Over time, they settled the islands of ɿlicronesia and Polynesia. Without a ɿompass or the other basic navigational ɿools, these early people proved to be ɿxtraordinary sailors. They guided double-ɿulled canoes, some 150 feet (45 m) long, ɿhousands of miles to fish or trade with ɿther islanders or to find new places to live. ɿhey read the stars, wind currents, the ɿolors of the water, and the flight paths of ɿirds at sea to sail around the Pacific.

People lived in widely separated ɿroups in the rain forest and the mountain ɿighlands of New Guinea. They developed ɿheir own languages and customs. For ɿxample, more than 700 different ɿanguages can be found in PNG.

Islanders living in Micronesia and ɿolynesia speak fewer languages. A single ɿasic language with different dialects ɿeveloped within the same island chain or ɿhroughout a larger area. Much later, as ɿhe islands came under colonial rule, ɿnglish became a common language.

In Oceania, ***pidgin*** (PIH·jen), a ɿixture of English and local languages, ɿs used more often than English. The ɿany versions of pidgin come from the ɿifferent island groups. In PNG pidgin, "good afternoon" is *apinun* (AH·pee·noon) and "that is mine" is *em bilong mi* (em BEE·long my).

With a population of 5.9 million, PNG has the most people in Oceania. The majority live in the mountain villages of the interior. Only 13 percent of the people live in cities such as its capital, Port Moresby.

The city with the largest population of Pacific Islanders is not even in Oceania. Auckland, New Zealand, has more residents from the islands than any city in the world. For people from many of the smaller islands, Auckland and other New Zealand cities offer greater job opportunities than their island homes.

Port Moresby, Papua New Guinea, is the capital and largest city of the most populous island in Oceania. **Where do most people live in PNG?**

LESSON 1 REVIEW

Fact Follow-Up

1. Contrast high islands and low islands.
2. What is an atoll?
3. What are the three major groups of the Pacific Islands?
4. How do scientists believe the Pacific Islands were settled?

Talk About It

1. How is Oceania both one of the world's largest regions and one of its smallest?
2. What island of Oceania would you most like to visit? Why?

Discussion Questions

1 If two cultures meet, what do you think would be the most important barrier they would have to overcome?

2 Why is language so important?

3 What is another example of a language that has been created for the purpose of trade?

4 What changes do you think will occur in the islands, even if the people return home?

Caption Answer

The people live in widely separated groups in the rain forest and the mountain highlands.

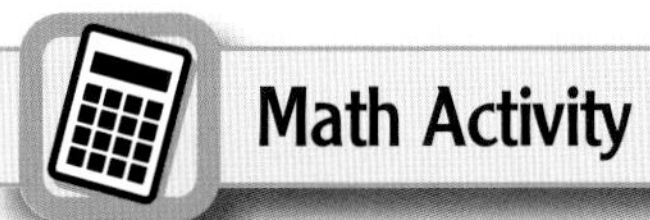

Math Activity

Island Population Density

OBJECTIVES: 1.01, 1.02, 1.03

Based on the information below, have students calculate the population density of each country. The area and 2005 population follow each country's name.

Papua New Guinea: 452,860 sq. km., 5,887,000
Tonga: 718 sq. km., 102,500
Fiji: 18,270 sq. km., 848,000
Tuvalu: 26 sq. km., 10,000; and
New Caledonia: 18,575 sq. km., 237,000

LESSON 1 REVIEW

Fact Follow-Up Answers

1. High islands are formed by volcanic eruptions. The soil is generally fertile. Low islands are formed by coral reefs. Few have soil in which plants can grow, and freshwater is lacking. Many more people live on high islands than low islands.
2. An atoll is a low island formed in a ring shape with a lagoon in the center. The lagoon was once a volcano, but the soil eroded over time and the volcano sank.
3. The three major groups of the Pacific Islands are Melanesia, Micronesia, and Polynesia.
4. They believe that people from Southeast Asia's islands came into New Guinea about 50,000 years ago. The people then spread into the Melanesian island group. Much later, they fanned out into Micronesia and Polynesia.

Talk About It Answers

1. The islands are small, but the ocean surrounding the island groups extends over a large area.
2. Students should choose one island and explain why they would choose to visit that island.

OBJECTIVES: 3.01, 4.01, 5.01, 13.01

Discussion Questions

1 If you were to leave home and go to a new land, what cultural values would you take with you?

2 What would you be willing to change?

Caption Answer

Congregations of Protestant and Catholic worshipers are common. On most Pacific islands, Sunday is a strict day of rest. In Western Samoa, some villagers attend three church services on Sunday.

Activity

Pacific Island Travel Brochure

OBJECTIVES: 11.01, 12.01, 13.03

Materials textbook, almanac, atlas, 9-inch by 12–inch white construction paper, colored pencils/markers

Directions Divide students into pairs. Assign each pair an island country. Each pair will create a travel/tourist brochure for their country. Each brochure should have a map, a flag, an imaginary hotel complete with amenities, and tourist attractions (things to do and see on the islands).

During the class presentations, students will try to "sell" their travel brochure to the class as "the place to vacation."

Students will vote or rank each of the presentations.

Extension This activity is suitable for novice and intermediate ELL students because they have a partner. ELL students should use an ELL-friendly Web site for research. The ELL student's partner should do more writing and the ELL student more illustrating.

LESSON 2 Government and Economy

KEY IDEAS

- Pacific Islanders lived in isolation until the 1600s, when they were drawn into contact with the rest of the world.
- Beginning in the 1960s, many of the islands gained independence from foreign rule.
- Islanders once lived by fishing and eating wild foods, but many islands now depend on tourism and exports.

KEY TERMS

copra
ecotourism
trust territories

John Uruo started his life on the island of Puluwat in the Caroline Islands (now the Federated States of Micronesia). At the age of eighteen, he left his home to go to college in the United States. He was the first person from his island ever to do so, and the islanders, most of whom are members of his extended family, were proud of him. At a feast held in his honor before he left, John told the islanders, "I go to jump over the wall."

The "wall" for John and many islanders was and still is their isolation, lack of education, poor health care, and lack of job choices. Eighteen years later, after John had finished college, married, and had two children, he returned to his home. By that time, Puluwat and the other Caroline Islands had become independent. John took a job working for the new government. Through his work, he hoped to help others "jump the wall," but without having to leave their island homes to do so.

Contacts from Beyond Oceania

Among the first Europeans to explore Oceania in the 1600s were Captain James Cook and Abel Tasman—both linked to European exploration in Australia and New Zealand. The first Europeans who came to stay were traders, whaling crews, and missionaries bringing the Christian religion.

The missionaries spread their faith. Today, congregations of Protestant and Catholic worshippers are common. On most Pacific islands, Sunday is a strict day of rest. In Samoa (formerly called Western Samoa), some villagers attend three church services on Sunday.

Missionaries preach to natives of the South Pacific in 1832. **What evidence exists today that missionaries visited Oceania?**

In the years before World War II, rance, the United States, Japan, and the Jnited Kingdom claimed some of the acific Islands. During the war years, many islands, such as Guadalcanal (one of the Solomon Islands) and Guam, became battlegrounds between Japanese and American soldiers. Thousands lost heir lives.

Today, it is still possible to see signs of those battles. In many places, tanks and bombers covered with vines startle isitors walking through tropical forests. The sunken wrecks of vessels rust in the vaters of the South Pacific.

Trust Territories and Independent Nations

When the war ended, islands held by apan such as Guam and Samoa became *trust territories,* territories supervised by other nations. Guam and American Samoa came under United States control. Other territories were put under the direction of New Zealand, Australia, the Jnited Kingdom, or France. Most of hese islands are independent now. None of the islands are considered to be trust erritories today.

Many islands gained independence in he 1960s and 1970s. Island nations often consist of numerous islands. Samoa Western Samoa) is made up of ten islands. Palau, with 26 islands, became a nation in 1994.

Other Pacific Islands remain under French or American control. Guam and American Samoa are territories of the United States. France has kept Tahiti and the other 130 islands that make up French Polynesia.

In some cases, local islanders have requested to remain a territory. The people are unwilling to surrender the financial aid and other advantages that come with being connected to a larger nation. The Northern Marianas Islands elected to become a commonwealth of the United States.

Both France and the United States also receive military or economic benefits from these islands. For example, Guam and American Samoa have been refueling bases for American ships or aircraft in the Pacific. Some of the islands France controls have been sites for nuclear testing. In 1995, France's decision to test nuclear weapons in the South Pacific angered many Pacific Islanders. This led to rioting in Tahiti, the government center of French Polynesia.

Democratic governments based on the British parliamentary system became common as islands gained independence. A few independent nations, such as Tonga and Samoa, choose kings from traditional ruling families.

The Solomon Islands received independence in 1978 from the United Kingdom. **What were the islands called that were formerly controlled by other nations?**

Discussion Questions

1 Do you think France has the right to conduct nuclear testing in its territories?

2 If you were a Pacific Islander, how would you handle it?

Caption Answer

Guam and American Samoa are territories of the United States. France has kept Tahiti and the other 130 islands of French Polynesia.

Background Information

The Challenge of Governing Papua New Guinea

Governing a nation divided by mountain ranges and scattered islands can be challenging. It's no wonder Papua New Guinea (PNG) has had problems becoming a unified nation with an effective government. PNG consists of half the island of New Guinea and 600 nearby islands. Some of its many ethnic groups live in almost complete isolation. Its people speak more than 700 different languages and have almost as many distinct cultures. Although the nation is rich in oil and copper, these resources have not led to a higher standard of living for most residents. One of PNG's problems has been political instability. In 1988, a secessionist movement began on Bougainville Island arising from islanders' anger with their share of revenues from a copper mining operation. The revolt lasted into the late 1990s.

Discussion Questions

1 Are there any food products we use as extensively as the islanders use coconut?

2 How would our lives change if we had a barter economy?

Caption Answer

The islanders drink the coconut milk, use coconut shells for cups, and use the husk fiber for rope or matting. Leaves are used for roofs, and smoke from bringing coconuts repells mosquitos.

Activity

Coconut: The Tree of Life

OBJECTIVES: 1.01, 1.03, 3.01, 5.01

On a large piece of paper, have students draw a tree with a trunk and two large branches, labeled as follows: trunk—Economy of Oceania; left branch—Farming; middle branch—Mining; right branch— Ecotourism. Students should then make "leaves" for the tree organizer by listing along each branch facts about each branch of the Economy of Oceania.

Extension Novice and intermediate ELL students should create pictures or simple descriptions on each leaf. Assign peer tutors as needed.

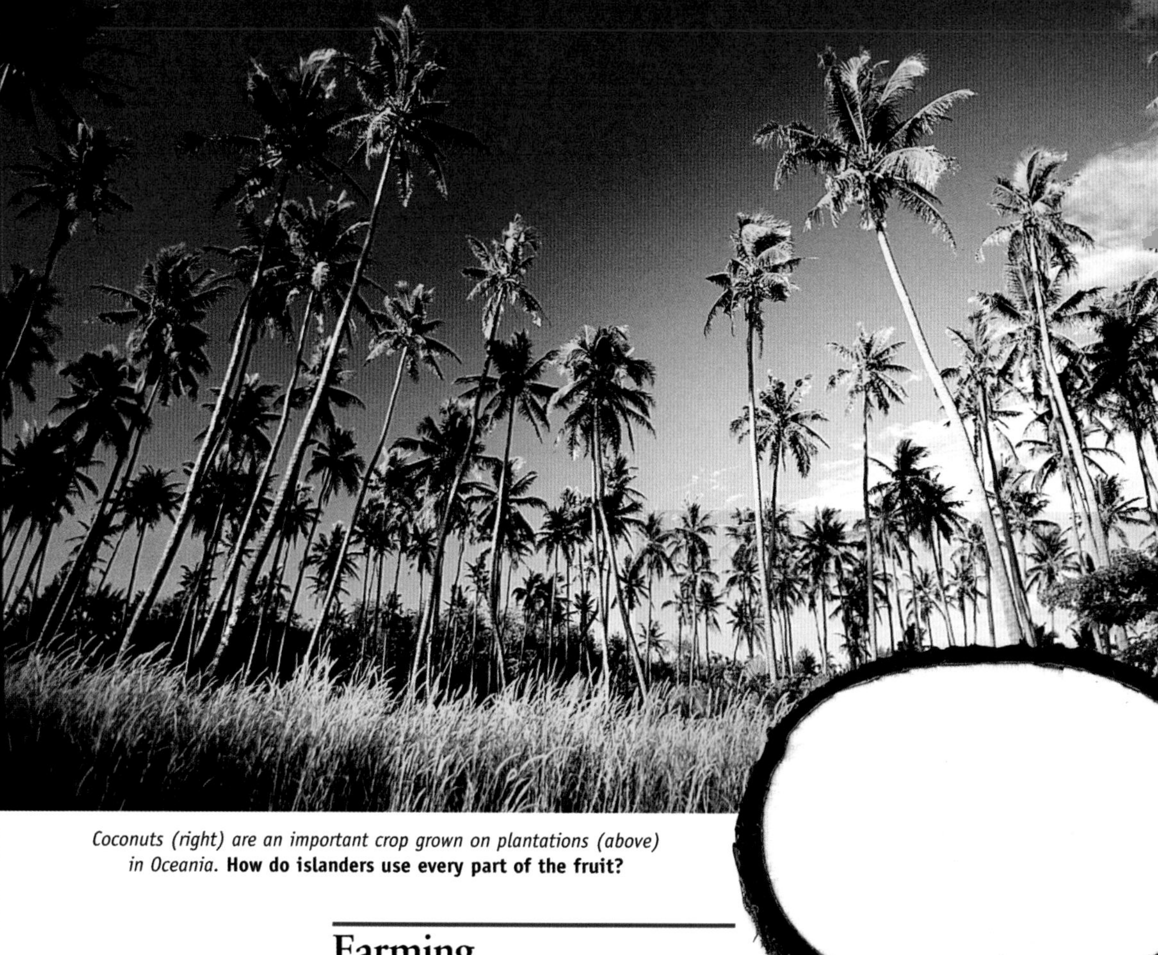

Coconuts (right) are an important crop grown on plantations (above) in Oceania. **How do islanders use every part of the fruit?**

Farming

For many centuries, most Pacific Islanders have supported themselves by subsistence farming or fishing. Without too much effort, islanders could catch their supper's main course from the sea and pick the side dishes from island fruit and coconut trees.

Islanders have long fed their families on coconuts and root crops such as yams, taro, and breadfruit. Many farmers also have raised pigs. On the larger high islands where volcanic soil allows more extensive farming, farmers grow such cash crops as bananas, coffee, sugarcane, and pineapples.

The coconut is one island crop that both subsistence and cash crop farmers like. The coconut palm grows easily on the soils of both volcanic islands and coral atolls. Once it reaches maturity in about eight years, the coconut palm produces about 50 coconuts a year for 60 years.

Islanders enjoy the liquid inside the green, young coconut as a refreshing drink. The nut's hard inner shell makes a good drinking cup, and the fiber of the husk becomes rope, brushes, and heavy matting. Leaves from the coconut palm are woven into thatch for roofs. Even the smoke from the burning coconut is useful. It makes an effective mosquito repellent.

The most important cash crop made rom coconut is ***copra*** —sun-dried oconut meat. The copra is pressed to xtract the oil, which is turned into soap, attle feed, skin-care products and other osmetics, margarine, and suntan lotions. Copra provides an export crop for slands with no other natural resources.

Subsistence farmers and fishermen have little contact with a money, or cash, economy. For these people, most goods are exchanged through barter. However, throughout Oceania, the barter system is disappearing. Mining, tourism, and government jobs have provided new ways to earn a living.

CONNECTIONS • GEOGRAPHY & THE ARTS •

Oceanic Art

Headdresses, canoe prows, and drums show how Oceanic people created art with objects from their everyday lives. Clay, feathers, bone, and shells decorated objects created by people of the South Pacific.

Bright blues, reds, and yellows express as much of the tropical surroundings of the art as the materials do.

Objects were made for special occasions. Chieftain stools, shell crowns, and ceremonial bowls show the rituals the people practiced.

In Polynesia, designs were carved into clubs and ceremonial staffs. Sculptures of gods were based on the human form but were often larger than life size, suggesting the supernatural.

In Melanesia, spiderwebs were used to make headdresses. In some parts of New Guinea, tree moss was formed into small spirit figures.

Grasses, bamboo, and fibers made figures, baskets, and masks. Teeth, both animal and human, decorated sculptures and were used for necklaces. Islanders also adorned costumes and headdresses with bird feathers and beaks.

Clay and stone formed pots and sculpture. Limestone was easy to carve, but even hard basalt was formed into ornaments and bowls. Clays of red, yellow, and white added color to the pottery.

Art from the prow of a canoe in the Solomon Islands

Art Activity

Nuts About Coconuts

OBJECTIVES: 4.02, 12.03, 13.03

Divide the class into six groups using information on uses of coconut.

Materials 1 coconut per group (complete with husk), 1 nail (12-penny or larger), palm leaves, paper cups, sweetened coconut, construction paper, hammer, Styrofoam, and popsicle sticks

Directions Have an adult crack open the coconut. Distribute chunks of coconut meat and a taste of milk to each student. (If a real one is not available, use canned and frozen coconut for tasting and cooking.) Shred husk and have some students braid strands; others can weave a thatch. Each group can build a hut from the popsicle sticks and add the thatch to make the roof.

Research soap/skin care products: Find as many products as possible that contain coconut. Each group can collect several recipes containing coconut, then select one to make. Each group will bring something to the "tasting party."

With a partner write a poem entitled "Ode to the Coconut" in which you explain the importance of the coconut in the lives of the islanders.

Extension Do not assign novice and intermediate ELL students the poem unless a partner does most of the writing and the ELL student illustrates it.

Discussion Questions

1 How has the use of natural resources in our region changed the environment?

Mining has increased the income of some islands, but mining can hurt the environment by polluting water supplies. Erosion can occur when trees are cut and not replaced.

Advertisement/Postcard

OBJECTIVES: 3.01, 3.03, 4.01, 4.02

Tourism is an important economic activity in Oceania. Have students pick one of the following ways to demonstrate what they have learned. Pick an area in Oceania. Do an advertisement for the area as a tourist attraction. The advertisement should reflect the idea of "ecotourism" and facts about the area. Design a postcard for an area in Oceania. On the back, in the upper left corner, write a two to three sentence description. Write a note to another person about the stay in the area reflecting facts learned. Share and display.

Extension Assign novice and intermediate ELL students a collage. Novice students should write one or two words on ten of the pictures they use; intermediate students should write a one or two sentence description of the collage. ELL students should use an ELL-friendly Web site for research.

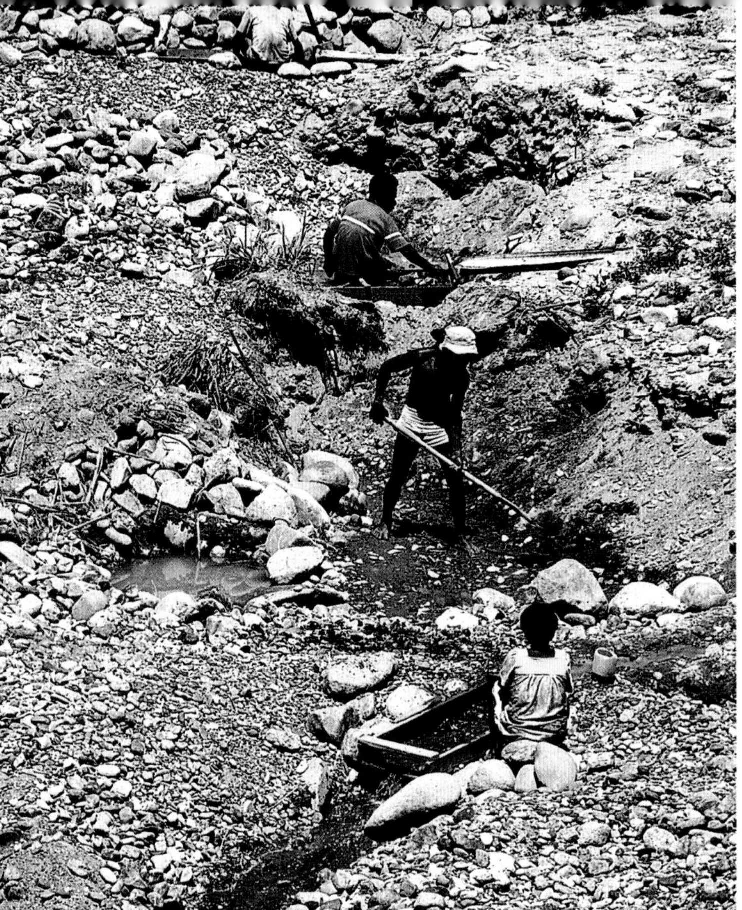

Miners pan for gold in Papua New Guinea. **How has mining helped and hurt the islands?**

Mining

A few island nations have seen their incomes rise through mining. Most mining occurs on Papua New Guinea, Nauru, and French-controlled New Caledonia.

Phosphate mining has given Nauru one of the highest incomes per person in all of Oceania. Its phosphates are sold as fertilizer for farms in Australia and New Zealand.

At independence in 1975, PNG was primarily a farming economy. Now four-fifths of its export income comes from copper, oil, and gold.

France operates nickel mines in New Caledonia. That mineral wealth is a mixed blessing to New Caledonians. Nickel mining has hurt the environment by polluting water supplies. Other mining islands suffer from erosion as trees are cut and not replaced. Rivers become polluted from runoff.

Tourism: Oceania's Fastest-Growing Industry

For many Americans, Europeans, and Japanese, the dream vacation is a carefree week on a Pacific island. Swimmers look for white sands and blue waters. Divers want the adventure of exploring the underwater world of coral reefs.

Today, many Pacific island nations rely on tourism as the mainstay of their economies. Tahiti is a good example. For decades, the economy of this French territory was based almost entirely on subsistence farming. Few people had jobs with a regular wage or salary.

Tahiti's first airport opened in 1961. Hotels, restaurants, and night clubs soon followed. In Papeete, the largest city on the island, tall buildings line the streets. Shops offer T-shirts of rock musicians and the latest French fashions. Cars and motorbikes clog traffic. Yachts from around the world anchor on the waterfront.

Tahiti's economy also changed because of the large French military force on the island. As the government center for French Polynesia, Tahiti now has jobs for hundreds of Polynesian office workers. Together the military and government offices have attracted a broad range of businesses—everything from construction companies to retail stores.

Although tourism has been an important moneymaker for many Pacific islands, it does have some drawbacks. When hotels, resorts, souvenir shops, and restaurants are first built, the visitors flood in. While this provides new jobs, it also takes a toll on the environment. Land is paved to make way for roads. Water becomes polluted. Environmental damage and overcrowding make scenic islands less attractive.

Activity

Nuclear Testing Debate

OBJECTIVES: 3.02, 3.03, 7.02, 8.03

In 1995, the decision by France to test nuclear weapons in the South Pacific angered many Pacific Islanders and led to rioting. Research the issue of nuclear testing and then stage a debate.

Resolved:

- Nuclear testing by France does not hurt the South Pacific.
- Nuclear testing by France does hurt the South Pacific.

Use the Guide to Student Debates in the Teacher's Edition.

Bora Bora, Tahiti's Marara Resort, is among many island tourist attractions in Oceania. **How could islands such as Tahiti improve their economies without the drawbacks of regular tourism?**

On some islands, government officials are working with investors and travel agents on a new kind of tourism. ***Ecotourism*** packages are trips that are carefully planned for vacationers to learn about the outdoors while doing activities that safeguard the environment. At the same time, governments and tourist agents have begun to put limits on the number of visitors and the number of hotels and resorts that can be built on islands.

What would YOU do?

Since tourism in Guam brings in more dollars than the United States military base, there is a move for independence. Some of the island's residents fear the move toward a tourist-based economy. Taxes will rise. Land prices will go up, making it hard for locals to own a home. Still, some say that independence from the United States is best. Which way would you vote?

LESSON 2 REVIEW

Fact Follow-Up

1. Describe Early European contacts with Oceania.
2. What were trust territories?
3. Describe agriculture in Oceania.
4. What were the most important mineral resources of Oceania?

Talk About It

1. Which problems facing people living in Oceania are caused by the physical characteristics of the islands?
2. What do you think is the single most important political or economic problem facing Oceania? Explain why.
3. Is tourism more of a burden or a benefit for Oceania? Explain your answer.

Discussion Questions

1. Could ecotourism be important in North Carolina?
2. How do you think environmentalists and people responsible for developing the economy need to work together in North Carolina?
3. What role do you think environmentalists have in shaping North Carolina's economy?

Answers will vary. Ecotourism puts less strain on the environment.

Editorial Cartoon

OBJECTIVES: 2.03, 3.02, 5.01, 7.02

Draw an editorial cartoon expressing an opinion on one of the following topics. Students may work in pairs or individually.

- **a.** Pollution caused by nickel mining
- **b.** Guam should/should not get independence from the United States.
- **c.** Disadvantages of tourism in Pacific Islands
- **d.** France's testing of nuclear weapons in the South Pacific

LESSON 2 REVIEW

Fact Follow-Up Answers

1. The first Europeans who came to Oceania were traders, whaling crews, and Christian missionaries.
2. Trust territories were territories supervised by other nations after World War II.
3. Islanders have long fed their families on coconuts and such root crops as yams, taro, and breadfruit. On high islands, the volcanic soil can support such cash crops as bananas, coffee, sugarcane, and pineapples.
4. The most important mineral resources of Oceania are phosphate, copper, gold, and nickel

Talk About It Answers

1. Important points: Students' responses should focus on physical characteristics. The islands are small and have few resources besides farming, and so employment is limited. Tourism is overwhelming some islands, and young people are leaving others.
2. Important points: Students should choose either one political problem or one economic problem and explain their choice. The region must find and develop resources without damaging the environment.
3. Important points: Students should state whether tourism is more of a burden or a benefit and give reasons for their choice. Tourism brings money, but it overwhelms the environment.

OBJECTIVES: 10.04, 11.02, 11.03, 12.03

Discussion Questions

1 What would you be willing to give up if you were to go "from the plastic age to the Stone Age"?

Caption Answer

Better roads, new air routes and airports, and construction of resort hotels have opened more of Oceania to the outside world.

Art Activity

Paper Fale Activity

OBJECTIVES: 1.01, 2.01, 3.01

Materials paper, scissors, stapler/staples, grass clippings, twigs, glue

Directions Cut on fold lines between A and E, E and I, I and M, D and H, H and L, and L and P. Fold on lines between "B/C" and "F/G", "F/G" and "J/K", "J/K" and "N/O" to stand up. Tuck center ends in. Bring end pieces around house. Staple. Using grass clippings, glue thatching onto roof and twigs under house's base as pilings/underpinning to create a fale.

For links to some photos visit **NCJourneys.com.**

A	B	C	D
E	F	G	H
I	J	K	L
M	N	O	P

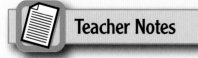

LESSON 3 Culture and Society

KEY IDEAS

- Tradition continues to shape daily life in Oceania, but contacts with the outside are weakening old ways.
- Differences between Samoa and American Samoa illustrate how island life is changing.
- Many young people leave the islands for greater economic opportunities and new ways of life.

KEY TERMS

matai
wayfinding

In 1992, sailors on eight double-hulled voyaging canoes from as far away as Hawaii and New Zealand met on Aitutaki in the Cook Islands. Their voyages were remarkable in several ways. The sailor built their boats entirely by hand using natural materials. They carved wooden hulls and lashed them together with coconut fiber ropes. No fiberglass or motors were allowed.

Most important, the sailors guided their canoes to the Cook Islands using traditional methods of navigation known as ***wayfinding.*** Developed by the Pacific Islanders hundreds of years ago, these skills enabled sailors to cross thousands of miles of uncharted oceans withou the aid of modern navigational tools.

Communications Bring Change

One visitor to Papau New Guinea observed that people he met had moved "from the Stone Age to the plastic age" in a single generation. Better roads, new air routes and airports, and construction of resort hotels have opened more of Oceania to the outside world.

These changes have had a striking impact on the islanders' ways of life. In some places, islanders who once ate yams, pineapples, and bananas now munch on French fries and double-decker cheeseburgers. They top off their snacks with soft drinks in plastic cups from fast-food restaurants.

Changes come from communications with the outside world through TV, the Internet, short-wave radios, tourists, and French and American military troops. Travel abroad by Pacific Islanders expose them to modern living. Islanders hope to gain from the new ways without losing al of their traditional ways of living.

Papeete, Tahiti, the capital of French Polynesia, shows many signs of modern life. **What has brought many changes to Oceania?**

Teacher Notes

Western Samoa Name Change

The eastern Samoan islands became territories of the United States in 1904; today they are known as American Samoa. The western islands became known as Western Samoa (now just Samoa). They passed from German control to New Zealand in 1914. New Zealand administered Western Samoa first under the League of Nations and then as a United Nations trusteeship until independence in 1962. Western Samoa was the first Pacific Island country to gain its independence.

In July 1997 the Constitution was amended to change the country's name from Western Samoa to Samoa. Samoa had been known simply as Samoa in the United Nations since joining the organization in 1976. American Samoa protested the move, feeling that the change diminished its own Samoan identity. American Samoans still use the terms Western Samoa and Western Samoans.

Contrasting Life in Oceania

The two Samoas, Samoa (Western Samoa) and American Samoa, are examples of contrasting societies in Oceania. Separated by just 80 miles (129 km), each is similar yet different. Samoa is an independent country that has kept many of the traditional ways. American Samoa is a territory of the United States, where change is taking place more rapidly.

Samoa

About 360 villages on four different islands are home to Samoans. Very few people live on the other six islands that make up the country. Unlike many island nations, Samoa's government has not encouraged a large tourist industry. With managed growth of resorts and hotels, Samoa hopes to hold on to traditional ways of life.

Most Samoans are subsistence farmers raising food for themselves and their families. Most food is grown in village gardens. Coconuts, yams, and bananas are the major crops.

As in most Pacific Islands, family ties are strong in Samoa. Within villages, families share work and food with one another. Almost everyone who lives in a village belongs to a large extended family, sometimes more than 100 people, most of whose members also live in the village.

Each family has its own *fale*, or house. Unlike many other kinds of houses, the fale has no walls. Samoans say it is the least private house on earth. Family life is lived in the open. When storms or heavy rains come, householders let down woven mats or blinds to keep out rain. Only then does a family experience privacy.

Within a village, each extended family chooses a ***matai***, or chief, to represent it. In Samoan society, land is traditionally held in common by all the members of an extended family group. It cannot be sold or given to others. One of the most important jobs of the *matai* is to make decisions about how this land will be shared. The *matai* also helps settle the conflicts that arise between villagers over land and other issues. The *matai* represents the family group on the village or district council.

Village women are likely to be found working together making such traditional crafts as *siapo* cloth from the bark of the mulberry tree. The women soften the mulberry branches with seawater, then strip them of their bark. After pounding the bark, the women weave it into cloth, mats, or baskets, which then are painted with natural dyes. Men wear the lavalava, a wraparound skirt made from *siapo* cloth.

For those who have always remained on the island, the Samoan way, called the *fa'a Samoa*, continues to be important. However, life is changing for young people. Every year, Samoans leave for American Samoa, where the job opportunities are more varied. Young islanders who have left to attend college are likely to settle as far away as New Zealand or the United States.

A thatched fale on Upolu Island shows how the people of Samoa try to keep traditions strong. **What are other examples?**

Customs

In traditional Melanesian society, a man's status was based not on what he owned but on what he could give away. Throughout Melanesia, pigs, certain kinds of seashells, and cassowaries (flightless birds) were part of a complex system of exchanges. Gift-giving feasts were a way for a person to gain respect and higher standing in the community.

Discussion Questions

1 In Melanesian society a man's social status is determined by what he gives away. What determines a person's social status in our society?

2 Is there anyone in our society having responsibilities similar to a matai? If so, how is that person selected?

Village women make such traditional crafts as siapo cloth from the bark of the mulberry tree. The matai, or chief, helps to settle conflicts.

Design for Masi or Wedding Cloth (Fiji)

OBJECTIVES: 12.02, 12.03

Materials Compass, pencils, 12 by 12-inch thick white paper, oil pastels, scissors

Directions Draw a circle 12 inches in diameter. Cut out circle. Fold in half. Fold in half again, then fold in half one more time. Unfold. This will give you eight slices to your circle.

In one section of your circle draw a very simple geometric design. Fill in designs with oil pastels. Limit the colors to three or four. The design will be most stimulating when no white is left.

Fold paper in half with the colored part on the inside. Using the handle of scissors, rub the colored part firmly. This will leave an impression of original design. Using impression as a guide, fill in new section with the same colors. Repeat the last three steps until entire design is filled with color. Note that the section that will be rubbed with handle of scissors will double in size each time.

Vignettes

OBJECTIVES: 11.01, 11.02, 11.03, 13.02

Assign each group an imaginary teen-ager, born and raised in Samoa. Give them this scenario: For the first time you are going to visit your aunt who lives in American Samoa. Prepare a series of letters or postcards describing to your family the cultural differences you are experiencing.

Pacific Realm Triarama

OBJECTIVES: 1.01, 1.03

Materials *Where the Forest Meets the Sea* by Jeannie Baker, (New York: Greenwillow Books, 1990, ISBN 0688063632.) 8½-inch by 11-inch sheets of construction paper; scraps of construction paper; colored pencils, markers, crayons; scissors; glue/glue sticks; various art supplies, such as yarn, modeling clay, tissue paper, clear plastic wrap, foil, chalk, and/or felt; found art items including twigs, leaves, grass clippings, sand, pebbles, buttons, eggshells, Styrofoam containers, packaging materials (shredded paper, bubble wrap, peanuts), plastic tubing, lightweight metals/magnets/washers, and string; and triarama pattern from the Teacher's Resource Guide

Directions Read aloud *Where the Forest Meets the Sea*, sharing collage illustrations as samples of how artists use texture and collage art to create three-dimensional effects as needed for a triarama. Students design triarama illustrating an aspect of the Pacific Realm (Australia, Melanesia, Micronesia, or Polynesia) by folding the right corner of an 8½-inch by 11-inch sheet of construction paper down to left-hand side of paper, forming square. Trim off the excess paper from the 11-inch side. Open the folded paper square, then fold the left corner down. Square paper should now have folded "X" line giving a center point on the square. With paper reopened cut along one folded line to the center of the square. Illustrate the uncut triangular portion of the square as the triarama's background. Overlap the two cut triangles to form the triarama's base; glue into desired overlap. Using paper scraps, art supplies, and found art items draw, cut out, and form three-dimensional illustrations of chosen Pacific region that has a tab at the bottom. Fold each tab and glue the three-dimensional illustration to the triarama's base so the feature is upright.

Wayfinding through the Ocean

Over 800 years ago, Pacific navigators (below) regularly sailed between Tahiti and Hawaii, a distance of 2,220 miles (3,574 km) by sea. The Pacific Ocean navigators relied upon the stars and a variety of clues from the natural world to chart their course.

At night, a certain kind of underwater light known as bioluminescence also guided them. This light can show the presence of land up to 100 miles (161 km) away.

The island sailors (far right) depended on their knowledge of water, waves, winds, ocean currents, birds, and sea creatures. The sea's color changes with its depth and is a different color close to land. Close to a coral reef, the water turns light green.

560 Chapter 27

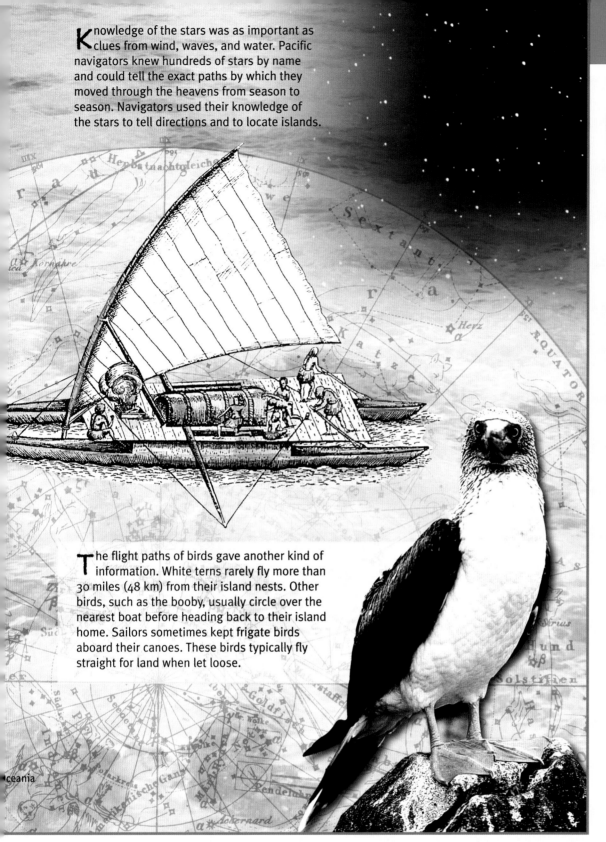

Knowledge of the stars was as important as clues from wind, waves, and water. Pacific navigators knew hundreds of stars by name and could tell the exact paths by which they moved through the heavens from season to season. Navigators used their knowledge of the stars to tell directions and to locate islands.

The flight paths of birds gave another kind of information. White terns rarely fly more than 30 miles (48 km) from their island nests. Other birds, such as the booby, usually circle over the nearest boat before heading back to their island home. Sailors sometimes kept frigate birds aboard their canoes. These birds typically fly straight for land when let loose.

Field Trip

After the study of wayfinding, take students to the Morehead Planetarium in Chapel Hill to learn more about astronomy and the solar system.

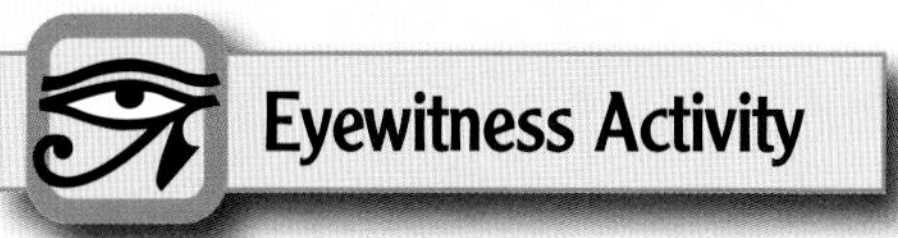

"Star Light, Star Bright..."

OBJECTIVES: 1.01, 1.03

Constellations can be mapped. Many images correlate with the star patterns in our planet's constellations. Have students carefully and closely (even using magnifying glass) examine background map on page 561 to identify any images they note. Use the internet to find maps of the contellations. Discuss with students that Southern Hemisphere constellations are different from those in the Northern Hemisphere. Remind students that most of the Pacific Realm is located in the Southern Hemisphere.

Extension For intermediate ELL students, model and provide additional explanations.

Discussion Questions

1 What have American Samoans gained by their willingness to work in factories?

2 What have they lost?

3 Do you think you would prefer to live in Samoa before Western influence?

4 How important to you is putting the needs of the group ahead of the needs of the individual?

Activity

Overview

OBJECTIVES: 1.01, 1.03, 2.01, 4.02

Have students design a question catcher about a country/island in Oceania. Write the names of the Pacific Islands on slips of paper. Allow students to draw the island they are to research. Design a question catcher to include important information about each country: capital, population, area, form of government, exports, languages, currency, flag, plants, animals, tourist attractions, historical events, topography (high or low), or life expectancy. Use the pattern in the Teacher's Resource Guide.

Residents of Pago Pago, American Samoa, lead less traditional lives than people of Western Samoa. **Why?**

American Samoa

The seven small islands that make up American Samoa were the site of a United States naval base. In the 1950s after the base closed, the United States encouraged American companies to build tuna canneries to provide a job source for Samoans.

Today, both the United States government and the tuna canneries are the major employers on the island. Far fewer American Samoans are farmers now. Most of the workers in the tuna canneries come from Samoa and are willing to do the smelly, unpleasant work of cleaning fish at the wages offered by the canneries. Most American Samoans work in government jobs.

Although American Samoans have welcomed modern consumer goods, they have also held on to many traditional beliefs and practices. Like the Samoans, they depend upon their *matais* to settle arguments and land rights issues. In American Samoa, *matai* have less influence than they once had. Fifty or a hundred years ago, the *matai* had the power of life and death over villagers, especially those who misbehaved. Today their influence is limited.

Other changes are coming. Younger generations learn through television and DVDs about other ways of life. Tourists and government officials who visit the islands bring still more foreign customs.

Island families have long taught their children to put the good of the group first. Islanders are expected to share whatever they have with one another, be it food or money. Those who refuse to do so are considered selfish. Today, traditional ways of sharing are breaking down as people become more involved in the money economy. Villagers are less willing to share their paychecks with those who do not work or cannot repay with money.

Right after high school, many young people from American Samoa leave their home islands. Because American Samoa is a United States territory, Samoans from there can easily move to the United States. Today, tens of thousands live in California, Washington State, and Hawaii.

LESSON 3 REVIEW

Fact Follow-Up

1. What is wayfinding? How does a wayfinder navigate?
2. How have improved travel and communications technology changed Oceania?
3. What is the function of a *matai?*
4. Contrast life in American Samoa and (Western) Samoa.

Talk About It

1. What do you think is the greatest challenge facing Samoans? Why?
2. Would you prefer to visit (Western) Samoa or American Samoa? Explain your choice.
3. Which traditional practices of Samoa do you think are most important to preserve for the future? Explain.

LESSON 3 REVIEW

Fact Follow-Up Answers

1. Wayfinding is a traditional method of navigation developed by Pacific Islanders hundreds of years ago. A wayfinder navigates by using knowledge of water, waves, winds, ocean currents, birds, and sea creatures.
2. Oceania has become a popular tourist destination. Tourism has brought hotels, resorts, souvenir shops, restaurants, more paved land, water pollution, and overcrowding. Communications technology and travel have "moved people from the Stone Age to the plastic age" in a single generation.
3. A matai is a chief chosen by each extended family. The matai makes decisions about how land will be shared, helps settle conflicts, and represents the family group on the village or district council.
4. Western Samoa is an independent country that has kept many of the traditional ways. The people are subsistence farmers who have controlled tourism. American Samoa is a territory of the United States, where change is taking place more rapidly. It has tuna canneries, which attract Samoan workers, and government jobs, which employ the American Samoans. Traditional ways are still present in American Samoa, but their influence is limited.

Talk About It Answers

1. Important points: Students should choose one challenge and explain why it was chosen. Western Samoa is in danger of losing its young people to American Samoa.
2. Important points: Students should state a preference and explain it. Western Samoa is a more traditional Oceanic nation.
3. Important points: Encourage students to list several practices and then limit the list to a few of the most important practices. Family ties and the tradition of the matai for conflict resolution are two possibilities.

Applying Decision-Making and Problem-Solving Techniques to World Issues

The Changing Pacific Islands

In this chapter you read about John Uruo who left his home in the Caroline Islands at the age of eighteen to go to college in the United States. As he left, John said "I go to jump over the wall."

Isolation was the wall, and the wall is crumbling as change comes to Oceania. Some areas, like American Samoa and Guam, have changed because of United States military and economic interests. Others are more traditional. One thing is certain: All will face change because of improved transportation, communications, and the movement of people and ideas.

What are some of the changes the people will face? Working with a partner, make notes from this chapter about some of the changes that have *already* come to the region. Then, brainstorm with your partner some changes you think *might* face the region in the years ahead.

When you have completed your two lists (changes that have already occurred and changes that might occur), compare your work with one or two other classmates. What can you learn from each other?

People and societies respond to change in at least three ways:

1. They can adopt the change outright.
2. They can adapt the change (or revise the change) to suit their own circumstances.
3. They can resist the change.

Your first list probably includes changes that have been adopted, adapted, and resisted. Does it? Discuss each change in the list with your partner and decide which of the three categories it fits.

How should the people of Oceania deal with the changes of the future? Should they adopt, adapt, or resist? Can they prepare for change?

To help you answer these questions, use the chart below for analyzing and evaluating change.

Analyzing and Evaluating Change in Oceania

Name of Island Nation: ____________________

Response	Change	Change	Change
Adopt			
Adapt			
Resist			

Teaching This Skill Lesson

Materials Needed textbooks, other references, paper, pencils

Classroom Organization whole class, pairs

Beginning the Lesson Refer to John Uruo mentioned in Chapter 27. Ask students what changes they think he might have faced when he moved from the Caroline Islands to attend college in the United States.

Lesson Development Write the following on the chalkboard:

- preparing for change
- adopting change
- adapting to change
- resisting change

Lead students to discuss how they think John Uruo might have responded to the changes he faced. Tell them they will be making inferences about how people living on the Pacific Islands described in this chapter might respond to changes. Place students in pairs or other small groups, assign each group a Pacific Island, and direct the groups to scan Chapter 27, making a list of changes that have *already* come about and another list of changes that *might* come about in the future. Each student, as a homework assignment, will construct a chart similar to the one on page 563 to analyze the changes that have *already* come about.

Conclusion Place students in their original groupings to compare the charts they have constructed. In a general class discussion, ask students to examine their second list (of changes that might come about in the future) and make some suggestions as to how residents of the Pacific Island nations might prepare for these changes.

Skill Lesson Review

1. How helpful was the chart in deciding which changes should be adopted, adapted, or resisted? *Important points: Students should compare the consequences chart to other graphic organizers.*
2. Are there other ways that you find useful for analyzing the potential consequences of change? What are they? *Important points: Encourage students to list a variety of methods of analyzing consequences. You might discuss the best outcome/worst outcome comparison.*
3. Are there any changes that cannot be resisted? Why or why not? *Important points: Encourage students to contribute to a class list, then narrow the list as they discuss each item on it. Changes brought about by natural disaster or war are hard to fight against.*
4. What other world areas that you have studied this year face similar challenges? *Important point: This is a challenge throughout Africa and Asia.*

Talk About It

1. Important points: Students should state whether the influence has been more positive or more negative and explain why. Outside influence has placed great stress on the environment and culture of the region. Yet outside influence has brought wealth to some parts of Oceania.
2. Important points: Students should choose one of the Five Themes and explain its choice. Region would help us see that although Oceania extends over a vast area, its islands have much in common.
3. Important points: Students should choose one aspect and explain its choice. Communication and medical care are two possibilities. They would be helpful without further harming the environment.
4. Important points: Encourage students to list several practices before choosing one and explaining it. The tradition of the matai to resolve disputes is a possible answer.
5. Important points: Students should choose one challenge and give reasons for choosing that one. Maintaining young people in the economy is essential for the region.
6. Important points: Students should take a position and support it with reasons. Holding territories may seem inconsistent with democracy. On the other hand, territories receive benefits from the countries that supervise them.
7. Important points: Students should comment on how houses are constructed and how they would get along in these environments.

CHAPTER 27 REVIEW

Lessons Learned

Lesson 1
People and Their Environment
Oceania is a vast region of small island groups located in the Pacific Ocean. Counting both water and land, the region is the earth's largest. If only the total land area is considered, it is a small region. Most of the people are Polynesians, whose ancestors began to settle islands 50,000 years ago.

Lesson 2
Government and Economy
Pacific Islanders were once in touch only with one another. Beginning in the 1600s, they were increasingly in touch with the world beyond the islands. These foreign contacts cost the islanders their independence and entangled them in world politics and wars. Only since the 1960s have the islands regained independence. Foreign contacts brought major changes to the islands' economies.

Lesson 3
Culture and Society
Traditional ways of life continue to command respect in the islands. Samoa (Western Samoa) reflects an effort on the part of native leadership to preserve traditional lifestyles while permitting some change. Neighboring American Samoa welcomes change that is rapidly weakening traditional ways. Many young people from the region are leaving the islands.

Talk About It

1. Has European (or Western) influence in Oceania been more positive or negative? Explain your answer.
2. Which of the Five Themes of Geography is most useful in analyzing Oceania? Why?
3. If you could export one aspect of our technological society to Oceania, which aspect would you choose? Why?
4. If you could import to the United States one traditional practice of Oceania, what would it be? Explain your choice.
5. What do you think is the most pressing challenge facing Oceania in the twenty-first century? Why?
6. Should the United States hold dependent territories in Oceania? Give reasons for your answer.
7. Suppose you were to visit a family in Samoa. How would you adjust to the lifestyle?

Mastering Mapwork

MOVEMENT

Use the map on page 547 to answer these questions:

1. What factors encourage the movement of goods, ideas, and people throughout Oceania?
2. What factors discourage the movement of goods, ideas, and people throughout Oceania?
3. Would the movement of people, goods, and ideas be easier in Melanesia than in Micronesia? Explain your answer.
4. What are some barriers to movement in New Guinea?

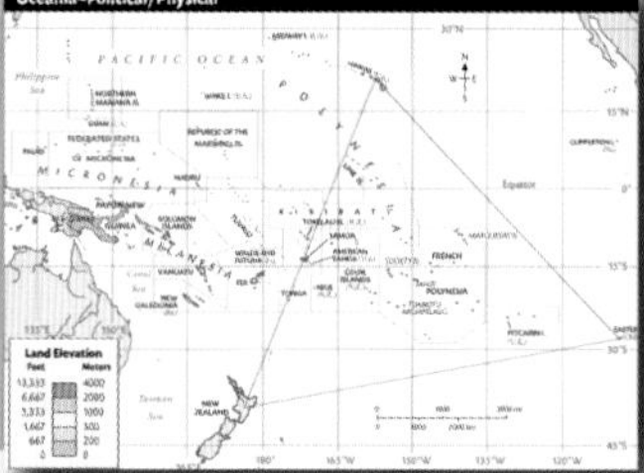

564 Chapter 27

Mastering Mapwork

1. Water and oceangoing shipping encourage movement.
2. Water and distance discourage the movement of goods, ideas, and people.
3. Important points: Students should choose a position and explain it. Melanesia covers more area than Micronesia, and the islands of Melanesia are larger.
4. High mountain ranges and the shape of the island itself—"elongated"—can be barriers to movement.

Go to the Source

Interpreting Statistics

Study the graph and statistics below from the South Pacific Tourism Organization (SPTO). Answer the questions using specific references to the data.

The SPTO is the mandated inter-governmental body for the tourism sector in the South Pacific. SPTO members include the Cook Islands, Fiji, Kiribati, New Caledonia, Niue, Samoa, Solomon Islands, Tahiti (French Polynesia), Tonga, Tuvalu, Vanuatu, and Papua New Guinea. China is also a country member of SPTO.

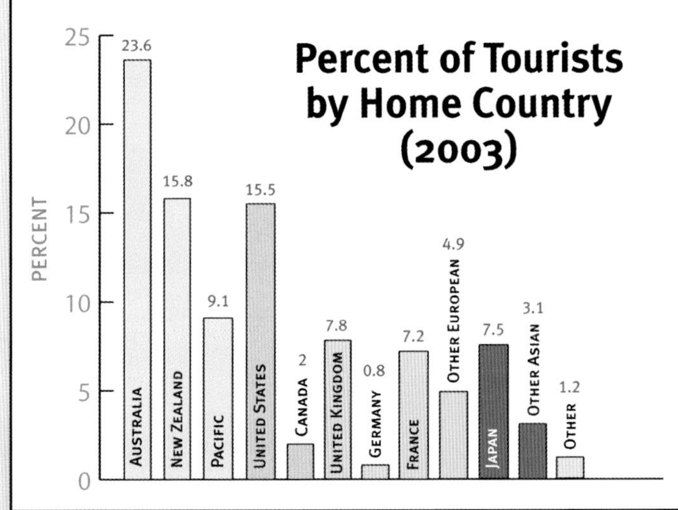

TOURISM FACTS

- Tourism was worth an estimated $1.23 billion (U.S. dollars) in 2003.
- Tourism accounts for up to 75 percent of foreign exchange.
- Tourism accounts for 50 percent of GDP.
- Tourism accounts for 12 percent of formal employment.

Go to the Source

Questions

1. From where are most of the tourists to the South Pacific coming? Why? Explain.
2. How important is tourism to the economies of countries in the South Pacific?
3. Consider the geography of the South Pacific region. Why do you think these countries rely so heavily on tourism?
4. What are some future issues that the region may face due to a rapid increase in tourism and dependency on tourism dollars?

Go to the Source

OBJECTIVES: 4.02, 5.01, 5.03, 5.04, 6.01. 6.03, 13.03 Skills 2.02, 2.05, 3.02, 4.05, 4.06

Because tourism is such a critical part of Oceania's economy, the South Pacific Tourism Organization both promotes tourism and facilitates cooperation among the nations of the region. For a link to these and more statistics and information from the South Pacific Tourism Organization visit **NCJourneys.com.**

ANSWERS

1. Most tourists are coming from Australia, New Zealand, United States, and Europe. The geographic proximity of Australia and New Zealand make the area an attractive destination. Many of these countries also have higher standards of living and incomes allowing more visitors from these areas.
2. Very important: $1.23 billion in 2003, and 50 percent of the region's Gross Domestic Product; 12 percent of employment
3. The region does not have large areas of land for farming or a large base of industry, so tourism makes up a large part of the economy. The warm and sunny weather and isolation are attractive characteristics for tourists.
4. An increase in the number of visitors can create great environmental impact such as water pollution and garbage disposal. Economic difficulties in other countries could keep tourists from visiting the region which will create economic and employment strains on the countries relying on tourist dollars.

How to Use the Chapter Review

There are three sections in the Chapter Review: Talk About It, Mastering Mapwork, and Go to the Source. Use the Vocabulary Worksheets and the Chapter Review Worksheet in the Teacher's Resource Guide for additional reinforcement and preparation for the Chapter Assessments. The chapter and lesson reviews and the Chapter Review Worksheets are the basis of the assessment for each chapter.

Talk About It questions encourage students to speculate about the content of the chapter and are suitable for class or small-group discussion. They are not intended to be assigned for homework.

Mastering Mapwork has students apply one or more of the Five Themes of Geography to maps within the chapter.

Go to the Source activities allow students to analyze a primary source that relates to the content of the chapter. The questions and activities familiarize students with different types of primary sources and also build content-reading skills.

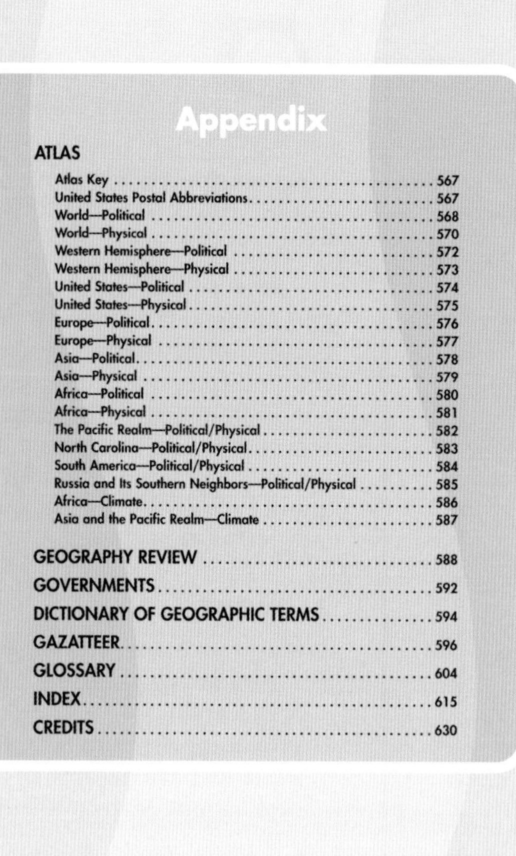

Appendix

ATLAS

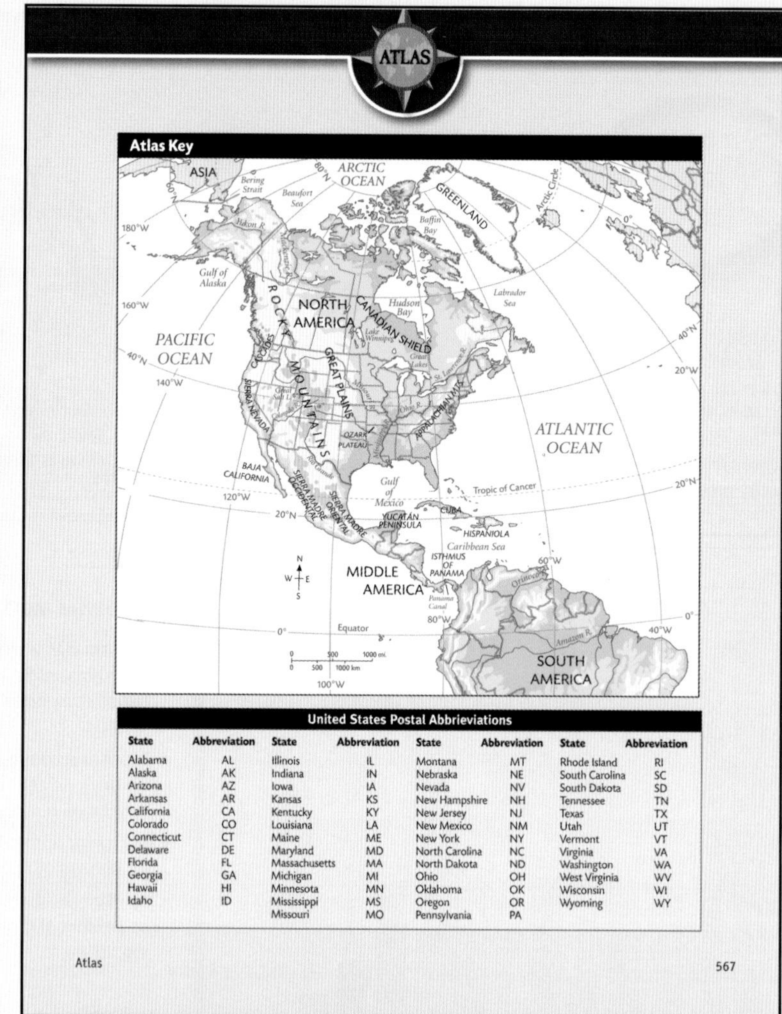

United States Postal Abbreviations

State	Abbreviation	State	Abbreviation	State	Abbreviation	State	Abbreviation
Alabama	AL	Illinois	IL	Montana	MT	Rhode Island	RI
Alaska	AK	Indiana	IN	Nebraska	NE	South Carolina	SC
Arizona	AZ	Iowa	IA	Nevada	NV	South Dakota	SD
Arkansas	AR	Kansas	KS	New Hampshire	NH	Tennessee	TN
California	CA	Kentucky	KY	New Jersey	NJ	Texas	TX
Colorado	CO	Louisiana	LA	New Mexico	NM	Utah	UT
Connecticut	CT	Maine	ME	New York	NY	Vermont	VT
Delaware	DE	Maryland	MD	North Carolina	NC	Virginia	VA
Florida	FL	Massachusetts	MA	North Dakota	ND	Washington	WA
Georgia	GA	Michigan	MI	Ohio	OH	West Virginia	WV
Hawaii	HI	Minnesota	MN	Oklahoma	OK	Wisconsin	WI
Idaho	ID	Mississippi	MS	Oregon	OR	Wyoming	WY
		Missouri	MO	Pennsylvania	PA		

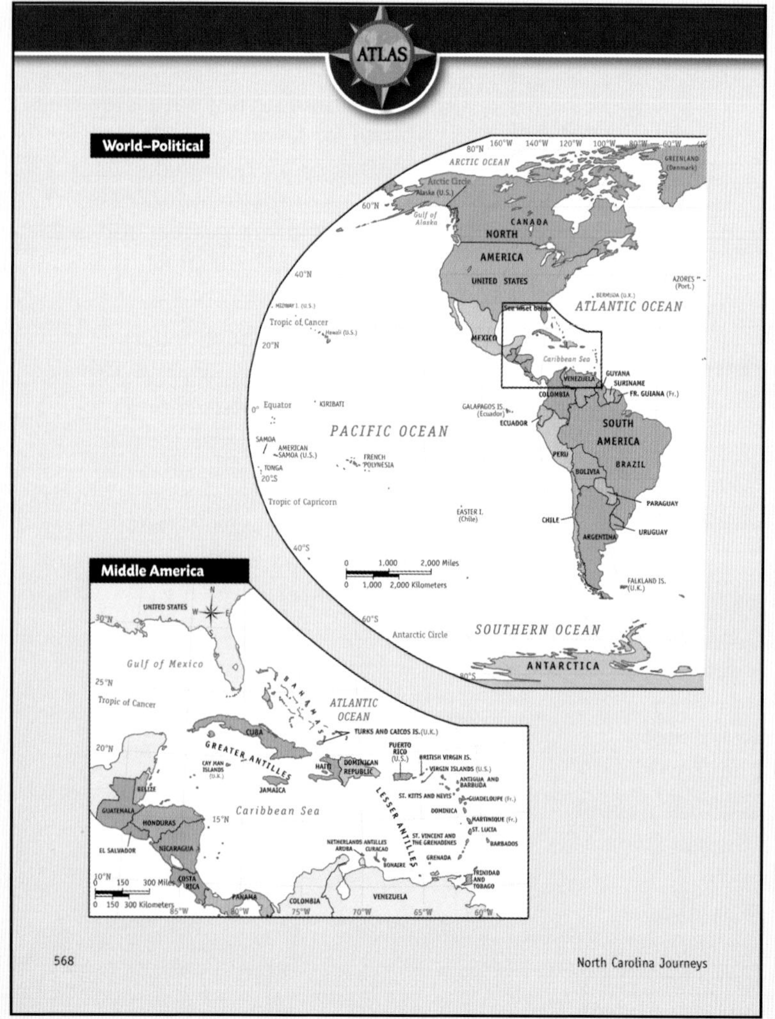

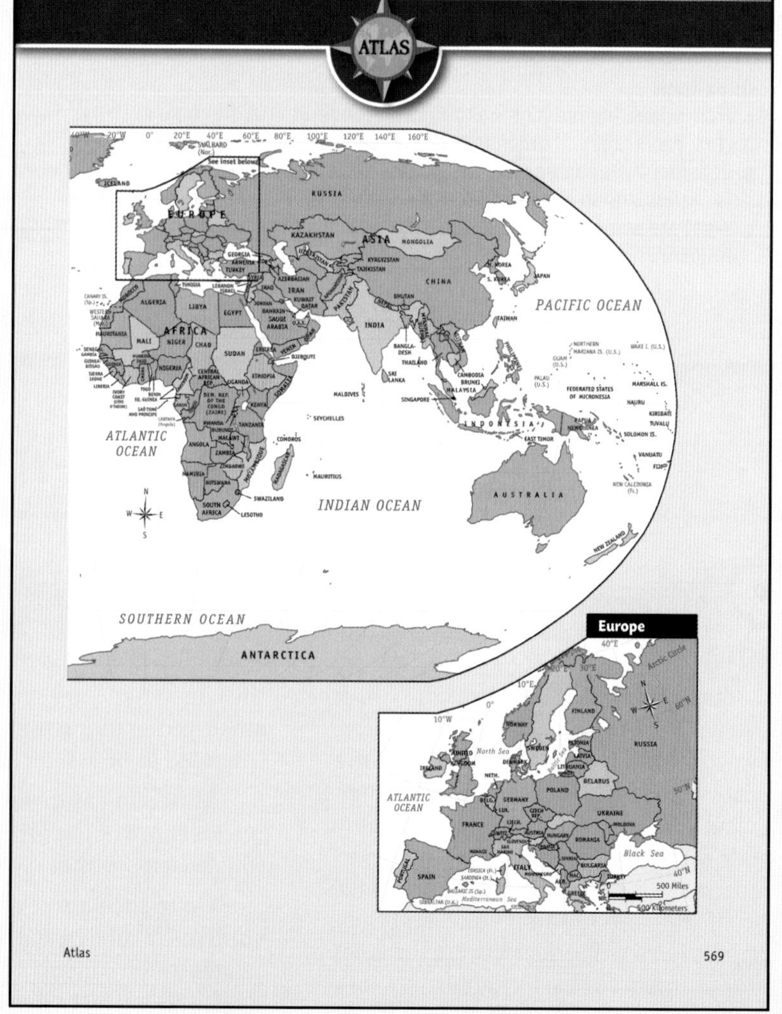

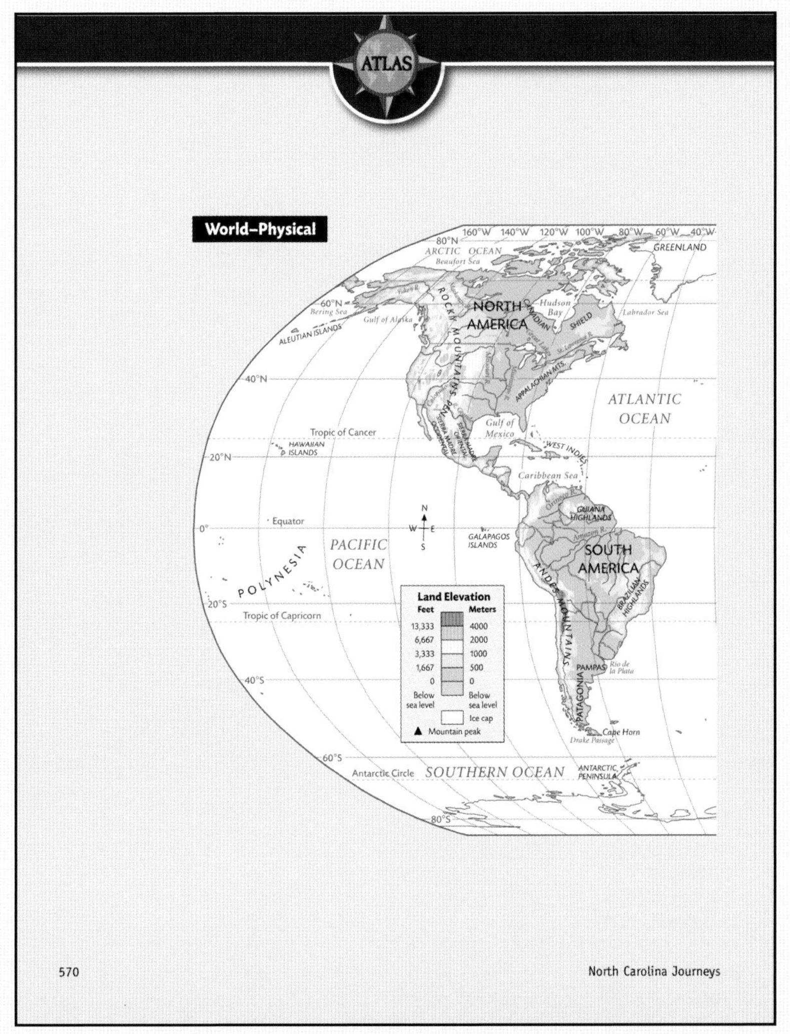
ATLAS
World–Physical
ARCTIC OCEAN
GREENLAND
NORTH AMERICA
Hudson Bay
Labrador Sea
Gulf of Alaska
ALEUTIAN ISLANDS
ATLANTIC OCEAN
Gulf of Mexico
Tropic of Cancer
HAWAIIAN ISLANDS
Caribbean Sea
Equator
PACIFIC OCEAN
POLYNESIA
GALAPAGOS ISLANDS
SOUTH AMERICA
Tropic of Capricorn
PAMPAS
Cape Horn
Antarctic Circle
SOUTHERN OCEAN
ANTARCTIC PENINSULA
Land Elevation
Feet
Meters
13,333
4000
6,667
2000
3,333
1000
1,667
500
0
0
Below sea level
Below sea level
Ice cap
Mountain peak

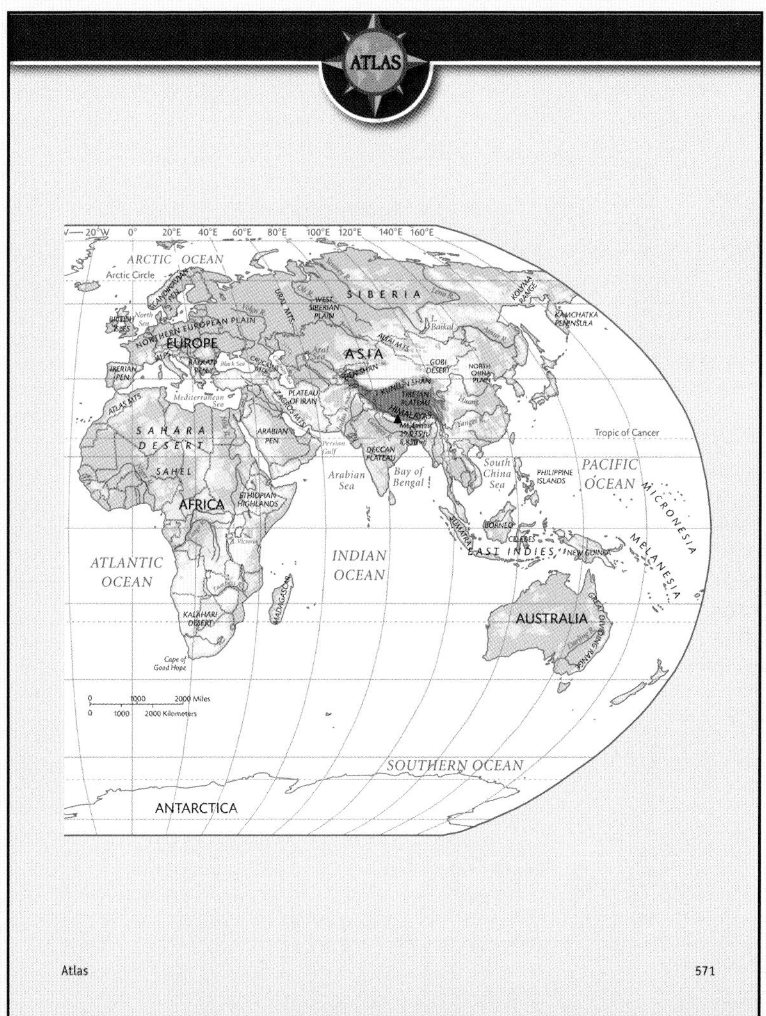
ATLAS
ARCTIC OCEAN
Arctic Circle
SIBERIA
EUROPE
ASIA
SAHARA DESERT
SAHEL
AFRICA
Arabian Sea
Bay of Bengal
Tropic of Cancer
PACIFIC OCEAN
ATLANTIC OCEAN
INDIAN OCEAN
AUSTRALIA
MICRONESIA
MELANESIA
SOUTHERN OCEAN
ANTARCTICA

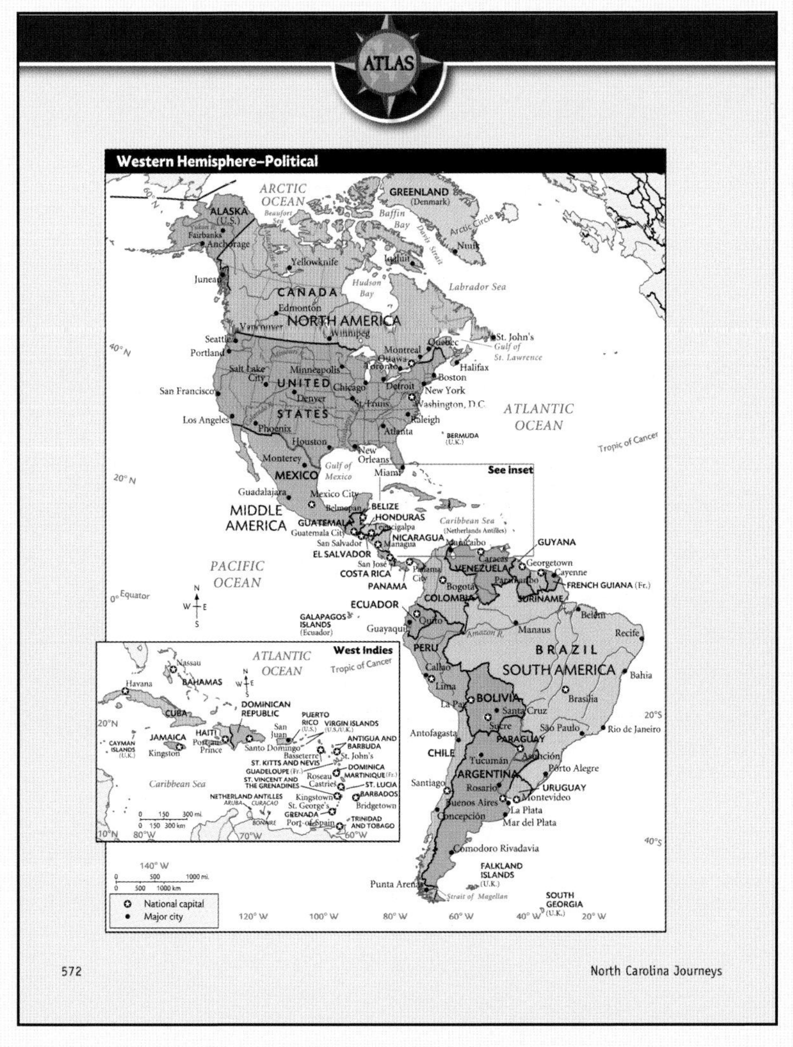
ATLAS
Western Hemisphere–Political
ARCTIC OCEAN
GREENLAND (Denmark)
ALASKA (U.S.)
CANADA
NORTH AMERICA
UNITED STATES
Labrador Sea
ATLANTIC OCEAN
Gulf of Mexico
MEXICO
MIDDLE AMERICA
PACIFIC OCEAN
See inset
SOUTH AMERICA
BRAZIL
West Indies
National capital
Major city

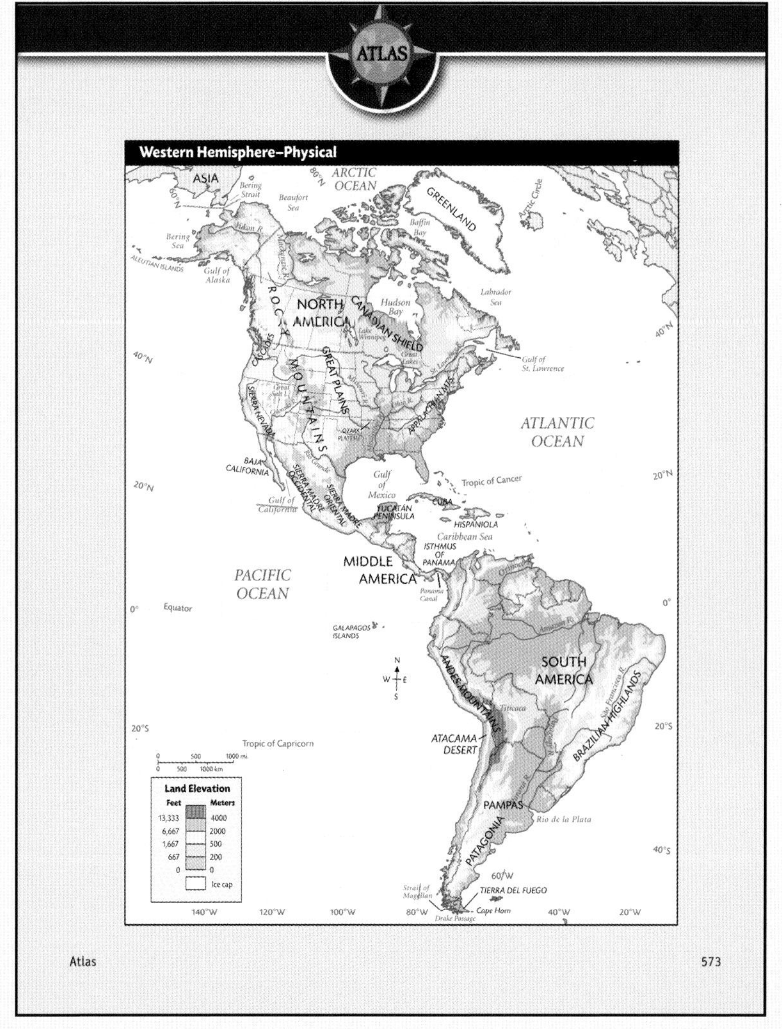
ATLAS
Western Hemisphere–Physical
ASIA
ARCTIC OCEAN
GREENLAND
NORTH AMERICA
Hudson Bay
ATLANTIC OCEAN
Gulf of Mexico
Tropic of Cancer
MIDDLE AMERICA
PACIFIC OCEAN
Equator
SOUTH AMERICA
ATACAMA DESERT
PAMPAS
PATAGONIA
TIERRA DEL FUEGO
Cape Horn
Land Elevation
Feet
Meters
Ice cap

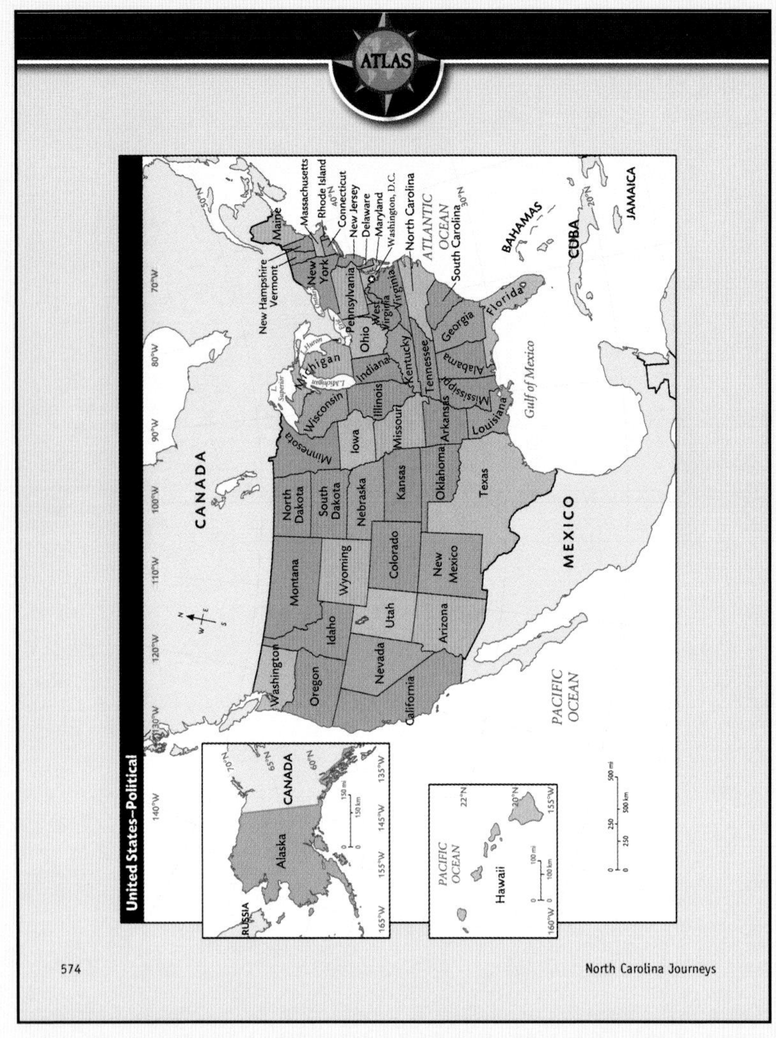
ATLAS
United States–Political
CANADA
MEXICO
Gulf of Mexico
ATLANTIC OCEAN
PACIFIC OCEAN
BAHAMAS
CUBA
JAMAICA
Washington
Oregon
California
Idaho
Nevada
Montana
Wyoming
Utah
Arizona
Colorado
New Mexico
North Dakota
South Dakota
Nebraska
Kansas
Oklahoma
Texas
Minnesota
Iowa
Missouri
Arkansas
Louisiana
Wisconsin
Illinois
Michigan
Indiana
Ohio
Kentucky
Tennessee
Mississippi
Alabama
Georgia
Florida
South Carolina
North Carolina
Virginia
West Virginia
Pennsylvania
New York
Vermont
New Hampshire
Maine
Massachusetts
Rhode Island
Connecticut
New Jersey
Delaware
Maryland
Washington, D.C.
Alaska
RUSSIA
Hawaii
574
North Carolina Journeys

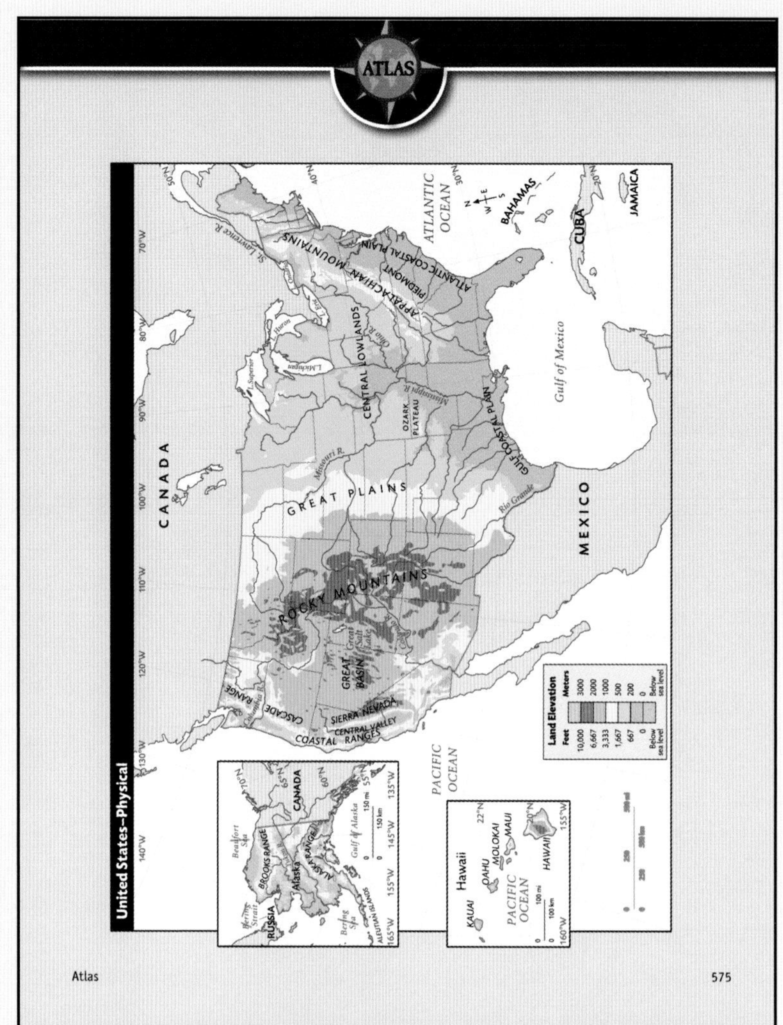
ATLAS
United States–Physical
CANADA
MEXICO
Gulf of Mexico
ATLANTIC OCEAN
PACIFIC OCEAN
BAHAMAS
CUBA
JAMAICA
APPALACHIAN MOUNTAINS
PIEDMONT
ATLANTIC COASTAL PLAIN
CENTRAL LOWLANDS
OZARK PLATEAU
GULF COASTAL PLAIN
GREAT PLAINS
ROCKY MOUNTAINS
GREAT BASIN
CASCADE RANGE
SIERRA NEVADA
CENTRAL VALLEY
COASTAL RANGES
Land Elevation
Hawaii
KAUAI
OAHU
MOLOKAI
MAUI
HAWAII
Atlas
575

ATLAS
Europe–Political
ICELAND
Reykjavik
Norwegian Sea
ATLANTIC OCEAN
NORWAY
SWEDEN
FINLAND
RUSSIA
ESTONIA
LATVIA
LITHUANIA
BELARUS
UKRAINE
POLAND
GERMANY
DENMARK
NETHERLANDS
UNITED KINGDOM
IRELAND
FRANCE
SPAIN
PORTUGAL
ITALY
AUSTRIA
HUNGARY
ROMANIA
BULGARIA
GREECE
TURKEY
MOLDOVA
North Sea
Baltic Sea
Bay of Biscay
Black Sea
Mediterranean Sea
AFRICA
National capital
International boundary
576
North Carolina Journeys

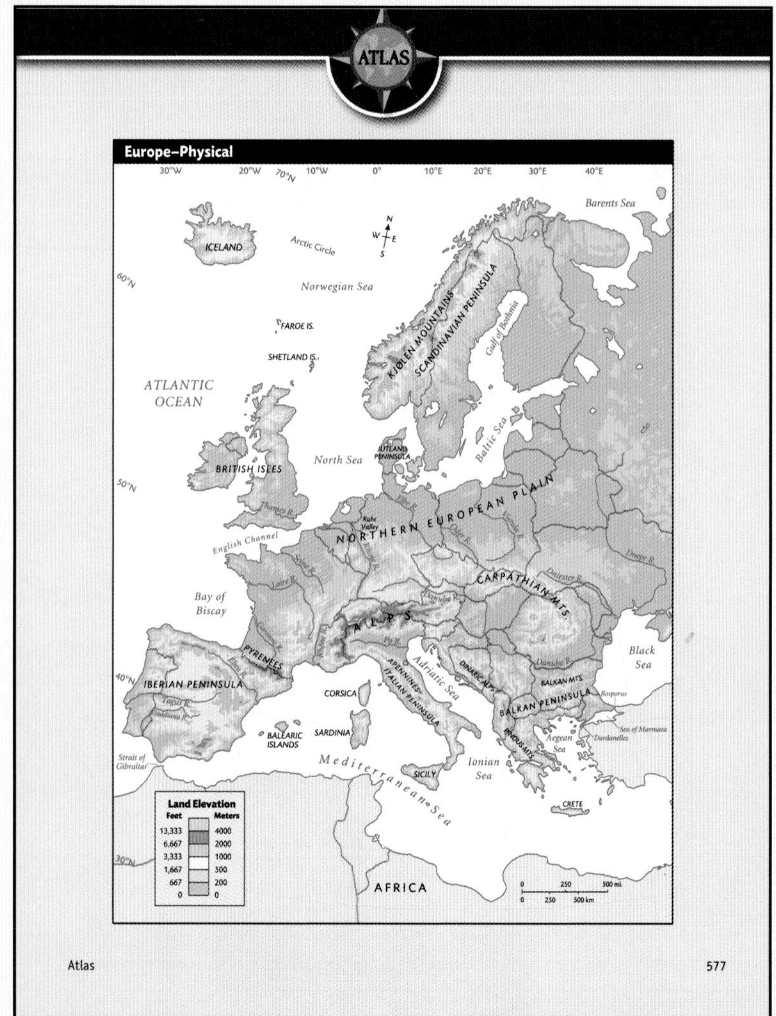
ATLAS
Europe–Physical
ICELAND
Norwegian Sea
ATLANTIC OCEAN
KJØLEN MOUNTAINS
SCANDINAVIAN PENINSULA
BRITISH ISLES
North Sea
NORTHERN EUROPEAN PLAIN
CARPATHIAN MTS.
ALPS
PYRENEES
IBERIAN PENINSULA
BALKAN PENINSULA
Bay of Biscay
Black Sea
Mediterranean Sea
CORSICA
SARDINIA
SICILY
CRETE
AFRICA
Land Elevation
Atlas
577

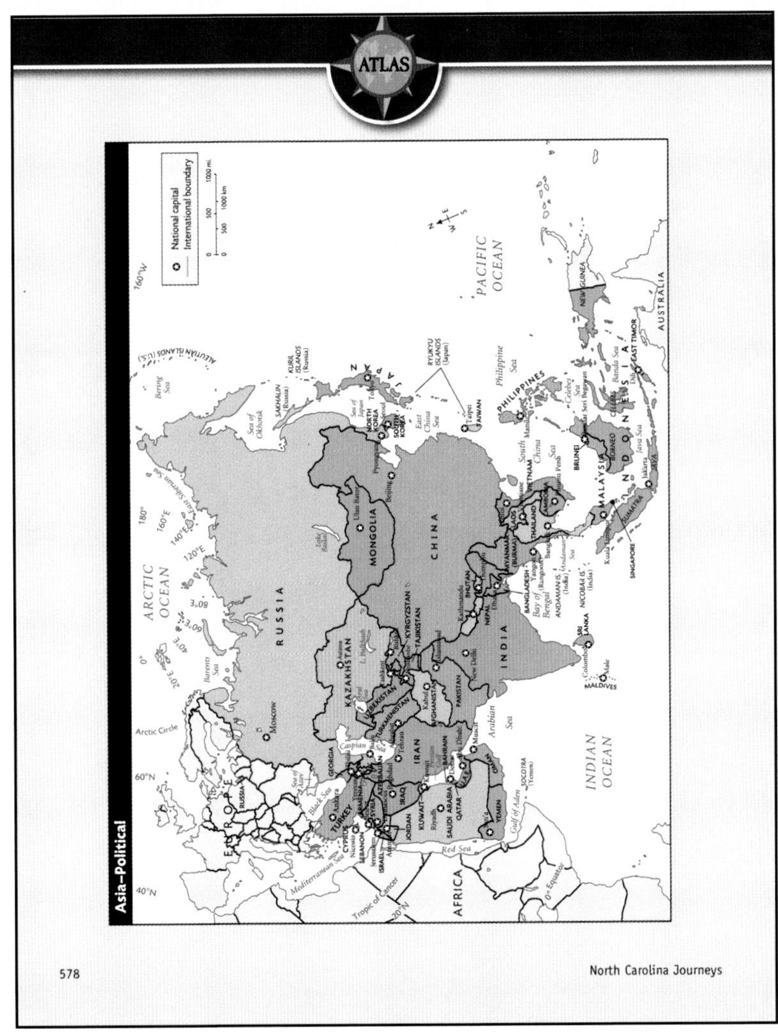
ATLAS
Asia–Political
National capital
International boundary
ARCTIC OCEAN
PACIFIC OCEAN
INDIAN OCEAN
RUSSIA
CHINA
MONGOLIA
KAZAKHSTAN
INDIA
IRAN
AFRICA
AUSTRALIA
578
North Carolina Journeys

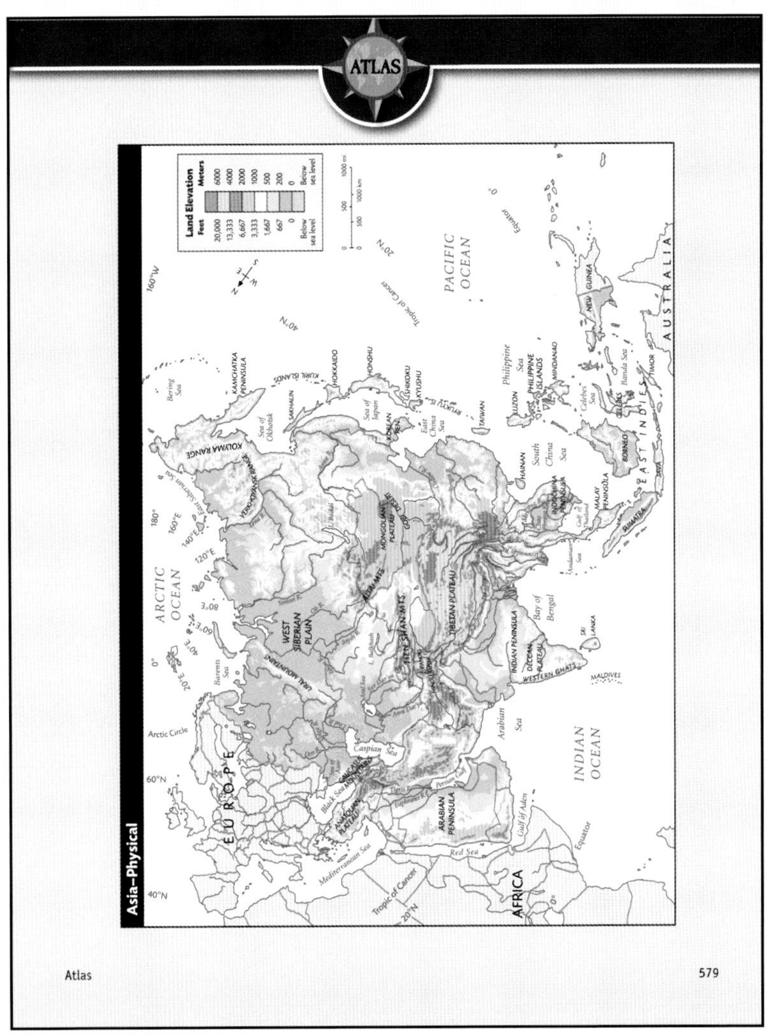
ATLAS
Asia–Physical
Land Elevation
ARCTIC OCEAN
PACIFIC OCEAN
INDIAN OCEAN
WEST SIBERIAN PLAIN
TIBETAN PLATEAU
ARABIAN PENINSULA
EUROPE
AFRICA
AUSTRALIA
Atlas
579

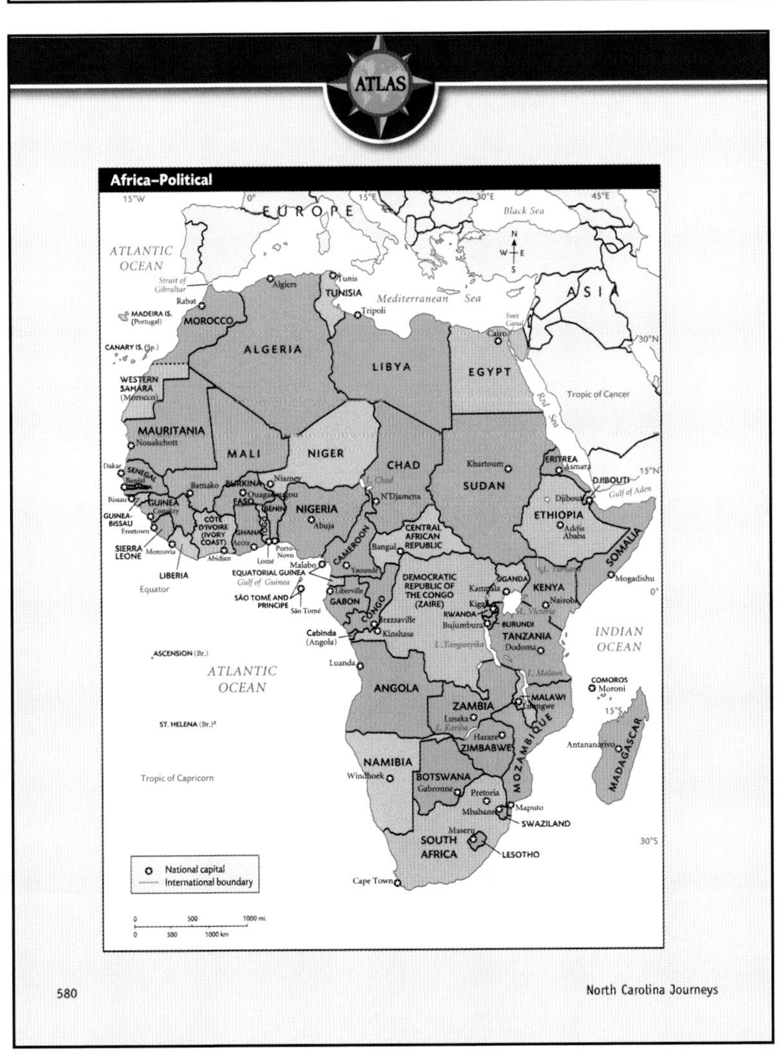
ATLAS
Africa–Political
EUROPE
ASIA
ATLANTIC OCEAN
INDIAN OCEAN
Mediterranean Sea
Black Sea
MOROCCO
ALGERIA
TUNISIA
LIBYA
EGYPT
WESTERN SAHARA (Morocco)
MAURITANIA
MALI
NIGER
CHAD
SUDAN
ERITREA
DJIBOUTI
ETHIOPIA
SOMALIA
NIGERIA
CAMEROON
CENTRAL AFRICAN REPUBLIC
GABON
CONGO
DEMOCRATIC REPUBLIC OF THE CONGO (ZAIRE)
UGANDA
KENYA
RWANDA
BURUNDI
TANZANIA
ANGOLA
ZAMBIA
MALAWI
ZIMBABWE
MOZAMBIQUE
NAMIBIA
BOTSWANA
SOUTH AFRICA
SWAZILAND
LESOTHO
MADAGASCAR
COMOROS
LIBERIA
SIERRA LEONE
GUINEA
GUINEA BISSAU
SENEGAL
Tropic of Cancer
Equator
Tropic of Capricorn
National capital
International boundary
580
North Carolina Journeys

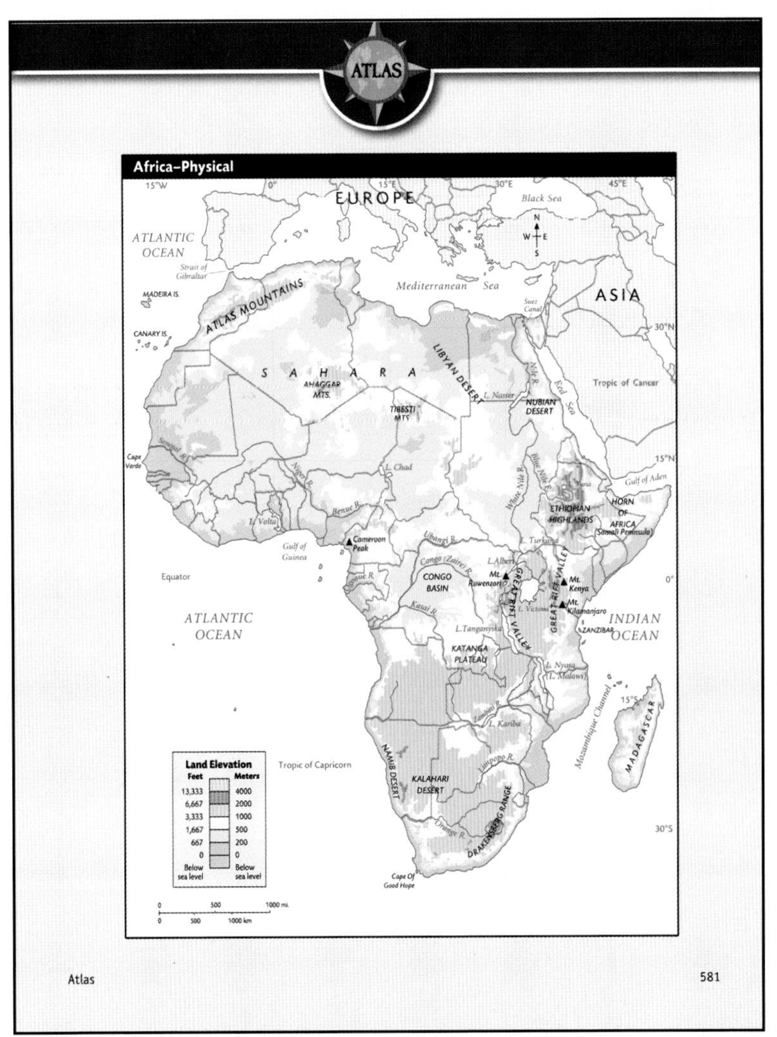
ATLAS
Africa–Physical
EUROPE
ASIA
ATLANTIC OCEAN
INDIAN OCEAN
Mediterranean Sea
Black Sea
ATLAS MOUNTAINS
S A H A R A
AHAGGAR MTS.
TIBESTI MTS.
LIBYAN DESERT
NUBIAN DESERT
ETHIOPIAN HIGHLANDS
HORN OF AFRICA (Somali Peninsula)
Cameroon Peak
CONGO BASIN
GREAT RIFT VALLEY
Mt. Kenya
Mt. Kilimanjaro
KATANGA PLATEAU
KALAHARI DESERT
NAMIB DESERT
DRAKENSBERG RANGE
MADAGASCAR
Cape Of Good Hope
Tropic of Cancer
Equator
Tropic of Capricorn
Land Elevation
Atlas
581

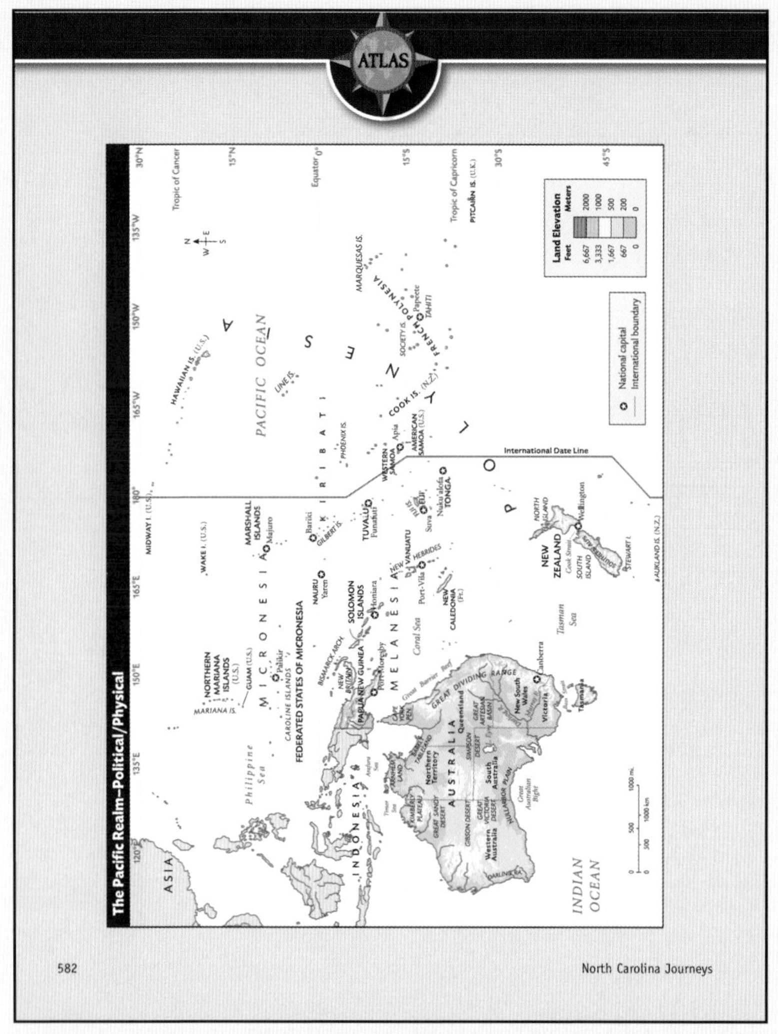
The Pacific Realm—Political/Physical
PACIFIC OCEAN
INDIAN OCEAN
AUSTRALIA
NEW ZEALAND
International Date Line
Land Elevation

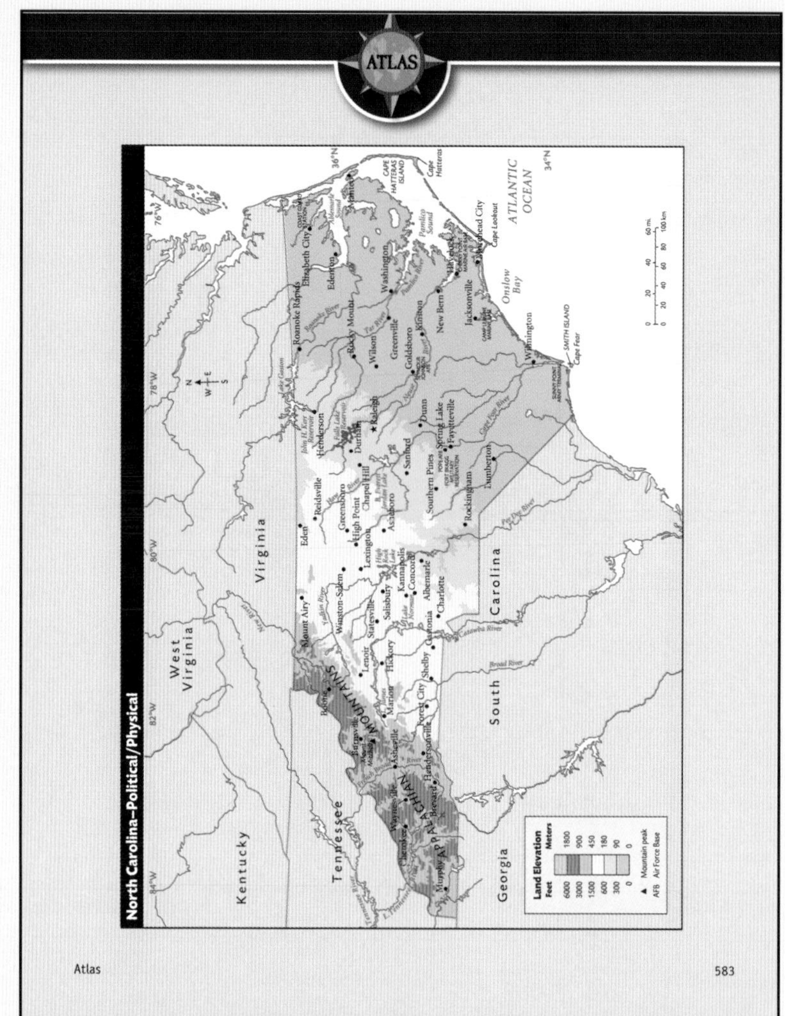
North Carolina—Political/Physical
Virginia
West Virginia
Kentucky
Tennessee
Georgia
South Carolina
ATLANTIC OCEAN
Land Elevation

South America—Political/Physical
VENEZUELA
COLOMBIA
ECUADOR
PERU
BRAZIL
BOLIVIA
PARAGUAY
CHILE
ARGENTINA
URUGUAY
GUYANA
SURINAME
FRENCH GUIANA (Fr.)
PACIFIC OCEAN
ATLANTIC OCEAN
Land Elevations

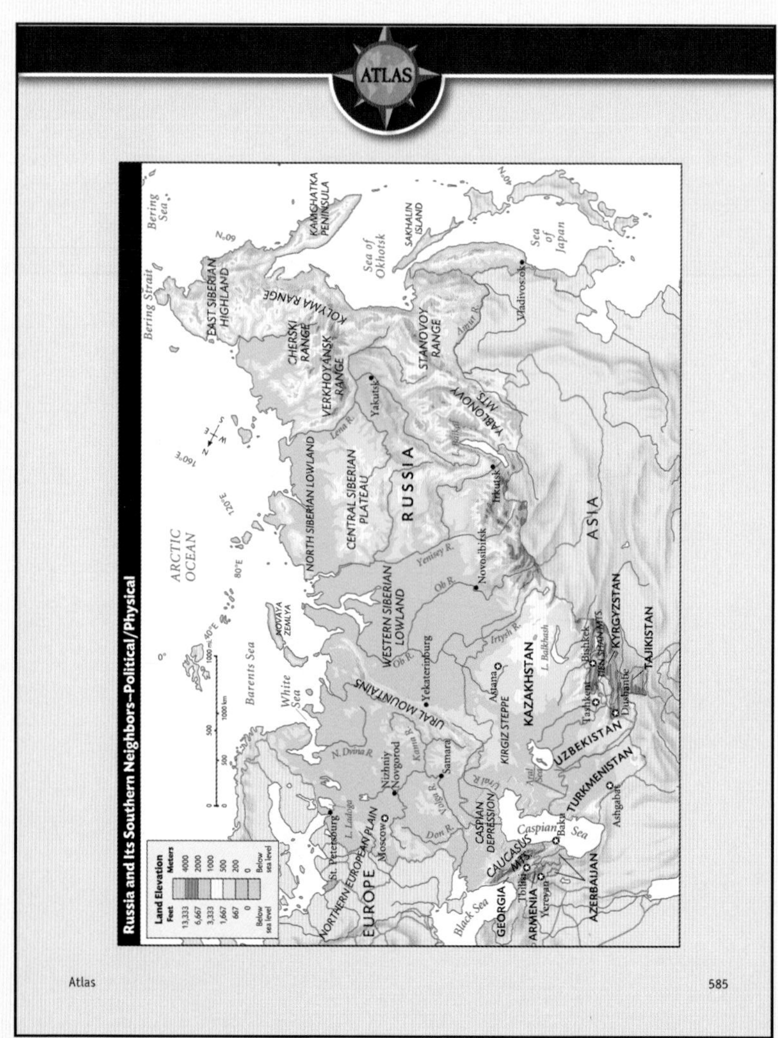
Russia and Its Southern Neighbors—Political/Physical
RUSSIA
ASIA
EUROPE
KAZAKHSTAN
ARCTIC OCEAN
Land Elevation

ATLAS

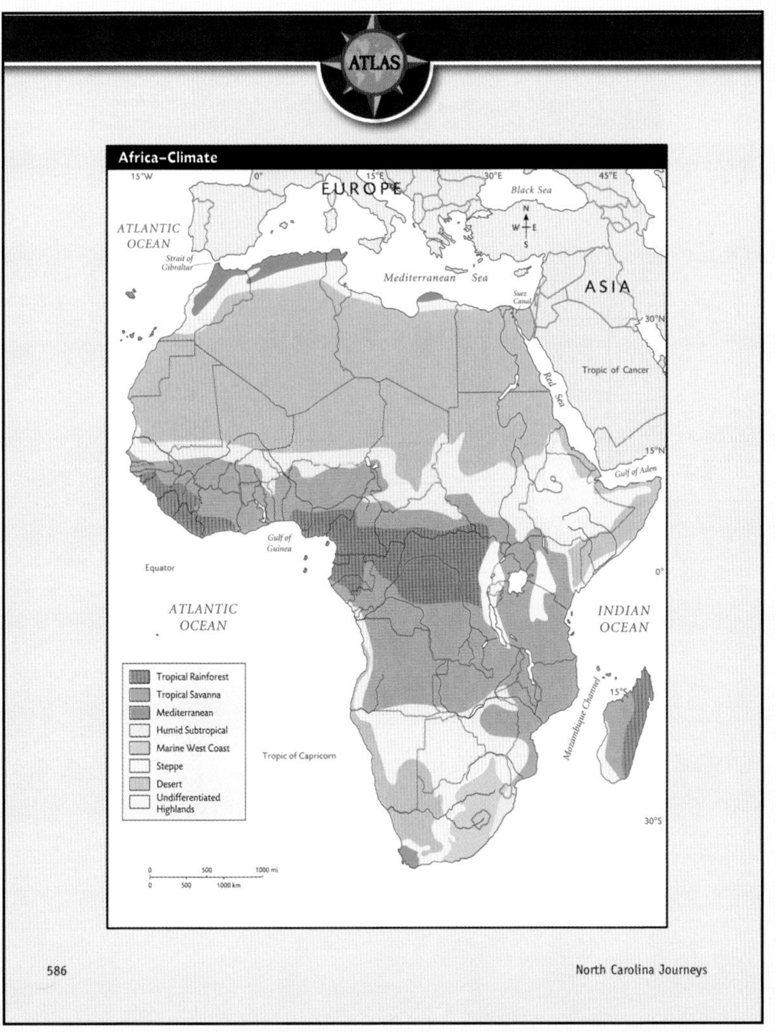

ATLAS

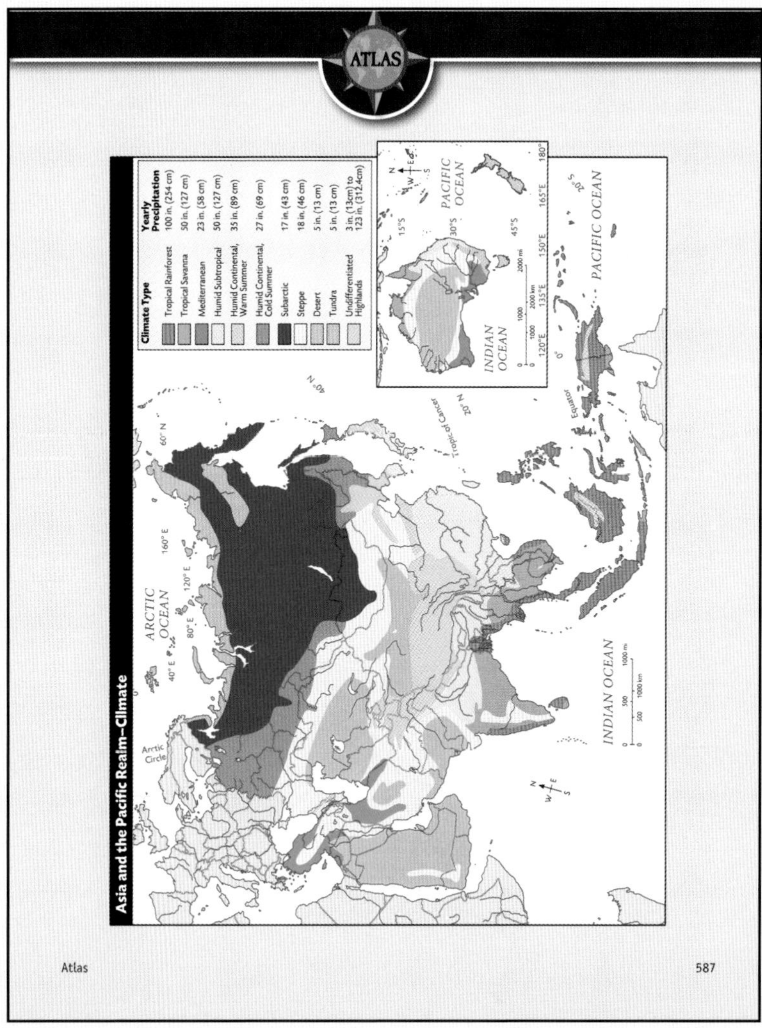

GEOGRAPHY REVIEW

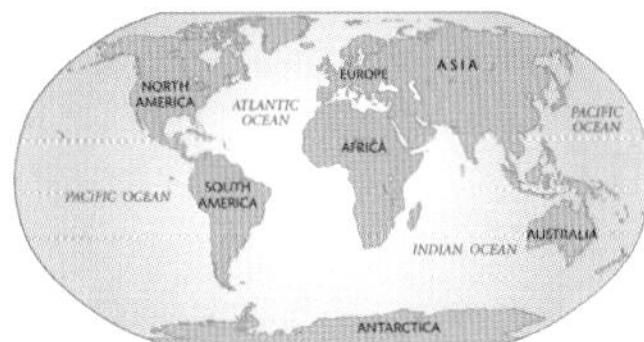

Geography helps make sense of the world around us. The word geography was adopted in the second century B.C. by the Greek scholar Eratosthenes and means "earth description." Geographers study the environment of the earth's surface and the relationship of humans to this environment, including both physical and cultural characteristics.

Geographers organize these characteristics by using the Five Themes of Geography: Location, Place, Region, Movement, and Human-Environmental Interaction (see the Skill Lesson "Using Geography's Five Themes" at the end of Chapter 1). Physical characteristics include the climate, landforms, and vegetation. Cultural characteristics include nations, settlements, modes of transportation, buildings, and other modifications of the physical environment. This lesson reviews geographic concepts relating to physical characteristics. The Dictionary of Geographic Terms in the Appendix reviews geographic descriptions of landforms.

Absolute and Relative Location

Relative location is the kind of location that most people understand. We use it when we describe a place in relation to other places. When you give directions to a store or say that Yanceyville is located in Caswell County south of the Virginia state line, you are using relative location.

What do we do if relative location cannot help us? Sailors on a ship, for example, cannot use landmarks to find their way. Today, sailors, airplane pilots, and others use an imaginary grid, made up of lines called latitude and longitude, superimposed on the earth. This grid allows us to locate any spot on the earth. To write a place's location, note its latitude, then its longitude. This is its **absolute location** (see the World–Physical map in the atlas to study this grid).

Parallels of Latitude Lines of latitude are imaginary circles drawn east and west around the globe. The Equator is the longest line of latitude, ringing the earth at its middle. The Equator divides the earth into two equal parts—the area from the Equator to the North Pole is the Northern Hemisphere, and the area from the Equator to the South Pole is the Southern Hemisphere. The Equator is given the latitude measurement of 0°. The symbol "°" is used for degree, the unit for measuring latitude and longitude.

Lines of latitude are called parallels because all points on any single line are the same distance from the Equator. The parallels give distance from the Equator in degrees. Each degree is equal to about 70 miles (113 km). There are 90 degrees of latitude between the Equator and each of the poles. The Equator is 0°, so the greater the number of degrees of latitude of a place, the farther that place is from the Equator. Durham, North Carolina, is located at 36°N. The "N" means north, indicating Durham is north of the Equator in the Northern Hemisphere.

Meridians of Longitude Lines of longitude, called meridians, like lines of latitude, are measured in degrees. Each meridian runs south from the North Pole to the South Pole. The prime meridian is the starting point for measuring longitude. It is assigned the longitude of 0°, and runs through at the Greenwich Observatory located on the outskirts of London, England.

Like the Equator, the prime meridian also splits the earth in half. High Point, North Carolina, is located at

GEOGRAPHY REVIEW

80°W. The "W" means west, indicating High Point is west of the prime meridian. The area of the earth west of the prime meridian is the Western Hemisphere. The area east of the prime meridian is the Eastern Hemisphere, shown with meridians of longitude in degrees east, or "E."

Time Zones and the International Date Line Longitudinal lines are used to determine time zones around the globe. For every 15 degrees of longitude, time changes by one hour. When it is 8:00 A.M. in North Carolina, for example, it is 7:00 A.M. in Illinois, 6:00 a.m. in Colorado, and 5:00 A.M. in California. The International Date Line is the imaginary line on or near the 180th meridian that marks the spot on earth where each new calendar date begins. The date just west of the line is one day later than it is just to the east. The date line moves away from the 180° meridian to avoid island groups in the Pacific. Although the Aleutian Islands of Alaska are split by the 180° meridian, all the islands observe the same date.

Climate

Climate is the weather pattern—both temperature and rainfall—of a place over a long period of time. Climate is affected by the tilt of the earth, latitude, elevation, and nearness to the sea. Weather is the day-to-day change in temperature and rainfall. Although in the summer the weather may be hot and humid in both North Carolina and at the Equator, the climates of North Carolina and the Equator are different.

The Tilt of the Earth and the Four Seasons The axis of the earth, an imaginary straight line that passes through both poles, is tilted to one side. As the earth orbits the sun in one year, every spot on the earth's surface is tilted away from and then back toward the sun.

The tilt causes some areas of the earth to get more direct sunlight than others. In these places, the rays of sun falling on the earth are very close together. In other places, the sun's rays do not beat down from directly overhead but strike the earth at an angle, spreading out and lessening the heat. We feel this same difference in the heat of the sun at noon and the cooler, slanting rays in the early morning or late afternoon.

Over a year's time, the changes in the earth's tilt affect the temperature of areas on the earth, giving us the four seasons of summer, autumn, winter, and spring. Between March and September, more sun hits the Northern Hemisphere. More sunlight in the north brings summer. Meanwhile, the Southern Hemisphere's sunlight is becoming more diffuse, or spread out. This is when the Southern Hemisphere has winter. The earth's tilt hardly affects the Equator because it continually receives direct sunlight. Seasons near the Equator are not hot or cold but are either rainy or dry.

At the poles, the sunlight lasts longer when that part of the earth leans toward the sun. The sun never sets on the North Pole during the summer. During those same months, the South Pole experiences a dark winter because the sun never rises. Even during the long days of polar summer, the temperature remains cool because the sun's rays are indirect.

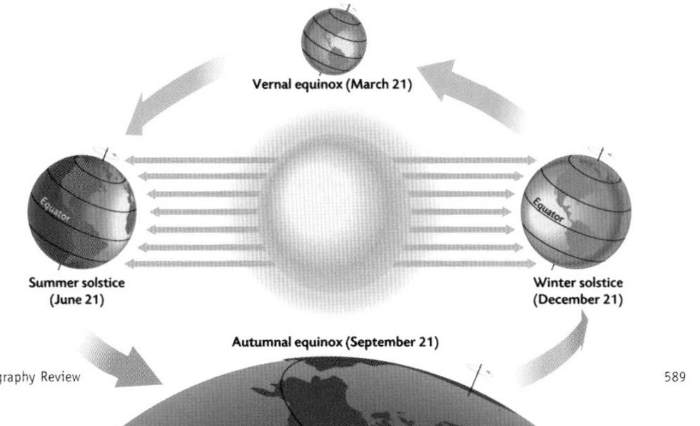

Latitude and Climate

In general, the greatest factor in determining a region's climate is the tilt of the earth, which causes sunlight to fall unevenly across different latitudes. The farther away you move from the Equator, the cooler the climate becomes. But climate regions also are defined by rainfall, not just temperature, so within the same latitude there may be more than one type of climate.

The Tropical Latitudes The north and south parallels of latitude at 23.5° mark the boundaries of the tropical latitudes, also called the Tropics. The northern boundary, 23.5°N, is called the Tropic of Cancer. The southern boundary, 23.5°S, is called the Tropic of Capricorn (see the World-Physical map in the atlas to locate the Tropics).

In the Tropics, temperatures stay hot all year. The area closest to the Equator is hot and mostly wet. Many of the world's rain forests are within 500 miles (805 km) of the Equator. This area has the **tropical rain forest** climate (see climate maps in the atlas to locate climate types). Plants here stay green and leafy. Another climate of the tropics alternates between rainy and dry seasons. This is called the **tropical savanna climate**.

The Temperate Latitudes The middle latitudes—from 23.5° to 66.5° in both the Northern and Southern Hemispheres—are called temperate. Places with temperate climates are cooler than the Tropics. Temperatures and rainfall vary greatly within these latitudes, so there are several types of temperate climates.

The temperate **Mediterranean** climate is characterized by hot and dry summers and mild and rainy winters. It is called Mediterranean because the regions surrounding the Mediterranean Sea in southern Europe and northern Africa have this type of climate. Another climate with mild and rainy winters is the **Marine West Coast** climate. In this climate summers are cool and rainy.

The **humid subtropical** climate has mild rainy winters and hot summers. But it has humid springs and summers. North Carolina enjoys this climate. The two **humid continental** climates both have cold and snowy winters. The continental climate to the north has a short, cool summer. The one to the south has a long, hot summer. Much of central and eastern North America have continental climates.

Within the temperate latitudes, near the border with the tropical latitudes are regions with dry climates. There are two kinds of dry climates: **desert** and **steppe**. Deserts are found in Africa at the edge of the Tropics near the 23.5° latitudes. Desert climates receive less than 10 inches of rain per year. Steppe climates, sometimes called semiarid regions, are not as dry as deserts. They are found in western United States and southern Russia. They receive between 10 and 20 inches (25.4 and 50.8 cm) of rainfall per year.

The Poles At the North and South Poles, from the latitudes 66.5° to the poles, water remains frozen because temperatures remain low. Weak sunlight produces a climate at the poles called **tundra**. This describes far northern Europe, Russia, Canada, and Alaska. Another cold climate is subarctic, covering much of Canada, Russia, and Alaska. Subarctic climates are warm enough for trees to grow.

Climate and Elevation

The final type of climate is characterized by elevation. All climates are changed by elevation, no matter the latitude. If you have stood at the top of a tall building, you know that temperature drops with higher elevation—a place's height above sea level. Going up 3,000 feet (900 m) takes you into a cooler climate.

The **highlands** climate varies with elevation. The Andes, the Alps, the Himalayas, and the Rocky Mountains have Highlands climate. Although parts of the Andes are near the Equator, its peaks are capped with snow year-round because the temperature at the summits rarely goes above freezing.

Rainfall in highlands areas can vary greatly. Mountain peaks can block rain from reaching the side of the mountain away from the wind. One side of a highland area may be very wet and the other side very dry. This is called the **rain shadow effect**. This effect happens in North Africa. The wind from the Atlantic Ocean carries lots of moisture. This moisture is dropped on the Atlas Mountains and never reaches the interior of the continent. The southwestern side of the mountains is very dry. The rain shadow effect has been one of the factors contributing to development of the Sahara desert.

Climate and Nearness to Water Like elevation, nearness to the sea can also modify a place's climate. Generally, places that are closer to oceans have milder winters, cooler summers, and more **precipitation**—rain, snow, hail, and sleet—than areas farther away from oceans. Oceans release stored heat in winter and cool the air during the summer. They also release much moisture into the air, which returns to the earth as rain. A good example of this is the **North Atlantic Drift**, or **Gulf Stream**, the ocean current that carries warm water

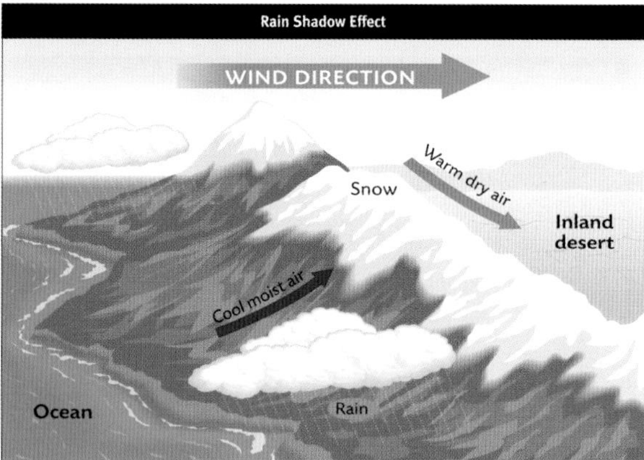

from the Gulf of Mexico to the western coast of Europe. With no high mountains to block them, the westerly winds bring warm weather and moisture to most of Europe.

The rain shadow effect causes an exception to this. In places where the wind is blowing out to sea over mountains, the land is very dry, such as on the Pacific Coast of South America.

Vegetation

Just as there are climate regions, there are regions of vegetation. Climate determines the plants that grow in a place. Vegetation maps follow climate maps. There are four broad types of vegetation—**forest, grasslands, desert**, and **tundra**. Forest and grasslands are found in highland, temperate, and tropical climates. Desert vegetation is found in dry climates. Tundra is mainly found in climate zones with the same name.

Forest Because forests are found in almost every climate except tundra, the types of forests change according to the climate. **Tropical rain forests** are found in the Tropics, especially near the Equator. **Deciduous forests** in temperate climates shed their leaves once a year during autumn. **Evergreen forests** keep their green leaves all year long. These forests appear throughout the temperate latitudes and provide much of the world's supply of lumber and paper. Evergreen forests include conifers, cone-bearing trees. Evergreen forests also thrive in humid temperate and dry temperate climates.

Grasslands Grasslands also change according to the climate. **Humid temperate grasslands** grow on plains in fertile areas well suited for raising grain. In the Americas these grasslands can be found in the wheat-growing areas of the United States. **Dry temperate grasslands** are important grazing regions. The pampas of South America are the best example of this vegetation. **Tropical grasslands** grow in humid areas such as the Deccan Plateau in India.

Desert and Tundra Desert vegetation of cactus plants and scrub brush grows in the dry regions of the Americas and in Southern Africa.

Plants of the polar regions grow on the treeless plain called **tundra**. Just as desert plants have long roots and thin leaves to adapt to a hot and dry environment, plants growing on the tundra adapt to the cold to survive. The far northern areas of Norden in Europe and the far northern areas of Russia, including parts of Siberia, have tundra vegetation.

There are many types of governments in the regions of the world we study. Many governments use similar terms to describe different functions and organizational structures. This guide reviews the basic structures of constitutional governments, including constitutional monarchies and republics. It also reviews non-constitutional governments, including autocratic and totalitarian regimes.

A constitution is a set of fundamental customs, traditions, rules, and laws that set forth the basic way a government is organized and operated. A nation may have a constitution, but that does not mean it has a constitutional government.

Constitutional Governments

A constitutional government is a government whose actions are limited by law and institutions. If a constitution permits unlimited political power held by one person, a few people, or only one political party, then it is not the basis of a constitutional government. If a constitution does not include ways to enforce limits on the power of government, it is also not the basis for a constitutional government. The separation of powers and the checks and balances system set forth in the United States Constitution are examples of limits of the actions of government. Each branch of the United States government—executive, legislative, and judicial—has the responsibility and the power to "check," or limit, actions taken by the other branches.

In a constitutional government, the constitution is considered a higher law. The constitution, or higher law, provides for the protection of the rights of the individual against unfair and unreasonable infringement by the government and other individuals. This typically includes establishment of a private domain into which the government may not intrude. The individual also typically has "due process of law"—the right to follow the formal procedures written into the law which protect the rights of both innocent and guilty from the arbitrary power of the state. In the United States, these rights are set forth in the Bill of Rights and the due process clause of the Fourteenth Amendment.

President George W. Bush addresses Congress. The United States is a republic with a presidential system of government. The president is not a member of Congress, but is elected by the people through the Electoral College.

Power is also limited by informal means. These include such group pressure as lobbying and demonstrations, and publicity given to government actions by the media. Another effective restraint is the awareness of citizens and public officials of the traditional limits of power on the government. When a person knows that they have certain rights they are more likely to both exercise them and protect them.

Nearly all constitutional governments are representative democracies. Most are either constitutional monarchies or republics.

Constitutional Monarchies and Republics

Some governments have a monarch as head of state and are called constitutional monarchies. Great Britain, the Netherlands, and Sweden are examples of this form of government. Australia, Botswana, and Canada, as members of the British Commonwealth, accept the British monarch as their own and are considered constitutional monarchies as well.

Constitutional states that have no monarch are called republics. Examples include Germany, the United States, Israel, and Venezuela.

In both constitutional monarchies and republics, the practice and process of governing is by representative democracy. The type of representative democracy is either a parliamentary system or a presidential system.

In a parliamentary system, the chief executive is chosen from among members of the legislative body and is directly responsible to them. Often, this chief executive is called the prime minister. Great Britain, India, and Japan are examples of parliamentary systems.

In presidential systems, the chief executive is not a member of the legislative body and is independently chosen. The president is not directly responsible to the legislature, and is removable by the legislative body only in extraordinary circumstances. A good example of the presidential system is the United States. France has a modified presidential system, combining a strong presidency with elements of a parliamentary system.

Constitutional governments may operate under either a unitary or federal system. In a unitary system, power is concentrated in a central government. France and Japan are examples of unitary systems. In a federal system, power is divided between a central government and territorial subdivisions. Australia, Canada, and the United States are examples of federal systems. In the United States, the Tenth Amendment reserves the rights not granted to the national government to the states and to the people, thus creating the federal system.

Non-Constitutional Governments

In non-constitutional governments there are no effective means available to the general public for limiting the powers of the rulers. In general, rulers are not effectively restrained by law in the exercise of their powers. Often, the government's rulings, actions, and decisions are made arbitrarily. In the Soviet Union under Joseph Stalin, for example, the fate of whole ethnic groups was decided by the dictator.

Under a non-constitutional government, any rights of the individual may be violated by the ruler or rulers. Typically there is no private domain where the individual is protected from the power of the state. Whatever rights the individual may be considered to possess, rather than being protected by stringent standards of due process of law, are subject to arbitrary deprivation. In Uganda, under Idi Amin, the people were terrorized by the Bureau of State Research, which arrested and tortured people at will.

Autocracies and totalitarian states are forms of non-constitutional governments.

Autocracies, or autocratic regimes, may take various forms. These are characterized by the unlimited power exercised by one person or a small group of people. Some autocracies are military, others are civilian. Many present-day autocracies call themselves republics, but many do not have the characteristics of a true republic. Examples of historic autocratic regimes are Haiti under the Duvaliers, the Philippines under Ferdinand Marcos, and Spain under Franco. Contemporary examples are Cuba under Fidel Castro and Libya under Muammar Qaddafi.

Dictatorships that attempt to exercise absolute control over all spheres of human life are called totalitarian dictatorships. The classical examples of totalitarian dictatorships are the Soviet Union under Josef Stalin, Germany under Adolf Hitler, and China under Mao Zedong. Contemporary examples are North Korea under Kim Il Sung and after his death under Kim Jong Il. Iraq under Saddam Hussein is another example.

Non-constitutional governments may also have constitutions that set forth the basic way they are—or are said to be—organized and operated. They also may be organized as parliamentary or presidential governments and may call themselves federal rather than unitary systems. These names, however, are used only to obscure the true nature of the autocratic or totalitarian state. One must study the actual functioning of a government on a daily basis to determine its true nature.

DICTIONARY OF GEOGRAPHIC TERMS

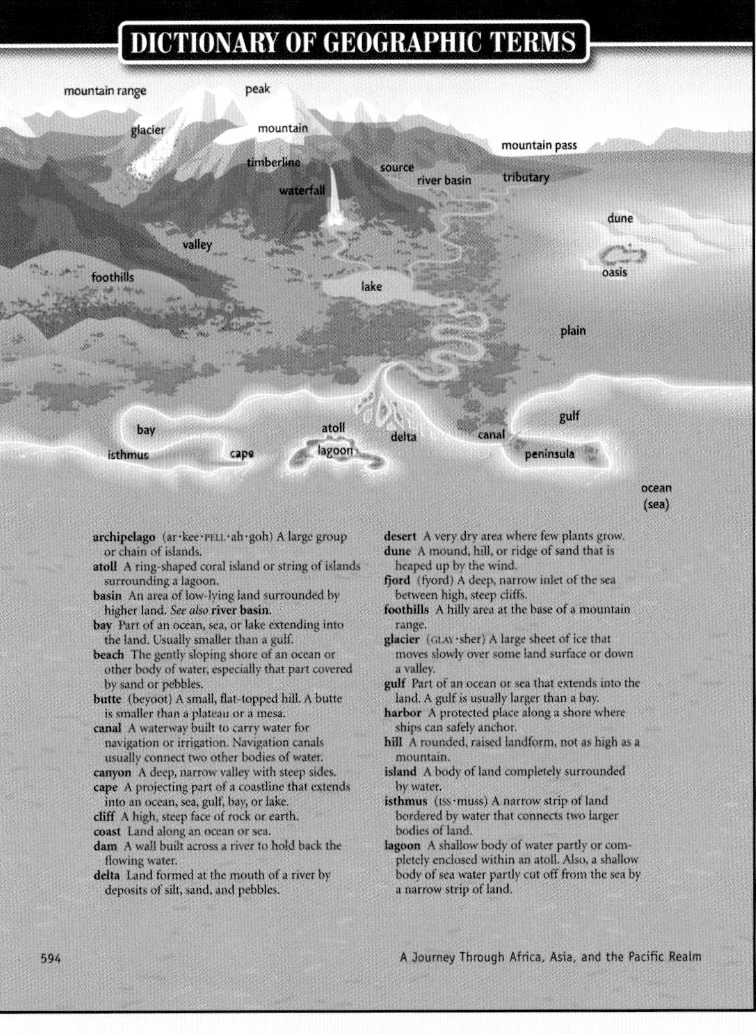

archipelago (ar·kee·PELL·ah·goh) A large group or chain of islands.
atoll A ring-shaped coral island or string of islands surrounding a lagoon.
basin An area of low-lying land surrounded by higher land. *See also* **river basin.**
bay Part of an ocean, sea, or lake extending into the land. Usually smaller than a gulf.
beach The gently sloping shore of an ocean or other body of water, especially that part covered by sand or pebbles.
butte (beyoot) A small, flat-topped hill. A butte is smaller than a plateau or a mesa.
canal A waterway built to carry water for navigation or irrigation. Navigation canals usually connect two other bodies of water.
canyon A deep, narrow valley with steep sides.
cape A projecting part of a coastline that extends into an ocean, sea, gulf, bay, or lake.
cliff A high, steep face of rock or earth.
coast Land along an ocean or sea.
dam A wall built across a river to hold back the flowing water.
delta Land formed at the mouth of a river by deposits of silt, sand, and pebbles.
desert A very dry area where few plants grow.
dune A mound, hill, or ridge of sand that is heaped up by the wind.
fjord (fyord) A deep, narrow inlet of the sea between high, steep cliffs.
foothills A hilly area at the base of a mountain range.
glacier (GLAY·sher) A large sheet of ice that moves slowly over some land surface or down a valley.
gulf Part of an ocean or sea that extends into the land. A gulf is usually larger than a bay.
harbor A protected place along a shore where ships can safely anchor.
hill A rounded, raised landform, not as high as a mountain.
island A body of land completely surrounded by water.
isthmus (ISS·muss) A narrow strip of land bordered by water that connects two larger bodies of land.
lagoon A shallow body of water partly or completely enclosed within an atoll. Also, a shallow body of sea water partly cut off from the sea by a narrow strip of land.

DICTIONARY OF GEOGRAPHIC TERMS

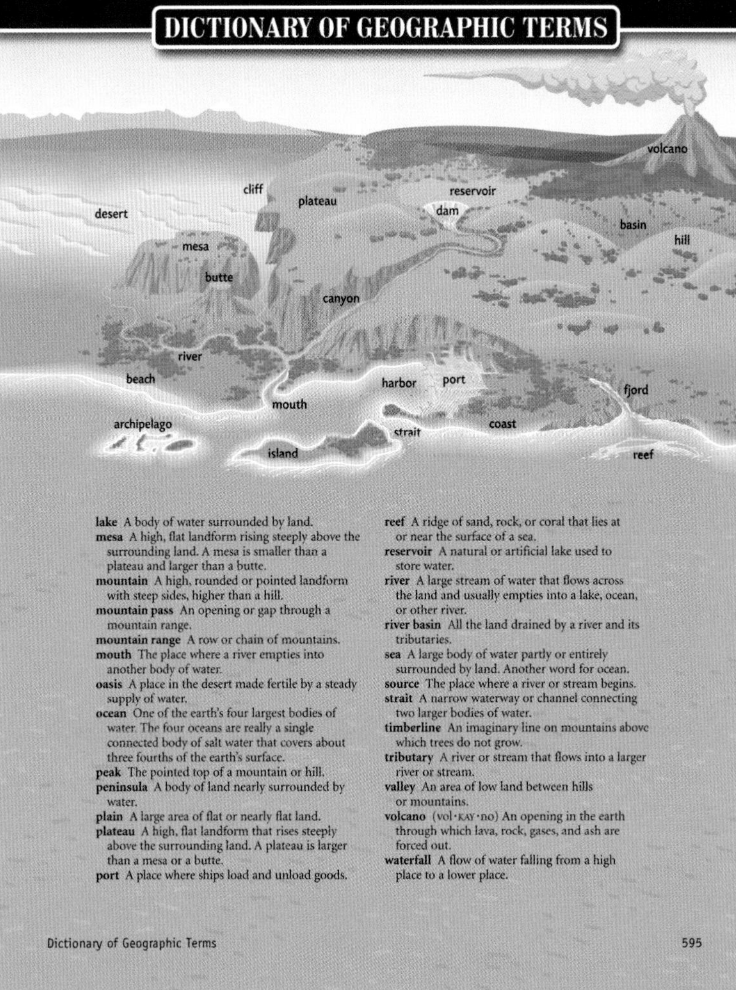

lake A body of water surrounded by land.
mesa A high, flat landform rising steeply above the surrounding land. A mesa is smaller than a plateau and larger than a butte.
mountain A high, rounded or pointed landform with steep sides, higher than a hill.
mountain pass An opening or gap through a mountain range.
mountain range A row or chain of mountains.
mouth The place where a river empties into another body of water.
oasis A place in the desert made fertile by a steady supply of water.
ocean One of the earth's four largest bodies of water. The four oceans are really a single connected body of salt water that covers about three fourths of the earth's surface.
peak The pointed top of a mountain or hill.
peninsula A body of land nearly surrounded by water.
plain A large area of flat or nearly flat land.
plateau A high, flat landform that rises steeply above the surrounding land. A plateau is larger than a mesa or a butte.
port A place where ships load and unload goods.
reef A ridge of sand, rock, or coral that lies at or near the surface of a sea.
reservoir A natural or artificial lake used to store water.
river A large stream of water that flows across the land and usually empties into a lake, ocean, or other river.
river basin All the land drained by a river and its tributaries.
sea A large body of water partly or entirely surrounded by land. Another word for ocean.
source The place where a river or stream begins.
strait A narrow waterway or channel connecting two larger bodies of water.
timberline An imaginary line on mountains above which trees do not grow.
tributary A river or stream that flows into a larger river or stream.
valley An area of low land between hills or mountains.
volcano (vol·KAY·no) An opening in the earth through which lava, rock, gases, and ash are forced out.
waterfall A flow of water falling from a high place to a lower place.

GAZETTEER

A

Abidjan The capital of the Ivory Coast.
Abu Dhabi The capital of United Arab Emirates.
Abuja The capital of Nigeria.
Accra The capital of Ghana.
Addis Ababa The capital of Ethiopia.
Afghanistan A small landlocked nation in the Hindu Kush Range on the northwestern edge of South Asia.
Africa The world's second largest continent. Africa lies south of Europe between the Atlantic and Indian Oceans.
Agra A city in central India and the site of the Taj Mahal.
Alexandria A city in Egypt founded by Alexander the Great.
Algeria North African country south of the Mediterranean Sea, west of Tunisia and Libya, north of Niger and Mali, and east of Mauritania, and Morocco.
Algiers The capital of Algeria.
American Samoa Island of Polynesia in Oceania. A territory of the United States.
Amman The capital of Jordan.
Amritsar City in northern India. The site of the Golden Temple, worship center of the Sikhs.
Anatolia A peninsula in western Asia.
Anatolian Plateau Temperate grassland in Turkey surrounded by mountains.
Angola Southern African country on the Atlantic Ocean north of Namibia, east of Zambia, and south of Democratic Republic of the Congo.
Ankara The capital of Turkey.
Antananarivo The capital of Madagascar.
Arabian Peninsula The great peninsula and subregion of Southwest Asia, south of Jordan and Iraq, north-west of the Arabian Sea, west of the Gulf of Aden, and east of the Red Sea.
Arabian Sea The northwestern part of the Indian Ocean, between the Arabian Peninsula and India.
Asia The largest continent, east of Europe and Africa, north of the Indian Ocean, and west of the Pacific Ocean.
Asian Pacific Rim The region of countries bordering on or located in the Pacific Ocean.
Asmara The capital of Eritrea.
Atlantic Ocean The body of water separating Europe and Africa from North and South America.
Atlas Mountains North African range that stretches from southwestern Morocco to northeastern Tunisia.
Australia The earth's smallest continent, bounded by the Indian and Pacific Oceans. It is also a country.

B

Baghdad The capital of Iraq.
Bahrain Southwest Asian island-country in the Persian Gulf northeast of Saudi Arabia.
Bali An island in the Malay archipelago in Southeast Asia and a center of Hinduism.
Baluchistan Plateau Arid region of South Asia bordering on Arabian Sea in southwest Pakistan and southeast Iran.
Bamako The capital of Mali.
Bandar Seri Begawan The capital of Brunei.
Bangalore See bengaluru.
Bangkok The capital of Thailand.
Bangladesh South Asian country east of India on the Bay of Bengal.
Bangui The capital of Central African Republic.
Banjul The capital of Gambia.
Bay of Bengal The northern part of the Indian Ocean, between Myanmar and the Indian subcontinent.
Beijing The capital of the People's Republic of China.
Beirut The capital of Lebanon.
Bengaluru Third-largest city in India, capital of the state of Karnataka, formerly called Bangalore.
Benin West African country on the Gulf of Guinea south of Niger, west of Nigeria, and east of Togo.
Bhutan South Asian country in the Himalayas on the northeast border of India.
Bissau The capital of Guinea-Bissau.
Black Sea An inland sea between Europe and Asia.
Bombay *See* Mumbai.
Bosporus Strait Narrow body of water connecting the Black and Marmara Seas.
Botswana Southern African country east of Namibia, north of South Africa, and southwest of Zimbabwe.
Brahmaputra River South Asian river flowing from the Himalayas in Tibet to the Ganges River delta in eastern India.
Brazzaville The port capital of Congo.
Brunei Southeast Asian country located in the northwestern part of the island of Borneo.
Bujumbura The capital of Burundi.
Burkina Faso West African country south of Mali and north of Ivory Coast, Ghana, Togo, and Benin.
Burundi East African country northeast of Lake Tanganyika, south of Rwanda, east of Democratic Republic of the Congo, and north and west of Tanzania.

C

Cairo The capital of Egypt and the largest city in Africa.
Calcutta See Kolkata.
Cambodia Southeast Asian country on the Gulf of Thailand lying south of Thailand and Laos, and west of Vietnam.
Cameroon Central African country on the Atlantic Ocean southeast of Nigeria, southwest of Chad, west of the Central African Republic, and north of Gabon, Congo, and Equatorial Guinea.
Canberra The capital of Australia.
Cape of Good Hope The southernmost point of Africa.
Cape Town The capital of South Africa.

GAZETTEER

Casablanca The seaport city of Morocco.
Caspian Sea The world's largest totally inland body of water, located in south-central Asia.
Caucasus Mountains A mountain range that forms part of the southern boundary between Asia and Europe.
Central Africa The region of Africa that includes the countries of Cameroon, Central African Republic, Chad, Congo, Equatorial Guinea, Gabon, São Tomé and Príncipe, and Democratic Republic of the Congo.
Central African Republic Central African country south of Chad, west of Sudan, north of the Democratic Republic of the Congo and Congo, and east of Cameroon.
Chad Central African country south of Libya, west of Sudan, north of Central African Republic, northeast of Cameroon, and east of Nigeria and Niger.
Cherrapunji City in northeast India that is one of the wettest places on earth. The average annual rainfall is about 450 inches (11.4 m).
Colombo Capital of Sri Lanka.
Comoros East African volcanic islands in Mozambique Channel between northeastern Mozambique and northwestern Madagascar.
Conakry The capital of Guinea.
Congo Central African country on the Atlantic Ocean west of Democratic Republic of the Congo, south of Central African Republic and Cameroon, and east of Gabon.
Congo River The second-longest river in Africa, flowing through the central part of the continent, and emptying into the Atlantic Ocean.
Cook Islands Island group of Polynesia in Oceania. A self-governing territory of New Zealand.
Cyprus Southwest Asian island-country in the eastern Mediterranean Sea, south of Turkey and west of Syria.

D

Dakar The capital of Senegal.
Damascus The capital of Syria.
Dar es Salaam The capital of Tanzania.
Dardanelles Strait The narrow body of water through Turkey separating Europe and Asia.
Darfur Region in western Sudan.
Darling River Joins with the Murray River to become Australia's most important river system.
Dead Sea A body of water between Israel and Jordan, and the lowest point on earth.
Deccan Plateau A high, rugged plateau in the center of the Indian subcontinent.
Democratic Republic of the Congo Central African country lying south of Central African Republic and Sudan, east of Congo, north of Zambia and Angola, and west of Uganda, Rwanda, Burundi, and Tanzania. A small westerly portion lies on the Atlantic Ocean. Formerly known as Zaire.
Dhaka The capital of Bangladesh.
Dili The capital of East Timor.
Djibouti East African country on the Gulf of Aden at entrance to Red Sea, southeast of Eritrea and northeast of Ethiopia. Its capital is also Djibouti.
Doha The capital of Qatar.
Drakensberg Mountains Range extending southwest to northeast in South Africa and Lesotho.
Dubai One of the seven emirates that make up the United Arab Emirates, located on the Persian Gulf on the Arbaian Peninsula in Southwest Asia.

E

East Africa The region of Africa that includes the countries of Burundi, Comoros, Djibouti, Eritrea, Ethiopia, Kenya, Madagascar, Mauritius, Rwanda, Seychelles, Somalia, Sudan, Tanzania, and Uganda.
East Asia The region of Asia that includes Japan, Mongolia, North Korea, People's Republic of China, Republic of China (Taiwan), and South Korea.
East Timor A country on the eastern part of Timor, an island in the Pacific Ocean in Southeast Asia.
Eastern Ghats A mountain range along the eastern edge of the Deccan Plateau in India.
Egypt North African country on the Mediterranean Sea east of Israel and the Red Sea, north of Sudan, and east of Libya.
Elburz Mountains A range in northern Iran, extending west to east parallel with the southern shore of the Caspian Sea.
Equatorial Guinea Central African country on the Gulf of Guinea south of Cameroon and west and north of Gabon.
Eretz Israel Meaning "Land of Israel," the official name for the original territory assigned to Israel under the Bristish Mandate for Palestine.
Eritrea Country in East Africa on the Red Sea, south and east of Sudan, and north of Ethiopia and Djibouti.
Ethiopia East African country south of Eritrea, west of Somalia, north of Kenya, and east of Sudan.
Euphrates River A river in southwestern Asia.
Eurasia A large landmass that includes the continents of Asia and Europe.

F

Federated States of Micronesia Formerly a United Nations trust territory administered by the United States, now independent. Island group of Micronesia located in Oceania. Includes the Caroline Islands.
Fertile Crescent A fertile region in the Middle East that stretches from the eastern Mediterranean Sea through the valleys of the Tigris and Euphrates Rivers to the northern end of the Persian Gulf.
Fiji Island of Melanesia in Oceania.

Freetown The capital of Sierra Leone.

French Polynesia Island group of Polynesia in Oceania. A territory of France.

G

Gabon Central African country on the Atlantic Ocean north and west of Congo, south of Cameroon, and south and east of Equatorial Guinea.

Gaborone The capital of Botswana.

Gambia A country in West Africa that consists of a narrow strip of land extending 200 miles (322 km) along the Gambia River. Bordered on three sides by Senegal and on the west by the Atlantic Ocean.

Gambia River West African river that rises in Guinea, flows through Senegal, and empties into the Atlantic Ocean at Banjul, Gambia.

Ganges River A river in northern India and Bangladesh that flows from the Himalayas to the Bay of Bengal.

Gaza Strip An area on the southeastern coast of the Mediterranean Sea in the Middle East and Southwest Asia, occupied by Israel since 1967. Governed by the Palestinian National Authority under the auspicces of the Oslo Accords.

Ghana West African country on the Gulf of Guinea lying south of Burkina Faso, west of Togo, and east of Ivory Coast. Site of ancient Ghana civilization.

Gobi A large desert in east-central Asia.

Golan Heights A border region between Israel and Syria that has been occupied by Israel since 1967.

Great Barrier Reef The largest coral reef in the world, along Australia's northeastern coast.

Great Dividing Range A range of low mountains extending down the eastern edge of Australia.

Great Rift Valley A series of valleys in Africa extending 6,000 miles (9,660 km) from the Mozambique Channel north to the Red Sea.

Great Sandy Desert One of the three main deserts of Australia, lying in the northern part of the country.

Great Victoria Desert One of Australia's three main deserts, lying in the southern part of the country.

Guam Island of Micronesia in Oceania. A territory of the United States.

Guangzhou A port city in southeastern China, also called Canton.

Guinea West African country on the Atlantic Ocean lying south of Mali and Senegal, north of Sierra Leone and Liberia, and west of Ivory Coast.

Guinea-Bissau West African country on the Atlantic Ocean lying south of Senegal and west of Guinea.

H

Hanoi The capital of Vietnam.

Harare The capital of Zimbabwe.

Himalayas The world's highest mountain range, part of the northern boundary of the Indian subcontinent.

Hindu Kush A mountain range in South Asia, forming the northwestern boundary of the Indian subcontinent.

Hiroshima A port city in southern Japan, on the island of Honshu.

Hokkaido Northernmost of the four main islands of Japan.

Hong Kong Until 1997, when it was returned to the People's Republic of China, Hong Kong was a British crown colony. Located on the southeast coast of China east of the mouth of the Zhu River.

Honshu The largest island of the Japanese archipelago.

Horn of Africa The easternmost projection of Africa, so called because of its resemblance to a rhinoceros horn.

Huang He (Yellow) River A major river in North China.

I

India Largest country of the South Asian subcontinent, south of Pakistan, China, Nepal, and Bhutan.

Indian Ocean The body of water south of Asia, located between Africa and Australia.

Indian subcontinent The large landmass that makes up South Asia.

Indonesia The largest nation in Southeast Asia, comprising Sumatra, Java, South and East Borneo, Sulawesi, west Timor, west New Guinea, the Moluccas, and many adjacent smaller islands.

Indus River A river that flows from Tibet, through the Hindu Kush, and into the Arabian Sea.

Indus-Ganges Plain A vast fertile plain lying south of the Himalayas on the Indian subcontinent.

Iran Southwest Asian country lying south of the Caspian Sea and Turkmenistan, west of Afghanistan and Pakistan, east of Iraq and Turkey, and north of the Gulf of Oman and the Persian Gulf.

Iranian Plateau Extensive highland area comprising central-eastern Iran and western sections of Afghanistan and Pakistan.

Iraq Southwest Asian country south of Turkey, west of Iran, northwest of Kuwait and the Persian Gulf, north of Saudi Arabia, and east of Jordan and Syria.

Irrawaddy River An important river in Southeast Asia.

Islamabad The capital of Pakistan.

Israel Southwest Asian country on the Mediterranean Sea lying south of Lebanon, west of Syria and Jordan, and northeast of Egypt.

Ivory Coast West African country on the Gulf of Guinea west of Ghana, east of Guinea and Liberia, and south of Mali and Burkina Faso.

J

Jakarta The capital of Indonesia.

Japan East Asian country consisting of an archipelago in the western Pacific Ocean. There are four main islands: Honshu, Shikoku, Kyushu, and Hokkaido.

Jeddah Second-largest city in Saudi Arabia.

Jerusalem Claimed by Israel to be its capital, yet not recongnized by the majority of the international community, including the United Nations. West Jersusalem is the seat of Israel's government; East Jerusalem is claimed by Palestinians as the desired capital for a future Palestinian state and the location of the Palestinian National Authority's goverment. According to the Oslo Accords, Jerusalem's status is to be determined by negotiation.

Johannesburg South Africa's largest city.

Jordan Southwest Asian country south of Syria, west of Iraq, north of Saudi Arabia, and east of Israel.

Jordan River River in Southwest Asia shared by Israel and Jordan.

K

Kabul The capital of Afghanistan.

Kalahari A desert region in southern Africa.

Kampala The capital of Uganda.

Karachi A seaport in southern Pakistan, located on the arm of the Arabian Sea just northwest of the mouth of the Indus River.

Karakoram Range Central Asian mountain range in northern Pakistan, northern India, and southern China.

Kathmandu The capital of Nepal.

Kenya East African country on the Indian Ocean lying south of Ethiopia, west of Somalia, north of Tanzania, and east of Uganda.

Khartoum The capital of Sudan, located where the White Nile and Blue Nile Rivers join to form the Nile River.

Khyber Pass A mountain pass in the Hindu Kush connecting Afghanistan and Pakistan.

Kigali The capital of Rwanda.

Kinshasa The capital of Democratic Republic of the Congo.

Kiribati Island group of Polynesia in Oceania.

Kolkata A large port city in northeastern India, on the Bay of Bengal, formerly known as Calcutta.

Korean Strait A strait separating Korea from Japan and connecting the East China Sea and South China Sea.

Kuala Lumpur The capital of Malaysia.

Kuwait An oil-rich country of Southwest Asia north of Saudi Arabia and south and east of Iraq. Its capital is also named Kuwait.

Kyushu Most southern of Japan's four main islands.

L

Ladakh Formerly independent monarchy located in northern India in the Himalayas.

Lake Nasser A lake in Egypt that was created when the Aswan High Dam was built on the Nile River.

Lake Nyasa A large lake in southern Africa, also called Lake Malawi.

Lake Tanganyika East-central African lake on the boundary between western Tanzania and eastern Democratic Republic of the Congo.

Lake Victoria The largest lake in Africa, located in the east-central part of the continent.

Laos Southeast Asian country lying south of China, west of Vietnam, and east of Thailand and Myanmar.

Lebanon Southwest Asia country at eastern end of Mediterranean Sea, south and west of Syria, and north of Israel.

Lesotho Southern African country completely surrounded by the country of South Africa.

Liberia West African country on the Atlantic Ocean between the Ivory Coast and Sierra Leone.

Libreville The capital of Gabon.

Libya North African country on the Mediterranean Sea lying west of Egypt, east of Algeria and Tunisia, and north of Chad and Niger.

Lilongwe The capital of Malawi.

Limpopo River A river that extends along the southern border of South Africa.

Lomé The capital of Togo.

Luanda The capital of Angola.

Lusaka The capital of Zambia.

M

Madagascar East African island in the Indian Ocean just east of Comoros.

Maghreb Arabic name for northwestern Africa, specifically Morocco, Algeria, Tunisia, and Libya.

Malabo The capital of Equatorial Guinea.

Malawi Southern African country east of Zambia, north of Mozambique, and south of Tanzania.

Malay Archipelago The largest island group in the world, extending from Southeast Asia into the Pacific Ocean.

Malay Peninsula A long peninsula extending into the Indian Ocean from Southeast Asia.

Malaysia An independent country in Southeast Asia consisting of eleven states of West Malaysia on the Malay Peninsula and two states of East Malaysia on the island of Borneo.

Mali A West African country in the Sahara Desert between Mauritania and Niger. Site of the ancient Mali civilization.

Manamah The capital of Bahrain.

Manila The capital of the Philippines.

Maputo The capital of Mozambique.

Marshall Islands Formerly a United Nations trust territory administered by the United States, now independent. Located in Oceania, part of Micronesia.

Maseru The capital of Lesotho.

Matadi The major port of Democratic Republic of the Congo.

Mauritania West African country on the Atlantic Ocean south of the Sahara Desert and Algeria, west and north of Mali, and northeast of Senegal.

Mauritius East African island-country in the Indian Ocean 450 miles (725 km) east of Madagascar.

Mbabane The capital of Swaziland.

Mecca A city in western Saudi Arabia, near the Red Sea. Mecca was the birthplace of Muhammad and is the holiest city of Islam.

Mediterranean Sea A large, almost landlocked sea between Europe, Asia, and Africa.

Mekong River An important river in Southeast Asia, flowing southwestward from western China into the South China Sea.

Melanesia One of the three main island groups in Oceania. The islands include Papua New Guinea, the Solomon Islands, Vanuatu, New Caledonia, and Fiji.

Melbourne Large port city on Australia's southern coast.

Mesopotamia The "land between two rivers," referring to the region between the Tigris and Euphrates Rivers in the Middle East. Mesopotamia was the birthplace of the Sumerian and Babylonian civilizations.

Micronesia One of the three major island groups in Oceania. The islands include the Northern Mariana Islands, the Republic of Palau, the Republic of the Marshall Islands, the Federated States of Micronesia, Nauru, and Guam.

Middle East The name traditionally given to Southwest Asia. Geographically a subregion of Southwest Asia that includes Israel, Jordan, Lebanon, Syria, and Iraq.

Mogadishu The capital of Somalia.

Mombasa The main port city of Kenya, on the Indian Ocean.

Mongolia East Asian country lying between China and Russia.

Monrovia The capital of Liberia.

Morocco North African country on the Mediterranean Sea and the Atlantic Ocean. Located north of Western Sahara (claimed by Morocco) and west of Algeria.

Moroni The capital of Comoros.

Mount Cook The highest mountain in New Zealand, on the central part of South Island.

Mount Everest The highest mountain in the world, located in the Himalayas on the border between Nepal and China.

Mount Fuji The highest mountain in Japan, located on the island of Honshu.

Mount Kenya The highest mountain in Kenya, located in the central part of the country.

Mount Kilimanjaro The highest mountain in Africa, located in northern Tanzania.

Mount Kosciusko The highest mountain in Australia, in the Great Dividing Range in the southeastern part of the country.

Mozambique Southern African country on the Indian Ocean and Mozambique Channel, north of South Africa and Swaziland, and east of Zimbabwe, Malawi, and Zambia.

Mumbai The largest city and chief port on India's western coast, formerly known as Bombay.

Murray River Joins with the Darling River to become Australia's most important river system.

Muscat The capital of Oman.

Myanmar Formerly Burma, a Southeast Asian country on the Bay of Bengal lying south of India and China, west of Laos and Thailand, and east of Bangladesh.

N

N'Djamena The capital of Chad.

Nagasaki A Japanese city on the island of Kyushu.

Nairobi The capital of Kenya.

Namib A desert that extends along the entire length of the southwestern African coast.

Namibia Southern African country on the Atlantic Ocean south of Angola and Zambia, west of Botswana, and north of South Africa.

Nauru Island of Micronesia in Oceania.

Nepal South Asian country on the northeast border of India in the Himalayas.

New Caledonia Island group of Melanesia in Oceania. A territory of France.

New Delhi The capital of India and one of the most populous cities in the world.

New Guinea An island of the Malay Archipelago in Southeast Asia. Includes the country of Papua New Guinea, which is part of Oceania.

New Zealand Country consisting of several islands in the southwestern Pacific. The major ones are North Island and South Island.

Ngorongoro Crater A conservation area in north-central Tanzania noted for its abundant wildlife.

Niamey The capital of Niger.

Nicosia The capital of Cyprus.

Nieu Island of Polynesia in Oceania. A self-governing territory of New Zealand.

Niger West African country south of Algeria and Libya, west of Chad, north of Nigeria, northwest of Benin and Burkina Faso, and east of Mali.

Niger River A river flowing from western Africa into the Gulf of Guinea.

Nigeria West African country on the Gulf of Guinea lying south of Niger, east of Benin, and west of Cameroon.

Nile Delta A marshy area in northern Egypt where the Nile River fans out before entering the Mediterranean Sea.

Nile River The longest river in Africa and the world's longest river.

North Africa The region of Africa along the Mediterranean coast in northern Africa that includes Algeria, Egypt, Libya, Morocco, and Tunisia.

North China A large, fertile region in northern China containing most of the country's population.

North China Plain A vast, fertile region of flat land that is watered by the Huang River.

North Island One of the two main islands that make up the country of New Zealand.

North Korea East Asian country lying south of China, north of South Korea, west of the Sea of Japan, and east of the Yellow Sea and Korea Bay.

Northern Mariana Islands An island group of Micronesia in Oceania. Formerly a United Nations trust territory administered by the United States, now a commonwealth of the United States.

Northern Tier A subregion of Southwest Asia that contains three non-Arab countries: Turkey, Iran, and Cyprus.

Nouakchott The capital of Mauritania.

O

Oceania Collective name for the islands of the central and southern Pacific Ocean, including Micronesia, Melanesia, and Polynesia.

Ogooue River Provides a vital transportation system for Gabon.

Olduvai Gorge A ravine in northern Tanzania, East Africa, not far from Mount Kilimanjaro. A site of rich fossil beds.

Oman Southwest Asian country at the southeastern edge of the Arabian Peninsula on the Gulf of Oman and the Arabian Sea.

Ottoman Empire Empire centered in today's Turkey from 1516 to 1918. At its height it included Southeastern Europe, the Middle East and North Africa.

Ouagadougou The capital of Burkina Faso. The site of the Pan African Film Festival.

Outback Isolated rural region of Australia.

P

Pacific Ocean The world's largest body of water, bounded by North and South America on the east and Asia and Australia on the west.

Pacific Realm Region of land in the Pacific Ocean, consisting of Australia, New Zealand, and the three island groups of Oceania.

Pakistan South Asian country on the Arabian Sea east and south of Afghanistan, southwest of China, west and southwest of India, and southeast of Iran.

Palestine The geographic region between the Mediterranean Sea and the Jordan River. Between 1920 and 1948, Palestine referred to the British Mandate for Palestine, covering all of what is now Israel, the West Bank, and the Gaza Strip. Other names for all or parts of this region, with different connotations, include: Canaan, Land of Israel/Eretz Israel, Judea, and the Holy Land.

Palestinian National Authority The autonomous government of the Palestinian regions of the West Bank and the Gaza Strip established under the Oslo Accords.

Palau Formerly a United Nations trust territory administered by the United States, now independent. Located in Oceania, westernmost archipelago in the Caroline chain, consists of six island groups totaling more than 300 islands.

Papua New Guinea Country on the island of New Guinea in the region of Oceania, part of Melanesia.

People's Republic of China East Asian country that covers most of the Asian continent. It is bordered by 14 countries. To the east it has a long Pacific coastline. Also referred to as China or Mainland China

Persia Western name for Iran until the 1930s.

Persian Empire A series of empires and spheres of influence centered in Iran (643 b.c. to a.d. 1935). The nations of Tajikistan, Uzbekistan, Turkmenistan, Afghanistan, Azerbaijan, and Kyrgyzstan were part of the empire at various times in their histories.

Persian Gulf A body of water between Iran and the Arabian Peninsula.

Philippines A Southeast Asian archipelago east of the Asian mainland between the South China Sea and the Philippine Sea.

Pitcairn Island of Polynesia in Oceania. A territory of Great Britain.

Phnom Penh The capital of Cambodia.

Polynesia One of the three main island groups in Oceania. The islands include Pitcairn, French Polynesia, Kiribati, Tokelau, Tuvalu, American Samoa, Western Samoa, Tonga, Cook Islands, Niue, and Wallis and Futuna.

Port Louis The capital of Mauritius.

Port Moresby The main seaport and capital of Papua New Guinea.

Porto Novo The capital of Benin.

Pyongyang The capital of North Korea.

Q

Qatar Southwest Asian country occupying a peninsula projecting into the Persian Gulf. Located north of United Arab Emirates and east of Saudi Arabia.

R

Rabat The capital of Morocco.

Rangoon The capital of Myanmar.

Red Sea A narrow sea between the

GAZETTEER

Arabian Peninsula and northeastern Africa.
Republic of China (Taiwan) East Asian country that lies off the coast of southeastern China, separated from the mainland by the Taiwan Strait.
Republic of Palau Island group of Micronesia in Oceania.
Riyadh The capital of Saudi Arabia.
Rub 'al Khali Desert in the southern Arabian Peninsula extending south from Saudi Arabia to Yemen, and from the northeast border of Yemen to Oman.
Rwanda East African country south of Uganda, west of Tanzania, north of Burundi, and east of Democratic Republic of the Congo.

S

Sahara The largest desert in the world, covering much of northern Africa.
Sahel A belt of semiarid grassland in Africa, south of the Sahara and north of the savanna.
Samoa Island of Polynesia in Oceania. Formerly Western Samoa.
San'a The capital of Yemen.
São Tomé The capital of São Tomé and Principe.
São Tomé and Príncipe An island nation of Central Africa located in the Gulf of Guinea.
Saudi Arabia Southwest Asian country on the Arabian Peninsula. Located north of Yemen, east of the Red Sea, southeast of Jordan, and south of Iraq.
Sea of Japan An arm of the Pacific Ocean separating Japan from the Asian mainland.
Senegal West African country on the Atlantic Ocean south of Mauritania, west of Mali, and north of Guinea and Guinea-Bissau.
Senegal River A river in West Africa.
Seoul The capital and largest city of South Korea.
Serengeti Plain A vast plain in East Africa, south of Lake Victoria.
Seychelles East African island-country in the Indian Ocean northeast of Madagascar and southeast of Somalia.
Shanghai The chief port and largest city of China.
Shikoku Smallest of the four main islands of Japan.
Sierra Leone West African country on the Atlantic Ocean bordered by Guinea and Liberia.
Sinai Peninsula A desert area in northeastern Egypt between the Mediterranean Sea and the Red Sea.
Singapore A country in Southeast Asia south of the Malay Peninsula, comprising the capital city of Singapore and several small islands.
Solomon Islands Island group of Melanesia in Oceania.
Somalia East African country on the Indian Ocean lying south of the Gulf of Aden and east of Kenya, Ethiopia, and Djibouti.
South Africa A country located at the southern tip of the African continent, on the Indian and Atlantic Oceans, south of Namibia, Botswana, Zimbabwe, and Mozambique.
South Asia Huge subcontinent that extends into the Indian Ocean. The region includes the countries of Afghanistan, Bangladesh, Bhutan, India, Nepal, Pakistan, and Sri Lanka.
South Island One of the two main islands that make up New Zealand.
South Korea East Asian country on the Sea of Japan lying south of North Korea and east of the Yellow Sea.
Southeast Asia The region of Asia that includes Brunei, Cambodia, Indonesia, Laos, Malaysia, Myanmar, Philippines, Singapore, Thailand, and Vietnam.
Southern Africa The region of Africa that includes Angola, Botswana, Lesotho, Malawi, Mozambique, Namibia, South Africa, Swaziland, Zambia, and Zimbabwe.
Southwest Asia The region of Asia that includes Bahrain, Cyprus, Iran, Iraq, Israel, Jordan, Kuwait, Lebanon, Oman, Qatar, Saudi Arabia, Syria, Turkey, United Arab Emirates, and Yemen.
Sri Lanka A small island-country southeast of India. Famous for its tea production.
Strait of Malacca A waterway between the Malay Peninsula and the island of Sumatra in Southeast Asia.
Sudan East African country south of Egypt, southwest of the Red Sea, west of Ethiopia, east of Chad and the Central African Republic, and north of Kenya, Uganda, and Democratic Republic of the Congo.
Suez Canal Canal across Isthmus of Suez in northeast Africa connecting the Red Sea with the Mediterranean.
Sumatra The westernmost island of Malaysia.
Swaziland Southern African country south of Mozambique and otherwise surrounded by South Africa.
Sydney Largest city of Australia, on the east coast.
Syria Southwest Asian country at the eastern end of the Mediterranean Sea, south of Turkey, west of Iraq, north of Jordan, and northeast of Israel and Lebanon.
Syrian Desert Large desert of northern Saudi Arabia, southeastern Syria, western Iraq, and northeastern Jordan.

T

Tahiti Island of French Polynesia in Oceania.
Taipei The capital of the Republic of China (Taiwan).
Tanzania East African country on the Indian Ocean south of Uganda and Kenya, north of Zambia, Mozambique and Malawi, and east of Rwanda, Burundi, and Democratic Republic of the Congo.
Tasmania An island south of Australia.
Taurus Mountains Mountain chain in southern Turkey that runs parallel to the Mediterranean coast.
Tehran The capital of Iran.

GAZETTEER

Thailand Southeast Asian country on the Gulf of Thailand lying west of Cambodia and Laos and south and east of Myanmar.
Thar Desert Desert in India and Pakistan between the Aravalli Range and the Indus River.
Three Gorges Dam Dam located on the Yangzi Tiver in China.
Thimphu The capital of Bhutan.
Tigris River A river in southwestern Asia.
Timbuktu A city in the West African country of Mali. Timbuktu was a major trade and Islamic cultural center from the eleventh through the fifteenth centuries.
Togo West African country on the Gulf of Guinea lying south of Burkina Faso, east of Ghana, and west of Benin.
Tokelau Island of Polynesia in Oceania. A territory of New Zealand.
Tokyo The capital of Japan, on the island of Honshu.
Tonga Island of Polynesia in Oceania.
Tripoli The capital of Libya.
Tropic of Cancer An imaginary line at latitude 23.5°N.
Tropic of Capricorn An imaginary line at latitude 23.5°S.
Tunis The capital of Tunisia.
Tunisia North African country on the Mediterranean Sea lying east of Algeria and northwest of Libya.
Turkey Southwest Asian (and southeastern European) country south of the Black Sea, north of the Mediterranean Sea, Syria, and Iraq, southwest of former republics of the Soviet Union, and west of Iran.
Tuvalu Island group of Polynesia in Oceania.

U

Ubangi River Central African river that forms section of boundary between Democratic Republic of the Congo and Central African Republic.
Uganda East African country lying south of Sudan, east of Kenya, north of Lake Victoria, Tanzania and Rwanda, and east of Democratic Republic of the Congo.
Ulan Bator The capital of Mongolia.
United Arab Emirates A group of small countries in Southwest Asia on the Arabian Peninsula, extending from Qatar to Oman south of the Persian Gulf.
United Kingdom The United Kingdom of Great Britain and Northern Ireland is a nation that lies to the northwest of the continent of Europe and east of Ireland. It is a union made up of four states: England, Scotland, Wales, and Northern Ireland.
United States of America Country in North America that extends from the Atlantic Ocean to the Pacific Ocean. It is bordered by Canada to the north and Mexico to the south.

V

Valley of the Kings An ancient burial place in Egypt near the Nile River.
Vanuatu Island of Melanesia in Oceania. Formerly New Hebrides.
Varanasi One of India's most ancient cities, on the Ganges River 400 miles (644 km) west-northwest of Calcutta. Holy City of the Hindus and the object of constant pilgrimages.
Victoria The capital of the Seychelles.
Vientiane The capital of Laos.
Vietnam Southeast Asian country west of the Gulf of Tonkin and the South China Sea, south of China, and east of Laos, Cambodia, and the Gulf of Thailand.

W

Wallis and Futuna Island group of Polynesia in Oceania. A territory of France.
Wellington The capital of New Zealand.
West Africa The region of Africa that includes the countries of Benin, Burkina Faso, Gambia, Ghana, Guinea, Guinea-Bissau, Ivory Coast, Liberia, Mali, Mauritania, Niger, Nigeria, Senegal, Sierra Leone, and Togo.
West Bank An area west of the Jordan River in the Middle East that has been occupied by Israel since 1967. Governed by the Palestinian National Authority under the auspices of the Oslo Accords.
Western Ghats A mountain range along the western edge of the Deccan Plateau in India.
Western Sahara An area of North Africa on the Atlantic Ocean claimed by Morocco, lying south of Morocco, southwest of Algeria, and west and north of Mauritania.
Western Samoa *See* Samoa.
Windhoek The capital of Namibia.

Y

Yamoussoukro The capital of Ivory Coast.
Yangzi River A major river in southern China.
Yaoundé The capital of Cameroon.
Yellow Sea An arm of the Pacific Ocean, between China and Korea.
Yemen Southwest Asian country on the Arabian Peninsula lying south of Saudi Arabia, southwest of Oman, and east of the Red Sea.

Z

Zagros Mountains Mountain system extending along and across the Iran-Iraq border.
Zaire *See* Democratic Republic of the Congo.
Zambezi River Southern Africa's longest river, flowing eastward through Zimbabwe and Mozambique, into the Indian Ocean.
Zambia Southern African country lying south of Democratic Republic of the Congo and Tanzania, west of Malawi and Mozambique, north of Zimbabwe and Namibia, and east of Angola.
Zimbabwe Southern African country north of South Africa, east of Botswana, south of Zambia, and west of Mozambique.

GLOSSARY

This glossary will help you understand the Key Terms in this book and other important social studies terms.

A

Aborigines The first inhabitants of Australia, who arrived there more than 50,000 years ago. There were hundreds of groups of Aborigines who spoke some 45 different languages by the time the Europeans settled in Australia. Because of the harsh treatment they received from later settlers, many Aborigines moved into the Outback. Today, they make up 1 percent of the population.
absolute location The unique spot on earth where a particular place is located, using coordinates of longitude and latitude.
Afrikaners South Africans of Dutch descent whose native language is Africaans.
age grade African system of training young people to become village leaders. Boys and girls are grouped according to age. They share experiences and responsibilities as they grow up together.
agriculture The science, art, or practice of cultivating the soil, producing crops, and raising livestock, and in varying degrees the preparation and marketing of the resulting products.
Ainu Descendants of the first settlers in the Japanese islands. About 20,000 live in northern Hokkaido.
air pollution The contamination of the air, especially caused by man-made waste.
altitude Vertical distance or extent.
ancestor veneration Belief that the spirits of a family's ancestors could help the family. Practiced in China. Includes home altars and offerings of food as signs of respect.
ancestors Those from whom a person is descended and who is usually more remote in the line of descent than a grandparent.
apartheid A policy of segregation and political and eco-nomic discrimination against non-European groups in South Africa. Apartheid ended there in 1993.
aquaculture Raising food products in water.
aquifers Geological formations under the earth's surface that hold water.
Arab A member of an Arab—speaking people.
arable Land fit for or used for the growing of crops.
Arab nationalism The idea, particularly widespread in the 1940s and 1950s, that Arabic-speaking people throughout Southwest Asia should be united into a single nation. It has not happened.
archipelago A large group or chain of islands. Japan is an archipelago.
arid Excessively dry; having insufficient rainfall to support agriculture.
arid China Thinly populated climate zone in western and northern China that is very dry. Less than 20 inches (51 cm) of rain falls each year. Arid China includes Tibet, Xinjiang, and Inner Mongolia.
armistice A temporary agreement to stop fighting.
arranged marriage A tradition in some African and Asian societies where the parents decide whom their children will marry.
Asian Pacific Rim A region of nations bordering the Pacific Ocean. The name is used especially for those Asian nations that are rapidly developing.
Association of Southeast Asian Nations (ASEAN) Organization of Brunei, Indonesia, Malaysia, Philippines, Singapore, and Thailand. It was set up in 1967 to resolve the region's social and economic problems, encourage cooperation between the six nations, and promote economic growth.
atmosphere The whole mass of air surrounding the earth.
atoll A ring-shaped island with a lagoon in the center. Early in its formation, the ring of coral surrounded a volcano, which over time became extinct. The volcanic soil eroded and the volcano eventually sank, leaving only the coral fringe.
authoritarian rule Refers to a concentration of power in a leader or an elite not constitutionally responsible to the people.
autocratic Kind of government in which one person has unlimited powers.
autonomous region A region having the right or power of self-government.

B

Berber A member of any of various non-Arab peoples living in northern Africa west of Tripoli.
Bhagavad-Gita A story from a religious poem known to hundreds of millions of Hindus.
biodiversity Biological diversity in an environment as indicated by numbers of different species of plants and animals.
biome A major ecological community type (for example, tropical rainforest, grassland, or desert).
biosphere The part of the world in which life can exist.
birthrate The ratio between births and individuals in a specified population and time.
bridewealth In some African societies, the tradition of the groom giving money, goods, cattle, or services to the bride's family.
British Commonwealth of Nations An association of countries that were once part of the British empire.
Buddhism A religion founded by Siddhartha Gautama, known as the Buddha (Enlightened One), in southern Nepal in the sixth and fifth centuries b.c. Buddhism teaches that meditation and the practice of good religious and moral behavior can lead to Nirvana, the state of enlightenment. Before achieving Nirvana one is subject to repeated lifetimes that are good or bad depending on one's actions (karma). Buddhism grew out of Hinduism. Buddhists believe in reincarnation and nonviolence, reject the caste system, and teach that all people are equal.
bullet train Japan's newest and fastest train, which reaches speeds of 170 miles per hour (274 km).
bunraku Japanese puppet theater featuring large costumed wooden puppets, puppeteers who are onstage, and a chanter who speaks all the lines.
bureaucracy A group of specialized government agencies, such as defense or treasury.

GLOSSARY

C

caliph The title used by any Islamic leader claiming to be the successor of Muhammad.
capital Money used for investing.
cardinal directions The directions north, south, east, and west.
cash crops Crops grown for sale or export. Under European colonial rulers, African farmers were forced to switch from subsistence farming to the production of cash crops.
caste system The rigid Hindu social structure evolved over thousands of years that limits the occupations of those within it and their association with the members of other castes. It is now outlawed in India.
castes The four Hindu social groups, or castes, from highest to lowest: the Brahmins (priests), Kshatriyas (warriors and rulers), Vaisyas (merchants, craftsworkers, and farmers), and Shudras (peasants and laborers). The Hindus believe that an individual is born into one of these groups through reincarnation. The Dalit fall outside of the caste system.
cataracts Large waterfalls or steep rapids.
censor To suppress or make illegal words, images, or ideas that are "offensive." Censorship can be carried out by the government, as in South Africa under apartheid, as well as private groups.
central economic planning Method by which economic goals are set by the government.
characters Language symbols that represent objects, ideas, or actions. The Chinese developed this system of writing many centuries ago.
Chiang Kai-shek Succeeded Sun Yat-sen as Nationalist Party leader in China. He proclaimed a new government in 1927. His aims were to stabilize and strengthen his government and destroy the Chinese Communist Party. Before the Japanese invasion of China in 1937, the Nationalists were firmly in control of China. But by the end of the war in 1945, the Communists had won a strong following among the farmers and had became the dominant force in China. In 1947, Chiang reestablished his government on Taiwan.
city-state An independent city that had its own government and controlled the surrounding land. Examples were the East African city-states of 500 a.d.–1500 a.d.
civil war An armed conflict between groups of people within a country.
civilians People who are not in the military but who all too often are killed in war. In the Korean War, about 3.5 million of the 5 million killed were civilians.
climate Average weather—temperature, wind velocity, precipitation—at a place over time.
coalition A temporary alliance of distinct parties, persons, or states for joint action.
Code of Hammurabi The laws put down by Hammurabi, ruler of Babylon, around 1750 b.c. Because his empire was so large and included so many people, Hammurabi sought to ensure order by posting his laws across the land. A stone tablet inscribed with the code, surprisingly advanced for one of the earliest known legal codes, is in the Louvre.
commerce The exchange or buying and selling of commodities on a large scale involving transportation from place to place.
commonwealth An association of self-governing autonomous states more or less loosely associated in a common allegiance (as to the British crown).
commune During Mao Zedong's tenure, a rural community where village farmers worked together and shared equally what they produced. Communes in China were not efficient.
communism Form of government in which the government alone decides how to use the resources of its country.
confluence A coming or flowing together, meeting, or gathering at one point.
Confucianism A belief system founded by Confucius, a Chinese philosopher, in the sixth and fifth centuries b.c. His teachings stressed the relationship between individuals, their families, and society, based on proper behavior and sympathetic attitude. Confucius's moral guidelines to restore harmony to his country influenced government leaders for thousands of years.
constitution The basic principles and laws of a nation, state, or social group that determine the powers and duties of the government and guarantee certain rights to the people in it.
constitutional monarchy A government with a democratic constitution headed by a monarch as the symbolic leader. Japan's

government is a constitutional monarchy.

continental drift The theory that the continents slowly and constantly move within the earth. Compare plate tectonics.

copra Sun-dried coconut meat, the oil of which is turned into soap, cattle feed, skin-care products and other cosmetics, margarine, and suntan lotions. Copra is the most important cash crop for the Pacific islanders.

corrupt When government or poltical officials abuse public power for private benefit. Corruption is the misuse of public goods by public officials, for personal gain.

cottage industries Small family businesses, where goods are made in the home. India's cottage industries are valuable to the nation's economy.

coup Short for coup d'é-tat (koo day-tah); the sudden overthrow or take over of a government by (usually) a small group of people, often military, or previously in other positions of power.

covenant A written agreement or promise between two or more parties. The Torah, Judaism's holy book, records how God made a special covenant with the Hebrew people.

"cram schools" Private schools in Japan that prepare students for the entrance exams of the top universities.

Cultural Revolution Chinese leader Mao Zedong's attempt, in 1965, to impose a utopian egalitarian (that is, social, political, and economic equality) program in China and spread revolution abroad. Massive purges took place. Political struggle, often violent, convulsed China in 1965–68.

culture The customary beliefs, social forms, and material traits of a racial, religious, or social group.

cyclones Fierce tropical storms with strong winds that trigger monster waves. They damage crops and kill many people. Cyclones advance at speeds of 20 to 30 miles (about 30 to 50 kilometers) an hour, and often bring heavy rain.

D

Dalit Those in Hindu society considered beneath the lowest social caste. They are seen as spiritually unclean, and they are the poorest and most ill-treated. Dalit work in jobs—street sweeping, for example—that others are forbidden to do.

Daoism A belief system founded by Lao-tzu in the sixth century b.c. Daoists believed that the best government was the one that did the least, that people should open themselves to nature and the wonders of the universe.

deforestation The removal of forests. Deforestation has contributed to erosion and the loss of soil. See reforestation.

deity God or Supreme Being; a god or goddess.

delta A normally triangular-shaped area of land at the mouth of a river. Made by the deposits of silt and sand carried by the river.

demand The quantity of a commodity or service wanted at a specific price and time. See supply.

democracy System of government in which power is held and exercised by the people.

density As regards to population, the average number of individuals per space unit (e. g., per square mile). Determined by amount of rainfall, farmland fertility, or availability of natural resources.

depleted Reduced in number or quantity so as to endanger the ability to function. South Asia's natural resources have been depleted over the centuries.

depression (economic) A period of low general economic activity marked especially by rising levels of unemployment.

desalination The process of changing salty seawater into freshwater that can be used for drinking and irrigation, also called desalinization.

desertification The process of grassland turning to desert because of human misuse or climate change.

developing (country) Poor one trying to build an economy and a higher standard of living.

Diaspora The dispersal of the Jews, initially from Palestine after the Romans sacked Jerusalem (a.d. 70) and crushed the Jewish revolt in 135. The term has come to refer to all Jews living outside Israel.

dictator Person who heads a government that exercises total authority over its people. An example was Adolf Hitler. See totalitarian.

diversify To engage in a variety of operations, usually for economic benefit. Saudi Arabia, for example, relied on oil money for years. But the oil is running out, so the Saudis are diversifying—building up a variety of other moneymaking industries.

diversity Differing from one another. Africa, for example, is a place of diversity because many different ethnic groups live there.

DMZ A demilitarized zone, within which no armed forces or fortifications are allowed. Peace zones in theory, DMZs are places of tension. One and a half million North and South Korean soldiers face one another on the border between the two countries.

double cropping A method of maximizing limited farmland. In southern China, for example, where the growing season is long, farmers plant a second crop between rows of the first crop. The second crop has already begun to grow by the time the first one is harvested.

domesticate To train or adapt animals to live in a human environment and be of use to humans.

Dreamtime The time of creation in the mythology of the Australian

Aborigine. The Aborigines' stories about Dreamtime explain how trees, rocks, water holes, and other parts of the natural world came to exist.

drought A long period—sometimes as long as a decade —of little or no rain.

E

earthquake A shaking or trembling of the earth that is volcanic or tectonic in origin.

"economic miracle" The phrase used to describe Japan's remarkable recovery since 1945, when the country was in ruins after World War II.

economy The structure of economic life in a country, area, or period based on the production, distribution, and consumption of goods and services.

ecosystem The complex of a community of organisms and its environment functioning as an ecological unit in nature.

ecotourism Vacations that are carefully planned to safeguard the environment.

ECOWAS The Economic Community of West African States, an organization of West African nations that hopes to increase trade among themselves.

elders In Africa, respected older leaders in their fifties who make laws for the village.

El Niño An irregularly occurring flow of unusually warm surface water along the western coast of South America that is accompanied by abnormally high rainfall in usually arid areas and that prevents upwelling of nutrient-rich cold deep water, causing a decline in the regional fish population. See la niña.

elevation Height above sea level.

embargo A legal prohibition on commerce.

emigration Moving away from one's country to live elsewhere. See immigration.

environment All the surroundings of a place, such as land, water, weather, plants, and the changes people have made.

epic poem A long narrative (story) about the deeds of heroes.

Equator Imaginary line circling the earth halfway between the North and South Poles, dividing the earth into two hemispheres.

escarpments Steep cliffs.

estuary A water passage where the tide meets a river current, especially an arm of the sea at the lower end of a river.

ethnic cleansing The forced removal or killing of one ethnic or religious group in an area or country by another ethnic or religious group in that area or country. *See* genocide.

ethnic group People with the same cultural background, united by language, religion, or ancestry.

ethnicity Refers to the affiliation of people with the same cultural background, united by language, religion, or ancestry.

exiled Banished or expelled from one's country. Australia's first European settlers were convicts from Great Britain exiled as punishment for nonviolent crimes.

export To carry or send (as a commodity) to some other place (as another country). See import.

extended family In some African societies, the tradition of several generations of relatives living together. The group might include a husband and wife, their unmarried children, and some of their married children with their families.

F

federal system A form of government, as in India, where power is distributed between a central authority and a number of states or territories. India has 28 states and seven territories.

fellaheen Egyptian name for farmers or peasants in an Arabic country (plural; singular form is fellah). Most fellaheen live in poverty.

fertigation The Israeli-inspired process of applying water and fertilizer directly to the roots of crops. Water is not lost to evaporation, and plants not normally suited to arid conditions can survive.

filial piety The respect and loyalty that children owe their parents. A great emphasis is placed on this in China.

Filipinos Natives of the Philippine Islands.

Five Pillars of Islam The five major religious practices of Muslims.

Five Themes of Geography Location, Place, Human-Environmental Interaction, Movement, and Region—the concepts used to describe a place on the earth and the people who live there.

forced migration The act of people involuntarily being moved from one place to another.

fossil fuels Nonrenewable fuels, such as coal, oil, or natural gas, formed in the earth from plant or animal remains.

fossil water Water collected millions of years ago in underground pools. Modern technology has enabled this water to be tapped and distributed to remote areas, especially significant in such dry Arab lands as Saudi Arabia.

free trade International business not restrained by government interference or regulation, such as protective tariffs, or import taxes. see tariffs.

G

GIS (geographical information systems) A computer system that records, stores, displays, and analyzes information about the features making up the earth's surface. GIS can generate two- or three-dimensional images of an area showing features as hills, rivers, roads, and power lines.

GPS (global positioning systems) Navigational aid that uses satellites to find absolute location.

genocide The international definition is from the Convention on the Prevention and Punishment of Genocide (1948). Genocide is the intent to destroy, in whole or in part, a national, ethnic, racial, or religious group by any of the following acts: killing members of the group; causing serious bodily or mental harm to members of the group; deliberately inflicting on the group conditions of life calculated to bring about its physical destruction in whole or in part; imposing measures intended to prevent births within the group; or forcibly transferring children of the group to another group.

global economy The ability to market products and services all over the globe, allowing businesses to develop partnerships and alliances throughout the world.

global interdependence The theory that every country in the world is affected by what happens in other countries; much of the inte-rdependence among nations is economic in nature, based on the production and trading of goods and services.

global warming The scientific theory that the earth is steadily getting hotter because the protective ozone layer is slowly but surely being eroded by man-made pollutants.

goods Something manufactured or produced for sale.

Gospels Books of the New Testament that contain the teachings of Jesus.

Great Barrier Reef Coral reef off the northeast coast of Queensland, Australia. It is the largest deposit of coral in the world, extending 1,250 miles (2,013 km). Designated a marine park in 1983.

great-circle route A circle on the earth's surface, an arc of which connecting two terrestrial points constitutes the shortest distance on the earth's surface between them.

Great Escarpment A steep wall of rock in Southern Africa that drops to a flat coastal plain.

Great Leap Forward Economic and social plan in the Peoples Republic of China from 1958-1962; the goal was to transofrm China from an agrarian economy to an industrial economy. The plan failed, resulting in wide-spread famine and other problems.

Great Wall Built during the Qin dynasty from 214 b.c. to prevent attacks by the Turks and Mongols. The wall, which took more than 300,000 workers 14 years to complete, stretches 1,500 miles (2,415 km) across northern China. Some 25 feet (7.5 m) high, it consists of a brick-faced wall of earth and stone, has a series of square watchtowers, and has been carefully restored. It is so large that it can be seen from space.

Green Revolution The name given to the dramatic rise in crop yields, which came about because of agricultural and cultivation innovations. Wheat production in India has tripled since 1967.

grid A network of uniformly spaced horizontal and perpendicular lines (as for locating points on a map).

Group of Eight (G-8) Organization of eight major industrial nations who meet periodically to discuss world economic and other issues. Established September 22, 1985. Members are Canada, France, Germany, Italy, Japan, Russia, the United Kingdom, and the United States.

H

habitat The place or environment where a plant or animal naturally or normally lives and grows.

hajj One of the duties of the Five Pillars Of Islam. A hajj is a pilgrimage to Mecca, which every Muslim should make at least once in his or her life.

han'gul A Korean alphabet developed in the 1440s that replaced a form of Chinese writing. Easier for Koreans to learn, han'gul helped increase literacy.

Han China's predominant ethnic group. More than 90 percent of Chinese are Han.

harambee Swahili word that means "let us all pull together." Popularized by Kenya's independence leader Jomo Kenyatta in 1963 urging workers to help build a strong economy.

hierarchy The classification of a group of people according to ability or to economic, social, or professional standing.

high islands Large rugged islands in Asia's Pacific Rim that are the result of millions of years of eruptions taking place on the ocean floor. The soil on these islands is generally fertile and supports tropical vegetation.

Hinduism A religion that includes many sects to which most Indians belong. Although many Hindus reject the caste system, it is widely accepted and classifies society at large into four groups: the Brahmins (priests); the warriors and rulers; the merchants, craftsworkers, and farmers; and the peasants and laborers. Central to Hinduism are the beliefs of reincarnation and karma.

Hindus The followers of the Hindu religion.

Holocaust The murder of more than 6 million European Jews by the Nazis during World War II.

homogenous society One in which the people belong to the same ethnic group, speak the same language, and share the same culture. Japan and Korea are homogenous societies.

Horn of Africa The easternmost part of Africa that extends into the Indian Ocean and looks like a rhinocerous horn. Includes the East African countries of Somalia, southeast Ethiopia, and Djibouti.

Human-Environmental Interaction One of the Five Themes of

Geography. Describes a place in terms of the environment's effect on humans who live there and how humans affect that environment.

humid China (monsoon China) Densely populated climate zone with two distinct regions. North China has a continental climate of warm summers and cold winters. South China has a subtropical climate of hot, humid summers and cold, damp winters. At least 20 inches (51 cm) of rain falls each year.

I

ideology A body of thought or theories about a culture.

ikebana The Japanese art of flower arranging.

imams The prayer leaders of a mosque. Also, Muslim leaders of the line of Ali held by Shiites to be the divinely appointed successors of Muhammad.

immigration The act of entering—and usually becoming established in—a country of which one is not a native for permanent residence. See emigration.

imperialism The control by one country of another through economic, political, or military means. Between 1880 and 1914, Britain, France, Germany, Portugal, Italy, Spain, and Belgium divided up and controlled the African continent.

import To bring (as merchandise) into a place or country from another country. See export.

infant mortality The number of infant deaths in a given time or place.

infrastructure The system of public works of a country, state, or region. Also, the resources—personnel, buildings, equipment—required for an activity.

intensive farming Using all available fertile land for agriculture. Practiced in China.

intermediate directions Directions between the cardinal directions—northeast, southeast, southwest, and northwest.

International Monetary Fund (IMF) An autonomous agency that has a functional relationship with the United Nations. It aims to promote international monetary cooperation and currency stabilization and expansion of international trade.

Islamists Those Muslims who want to create governments based on conservative Islamic traditions. They demand a strict moral code and religious observance.

Islamization To make Islamic; to convert to Islam. In the 1980s, for example, Pakistan's leaders campaigned to give Islamic law and customs greater emphasis in their nation's government. Islamists (conservative Muslims) throughout the Muslim world try to erase what they call dangerous Western influences.

isolationism A policy of national isolation by abstention from alliances and other international political and economic relations.

J

Japan Incorporated Refers to the combination of government, business, and labor leaders in Japan who have cooperated to maximize that country's greatest resource—its people—and created Japan's global economic success.

juche North Korea's self-sufficiency ideology adapted by Kim Il-sung. It was a philosophy, a rallying call for nationalists, a legitimization of Kim Il-Sung's own position, and a tool to justify non-alignment with either Russia or China.

jute The glossy fiber of either of two East Indian plants used chiefly for sacking, burlap, and twine.

K

kabuki Traditional Japanese popular drama with singing and dancing performed in a highly styled manner.

kami Spirits. Early Japanese believed that kami lived in natural objects, such as rocks or weathered trees. The religion that grew out of this reverence for nature was Shinto.

kana A Japanese system of writing with symbols.

karma The Buddhism and Hinduism concept that everyone's fate is determined by one's actions. How a person acts in this existence will determine the nature of the person's next existence.

kgotla In Botswana, a public discussion in which anyone can give their views on issues. The kgotla reflects the success of democracy in Botswana.

kimono Traditional Japanese clothing—a long robe-like garment that wraps across in the front. It is tied in place with a sash, or obi, in the back.

Kurds Members of a pastoral and agricultural group who inhabit a plateau region in adjoining parts of Turkey, Iran, Iraq, Syria, Armenia, and Azerbaijan. All want a homeland of their own.

L

landlocked Enclosed or nearly enclosed by land.

La Niña An irregularly occurring flow of unusually cold ocean temperatures in the eastern equatorial Pacific that is accompanied by wetter than normal conditions across the Pacific Northwest and dryer and warmer than normal conditions across much of the southern tier; winter temperatures are warmer than normal in the Southeast and cooler than normal in the Northwest. *See* el niño.

latitude Distance north or south of the Equator, expressed in degrees (°).

leaching The process by which heavy rains cause the nutrients in the soil to dissolve and wash away. This action quickly wears out the soil.

life expectancy The average life span.

lineage A group of people who trace

their descent from a single ancestor.

literacy rate The degree to which a group of people can read and write.

Location One of the Five Themes of Geography. Describes a place by its nearness to other places (relative location) or by its exact latitude and longitude (absolute location).

longitude Distance east or west of the prime meridian, expressed in degrees (°).

low islands Small flat islands in the Pacific Ocean that are coral reefs created by the gradual buildup of the skeletons of tiny sea creatures. Nearly all freshwater comes from rainfall, and few islands have soil in which plants can grow.

M

Maghreb Arabic name for northwest Africa: Morocco (including Western Sahara), Algeria, and Tunisia.

Mahabharata A famous Indian epic, which is the world's longest poem. Part of it describes the struggle between two related families for the throne of an Indian kingdom. Other parts tell how rulers should govern, recount ancient legends, and teach about religion.

Mandarin The group of closely related Chinese dialects that are spoken in about four fifths of the country. Mandarin is China's official language.

Mandate of Heaven Chinese theory explaining the duration of dynasties: Heaven gave an emperor the mandate, or right to rule. If he was just, he and his line stayed in power. If he ruled unwisely, he lost Heaven's favor and thus his mandate.

mansa Any leader of the West African kingdom of Mali during the Middle Ages. Most mansas followed the Muslim faith.

Mao Zedong (1893-1976) Chinese Communist leader, first chairman (1949) of the People's Republic, and cofounder of the Chinese Communist Party (CCP) in 1921. Mao's Communists successfully resisted the Japanese between 1937 and 1945, and after their collapse overwhelmed the Nationalist regime of Chiang Kai-shek. Mao remained chairman of the CCP's politburo until his death. He endured much criticism for his "Great Leap Forward" and "Cultural Revolution" campaigns.

map projection A way of representing a three-dimensional object on a two-dimensional surface.

matai The chief of any extended family in Western Samoa villages. He helps settle conflicts, represents the family on the village council, and makes decisions on sharing the family land.

matrilineal A group of people who trace their descent through the mother's family.

Messiah To the Jews, the leader God had promised would save the Jews. To Christians, the person of Jesus Christ.

mixed economies A combination of government ownership and private enterprise.

monarchy Undivided rule or absolute sovereignty by a single person.

monotheism Belief in one god.

monsoon A seasonal wind, especially in the Indian Ocean and southern Asia, that blows between the ocean and nearby land bringing very heavy rainfall.

mosques Muslim houses of worship.

Movement One of the Five Themes of Geography. Describes a place by its movement of people, goods, and ideas.

mudang In Korea, a spiritual medium—an individual held to be a channel of communication between the earthly world and a world of spirits. Spirit worship is Korea's oldest religion.

muezzin A Muslim who calls the hour of daily prayers from the tower of a mosque.

multinational Of or relating to more than two nationalities (a multinational society) or more than two nations (a multinational alliance); or having divisions in more than two countries (a multinational corporation).

N

National Diet The Japanese legislature, which consists of the House of Representatives and the House of Councillors. Both houses are elected by the people.

nationalized Ownership of industries taken over by the government.

noh Classic Japanese dance-drama having a heroic theme, a chorus, and highly stylized action, costuming, and scenery. A forerunner of kabuki.

nonalignment A country's policy of avoiding alliances with any superpower. After independence in 1947, India refused to line up with either the United States and the Soviet Union, and became a leader of nonaligned nations.

nonrenewable resource Fuel, such as coal, gas, and natural gas, formed in the earth from plant or animal remains.

nonviolent resistance Peaceful, nonviolent ways of protest. Used and taught by Gandhi in his leadership to lead India to independence from Great Britain. Based on Hindu, Buddhist, and Christian teachings.

O

oases Fertile or green areas in the desert nourished by underground wells or springs. The only places people can live in the Sahara Desert.

oligarchy A government in which a small group exercises control, especially for corrupt and selfish purposes.

OPEC (Organization of Petroleum Exporting Countries) Members include Arab and non-Arab nations from around the world, although not all oil-exporting nations in the world are members.

opium A drug derived from poppies

and sometimes used in medicine.

origami The Japanese art or process of folding squares of paper into representational shapes.

Ottoman Empire Empire centered in today's Turkey from 1516 to 1918.

Outback Desert and semiarid areas in Australia's interior. Temperatures soar over 120° F (49° C) in the summer.

P

pacifists Anyone who opposes all war. In large part because of the atomic bombs dropped on Hiroshima and Nagasaki, many Japanese are pacifists.

Palestinian National Authority The autonomous Palestinian government established to implement the Israeli-Palestinian agreements (the Oslo Accords). It governs parts of the West Bank and the Gaza Strip. Also called the Palestinian Authority.

parliamentary government A system of government having the real executive power vested in a cabinet composed of members of the legislature who are individually and collectively responsible to the legislature.

partition To divide (as a country) into two or more territorial units having separate political status. In 1947, the United Kingdom partitioned India. The new country was called Pakistan.

patriarchal Refers to a system of social organization where the father is head and ruler of his family and descendants.

patrilineal A group of people who trace their descent through the father's family.

Persian Empire A series of empires and spheres of influence centered in Iran (643 B.C. to A.D. 1935).

pharaohs Rulers of ancient Egypt.

pidgin A simplified speech used for communication between people with different languages. In Oceania, pidgin is used more often than English.

Place One of the Five Themes of Geography. Describes a spot on the earth by its physical (landforms, climate, and vegetation) and human (culture, government, and economy) characteristics.

plantations Large farms specializing in one or two crops. European powers in the 1800s colonized Southeast Asia and set up profitable plantations

plateau Flat or gently rolling land that is higher than nearby areas. Most of Africa, for example, is plateau.

plate tectonics A theory in geology that (1) the lithosphere (outer part of the solid earth composed of rock similar to that on the surface; usually considered to be about 50 miles [80 km] thick) of the earth is divided into a small number of plates that float on and travel independently over the mantle (the part of earth that lies between the lithosphere and the central core) and that (2) much of the earth's seismic activity occurs at the boundary of these plates. See continental drift.

poaching Taking game or fish illegally.

polytheism Belief in more than one god.

population age-sex structure Population figures based solely on age and gender.

population density The number of people living in a square mile or kilometer of land.

population distribution The statistical detailing of distinct populations within a certain area, state, or country, usually expressed in map or graph form.

population explosion The dramatic multiplication of people in any given area, partly because people are living longer.

population growth rate The percentage of population increase in a specific place over a specific period of time.

precipitation A deposit on the earth of hail, mist, rain, sleet, or snow.

president Head of the executive branch.

presidential government A system of government in which the president is constitutionally independent of the legislature.

primary economic activities Those activities in which workers and the environment come into direct, active contact; for example, farming, fishing, and mining.

prime minister Chief executive of a parliamentary government.

privatized Government-run industries sold to private owners.

protectorate A relationship of protection and partial control taken by a superior or stronger power over a dependent or weaker country or region.

purdah Strict seclusion of women from public observation among Muslims and some Hindus, especially in India.

pyramids Huge stone tombs built by the Egyptian pharaohs for themselves. Many still exist. A typical pyramid had a square ground plan, four outside walls in the form of triangles that met in a point at the top, and inner chambers.

Q

Qin dynasty (chin) China's first imperial dynasty (221–206 b.c.). Writing and measurement systems were standardized, state roads and canals were built, and border defense was consolidated into what became known as the Great Wall. On the less favorable side, the dynasty is identified with injustice, oppression, and a literary inquisition (an investi-gation with little regard for human rights) that came to be known as "the burning of the books."

quaternary economic activities Those activities responsible for collecting, processing, and manipulating information; for example, business management and data processing.

Quran Islam's holy scripture.

R

racism The belief that one race is superior to another.

rain shadow effect Exists when mountain peaks block rain from the leeward side.

rajahs Early South Asian Aryan rulers. The name comes from a Sanskrit word that means "king."

Ramayana A famous Indian epic poem. It tells the story of Rama, the ideal son, husband, and warrior-king.

redistribution of wealth The shifting wealth from a rich minority to a poor majority. Income redistribution has been the focus of some international development efforts.

referendum An issue decided by all voters.

reforestation The action of renewing forest cover by planting seeds or young trees. See deforestation.

refugee A person who flees to a foreign country or power to escape danger or persecution.

regime A government in power; administration.

Region One of the Five Themes of Geography. Describes a place in terms of its shared characteristics that distinguishes it as part of a broad geographical area.

reincarnation The belief that the soul is reborn after death in human—or some other form. The cycle of birth, death, and rebirth continues until the soul becomes perfect and is unified with the Universal Spirit.

relative location Approximate location found by using nearby references.

relief The elevations of land surface.

religion A personal set or institutionalized system of religious attitudes, beliefs, and practices.

renewable resource One that is capable of being replaced by natural ecological cycles or sound business practices. See nonrenewable resource.

representative democracy That system of government in which the many are represented by persons chosen from among them, usually by election. See republic.

republic Form of government in which people elect their leaders by voting.

revolution The overthrow of an existing government by those subject to it.

Ring of Fire Refers to the location of the most volcanic and earthquake activity in the world. The Ring of Fire includes the Asian islands of Japan, the Philippines, and Indonesia. It circles eastward toward North America and extends southward along the western coast of the Americas.

rural Open land usually used for agriculture.

S

Sahel The semiarid grassland that stretches up to 700 miles (1,127 km) across the African continent between the desert and the savanna. The Sahel receives less rain than the savanna but more than the desert.

samurai The warrior aristocracy of Japan. In the 1200s, these powerful military leaders challenged the emperors' authority to the point where the emperors ruled in name only.

sanctions Measures taken by one or more nations to apply pressure on another nation to conform to international law or opinion. Such measures usually include restrictions on or withdrawal of trade, diplomatic ties, and membership in international organizations.

Sanskrit An ancient Indo-Aryan language that is the classical language of India and of Hinduism.

savannas (grasslands) Large open areas of grass with few trees or bushes. They make up the most extensive vegetation zone south of the Sahara Desert.

scale Relative size as shown on a map, such as one inch = 100 miles.

seasons The four quarters into which the year is divided: spring, summer, autumn, winter.

secondary economic activities Those activities in which workers take raw materials and produce something as a finished product; for example, manufacturing.

sects Organized religious groups. In Southwest Asia there are two main sects, Sunni and Shiite.

secular Not controlled by a religious body or concerned with religious or spiritual matters.

semi-colonial status Technically independent but actually under foreign domination. This is what happened to China, for example, when that country turned over so many rights and powers to other nations in the 1800s. The Chinese came to resent foreigners in their land.

shanty towns Slum settlements usually on the outskirts of cities. A living situation worsened by the massive migration of rural people to the cities.

Shariah Law code drawn from Islam's holy scripture, the Quran.

shifting agriculture Method of farming that some Africans use to cope with land that is soil poor. Minerals and fertilizers from burned trees and underbrush are applied to the soil. When that soil loses its fertility, the land is abandoned in favor of new fields, where the process is repeated.

Shiite The Muslims of the branch of Islam that believes the only rightful successors of Muham-mad were his daughter and son-in-law. Although a majority sect in Iran, Shiites are in the minority of Muslims elsewhere. Also called Shi'a or Shia.

Shinto The ancient native religion of Japan, established long before the introduction of writing to Japan in the fifth century A.D. Shinto stresses belief in many spirits of natural forces, known as kami, and

venerates the emperor as a descendant of the sun goddess.

socialism Any of various economic and political theories advocating collective or government ownership and administration of the means of production and distribution of goods.

socialist One who advocates or practices socialism: a system or condition of society in which the means of production are owned and controlled by the state.

souk A marketplace in Southwest Asia or North Africa.

South Asia Peninsula region (often called a subcontinent) located between Southeast and Southwest Asia. Countries include India, Pakistan, Bangladesh, Afghanistan, Nepal, Bhutan, and Sri Lanka.

Special Economic Zones (SEZ) Areas set aside in China for foreign investors to set up businesses with little government intervention. The SEZ provided jobs and introduced Chinese to advanced science and technology.

spheres of influence Areas in China in the 1800s where Europeans could open mines, build railways, and conduct other business with little Chinese interference. This was possible because European nations had signed treaties with China that gave them special rights.

Spice Islands Name for the archipelago of Indonesia five hundred years ago. The place Columbus was looking for in 1492.

stalemate A situation where no progress can be made; a deadlock or an impasse, particularly in diplomatic negotiations.

standard of living In economics, the measure of consumption and welfare of a country, community, class, or person. Individual standard-of-living expectations are heavily influenced by the income and consumption of other people in similar jobs.

stations Large ranches in the Australian Outback, which often are hundreds of miles from the nearest city.

strait A narrow body of water that connects two larger bodies of water. The Dardanelles Straits, for example, link the Black Sea to the Mediterranean Sea.

subcontinent A distinct landmass that is smaller than a continent. South Asia is considered a subcontinent.

subregion A subdivision of a region; one of the primary divisions of a biogeographic region.

subsistence agriculture Farming or a system of farming that produces a minimum return to the farmer.

subsistence farmers *See* subsistence agriculture.

suburban Of, or relating to, an outlying part of a city or town. See urban.

sumo Japanese wrestling, which is one of the world's oldest sports. Sumo has rituals that link it to Shinto and other traditions.

Sun Yat-sen (1866–1925) Chinese revolutionary and founder of the Nationalist Party. Anti-Communist, he wanted to build a strong modern China by blending Chinese and Western ideas about government. In 1912 he was elected president of the new Chinese republic but was sent into exile a year later. Three years after Sun's death, Chiang Kai-shek unified China under a Nationalist Party government inspired by Sun's Three Principles of the People, which called for nationalism, democracy, and social reform.

Sunni The Muslims of the branch of Islam that adheres to the orthodox tradition and acknowledges the first four caliphs as rightful successors to Muhammad. The vast majority of Muslims in Southwest Asia and beyond are Sunni.

supply The act or process of filling a want or need; the quantities of goods or services offered for sale at a particular time or at one price. See demand.

sustainable resource A resource harvested or used in such a way that it is not depleted or permanently damaged. See nonrenewable resources.

symbols Anything that stands for something else, such as a blue line standing for a highway on a map.

T

tariff A tax placed on a product when it is imported into a country.

territory A geographical area dependent on an external government but having some degree of autonomy

terrorism Generally thought to be the use, or threatened use, of violence, including killing or injuring people or taking hostages, to intimidate a government in order to achieve a goal, usually political. Terrorist acts take many forms and occur all over the world. They are not confined to one place, one religion, or one form.

tertiary economic activities Those activities promoting, distributing, selling, or using what is made from raw materials; for example, education, finance, office work, and retailing.

theocracy A government that claims to rule with divine authority. Iran is an example.

Three Principles of the People Sun Yat-sen's organizing ideas for a modern Nationalist Party: nationalism, democracy, and social reform.

time zone A geographical region within which the same standard time is used.

topographic Of, relating to, or concerned with topography.

topography The art or practice of graphic delineation in detail usually on maps or charts of natural and man-made features of a place or region, especially in a way to show their relative positions and elevations.

Torah The holy book of Judaism.

tornado A violent destructive swirling wind accompanied by a funnel-shaped cloud that progresses in a narrow path over the land.

totalitarian Of or relating to a political regime based on subordination of the individual to the state and strict control of all aspects of the life and productive capacity of the nation, especially by coercive means. See dictator.

trade Dealings between persons, groups, or countries; the business of buying and selling or bartering commodities.

trading partners Countries that trade with each other. (

tramping New Zealand term for mountain hiking.

transnational Extending or going beyond national boundaries. Transnational corporations are those that do business with other countries.

Tropics, the The region lying between the Tropic of Cancer (23.5°N) and the Tropic of Capricorn (23.5°S). It is generally hot year-round. Most of Africa is in the Tropics.

truce accord An agreement for a temporary cessation or suspension of hostilities; an armistice.

trust territories Territories of the United Nations supervised by other nations. There are no longer any trust territories. The Federated States of Micronesia, the Republic of the Marshall Islands, the Republic of Palau, and the Northern Marianas Islands are former trust territories of the United States.

tsetse fly Insect that spreads a deadly sleeping sickness among people and cattle. Found primarily south of the Sahara Desert in Africa.

tsunami A huge destructive ocean wave (tidal wave) caused by underground movement or volcanic eruption. Tsunamis flood coastal villages and sweep people off shorelines.

typhoon A great hurricane-like wind and rain storm that destroys property and takes lives along the coasts of East and Southeast Asia.

U

unitary Of or relating to a unit. The emphasis is on a group rather than an individual.

urban Of, relating to, characteristic of, or constituting a city. See rural.

urbanization Process by which the proportion of a population living in or around towns and cities increases through migration as the agricultural population decreases. A relatively recent phenomenon, dating back only about 150 years to the beginning of the Industrial Revolution.

V

vegetarian Refers to anyone who does not eat meat, whose diet consists wholly of vegetables, fruits, and sometimes eggs or dairy products.

Vietnam War The struggle between Communist North Vietnam and anti-Communist South Vietnam. The United States supported South Vietnam; China and the Soviet Union assisted North Vietnam. In 1975, South Vietnam collapsed in defeat and a harsh Communist-led dictatorship was imposed on the country.

volcano A vent in the crust of the earth from which usually molten or hot rock and steam come forth.

voluntary migration To move from one country, place, or locality to another as an act of free will. See forced migration.

W

wadis Dry streambeds found throughout desert regions. Water is often found under wadis.

water pollution The contamination of waters, especially with man-made waste.

watershed A region or area bounded peripherally by a divide and draining ultimately to a particular watercourse or body of water.

wayfinding Traditional methods of navigation developed by the Pacific islanders hundreds of years ago. Wayfinding allowed sailors to cross thousands of miles of uncharted oceans without the aid of navigational tools.

weapons of mass destruction Munitions with the capacity to kill large numbers of living beings, including nuclear, biological, chemical weapons.

weather State of the atmosphere with respect to heat or cold, wetness or dryness, calm or storm, clearness or cloudiness.

windward Being in or facing the direction from which the wind is blowing.

World Bank An autonomous agency that has a functional relationship with the United nations. Provides loans and technical assistance for economic development projects in developing member countries; encourages co-financing for projects from other public and private sources.

World Trade Organization (WTO) An international agency that promotes trade between member nations, administers global trade agreements, and resolves disputes when they arise.

Z

zero growth No increase in population in a specific area over a given time.

Zionists Jewish nationalists since the 1890s who first wanted the establishment of a Jewish national or religious community in Palestine and then were determined to create a Jewish homeland in Israel, where Jews could live without persecution.

A

B

C

S

T

U

V

W

X

Y

Z